CULINARIA

Italy

CULINARIA
Italy

PASTA · PESTO · PASSION

CLAUDIA PIRAS

EDITOR-IN-CHIEF

RUPRECHT STEMPELL

PHOTOGRAPHY

h.f.ullmann

Abbreviations and Quantities

1 oz	= 1 ounce = 28 grams
1 lb	= 1 pound = 16 ounces
1 cup	= 8 ounces ★(see below)
1 cup	= 8 fluid ounces = 250 milliliters (liquids)
2 cups	= 1 pint (liquids)
8 pints	= 4 quarts
	= 1 gallon (liquids)
1 g	= 1 gram
	= 1/1000 kilogram
1 kg	= 1 kilogram
	= 1000 grams
	= 2¼ lb
1 l	= 1 liter
	= 1000 milliliters (ml)
	= approx. 34 fluid ounces
125 milliliters (ml)	= approx. 8 tablespoons
1 tbsp	= 1 level tablespoon
	= 15–20 g ★(see below)
	= 15 milliliters (liquids)
1 tsp	= 1 level teaspoon
	= 3–5 g ★(see below)
	= 5 ml (liquids)

Where measurements of dry ingredients are given in spoons, this always refers to the prepared ingredient as described in the wording following, e.g. 1 tbsp chopped onions BUT: 1 onion, peeled and chopped.

★The weight of dry ingredients varies significantly depending on the density factor, e.g. 1 cup flour weighs less than 1 cup butter.

Quantities in recipes have been rounded up or down for convenience, where appropriate. Metric conversions may therefore not correspond exactly. **It is important to use either American or metric measurements within a recipe.**

Quantities in recipes
Recipes serve 4 people, unless specified otherwise.
Exception: Recipes for drinks (quantities given per person).

PANINI – the different typeface indicates that this topic is relevant to an area wider than the region in question.

WARNING:
A number of recipes include raw eggs. It is advisable not to serve those dishes to very young children, pregnant women, elderly people or anyone weakened by serious illness. If in any doubt, consult your doctor. Of course, be sure that all the eggs you use are as fresh as possible.

© 2004 Tandem Verlag GmbH
h.f.ullmann is an imprint of Tandem Verlag GmbH

Art Director:	Peter Feierabend
Layout:	Michael Ditter
Project management:	Birgit Gropp
Assistance:	Freia Schleyerbach
Editor:	Daniela Kumor
Translation from Italian:	Giorgio Sinigalia, Peter Schelling, Stefanie Manderscheid
Travel organization (photography):	Bettina Dürr, Nina de Fazio
Photographic assistance:	Benjamin Holefleisch
Food stylist:	François Büns
Maps:	Studio für Landkartentechnik, Detlef Maiwald
Picture editor:	Mitra Nadjafi

Original title:	*Culinaria Italia – Italienische Spezialitäten*
ISBN	978-3-8331-1049-8

© 2008 for this edition: Tandem Verlag GmbH
h.f.ullmann is an imprint of Tandem Verlag GmbH

Special edition

Translation from German:	Susan Ghanouni, Harriet Horsfield, Judith Phillips, Elaine Richards, Rae Walter, in association with First Edition Translations, Cambridge, UK
Typesetting:	The Write Idea, in association with First Edition Translations
Project management:	Béatrice Hunt, for First Edition Translations
Project coordination:	Nadja Bremse-Koob
Cover design:	Peter Feierabend, Claudio Martinez
Photographs on front and back cover:	Tandem Verlag GmbH/Ruprecht Stempell

Printed in China

ISBN 978-3-8331-4889-7

10 9 8 7 6 5 4 3 2

From an idea and original concept by Ludwig Könemann

www.ullmann-publishing.com

CONTENTS

L'ARTE DELLA CUCINA ITALIANA

Whether a gastronomic tour of Italy, an elegant meal at the home of an Italian acquaintance, or "cooking Italian" back in one's own kitchen, the prospect is mouth-watering. It evokes memories, perhaps of holidays past, and the remembered flavors of culinary delights enjoyed in that land fringed with mountains, the land where the lemon tree blooms. Fine antipasti, and pasta of every shape and form, delicious sauces, fresh fish and seafood, crisp salads, fruit, and vegetables, straight from the garden; and pork, beef, wild boar, lamb, and even kid, all of the highest quality straight from the butcher. Last but not least are Italy's baked goods and desserts, from the savory focaccia to sugar-sweet confections such as cassata.

The popularity of *la cucina italiana* has never been greater. This is true not only of cooking in Italy itself, where traditional recipes are enjoying something of a renaissance, but also in other countries where there has been a revolution in what is called "Italian cuisine." The days when this meant simply pizza, spaghetti, and cheap Chianti in wicker-clad bottles, are long gone. Now, ambitious food retailers, excellent chefs, gastronomic experts, and whole armies of talented home cooks have ensured that authentic Italian specialties are known and available far beyond their·country of origin. The customer asking for arborio or carnaroli rice by name has surely been exploring the art of making a good risotto; the one requesting a particular prosecco has perhaps spent the previous evening discussing that very winemaker. Today, almost everyone knows that freshly grated parmesan tastes better than the ready-grated packet variety, convenient though this is.

What is the key characteristic that makes Italian cuisine what it is? What particular charm has aroused such lively interest? Italian cuisine is not a single entity. There is great variety in a country of Italy's size; it is about 750 miles (1200 kilometers) from the Alpine peaks of the north to the toe of the "boot." The country also has two large islands, Sicily and Sardinia. Its changing geography from north to south results in a fascinating profusion of different foods; the distinct microclimates produce a great range of different sausages, hams, and cheeses – as well as the rich palette of Italian wines. The changing historical fortunes of the various regions have also left their mark on the cuisine. Sicilian cooking, for example, still reflects a degree of Arab influence to this day, and the Austro-Hungarian dish of goulash can still be tasted in Trieste.

Italian cuisine, then, cannot be seen as a unified tradition; on the contrary, each region has its own colors. Certain features are common to every city and province, such as the insistence on highest quality produce, and the love, care, and enthusiasm employed in preparing it.

People frequently travel long distances and pay slightly higher prices to buy from a favorite retailer or producer. All over Italy there are specialist producers dedicated to traditional methods. In Tuscany, for example, there are pork farmers devoting their efforts to preserving the *cinta senese* breed of pigs. These pigs lead a semi-wild existence, so keeping them is very cost-intensive, but their meat is of high quality and incomparable flavor. Although the producers realize that theirs is a niche product, they find that more and more consumers are looking for quality rather than quantity. Another example of this trend is the fact that cheese merchants are choosing to stock raw milk cheeses from small-scale cheese-makers – despite the distinct lack of enthusiasm shown by the food control legislators of the European Union for such resolutely noncompliant products.

The Italian table presents us with a veritable feast. The regional variation, the high quality of the produce, and a sense of tradition are its mainstays. Yet these alone are not enough: perhaps the true foundation on which this richly laden table rests is the Italian attitude to food and drink. Food in Italy means pure enjoyment, daily celebrated as a feast for the senses, in the company of family or friends, at home or in a good restaurant.

But now it is time to set out together on a journey of discovery. It will take us through 19 regions of this enchanting country that never loses its magic. Take a look inside the cooking pots, taste the wines, and meet interesting people. Listen to tales about our daily bread, tales from the earnest to the amazing. Did you know how to cheat the Devil with a cheese? Or how you can use a cake to save your life? *Culinaria Italy* will reveal this and more.

We hope you enjoy reading this book and sampling the many recipes it contains.

Good luck and *buon appetito!*

Claudia Piras

FRIULI VENEZIA GIULI

FRIULI

BEAN SOUPS

THE BIGGEST FRICO IN THE
WORLD

PORK

CORN

THE COAST

WINEGROWING IN THE
BORDERLANDS

SWEET DELIGHTS

GRAPPA

Friuli
Venezia Giulia

Jôf di Montasio
2753 m

Carnia

San Daniele
del Friuli

Udine

Gorizia

Pordenone

Laguna di
Marano

Grado

Trieste

Friuli lies away from the usual tourist track. The visitors who do reach this Alpine region bordering the former Yugoslavia choose it for its unspoiled natural beauties and relief from the hubbub of tourist hordes – and especially for its excellent cuisine and famous wines. For the gourmet, a place-name such as San Daniele del Friuli is synonymous with its famous hams, and Carnia in the far north with its delicious bacon and wonderful Montasio cheese, while Collio, Grave del Friuli, and Colli Orientali are music to the ears of those who love good wine. Winegrowers in the Friuli region made an early decision to aim for quality by consciously reducing the size of their yield. They are now among the best producers in Italy.

The region's cuisine keeps alive its Central European past. Trieste played a significant role in that history as a major trading port for the Danube area and Austrian monarchy. Faithful to the name the city had acquired as a "town of many peoples," its dishes mingle Austrian, Hungarian, Slovenian, and Croatian influences as well as local cooking traditions. In the beer halls, the clientele can enjoy Viennese sausages, goulash, and Bohemian hare, washed down with potent wine or beer, that "un-Italian" drink. Desserts of the flour-based type, including strudel, round off the meal.

The area known as Venezia Giulia has a cuisine that embraces and assimilates foreign influences; Friuli itself, the rest of the province, is more traditional. There, the simplest of ingredients are transformed into delicious dishes. The staple ingredient is polenta. Other regions may dismiss it as no more than the food of the poor, but between Udine and Tarvisio, Gorizia and Cortina d'Ampezzo it makes its appearance in innumerable variations: stirred, baked, served with sausage, with cheese, with fish, or with meat. The people of Friuli love their uncomplicated cuisine and regard it with pride. Spicy dishes often accompany pork, slowly roasted in traditional style over the *fogolar*, the open hearth in the kitchen. The appreciation of simple but flavorsome dishes, typical of this region, has produced true classics such as *jota*, a hearty bean soup with lashings of bacon, and *brovada*, turnips bottled in marc.

Previous double page: Caterina Castellani has been involved in the production and ripening of San Daniele hams for 50 years.

Left: The grapes that ripen on the fertile plains of Friuli not only produce impressive wines, but also various types of grappa, as here at Grave del Friuli.

Frico is a cheese dish, fried like a pancake until hardened and crisp. It is typical of Carnia. Potatoes and other ingredients can be added, making the finished dish somewhat like a cheese omelet. There are endless variations – almost every village and mountain valley has its own special recipe. Highly nourishing, *frico* used to be popular as a food for shepherds and forest workers to take with them. Today, it is often served as a starter, usually with a salad.

The biggest *frico* in the world was made by the Udine Association of Chefs. The frying pan was specially made in Austria, and measured 10 feet (3 meters) across. It weighed over ⅔ ton (600 kilograms). The huge *frico* cooked inside it weighed more than ⅓ ton (300 kilograms).

BEAN SOUPS

Beans are popular throughout Friuli. The robust dish *jota* comes from Trieste. Once thought of as a pauper's dish, it is now becoming a recognized culinary specialty: regaining its position, in fact, for the people of Trieste like to point out its honorable origins. Its name apparently derives from the late Latin word *jutta*, meaning a stock or liquid soup. Its history may go back still further to the food enjoyed by the Celts.

Jota is a specialty of Venezia Giulia and of Trieste in particular. The rest of Friuli has its own specialties using beans. *Minestra di fagioli e orzo* is a magnificent dish, although it does take time to prepare. The beans are cooked twice, each time in fresh water. Finally, milk and pasta or rice are added to make a splendid, filling soup.

JOTA
Bean stew
(Illustration above)

1 1/2 CUPS/250 G DRIED LIMA BEANS
GENEROUS 1/2 LB/250 G POTATOES
10 OZ/300 G BACON
1 1/2 CUPS/200 G SAUERKRAUT (FERMENTED WHITE CABBAGE)
1 BAY LEAF
3 TBSP OLIVE OIL
1 CLOVE OF GARLIC
2 TBSP FLOUR
SALT AND PEPPER

Soak the beans in water overnight. Then drain and place in a saucepan with the potatoes. Dice and add the bacon. Add water to cover, and bring to a boil. When cooked, pass half the potatoes and beans through a sieve and return to the pan. Cook the sauerkraut in a little water with the bay leaf for a few minutes, shaking the saucepan occasionally.

Peel and chop the garlic coarsely. Heat 2 tablespoons of the oil, brown the garlic and then remove. Mix the flour into the hot oil, and cook gently for 2–3 minutes, stirring. Add the sauerkraut and cook gently for about 5 minutes. Transfer to the saucepan containing the beans, potatoes, and bacon. Add the remaining oil. Cook for another 30 minutes, adding more water if necessary. Season with salt and pepper, and serve hot.

MINESTRA DI FAGIOLI E ORZO
Bean soup with orzo

1 CUP/200 G DRIED BEANS
1/2 CUP/80 G PASTA PELLETS (ORZO)
1/2 ONION, CHOPPED
1 CLOVE OF GARLIC, CRUSHED
1 STALK OF CELERY, SLICED
2 POTATOES, DICED
1 CARROT, DICED
2 BAY LEAVES
1 HAM BONE
2 CUPS/500 ML MILK
SALT

Soak the beans in water overnight. Drain and place in cold water with the pasta pellets. Add the onion, garlic, celery, potato, carrot, bay leaves, and ham bone, and bring to a boil. Reduce the heat and simmer for 1½ hours. Then add the milk. Season with salt, and continue simmering for another ½ hour. Remove the ham bone and bay leaves, and serve with slices of toasted bread.

In Friuli, the soup is left to stand for a short while before serving, until it has thickened to the point where it could be cut with a knife.

FRICO CON PATATE
Cheese and potato fry

1 ONION
4 MEDIUM SIZED POTATOES
1 TBSP BUTTER
1–2 CUPS/250–500 ML OF STOCK
14 OZ/400 G MONTASIO CHEESE

Chop the onion, peel the potatoes and slice them thinly.
Melt the butter in a frying pan and lightly sauté the onions.
Add the sliced potato and toss briefly in the butter. Pour on
the stock, and cook gently until the potatoes are soft.
Meanwhile grate or dice the cheese. Once the potatoes are
cooked and all the stock absorbed or evaporated, scatter the
cheese on top and let it melt. Brown slowly, pouring off the
excess fat from the cheese. The *frico* is ready when the edge
is browned. Serve hot.

Below: The Udine Association of Chefs made an enormous
frico, a fried cheese dish, in an attempt to get into the
Guinness Book of Records.

MONTASIO

Montasio cheese has a long tradition reaching back to
around the year 1200, when the Benedictine monks
began making this cow's milk cheese in Giulia and the
Alpine valleys of Carnia. According to old trading
documents, it has been one of the region's exports
since the 18th century. A consortium for the protection of *Montasio* and the preservation of the traditional
method of production was set up in 1984, and two
years later, the cheese was awarded the DOC appellation. Today, *Montasio* may only be produced within a
legally defined, controlled geographical area covering
Friuli, Venetia Giulia, and the Veneto provinces of
Belluno, and Treviso, together with parts of Padua
and Venice.

There are three varieties of *Montasio*: fresh, which is at
least two months old and has a correspondingly mild
flavor, *Montasio mezzano*, matured for five to ten
months and with a stronger flavor, and *Montasio stravecchio*, over ten months old, whose flavor is tangy but not
harsh. Young *Montasio* is suitable as a starter or as an
ingredient in a main dish. The oldest type (*Montasio
stravecchio*) can be grated to use as an alternative to
parmesan. All three are delicious as a small snack, and
irresistible served on a slice of bread.

15

PORK

Pork has always been popular in Friuli. It is still the custom for many families to rear their own pig, calling in the services of a peripatetic butcher and sausage manufacturer, called the *purcitar*, to process the meat. The slaughter of a pig remains to this day a ceremony with its own traditional rituals. The children are even granted a day off school, and everyone, young and old, impatiently awaits the arrival of the *purcitar*. A toast is drunk in wine or grappa, which is highly popular in Friuli, and events can begin.

Every part of the pig is used to prepare sausages and pork products, following traditional recipes. Use is even made of the blood and organ meat. They are mixed with raisins and pine nuts to create the typical Friuli delicacies *sanguinaccio* (other local names for blood sausage are *mule* or *mulze*) and *pan de frizze dolce* (a type of sweet bread with crackling).

Musetto is a boiled sausage popular in Friuli. The sausage meat is made of finely ground pork flavored with white wine or Marsala, together with rind and snout (hence the name, *muso* being the Italian for snout). It is richly seasoned with nutmeg, cinnamon, coriander, allspice, and pepper. The casings used are beef intestines, which accounts for the long, tapering appearance that is characteristic of *musetto*. It is not unlike *zampone*, a robust dish of stuffed trotter from Emilia-Romagna. The difference is that, in Emilia-Romagna, *zampone* is usually served with *bollito misto*, whereas in Friuli, *musetto* is mainly eaten with *brovada*. This is turnip marinated in marc and then allowed to ferment. *Musetto* and *brovada* are combined in a hearty one-pot meal.

The better cuts of meat are used to make salami, including the specialty garlic salami. Pork products are still made in the traditional way, and a noted center for this is the small town of Sauris in Carnia, a northern region with an Alpine character. At some time in the past, people arrived here from Tyrol and Kärnten in Austria and from southern Germany, and one particular precious recipe that they brought with them was the method of making bacon, famous today across the whole of Friuli. The manufacture of bacon begins with the outer part of the ham joint, which is streaked with fat. This, the side of bacon, is salted and left to absorb the salt for seven or eight days. The next stage is the smoking: it is hung for a day in a smokehouse heated with juniper wood, and finally matured for about ten months. The method used to produce Sauris bacon is the same, except that the maturing period is 18 months. *Pancetta*. bacon made from belly of pork, is also produced here. *Pancetta* is smoked for 12 hours, and matures in "just" seven months.

The hams and sausages of Sauris are the pride of the town, and customers often travel long distances to buy Carnian specialties from one of the small firms producing them. The producers, aware of this, do their utmost to maintain their excellent standards of quality. The pork they use comes exclusively from Friuli; the animals are carefully tended and given the very best feed: corn, fruit, and grain, enriched with whey. The fact that Carnia is a cheese-producing area means that whey is abundantly available.

The specialties for which Sauris is known make a delicious wholesome but simple meal with bread. The combination tastes still better if the bread is a full-flavored one with caraway seeds.

SALSICCE AL VINO
Pork sausages in wine
(Illustration left)

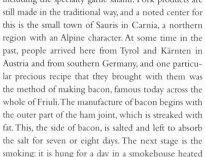

4 SALSICCE
1 TBSP WHITE WINE VINEGAR
1 GLASS OF DRY WHITE WINE

Prick the *salsicce* a few times all over. Begin to fry them lightly, and sprinkle them with the white wine vinegar. When this has been absorbed or evaporated, pour on the wine and continue cooking. Serve the *salsicce* with slices of polenta, toasted under the broiler or in the oven.

SAN DANIELE HAM

Friuli is one of the few regions of Italy that can boast a DOC ham – one whose place of origin is legally defined and controlled – *Prosciutto di San Daniele*. According to EU regulations, such controlled-origin hams may only be produced from fresh cuts of locally produced meat. In Friuli, the excellent *prosciutto* is mainly produced using leg meat from Valpadana pigs. These pigs can reach nearly 440 pounds (200 kilograms) in weight, which means that the yield in ham is correspondingly high.

Production methods have changed little with the passage of time. The selected cuts of meat are first trimmed, and the fat and rind removed. They are then sorted by size and weighed. The curing time depends on the weight, so, for example, a ham weighing around 29 pounds (13 kilograms) has to be cured for 13 days under a layer of salt (possibly a day or two longer). This is nevertheless quite short compared with some other methods of ham production. After curing, the ham is pressed and sheds its remaining moisture content, becoming more compact. This process accounts for the typical shape of the hams. They then spend at least ten months, often 12 to 13 months, maturing in warehouses around San Daniele. The climate in this area is particularly well suited, with mountain air and a fresh sea breeze.

PROSCIUTTO DI SAN DANIELE CON FICHI
San Daniele ham with figs
(Illustration in background)

Wash some fresh figs and slice them in half lengthways. Slice the ham by hand, cutting it as thinly as possible. Arrange on a large serving platter.
If liked, a large, ripe, sweet melon may be used instead of figs.

Only a ham with the stamp of quality is a genuine San Daniele product. The riband is a further guarantee of controlled origin.

The regal hams of San Daniele have to be matured for at least ten months if their unmistakable flavor is to develop fully.

CORN

The 17th century was a time of hardship for the farmers of Friuli. The powerful city-state of Venice then ruled over the area, and not only did it show little interest in its hinterland; it drafted in the men of the region, the *friulani*, as soldiers to defend Venice from the Turks. The result was a lack of workers, with fields lying untended. Those few inhabitants who did not have to serve in Venice were hard put to find food. Famine was a common occurrence. Golden corn on the cob proved their salvation.

The great voyages of exploration of the 15th and 16th centuries did more than change men's geographical image of the world; they brought innovations in cooking too. Tomatoes, potatoes, beans, and of course corn appeared. These were at first regarded with scepticism by botanists and naturalists – some held them to be inedible if not actually poisonous – but they gradually came into use as food.

Corn (*Zea mays*) has a long history as a cultivated crop. It originates from the continent of America. Researchers have found evidence of its cultivation in the Tehuacán valley in Mexico as far back as the 5th century B.C. It was revered by the Aztec and Maya civilizations, and the corn god occupied an important place in the religious hierarchy.

Venetian merchants were already importing corn in the 16th century, but the real breakthrough did not come until a hundred years later, when it began to be cultivated in increasing quantity. It must have been around that time that corn arrived in Friuli. This foreign cereal plant brought an end to want and hunger in the region as farmers discovered it to be a useful source of nutrition, as well as an undemanding and easy crop to grow.

The region's cooks soon agreed on the best method of preparing it: following the long-established method used for lima beans, chickpeas, and buckwheat, it was ground into flour and turned into a thick porridge or pudding. The Venetians called this new corn *grano turco*, Turkish corn, since many foreign imports came via the East. In Friuli, it was called *blave*.

Polenta made from the corn soon became a highly popular dish in Friuli and the whole of northern Italy, eclipsing other types of cereal pudding, and even, in some areas, the traditional bread. A daily helping of polenta was often the only food eaten by poor mountain peasants.

Useful as it had been in preventing famine, corn had one big disadvantage, especially if it was the only foodstuff: it contains no niacin that can be used by the body. The medical significance of niacin is that it prevents pellagra. Large sections of the population were released from hunger only to suffer from this disease. It causes general weakness, impaired memory, and skin and nervous symptoms.

The modern balanced diet has thankfully put an end to this risk, and polenta features prominently on northern Italian menus. It is not for nothing that the Veneto is the largest corn-producing area in Italy, closely followed by Friuli, Lombardy, and Piedmont.

Corn is an undemanding crop that does not need special conditions, but it prefers warm, mild locations and humus-rich soils with good water retention.

Harvest time is in October. The cobs are removed from the plant and stored with their outer leaves intact, to prevent the kernels from drying out.

For some years, the farmers of these regions have been using traditional strains of corn with a more pronounced flavor, rather than hybrid varieties. This gives local traditional corn-based dishes a characteristic taste that is enjoying continued – or at least rediscovered – appreciation.

POLENTA PASTICCIATA AI GAMBERI
Polenta with shrimp
(Illustration below)

POLENTA (SEE BASIC RECIPE RIGHT)
BUTTER
GENEROUS 2 LB/1 KG SHRIMP
1 HANDFUL OF FRESH MUSHROOMS
1 CLOVE OF GARLIC, CHOPPED FINELY
1 TBSP CHOPPED PARSLEY
3/4 CUP/200 ML WHITE WINE
4 CUPS/1 LITER VEGETABLE STOCK
FRESHLY GROUND PEPPER
NUTMEG

Prepare the polenta to a soft consistency. Cool and cut into slices, and place them on a greased baking sheet so that the slices cover it completely, overlapping slightly. Preheat the oven to 350–375 °F (175-190 °C).
Clean the mushrooms and chop finely. Peel the shrimp and sauté them in a little butter in a saucepan. Add the mushrooms, garlic, and parsley. Pour on some of the white wine and vegetable stock, and bring to a boil. Add the rest only if needed. Season with freshly ground pepper and nutmeg, and arrange on top of the polenta slices. Bake for a few minutes in the preheated oven.

POLENTA AL BURRO
Polenta with butter

Prepare polenta to a firm consistency, and slice.
Grease a baking sheet with butter or lard, and arrange the polenta slices on it, side by side. Scatter with grated cheese and cinnamon, and sprinkle with melted butter. Bake in a preheated oven at 350–375 °F (175–190 °C).

FRIULIAN POLENTA

Following the arrival of corn in northeastern Italy in the 16th century, it quickly became an important staple food – especially in those areas of Carnia where people were poor and the task of feeding their families placed constant demands on the cooks. They now ate polenta at every meal: with milk for breakfast, with cheese at midday, and in the evening, as a porridge with vegetables, bacon, or butter.
Polenta accompanies almost all traditional dishes in Friuli to this day. There are three types: the traditional, yellow polenta, which can be served in a host of different ways; white polenta, made of light-colored corn flour, which is excellent served with broiled or baked fish, and can be broiled in its own right; and black polenta made from buckwheat. This last has a unique, slightly bitter flavor and is best simply served with butter and sardines.

BASIC RECIPE FOR POLENTA

SALT
1 CUP/250 G POLENTA FLOUR

Add a pinch of polenta flour to 3 cups/750 ml of salted water and bring to a boil. Slowly sprinkle in the rest of the polenta, stirring constantly. Stir more vigorously as the polenta thickens, to ensure an even consistency. Crush any lumps that form, by pressing them against the side of the saucepan. Once all the polenta has been added, reduce the heat and simmer for 45 minutes, stirring constantly. Take care during this time, as the polenta is very hot and can spurt out of the saucepan. The bottom of the saucepan becomes encrusted during the cooking. The polenta then begins to lift away from the encrusted base of the pan. This indicates that it is ready. Turn it out onto a board and smooth it flat with the back of a knife. Polenta can be cut with kitchen string when hot, and with a knife when cold.

GNOCCHI DI POLENTA
Polenta gnocchi

Dice leftover polenta and pour on boiling salted water. When heated through, drain and place on deep pasta plates. Top with grated smoked ricotta.

EVENING BY THE FOGOLAR

In Friuli there is a type of fireplace called a *fogolar*. This is more than just a fire for cooking food; it forms part of a traditional life style with a long history. It is the focus and meeting place where friends gather to eat, drink, talk, and argue, and it creates a cosiness that is all the more attractive on cold winter nights. It consists of a hearth where food is grilled over a wood fire, and often occupies the center of the kitchen, crowned by a massive flue. Here, people often cook a simple meal of pork, chicken, beans, root vegetables, or polenta – warming, nourishing food that is hardly *haute cuisine*, but is nonetheless delicious and makes for a delightful and often stimulating evening.

THE COAST

Friuli boasts an interesting coastline in addition to the beauties of its inland areas. There are two lagoons, Laguna di Grado and Laguna di Marano, both well worth a visit. The sleepy fishing port of Marano is one of the few places in Italy that cherishes unspoiled tradition, despite the proximity of Lignano Sabbiadoro and Bibione with their throbbing nightlife. Marano, in contrast, still has some old houses in the Venetian style, with gaily painted façades. There are even some traditional fishermen's straw-thatched dwellings – *casoni* – to be seen around the Laguna di Grado and the fishing village of Portogruaro.

The scenery of the lagoons is likewise more natural here than elsewhere. Between the distant shores lined with fishermen's houses, the broad expanse of the water is dotted with small, shrubby islands. As the tide ebbs, the sandbanks and mudflats are exposed, with their lush and varied growth of algae and other plant life.

In the historical past, the local center for this coastal region was the ancient Roman city of Aquileia. The settlement of the lagoons came about as the result of other events. Aquileia was a Roman Imperial trading city, whose citizens practiced a luxurious life style and a tolerance that enabled the early Christians to become established here; it became a stronghold of Christianity. It was destroyed and razed to the ground by the invading Huns. Most of the population fled to the islands of the lagoons, where they found abundant fish and marshland birds, though they lacked drinking water. Initially, they lived mainly on fish. As it is still done in the most northern part of Europe, they used the fish oil both for food and for practical purposes: to lubricate their tools, as fuel for their lamps, and to paint the hulls of their boats to make them watertight. It was a long time before Aquileia recovered from its destruction by the Huns. It began to regain some of its former glory in the Middle Ages, and became the seat of influential patriarchs with almost as much power as the pope in Rome.

The number and variety of fish around the coasts and lagoons of Friuli equal other parts of the Adriatic. Eel are a specialty of the calm waters of the lagoons. Fish varieties caught farther out to sea include mullet, sea bass, and gilt head bream. The fishermen's lives and methods have changed radically since the days of these first settlers; no longer do they set out to sea in traditional fishing smacks under sail, but in fast, powered boats. Traditional clothing has long since given way to T-shirts and blue jeans. In one respect, though, little has changed: fishing is a man's job, and the women's involvement starts with the fish soup. Locals claim that they can still identify distinct types among the fishermen: tall, muscular, ash blond men of Dalmatian ancestry; blond, blue-eyed fishermen from Caorle or Istria, who are seen as lively and always ready for a joke; dark-eyed and fiery men of Romagnan stock, nevertheless friendly and tolerant, and delighting in the sensual pleasures of life; and, lastly, the Venetians, reddish of face, typically with green or hazel eyes. They are seen as agreeable, cheerful, and a little garrulous, yet patient, peaceable, and full of common sense.

ANGUILLA AI FERRI
Grilled eel
(Illustration far left, behind)

2 GUTTED FRESHWATER EELS, I I/4 LBS/600 G EACH

For the marinade:
OLIVE OIL
VINEGAR
SALT AND PEPPER

8 BAY LEAVES
CHOPPED PARSLEY
GRILLED SLICES OF POLENTA

Wash the eels, carefully cleaning off all the slime. Remove the heads, tails, and backbones, and cut into pieces about 3 inches/8 cm long. Open out and press as flat as possible. Mix the marinade ingredients and place the eels in it for several hours to absorb the flavors. Then remove and lay the pieces on a hot grill, skin side down. Scatter with bay leaves and cook for about 15 minutes. Turn and cook for another 10 minutes. Season with salt and pepper, and sprinkle with parsley. Serve with grilled polenta.

ANGUILLA FRITTA
Fried eel
(Illustration far left, in foreground)

4–5 GUTTED EELS, I/2 LB/250 G EACH

For the marinade:
OLIVE OIL
LEMON JUICE
SALT AND PEPPER

ALL-PURPOSE FLOUR
OIL FOR FRYING
GRILLED OR ROASTED SLICES OF POLENTA

Choose small eels if possible. Wash them and clean thoroughly of slime. Remove the heads, tails, and fish bones and cut the eels into roughly 2 inch/5 cm pieces. Mix the marinade and leave the eel in it for at least 2 hours to absorb the flavors.
Drain the eels and coat in flour. Heat a generous quantity of oil, fry the eel, then remove and drain on paper towels before serving. Accompany with grilled or roasted polenta slices.

RISOTTO ALLA MARANESE
Seafood risotto
(Illustration left, center)

I/2 LB/200 G PREPARED SQUID
I/4 LB/100 G PREPARED SHRIMP
6–7 TBSP OLIVE OIL
I CLOVE OF GARLIC, CHOPPED FINELY
3–4 TBSP CHOPPED PARSLEY
SALT AND PEPPER
I LB/500 G MUSSELS
I GLASS DRY WHITE WINE
I 3/4 CUPS/300 G RISOTTO RICE
VEGETABLE STOCK

Wash and slice the squid, not too finely. Wash the shrimp. Sauté both briefly in half the olive oil, with the garlic and parsley. Wash and clean the mussels, discarding any that are open. Cook them in the remaining oil until the shells have completely opened. Discard unopened mussels. Remove the flesh from the shells and add it to the shrimp and squid. Strain the cooking juices from the mussels through muslin, and add it to the seafood. Pour on the white wine. Add the rice, and simmer until tender. Add vegetable stock from time to time to prevent drying out. Allow the risotto to stand for a few moments before serving.

SCAMPI FRITTI
Fried shrimp

24 SHRIMP
2 EGGS
SALT AND PEPPER
OLIVE OIL FOR FRYING
2 TBSP ALL-PURPOSE FLOUR

Wash the shrimp and remove from their shells, discarding heads, tails, and innards. Beat the eggs and season with salt and pepper. Toss the shrimp in flour, then dip in egg and fry in the hot oil for a few minutes. Drain on paper towels and serve hot.

CODA DI ROSPO AL VINO BIANCO
Monkfish in white wine

4 PORTIONS OF FILLETED MONKFISH
I ONION, CHOPPED
2 CLOVES OF GARLIC, CHOPPED
I STALK OF CELERY, CHOPPED
I SPRIG OF ROSEMARY, CHOPPED
3 SPRIGS OF FLAT LEAF PARSLEY, CHOPPED
6 TBSP OLIVE OIL
SALT AND WHITE PEPPER
ALL-PURPOSE FLOUR
I CUP/250 ML DRY WHITE WINE

Preheat the oven to 400 °F/200 °C. Wash the fish and pat dry. Briefly sauté the onion, garlic, celery, rosemary, and parsley in the olive oil in an ovenproof pan or casserole. Season the fish with salt and pepper, toss in flour, and sauté on both sides. Pour on the white wine, and bake for about 20 minutes. Then remove the fish and keep hot. Reduce the cooking liquid, strain it, and pour over the fish. Serve immediately.

MISTO DI PESCE CON SALSA D'AGLIO
Fried fish in garlic sauce

4 SMALL, GUTTED PLAICE
4 SMALL, GUTTED RED MULLET
4 PORTIONS MONKFISH OR OTHER MARINE FISH, AS AVAILABLE
SALT
ALL-PURPOSE FLOUR
OLIVE OIL
LEMON WEDGES

For the sauce:
2 CLOVES OF GARLIC
I BUNCH OF PARSLEY
6 TBSP OLIVE OIL
JUICE OF I LEMON
SALT

Wash the fish and pat dry. Rub the inside of the plaice and red mullet, and the outside of the monkfish, with salt, and coat them lightly in flour.
Crush the garlic and mix it with the parsley, the 6 tablespoons of olive oil for the sauce, and the lemon juice. Season with salt, and add more olive oil if necessary.
Heat olive oil in a skillet and sauté the fish for about three minutes on each side. Arrange on a plate to serve, garnished with lemon wedges and accompanied by the sauce.

WINEGROWING IN THE BORDERLANDS

There is always a fascination about wine grown in border regions that have seen the passage of many peoples. This region in the far northeast of Italy is no exception. From the earliest times, viticulture in this area has been influenced by Romans, Celts, Furlani, and Illyrians. This tract of country saw successive kingdoms come and go – Gothic, Lombard, Carolingian and Frankish rulers were followed by centuries of tension between the Habsburg Empire and Venice. Signs of Habsburg influence can mainly be found in the modern province of Gorizia; the social, political, and cultural sway of Venice has left its mark on Grave and Colli Orientali, areas where the production of red wines predominates. In modern times, vineyards in Collio, a region of hills, are owned and worked by winegrowers from Friuli and from Slovenia, with large estates on both sides of the border.

Single-variety white wines of the highest quality are produced in Collio from Chardonnay, Sauvignon, and Ribolla grapes.

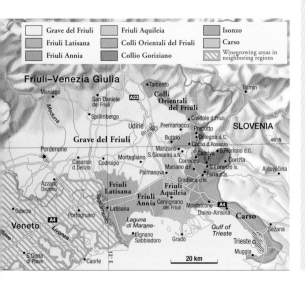

Friuli-Venezia Giulia

Grave del Friuli	Friuli Aquileia	Isonzo
Friuli Latisana	Colli Orientali del Friuli	Carso
Friuli Annia	Collio Goriziano	Winegrowing areas in neighboring regions

WHAT DOES THE LABEL TELL US?

1 Producer country

2 DOC classification (or other classification: DOCG, IgT, or VdT = Vino da Tavola)

3 Producer or estate

4 Address of producer or bottling address (second applies if the wine is not made and bottled by the winegrower)

5 Grape variety (only applies to DOC wines, where the variety is specified)

6 Year

7 Classification

8 Alcohol content as alcohol by volume

9 Capacity of contents (e = EU standard bottle)

10 Producer bottled (wine made and bottled by the winegrower)

Colli Orientali
Although "Colli Orientali" means "Eastern Hills" this is not the easternmost winegrowing area of Friuli; Collio and Carso lie farther to the east. It surrounds the regional capital, Udine, in a crescent, and the area occupies the northwestern part of the range of hills to which Collio too belongs. The gentle hills in the central part of the area offer the right climatic conditions for fine, elegant white wines. The southern part, facing the Adriatic, is suitable for creating great, powerful, red wines. Some of these are among the best products of Italian winemaking today. The regions Romandolo (for sweet wines), Cialla and Rosazzo which were once part of the Colli Orientale, have been classified since 2001 as independent DOCG wine – producing areas.

Collio
Collio is the most famous winegrowing area in Friuli. The name means "hill." It does not lie entirely in Italy, since over half the area belongs to Slovenia. There, the area is called Brda; historically, it is a relic of the Austro-Hungarian Empire, which formerly ruled the entire region. Many Collio winegrowers also own vineyards on the Slovenian side,

but they are allowed to market their wines with an Italian label, thanks to a legal exception made under EU regulations.
White wines are the great specialty of Collio: varietal wines made from Chardonnay, Sauvignon, and Ribolla grape varieties, and blended wines using several types. The hills of central Collio are among the few really excellent white wine producing areas in Italy. The southern slopes around Capriva and Cormóns also produce outstanding red wines, particularly those based on Merlot.

Isonzo, Carso, and the river plains of Friuli
The remaining areas of Friuli have to struggle to establish a reputation for themselves in competition with the top wine-

growing areas of Collio and Colli Orientali. Nevertheless, they include the Grave region, which accounts for most of Friuli's wine production in terms of quantity. The Isonzo region in the south of Collio offers the delightful surprise of some outstanding Chardonnay and Sauvignon Blanc. And to the north of Trieste, in the limestone karst area of Carso, minute amounts of highly individual wines of marked character are being made from the local varieties Terrano and Vitovska.
Latisana, Aquileia, Annia, and Lison-Pramaggiore are generally known for clean-tasting, respectable mass-production wines.

The winegrowing potential of this territory between the Alps and the Adriatic has only recently been developed, unlike other Italian regions. It offers travelers a beauty of landscape as yet unspoiled by mass tourism, and enjoys a climate with abundant sunshine, adequate rainfall, and a wide range of soil types, ideal for viticulture. It allows the cultivation of a number of grape varieties, both native and imported. The region initially established its reputation for its white varieties, especially Pinot Grigio, Chardonnay, and Sauvignon Blanc. Until a few decades ago, the vineyards here were mainly stocked with red varieties, but the market for the great, well-known red wines was dominated by Tuscany and Piedmont. The market for white wines, on the other hand, was growing exponentially, and the only internationally significant Italian wines in this category were from the Alto Adige.

Recent years have seen a return to red wines in all markets, and many winegrowers in Friuli have consequently begun to concentrate again on the red varieties. The region had a good foundation from which to begin. French varieties such as Cabernet Sauvignon and Merlot had been planted immediately after the great phylloxera disaster of the 19th century. Merlot has been the most widely grown variety in Friuli ever since the beginning of the 20th century, and excellent results have been achieved through the careful work done in both cultivation and winemaking. The finest growths of these two varieties correspond to what wine-drinkers have been looking for in the 1990s: they combine the structure and finesse of the great European wines with the juiciness and fruit of those from California and Australia.

Another great benefit of this region is the existence of many native varieties, still to be found here and there, having survived the years of mass wine production in some forgotten corner of an unworked vineyard. In the 1980s, a small group of winegrowers began to devote more attention to the Schioppettino, Refosco, Pignolo and Tazzelenghe vines they had. From these grapes, they made some powerful and highly individual red wines of great character.

There is also increasing use of native white varieties, especially Ribolla Gialla in the Collio region on the Slovenian border. This produces fine, fresh wines with good acidity, either as a single-variety wine or as part of a blend. Sweet wines produced from the Picolit and Verduzzo varieties are a specialty of the region. On the whole, the ones made from Verduzzo grapes, especially those from Ramandolo, are of much better quality.

Left: Collio produces excellent white wines, both varietal and blended types. In addition, the region has for some years been producing some respectable reds, some from French grape varieties such as Merlot, and others from local ones like Refosco.

SWEET DELIGHTS

The rule that a dessert wine is the right accompaniment to a sweet dessert dish applies in Friuli just as surely as elsewhere. A meal here might culminate in a slice of the traditional Friulian sweet yeast bread, *pinza*, or with *presniz* – made of pastry whorls generously filled with walnuts, hazelnuts, almonds, pine nuts, and raisins soaked in rum.

ITALIAN DESSERT WINES

Italy has a whole range of different types of dessert wine, though their reputation lags behind that of their French, German, and Austrian equivalents. Wine from selected, ripe grapes, and wine made from frosted ones, were known as long ago as Imperial Roman times. It was also common to sweeten dry ones, perhaps by adding honey. Even famous dry wines like Frascati, Orvieto, and Soave were produced in the sweet style, *abboccato*, for centuries.

Four main classes of sweet wine types are known in Italy today. Recioto, a type of *vin de paille* or "straw wine" is mainly produced in the Veneto. The grapes are left to dry out on wooden trestles for a few weeks after harvesting, before being pressed in the normal way. The wines have an intense sweetness, yet are light and fruity in flavor, ideal to accompany a light sweet course. Vin Santo is a very different wine. It comes mostly from Tuscany, though also from the Trentino region. For this, the grapes are air-dried, and the wines stored for a long period in small, hermetically sealed wooden casks in a warm loft. This gives the wines an oxidized character sometimes reminiscent of sherry.

The most popular Italian sweet wine is certainly the sparkling Moscato d'Asti, along with Asti and Asti Spumante. The natural sweetness of the grapes is preserved by interrupting the fermentation process in the tank. This is done either by cooling the wine or by filtration. A good Moscato d'Asti is excellent with fruit salad or very light desserts, such as sorbets or fruit tarts. In Sicily, sweet wines are generally made from overripe grapes of the Moscato or Malvasia varieties. These have sufficient depth to drink with more substantial, creamy desserts, such as chocolate torte or cheese cakes. Wines from late-harvested grapes and selected ripe grapes (Spätlese and Auslese) in the tradition of the German-speaking countries are found in the Alto Adige region. The grape varieties used are also German.

The conditions of the Italian climate are not usually suited to noble rot, as for the grapes used in making French Sauternes and the Beerenauslese type of German and Austrian wine. A few winemakers are therefore using special chambers in which they recreate the climatic conditions, so that the harvested grapes can continue ripening under the appropriate high levels of humidity.

PINZA
Sweet yeast bread

GENEROUS 2 LB/I KG ALL-PURPOSE FLOUR
2 1/2OZ/70 G FRESH YEAST (IF USING ACTIVE DRY YEAST, FOLLOW MAKER'S INSTRUCTIONS)
I CUP/250 ML MILK
I 1/3 CUPS SUGAR (PREFERABLY SUPERFINE)
3 1/2 OZ/100 G BUTTER
6 EGGS
SALT
RUM
I VANILLA BEAN

Mix together a generous ½ lb/250 g of the flour with the yeast and lukewarm milk to a batter. Leave to rise for 1 hour, then add another ½ lb flour, ½ cup/100 g sugar, 3 tablespoons/40 g melted butter, and 2 eggs. Mix carefully and leave for 2 hours. Preheat the oven to 400 °F/200 °C. Add and knead in the remaining flour, butter, sugar, 3 eggs plus 1 egg yolk, a pinch of salt, a dash of rum, and the pulp from the center of the vanilla bean. Leave to rise, then knead again and shape into a loaf. Place on a baking tray and bake for 30 minutes at 400 °F/200 °C. Reduce the oven temperature to 350 °F/180 °C and continue baking for about another 10 minutes until the crust has browned.

PRESNIZ
Pastry whorl dessert
(Illustration left)

For the pastry:
GENEROUS 2 CUPS/250 G ALL-PURPOSE FLOUR
I CUP/250 G BUTTER
5–6 TBSP MILK
JUICE OF I LEMON
I EGG
SALT

For the filling:
WALNUTS
HAZELNUTS
CHOPPED ALMONDS
PINE NUTS
RAISINS SOAKED IN RUM
CANDIED FRUITS

FLOUR FOR WORK SURFACE
BUTTER FOR GREASING PANS
I EGG, BEATEN
CONFECTIONERS' SUGAR

Rub the butter into half the flour, and leave to stand overnight. Mix the remaining flour, milk, lemon juice, egg, and salt in a second bowl. Leave to stand for 1 hour. Then knead the two mixtures together, and roll out thinly into a rectangle on a floured cloth. Preheat the oven to 400 °F/200 °C.
Scatter the nuts and fruits for the filling over the pastry. Use the cloth to help roll up the pastry into a sausage shape. Then slice into rounds. Grease a baking dish with butter and lay the slices side by side to fill the dish. Brush the top with the beaten egg and bake for about 40 minutes. Sprinkle with confectioners' sugar before serving.

Tajut

The time-honored custom of *tajut* or *cajut* is one of the oldest drinking habits in Friuli. It dictates that, when two friends meet in the street, one stands the other a glass of wine. The recipient must respond by providing the second glass. In small villages in Friuli, several friends are likely to wander by and join the group, each receiving a drink and standing a round. Not surprisingly, *tajut* calls for a good deal of time – and for prior drinking practice. Fortunately for the drinkers, the wine is served in small glasses, thus averting the hangover that would otherwise have followed the sociable get-together.

Background: The custom of *tajut* is beginning to die out in Friuli. Here, Gianni is waiting for his friends outside a small *trattoria*.

GRAPPA

The origins of grappa, a clear spirit distilled from marc, lie shrouded in the past. It is made from the remains of the grapes after pressing, the Italian word *grappa* literally meaning "grape stalk". There is an early written record of this alcoholic product of the Alps and Alpine foothills, that dates from 1451. A native of Friuli by the name of Enrico made mention of a brew called *grape* in his last will and testament. The original use of grappa was to provide a sense of Mediterranean warmth in the chill climate of northern Italy.

Its career has led upward ever since, and grappa now enjoys a good reputation and a place in the European pantheon of fine food and drink. Huge differences in quality exist, as a result of rising demand, and a correspondingly wide spectrum of prices. These range from fairly cheap, industrially produced spirits made by a continual process to the more expensive products of traditional distilleries, which have greater sophistication. Here, individual batches are distilled, each of which is attended to with a craftsman's care. Single variety grappa has gained currency in recent years, though critics point out that this is only justifiable where the grape variety is a highly aromatic one such as Moscato, or muscat. Opinion also differs on whether grappa should be aged. The quality of the marc is certainly the main determinant of quality, along with the skill of the distiller. No amount of maturation in the cask can make up for poor quality grapes. Maturation does however harmonize and refine the flavors and aromas. A riserva or stravecchia is aged for at least twelve months, of which six are spent in the wooden cask. Oak casks give them their typical golden hue.

Young grappa is at its best when drunk slightly chilled, at 46–50 °F (8–10 °C) out of tall-stemmed glasses. Aged varieties are better drunk from a brandy glass at 61–64 °F (16–18 °C). Whatever its age (or even flavoring), however, grappa must always be crystal clear. Cloudiness or impurities are a sign of poor quality, as are a sooty, acrid or rotten odor.

In the Sibona grappa distillery in Piobesi d'Alba, Piedmont, the stills are used to make separate batches of spirit. The grape residue for each batch is heated by means of a waterbath.

Romano Levi's distillery in Neive, Piedmont, is of the traditional type, so the separate-batch method is used. Heating is done using the dried residue of the previous year's marc as fuel. The grappa is of the highest quality.

The furnace is burning fiercely, but excessively high temperatures will impair the marc. It is therefore heated inside a bath.

The marc is loaded into the heating vessel. Good quality marc comes from good, ripe, fresh grapes.

The distiller now seals down the lid. The furnace is stoked high, and heating of the still can begin.

The alcohol and aromatic substances rise as they vaporize, and enter the condensing coil, where the distillate liquesces.

THE MANUFACTURE OF GRAPPA

The process by which grappa is made begins with marc, the skins of the grapes that have been pressed. For the production of good grappa, the marc should still be as fresh and moist as possible. Mold and acidifying bacteria have not yet had a chance to multiply if the marc is fresh. The marc from red grapes will already have been fermented as part of the red wine production process, so it is ready for distillation. In white wine production, there is less skin contact, and the must is separated off before fermentation of the wine. The skins have still to be fermented before the marc can be distilled.

Care must be taken when heating the marc, or it will thicken and burn onto the bottom of the still. This has an adverse effect on flavor. There are two methods of preventing this: the first is to place the still inside a second container filled with water, so that the marc is heated in a *bagnomaria* or waterbath; the second is to heat it by means of steam. Both ensure that no direct heat reaches the marc, and that the temperature remains below 212 °F (100 °C).

Each of the various individual substances contained in the marc boils at its own particular temperature. Methyl alcohol, along with certain other alcohols (called polyhydric alcohols), is the first to evaporate from the bubbling mixture being distilled. Together these make up the *testa* or "head" of the distillate, which is an evil-smelling, poisonous mixture. Frustratingly for the distiller, the very next stage contains the alcohol that is wanted, as well as all the precious aromas that give the grappa its character. This demands considerable experience on the part of the distiller, who needs to have a good "nose" so as to separate off the *testa*, but capture the "heart" of the grappa, (*il cuore* as it is called in Italian). Only by acting at exactly the right moment can this be done, and the spirit collected free of impurities.

The distillation process is followed through observation portholes.

In the large grappa distillation plants, the process runs continuously, but the small, traditional distillers prepare each batch individually. The stills are emptied completely after each process, and refilled with fresh marc. The used marc is pressed and laid out to dry, to be used as fuel the following year. The ashes of the burnt marc are used in their turn, to fertilize the vines. It is hard to imagine a more efficient re-use of waste. A spirit that has been distilled with so much care needs to be truly appreciated and carefully handled. The connoisseur should store grappa in a cool, dry place. It is best to finish a bottle fairly quickly once opened; the delicate, volatile bouquet will not last beyond about three months.

Left: Grappa has made a remarkable transition from a spirit drunk by peasants to the height of fashion. The delightful bottles no doubt contributed to its success.

27

Grappa is traditionally drunk young and crystal clear. The variety chosen is a matter of taste.

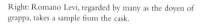

Right: Romano Levi, regarded by many as the doyen of grappa, takes a sample from the cask.

Italian bars usually serve grappa in small, heavy-bottomed glasses, but a whole variety of specialized shapes can be found for the enjoyment of this drink.

TYPES OF GRAPPA

Interest in grappa was muted until recently. Especially in the more exalted gastronomic circles, it was thought of as merely a peasant drink. Its popularity has now risen to levels that would have been impossible without gifted distillers like Romano Levi, Luigi Orazio Nonino, Bruno Pilzer, Gioachino Nannoni, and certain others. Distillers of grappa used to travel from one vineyard to the next, distilling on the spot to provide the winegrowers with a potent drink to keep out the cold; now, modern distilleries are specializing. They are producing fine quality grappa, often from single grape varieties – Moscato or Traminer – capable of satisfying the highest expectations.

Distillation of grappa is not limited to Piedmont and Friuli: marc is widely available, since winemaking is carried on in most regions of the country. The most important areas of grappa production are Lombardy, Val d'Aosta, the Veneto, Trentino, and Alto Adige. Any grappa simply described as "Italian" is probably a blend of spirit from several regions. In Friuli, grappa made using marc from the sweet, low-yield grape variety Picolit is a specialty.

A TRADITIONAL DISTILLERY

Romano Levi is one of the best-known grappa distillers in Italy; certainly the one most pictured. His tiny distillery is located in Neive, Piedmont. It has the quaintness and reverence of age. He learned the craft from his father, eventually took over the distillery himself, and has altered nothing in the centuries-old production process. Watching him at work, it is clear to see that he would never dream of changing his methods – and their success proves him right. His output is only a couple of thousand bottles a year, but his products are known and appreciated far beyond Piedmont or even Italy. A number of customers travel far to buy from him. His grappa may not necessarily have the clarity of others, as is well known. Nor does he take that great an interest in flavor; this he happily admits himself. But there is great attraction in the personal attention he devotes to the bottles, lovingly created by him and adorned, once filled, with handwritten labels. They are a collector's item.

VENICE AND
THE VENETO

VENEZIA
VENETO

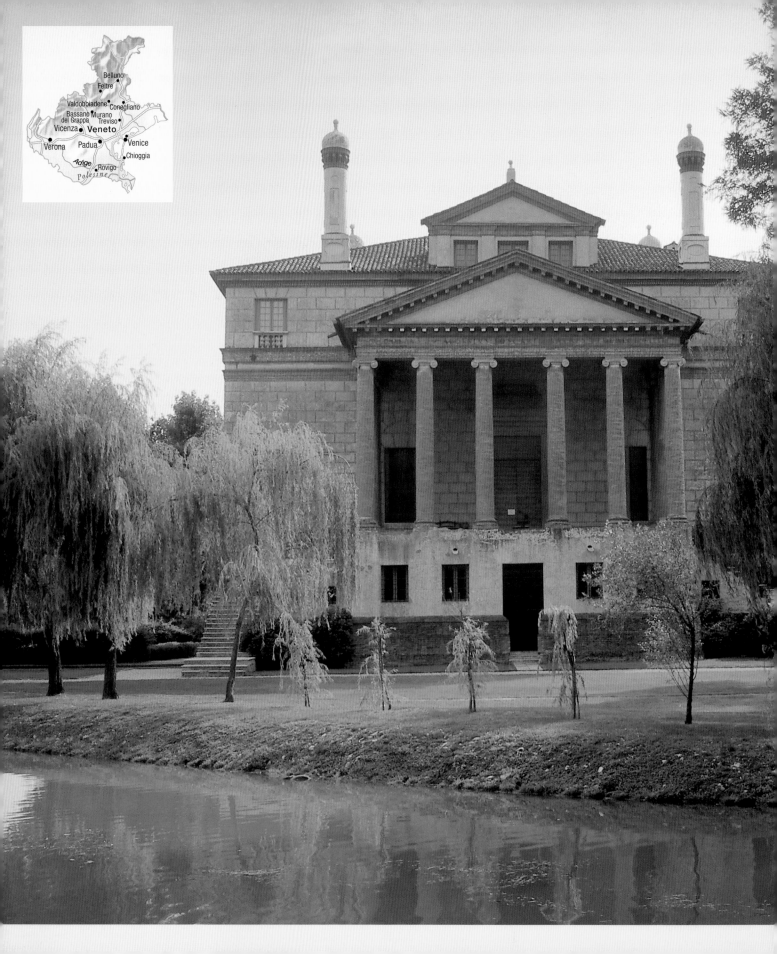

The city of Venice and the Veneto region, whatever the political links between them, are strikingly different in atmosphere and association. The city itself, truly the *grande dame* of the Adriatic, graces many a photograph album. Its romance never ceases to fascinate; the Veneto, in contrast, calmly boasts the finest of Palladian villas. These were mainly built as summer residences for the rich Venetian aristocracy eager to escape the heat and stench of the city's canals and alleyways. The healthy climate on the banks of the river Brenta provided an ideal retreat in the hottest months. The region is more than a backdrop for Venice, the former trading and seagoing power. In the territory from Padua to Verona – city of the once-powerful and dreaded Sforza family – and on to the eastern shores of Lake Garda, another Italy is revealed, with a character all its own. Venice, the *Serenissima*, seems part of a different world.

The cuisine of Venice likewise differs from that of the Veneto. Risotto is common to both, but the added ingredients on the coast are fish and seafood; away from the Adria, we find pumpkin, asparagus, radicchio, and frogs' legs being used. Beans and legumes feature in both areas; the traditional dish of *pasta e fagioli* combines pasta with beans. It is served lukewarm, usually with a dash of olive oil. *Risi e bisi*, a dish of rice with tender, young peas, has gained a place on menus both within and beyond the region.

Otherwise, the Veneto tends to favor heavier dishes, while some of the food served in Venice reflects the former glories of the *Serenissima*. Exquisite menus are created, with the use of exotic spices and fine sauces. Yet simple and traditional foods like stockfish or the dish of marinated anchovies or sardines called *sarde in saor* are not forgotten. In the Veneto, less fish is eaten. Meat and sausage are preferred, such as *sopressata*, a coarse-textured, pressed meat sausage, and garlic salami. The region is also one of the main producers of fine vegetables. Red radicchio from Treviso is one such specialty; asparagus from Bassano del Grappa is another.

Previous double page: Harry's Bar is one of the icons of Venetian gastronomy.

Left: The villas built by the architect Palladio (1508–1580) are world famous. Shown here is the Villa Foscari (built around 1560), also known as the Villa Malcontenta.

HARRY'S BAR

The history of the legendary Harry's Bar goes back to 1930, to the counter of another bar entirely: that of the eminent Hotel Europa-Britannia. There, Giuseppe Cipriani was mixing cocktails for a handful of guests able to defy the Great Depression. There were three Americans among them: a somewhat reserved young student, Harry Pickering, his aunt, and her lover. The trio made a few excursions now and again into St. Mark's Square, but otherwise saw little of the city, preferring to spend their time in the bar of the hotel. Their day began around 11 in the morning, when they ordered aperitifs before eating lunch on the terrace. They returned to the bar for drinks in the afternoon, and once more in the evening. Some two months later, an argument took place, and the aunt left, together with her young lover. Harry remained behind with a mountain of unpaid bar bills.

Harry's visits to the bar became fewer and fewer. On one of his rare appearances, Giuseppe Cipriani tried to discover the reason for this change in habits. Pickering had been one of his best customers; could he be ill, or in financial straits? The problem turned out to be financial. Giuseppe took pity on the young man, and lent him his hard-earned money – the not inconsiderable sum of 10,000 lire, which he had been saving to buy a bar of his own. The checks were all paid, and Pickering disappeared across the Atlantic, apparently for good. A few months later, however, he was back, to repay the debt – and gave Cipriani an extra 30,000 lire as an expression of thanks. The amount was enough to enable them jointly to open the bar that Giuseppe had dreamt of for so long.

As a mark of gratitude to Mr. Pickering, the name "Harry's Bar" was chosen. It was Giuseppe's wife Giulietta who found the premises: it was a former shop at no. 1323, Calle Vallaresso, near the landing stage where the boats stop for S. Marco. Just 485 square feet (45 square meters) in size, it was tucked away in a cul-de-sac, away from the bustle of St. Mark's Square itself.

ROSSINI
(Illustration above right)

Serves 1

SCANT 1/4 CUP/50 ML ICE-COLD STRAWBERRY PURÉE
2/3 CUP/150 ML WELL CHILLED PROSECCO DI CONEGLIANO

Place the strawberry purée in a chilled glass. Top up with prosecco, stir quickly, and serve immediately.

TIZIANO
(Illustration below right)

Serves 1

SCANT 1/4 CUP/50 ML COLD RED GRAPE JUICE
2/3 CUP/150 ML WELL CHILLED PROSECCO DI CONEGLIANO

Put the grape juice into a chilled glass. Top up with prosecco, stir quickly, and serve immediately.

BELLINI

Serves 1

SCANT 1/4 CUP/50 ML ICE-COLD PURÉE OF UNPEELED WHITE PEACHES
2/3 CUP/150 ML WELL CHILLED PROSECCO DI CONEGLIANO

Place the purée in a chilled glass. Top up with prosecco, stir quickly, and serve immediately.

Giuseppe Sereno, barman at Harry's Bar, mixes a Bellini, a drink made of white peach purée and well chilled Prosecco di Conegliano.

Carpaccio di Cipriani

Beef carpaccio, Cipriani style
(Illustration in background)

1/4 cup/60 ml freshly made mayonnaise
2–3 tbsp single cream
1 tsp mild mustard
1 tsp Worcester sauce
Tabasco; salt
10 oz/300 g fillet steak
Rocket salad (arugula) to garnish

Mix the freshly made mayonnaise, cream, mustard, and Worcester sauce until blended and creamy. Season with Tabasco and salt, and leave to rest for 15 minutes for the flavors to mingle.
Place the fillet steak in the freezer just long enough to become lightly frozen. Then cut the meat into wafer-thin slices and arrange on 4 individual plates or one large one. Pour over the mayonnaise sauce and garnish with rocket.

This made it ideal to attract a regular clientele, rather than passing custom. The choice proved a perfect one. Harry's Bar was an instant triumph as fashionable customers streamed in. It continued to be a favorite haunt of the contemporary jet set as time went on, for Harry's Bar has lost none of its appeal to the beautiful, rich, and famous. The list of such names is endless, including Ernest Hemingway, Somerset Maugham, the Rothschilds, Arturo Toscanini, Orson Welles, Aristotle Onassis, Maria Callas, Truman Capote, Peggy Guggenheim, Charlie Chaplin, Barbara Hutton, and even royalty, such as King Alfonso XIII of Spain, Queen Wilhelmina of the Netherlands, King Paul of Greece, Princess Diana and Prince Charles.

From the outset it was not only the drinks that exerted such attraction; delicious food accompanied them. Among the drinks dispensed by Giuseppe at the bar were simple but inspired creations such as Bellini and Tiziano. His most famous invention is probably a culinary one. One of the regular customers at Harry's Bar

during the 1950s was Amalia Nani Mocenigo, a lady from the highest ranks of the Venetian nobility. Her doctor had prescribed for her a diet rich in raw meat to counter slight anemia, and Giuseppe now created a unique dish of quite elegant simplicity. An exhibition of the works of the Renaissance Venetian artist Vittore Carpaccio, a painter famous for his brilliant reds, was taking place in the city at that time, and it was decided to name the dish after him. It consists of wafer-thin slices of raw fillet steak in a sauce of mayonnaise, lemon juice, Worcester sauce, cream, salt, and white pepper. Today this dish can be found on almost every Italian menu at home and abroad – albeit with variations. The original may still best be enjoyed at 1323 Calle Vallaresso.

Giuseppe Cipriani died in 1980, and the management of the bar passed to his son, Arrigo. The bar in fact bears his name, and always has done – Arrigo is the Italian equivalent of Harry. A lawyer, he had worked in the bar in his youth as often as he could, at the request

of his father. He took loving care of the small establishment, changing nothing. The one concession to modernity is a computerized cash desk. For maintaining its character he has earned the gratitude of his customers, and Harry's Bar seems proof against the tyranny of changing times and fashions.

THE OSTERIA DA FIORE

In the dark recesses of Calle del Scaleter, in the Sestiere San Polo area of the city, lies an outwardly unremarkable small establishment, a former wine shop that is now Maurizio Martin's restaurant, the Osteria da Fiore. This tiny, tucked-away gem is well worth the search. The restaurant seats just 40 people, and its decor, in the traditional style, is both pretty and unassuming. Above all, there is no better place to taste traditional Venetian fish dishes.

Mara Martin, who heads the kitchen, uses only freshly caught fish from the lagoon, such as gilt head bream, sea bass, and turbot, as well as seafood, including squid, octopus, and local varieties of mussel. Any lingering doubts over dried cod – the centuries-old staple of stockfish – are dispelled here by a delicious pureed dried cod dish that taunts the taste buds. Another of Mara Martin's specialties is *risotto nero*, in which the rice is colored by the ink from the octopus. The Osteria da Fiore is equally happy to entertain guests who simply want a glass of wine and a selection of tempting morsels.

Risotto nero
Octopus risotto with ink
(Illustration below left)

Serves 4–6

Generous 1 1/2 lbs/750 g octopus with ink sacs
2 cloves of garlic
7 tbsp olive oil
Juice of 1 lemon
1 onion
1 cup/250 ml dry white wine
2 cups/750 ml fish stock (homemade or bought)
1 1/2 cups/250 g vialone rice
Salt and freshly ground black pepper
1 bunch of flat leaf parsley, chopped

Clean the octopus and place the intact ink sacs carefully in a bowl. Slice the octopus body and tentacles finely.

Chop the garlic finely and mix with the olive oil and lemon juice. Pour the mixture over the octopus and marinate for 20 minutes. Heat the fish stock and keep hot.

Chop the onion finely and sauté lightly in 4 tablespoons of olive oil in a saucepan. Drain the octopus, reserving the marinade. Add the octopus to the saucepan, stirring to seal on all sides. Then add the marinade and the white wine.

Open the ink sacs and carefully pour the ink into the saucepan. Simmer for 20 minutes, adding some of the hot fish stock from time to time. Add the rice and cook until it is tender and has absorbed the liquid. Stir it constantly, gradually adding the remaining fish stock. Season with salt and pepper, and garnish with chopped parsley.

Risotto nero –
Octopus risotto with ink

Baccalà alla vicentina –
Dried cod Vicenza style

Baccalà mantecato
Puree of dried cod
(Illustration above)

1 DRIED COD, SOAKED
EXTRA VIRGIN OLIVE OIL (1/4 THE WEIGHT OF THE PIECE OF COD)
SALT AND PEPPER
NUTMEG
3 CLOVES OF GARLIC
1 SMALL BUNCH OF PARSLEY

Wash the cod and boil for 20 minutes. Drain it and remove any bones. Then cut into pieces. Using a blender, mix with the olive oil and a seasoning of salt, pepper, and grated nutmeg until creamy. Chop the garlic and parsley and stir into the fish puree. Serve either cold or lukewarm, with hot polenta.
Stockfish (dried cod) is dried in the sun. Unless bought ready-soaked, it must be prepared before use. It needs to be beaten with a meat mallet and soaked for 2–3 days in enough water to cover it, changing the water daily.

Baccalà alla vicentina
Dried cod Vicenza style
(Illustration left)

GENEROUS 2 LBS/1 KG SOAKED DRIED COD
6–7 TBSP EXTRA VIRGIN OLIVE OIL
3 CLOVES OF CHOPPED GARLIC
2 TBSP CHOPPED PARSLEY
SALT AND PEPPER
1 ONION, FINELY CHOPPED
4 CUPS/1 L MILK
NUTMEG
3 SARDINES
GRATED PARMESAN

Wash the dried cod and pat dry. Cut into pieces Place half the olive oil, the garlic, and 1 tablespoon of parsley in an oven-proof casserole. Then add the fish and seal on all sides. Season lightly with salt and pepper, and add the finely chopped onion. Remove from the heat and take out the garlic.
Warm the milk slightly and pour over the fish to cover completely. Grate in a little nutmeg, and simmer for about 2 hours until the milk is nearly all absorbed.
Meanwhile, preheat the oven to 430 °F (220°C). Heat the remaining olive oil in a small saucepan and soften the sardines in it, removing any bones. Pour over the cod. Sprinkle with the remaining parsley and grated Parmesan. Bake in the open casserole for about 10 minutes. Cut out crescent-shaped pieces of polenta and bake these to serve with the fish.

VENICE AND THE AUSTRIANS

Venice, the *Serenissima Dominante*, once ruled lands extending from Istria to Byzantium and from Dalmatia to the Levant. Many times in its history it has been "in peril" – yet it has always survived with a legendary tenacity. The decline of this proud, aristocratic republic may be traced to the invasion of Napoleon on 12 March 1797. Even then, it had an air of decay. The last Doge, Ludovico Manin, abdicated. Soon after, Venice was handed over by Napoleon to the Austrians. The French returned in 1806, and carried off everything they could carry. The Congress of Vienna once more assigned Venice to the Austrians, who continued to hold it for 50 years. During this time, they imported the pigeons, and transformed the former monarch of the seas into a sleepy, provincial town. In 1866, Venice fell to the newly created kingdom of Italy. The Venetians are not by nature rebellious – they are said to tread warily in political matters – but a citizens' revolution against the Austrians was attempted. On 22 March 1848, Daniele Manin (coincidentally a namesake of the last Doge) climbed onto a table in front of the Caffè Florian on St. Mark's Square and proclaimed the republic. His attempt ended in failure, but illustrates the fact that Venice's cafés and hotels do serve as places of assembly where resistance may grow. Venetians can spend days at a time sitting in cafés – some even used to have their post directed there. The city was bombarded by the Austrian General Radetzky to bring it into submission.

During that bombardment, the populace had to abandon its outer sectors, and seek refuge elsewhere. The more affluent of them chose the elegant Hotel Danieli. The opponents of Austria-Hungary made the Caffè Florian their meeting-place, duly coming under observation there by the Austrian Imperial and Royal secret police.

Fegato di vitello alla veneziana
Calf liver Venetian style
(Illustration above)

1 LB/500 G ONIONS
5 TSP/25 G BUTTER
3–4 TBSP OF OLIVE OIL
1 TBSP CHOPPED PARSLEY
2 BAY LEAVES
1 LB/500 G CALF LIVERS
4 TBSP MEAT STOCK
SALT AND FRESHLY GROUND BLACK PEPPER

Peel and slice the onions into rings. Melt the butter in a skillet with the olive oil. Peel the onions and cut them into fine rings. Add the onions, bay leaves and parsley. Cover and cook gently for about 10 minutes. Cut the calf liver into 4 slices. Add to the onions, raise the heat, and add a little meat stock. Cook not too fiercely for 5 minutes. Remove from the heat, season with salt and freshly ground pepper, and serve with slices of polenta.

PANINI

Salmone
Small *tartine* usually in the form of an open, filled bread roll. Generously buttered, the salmon complemented by a squeeze of lemon juice.

Arrostino e zucchini
Roast meat with either sliced zucchini and thyme, or julienne strips of zucchini to add a crisp, fresh note.

Primavera
The Italian version of the sandwich, the *tramezzino* is made from sliced white bread, usually untoasted. Here, the filling is ham with lettuce salad.

Gorgonzola e tartufo
The wonderful flavor of truffles contrasts with the strong taste of Gorgonzola cheese. Another combination is Gorgonzola with chestnut honey.

Insalata di gamberetti
This *tramezzino* has a shrimp and lettuce filling, often with mayonnaise. It is served cold.

Salmone e insalata
Crisp lettuce, usually frisée, and smoked salmon are used together to create a light, elegant note.

Tonno e carciofini
A real classic among *tramezzini*, with a filling of tuna and hearts of artichoke. Succulent and flavorsome.

Carciofini e Würstel
Italian-style small sausages with a German name in a very Italian combination.

Spinaci e mozzarella
Fresh Mozarella cheese with cooked spinach, seasoned with a little lemon juice and pepper, makes for a light, very digestible snack.

Piadina caprese
Piadina is a type of flat bread from Romagna. Here, it is filled with tomatoes and mozarella cheese.

Carciofini e salame
This small baguette has a piquant filling of strong salami and artichokes.

Prosciutto e formaggio
This type of *panino* is best eaten hot. The cheese then melts, so that its flavor mingles with that of the ham

Mozzarella e acciughe
This combination dates back to ancient Rome. The piquancy of the anchovies is tempered by the mellow cheese.

Parmigiana di melanzane
A southern Italian specialty fit for a king. Fried eggplant is baked with a melting cheese and tomatoes.

Croissant al prosciutto e formaggio
This combination with ham and cheese demands a hot, buttery tasting croissant. *Mignon croissants* are the type usually used.

Fiore di zucca
This recipe calls for zucchini flowers, stuffed with mozzarella cheese and an anchovy. They are then fried in light batter.

Speck e brie
Speck is the name given to a delicious smoked ham from the Trentino region.

Piadina mozzarella e funghi
Piadina, with toasted cheese and mushrooms, makes a delicious, quick snack.

Pomodorini
This combination of buffalo-milk mozzarella and tomatoes is called *Caprese* in Italy. Capri is the place where it tastes best.

Bresaola, racletta e rucola
Wafer-thin *bresaola* air-dried beef is served with fresh cheese, rocket salad (arugula), and a dash of lemon juice.

Mozzarella e prosciutto
A cheese and ham combination. If you wish to make a more nourishing tramezzino, wholemeal bread (*pane integrale*) can be used.

Mozzarella e pomodoro
Completely fresh mozzarella is the key to this combination – cheese straight from the refrigerator is simply not as good. It tastes delicious with tomatoes.

Uovo e tonno
Sliced, hard cooked eggs add just the right consistency to tuna canned in oil, and enhance the flavor.

Prosciutto cotto, formaggio e pomodori
Many Italians who go out to work eat bread rolls or *tramezzini* at midday. The fillings usually include vegetables to make the meal complete – here, ham, cheese, and tomatoes.

Italian bars, motorway eating places, and snack bars serve sandwiches and *panini, tramezzini,* or *crostini* to go with the usual *espresso*. They are often magnificent artistic and culinary creations. The fillings reflect the regional choice of ingredients in the combinations offered: local sausage, cheese, tomatoes, ham, anchovies, tuna, and shrimp.

VENETIAN MASKS

The masks that featured in the original Venetian carnival are more than just imaginative items of costume: they represent a set tradition, and several have a long history. Some are a reminder of events in the city's history; the Plague Doctor is one such. It harks back to the devastating plagues of the 16th and 17th centuries. Others, like *Pantalone* and *Arlecchino* derive from characters of the *Commedia dell'arte*. They still have an essential place in the staging of carnival folly, long after Goldoni's theater reforms.

Bauta

Bauta was one of the most popular Venetian costumes. It featured a three-cornered hat and black veil with a white face mask, and could be worn by women as well as by men.

Arlecchino

Arlecchino is Harlequin, a typical *Commedia dell'arte* figure. The character is an impudent prankster, and wears a black face mask and soft hat above a costume made up of brightly colored patches.

Moretta

Moretta is the name for an oval, black face mask worn by a woman. It was kept in place by means of a knob at the back, which the wearer held between her teeth.

Pantalone

This is another typical *Commedia dell'arte* character, an ill-tempered old man whose face expresses his avarice. The figure symbolizes a self-made rich Venetian merchant.

The Plague Doctor

This costume is a reminder of the terrible plagues that affected the city during the Middle Ages and Renaissance. The doctor carries a wooden stick like the one used in those times to push back the bedclothes without having to touch the patient. Another feature is the mask, which is beaked. The beak used to be filled with sweet-smelling herbs to counter the stench of the plague.

Commedia dell'arte, The Pantaloon and Harlequin figures of old Italian comedy: Color lithograph, from a 17th century original illustration: from a history of grotesque comedy, "Floegels Geschichte des Grotesk-Komischen" ed. Friedrich W. Ebeling, 4th edition, Leipzig 1887, Plate 3.

CARLO GOLDONI

Carlo Goldoni, the great reformer of Italian theater, was active in the middle of the 18th century. His reforms ensured that the ancient *Commedia dell'arte*, with its highly stylized characters such as *Capitano, Arlecchino,* and *Colombina,* went out of fashion. This opened the way for new characters. Goldoni himself was a true Venetian. As such, he loved good food and drink. He also loved his home city, though he left it in despair for Paris at the age of 55, following a quarrel with his theater colleagues Chiari and Gozzi. Goldoni's plays repeatedly show Venetian life. His 1756 comedy "Il campiello" (The Square), for example, contains the character of a *fritoler,* a woman who fries the delicious *fritole* sweetmeats. His "Le baruffe chiozzotte" (Quarrels at Chioggia), first performed in 1762, just before his departure for Paris, turns on a slice of fried melon. The melon proves to be a source of strife when a gondolier gives it to a young woman, one of a number of lovers. The couples are thrown into argumentative chaos by this innocent act.

Pietro Longhi (1702–1785), *Portrait of Carlo Goldoni,* 1760, Museo Correr, Venice

CARNEVALE

Despite the enormous interest excited by Venice's modern street carnival, some of the city's most devoted citizens insist on preferring the ancient customs, which are quite unlike the tourist event in St. Mark's Square. *Carnevale* in Venice used to be celebrated in great style. Vast sums were spent on costumes and on balls – with fierce competition between societies and associations as to whose would be the most glamorous, would have the most elaborate setting, or would be able to serve the most opulent meal.

For the inhabitants of this city, festivals offer a magnificent opportunity for indulgence in good food. In the past, though not today, their love of such creature comforts brought them considerable moral criticism. The ecclesiastical authorities reproached them from time to time for their eagerness to move on from the sermon or ceremony to the table on the feast days of the church. "Gluttony is the greatest sin of the Venetians," wrote the city chronicler Pietro Gasparo Morolin in 1841.

Special foods, whether unusual or traditional, were indeed the focus of the various occasions of the church year, as well as the carnival. According to the writer Tommaso Locatelli, Venice in 1830 resembled a festival ground – and this was at a time of serious economic and political difficulties in the city. "Spits were turned and fish grilled in preparation for that great communal dinner." Delicacies eaten during the carnival included *galani*, strips of sweet pastry, crisply fried and dusted in sugar, and *fritole* or *fritelle*, carnival doughnuts. Other sugary delights to sustain participants in the carnival through long nights of celebration were *zaleti* and circular *buranelli* from the island of Burano, still popular today. A specialty traditionally eaten on 21 November, the day of the *Madonna della Salute*, was – and occasionally still is – *castradina*, salted, lightly smoked and air dried lamb prepared as a stew. Fortunately, the eating of *baccalà*, an extremely popular dish, was not limited to any particular feast day. It was enjoyed all year round in various guises. Another year-round dish was the delicious *fegato alla veneziana*, liver with onions. The calendar is less strictly observed today than it was, and the tiny doughnuts for which Venice is famous, *fritole*, can now be purchased and eaten whatever the season of the year.

Left: Far from being a riotous event, the carnival in Venice has a seriousness and solemnity not found in those of other countries and cities.

Doughnuts

The cheerful hiss of doughnuts frying in deep pans of hot fat is a sound that evokes the pleasures and the magnificence of carnival in the time of the Doges. *Fritole* were made of yeast dough, of flour, yeast, sugar, and a dash of grappa or anise, with the occasional addition of raisins, golden raisins, or pine nuts. They were deep fried in fat and sold on the streets.

The makers and sellers of these delicacies, the *fritoler*, were constantly inventing new variations on their wares. Sometimes they added rice, sometimes melon flowers, sometimes salt or fish, or even the powerfully flavored *baccalà*.

Towards the end of the 18th century, the *fritoler* of Venice achieved such economic significance that they banded together in a guild, the *corporazione dei fritoler*.

The most famous Venetian doughnut maker was probably a man named Zamaria. He even appears in an early 19th century print, cooking his wares. The self-confident title of the print is, "Here is Zamaria at work."

Zaleti
Polenta flour buns
(Illustration left)

2 TBSP RAISINS
1 SMALL GLASS OF GRAPPA
1 CUP/250 ML MILK
6 1/2 TBSP/100 G BUTTER
2 CUPS/250 G POLENTA FLOUR
2 1/2 TSP BAKING POWDER
A PINCH OF SALT
2/3 CUP/120 G SUGAR
1 TBSP/30 G SUPERFINE SUGAR, FLAVORED
WITH A VANILLA BEAN

Soak the raisins in grappa. Warm the milk and melt the butter in it. Mix the flour, baking powder, salt, and sugar in a bowl. Pour in the milk and butter, and mix to a smooth dough. Add more milk if needed. Stir in the soaked raisins. Preheat the oven to 355°F (180°C).
Line a baking tray with parchment. With floured hands, take out portions of dough and shape into elongated buns about 4 inches (10 cm) long by 1 inch (2 cm) wide. Bake in the preheated oven for about 15 minutes. Sprinkle immediately with vanilla flavored sugar and leave to cool.

Deep-fried buns have always been popular in Italy. In times gone by they were often sold by traders on the street.

Fritole
Doughnuts

1/2 CUP/50 G GOLDEN RAISINS
1 2/3 CUPS/200 G ALL-PURPOSE FLOUR (PLUS A LITTLE EXTRA)
SALT
1/3 CUP/60 G SUGAR
1 EGG
1/3 OZ/10 G FRESH YEAST (IF USING ACTIVE DRIED YEAST, FOLLOW MAKER'S INSTRUCTIONS)
3/4 CUP/200 ML MILK (NOT TOO COLD)
PEANUT OIL
GENEROUS 1/4 CUP/50 G CONFECTIONERS' SUGAR FLAVORED WITH A VANILLA BEAN

Soak the golden raisins in lukewarm water, then drain and toss in a little flour to coat. Sieve the flour into a mixing bowl and add a pinch of salt, sugar, the egg, and the golden raisins. Mix the yeast with half the milk. Pour into the bowl with the other ingredients and stir in. Then knead to a smooth dough, gradually adding the remaining milk . Leave in a warm place to rise for about 1 hour.
Heat the oil (about 1 inch/2 cm deep in a deep pan). Fry the dough a small spoonful at a time until browned on both sides. Lift out with a slotted spoon and drain on paper towels. Sprinkle the doughnuts with confectioners' sugar to serve.

PANDORO

Pandoro, a Venetian specialty (illustration in background), is closely related to the *panettone* of Milan, and is mainly eaten at Christmas time. Both have a long history. *Pandoro* may go back to *nadalin*, a typical home-baked Christmas cake, or to the *pan de oro*, a type of golden bread served at the end of the meal by well-to-do patrician families. At the height of the city's splendor, the cake was finely dusted with real, powdered gold. Today it is vanilla flavored confectioners' sugar that covers the golden brown surface of the *pandoro*. A portion of this sugar is sold packed inside every box, and helps give a Christmas feel to this delicious and light-textured cake.

Most *pandoro* today is commercially made, but the factories do try to maintain the old recipes. The ingredients used are the traditional flour, sugar, eggs, butter, and brewers' yeast, and nothing else, and the characteristic shape – a flattened cone with the ribbed sides running to an eight-pointed star at the top – has been preserved over the years.

MURANO GLASS

The island of Murano lies more than a mile (2 kilometers) north of Venice. Its fame rests on its glass, and can ultimately be traced to the fear of fire. Glassware was originally produced on the main island of Venice. It was a precious commodity that brought both riches and reputation to the *Serenissima*. The furnaces needed for glassblowing represented a considerable fire risk,

Murano, a small group of islets, has a population of around 5,000. Like most destinations in Venice, it is best reached by means of the *vaporetto*.

however, especially as open furnaces were used, and so, in the 13th century, the decision was made to transfer the Venetian glassblowers entirely and almost overnight to Murano. The islanders of Murano were given special privileges to ease the transition. For example, their daughters were permitted to marry into the Venetian nobility. With these privileges came restrictions; the glassblowers were forbidden on pain of death to leave, so that they would never divulge the secrets of their trade.

Today, we tend to think of Murano glass as brightly colored and ornate, but the fame of Venetian glass production was originally based on the particularly fine glass developed and made there in the 16th century. Murano became the supplier of incomparably light and elegant crystal glassware to the courts of

Gianni Seguso's glassworks are on Murano, on the Fondamenta Serenella. Here, he and his craftsmen create fine quality glassware by the traditional methods of the glassblower's art.

The glassblower's most valuable tool is the blowing iron (background). The end of this is used to gather the required mass of glowing, semi-molten glass.

A wooden mold or matrix is bathed in water and used to create the shape. The glassblower turns the molten glass on the mold.

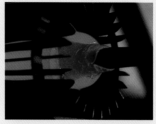

Different molds are employed to decorate and shape the glass. This one produces a ribbed effect.

The glassblower rolls the hot glass across the grid of the mold, in order to produce evenly spaced ridges.

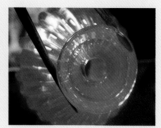

The glassblower can further refine the shape using a wet wooden rod. Here, the circular base of a vase is being formed.

Europe. Despite the precautions taken, the secret of this precious clear glass filtered out to their competitors. Bohemian glassblowers in particular possessed the skill to produce glass of a quality to rival Venice. It was time for the men of Murano to invent something new. In the 17th century, the *soffiatori di vetro*, the glassblowers, developed a novel method of production, and launched onto the market their *reticello* glassware, soon highly sought after across Europe. This style features a network or lattice effect, of which Murano is still the leading producer. The creation of this latticework glass involves decorating the inside of a bulb of plain glass with opaque white or colored threads. The bulb of glass is blown and encased in a further layer, and the glassblower intertwines the threads into an amazing network with a few deft turns of the blowing iron.

The fine reputation of Murano glass has suffered somewhat since the 19th century, partly because of low-priced competing glassware from Hong Kong and Taiwan, and partly because of the manufacture of cheap, tasteless souvenirs in Murano itself. Individual items of high quality craftsmanship do not provide the income to remain competitive, and so most of the 50 glassworks in Murano make the sort of product that appeals to popular taste, the type seen on sale on every street corner.

A few outstanding representatives of the glassblower's art have ensured by their traditional craftsmanship that Murano has regained its name for glassmaking of the highest caliber. They measure their own achievements against the finest work of the past, in the conviction that their craft had reached its best at the time of the

Renaissance. They are now trying to take up and continue these older traditions, though some of the shapes and designs they produce are extremely modern. Glass houses such as Tagliapietra, Venini, Barovier & Toso, and Salviati have been in the vanguard of this development. Their workshops and sales rooms are well worth a visit, even for the most discriminating connoisseur.

Below: Murano is as synonymous with glass as Brussels is with lace. There are still glassworks on the island that seek to preserve the old, pre-industrial standards of quality, maintaining the high reputation of Murano glass.

A demonstration of the *bigolaro* at the Volpato delicatessen in Mestre. The dough is forced through the holes that shape it into noodles.

The fresh pasta lands on a sieve and is then laid out and allowed to dry out before being cooked.

BIGOLI – HOME-MADE PASTA

Before the invention of pasta machines and factory-produced noodles, long types of pasta were made at home using a traditional kitchen implement called a *bigolaro*. This is still sometimes done today. The pasta-making part of this machine is attached to one end of a three-foot (1 meter) long stool. A tube some 4 inches (10 centimeters) in diameter dispenses the pasta. The tube has interchangeable inserts, with holes of various sizes for the different shapes and thicknesses of the noodles. The pasta dough goes into the top of the tube and the cook turns a handle to force it through. By changing the insert, the cook can make thick or thin noodles (*bigoli*), *bigoli* with a hole down the middle, and so on, and cut them to the desired length.

The pasta was laid on a mesh of canes slung between two chairbacks to dry. Families used to lend their *bigolaro* to others who did not own one, or would make their pasta at the home of someone who had a machine. The customary way of thanking the owner of the *bigolaro* for their generosity was to give them some of the pasta. *Bigoli in salsa* is a typical Venetian dish. The combination of fresh pasta with a sauce of anchovies, olive oil, and onions is delicious.

BIGOLI IN SALSA
Pasta with anchovy sauce
(Illustration below)

4 SALTED ANCHOVIES
14 OZ/400 G BIGOLI (SPAGHETTI OR TRENETTE)
SALT
4 TBSP EXTRA VIRGIN OLIVE OIL
2 ONIONS
FRESHLY GROUND PEPPER
1 BUNCH OF FLAT LEAF PARSLEY TO GARNISH

Wash the anchovies, removing any bones. Cut small. Peel the onions and slice finely. Boil the pasta in plenty of salted water until *al dente* – just firm to the bite. Meanwhile, gently heat half the olive oil in a skillet and sauté the onions until soft, without browning. Add a little water if necessary. Add the anchovies and cook gently until they disintegrate. Remove from the heat. Stir in the remaining olive oil. Transfer the pasta to plates and pour over the sauce. Season with freshly ground pepper and garnish with whole parsley.

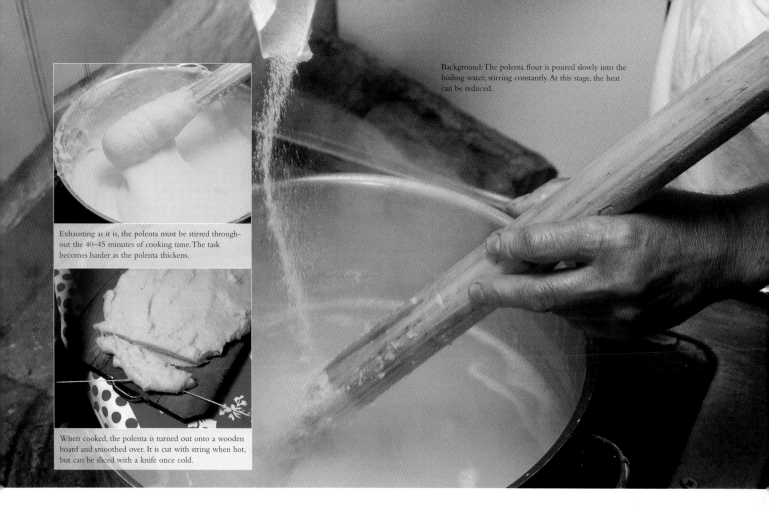

Exhausting as it is, the polenta must be stirred throughout the 40–45 minutes of cooking time. The task becomes harder as the polenta thickens.

When cooked, the polenta is turned out onto a wooden board and smoothed over. It is cut with string when hot, but can be sliced with a knife once cold.

VENETIAN POLENTA

Polenta is a simple, even modest dish, yet it occupies an important place in the cuisine of Venice and the Veneto. The variations are almost endless. It can be eaten hot or cold, broiled, grilled, or cooked in the oven, served as a first course or baked main course, and accompanied by egg, fish, meat, or cheese.

Puddings made of ground millet, barley, or even beans were already well established in Venice, the Veneto, and Friuli, before corn swept onto the scene. Polenta from corn flour is still the most popular type, and the dish is felt to express family togetherness. The appetizing sight of a hot, golden, steaming meal of polenta creates a sense of warmth and comfort on cold winter days – a sense of home.

Polenta smells and tastes most appealing when cooked in the traditional way over a charcoal fire, when it absorbs the flavor of the smoke. It has to be prepared in a deep copper pot with a rounded cauldron base and no coating of zinc. This is because of the high cooking temperature, which would melt the zinc. The pot is either suspended over the fire by a chain, or can be placed directly on the hob. The metal rings of the hob can be removed as necessary to create a hollow where the cauldron can rest.

The pot is half filled with salted water. When this has boiled, the polenta flour is stirred in, adapting the amount to the consistency wanted. For a firm polenta, this is about 3 cups (350 g) of the flour, with about 2 teaspoons of salt. For a looser consistency, slightly less polenta flour or semolina is used. The fineness of the flour also affects the result: fine flour gives a smoother texture. The flour must be dry and free of lumps, and no more than a year old.

Cooking polenta is hard work. The mixture must be stirred constantly in slow, even, circular movements, occasionally switching direction to help the flour and water to blend thoroughly – and to ease the strain on the cook, especially towards the end of cooking, when the mixture is becoming stiff. A wooden stirring stick called a *mescola* is used for this task. One way of easing the effort is to call on many cooks to help; they will certainly not spoil the broth.

It takes about 40–45 minutes for the polenta to reach its optimum consistency. The cauldron is then lifted and swung toward a waiting wooden board for the contents to be tipped out. The polenta spreads across the board, helped along by smoothing it with a wetted knife. While it is still hot, polenta can be cut with a taut piece of string. When it has cooled down, it can be cut with a knife.

Special stirring machines are available today. These are fastened to the side of the pot, and achieve very respectable results, though they can never create the sense of affinity that develops when cooks stir the polenta themselves. When an artificial stirrer is used, many people also miss the togetherness of sitting around the kitchen with the aroma of cooking polenta wafting around them and their mouths watering in anticipation of a delicious meal.

LIFE ON THE LAGOON

The conduct and pace of life in Venice and on its neighboring islands are set by the surrounding water. In summer, as tourists delight in the vision of the canals sparkling in the midday sun, locals bemoan the stagnant reek in the side canal under their bedroom window. A change of season, and the worry is the threat of flooding, called *acqua alta*, arriving long after the tourists have returned to Tokyo, Toronto, Texas, or Telford, and bringing devastation to homes and business premises.

Yet it is equally to the lagoon that many Venetians owe their living. Some 30 miles (50 kilometers) long by 9 miles (14 kilometers) wide, dotted with innumerable islands, it supports a whole armada of fishermen, and Venice has the highest per capita consumption of fish and seafood of any Italian city. Everything has to be transported by boat in Venice and the surrounding area, making boatbuilding an important branch of local industry. Many of its inhabitants make their living as masters of vessels.

Malicious tongues claim that Venice is so beset by vanity that it banishes the less agreeable aspects of human existence from its shores. Death, for example, since the dead of the city are buried on a separate, burial island, the Isola di San Michele. It is easy for the city authorities to set aside a particular area; the number of reasonably inhabitable islands of all shapes and sizes is well nigh inexhaustible. A place was found in the 15th and 16th centuries to serve as a quarantine island, the Isola Lazzaretto Nuovo. This is where ships discharged passengers and crew showing symptoms that might indicate unwelcome illness. Burano is a fishermen's island and Murano belongs to the glass-blowers. Sant'Erasmo and Vignole are the city's kitchen garden, where its vegetables are grown. A visit to the island of Torcello can take in the restaurant Locanda Cipriani on the Piazza Santa Fosca.

Various means of transport are available to take the visitor around the lagoon and its islands. *Vaporetti* are motor-launches plying fixed routes to various destinations around the city like buses. Over longer distances, there are larger boats, two decks high, the *motonave*. The ferries are called *traghetti*, and there are also water-taxis, called *motoscafi*. Finally, Venice would not be Venice without its gondolas. With these, too, there is more than one type. The tourist gondolas can be booked for sightseeing trips, complete with musical accompaniment. Other gondolas, the *gondole traghetti*, are used by locals as ferries to cross the canals. They are inexpensive, but passengers need a good sense of balance if they are not to be seasick.

The Venetian lagoon extends between the rivers Brenta, Bacchaglione, and Sile, covering an area of about 225 square miles (58,660 hectares). Half of this area is tidal, the rest is the *Laguna Morta*, the dead lagoon. It is by no means empty of life, but is a fishing area. The catch can be plentiful, and is often to be found on the tables of the city's restaurants by the following lunchtime.

Above and background: Chioggia, situated on the lagoon some 28 miles (45 kilometers) south of Venice, is the unknown little sister of Venice itself. It is a place of greater simplicity – its palaces are less magnificent than those in the city of the Doges, and its campanile less impressive – yet the old town in particular has a charm of its own.

THE FISH MARKETS

The *mercato ittico all'ingrosso di Chioggia* is the country's largest fish market. It supplies fresh fish and seafood to the whole of northern Italy. The wholesalers' market is for the trade only, but consumers do have access to the retail market, the *mercato di pesce al minuto*. Fish is sold here twice a day, between five and six in the morning and around three in the afternoon. The fishermen bring in their catch and transfer it from the harbor to the floor of the market in large tubs. What follows is a selling process that seems entirely straightforward to the initiated, but may strike the observer as quite mysterious: instead of a noisy auction, there is a whispering process. One tradesman will whisper a price to a fisherman with a catch to sell. He may be surrounded by several other would-be buyers, but they cannot hear what is being said. If the offer is satisfactory, the fisherman nods his acceptance. If it is too low, he protests out loud. That is the sign to the others to whisper their offer for the catch – until the fish is finally sold.

Above and below: The fish market in Chioggia is famous for its great variety of fish and seafood.

HOW TO TELL IF FISH IS REALLY FRESH

It is best to buy fish from a retailer you know and trust. If the fish is being sold whole, check that the eyes are clear and the gills bright red. Whether whole or filleted, the fish should have an appetizing smell of the sea. A "fishy" smell is to be avoided, as it is a sure sign that the fish is old. If you are able to, try the thumb test: quickly press the fish with your thumb. The flesh should spring back into shape almost at once. If the hollow left by the pressure remains, forget that fish and look for another retailer. Some types of fish are not sold freshly caught, so the above will not apply. Tuna and swordfish, for example, are "hung" for a while to tenderize them and develop their flavor.

The eyes should be bright and "lively," not dull.

The flesh should be firm and resilient, and not yield to pressure.

The gills should be red, and there should be no offensive smell.

Trade in fish takes place twice a day. The night's catch is sold in the morning, and the day's catch in the afternoon.

Orata, Marmora, Pagello (porgy)
The various types of porgy, gilt head bream *(orata)*, striped bream *(marmora)*, and sea bream *(pagello)* are all extremely suitable for baking.

Sardina, Sardella, Acciuga (sardine)
These tiny herring are popular all over the Mediterranean. Their flesh is oily, and tastes best freshly broiled and sprinkled with lemon juice. They are also good preserved in vinegar or oil.

Pesce San Pietro (John Dory)
Also called Peter-fish, this is quite expensive in practice, as the flesh accounts for only a third of its weight. It is best broiled, to preserve its excellent flavor.

Branzino, Spigola (sea bass)
Sea bass is probably the Italians' favorite fish. Its fine-textured but firm flesh can be prepared in many ways. A particularly delicious method is to bake it in a salt crust or wrapped in foil.

Triglia (striped mullet, goatfish)
Mullet, like salmon, is a good fish for making delicate pasta sauces. It is also good fried, broiled, boiled, or in fish soups.

Muggine (gray mullet)
The flesh of the mullet is good to eat, but it is most valued for its roe. *Bottarga di muggine* is regarded as a delicacy in Sicily and Sardinia, and is also expensive in the rest of Italy.

Anguilla, Bisato (eel)
Eels can live in salt or fresh water. The young elvers or glass eels are a traditional Christmas dish in many parts of Italy.

Salmone (salmon)
For those who know salmon mainly as prepacked, smoked fish from a supermarket shelf, fresh salmon can be a revelation. The delicate, pink flesh is delicious broiled or when served with pasta.

Palombo (shark)
Adriatic sharks are not particularly good to eat, and have tended to disappear from most of the region's menus. It can still sometimes be found in Venice, under the name *vitello di mare* (sea veal).

Rombo (turbot)
In Italy, turbot *(rombo chiodato)* and brill *(rombo liscio)*, both flat fish, are eaten. They are filleted and steamed or poached in a sauce.

Rospo, Rana pescatrice (monkfish)
The monkfish or angler fish lives on the sea floor. As food, the tail flesh *(coda di rospo)* is much in demand, and has hardly any bones. Cooked, it tastes a little like lobster.

Tempting sardines

Sarde in saor is a fishermen's dish, but it is also a delicious one for mere landlubbers. Sardines and anchovies are the fish usually used. They are tossed in flour and fried in oil until golden. They are then lifted out, and layered in an earthenware dish. A finely chopped onion is fried without browning. White wine and vinegar are added, and the whole, with the cooking juices, is poured over the fish. An ancient Byzantine and Roman way of serving them was with raisins and pine nuts, especially in winter. They are a fairly high-calorie addition, but turn the dish into a feast. *Saor* can be refrigerated. It is served in Venetian restaurants, and is an excellent appetizer, accompanied by an aperitif. It is quite a match for the fish tapas of Spain.

Sarde in saor
Marinated sardines

1 1/4 LBS/600 G FRESH SARDINES
ALL-PURPOSE FLOUR
1 1/4 LBS/600 G ONIONS
1/2 CUP/125 ML OLIVE OIL
1 GLASS OF RED OR WHITE WINE VINEGAR
SALT AND PEPPER
2 TBSP RAISINS
2 TBSP PINE NUTS

Clean and gut the sardines and cut off the heads. Wash the fish thoroughly. Pat dry and toss in flour. Heat half the olive oil in a skillet and fry the fish quickly until crisp, then drain on paper towels. Wipe the skillet clean.
Cut the onions into fine rings. Heat the remaining oil and sauté the onions until translucent. Pour on the vinegar and stir. Finally, season with salt and pepper, and add the raisins and pine nuts.
Place the sardines in a shallow dish, and pour on the marinade. Cover and transfer to the refrigerator to absorb flavors for 2 days.

SEAFOOD

Seafood – all the creatures of the deep apart from fish – is extremely popular in Italian coastal regions, and it is hardly surprising that there is such variety. A glance at the market stalls shows four main groups. First come the crustaceans, all the many types of shrimp and crayfish, as well as the crabs, then shellfish like mussels, clams, and scallops. Then there are the limpets and murex shells, and finally, squid, cuttlefish, and octopus. These delicious creatures are so different, but one thing is common to them all: the fact that they are all best eaten perfectly fresh. They then need almost no flavoring or elaborate preparation, so that the tangy freshness of the sea can be fully appreciated. Gentle cooking methods such as steaming, poaching, or light broiling are best.

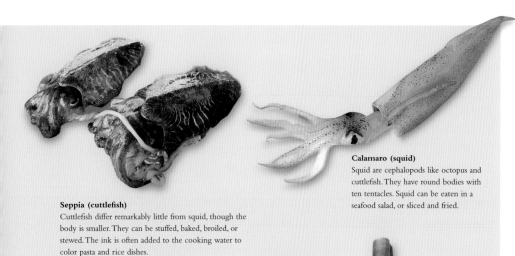

Seppia (cuttlefish)
Cuttlefish differ remarkably little from squid, though the body is smaller. They can be stuffed, baked, broiled, or stewed. The ink is often added to the cooking water to color pasta and rice dishes.

Calamaro (squid)
Squid are cephalopods like octopus and cuttlefish. They have round bodies with ten tentacles. Squid can be eaten in a seafood salad, or sliced and fried.

Lumaca di mare (red abalone)
The meat is difficult to extract from the shells, but it is firm and full of flavor.

Vongola, Arsella (hard clam, Venus clam)
There are two varieties, *vongola verace* and *vongola gialla*. Both are good with pasta or as a main course.

Cozza, Mitilo (mussel)
Mussels are served cooked, though they used to be eaten raw like oysters. *Cozze* are good boiled and taste excellent with pasta dishes.

Cannolicchio, Cappalunga (razor shell)
The two halves of the shell look like a razor, and are nearly as sharp. The shellfish can be broiled, or eaten in a seafood salad.

Dattero di mare (date shell)
A type of mussel that really does look like fresh dates. They are difficult to gather, because they secrete an acid to help embed themselves in the rock, making them very hard to dislodge. They can be eaten raw.

Capasanta, Conchiglia di San Giacomo (scallop)
Scallops are popular all over Italy, especially in seafood salads. They can also be stewed in white wine, and they make a delightful alternative stuffing for light, tender meats.

Scampo (tiger shrimp)
Shrimp, true lobsters and spiny lobsters are all closely related, so the terms tend to overlap. Freshly broiled, shrimp are a delight. Another excellent use is in fish soups.

Cannocchia (mantis shrimp)
These long shrimps can be boiled and eaten with parsley, garlic, and lemon juice. They make a fine ingredient for fish soups, and in seafood salads.

Granchio (crab)
Depending on size, crabs can be used in fish soups, stuffed, or served alone as a delicacy, seasoned with lemon juice and salt.

Grancevola (spider crab)
Spider crabs are cooked whole. The top shell is then removed and the flesh lifted out of the body cavity and claws.

CRABS

A huge variety of crabs and crustaceans lives around the
Adriatic coast of Venice and the Veneto, yet all of them
can be linked to one ancestor, the crab – *granchio* or
granzo in Italian. Crustaceans are normally protected by
their hard shell of chitin, and this does also make them
difficult to eat and to handle in the kitchen. They do
however need to shed their outgrown shells at certain
seasons of the year, and the shell becomes softened at that
time. The male casts its shell twice a year, in spring and
autumn; the female, once, in the autumn. These soft-
shelled crabs are seen as a specialty, and are prized by the
canny fishermen of Venice and Chioggia, who diligently
seek them out.
The female is called *manzaneta*. In the kitchen, it is
boiled and prepared with oil, lemon juice, salt, pepper,
parsley, and garlic. The male, *moleca* in the Venetian
dialect, is a still more delectable morsel. It is dipped in
beaten egg and fried in oil.

Right: The fishermen of Venice use creels, which are
dragged across the floor of the lagoon, to catch crustaceans and crabs.

GRANZOLE OR MOLECHE RIPIENE
Stuffed crabs

2 EGGS
SALT
1 1/4 LBS/600 G LIVE CRABS
ALL-PURPOSE FLOUR
EXTRA VIRGIN OLIVE OIL OR PEANUT OIL FOR FRYING

Begin beating the eggs together, add a pinch of salt, and
whisk. Wash the crabs in salted water, drain, and place in
a bowl with the beaten eggs. Cover with a plate and
weight it down. Leave in a cool place for at least 2 hours.
The crabs will drink in the mixture.
At the end of the 2 hours, place the crabs one by one
with the bread first in a big pot full of boiling water.
Leave them in for 1–2 minutes, drain them, break off the
legs, toss them in flour, and fry them in the hot oil.
Drain on paper towels. Serve hot and crisp.

INSALATA DI MARE
Seafood salad
(Illustration left)

2 CLOVES OF GARLIC
JUICE OF 2 LEMONS
1 1/4 LBS/600 G SEAFOOD, WASHED AND CLEANED (E.G.
SHRIMP, MUSSELS, BABY OCTOPUS, SMALL SQUID, CLAMS)
GENEROUS 1/4 CUP/90 ML OLIVE OIL
2 TBSP FINELY CHOPPED FLAT LEAF PARSLEY
SALT AND PEPPER

Pour the lemon juice over the garlic and leave to infuse for
1 hour. Then remove the garlic.
Meanwhile cook the seafood in a little water. Discard any
mussels that are open when raw, or that do not open once
they have been cooked.
Mix the lemon juice, olive oil, parsley, salt, and pepper.
Turn the seafood in the sauce until coated, and leave in a
cold place for the flavors to mingle and develop. Mix once
more before serving.

ZUPPA DI COZZE E VONGOLE
Mussel and clam soup
(Illustration right)

2 CLOVES OF GARLIC
4 TBSP EXTRA VIRGIN OLIVE OIL
GENEROUS 1 LB/500 G MUSSELS
GENEROUS 1 LB/500 G HARD CLAMS
1 GLASS DRY WHITE WINE
3 TBSP CHOPPED PARSLEY
WATER OR FISH STOCK
4 SLICES LIGHTLY TOASTED WHITE BREAD
FRESHLY GROUND PEPPER

Chop the garlic a few hours in advance if possible, and stir
it into the olive oil to flavor it. Wash and scrub the mussels
and clams, discarding any open ones.
Heat the olive oil in a deep pan. Sauté the garlic, but do not
let it discolor. Add the mussels and clams to the pan and

Zuppa di cozze e vongole – Mussel and clam soup

begin cooking. Pour on the white wine, sprinkle in the
parsley, and continue to cook all together until the mussels
and clams have all opened. Discard any that remain closed
when cooked. Pour in water or fish stock as needed.
Transfer the mussels and clams to a bowl and pass the cooking liquid through muslin or a fine sieve to remove any
vestiges of sand.
Return the mussels and clams to the cooking liquid. Place a
piece of toasted bread in each soup plate, pour on the hot
mussel soup, and season with pepper.

VEGETABLES FROM THE PO VALLEY

RADICCHIO FROM TREVISO

It would be little short of a crime to describe radicchio from Treviso and Castelfranco as just "lettuce." Here in Italy, this delicious specialty is a vegetable in its own right, not a mere garnish. It is often eaten raw, sometimes broiled, roasted, or stuffed. An annual gathering even takes place in its honor near Treviso, at which the best gastronomic experts of the area assemble and rejoice in having available to them in the kitchens the finest radicchio in all Italy. A consortium dedicated to its supervision and protection has been created, to which eight precisely defined geographical communities belong.

A number of varieties of radicchio exist. *Radicchio variegato di Castelfranco* has a full, round head with loosely packed, creamy colored leaves splashed with red to violet variegation. Only small quantities are grown, so it is little known outside the area of production. The cultivation of this Castelfranco variety, like that of other types of radicchio, is labor and cost-intensive. The plants are biennials, related to chicory and endive. Sowing takes place in April, and the plants are thinned out about six weeks later. The leaves are removed in August to encourage new growth, and the Castelfranco transplanted into boxes before the arrival of the first frosts. These are placed in a darkened greenhouse, with the result that the plants cannot make enough chlorophyll to become green, and develop their characteristic pale color. Castelfranco is in season from December to April.

Radicchio di Treviso rosso tardivo has an elongated shape and purplish-red leaves with striking, thick, white ribs. It too is sown in April and thinned out six weeks later. The plants are bound up in September to blanch them by preventing light from reaching the inner leaves. They are dug up in the autumn and placed in water-tubs. This type of radicchio also goes to market from December onward. It is first stripped of its outer leaves, and then thoroughly cleaned, leaving just the tender heart. If it is to be eaten raw, as a salad vegetable, a dressing of robust wine vinegar and good olive oil is added to bring out its slightly bitter flavor. The dainty shape of the head would grace any plate, and it is never sliced or shredded, like lesser saladstuffs. *Radicchio di Treviso,* if it is the genuine article, should be served whole.

Radicchio di Treviso rosso precoce likewise has an elongated shape. The head is more compact and the veining of the leaves more delicate. It is also crisper than other varieties. The method of cultivation is the same as for the *tardivo* variety from Treviso.

Radicchio di Treviso rosso tardivo has purplish-red, loosely packed leaves with bold, white ribs. It is available from December to April.

Radicchio variegato di Castelfranco has a fairly compact heart and looser outer leaves. The pale color and splattered, red variegation are distinctive. It is available from December to April.

Radicchio di Treviso rosso precoce is a crisp variety with a compact head of closely-packed leaves characterized by their thick, white ribs and fine, white veins.

Radicchio di Chioggia is rounded and compact with dark purple leaves. It can be grown all year round. Its other name is *Rosa di Chioggia*.

Beans from the Veneto

Beans and pasta make a delicious combination, as connoisseurs will know. *Pasta e fasoj* – the Venetian name for this well-loved dish – is a true regional classic that owes its fine reputation to the many excellent varieties of tender beans grown between Lamon, Belluno, and Feltre. One such variety is the borlotto bean, perhaps the best variety in Italy, with its red freckled skin and good flavor. The beans are quite large and are usually sold dried.

Cannellino beans come originally from Tuscany, though they are now grown all over Italy. Delicate in shape and light in color, they are much used in gastronomy. They too are mostly sold dried. The beans produced in Lamon are similarly regarded as particularly fine and flavorsome.

The Italian name *fagiolini* refers to green beans. These are picked young and steamed to serve cold as a summer salad or hot to accompany a main dish. Varieties include Contender, the smallest, Bobis, slightly larger, and Stringa, like a pole bean or runner bean, which can grow to a length of 20 inches (50 centimeters). There are also white varieties of *fagiolini*, like Burro di Roquencourt – originally developed in France – and Meraviglia di Venezia, the "Venetian Wonder," a mangetout type. Beans are some of the oldest known foodstuffs, and have never been entirely forgotten by the great chefs. Now, the humble bean has made the transition from pauper's dish to the most exclusive menus, not only in Italy. There is even a delicious bean accompaniment for beluga caviar.

Borlotti beans are much esteemed. Spattered with red when raw, they turn green on cooking. This variety is ideal for salads, soups, and sauces.

Asparagus is grown around Bassano del Grappa, situated at the end of the Valsugana valley. Although the green type is grown, the area is best known for its white asparagus. Bassano asparagus enjoys DOC recognition.

Asparagus from Bassano

Asparagus enjoys great popularity in Italy. Three types are grown: green asparagus, produced mainly in Piedmont and Emilia-Romagna, a purple variety from Campania, often called *asparago napoletano* because it comes from that region, and white asparagus, which is grown almost exclusively around Bassano del Grappa on the River Brenta, in the Veneto. There is an annual asparagus festival in Bassano, for which the restaurants produce their latest culinary creations using asparagus, and their patrons vote to decide which is the best restaurant of the day.

White asparagus has to be blanched as part of the cultivation process. Earth is banked up around the plants, or dark plastic sheeting used, to prevent light reaching the emerging asparagus tips. This prevents them from synthesizing chlorophyll, and so keeps them white. Usually, only the first crop is blanched, with increasing amounts of the rest grown as green asparagus. This has the same, typical asparagus flavor, though it is generally less intense.

Squash and pumpkins

The squash and pumpkin family is large and very varied, and much eaten in Italy. Even the well-known garden pumpkin with its orange flesh and green skin is widely enjoyed; in Venice and Chioggia, it is often served with pickled vegetables. In times past, traveling merchants plied their wares throughout Venice and the surrounding area, selling chestnuts, sweet potatoes, baked apples and pears, and slices of roasted pumpkin, *zucca barucca*. This variety has a spreading, squat shape like the turban of one of the Turkish ambassadors depicted in a painting by Vittore Carpaccio. It has a more pronounced flavor than other, more traditional members of this family of vegetables.

Asparagi in salsa

Asparagus with anchovy sauce
(Illustration below left)

GENEROUS 3 LBS/1.5 KG WHITE ASPARAGUS
SALT
4 HARD-BOILED EGGS
JUICE OF 1 LEMON
EXTRA VIRGIN OLIVE OIL
2 ANCHOVY FILLETS
1 TSP CAPERS
PEPPER

Peel the asparagus and tie in small bundles. Stand the
bundles upright in a tall saucepan of boiling salted water,
and cook for 10–20 minutes, according to thickness.
Remove and drain the asparagus, and untie the bundles to
let it cool.
Cut the boiled eggs in half and pass the yolks through a
sieve. Mix them with 2 tbsp lemon juice and enough olive
oil to create a liquid sauce. Chop the anchovies, capers, and
egg whites finely, and stir into the sauce. Season with salt
and pepper, and pour over the asparagus.

Zucca al latte

Pumpkin in milk

GENEROUS 2 LBS/1 KG YELLOW PUMPKIN
SALT
1/4 CUP/50 G SUGAR
GROUND CINNAMON
MILK

Preheat the oven to 350 °F (180 °C). Wash and peel the
pumpkin, and cut into pieces. Place in an ovenproof dish
(preferably terra cotta), season with salt, and bake.
Sprinkle the cooked pumpkin with sugar and cinnamon,
and serve on dessert plates. Pour over hot or cold milk
according to season.

Fasoj in salsa

Beans with anchovy sauce
(Illustration below right)

1 1/4 LBS/600 G FRESH BROAD BEANS OR 3/4 CUP/200 G DRIED
LIMA BEANS
1 CLOVE OF GARLIC
5 TBSP EXTRA VIRGIN OLIVE OIL
4 ANCHOVY FILLETS
1 TBSP CHOPPED PARSLEY
5–6 TBSP RED WINE VINEGAR
SALT
FRESHLY GROUND PEPPER

Shell the beans if using fresh. Cover with water, add a little
salt, and cover. Bring slowly to a boil. If using dried beans,
soak for at least 12 hours in lukewarm water before cooking. Remove from the heat when cooked, without draining.
Cut the garlic clove in half and sauté it lightly in a little
olive oil in a small saucepan. Add the anchovy fillets and
cook them until they melt. Add half the parsley, the vinegar,
salt, and a little pepper, and cook together for a few
minutes.
Drain the beans, transfer to a dish, and pour over the sauce.
Add a seasoning of pepper, cover, and leave to stand for
about 1 hour.
Sprinkle with the remaining parsley and serve lukewarm.

Risi e bisi

Rice with peas
(Illustration facing page below left)

2/3 CUP/50 G FINELY DICED BACON
2 ONIONS
8 TSP/40 G BUTTER
SCANT 1 LB/400 G FRESH, SHELLED PEAS
2 TBSP CHOPPED PARSLEY
4 CUPS/1 LITER CHICKEN STOCK
GENEROUS 1 CUP/200 G VIALONE RICE
SALT
1/2 CUP/50 G GRATED PARMESAN OR GRANA PADANO CHEESE

Dice the onions finely. Heat the stock. Melt half the butter
in another pan and sauté the diced bacon and onions without browning. Add the peas and 1 tablespoon of parsley. Add
one ladle of the stock, cover, and cook for 15 minutes. Add
the rice and a seasoning of salt. Cook gently over a low heat
for 20 minutes, little by little adding just sufficient hot stock
to keep the rice moist. Stir in the grated cheese and the
remaining butter and parsley. Leave to stand briefly before
serving.
Like risotto, this dish should be slightly moist, but not wet.
A further refinement is to boil a few pea pods in the
chicken stock and purée them, then pass them through a
sieve onto the rice.

Fasoj in salsa – Beans with anchovy sauce

Asparagi in salsa –
Asparagus with anchovy sauce

Radicchio rosso di Treviso al forno
Radicchio Treviso style
(Illustration below right, background)

1 1/4 LBS/600 G RADICCHIO ROSSO
EXTRA VIRGIN OLIVE OIL OR PEANUT OIL
SALT AND PEPPER

Wash the radicchio and cut it in half or quarters, depending on size. Pat dry with paper towels. Place it in a flameproof baking dish or iron skillet, then drizzle with olive oil, season with salt and pepper, and broil for about 5 minutes with high heat, turning frequently. The radicchio is ready when cooked through and slightly crisp. Serve hot, immediately. Peanut oil is often used in place of olive oil in traditional Venetian cuisine, because of its more subtle flavor.

Pasta e fagioli alla veneta
Pasta with beans

1 1/2 CUPS/250 G DRIED BEANS (BORLOTTI OR LIMA BEANS)
1/3 CUP/30 G DICED BACON
1 ONION
1 CARROT
1 STALK OF CELERY
2 OZ/60 G BACON RIND
4 OZ/120 G TAGLIATELLE
SALT AND FRESHLY GROUND BLACK PEPPER

Soak the beans for at least 12 hours in advance in lukewarm water.
Chop the onion, carrot, and celery, and sauté them lightly with the diced bacon, over a low heat. Remove the pan from the heat and cool a little. Dip the bacon rind briefly in hot water to melt off some of the fat. Drain the beans and add them to the pan, together with the bacon rind. Cover with water and simmer. Froth will rise during the early stages of cooking. Skim this off with a slotted spoon. When the beans are cooked, pass about one third of them through a sieve, and return to the pan.
Now add the pasta and cook until al dente. Add a little more boiling water if the bean liquid is too thick. Season with salt and pepper. Remove the pan from the heat, take out the piece of bacon rind, and cut it into fine strips. When the fat begins to collect on the surface, transfer the pasta and beans to individual soup plates or a serving dish. Season generously with black pepper.
The traditional method of making this dish in the Veneto calls for pork fat only. In Liguria and Tuscany, a dash of olive oil is added just before serving, but this is not normally done in the Veneto.

Radicchio rosso di Treviso al forno –
Radicchio Treviso style

Risi e bisi –
Rice with peas

HUNTING AND FISHING IN THE VALLE SALSA

Valle Salsa is a name given to the delta of the River Po – it means "salt valley." As the river approaches the sea, the fresh and the salt water mingle, with a gradual increase in salinity. These waters are full of fish, and cover several square miles. The inflow and outflow of the water is controlled by a complex system of locks and dykes. Some of the pools are artificial, and there has been fishing here since time immemorial. The water at this point is more fresh than salt. Here, pike, carp, sturgeon, trout, tench, and pike-perch abound. The fish have no means of escape, so are fairly easy to catch. Large nets are let down into the water, suspended on crane-like structures and extending down to the river bed. Bait is attached, and then the only thing to do is to wait. By the next morning – if not before – a net full of fish can be hauled out.

In the southern section of the delta, where the water starts to become saltier, fishermen farm mussels and clams, or marine fish such as mullet, sea bass, gilt head bream, and sole. The area also offers crabs and shrimp. Eel, which is extremely popular all over Italy, is caught in great numbers across the whole delta region. The natural fauna of this broad, flat land includes frogs and the like.

The area around the river mouth was once sea marsh. The reclaimed fields and meadows won back from this boggy terrain were famed for their fertility, but life at the end of the 19th century was not always easy for the local populace. Sickness and a variety of risks to health were inevitably linked to a marshland existence, and infections were common, including malaria. The people of this tract of country remained there, however, because a good living could be made from agriculture and fishing. The Valle Salsa provided its inhabitants with a wide range of food in their immediate, natural environment, a distinct benefit in those times.

The *potentes*, the region's landowners, did no more than to order the peasants to tend the land: the meadows were to be grazed, woodland cleared, and acorns collected. In return, they granted the people the right to grow their crops on the land and to fish the waters. Fishing was of great economic importance in this region even then, as the peasants had to pay their fishing dues – *pisces amisseros* – in kind.

Hunting, too, has been carried on here since anyone can remember. Rights had to be formally agreed, on account of the sheer quantity of game involved, but a spoken agreement was enough, and order otherwise maintained by observing tradition. The number of game birds inhabiting the river flats was and is considerable: mallard, teal, wigeon, tufted duck, snipe, coot, curlew, and water rail, and many other wetland birds,

Right: Duck are hunted along the banks and in shallow waters. The hunting dog retrieves the birds without damaging them.

The mallard *(Anas platyrhynchos)* is a widely distributed species of duck. Italian huntsmen call the bird *anatra selvatica*.

The men lie in wait for the duck inside a cover of reeds. They kill them – using small shot – in the air, not on the water.

hotly disputed between the huntsmen on the one hand and ornithologists and nature protectionists on the other. The region's cuisine is known for the unusual game among the specialties it offers. These are often flavored with the wonderful white truffle, which grows in a few places between the Brenta, the Adige, and Po rivers.

The delta today attracts much tourism. Marked foot-paths, bridle-paths, and cycle paths have been laid out, thanks to the relevant authorities, and excursions to historic sites put in place. But the visitor seeking no more than peace and quiet will be fascinated by the mysterious magic of the silence and expanse here in this flatland running down to the sea.

ANATRA ALLA VALLESANA
Wild duck with herb and anchovy sauce
(Illustration above)

Serves 6

FRESH SPRIGS OF THYME AND MARJORAM
3–4 PEPPERCORNS
1 GLASS OF WHITE WINE VINEGAR
2 WELL-HUNG, OVEN-READY WILD DUCK
CORN OIL OR PEANUT OIL
1 ONION
CHICKEN (OR OTHER POULTRY) STOCK
4 ANCHOVY FILLETS
1 GLASS OF WHITE WINE VINEGAR

Set aside some of the herbs for garnish, and chop the rest. Crush the peppercorns and mix with the vinegar, then marinate the duck in this mixture for at least 12 hours, turning frequently, to reduce the "gamey" flavor.
Drain off the marinade and joint the duck. Brown the pieces in oil.
Chop the onion and begin cooking it in a little oil and stock in a saucepan. Add the anchovies and melt them. Then add the pieces of duck, and pour on the white wine. Boil until the wine has evaporated, then cover and cook the

duck gently until done, adding hot stock little by little as required to prevent drying out.
Arrange the pieces of duck on a serving dish and pour over the cooking juices. Garnish with herbs, and serve with slices of toasted polenta.

BISATO SULL'ARA
Baked eel with bay

Serves 6–8

1 LARGE EEL (ABOUT 2 1/2 LBS/1.25 KG) OR 2 SMALLER EELS
(1 3/4 LBS/800 G EACH)
COARSE SALT
FRESHLY-PICKED, LARGE BAY LEAVES

Preheat the oven to 400 °F (200 °C). Skin and clean and gut the eel, then rub with a kitchen cloth to remove some of the shine. Cut into pieces about 3 inches/7.5 cm long, and layer with the salt and bay leaves in an ovenproof dish. Bake uncovered for about 30–40 minutes. Test occasionally with a skewer to see whether the eel is cooked.

WINES OF THE VENETO

The Veneto is one of the most important wine-producing areas of the Italian mainland. It lies only just behind the leaders, Sicily and Apulia, in vineyard area and production figures, but is far better known than its southern rivals. In terms of both quality and reputation, the region has a marked east-west divide. The province of Verona produces some of the most prolific and popular wines of Italy, Soave, Valpolicella, and Bardolino, as well as one of the country's great red wine types, Amarone. The wines of Breganze, Colli Berici, Lison-Pramaggiore, and even the Piave valley, on the other hand, are generally little known. Prosecco from this eastern part of the region is a solitary exception, though quality does not always live up to expectations. The region extends from Lake Garda in the west, along the foothills of the Alps, to the Adriatic lagoons

Background: The best Soave comes from the area around the Castello di Soave in the Verona region.

Valpolicella

The vineyards that produce this wine, one of Italy's most famous reds, lie on the slopes of the Alpine foothills north of Verona. The grape varieties used are Corvina or Corvinone, Rondicella, and Molinara, with small quantities of other, native varieties. The bouquet is reminiscent of sour cherries, and the flavor dry, fruity, and not too heavy. The best are those from the Classico zone, around the small towns of Fumane, Negrar, and San Pietro. The wine is especially suitable as a partner for rich pasta dishes.

Amarone

Amarone wine is one of the most intense and powerful types that Italy produces, and accordingly high in alcohol. Valpolicella grapes are hung or spread out to dry in well-ventilated storage areas for two to three months. The drying process concentrates the juice, giving the resulting wines an alcohol content of up to 16 percent. Well-made Amarone has a rich bouquet and full flavor. It can age for many years in the bottle. Recioto, the sweet version of Amarone in which the sugar has not all fermented to alcohol, is historically speaking older than Amarone, but has been rather forgotten in recent years.

Bardolino

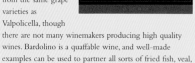

This light, fruity red comes from the southeastern shores of Lake Garda. It is in principle made from the same grape varieties as Valpolicella, though there are not many winemakers producing high quality wines. Bardolino is a quaffable wine, and well-made examples can be used to partner all sorts of fried fish, veal, and pasta dishes.

Soave

The best-known Italian white, Soave comes from a wine-producing region east of the city of Verona. It is made from the Garganega, Trebbiano di Soave, Chardonnay, and Pinot Blanc varieties, and is best drunk to accompany starters, fish, and shellfish. The differences in quality between the best examples and the rest can be striking. The better wines come from the slopes of the Classico zone comprising Soave and Monteforte.

between Venice and Trieste. Vineyard slopes are mainly south-facing, and protected by the mountains. The region's really fine quality wines come only from these hills, whereas the bulk quantity wines come from the plain that lies between the foothills and the River Po or the River Adige. Soil types range from glacial gravels through weathered dolomite rocks to the fertile soils of the plain.

The grape varieties do not appear in the DOC names, which means that the most important varieties, other than Prosecco, are not generally familiar names. They include Garganega and Trebbiano, both white, the basis for Soave, Gambellara, and Bianco di Custoza, and the red varieties Corvina and its sport Corvinone, the main component of Valpolicella and Amarone, its dried grape variant.

From Lake Garda to Verona

The region's range of wines begins with the mainly white wines of the west. The DOC region of Lugana extends across the border from Lombardy, followed by Bianco di Custoza and the light, quaffable red, Bardolino, which all predominate in the vineyards of the southeastern corner of Lake Garda. To the north of Verona, historic city of opera, lie the vineyards that

produce Valpolicella. This, like Bardolino, is made from the Corvina grape among others, but the result has more power and body.

It is an ancient tradition to take some of the grapes from the Valpolicella harvest and spread or hang them on wooden trestles to dry. Nowadays this is usually done in climate – controlled drying rooms. The wine from these is not made until December or January, when drying has increased the sugar content. Since usually not all the sugar is converted to alcohol, the resulting wine is sweet and full. It is called Recioto della Valpolicella. Sometimes, the natural yeasts do succeed in converting the sugar in these partially dried grapes to alcohol, producing powerful, markedly alcoholic, full-bodied wines. These began to be systematically made in the 1950s, under the name Amarone or Recioto Amarone. A third variant of this powerful Valpolicella wine type is *ripasso*, a method developed in the 1970s and 1980s. For this, fully fermented Valpolicella was added to the pressed grape skins from the fermented Amarone. These still contained sugar and yeasts, so that a further process of fermentation occurred. The wines produced by this method are often labelled Valpolicella Superiore or as Vino da Tavola.

Vicenza and Treviso

Moving eastward from Verona, the next wines are white: this is the home of Soave, and again, there is a sweet Recioto version. Soave, the best-known Italian wine along with Chianti, has long had to do battle against the image of being a cheap, mass-produced wine. A large number of winemakers have in fact striven to create genuinely good, dry and soft wines, some with a surprising capacity for aging. However, the negative image that this wine often has worldwide no doubt accounts for the fact that their achievements have so often not been recognized.

Gambellara is the twin of Soave, an otherwise little known wine from the neighboring province of Vicenza, not much associated with any great names. Mass production wines predominate from here on, from vast expanses of vineyard that stretch on toward the border with Friuli – and amid this anonymous profusion, a few islands of quality can be distinguished. Those worthy of note include the wines of Breganze, those of Colli Berici and Colli Euganei near Padua, and the Montello winegrowing region south of the small towns of Conegliano and Valdobbiadene, home of Prosecco. In recent years increased efforts to improve quality have been made in the huge wine-producing region in Piave.

PROSECCO

Prosecco is in fact the name of a grape variety, rather than that of a wine or wine-producing region. This delightfully sparkling white wine has risen greatly in popularity throughout Europe in the 1990s. The variety is not in itself remarkable; it is not over-endowed with the qualities of flavor and aroma that usually go with popularity. Its bouquet is somewhere between neutral and slightly fruity, certainly not rich and complex, and tasting the wine reveals few outstanding characteristics.

The origins of this grape are obscure. Some believe it to have come from a village of that name near Udine, and to resemble an old, native Friulian variety, while others think that it comes from Dalmatia. The reason for its cultivation in Treviso province lies in the series of very cold winters at the end of the 18th century, when the area's vineyards were almost completely destroyed by frosts, and this variety spread because it was hardy. The history of Prosecco begins in earnest in the 19th century, with the foundation of a *società enologica*, an enological society, by Antonio Carpené and his three partners. The society's aim was to bring champagne production to Italy.

The champagne idea did not materialize, but Prosecco di Conegliano-Valdobbiadene – to give it its full DOC name – did, and gradually became Italy's most popular sparkling wine. Winemakers, incidentally, do not always use the full name on their labels. It is produced by means of a second fermentation of the base wine in large pressure tanks. After aging for one month and attaining a bottle pressure of at least three atmospheres, the wine earns the right to the designation Spumante; it is otherwise termed Frizzante. Although Spumante commands the higher price, the difference in quality of the wine itself does not always correspond to this price difference.

Even the much-vaunted Cartizze from the steep slopes above Vidor, between Conegliano and Valdobbiadene, is not usually a better product than others from the same winegrower that do not happen to have this extra declaration of provenance on the label. DOC wines are not the sole type that emerge from the northeastern reaches of the Veneto; there are numerous imitations, which, being Vino da Tavola, can contain wine from other parts of the region and even beyond – even from distant Apulia.

Gregorio Bartolin produces an excellent Prosecco on his Ca' Salina estate at San Stefano di Valdobbiadene.

This refreshing, harmonious Prosecco is nowadays made in modern fermentation tanks. They are fitted with accurate pressure gauges.

Right: The range of Prosecco offered by the house of Ca' Salina includes a Brut, an Extra Brut, and a Rosé. The charm of Prosecco lies in its fine bubbles (far right).

The corks are inserted by machine (above) and secured with wire cages on account of the pressure (background).

TRENTINO
ALTO ADIGE

Lagundo (Algund)
Bressanone
(Brixen)
Meran
(Merano)
Bolzano
Hocheppan Castle
(Bozen)
Caldaro (Kaltern)
Trent/
Alto Adige
Trento (Trient)
Riva
del Garda
Castel
Beseno
Rovereto

Always overshadowed by the glories of the Alto Adige, the Trentino is no rich man's country; the peasant inhabitants of the land around Trento and Lake Garda have always had to struggle for their existence, tilling a harsh and infertile soil. Creature comforts counted for little, and regional specialties were therefore few. The main aim was to see the family fed, and the modest kitchen facilities that the houses afforded left no room for experimentation in cuisine. A historical event was to change all this. Around the year 1550, with the convening of the Council of Trient, the prelates of the Church arrived with their retinues of able cooks, and the art of cooking in the region was roused from its slumbers. Elaborate new recipes now found their way into the repertoire. Cooking methods for freshwater fish were learned from the ecclesiastical cooks. Only a few of these culinary secrets have been handed down. Two of them are *gnocchi con la ricotta* and *pollo ripieno alla trientina*, stuffed chicken Trento style. The Council of Trent was not the only influence on local cuisine. Later, dishes from the Republic of Venice were adopted, and further ideas from the Habsburg Empire.

The cuisine of the Alto Adige – sometimes called South Tirol – looks to a different tradition, one of Alpine specialties. It looks to the northeast corner of Europe, and bears elements of Slav, Austrian, and Hungarian cookery. One such dish is goulash, a regular Sunday treat. Others are the farinaceous dishes and strudels that betray Austrian influence. Potatoes, sauerkraut, and dumplings can be found on almost every menu. Many families make their own sauerkraut – which most Italian-speaking locals call *crauti*. In this region, lard is added. Dumplings are served as an accompaniment to a main dish (they are called *canederli* in the Trentino). The basic ingredient is leftover bread. Universal Italian ingredients like pasta, tomatoes, and olive oil have made their mark here, too, and it is this harmonious coexistence that makes the cuisine of the Alpine region so interesting.

Preceding double-page: The Franciscan bakery in Bolzano is the ideal place to try the local bread specialties, including "Schüttelbrot."

Left: Alto Adige and the Trentino are two very different regions, yet they have in common an impressively beautiful landscape, as here, at Castetel Beseno (Trentino).

CABBAGE AND POTATOES

Cabbage is grown all over the Alpine region and its foothills, as well as the Alto Adige and Trentino. White cabbage in particular plays an important part in the diet, and has the added advantage that it can be preserved for months as sauerkraut. This benefit was an important one in times past when preparing for a long winter. The traditional method is to slice the cabbage finely with a special knife, and layer the strips in a wooden barrel with coarse-grained salt, caraway seeds, and other flavorings like juniper and coriander. Once full, the barrel is closed with a lid of slightly smaller diameter. This is then weighted down with a large stone. Fermentation begins within a few days, forming lactic acid. The moisture is carefully spooned away. About four weeks later, the sauerkraut is ready to be used as required.

The popularity of sauerkraut has continued to this day, though not everyone now makes their own at home in a wooden barrel. Many of the Alpine dishes of the Alto Adige have sauerkraut as an accompaniment. Its popularity extended far beyond the Alps, however, for another of its benefits is to health. It has a high vitamin C content, so much so that it was taken to sea as provisions for long voyages, to protect the sailors against scurvy, the disease caused by vitamin C deficiency. It also contains vitamins B and K and the minerals iron, potassium, and calcium – and the bacteria responsible for the fermentation process are beneficial to the stomach and digestive tract, especially if the sauerkraut is eaten raw.

Potatoes have been long established in the Trentino and Alto Adige. It is even claimed that people in this region were the first to adopt it, and were soon thereafter making bread from it. Certainly it proved versatile, and was long a major item in local cuisine. It could be boiled and eaten with milk or cheese, and cold leftovers could be sliced and made into a salad with a salt and vinegar dressing. As a crop, potatoes are undemanding, and will grow even in the poorest soil. They are also a very healthy foodstuff, and contain plenty of protein, minerals, and vitamins.

The main use of potatoes in the Alto Adige and northern Trentino today is for potato dumplings – gnocchi – which are widely popular. On the other hand, polenta made with potatoes is a dish that is mainly confined to the area around Trento. It is served with local cheese or mixed pickled vegetables.

Fresh white cabbage is needed to prepare homemade sauerkraut.

The cabbage is grated or sliced finely.

Then the cabbage is layered into the sauerkraut pot with salt.

Caraway seeds and juniper berries may be added.

The cabbage is pressed down and weighted with a glass jar or a lid.

When the sauerkraut is ready, it can be used a portion at a time.

GNOCCHI CON LE PRUGNE
Potato gnocchi with plums
(Illustration in background)

GENEROUS 1 LB/500 G POTATOES
SALT
1 1/4 CUPS/150 G ALL-PURPOSE FLOUR
1 EGG
20 PITTED PLUMS
1 CUP/200 G BUTTER
1 CUP/100 G FRESHLY GRATED PARMESAN OR GRANA PADANO

Boil the potatoes, remove the skins, and pass through a sieve. Add salt, and mix to a dough with the flour and egg. Shape into large gnocchi, and stuff each with a pitted plum. Boil the gnocchi in plenty of salted water. They rise to the surface when cooked. Lift them out immediately. Serve with butter and grated cheese.

ZUPPA DI CRAUTI
Sauerkraut soup

2/3 CUP/50 G DICED BACON
1 ONION, DICED
2 TBSP BUTTER
3 1/4 CUPS/800 ML STOCK
2 CUPS/260 G SAUERKRAUT
1 MEDIUM-SIZED POTATO
4 LARGE SLICES/150 G WHITE BREAD (3 CUPS WHEN DICED)
SCANT 1/2 CUP/100 ML SOURED CREAM
SALT AND PEPPER

Sauté the bacon and onion in 1 tablespoon of the butter. Add the stock and sauerkraut, and simmer for 30 minutes. Peel the potato and grate it (raw) into the soup. Bring to a boil. Dice the bread and fry it in the remaining butter. Remove the soup from the heat, and while it is still hot but not boiling, add the soured cream. Season with salt and pepper. Scatter with the croutons to serve.

GNOCCHI DI PATATE CRUDE
Raw potato gnocchi

GENEROUS 2 LBS/1 KG POTATOES
GENEROUS 2 CUPS/250 G ALL-PURPOSE FLOUR
SALT
6 1/2 TBSP/100 G BUTTER
5 OZ/105 G SMOKED RICOTTA CHEESE

Peel and grate the potatoes and mix with the flour. Shape into gnocchi as described in the recipe opposite, and cook in plenty of boiling, salted water. Serve with melted butter and ricotta.

Avezzana is one of the many potato varieties that grow around Avezzano in L'Aquila province, Abruzzi.

The very early variety **Agata** tends to remain firm when boiled. It is mainly grown in Emilia-Romagna.

In the potato-growing area around Viterbo in Lazio, a large range of varieties is cultivated. These are grouped together under the name **Viterbese**.

Pastagialla has yellowish flesh, and tends to remain firm when cooked. The whitish *pastabianca*, on the other hand, is floury.

Sieglinde is an early variety with yellowish flesh. It grows particularly well in Apulia and Sicily.

Locally grown potatoes play an important role in the recipes of this Alpine region, although potatoes are also grown farther south.

GNOCCHI CON LA RICOTTA
Gnocchi with ricotta

GENEROUS 2 LBS/1 KG POTATOES
GENEROUS 2 CUPS/250 G ALL-PURPOSE FLOUR
SALT
6 1/2 TBSP/100 G BUTTER
10 OZ/300 G SMOKED RICOTTA

Boil the potatoes and remove the skins while they are still hot. Pass them through a sieve or potato ricer. Gently work together the potatoes and flour to a smooth dough. Add a little salt. Shape pieces of the mixture into long rolls, about as thick as a finger, and cut into lengths about 1 inch/3 cm or so long. Place each on top of a fork, and press lightly with your thumb, rolling the edges slightly upward to create a rounded, dished shape.
Cook the gnocchi in plenty of boiling, salted water for a few minutes. Lift them out with a slotted spoon when they rise to the surface, and drain thoroughly. Serve with melted butter and ricotta cheese.

BREAD, DUMPLINGS, AND THICK SOUPS

Robust country bread is an essential element in the food of the Alto Adige. Even the names sound Austrian. Dunked into soups, or eaten to accompany the meal, there is always bread on the table. There is black whole wheat or rye bread, and a few bread varieties entirely special to the area – *Schüttelbrot*, *Vorschlag*, and *Paarl*. *Schüttelbrot* is a hard, unleavened bread that needs to be snapped in pieces like crispbread. *Vorschlag* is leavened, some 10 inches (25 centimeters) in diameter, and made of a mixture of rye and wheat flours. *Paarl* comes from the Val Venosta. The loaves come in pairs (the name means "pair") and consist of a sourdough rye bread. The pairs of loaves are an everyday reminder of the marriage partnership, and in the past, the loaves used to be baked singly if one of the spouses had sadly died.

The bread of the Alto Adige is often flavored with caraway, fennel, or aniseed. A still more typical addition is a native, white-flowered plant about 16 inches (40 centimeters) high, called "bread clover" (*Trigonella caerulia*). The country women often grow this in their gardens, and townsfolk buy it from a herbalist, pharmacist, or health food outlet. A relative of fenugreek, it has a savory, almost spicy aroma.

In every country wine bar, a basket of various local breads is the first thing to be put on the table. These will always include Schüttelbrot and Paarl, which is traditionally flavored with "bread clover".

Bread is not only eaten at meals in its own right; it serves another purpose in the kitchens of Alto Adige: leftover bread and stale rolls are the basic ingredient in dumplings. Various other ingredients provide variety. The more substantial additions include bacon and cheese, and the lighter, but equally traditional ones are onions, spinach, mushrooms and the like. Beet dumplings are a great specialty. They are eaten with brown butter and grated parmesan.

Flour and the various grains are not only made into bread – or indeed dumplings – here. They are also used in delicious, thick soups. One tasty example of this is barley soup, which uses pearl barley, vegetables, and bacon. Flour-thickened soups include the simple, traditional one made just with flour with butter or lard, salt, and water. Other recipes recommend milk instead of water, or the addition of onions.

CANEDERLI
Bacon dumplings

6 SLICES/250 G STALE WHITE BREAD OR ROLLS (5 CUPS WHEN DICED)
3 EGGS
1 CUP/250 ML MILK
1/4 LB/100 G BACON, FINELY DICED
1 ONION
1 BUNCH OF FLAT LEAF PARSLEY
2 OZ/50 G SALAMI
6 TBSP ALL-PURPOSE FLOUR
SALT AND PEPPER
GRATED NUTMEG

Dice the bread or rolls, and place in a bowl. Mix the eggs and milk, pour over the bread, and leave to stand for 20 minutes, stirring occasionally.
Dice the onions finely. Chop the parsley. Sauté the diced bacon until the fat runs, then add the onion and half the parsley, and sauté for 2 minutes.
Dice the salami finely and add to the pan, along with the remaining parsley. Stir to mix, then add all to the soaked bread. Fold in the flour, and season to taste with salt, pepper, and nutmeg.
Bring about 3 pints/1.5 liters of water to a boil. With wet hands, form 10 evenly sized dumplings and cook until done.

Crispy Schüttelbrot can be stacked upright in racks.

ZUPPA DI FARINA TOSTATA
Flour soup
(Illustration below)

6 1/2 TBSP BUTTER
2 1/2 CUPS/300 G ALL-PURPOSE FLOUR
4 CUPS/1 LITER HOT MILK
SALT

Melt the butter in a saucepan and slowly blend in the flour until it begins to brown. Gradually add 4 cups/1 liter of water and the hot milk, stirring to blend and avoid lumps. Season with salt. Boil for about 20 minutes until the soup is creamy. Serve hot.

Canederli di pan grattato
Bread dumplings
(Illustration right)

3 CUPS/150 G DICED STALE WHITE BREAD
MILK
2 EGGS
BUTTER
1/2 ONION, CHOPPED
1 TBSP CHOPPED PARSLEY
1 CUP/50 G BREADCRUMBS
SALT AND PEPPER
GRATED NUTMEG
GRATED CHEESE

Soak the diced bread in milk. Beat together the eggs and
1/3 cup butter, and mix in the onion and parsley. Squeeze
out the bread and pass it through a sieve. Add the egg
mixture and the breadcrumbs. Season with salt, pepper, and
nutmeg, and leave to stand for a few minutes.
Shape the mixture into dumplings, and boil them in plenty
of salted water. Serve with melted butter and grated cheese.

Strangolapreti
Spinach dumplings

Serves 4–6

6 SLICES/250 G STALE WHITE BREAD (5 CUPS WHEN DICED)
2/3 CUP/150 ML MILK
GENEROUS 1 LB/500 G FRESH SPINACH
2 EGGS
4–5 TBSP ALL-PURPOSE FLOUR
SALT AND PEPPER
GRATED NUTMEG
3 1/2 TBSP/50 G BUTTER
A FEW SAGE LEAVES
1/2 CUP/50 G FRESHLY GRATED PARMESAN

Cut the bread into small dice, pour over the milk, and
stir well. Cover, and leave to soak for at least 2 hours.
Wash the spinach, and remove the stalks. Blanch for
2 minutes in plenty of boiling, salted water. Rinse in cold
water, drain, and cool. Then press to remove all moisture,
and chop very finely. Mix into the soaked bread, then
thoroughly knead in the eggs and flour. Season with salt,
pepper, and nutmeg.
Bring approximately 4 pints/2 liters of salted water to a boil
in a large saucepan. Shape a test dumpling between two
tablespoons, drop it into the water, and cook for about 5
minutes until done. If it is too dry, add more milk to the
dumpling mixture, and if too wet, more flour. Then shape
the remaining dumplings and lower them into the boiling
water to cook.
Lift them out with a slotted spoon, drain, and transfer to a
warmed dish. Melt the butter in a skillet and sauté the
sage leaves. Then add the dumplings to the pan and turn
until well coated with the butter. Serve, sprinkled with the
grated cheese.

Right: The frescos in Hocheppan castle chapel. The love of
dumplings in this region is nothing new! The frescos in the
castle chapel were painted in about A.D. 1200. Depicted
below the Virgin and Christ Child is a woman in a green
dress, eating dumplings out of a pan.

Beer

Alto Adige is Italy's beer country. The crystal-clear water that flows from the Eastern Alps above Merano made this an ideal area for the industry, as did the easy availability of natural mountain ice, which could be collected in winter to cool the cellars in summer. It is then no surprise that the art of brewing beer in this area dates back to the period between 985 and 993. Small brewers supplied private customers as well as coaching inns and the like. Sadly, almost none of the highly traditional small breweries has survived.

The one exception is the firm of Forst, founded by two entrepreneurs from Merano in 1857. It enjoys a very good annual turnover.

A man called Josef Fuchs took over the brewery in 1863, and founded a brewing dynasty that is now in its fourth generation. The family adheres resolutely to its motto of "quality respects nature – beer is nature." The beautiful building that houses the brewery is not called anything so prosaic; it is called the "Forst" after the firm itself.

It produces an annual 18,492,600 gallons (700,000 hectoliters) of beer. The building also contains a restaurant, with rooms that can be booked for functions and weddings. The Forst beer then flows, as can be imagined. A range of beers is offered: a fresh, dry Pils, the exclusive V.I.P. Pils, the elegant, dry Forst Kronen, the Forst Premium, with its refreshing, fine effervescence, Forst Sixtus, a special Doppelbock beer that recalls the historic, monastic tradition of brewing, and Luxus Light, with a reduced calorie and alcohol content. The company is also the general representative in Italy for the British brewery names Allsopps, Arrol's, and John Bull. The Forst brewery has a second string to its bow. Having bought some springs on the Vigiljoch, it bottles the mineral water Merano Acqua minerale naturale San Vigilio.

The brewery's turnover is not the only sign that beer is gaining in popularity in Italy. The evidence is there to be seen, from Lake Como to Rome, that people are discovering the delights of a cold beer on a hot summer day, and finding that it tastes at least as delicious as a glass of red wine with pizza or a snack.

The Forst brewery at Tel (Töll) in Lagundo (Algund), Merano, is steeped in tradition. The brewing and bottling of the various beer types produced here, from Pils and Märzen to Bock, are done using ultra-modern equipment. The delightful rooms belonging to the brewery's own restaurant can be hired for private functions. Beer is then dispensed.

BARLEY

Wheat and barley are the two oldest plants under cultivation. Archaeological digs have even uncovered flat bread made from a mixture of wheat and barley and dating back to the Stone Age. It is not clear whether the grain was wild or cultivated. Barley grain is much like wheat, but the shape is more elongated and runs to a point. It is easy to grind into flour, but does not make very good bread, so acquired a reputation as nutritious but coarse and difficult to digest. It is usually mixed with other types of flour, such as wheat flour, to make it easier to use.

Barley is hardy and robust, able to cope with the most difficult climates. It was possible to grow it in a great range of places from ancient Egypt to China and from the Arctic Circle to the tropical plains of India. Although its cultivation has declined in many parts of Europe, it is still much in evidence in northern Africa and Middle Eastern countries, where it is a major part of the diet and is still of economic value.

The main barley-growing regions in Italy are Alto Adige and Friuli. The round, white grain is added to soups as pearl barley. Genuine South Tirolean barley soup is a typical local dish, and a nourishing one for mountain-dwellers during the long months of winter.

Minestra d'orzo
Barley soup

Generous 1 cup/200 g pearl barley
2 cups/500 ml stock
5 oz/150 g Belgian endive
1 carrot
1 stalk of celery
1/4 lb/50 g diced bacon (belly bacon is best)
3 1/3 tbsp butter

Soak the pearl barley in cold water for at least 1 hour.
Then pour off the water and place the barley in a
saucepan with the stock. Heat. Cut up the endive and
stir in. Simmer for about 1 hour.
Cut up the carrot and celery. Melt the butter in
another saucepan and brown the bacon and vegetables.
Add the barley and stock, and boil the soup for
another 30 minutes. Serve hot.

FAREWELL TO WINTER

Along the "Wine Road" of Alto Adige, the wine villages are strung out like pearls: Eppan, Tramin, Girlan, Kaltern, Kurtatsch, and Margreid. This area appears to have been inhabited since the earliest times, and the old rituals and traditions are preserved here. A multitude of wine festivals takes place here, and Shrove Tuesday is celebrated with carnivals like the large procession through the streets of Tramin. The terrifying masks parading among the gaily decorated floats recall the carnival costumes of the old Alemannic celebrations. The origins of this procession, which here in Alto Adige is called the Egetmann parade, are altogether darker. It goes back to a pre-Roman fertility cult, in which winter was driven out every year with various rites and a great deal of noise, and the nature spirits asked to send a good growing season and an abundant harvest in the vineyards.

Right: The Egetmann parade happens only every two years. Spectators are advised to wear old clothes – the proceedings involve smearing people with rust or shoe cream.

A Lenten carnival dish

Smacafam is a dish that was traditionally eaten in the closing days of the carnival. It is a baked mixture of buckwheat, corn, or wheat flour, bacon and sausages; the exact ingredients varied according to region. In some places, a sweet version of this traditional favorite is enjoyed.

Smacafam
Buckwheat bake

Serves 6

2 cups/500 ml milk
Generous 2 cups/250 g
buckwheat flour
1 small onion
Salt and pepper
4 tsp/20 g shortening
1–2 well hung salsicce
sausages

Preheat the oven to 375 °F (190 °C). Gently heat the milk in a saucepan, and stir in the flour to create a smooth, soft batter, still fluid rather than stiff. Chop the onion finely and stir into the batter. Season with salt and pepper.
Grease a baking dish with lard and transfer the batter to the dish, to a depth of about 1 inch/2 cm. Break the sausage into pieces and distribute over the batter. Bake until brown (about 1 hour or less). Serve hot.

BOLZANO/BOZEN

Austrian as it seems to Italians, there is a Mediterranean feel to Bolzano (whose German name, Bozen, is also much used). Temperatures are mild during most of the year, though winter itself is cold. Its famous fruit market is held in the town square just as it was 700 years ago, when this town achieved importance as a trading place for goods from southern Germany and Lombardy, and with as much haggling and energetic debate. In the shadow of the parish church, all is color and bustle.

The modern face of the city is open and cosmopolitan, and no more than 80 years old; there has been much change. The original town of Bozen was German-speaking. It was a sleepy South Tirolean location half-forgotten by its Habsburg rulers in distant Vienna. The Peace of Paris in 1919 obliged Austria to hand

over South Tirol (as this region was then called, and indeed sometimes still is) to Italy, then a relatively new country. Bozen then began to undergo a degree of Italianization. Mussolini's seizure of power led to an influx of Italian workers, merchants, and officials. Only the city center with its signs in both languages now retains any character of the former town. The outskirts, which sprawl as best they can between the rivers Talvera and Isarco, contain the same anonymous apartment blocks as the residential suburbs of most of Italy. Today's Bolzano is a location for industry, and a provider of jobs in the region – a role it has always had. It attracts people from the Alpine valleys looking for work.

Bolzano, the modern capital of Alto Adige, lies at the confluence of the Adige, Talvera, and Isarco rivers. Trade fairs and commerce have taken place here since the 12th century. The fruit market illustrates the town's talent for trade.

THREE LOCAL LANGUAGES

There are three languages spoken in the Trentino and Alto Adige: Italian, German, and Ladin. All three are officially recognized by the region's Statute of Autonomy. This official protection enables the Ladins in particular, some 40,000 in number, to preserve their language and culture from oblivion. The Ladins are descended from the original Rhaetian inhabitants of this area in pre-Roman times. They avoided Romanization by largely maintaining their own language. Certain elements were absorbed from Latin, so that Ladin became what linguists have defined as a "Romance idiom built on a Rhaetian substrate." It is related to the Romansh language spoken in Switzerland, and to the Friulian dialect encountered in northeastern Italy.

COUNTRY BACON

The cuisine of the Alto Adige is much influenced by that of the German-speaking countries that surround it, so the region's specialties are quite unlike those of the rest of Italy, and little to be found there. The bread called Schüttelbrot is an example. It is flavored with caraway, a spice hardly used in Italian cooking south of the Alps. Meat recipes, too, are different from Mediterranean ones. The people of the Trentino and Alto Adige enjoy pork, usually smoked, although it is also eaten unsmoked, as in the Lombard dish *bollito* or a pork roast.

Pork fat is turned into lard and used for frying. Two specialties made in this way are *Strauben* and *Kniekiachl*. The first are swirls of pancake batter, poured in a spiral into the hot fat; the second are made from yeast dough, by taking an apple-sized portion and pulling it into a cup shape, which is then fried and basted in lard, and filled with cranberry jam.

The country bacon of Alto Adige, *speck*, is a typical local product of excellent quality. The process involves first curing the legs of pork in salt and spices, using varying combinations of bay, juniper, pepper, nutmeg, cinnamon, and coriander. Each producer has a jealously guarded recipe. The next step in the process involves smoking and maturing.

The sides of bacon used to be hung in the chimney space above the domestic fire to be smoked, but today, smoking is done either by a cold smoking process, or at temperatures not exceeding 20 °C (68 °F), in well-ventilated smokehouses. This recreates the conditions of the chimney. Smoking takes about ten days, and during this time, the bacon absorbs the aromas of the wood. Juniper and pine wood are the types most used. Maturation takes about 20 weeks, and demands great skill. Good ventilation and a constant temperature are important, and the cool mountain climate of the region provides almost ideal conditions, whether the bacon is lean or fat. Each type of *speck* is able to develop the right consistency, which is neither too soft nor too hard.

A consortium of bacon producers for Alto Adige, the *Consorzio produttori speck dell'Alto Adige*, was formed in 1987. Its aim is to ensure today's consumers a bacon product that tastes as good as the traditional country bacon, despite the fact that industrial production methods have replaced the small-scale, handmade approach. All genuine bacon from Alto Adige bears a mark of quality, the emblem of the Consortium, stamped on the rind.

Local country bacon is an essential part of any snack or supper here. And in October and November, when the parties of revelers set out from inn to inn to taste the new wine after the harvest, they too welcome a tasty snack. There is bread, cheese, sausage, and, it goes without saying, *speck*.

Country bacon from the Val Pusteria valley in Alto Adige is a delicious and sustaining delicacy. Its worth is appreciated well beyond the local region.

POLENTA

One of the staples of people's diet in all the Alpine regions was always polenta. It is a simple dish, a pudding of buckwheat or barley flour, with the possible addition of potatoes or yellow pumpkin. Wheat flour only began to be used around 1650. Poorer people in the community would eat polenta instead of bread, serving it either on its own or with milk, cheese, or sausage.

Menus in Alto Adige still feature a number of polenta dishes. *Polenta nera* or "black polenta" is a delicious type, made of buckwheat flour, and served with anchovies "melted" in butter. Meat or game can be used, for a more elaborate meal. *Mosa* is a type of polenta made with milk, using one-third corn and two-thirds wheat flour. The flours are stirred into the boiling milk, and the resulting *polentina* is often served with melted butter.

SOUTH TIROLEAN VESPER

This meal (background) is an afternoon snack or early supper eaten in Alto Adige. It consists of smoked sausages, thin, crisp *Schüttelbrot*, boiled potatoes, wine, and *speck*. This may be the belly bacon or the smoked ham type, according to individual preference. If the meal is eaten out of doors, many people carve off wafer-thin slices or matchsticks of *speck* with their own pocket knives.

POLENTA NERA
Buckwheat polenta with anchovies
(Illustration above)

2 1/2 CUPS/300 G BUCKWHEAT FLOUR
6 1/2 TBSP BUTTER
10 ANCHOVY FILLETS IN OIL
GRATED PARMESAN OR GRANA PADANO
SALT

Bring 4 cups/1 liter of salted water to a boil in a saucepan. Just before it boils, add the flour, stirring every addition. Boil for 40 minutes, stirring constantly. Transfer the cooked polenta to a buttered ovenproof dish. Preheat the oven to 465 °F (240 °C).
Cut the anchovies into pieces and sauté briefly in a little butter. Place on top of the polenta and sprinkle with grated cheese. Brown in the oven for 5 minutes.

POLENTA CON LA ZUCCA
Polenta with pumpkin

Peel a pumpkin weighing about 1¼ lb/600g and boil it in plenty of salted water until tender. Puree it. Boil the puree, together with corn polenta flour, in salted water for 50 minutes, stirring constantly (see recipe on page 19). Turn out onto a board and cool. Slice and serve with hot milk.

POLENTA CON LA CIPOLLA
Polenta with onions

Prepare a firm polenta (see recipe on page 19), and cool. Cut into slices of a finger's breadth. Chop onions finely and cook lightly in olive oil. Season with salt and pepper. Toast the polenta, top with onion, and serve hot.

ASIAGO

The Asiago plateau has been used to pasture cows for around a thousand years. A cheese that bears its name is still made from the delicious milk produced by these cows in such a natural, organic context. *Asiago* received DOC status in 1978, and the consortium for its protection was founded a year later. It keeps strict watch over compliance with the production regulations, and now comprises about 100 dairies and warehouses. *Asiago* is by law required to come only from an area covering the provinces of Vicenza and Trento, and certain parts of Padua and Treviso.

This cheese specialty is available in a number of different types. It is rich in enzymes and protein, but has only a moderate fat content. *Asiago pressato* is a young cheese, made from whole milk and matured for 20 to 40 days. It has a mild flavor and pale color. *Asiago mezzano* uses a mixture of whole and skimmed milk, matures for at least three months, and has a more pronounced flavor than the younger version. *Asiago vecchio* has a maturation time of at least a year, and a characterful flavor. There is also an

Asiago stravecchio, which matures for over a year, developing into a compact and extremely flavorful morsel. *Asiago* can be used in many ways in cooking. The younger types can be eaten with bread as a snack or appetizer, the older varieties either grated over pasta or served with a cheese board and accompanied by a robust red wine – the perfect choice to round off an evening meal instead of a sweet course.

APPLES

Both the Trentino and Alto Adige are agricultural in character. Dairy farming, including on the mountain pastures, winegrowing, cereal crops, and fruitgrowing are all long established as important contributors to the local economy. Half of all Italian apples come from its small area of orchard in the Val di Non. The wide range of varieties and storage techniques ensures that the quantity and choice of apples in Italian markets is abundant from June to September. Much of the crop is exported to the rest of Europe. The fruit farmers of the Trentino and Alto Adige were incidentally the first to improve their methods so as to reduce the need for herbicides and pesticides.

The apple varieties grown here are so numerous that it is almost impossible to name them all. The category that includes Red Delicious and Golden Delicious is a significant one. The variety Stark Delicious, also called *delizia*, deserves special mention. It is a sub-variety of Red Delicious with a rich red skin. It keeps very well, although it does tend to become soft and sleepy in texture towards the end of its storage life. Golden Delicious has a golden green, slightly freckled skin, with a reddish tinge on its "sunny side." It has juicy, sweet, crisp flesh, and is one of the most popular apple varieties that the region exports. *Renetta del Canada* is also widely grown here. All three varieties ripen within a short time of each other, and are ready for picking from September 20 to early October.

Members of the umbrella organization Melinda, Val di Non, which comprises 16 local apple consortia, have to observe strict criteria. These not only relate to growing methods, but to the timing of the harvest. Agronomists and food chemists decide the correct moment for harvesting each variety and each orchard, based on an analysis of exactly when the starch in the apple has been converted into sugar. They set a final date for the completion of harvesting, to ensure that apples picked later do not become overripe and spoil too soon. The demanding time limits that this imposes on the apple growers of the consortium mean a period of hectic activity in the orchards. On average 275,000 tons (250,000 tonnes) of fruit has to be expertly picked and transferred to interim storage with as little time wasted as possible. From there they are taken to the centers in Italy or abroad. It is vital to transport them to cold storage as quickly as possible, within 12 hours. Every hour of warmth and daylight beyond that shortens storage time by three weeks.

Morgenduft (Mela imperatore) is a finely scented apple with a sweet, sharp aroma and fresh character. It is especially good for stewing and baking.

Golden Delicious is greenish-yellow, becoming golden yellow with a slight rosy blush as it ripens. It has a delicately juicy, sweet flesh.

Granny Smith has risen to fourth place among the apple varieties most grown in Alto Adige. It is crisp and juicy, with a sharp flavor and firm flesh.

Idared, a bright red variety, originates from the USA and Canada. It has a sweet but sharp flavor, keeps well, and is well suited for use in stewing or baking.

Gloster is a refreshing apple with a mild flavor and delicate, fruity acidity. It is easily recognized by its shape, tapering toward the base.

Jonathan has long been one of the most popular varieties. It has a sweetish, delicate acidity, and is related to Jonagold, another popular apple.

Alto Adige grows more apples than the Trentino; the ratio of production between the two is 70:30.

Renette du Canada is a dry, rough-skinned apple. It is greenish-yellow, ripening to rusty red.

Royal Gala is a crisp apple with low acidity and a sweet aroma. It is a cross between Kidds Orange and Golden Delicious.

Elstar is juicy, refreshingly sharp, and aromatic. Unfortunately, it cannot be stored for long periods.

Delicious ways with apples

Apple fritters are popular everywhere. This simple, easy-to-prepare treat consists of apple slices – usually Golden Delicious – that are coated in batter before being deep fried in oil or shortening.

Fritelle di mele
Apple fritters
(Illustration left)

Serves 6–8

1 TSP DRIED YEAST (IF USING ACTIVE DRIED YEAST, FOLLOW
MAKER'S INSTRUCTIONS)
3 1/2 TBSP BUTTER
1/2 CUP/125 ML MILK
SCANT 1/2 CUP/50 G ALL-PURPOSE FLOUR
3 EGGS, BEATEN
SCANT 1/2 CUP/50 G CONFECTIONERS' SUGAR
8 APPLES
VEGETABLE OIL FOR FRYING

Dissolve the yeast in a little warm water. Melt the butter and mix thoroughly to a smooth batter with the milk, flour, beaten eggs, yeast, and ¼ cup of the sugar.
Peel and core the apples using an apple corer. Slice into thin rings, and sprinkle with the remaining sugar. Dip the apple rings into the batter one by one and deep fry them until golden brown, in batches.
Drain on paper towels and serve hot.

Sweet temptation at Christmas

Zelten is a specialty of both the Trentino and Alto Adige, yet each area has its own interpretation. In Alto Adige, it consists mainly of dried fruit – figs and raisins – and candied citrus fruit, as well as hazelnuts, almonds, and pine nuts. Only a small amount of flour is added. In the Trentino, the quantity of flour equals the quantity of fruit and nuts.
This specialty is eaten on Christmas Day itself in Alto Adige. Stored in the right conditions, it will keep until Easter.

Zelten
Christmas cake

For the cake mixture.
SCANT 1/2 CUP/50 G RAISINS
1 1/4 CUPS/200 G DRIED FIGS, CHOPPED
SCANT 1 CUP/100 G CHOPPED FILBERTS
GENEROUS 1/3 CUP/50 G CHOPPED
ALMONDS
GENEROUS 1/3 CUP/50 G PINE NUTS
3/4 CUP/100 G DICED CANDIED FRUITS
1/2 GLASS GRAPPA
1/3 CUP/80 G BUTTER
2/3 CUP/120 G SUGAR
2 EGGS

1 2/3 CUPS/200 G ALL-PURPOSE FLOUR
5 TSP/10 G BAKING POWDER (OR MANUFAC-
TURER'S SPECIFIED AMOUNT FOR 1 LB
FLOUR)
GENEROUS 1/4 CUP/70 ML MILK

BUTTER AND FLOUR FOR BAKING PAN
1 EGG YOLK
ALMONDS, FILBERTS, AND CANDIED FRUITS
TO DECORATE

Soak the raisins in lukewarm water, and drain. In a bowl, soak the raisins, figs, chopped filberts and almonds, pine nuts and candied fruits in the grappa.
Mix the baking powder evenly into the flour. Preheat the oven to 350 °F (180 °C). Melt the butter in a bowl over hot water, add the sugar, and beat together until smooth and creamy. Then blend in the eggs, followed by the flour and baking powder. Add milk to soften the mixture. Add the soaked fruit and nuts, and mix well.
Butter a cake pan and coat the inside with flour. Transfer the mixture to the baking pan, and brush the top with egg yolk. Bake for about 45 minutes. Decorate the top of the cake with almonds, filberts, and candied fruits. Serve cold, in thin slices.

Pasta di strudel classica
Strudel pastry

GENEROUS 2 CUPS/250 G ALL-PURPOSE
FLOUR
1 EGG
3 TBSP WATER
1/4 CUP/60 G BUTTER
1 PINCH OF SALT
2 TBSP BUTTER, MELTED
CONFECTIONERS' SUGAR

Place the flour in a heap on a clean work surface and make a well in the center. Separate the egg and set the yolk aside. Soften the butter, and add in flakes to the well in the flour, together with the egg white and a pinch of salt. Mix into the flour, and knead to a smooth, elastic dough. Shape into a ball and leave to rest. Preheat the oven to 350 °F (180 °C). Spread a clean kitchen cloth over the work surface, dust it lightly with flour, and place the pastry on top. Roll out the pastry as thinly as possible, pulling and stretching it over the back of your hand until it is so thin as to be almost transparent. Brush it with melted butter, and spread the chosen filling on top. Then carefully roll up the strudel, using the kitchen cloth. Transfer to a greased baking sheet, brush with melted butter, and bake until golden. Sprinkle with confectioners' sugar and serve warm.

Ripieno per strudel
Strudel filling

GENEROUS 1 LB/500 G APPLES
1 TBSP/15 G SUGAR
CINNAMON
1 SMALL GLASS OF WHITE WINE
GRATED ZEST OF 1 LEMON

Peel, quarter, core, and slice the apples thinly. Add the sugar, cinnamon, white wine, and lemon zest, and boil until disintegrated. Cool, then spread on the thinly rolled out strudel pastry.

The Vernatsch grapes for St. Magdalener also grow in the steep vineyards of the Bozner Leiten slopes.

FINE WINES FROM THE ALTO ADIGE

Most of the region's winegrowing is located in the valley of the river Adige (Etsch in German), with a small proportion of vineyards along its tributary, the Isarco (Eisack), on steep terraces to the north of Bolzano (Bozen).

Much German is spoken here, and German traditions are still a strong influence on winegrowing. The grape varieties, for example, are Riesling, Silvaner, Müller-

There are tiny country inns called "Buschenschänken" attached to individual farms (above). Many winegrowers make some wine themselves from the grapes they harvest, and sell the wines from their own production in cosy rooms like this (background).

Kalterer See Auslese and Vernatsch Alte Reben

Kalterer See was for many years the Alto Adige's wine lake, producing uncomplicated, quaffable wines, often pale and with a sweet after-taste, and largely responsible for the poor image of the region's wines. The variety used is Vernatsch. Many local producers, including some of the excellent cooperatives, have made great efforts in recent years to turn Kalterer See back into a high quality product. Discredited names are helped toward oblivion by marketing the wines under their variety name, Vernatsch.

Lagrein

Modern Lagrein can be a deeply colored wine, with dark-berried aromas, good body and mouth feel, and even a capacity for aging. Tasting these wines, especially the barrique-aged ones, it seems incredible that winegrowers here so long continued to use this grape only for the rosé wine, Kretzer. It had been thought that only the Gries vineyard in Bolzano was suitable for growing Lagrein, but a number of wineries in the Upper Adige have since proved this idea mistaken.

Pinot nero

French in origin, this grape is considered the most difficult of the world's great red varieties. It has not been distinguished by much success in Italy generally, but Alto Adige is an exception. In this region, especially around the village of Mazzon on the left bank of the Adige, magnificent Pinot Noir is grown. With low yields, they produce intensely colored, full-flavored wines with a pronounced bouquet. They make an excellent accompaniment to game.

Südtiroler or Alto Adige (Chardonnay and Pinot Bianco)

Pinot Bianco and Chardonnay used to be confused with each other in the Alpine region and in northern Italy for many years. The wines that feature under the designations *Südtiroler* or Alto Adige have been grown in the region for some one hundred years, but it is only with the advent of modern methods of winemaking and maturation that it has been possible to make of them fruity, yet full and powerful white wines. Barrique fermentation particularly suits the Chardonnay grape, resulting in a very quaffable wine.

Thurgau, Traminer, and Trollinger – here called Vernatsch or Schiava. The way the vineyards are denoted is another, as is the fact that almost all wines are classified as quality wines – here, DOC. Grape harvesting practices too are similar to those followed in Germany, such as the Auslese practice of using selected ripe grapes.

The center of good quality wine production lies along the upper reaches of the Adige, on a mountainside terrace above the river valley between Bolzano (Bozen) in the north and Ora (Auer) in the south. Other, smaller centers of good quality can be found in the Terlan, Meran, and St. Magdalena area and on the left bank of the Adige at Mazzon. Wide as the distribution of German grape varieties is, the best wines are now being made mainly from French varieties such as Cabernet Sauvignon, Chardonnay, and Pinot Noir (also called Pinot Nero and Spätburgunder). This has happened as a result of the leap forward in quality in Alto Adige and other Italian wines during the 1980s. Native varieties have only achieved a share of the limelight in recent years. They have yielded some truly convincing wines that have earned them popularity with consumers. The red wine, Lagrein, has been the star performer here. This grape was previously known mainly for producing a thin, unremarkable rosé, Kretzer. It is a variety that dates back in this region to the 17th century, and its name suggests that it may originate from the Lagarina valley, Valle Lagarina, in the Trentino.

The rise of the modern French varieties had threatened to eclipse Lagrein, but in recent years, a series of winegrowers and winemakers have shown that it is capable of producing powerful wines with an intense color and good balance between soft fruit and hard tannins. Remarkably, one of the best vineyard sites for this variety turned out to be one in Bolzano itself. This is the Gries vineyard, an isolated, flat site in the densely built-up city.

Another interesting feature here in Alto Adige has been the importance of the large houses and cooperatives in developing modern, good quality wine production. Unlike the rest of Italy, where such bodies are still turning out mainly simple, cheap, mass wines to satisfy a demanding market, some of the Alto Adige cooperatives are leaders in the field, with top wines that fetch prices many a renowned winegrower can only dream of.

KALTERER SEE AND ST. MAGDALENER

The most widely grown grape of Alto Adige is the red variety Vernatsch in its various guises: in Trentino, it is called Schiava, and elsewhere – in Germany – Trollinger. Used to make the wine known as Kalterer See, it became the most popular type produced by Alto Adige winegrowers, but simultaneously suffered by becoming a symbol of the decline in quality that took place in the 1970s. When people spoke of the Alto Adige wine lake, what they had in mind were huge quantities of characterless, sweet Kalterer See Auslese wines, which only rarely deserved their designation "quality wine." A striking change has come about in this wine, too. Both Kalterer See – from around the lake of that name – and St. Magdalener – the red wine made from the Vernatsch grape, and grown in vineyards north of Bolzano – are today made by the most modern methods. Both now produce dry wines with pronounced aromas, light but characterized by soft body, and sometimes a slight bitterness in the after-taste, ideal drinking with light, summer foods.

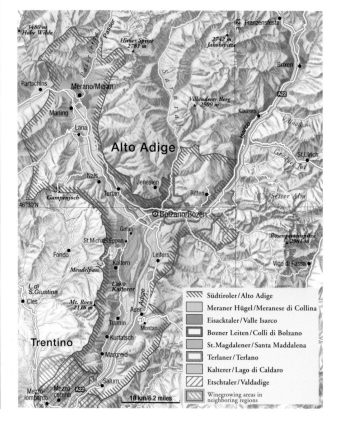

Südtiroler / Alto Adige
Meraner Hügel / Meranese di Collina
Eisacktaler / Valle Isarco
Bozner Leiten / Colli di Bolzano
St. Magdalener / Santa Maddalena
Terlaner / Terlano
Kalterer / Lago di Caldaro
Etschtaler / Valdadige
Winegrowing areas in neighboring regions

Oglio

11°E

Val d'Isole

Passo del
Tonale

Madonna
di Campiglio

Alto Adige

11°30'

Cavalese

Val di Fiemme

Mezzo-
corona

Sarvi

3556 m
Cima Presanella

Mt. Adamello
3554 m

Lombardy

Pinzolo

Cima Tosa
3159 m

Brentagruppe

Mezzo-
lombardo

S. Michele
all'Adige

Faedo

Cembra

Mt. Croce
2490 m

Cima d'Asta
2847 m

La Paganella
2125 m

Val d'Adige

Mt. Cave Alto
3462 m

Molveno

Lago di
Molveno

Lavis

Valle Rendena

Val di Cembra

Stenico

Vezzano

Civezzano

2383 m

Maso

Strigno

Mt. Frizzon
3899 m

Tione
di Trento

Valle Giudicarie

Lasino

Trento

Pergine
Valsugana

Levico
Terme

Bergo
Valsugana

Valle Sugana

Brenta

46°N

Trentino

2176 m

A22

Lago di
Caldonazzo

Caldonazzo

2336 m
Cima Dodici

3830 m
Cornone di
Blumone

Sarca

Arco

Nogaredo

Lavarone

2059 m

Rovereto

Folgaria

Valli

Riva del Garda

Chiese

Isera

Mori

Pasubio
2235 m

Veneto

Bagolino

Lago di Ledro

Torbole

Etschtaler / Valdadige

Casteller

1977 m
Mt. Caplone

Limone
s. Garda

Teroldego Rotaliano

KaltererSee / Lago di Caldaro

Anto

Lago
d'Idro

Malcesino

Adige

Ala

Monte Baldo

Avio

Trentino

Trento Spumante

Idro

Lago
di Valvestino

Lake Garda

South Tyrol / Alto Adige

2200 m

Mts. Lessini

Winegrowing areas in
neighboring regions

Gargnano

10 km/6.2 miles

TRENTO TALENTO

Trento is Italy's secret capital of sparkling wine. Wineries making sparkling wine from base wines produced all over northern Italy were established here at the beginning of the 20th century. More recently, the Franciacorta area has begun to produce sparkling wines by the Champagne method, and is now altogether more successful. Wines produced in the region from Chardonnay and Pinot grapes have been permitted to bear the DOC classification Trento since 1993. In the mid-1990s, the main Italian wineries producing sparkling wine banded together to found an umbrella organization that they called *Talento*, talent. The other name they considered was *Classimo*, from the term *metodo classico*, the traditional "méthode champenoise" of bottle fermentation. Many sparkling wines from Trento now call themselves *Trento talento*.

KNOWLEDGE AND INSTRUCTION IN WINEGROWING – SAN MICHELE

The agricultural research institute or *Istituto agrario* of San Michele is regarded as one of the most important teaching institutions for winegrowing in Europe. It was founded in 1874 by a decision of the Tirolean parliament of that time. It engages in both teaching and research, instructing winegrowers and those working in agriculture, and carrying out agricultural, viticultural, and environmental research. It also produces almost a quarter of a million bottles of still and sparkling wine with the regional classifications Trento and Trentino metodo classico. These include both traditional Trentino wines and more exotic ones, such as a white blend of Sauvignon blanc, golden Muscat, Traminer, and Riesling.

Background: Mountains and vineyards characterize the scenery of the Trentino-Alto Adige region, as here at Callio. The grapes are usually trained over pergolas.

QUALITY WINE PRODUCTION IN THE TRENTINO

The Trentino, southern half of the region Trentino-Alto Adige, is largely mountainous, characterized by the towering peaks of the Dolomites and the Rhaetian Alps. Yet winegrowing is more important than one might think; the valley of the Adige and some of the side valleys offer good vineyard locations. Vines may well have been introduced here by the Etruscans, before the time of the Romans, but until very recently, the Trentino was known only for its trade in casked wine, including that from other regions of Italy. The pergolas that extend to left and right of the motorway present a typical picture of the region's vineyards. They ensure generally high yields, but promise little in terms of quality. Three quarters of the province's grape production is not vinified by the winegrowers themselves, but it goes to the huge tanks of the cooperatives and bulk suppliers. Vineyard land, in sharp contrast to this dismal portrait of the quality and value of the wines, fetches huge sums. The rampant urbanization of the Adige valley puts land at a premium, and stifles any desire to take the risks associated with quality wine production and the low yields it involves.

It is all the more important in the light of this to acknowledge the step taken by those winegrowers who have taken the difficult route, and are pursuing quality in cultivation and winemaking methods – with notable results. The best known of the region's products are its white wines, made from Chardonnay or Pinot Grigio. Many wine-lovers consider the reds of the Adige valley to be better. One in particular carries conviction: the native variety Teroldego – pronounced with the stress on the first "o" – that is grown on the Campo Rotaliano at Mezzocorona and at San Michele, on gravel and alluvial soils. This produces wonderfully complex and powerful wines with aromas of liquorice, plums, cherries, or violets.

Apart from Teroldego, most other wines are sold under the regional name Trentino together with the name of the variety. The best of these are Cabernet and Merlot, but the easy-drinking, slightly rustic native variety Marzemino is also sometimes worthy of attention. Nosiola, the most important white variety, is only grown here. In the Sarca valley, the valley of the lakes that opens onto Lake Garda, this grape is made into a good, sweet Vin Santo. Last but not least, mention needs to be made of sparkling wine production. A number of bulk winemakers in and around the city of Trento specialize in this.

Spumante Trento
Franciacorta and Trentino are the only two classifications of origin applied to sparkling wines. The grapes used are the traditional Champagne varieties, and the best wines made by the bottle fermentation method. Trento Spumante seldom attains the complexity of Franciacorta, but the wines are nevertheless pleasant, fresh, and fruity, and are best suited for drinking as an aperitif.

Trentino (Cabernet)
Trentino is the province's equivalent to the designation Alto Adige (German Südtiroler). Here, too, a number of varietal wines are sold under the common regional name. One of the most interesting developments of recent years has been in Cabernet Sauvignon. The wines may not achieve the greatness of the Bordeaux product, and the growths may not equal those of California, but their fruit character and good structure make them pleasing nonetheless, and a particularly agreeable accompaniment to red meats and game.

Teroldego Rotaliano
Teroldego is one of Italy's most remarkable varieties. It is only on the alluvial plain of the Campo Rotaliano and San Michele that it grows well enough to produce wines worthy of note. Like Lagrein in Alto Adige, which it is probably related to, it results in full, intensely colored wines with capacity for aging, suitable for drinking with the whole range of richly flavored meat dishes.

Nosiola
The Nosiola grape was long thought of simply as one for blending or distilling. It does, however, make thoroughly respectable wines. In the Cembra valley, it is often blended with more aromatic varieties. In the Sarcatal, the valley of the lakes, that drains into Lake Garda from the north, it is used to make a wonderful sweet and semisweet Vin Santo.

LOMBARDIA

Lombards, especially those in the bustling city of Milan, stand accused of having contributed little to Italy's stock of culinary specialties, and of being so industriously devoted to their work that they have no time for a long, leisurely meal or a good glass of wine. The secrets of this region's cuisine do seem at first glance less easy to unlock – yet a closer look at the foods bubbling away in its kitchens reveals certain characteristics in common among the nine provinces that make up the region. Rice is popular everywhere, in nourishing soups and in light, separate-grained risottos that are often preferred to pasta. Another feature found throughout Lombardy is the habit of rounding off a meal with a piece of cheese – *robiola* or *grana padano*. Butter is used more often than vegetable oils, and sauces are frequently made with generous amounts of cream. There is, then, a culinary tradition with its own customs and preferences. That might even be said to include the Lombard tendency to spend less time on food – certainly during the working week – than other regions do. Risotto with ossobuco fits this pattern; it saves time, because it is a starter and main course in one. *Casoeula* is another dish that is simple to prepare and quick to eat, as the meat and vegetables are first cut into bite-sized pieces before being cooked together in the same pot.

This sort of "fast food" can be set aside, though, when occasion demands. When the calendar indicates a particular feast day, or when some personal celebration falls due, people spare neither time nor effort in preparing delicious specialties, and delight in enjoying them. The table groans beneath the weight of meat and game, accompanied in Bergamo, Brescia, and Valtellina by polenta. In Mantua, a favorite dish for special occasions is one that used to be served at village festivals – *tortelli di zucca*, ravioli with pumpkin filling, served with melted butter. This is followed by stuffed turkey, stuffed chicken, or a tempting mixture of stewed meats. The accusation is quite mistaken: the people of Lombardy do know how to feast just as well as other Italians.

Previous double page: Christmas would not be the same without panettone. Here, fresh panettone is being offered in the Marchesi bar and *pasticœria*, Milan.

Left: Lago d'Iseo, 40 miles (25 kilometers) long, is one of Italy's most beautiful lakes. The mountainous island of Montisola lies roughly at its center.

ASPARAGUS

Asparagus occupies a significant place in Lombard cuisine. The first tender shoots of spring are eagerly awaited. Whereas places like Bassano del Grappa are committed to white asparagus, green is the preferred type in Lombardy in general. The flavor is delicious, and it is very much easier to grow, as it does not have to be blanched – this is the process of earthing up the young plants or covering them with dark plastic to prevent them from making chlorophyll and becoming green. In contrast, the green asparagus can simply be left to grow in the sunlight. Other nations in history have shared this liking for green asparagus: the ancient Egyptians, Greeks, and Romans.

Asparagus has excellent health-giving benefits. It is low in calories, but rich in vitamins A and B and in minerals; it also has diuretic properties. It tastes best when very fresh, so care should be taken when purchasing to choose smooth, firm, asparagus with clean, unblemished stems, and to avoid any that seems wet. The tips should be compact and straight. If stored at all, it should be kept in cool, dark conditions. A good method is to wrap it in a damp cloth and keep it in the vegetable compartment at the bottom of the refrigerator.

Asparagus can be used to make delicious soup, or as the filling for asparagus omelet. Steamed and tossed in butter, it makes an incomparable vegetable accompaniment. Simply simmering in salted water for 20–25 minutes is an ideal alternative for the calorie-conscious. Asparagus pans are tall and straight.

ASPARAGI AL BURRO
Asparagus with butter

GENEROUS 3 LBS/1.5 KG GREEN ASPARAGUS
1 1/2 CUPS/150 G FRESHLY GRATED PARMESAN OR GRANA PADANO
6 1/2 TBSP/100 G BUTTER

Peel the asparagus if necessary, and cut off the woody part of the stem. Tie the asparagus into a bundle and place upright in a deep saucepan, in plenty of boiling, salted water. Cover and simmer for about 20 minutes. Drain and arrange on warmed plates, and sprinkle with the cheese. Have ready some melted, browned butter, slightly cooled, to pour over the asparagus.

Green asparagus is easier to harvest than white, because it has not been earthed up or covered with plastic sheeting. However, it still demands hard work

A special tool is used to harvest the asparagus – one by one, by hand. First, the spear has to be freed of surrounding earth.

Agricultural standards lay down that the asparagus must be green for at least two thirds of its length if it is to be sold as "green asparagus."

SAINT BERNARD

The history of Bernard of Clairvaux illustrates the power of a single wise man to bring about radical change in the fortunes of a city and an entire region. The year is 1134, and Milan is welcoming the arrival of the abbot Bernard with great pomp. Soon to be declared a saint, Bernard had been sent by Pope Innocent II to settle a theological dispute and to set Milan back on the path of Rome. Every day in the church of S. Lorenzo, he received many citizens of Milan who came begging him to found a monastery. Bernard finally agreed to this request, and set about finding a suitable site. He made the deliberate decision to establish it on a patch of boggy ground outside the walls of the city. This was to become the Cistercian monastery of Chiaravalle.

In the *Legenda Aurea*, the medieval collection of legends of the saints by Jacobus de Voragine, there is an interesting anecdote about the founding of the monastery: "St. Bernard had built a monastery, and it was visited by such a plague of mosquitoes that the brothers suffered greatly. Then St. Bernard spoke and said, 'I will place the church's ban on them.' The very next morning, they were all found dead."

Despite the apparent Divine assistance in matters of combating insects, St. Bernard and his monks found themselves with much other work to do. They carried out their religious duties, and also saw it as their duty to assist the peasants in reclaiming land for the cultivation of crops, regulating water supply and drainage, and establishing large, meticulously organized farms that remain to this day the linchpin of agriculture on the Po plain. The monks of the order helped to create accurately laid out terraced fields, kept under constant irrigation so that they produced vital fresh fodder for cattle-rearing even in the midst of winter frost and ice.

A number of further benefits followed in the wake of the field improvements. The complete draining of parts of the marshes reduced the risk of malaria; the increased crop yields raised the living standards of the local population; and larger herds of cattle could be kept on the new meadows. Cattle farming in its turn brought new opportunities, such as the need for dairy workers to process butter and cheese. One new product was a medium fat cheese made from milk that had been heated. It had excellent keeping qualities. Later, it became known under the name *grana padano*. The range of food being produced in this tract of countryside was soon sufficient to prosper the nearby city of Milan as well.

Perugino, *The vision of St. Bernard*, c. 1490/94, oil on canvas, 173 x 170 cm, Alte Pinakothek, Munich
The Virgin Mary accompanied by angels appearing to St. Bernard.

ASPARAGI ALLA MILANESE
Asparagus with fried egg
(Illustration below)

3 LBS/1.5 KG GREEN ASPARAGUS
SALT
FRESHLY GRATED PARMESAN OR GRANA PADANO
4 EGGS
BUTTER

Peel the asparagus if necessary and cut off the woody ends.
Tie the asparagus into a bundle, and place in a deep
saucepan with plenty of boiling salted water. Cover and
cook for about 20 minutes. Drain and arrange on warmed
plates, or one large serving dish. Sprinkle with the grated
cheese. Fry the eggs lightly in the butter and place carefully
on top of the asparagus.

The asparagus season begins when the new
shoots appear from the soil in April. Green
asparagus is the type preferred in Lombardy.

RISOTTO ALLA MILANESE

Rice and rice dishes have an important place in the cuisine of northern Italy, and saffron an equally essential one in *risotto alla milanese*. Milanese chefs prefer to use Carnaroli rice for this dish, whereas Vialone nano is the variety normally used for Venetian risottos. The famous Milanese risotto derives its golden color from the precious spice saffron, still an expensive luxury. This color is also the reason that the dish is sometimes called *risotto giallo* or yellow risotto.

Some historians claim that saffron made its first appearance in the Lombard capital in the 13th century, though it is not known how, or by what route. What is known is that Pope Celestine IV, a native of Milan whose papacy lasted just from October 28 to November 10, 1241, often used the spice. Prepared from the stigmas of the saffron crocus (*Crocus sativus*), it was sent to him from Abruzzi, and used by him not only for cooking, but to mix with the other precious essences of lilies, roses, and lavender with which he scented his daily bath.

Risotto alla milanese
Saffron risotto
(Illustrations right and below)

5 TBSP/75 G BUTTER
2 OZ/50 G BEEF BONE MARROW (OPTIONAL)
I SMALL ONION, CHOPPED FINELY
2 CUPS/350 G RICE (CARNAROLI OR VIALONE)
I GLASS DRY WHITE WINE
I PINCH OF POWDERED SAFFRON OR A FEW STRANDS
About 3 PINTS/1.5 LITERS MEAT STOCK
SALT AND PEPPER
1/2 CUP/50 G FRESHLY GRATED PARMESAN

Melt 2 tablespoons/50 g of the butter and the bone marrow in a saucepan or large skillet, and sauté the onions until transparent. Add the rice, and turn it constantly in the fat, using a wooden spoon, until translucent. Pour on the wine and cook until completely reduced. Then stir in the saffron. Heat the stock, and add it gradually to the rice, stirring constantly, ensuring that the rice can absorb each addition.

Season with salt and pepper. Just before the rice is cooked, stir in the grated Parmesan and the remaining butter, cover, and leave for a few minutes to rest and develop the right consistency.

The bone marrow is not an essential ingredient, but does give a wonderfully creamy texture.

Risotto alla monzese
Pork sausage risotto

1/2 LB/200 G SALSICCE SAUSAGES
1/2 ONION
I 3/4 CUPS/300 G CARNAROLI RICE
I GLASS DRY WHITE WINE
2 CUPS/500 ML MEAT STOCK
SALT AND PEPPER
1/2 CUP/50 G FRESHLY GRATED PARMESAN OR GRANA PADANO

Strip the skin from the *salsicce* and slice them. Chop the onion finely, and sauté in the butter until golden. Add the *salsicce* and sauté, and then the rice, turning it with a wooden spoon until coated and translucent. Pour on the wine and reduce. Heat the stock separately, and add it gradually, ensuring that the rice can absorb each addition. Just before the rice is cooked, season with salt and pepper. Stir in the grated cheese, cover, and leave to stand for 2–3 minutes before serving.

Risotto al salto
Rice tarts

I LB/450 G COLD RISOTTO ALLA MILANESE (SEE LEFT)
8 TSP/40 G BUTTER
I TBSP EXTRA VIRGIN OLIVE OIL
FRESHLY GRATED PARMESAN OR GRANA PADANO

Shape left-over *risotto alla milanese* into 4 roughly equal round, flat portions, and place on baking parchment. Melt the butter in a skillet, and slide the tarts gently into it, without breaking them. Fry the underside until a light crust forms, shifting them during cooking to prevent them from burning. Turn out onto a plate and slide them back to cook the other side, adding a little olive oil. Sprinkle with grated cheese before serving.

Vialone and Carnaroli are the best types of rice for risotto. For Milanese risotto, the other ingredients are bone marrow, butter, stock, wine, onion, saffron, and Parmesan.

Melt the butter and bone marrow in a skillet. Add the onion as soon as the butter becomes frothy. Sauté until translucent but not colored.

Sprinkle in the rice and stir until translucent, but do not allow it to brown. Pour on the white wine and continue stirring to prevent the rice sticking.

The risotto should be creamy and moist but not wet. Leave to stand before serving, to achieve the right consistency.

TRIPE

Tripe *(trippa)* – at least in most Italian regions – normally means the fore-stomach of ruminants, but in Lombardy it includes the upper part of the small intestine. Beef or veal may be used. In Lazio, the whole of the small intestine is included, and is called by the local name *paiata* or *pagliata*.

In Lombardy, the intestine is opened out to clean it thoroughly. It has a ridged, wavy surface, full of glands and full of flavor, and is an important ingredient of the classic Lombard dish of mixed tripe called *busecca*. If the idea of preparing it is unpleasant to them, it is possible to buy the tripe ready prepared – even ready parboiled – from a butcher they know and trust. Tripe prepared according to a local recipe can be sampled in one of the region's good restaurants. It makes a delicious starter or main course.

Tripe is rich in mineral content, especially phosphorus and calcium, though it is also high in cholesterol. That need not matter, as it is not eaten every day.

TRIPPA IN UMIDO DI MEZZANOTTE DELLA VIGILIA DI NATALE
Stew of tripe and vegetables

GENEROUS 4 LBS/2 KG BEEF TRIPE
SALT
1/4 LB/100 G BACON, DICED
2 CLOVES OF GARLIC
1 BUNCH OF PARSLEY, CHOPPED
1 STALK OF CELERY
4 CARROTS
GENEROUS 1LB/500 G ONIONS
MEAT STOCK OR WATER

Wash the tripe and boil it for 2 hours in salted water. Then cut into roughly 1 inch/3 cm pieces. Crush the garlic and parsley into a paste, then heat this in a saucepan. Slice and add the vegetables, and cook lightly before adding the tripe. Add water or stock to cover, and simmer for 4–5 hours over a low heat. Top up the liquid from time to time. At the end of the cooking time, the liquid should all have been absorbed. Serve with polenta or slices of corn bread. Another suitable accompaniment is boiled garbanzo beans with a little oil, salt, and pepper.

After 15 minutes, add the saffron. This can be dissolved in a little stock, but no more stock is added from this point on.

The gradual, even addition of the stock is the key to making a good risotto. Each time the rice becomes dry, add just enough liquid to cover.

Just before the end of cooking, add the remaining butter and the Parmesan. Leave the risotto to stand, so that the rice can swell and separate while remaining creamy.

COTOLETTA ALLA MILANESE

The term *cotoletta* may be a corruption of the southern Italian word *costoletta*, meaning ribs or cutlet, or may come from the French *côtelette*. France is, after all, nearer than southern Italy. Though the origin and the spelling of the name are uncertain, the dish itself is not: it is a portion of meat fried in breadcrumbs, and in its most famous form, it is called *cotoletta alla milanese*. The idea has been extended of late, and chicken, turkey, or even vegetable slices *alla milanese* have been with us for some years now. In dishes like these, the name describes the manner of preparation, and simply tells us that the food has been fried in breadcrumbs.

The origin of the dish is as obscure as that of the name and its spelling, with both Austrians and the Milanese claiming to have invented it. One explanation is that the Austrians passed on to the Milanese the art of preparing meat in breadcrumbs during the one and a half centuries of Austrian rule. The difficulty with this is that the method of preparing Viennese Schnitzel is not the same: the *cotoletta* is dipped first in flour, then in egg and finally in breadcrumbs. Nor is the same cut of meat used: the *Schnitzel* uses leg and not loin. Finally, it is fried in shortening or, today, in oil.

Proof that the *cotoletta alla milanese* is a Milanese invention is in fact provided by two historical documents. The first is a "menu" of 1134, for a meal given by an abbot to the choristers of Sant' Ambrogio. The list of dishes includes *lumbulos cum panitio*, sliced loin in breadcrumbs. This evidence of Lombard specialties is quoted in Pietro Verri's *Storia di Milano*. The second item of proof is a letter written by the Austrian general, Field Marshal Radetzky, to the Imperial staff officer, Baron Attems. After various comments and pieces of information, the general writes of the *cotoletta* and describes the method of preparation, speaking of it as a new discovery. Would he have praised it as a novelty if Viennese Schnitzel had been familiar to him already from home? Perhaps it was the Austrians who learned the dish from south of the Alps – the Milanese at least believe so. Should you put the matter to the test and discuss it with a Lombard chef, you will be assured that this dish is an utterly original Milanese invention.

MONDEGHILI
Meatballs

1 STALE WHITE BREAD ROLL
1/2 CUP/125 ML MILK
1/4 LB/100 G SALSICCE SAUSAGES
1/4 LB/100 G MORTADELLA
SCANT 1 LB/400 G MIXED GROUND MEAT
2 EGGS
1 TBSP CHOPPED PARSLEY
1 CLOVE OF GARLIC, CHOPPED
SCANT 1/2 CUP/40 G GRATED PARMESAN
GROUND NUTMEG
SALT AND PEPPER
BREADCRUMBS
3 1/2 TBSP/50 G BUTTER

Soak the roll in the milk and squeeze out. Chop the *salsicce* and mortadella, and mix well with the ground meat in a bowl. Beat the eggs and add to the meat, together with the parsley, garlic, cheese, and soaked bread roll. Season with nutmeg, salt, and pepper, and mix thoroughly with a wooden spoon. Loosely shape the mixture into small meatballs and toss in the breadcrumbs. Fry them in butter, and serve hot with a salad. The meatballs can also be eaten cold, in summer.

Mondeghili are a traditional way of using leftovers, so the ingredients can be varied to include the remains of a roast, the meat from soups, or sausagemeat. These meats should be ground before making the meatballs.

SCALOPPINE AL LIMONE
Veal cutlet with lemon sauce
(Illustration below)

4 VEAL CUTLETS
2 UNWAXED LEMONS
6 TBSP OLIVE OIL
WHITE PEPPER
1 TBSP BUTTER
SALT

Slice the cutlets in half and beat them out to a thickness of 1/4 inch/0.5 cm. Finely grate the zest of one lemon, and squeeze the juice. Beat together the lemon juice and 4 tablespoons of olive oil, season with pepper, and stir in the lemon zest. Pour over the meat, cover, and marinate for at least 1 hour in the refrigerator, turning once.

Heat 2 tablespoons of olive oil in a skillet. Take out and drain the cutlets, reserving the marinade, and fry for about 2 minutes each side. Lift out, cover, and keep hot.

Pour the marinade into the skillet. Squeeze the second lemon and add the juice to the pan. Boil rapidly, add the butter, and season with salt and pepper. Return the cutlets to the skillet and heat through. Serve immediately on warmed plates, with the sauce poured over.

OSSOBUCHI ALLA MILANESE
Braised knuckle of veal
(Illustration right, behind)

3 1/2 TBSP/50 G BUTTER
4 THICK SLICES OF VEAL KNUCKLE
SALT AND PEPPER
1 GLASS DRY WHITE WINE
1/2 CUP/125 ML CHICKEN STOCK
4–5 TOMATOES, SKINNED AND DICED
1–2 SLICES/20 G RAW SMOKED HAM
1 CARROT
1 STALK OF CELERY
1 SMALL ONION
1 TBSP CHOPPED PARSLEY
GRATED ZEST OF 1 LEMON

Melt half the butter in a shallow saucepan, and briefly fry
the knuckle of veal on both sides to seal. Season with salt
and pepper, then lift out and keep hot.
Heat the chicken stock separately. Pour off the fat that has
collected in the veal saucepan, then replace it on the heat
and pour in the white wine to deglaze, stirring to dissolve
the solidified cooking juices. Reduce almost completely
before adding some of the chicken stock. Add the tomatoes
and knuckle of veal, cover, and simmer for about 1½ hours,
adding more stock from time to time, and seasoning with
salt and pepper. Cut the ham into thin strips. Chop the
carrot, celery, and onion finely. Melt the remaining butter in
a saucepan, sauté the ham briefly, add the vegetables, and
cook gently for 1 minute. Add the parsley and lemon zest.
Then transfer the mixture to the pan with the knuckle of
veal, and continue cooking for 10 minutes. Serve the meat
on warmed plates with the sauce poured over.
This dish is traditionally served with *risotto alla milanese* (see
p. 90). Mashed or duchesse potatoes make a suitable alternative, as do vegetables sautéed in butter.

ARROSTO DI MAIALE AL LATTE
Leg of pork in milk

GENEROUS 2 LBS/1 KG LEG OF PORK
1 CLOVE OF GARLIC
2 CUPS/500 ML DRY WHITE WINE
ALL-PURPOSE FLOUR
3 1/2 TBSP/50 G BUTTER
1 SPRIG OF ROSEMARY, CHOPPED
3 CUPS/750 ML MILK
SALT AND FRESHLY GROUND BLACK PEPPER

Place the meat in a large dish, slice and add the garlic,
pour on the wine, cover, and marinate for 2 days in the
refrigerator.
Lift out the meat, carefully pat it dry, and dust it lightly with
flour. Heat the butter in a large saucepan, add the rosemary,
and brown the meat on all sides. Pour on the milk, and
season with salt and pepper. Cover and braise for 2 hours,
until tender.
Place the meat on a warmed dish and keep hot. Boil the
cooking liquid until reduced to a creamy consistency. Slice
the meat and serve hot, with the sauce poured over.

COTOLETTE ALLA MILANESE
Cutlets Milan style
(Illustration above, foreground)

4 THIN VEAL CUTLETS
SALT AND PEPPER
A LITTLE FLOUR
1–2 EGGS, BEATEN
BREADCRUMBS
6 1/2 TBSP/100 G BUTTER
LEMON WEDGES TO GARNISH
PARSLEY TO GARNISH

Carefully beat out the cutlets thinly. Season with salt and
pepper. Dip them first in a little flour, then in beaten egg
and finally in breadcrumbs to coat. Press the breadcrumbs
into place with your hand. Melt the butter in a skillet and
cook the cutlets for a few minutes on each side, until the
coating is golden and the meat inside tender. Lower the
heat and turn the cutlets once more before serving,
garnished with lemon wedges and parsley.

93

PECK, FINE
FOOD
MERCHANTS

It would fill an entire book to tell the whole story of Milan's traditional delicatessen store, Peck. Such a book has in fact been written, by author Davide Paolini. His compendium about this gourmets' temple has been published by the Milan publishing house of Mondadori. It will be in order, then, for us to present a rather shorter account.

In 1883, a young man by the name of Peck, who ran a successful sausage business in Prague, opened a branch in Milan to sell mainly German specialties, such as smoked sausage, meat, and ham. He soon reaped the rewards of his enterprise, and his small store became the gastronomic hub of Milan. Peck even became a supplier to the court of Milan and to a

number of the city's noble and respected families. He retired in 1918, handing on the ownership of the store to Eliseo Magnaghi, who moved it to new and very central premises in the Via Spadari. While continuing to sell German sausage and meats in the Peck tradition, Magnaghi also introduced new lines, in particular, fresh, homemade pasta and ready-made meals to take away. The well-heeled soon recognized the advantages of having the Peck ravioli – famous to this day – delivered to their doors, rather than spend time and effort preparing their own. The new management also opened an area to the rear of the store where the specialties of the house could be sampled, and this delightful corner quickly became a meeting place for the intelligentsia of the time. Artists, journalists, army officers, poets, actors, and the great and the good of the city sat around the small tables. Regular customers included d'Annunzio, Bacchelli, Vergani, Monelli, and Marchi. Peck received a further boost to its popularity when the film director, Mario Mattioli, set several scenes of his 1937 film, *Felicita Colombo* in the store. The film told the story of a rich Milanese woman who

ran a grocery business. Following Eliseo Magnaghi's death, the management of the store passed to his daughter Emi, who ran it for 24 years.

The third epoch in the store's history began in July, 1956, with the Grazioli brothers. This was the dawn of the Italian economic miracle that was to make Milan the richest city in Italy, and the firm's new policy took account of that situation. Three further stores were opened: the *casa del formaggio* in Via Speronari (which dealt in cheese), the *bottega del maiale* opposite the main store (dealing in pork and sausage), and the *rosticceria* in Via Cantù (a snack bar, in today's language, selling roast meat). The kitchen and storeroom areas of the building were renovated, and modern technical equipment installed. These changes enabled Peck to introduce a vastly increased range of ready made foods, and its customers responded with enthusiasm. Giovanni and Luigi Grazioli carefully observed the changes in their fellow citizens' eating habits and needs; the demands of work in this booming city meant that people had little time for a protracted lunch with several courses. Peck therefore began to offer tastefully made small snacks –

Peck in Milan is both a delicatessen and a restaurant with a Michelin star. Specialties here include asparagus (in spring), ravioli with red abalone, and sole in curry sauce.

into the main building during the refurbishments. New ventures have been developed: catering by Peck has become an essential feature of every important Milan party, there is a Christmas gift service, and exports are rising constantly. The main countries, in order of sales volume, are Germany, Great Britain, Austria, France, the USA, and Hong Kong.

The Stoppani brothers – four of them – run the business with great energy and devotion. Angelo, the eldest, is responsible for sausage and meat products and for imports; Mario, next in age, takes care of wines and catering; Remo, the third brother, looks after cheeses and exports, and Lino, the youngest, does the management and bookkeeping. Typically for an Italian family enterprise, they are also supported by Mario's sons Andrea, Stefano, and Paolo. There are four grandchildren studying and gaining experience elsewhere before entering the family business. They frequently help out serving food or behind the counter.

It would be impossible to list all the products so attractively and appetizingly set out for sale in Peck's 35,520 square foot (3300 square meter) retail area. It includes sausage, cheese, fruit, vegetables, pasta – both *pasta secca* and *pasta fresca* – bread, fish, seafood, smoked salmon, truffles, mushrooms, caviar, fresh meat, meat products, pastries, ready-made dishes to take away, wines and spirits, all in an incredible range of varieties. In other areas of the store, chefs can be watched at work over sizzling pans, or customers can sit and relax over an ice cream or coffee, to recover from their tour of the counters. Even those who wish to observe rather than buy will find their visit an unforgettable experience. This is a place where customer service is writ large.

open sandwiches and filled rolls – that established a new lunch trend. Employees of neighboring businesses and offices would hurry in to Peck in their lunch break, have a *panino* made up to order from the huge range of fillings and dressings, and hurry out. This venture into fast food did not distract the Grazioli brothers from their trade in quality sausages, hams, and cheeses, nor from an emphasis on good service designed to make the store a welcoming one even for less affluent customers. Peck maintains not only its exclusive image, but a policy of making sure its doors are open to everyone. That policy believes that everyone should feel able to visit the store – even those whose budget only runs to a quarter of ham once a year must never be treated condescendingly. They must know that they are welcome. The Grazioli brothers were well aware that not everyone in the rich city of Milan shared its prosperity, and wanted the delights they sold to be available to them all nonetheless. A further change in ownership occurred on September 1, 1970. The Graziolis chose the sons of the Stoppani family from Corticelle Piave in the province of

Brescia, convinced that only they would be able to continue the business in the established spirit and to the standards that had been set. The Peck enterprise took a further leap forward under the management of the Stoppani brothers. The first step was to modernize the *rosticceria* and the *bottega del maiale*, followed four years later by the main store in the Via Spadari. They also acquired further premises: a wine store in the Via Victor Hugo, where in 1982 they opened a wine and snack bar serving hot and cold food, and the Peck restaurant, also in the Via Victor Hugo, opened a year later. The restaurant's excellent cuisine earned it a Michelin star in 1986. The new building in the Via Spadari was begun in 1988, and the gleaming new gourmets' temple formally opened in 1996.

The elegant, three-story main building is the heart and the control center of the Peck enterprise. Its activities have now extended to include high quality snack bars at the Linate, Malpensa, and Fiumicino airports, six outposts in Japanese Takashi stores, and a restaurant in Tokyo. The *casa del formaggio* and *bottega del maiale* no longer exist as separate stores, but were incorporated

CHEESE AND SAUSAGE VARIETIES

Stracchino or Crescenza

Crescenza cheese derives its other name, *stracchino*, from the way the milk to make it was originally obtained: it was the milk of *vacche stracche*, cows exhausted by the journey back down the mountain from the summer meadows. *Stracco* is local dialect for "exhausted" – and *stracchino* is "little exhausted one."

Small and medium-sized producers of specialist cheeses in the Alpine regions face a difficult struggle to maintain their existence in competition with the varied palette of factory-made dairy products. Unfortunately, European Union regulations often only serve to hasten their demise, by making often contradictory demands, imposing quotas and limits, or fining them for not fulfilling certain norms, despite the fact that theirs are high quality, often imaginative, products. *Stracchino* is one of these threatened products. It is a rectangular cheese made from whole milk. It is a rich cheese, pearly white in color, with a soft, creamy texture and remarkable, delicate flavor.

Taleggio (DOC since 1988)

This is a square cheese weighing about four pounds (2 kilograms). It is a typical Lombard country soft cheese. The rind is brownish and tends to form a mold. Directly beneath this rind, the cheese is soft and soft textured, but in the center, it is whitish and crumbly. The first mention of *taleggio* dates from around 1200, and the method of production has changed little since then, apart from the use of selected enzymes to ensure the quality of the end product. The cheese is still only made from cow's milk. The curd takes 18 hours to form, and the cheese must mature for at least one month before being ready to eat.

Taleggio is mild with a slight sourness, becoming quite piquant as it ages. It should not be kept for long periods because it spoils easily. A slice of *taleggio* rounds off a meal. It also goes well with hot polenta, and tastes delicious eaten with ripe pears.

Gorgonzola (DOC since 1955)

Gorgonzola is a very old cheese specialty, and originates from the town of Gorgonzola in Lombardy. First written records of it are from the 11th and 12th centuries. A blue-veined cheese, it is produced today across a wide area of Piedmont and Lombardy, and is popular both in Italy and abroad. The region produces around three million Gorgonzola cheeses per year, which are exported to the rest of Italy, France, Germany, Switzerland, the USA, and Canada packed as portions in colorfully printed foil wrappers, which must bear the brand figure of the consortium to be genuine. It has a strong, piquant flavor with a hint of bitterness, and is a true all-round cheese. Gorgonzola makes a good partner to eat with polenta, tastes good with egg and with nuts, and can be used for creams and sauces. It is delicious with a robust red wine.

Provolone valpadana (also DOC)

This hard cheese with its characteristic shape – round, pear-shaped, or sometimes cylindrical – originally comes from Basilicata in the south, but is also made in northern Italy today, especially in Lombardy. *Provolone* is sold in various sizes, and is made by a similar *pasta filata* process to mozzarella. The curd is scalded – it is heated until it begins to melt and become stringy (*filata*), and then wrapped around itself until it assumes its round shape. It is dipped in brine and hung up on a cord to ripen, which takes about a year. The rind is coated in wax to protect it from drying out. *Provolone* comes in various flavor categories from *provolone dolce*, which is mild and buttery, to piquant (*provolone piccante*). The mild version makes a good end to a meal, and the piquant one is often used grated. A smoked version is available in Lombardy.

Grana padano

Grana padano is often compared to *parmigiano reggiano*, despite the differences between them in the method of production and region of origin. *Parmigiano reggiano* comes exclusively from Emilia-Romagna, and *grana padano* from the Veneto, Trentino, Piedmont, or Lombardy. *Parmigiano reggiano* may by law only be made from the milk of cows that have been fed on grass or hay, whereas other types of fodder are permissible for *grana padano*. This does not mean that it is in any way inferior. Its manufacture is supervised by a consortium, and only cheeses bearing the official brand mark *grana padano* are the genuine article. The milk from which it is made comes from two consecutive milkings, and is allowed to stand and partially skimmed to produce a cheese with just 30 percent fat in dry matter. The milk is then heated and micro-organisms added. The cheeses are matured for 1–2 years. *Grana padano* has a granular texture, and can become dry and crumbly. It forms a thick, smooth rind. The cheese has a harmonious flavor, not too salty and not too mild, with a slight piquancy and a nutty quality. It can be eaten as an appetizer, or used for grating over pasta dishes or green salads.

Grana Padano

Gorgonzola

Provolone piccante

Stracchino or Crescenza

Taleggio

Salametto

Salame di Varzi

Salsiccia luganega

Salame di Milano

Cacciatorino

Salame di Varzi

Around Pavia, south of the River Po, are a number of
villages where sausages are still smoked in the traditional
way. This is the area where *salame di Varzi* is made. Only the
finest pork is used to make this sausage, and only wine,
pepper, salt, and saltpeter are added. The sausage is matured
for three to four months. This comparatively long maturation brings out the flavor. A whole *salame di Varzi* as sold is a
medium-sized, coarse-grained sausage weighing about
2 pounds (1 kilogram). It has been a DOC designated
product since 1989.

Salsiccia luganega (or luganiga)

Sausages called *salsiccia* are usually of fresh meat, and cooked
or heated in water before serving. The meat is a finely
ground mixture of fat and lean pork, flavored with pepper
and spices. *Luganiga* or *luganega* is an example of this type.
The meat is filled into long casings, divided into sections
and sold by length rather than weight. *Luganiga* is often
served with polenta in northern Italy. It can be fried,
broiled, or braised as well as boiled.

Salame di Milano

This fine-textured salami made from pork, pork fat, beef,
and spices is matured for about 3 months and weighs up to
about 3 pounds (1.5 kilograms). It has an essential place in
any *antipasto misto* starter of mixed sausage, and is popular
well beyond its place of origin. It is probably one of Italy's
best-known food products, along with Parma ham. The
imitations available elsewhere do not necessarily do justice
to the original.

Cacciatorino

This small, well-hung variety of salami consists of two thirds
lean pork, tender veal, and various types of fat. It was originally devised as a convenient type of sausage for those working out in the forests to take with them as supplies. That
may be the source of the name, *cacciatorino*, "small hunter."

Salametto

Salametto is a small, well-hung sausage, similar to *cacciatorino*.
It, too, can be taken as provisions for an excursion into the
countryside.

DOC or DOP?

More and more Italian food products in recent years
have begun to bear the designation DOP instead of
the usual DOC. DOP is a mark awarded by the EU,
and stands for *denominazione di origine protetta*
(protected designation of origin). All Italian DOC
products are recognized as DOP, and the DOC mark
continues to be a valid symbol.

COLOMBA PASQUALE

Pavia is the home of a version of panettone, the *columba pasquale*, that is baked in the stylized form of a dove. There is a story behind it, and if this is to be believed, we owe this specialty to a cruel king and twelve beautiful maidens.

Alboin, ruler of the Langobards, had long laid siege to the city of Pavia, and had at last taken it. It is said that he demanded not only the gold and treasure usually paid to the conqueror, but twelve beautiful maidens in addition. The maidens selected were in no doubt of the fate that awaited them and their virtue. They wept inconsolably – all but one, who refused to spend the last hours before her doom in anything as useless as weeping. She sent for honey, flour, and candied fruits, and baked a cake shaped rather like a dove. She then waited with the other maidens for her turn to be called to the royal chamber. When the moment arrived, she presented him with her cake. Filled with suspicion, probably expecting to be poisoned, he demanded that she eat some herself, which she gladly did. He then ventured to try some himself. Perhaps he was all too used to poor food; this cake, in contrast, was delicious, and he ate it all. As a mark of his appreciation, he granted the girl her freedom.

The basic mixture is a yeast dough with candied peel, raisins, and candied fruits.

The paper cake molds are only partly filled. They are baked in these molds.

The wrapper is kept on when the cake comes out of the oven.

PANETTONE

The first indications that a special type of bread was eaten on certain religious feast days – especially Christmas – come from the 11th century. These record how the whole family would gather around the decorated hearth on the feast day, and the head of the household would cut a large loaf. The crust was kept to one side, because it was said to have healing powers, especially for sore throats. This description of the large loaf and the customs associated with its use bears a close resemblance to the cake later to become known as panettone. The name comes from the Milanese dialect, which loves to attach diminutive – or magnifying – endings to words.

At the time of the Milanese Duke Ludovico il Moro (1452–1508), panettone was made just as it is today, as a tall coffeecake. It began as the traditional Christmas cake of Milan, soon endeared itself to the people of Lombardy, and spread to take an essential place on Christmas tables in the whole of Italy. It is now continuing its advance into other parts of Europe and perhaps beyond.

The cake is made from a yeast dough, to which candied citrus peel, raisins, and candied fruits are added. It is baked in paper molds, but only a little of the mixture is filled into each to allow for expansion during baking. It rises well above the top of the mold. It is not turned out of the paper mold once baked; instead, this is left on as a mark of identification, and also to prevent it from drying out.

Until very recently, workers right across industry, whether metalworkers on a huge site, employees of a smaller, specialist factory, or craftsmen in a small workshop, could be observed hurrying home shortly before Christmas with a panettone in one hand and a bottle of Spumante (more often than not a sweet muscat) in the other. These were the Christmas gifts of the factory owners to their workforce.

Another delightful custom associated with panettone has to do with the *panettone di San Biagio*. It is one still observed by many families in Milan, who keep one whole panettone until February 3, the saint's day of St. Blasius. Popular tradition has it that those who eat the stale panettone with its hard crust will be spared from sore throats during the year to come. Bad throats, it must be remembered, are no rarity during the cold, misty northern Italian winter.

Left above and below: Panettone tastes best when really fresh. The Marchesi bar and *pasticceria* in Milan serves excellent panettone. It is as delicious for breakfast as eaten in the afternoon with a glass of Spumante. The usual way to eat this cake is to break off pieces by hand.

SWEET CONFECTIONS

CREMA DI MASCARPONE
Mascarpone cream
(Illustration below)

3 EGGS
1/2 CUP/100 G SUPERFINE SUGAR
1/2 CUP/100 G MASCARPONE
1 SMALL GLASS OF RUM

Separate the eggs, and beat together the yolks and sugar in a bowl. Add the mascarpone, and beat in thoroughly with a balloon whisk. Flavor with rum. Whisk the egg whites until stiff, and fold into the mascarpone mixture. Transfer to dessert dishes, and leave for a few hours in the refrigerator to chill and become firm. Serve with shortbread biscuits.

ROSUMADA
Red wine with egg

4 EGG YOLKS
1/4 CUP/50 G SUPERFINE SUGAR
3–4 GLASSES OF RED WINE (BARBERA OR BARBARESCO)

Beat together the egg yolks and sugar in a bowl until light and frothy and almost white in color. Add the red wine gradually, continuing to beat with a balloon whisk. Pour the creamy mixture into attractive, robust glasses to serve. *Rosumada* is a typical Milanese drink, often taken during the morning or afternoon. In the summer, ice cold water or milk are often used instead of the wine.

SBRISOLONA
Almond cake

Serves 6–8

2 1/2 CUPS/300 G ALL-PURPOSE FLOUR
GENEROUS 3/4 CUP/100 G CORN (POLENTA) FLOUR
6 1/2 TBSP/100 G BUTTER
6 1/2 TBSP/100 G SHORTENING
GENEROUS 1 1/2 CUPS/200 G CHOPPED ALMONDS
1 CUP/200 G SUGAR
2 EGG YOLKS
GRATED ZEST OF 1 LEMON
A FEW DROPS OF VANILLA

Preheat the oven to 320 °F (160 °C). Sift both flours into a bowl. Mix and then knead in the butter and shortening. Add the finely chopped almonds and sugar and mix together. Add the egg yolks, lemon zest, and vanilla, and knead until smooth.
Place the mixture in a greased springform cake pan, smooth over the top, and bake for about 45 minutes. Leave to cool in the tin for about 10 minutes before turning out onto a cake rack. The cake can be kept for several days.
This cake is particularly popular in the province of Mantova. Its Italian name stems from the fact that it crumbles easily when cut (*sbriciolare* means to crumble).

Monte bianco
Chestnut purée with cream

Serves 6

1 1/4 LBS/600 G FRESH CHESTNUTS
2 CUPS/500 ML MILK
1 VANILLA BEAN
SCANT 1 CUP/100 G CONFECTIONERS' SUGAR
1/2 CUP/50 G COCOA
GENEROUS 1 TBSP RUM
3/4 CUP/200 ML WHIPPING CREAM

Preheat the oven to 480 °F (250 °C). Slit the skins of the chestnuts with a sharp knife and bake for about 20 minutes until the shells split open. Rinse briefly in cold water and remove the skins while still hot.
Place the chestnuts, milk, and slit vanilla bean in a saucepan and boil until tender (about 45 minutes). The milk will be almost completely absorbed.
Take out the vanilla bean, and purée the chestnuts. Add the confectioners' sugar, cocoa, and rum, and blend in until smooth.
Whip the cream stiffly. Serve the purée in dessert dishes, topped with cream.

THE LOMELLINA PLAIN

About 19 miles (30 kilometers) south of Milan, between the rivers Po, Ticino, and Sesia, stretches the flat expanse of the Lomellina plain. This area, once nothing but marshland, is the grain and rice field of Italy. Land reclamation by monks around the year 1000 gradually made it cultivable, and rice began to be imported from Spain in the 15th century. The design of the irrigation system for the rice fields is attributed by some to Leonardo da Vinci.

The Lomellina plain is also a center for salami production. The pig industry developed here in tandem with the manufacture of cheese – Grana Padano and Gorgonzola – since the byproducts could be used to feed the pigs. Among the agricultural workers, piglets were in effect a unit of currency, and this enabled them to build up their own breeding herds of pigs. Slaughter day brought a midday meal of pork and onions on a bed of polenta, and an evening feast of pork ribs, salami, risotto, cabbage, and trotters. Sausages of various sorts were made and preserved in fat for months, to be eaten at pre-ordained times. Kidneys were eaten with truffles, and loin hung for a week before being braised in good wine – wine that was also used in making the sausages.

Beef is also widely enjoyed here. It is usually stewed or braised as a ragout. Organ meat (referred to as the "fifth quarter" of the animal) is much in demand. Other meats that often feature in the cuisine of this area are eels and frogs, which frequent the flooded rice fields. Eel in red wine, and eel cooked in the fire in an earthenware pot with parsley and lemon, are both specialties of the region.

Oca farcita
Stuffed goose

Serves 6–8

1 CUP/100 G PITTED PRUNES
1 CLEANED, OVEN-READY GOOSE (ABOUT 7–9 LBS/3–4 KG)
GENEROUS 1/2 LB/300 G SALSICCE
2 APPLES (PREFERABLY RENETTE)
2 CUPS/200 G ROASTED, PEELED CHESTNUTS
10 BLANCHED FILBERTS
SCANT 1/2 LB/200 G BACON OR HAM
4 TSP/20 G BUTTER
STOCK OR WATER

Soak the prunes in lukewarm water for half a day. Rinse the goose, and remove the breastbone to make the bird easier to stuff. Preheat the oven to 400 °F (200 °C). Coarsely chop the sausage, apples, chestnuts, prunes, and filberts, and mix by hand. Stuff the goose with the mixture, and sew up the opening with kitchen thread. Lay slices of bacon or ham over the goose, place in a roasting pan, and roast for about 3 hours, turning occasionally, and basting with hot stock or water as necessary.

Right: The Lomellina plain is the center of goose breeding in Italy. Some restaurants offer menus exclusively made up of goose dishes – even the desserts.

Geese cannot be kept indoors like chickens. The farmer must ensure that the birds have sufficient meadowland at their disposal to give them the freedom they need.

GEESE

Ludovico Sforza, called il Moro, Duke of Milan (1452–1508), was not only the patron of Bramante and Leonardo and active in the building of the castle; he was concerned with the problems of agriculture in his territory. He established basic conditions to promote the breeding of geese on the Lomellina plain with the consent and active support he gave to the founding of a Jewish settlement near Mortara. Since the Jews are forbidden to eat pork, but geese were declared to be kosher, these proved an ideal food solution.

With geese (as with pigs) all parts of the creature can be used. The feathers are useful to stuff pillows, their fat as a fine cooking ingredient, their meat is delicious and nourishing, and the livers can be made into pâté. The conditions for keeping them are also similar to those needed for pigs.

From the point of view of cooking, goose is handled much like duck. Goose must always be cooked right through, on account of the high fat content. This fat content gives it the reputation of being heavy and difficult to digest, but the slur is undeserved: goose can be wonderfully light and tender if the fat is properly removed during the cooking process.

Geese on the Lomellina today are bred mainly for their livers. In France, the rich livers of fatted geese, known there as *foie gras*, have always been an acknowledged delicacy; this is being rediscovered in Italy. There are further specialties too, such as a delicious goose salami from Mortara. *Salame d'oca* is made with a mixture of goose meat and fat, with the skin of the neck as the casing.

Like turkey and capon, goose is frequently eaten at Christmas. It may either be roasted whole or jointed and braised.

PETTO D'OCA IN CRESCIONE
Goose breast with watercress
(Illustration below)

1/3 CUP/40 G GOLDEN RAISINS
1/2 GLASS OF BRANDY
2 TBSP/30 ML OLIVE OIL
1/2 BREAST OF GOOSE (ABOUT 1 LB/400 G)
2 CUPS/500 ML VEGETABLE STOCK
1 CARROT, FINELY CHOPPED
1 CELERY STALK, FINELY CHOPPED
4 BUNCHES OF WATERCRESS
1 TSP BALSAMIC VINEGAR
SALT
SEEDS OF 1 POMEGRANATE
SCANT 1/4 CUP/20 G ROASTED PINE NUTS

Soak the golden raisins in brandy for about 3 hours. Preheat the oven to 350 °F (180 °C). Heat some of the oil in a casserole, and brown the meat on all sides. Pour on the stock, add chopped vegetables cover, and transfer to the oven to cook. Top up as necessary to ensure that the meat is always one-third covered by the stock. As soon as the goose is cooked, but still slightly pink in the middle, it is ready. The temperature in the center should be 146 °F (63 °C) when measured with a meat thermometer.

Wash the watercress and pat dry. Make a dressing by whisking together olive oil and balsamic vinegar, and a little salt. Arrange the cress on plates to serve, and sprinkle with half the dressing.

Slice the goose and lay it on top of the cress while lukewarm. Scatter with golden raisins, pomegranate seeds, and pine nuts, and sprinkle on the remaining dressing.

THE RISTORANTE

Good home cooking is highly valued in Italy, but it is becoming increasingly fashionable to eat out in restaurants – no more so than in the prosperous cities of the north. Many women in the regions here go out to work, and no longer see the care of the children, the home, and the cooking as their only role. When the industrious men and women of Lombardy return home to find no miraculously-produced meal waiting on the table, there is always the restaurant on the corner. Likewise, when a special occasion calls for a celebration, it is to a carefully chosen restaurant – one noted for its good food, or discovered by means of previous visits and "test meals" – that people invite their friends and relations.

In the south of Italy, matters are rather different. Many generations of the same family still usually live together, and if *mamma* has no time to go to the market, *nonna* (the grandmother) will go instead. It is still *nonna* who knows the best recipes and practical cooking tips, and passes them on to the next generation. Celebrations are family occasions, and in the south, this takes place at home. People visit each other, and enjoy a feast together, which may sometimes continue for days.

A visit to a restaurant in Italy requires time. A meal consisting of a single, quickly-consumed course, perhaps followed by a dessert, is largely unknown. Instead, there is a dinner of at least four courses: *antipasto, primo piatto, secondo piatto*, and *dolce* – that is, hors d'oeuvres, first course, second course, and dessert. The meal may be extended by inserting further courses in between these.

It is best to ask the advice of the waiter or wine waiter about the choice of wine. It does not necessarily need to be a bottle, as many Italian restaurants have good regional house wines available by the glass or carafe, which may provide a delicious insight into the wine culture of the area.

The *antipasto* usually consists of smaller items to stimulate the appetite and accompany the aperitif. The popularity of the traditional Italian plate of such delicacies as stuffed mushrooms, preserved or cooked vegetables, juicy olives, sausage and cold meats, called *antipasto misto*, is as great as ever, varying according to taste and season. Restaurant guests can often select their own from a glass counter; elsewhere, the waiter may bring an *antipasto* trolley to the table. On the coast, this course often consists of seafood, *antipasto misto di mare*. It is a mixture of very fresh shellfish and crustaceans in a simple dressing of oil and lemon juice.

The *primo*, or first course, is usually a pasta or rice dish. Half portions can be ordered if an entire plate of spaghetti seems too daunting.

Il secondo, the second course, consists of meat or fish. This is served alone on the plate, apart from the garnish, so it is normal to order an accompaniment, called *contorno*. This is usually lightly cooked vegetables, and, in the north, polenta.

Finally comes the sweet dessert. A selection of cheeses or fresh fruit in season may be offered as an

alternative. Italy has some wonderful regional sweet dishes, so sampling them is particularly recommended if at all possible.

A little help with digestion is welcome following all these delights, and a number of digestive drinks exist – all claimed by their adherents to be most beneficial to the stomach. In the north, a good measure of grappa is usual; traveling south, the choice changes to liquor made with herbs. An espresso is often taken to round off the meal.

Hors d'oeuvres
Usually cold regional delicacies. These are eaten to stimulate the appetite and prepare the palate for the courses to come.

First course dishes
The *primo* almost always consists of pasta, rice, or gnocchi. The intention is the satisfy hunger and set the eater at ease to enjoy the main course.

Fish main courses
For the main course, there is a choice between fish and meat. The two categories are listed separately. The waiter or innkeeper often advises the customer about the options, especially any freshly arrived ingredients. Smaller portions are served if the fish is to be eaten as an additional course before a meat dish.

Meat main courses
Italian menus are often negotiable. If the customer would like the food prepared differently from the options listed, it is possible to consult the waiter about alternatives. The customer's wishes are often met. Meat may be served as the sole main course, or to follow a fish course.

Extras
Complete meals with vegetables are not served in Italy: the fish or meat arrives without any accompaniments, and these are ordered separately.

MENU

Antipasti

Bresaola condita	EUR	9,00
Insalata frutti di mare	EUR	9,00
Insalata Caprese	EUR	8,00
Vitello tonnato	EUR	9,00

Primi Piatti

Spaghetti alla trapanese	EUR	10,00
Penne all'arrabbiata	EUR	8,00
Pappardelle sulla lepre	EUR	14,00
Gnocchi con la ricotta	EUR	10,00
Risotto nero	EUR	11,00

Secondi di Pesce

Baccalá alla vicentina	EUR	19,00
Filetti di lavarello in carpione	EUR	20,00
Involtini di pesce spada	EUR	22,00
Triglie in cartoccio	EUR	19,00
Calamari ripieni in teglia	EUR	17,00

Secondi di Carne

Cinghiale alla cacciatora	EUR	19,00
Scaloppine al limone	EUR	18,00
Bue brasato al Barolo	EUR	19,00
Saltimbocca alla romana	EUR	18,00
Coniglio con olive taggiasche	EUR	19,00

Contorni

Radicchio al forno	EUR	7,00
Melanzane alla menta	EUR	5,00
Puntarelle in salsa di alici	EUR	5,00
Insalata mista	EUR	4,00

Dolci

Macedonia di frutta		EUR	7,00
Tiramisù		EUR	7,00
Zuppa Inglese		EUR	8,00
Frutta varia di stagione		EUR	5,00

Formaggi

Ricotta fresca		EUR	6,00
Selezione di formaggi		EUR	10,00

Vini

Rosso della casa	½ lt	EUR	10,00
	¼ lt	EUR	5,00
Bianco della casa	½ lt	EUR	10,00
	¼ lt	EUR	5,00

Bibite

Acqua naturale	½ lt	EUR	2,00
Acqua gassata	½ lt	EUR	2,00
Coca Cola	33 cl	EUR	3,00

Birre

Nastro Azzurro	33 cl	EUR	3,00
Heineken	33 cl	EUR	4,00

Digestivi

Grappa		EUR	5,00
Amaro		EUR	5,00
Coperto e servizio		EUR	3,00

Sweet desserts
The meal ends with a sweet dessert or piece of fruit in season (*frutta varia di stagione*), or fruit salad (*macedonia di frutta*).

Cheese
Another popular end to the meal is cheese. The cheese board (*selezione di formaggi*) usually consists of regional specialties, and may feature some new discoveries that are not available in the stores.

Wine
The house wines of many Italian restaurants can be heartily recommended, as these are often good regional wines, and may be more enjoyable than the bottled ones.

Soft drinks
Mineral waters and internationally known soft drinks appear on all Italian menus. The waiter will ask "naturale o gassata?" if mineral water is ordered. This means "still or fizzy?"

Beer
The beers offered usually include some international ones and one or two local varieties. If the quantity is given as 33 cl, bottled beer is meant. Draft beer comes in multiples of 100 centiliters – the choice here is between *birra piccola* (0.2 liters, or just under ½ pint), *media* (0.3–0.4 liters, roughly ½–¾ pint), and *grande* (up to 1 liter, or about 2 pints).

Digestifs
The choice of alcoholic aids to digestion includes marc (*grappa*), anis (*sambuca, mistrà, sassolino, etc.*), regional bitters (*amaro*), and various liquors based on herbs (*centerbe, genepy*).

Cover and service charge
In some restaurants, the prices charged for the food itself exclude the cost of the service and basic table items such as oil and vinegar, bread, olives to nibble while waiting, provision of cutlery, and the like. The service charge (*coperto e servizio*) is levied to take account of these. Other restaurants charge inclusive prices for the food. If the menu does not make clear which is being done, the best solution is to ask the waiter. Even if service is included, the staff are always happy to receive a tip from satisfied customers. The amount is usually five to ten percent of the total bill, though up to 15 percent might be given if service is exceptional.

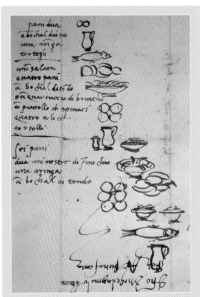

Michelangelo Buonarotti, *Three lists of foods*, pencil, 21.3 x 14.5 cm, Archivio Buonarotti, Florence.

THE ITALIAN MENU

In many restaurants, a menu exists, yet the customers hardly look at it. It seems puzzling that anyone bothered to write it. Instead, guests consult the menu of the day, or seek the advice of the waiter or innkeeper. This is regarded as a more reliable way of finding out the best dishes to choose. The freshest options of the day are usually chalked up on a slate, reasonably legibly and interspersed with dialect terms. No-one need hesitate to ask if the information is not clear: extensive discussion with the staff is all part of the accepted proceedings when visiting a restaurant, and some restaurants even dispense with a written menu altogether. Instead, the waiter arrives at the table and lists what is available. Sometimes, the chef will also offer the customers advice at the table, or ask what they would like. Those from outside the area can ask for a description of the regional specialties. The different terms and culinary traditions of the Italian regions make this a necessity, and no customer should feel embarrassed about asking what ingredients or methods of preparation are involved. This will not be seen as indicating a lack of confidence in the cook, but as the guest's natural interest in ensuring an enjoyable evening. If the dishes described do not appeal, it is still no problem. The customers can describe what they want, and can even ask the kitchen whether the necessary ingredients are available. They can say how they would like these prepared: would they like their spinach with onions and garlic, or without? Do they enjoy piquant food, or do they dislike *peperoncini*? These details are matters the cook cannot know, and are not seen as awkwardness on the part of the customers, simply as indications to help ensure satisfaction.

A BRIEF GUIDE TO MENU TERMS

al forno: oven-baked
alla casalinga: housewife style
alla griglia: broiled
all'uovo: with egg
al pomodoro: with tomatoes
arrabbiato: piquant; with *peperoncini*
arrosto: roast
bollito: boiled

brasato: braised
con aglio: with garlic
con cipolla: with onion
con latte: with milk
con limone: with lemon
con olio: with oil
con panna: with cream
cotto: cooked
crudo: raw
fritto: fried
gratinato: topped with toasted cheese

in agro: in lemon or vinegar
in agro-dolce: sweet and sour
in brodo: in stock
in marinata: marinated
in padella: pan-fried
in umido: braised or poached in a gravy or sauce
magro: lean
ripieno: stuffed
sott'aceto: preserved in vinegar
sott'olio: preserved in oil

A DAY IN THE LIFE OF A CHEF

A strict hierarchy exists in the upper echelons of gastronomy. The regular cooks in the bottom ranks have immediately over them the *demi-chef de partie* and *chef de partie* (senior chefs). They in turn are under the authority of the *sous-chef* (deputy kitchen chef), and above them is the *chef de cuisine* (kitchen chef), or catering manager of a large establishment.

The kitchen chef is the unquestioned authority in the kitchen domain. Only the chef or deputy chef (if the chef is absent) has the right to taste the food and make any decision to adjust the seasoning. On the other hand, it is only the combined skill of the entire team that enables a kitchen chef to reach the highest ranks of international gastronomy, however versatile and gifted that chef may be. Unless the staff includes specialist buyers, the chef's day begins extremely early, with a visit to the vegetable or fishmarkets around three or four in the morning to select the ingredients for the day. During the course of the morning, goods ordered the previous day are delivered. All orders are prefaced by the negotiation of prices and the calculation of the quantities required. Does the chef need a haunch of venison for 20 evening guests, or for a party of 60 businessmen? As the goods arrive, the chef inspects them and checks the quality. Meat and dairy products must be genuinely fresh, and the prices and quantities must tally with the order. The next stage is to discuss the forthcoming menu, and to establish with the service personnel whether there are any guests with special requirements to be catered for. Between eleven and half past, the preliminary cooking begins. Sauces are prepared, and meat put into the roasting ovens. The chef takes part in the preparation, samples the food, and above all, coordinates activities. There is a break after the work of lunch is done.

The chef goes into the restaurant to check that all is in order. In the afternoon, the preparations for the evening are made.

The chef is also responsible for drawing up new menus. This includes decisions about prices and suitable wines to accompany the food. Stocks of drinks, foodstuffs, and kitchen equipment must be maintained. The chef also has the final authority in staffing decisions within the kitchen domain, draws up work rotas, and decides who shall and shall not be allowed to cook in that kitchen.

Below: Complete concentration in the kitchen of Antonio Marangi, chef of the Milanese restaurant Giannino.

Separator pan (casseruola con 4 cola-pasta a spicchio e coperchio)
For boiling different types of pasta with different cooking times.

Sauté pan (sauté a sponda dritta)
Food inside is kept constantly moving by circular, controlled agitation of the pan. This cooks it evenly and preserves flavor.

Spaghetti saucepan (pentola cilindrica)
For boiling all pasta with a long noodle shape, *bucatini* and *trenette* as well as spaghetti. Also for making stock.

Colander (colapasta sferica 3 piedi)
A freestanding steel colander for draining pasta is more hygienic. Plastic softens and distorts with heat over time.

Non-stick roasting/broiling pan (rostiera antiaderente)
Ideal for oven cooking of meat and vegetable dishes.

Couscous pot (pentola per cous cous)
Used in Sicily and the Sardinian island of Carloforte for the Arab-Sicilian dish *cusucusu* and the Tunisian *cashka*.

Frying and gratin dish (tegame svasato a 2 manici)
For frying small fish, omelets, and foods requiring short cooking times.

Shallow saucepan (casseruola bassa)
Useful for pot-roasting, involving long, slow cooking.

Perforated insert for pasta pot (scalda-pasta a 1 manico con fondo piano)
Enables cooked pasta to be lifted free of the water.

Handled saucepan (casseruola fonda a 1 manico)
For making sauces, cooking polenta, or use as steamer base.

Saucepan (casseruola fonda a 2 manici)
Versatile saucepan for making stock, boiling, braising, and pot-roasting meat.

Nonstick skillet (padella antiaderente)
For low-fat frying on a high heat. Also for sautéing cooked vegetables in olive oil and garlic.

Skillet (padella a sponda obliqua medio peso)
Stainless steel or copper make the best pans.

Fish kettle (romboniera con griglia e coperchio)
This type is for cooking turbot.

Fish kettle (romboniera con griglia e coperchio)
Note the inner steaming platform on which the fish rests.

Deep fryer (padella per fritto alta con paniere)
The frying basket allows fried food to drain.

Long fish kettle with steaming plat-form (pesciera con griglia e coperchio)
For poaching or steaming whole, long fish.

Fine-mesh chinois or tammy strainer (chinois a maglia fine)
Conical strainer for soups and sauces at the end of preparation.

Fine-mesh bowl strainer (colino semi-sferico a rete fina)
Sieve for stocks, soups, and sauces.

Flat perforated spoon (schiumarola a rete fine)
Fine-mesh version for lifting and draining a range of deep-fried food, such as vegetables, mozzarella fritters, and fish.

Ladle (mestolo fondo)
For stirring and serving soups cleanly and without drips.

Fish slice (paletta con fori per pesce)
This slotted lifting spatula keeps the fish whole and allows cooking liquid to drain.

Cooking fork (forchettone unipezzo a 2 denti)
For turning roasts and holding meat in place while carving.

Basting spoon (cucchiaione fondo)
A versatile utensil. Useful when making *quenelles*, which are shaped between two oiled spoons.

Perforated spoon (schiumarola)
Has many uses. Can be used to lift cooked gnocchi individually out of the water.

Spatula (palettina senza fori)
Useful for lifting food out of baking dishes without crumbling.

Wooden pizza lifter (pala piatta rettan-golare per pizza)
A large, flat, wooden scoop with a handle for reaching into deep pizza ovens.

Mandoline grater (tagliaverdure a mandolino)
For grating vegetables quickly by hand.

Waffle iron (tostatore in alluminio per gauffres e cialde)
For *cialde alla fiorentina* and *brigidini*.

Hand molds for pastry shapes (stampo per crostatine in lega di ottone)

Stamper (stampo per passatelli)
The *passatelli* can be pressed straight into the stock beneath.

Chestnut roaster (padella per castagne)
For dry-roasting chestnuts.

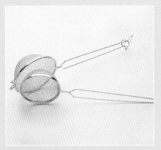

Mesh ladle for nest pasta (paniere per nidi, filostagno)
May be used for preparing nests of tagliatelle, for example.

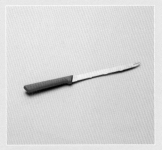

Citrus knife (tagliamino)
A long, thin, serrated knife for cutting lemons. The forked point can be used to lift individual slices.

Nutmeg and lemon zest grater (grattugia per noce moscata e buccia di limone)
Many recipes call for grated nutmeg.

Rolling pin (mattarello)
Used mainly in the preparation of fresh pasta (*pasta fresca*) and the dough for tortellini, ravioli, *quadrucci*, and tagliatelle.

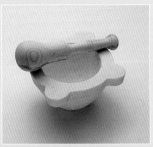

Mortar (mortaio in marmo)
It is better to use a pestle and mortar to make pesto, because the metal blades of food mixers discolor the basil.

Meat grinder (tritacarne)
Ground meat hamburgers or *polpette* and meat balls of all sorts are popular in Italy too.

Mixing bowl (bacinella bombata)
Useful for whisking egg white or cream, and for puréeing fruit.

Lemon press (spremi spicchi per agrumi)
Allows juice to be squeezed over meat and fish without soiling the hands.

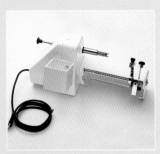

Apple peeler (pela e affetta mele "Kali")
Peels and cores apples neatly in an instant.

Potato ricer (schiacciapatate professionale)
For crushing boiled potatoes, as when making gnocchi.

Flour scoop (paletta per la farina)
Flour is in constant use in the Italian kitchen, and does not stick to a wooden scoop.

Tomato slicer (affettapomodori "Econo pro")
Instantly cuts tomatoes into even slices.

Spaghetti tongs (molla per spaghetti)
Lifts and serves spaghetti cleanly and easily.

Snail tongs (molla per lumache)
Used to hold the snail and keep the hands clean.

Fish scaling knife (squamapesce)
For removing the scales from fish.

Balloon whisk (frusta)
For whisking egg whites, beating sauces and gravies, and preventing lumps.

VIRTUOSO DELIGHTS OF CREMONA

The city of Cremona, an important inland port on the River Po, is of course memorable for its contributions in the sphere of music. Antonio Stradivarius, who gave the world his universally famous violins, was a son of Cremona. It has also bestowed the gift of two culinary specialties: *torrone*, a sweet and sometimes sticky candy made of honey and almonds, and a combination of candied fruits in hot mustard, called *mostarda*. Cremona's claim to be the originator of *torrone* does not stand up to scrutiny, however.

TORRONE

The invention of *torrone* is often said to go back to 1441, to the marriage of Bianca Maria Visconti and Francesco Sforza in Cremona. The account claims that, on October 25 of that year, the town's confectioners made an enormous cake of honey and almonds for the wedding breakfast. The cake was in the form of the *torrazzo*, the tall tower on the city's main square. The banquet was held in that very square, which meant that the cake was doubly impressive, because the diners could compare it with the original.

Farther back in time, the Romans used to eat a cake of honey and almonds as a finale to their dinners. There is another early record of this candy dating from the period between 1100 and 1150. A certain Gherardo, citizen of Cremona, was translating a book by a medical doctor, Abdul Mutarrif, whose practice was in Córdoba, Spain. In this work, *De medicinis et cibis simplicibus*, the scholar not only praised the beneficial properties of honey, but spoke of an Arab sweetmeat called *turun*. It seems more likely that this, rather than the *torrazzo* of Cremona, is the true origin of the name *torrone*. Nevertheless, Cremona does produce an extremely delicious *torrone*.

MOSTARDA

The Italian word *mostarda* comes from the French *moutarde* (mustard). This in turn comes from *moult ardent* (hot juice). It used to be the practice to mix mustard seed with grape juice to create a hot seasoning. *Mostarda di Cremona* consists of candied fruits such as cherries, figs, and pears, preserved in a mixture of sugar syrup and white mustard. The result is a highly piquant accompaniment for boiled meat, game, or poultry.

Today, *mostarda di Cremona* is mainly commercially produced. The factories do not use candied fruits, but a stewed fruit mixture that is mixed with mustard sauce. The piquancy of the mustard has been considerably reduced to meet the demands of customers' palates. As with other commercially made mustard products, the flavors and aromas are always best when the *mostarda* is freshly opened, not after it has been kept for any length of time.

Mostarda di Cremona is a piquant accompaniment to other dishes. Tuscany has a similar specialty, called *mostarda all'uso toscano*.

Torrone comes in all sorts of regional variations, sometimes even coated in chocolate.

The imposing campanile and cathedral with its surrounding towers is one of the most famous and impressive sights of Cremona.

BISCOTTI – COOKIES

Biscotti feature prominently on the Italian culinary scene. Every region has its own varieties, shapes, bakers, and, occasionally, factories. The annual production of *tenerezze, mattutini, gocciole,* and other cookies by companies such as Mulino Bianco and Varesi (both part of the Barilla Group) is measured in tons. The basic mix can be variously of the biscuit, yeast, or shortbread type, with or without egg, sweetened with sugar or with honey; it may contain cocoa or chocolate, have a jam or cream filling, or include almonds, filberts, or dried fruit. Cookies are mainly eaten at breakfast in Italy, where it is the custom to eat cake or to dunk one or two *biscotti* into hot milky coffee, or *caffè latte* as it is known there.

LAZZARONI AND AMARETTI

A great variety of different types of amaretti and the smaller amarettini can be found, from the tiny, hard cookies to the large and succulent macaroons with their rounded tops. An espresso ordered in a northern Italian bar will usually arrive accompanied by a cookie of this kind, a special pleasure if it is one of the original Amaretti di Saronno. Amaretti from the town of Mombaruzzo in Piedmont are another type considered to be particularly delicious. They are wrapped by hand in colored paper, like pieces of candy.

The history of amaretti stretches back to the end of the 18th century, to the time when coffeehouses were becoming increasingly popular, and were often meeting places for men of ideas – the scene of lively debate between artists, scholars, and the proponents of various contemporary political causes. Some of the coffeehouses in Milan belonged to the Lazzaroni family. Carlo Lazzaroni (1774–1835), founder of the Amaretti di Saronno dynasty, gradually bought up small bakeries in his home town of Saronno, which had been making almond macaroons for generations, and began to sell their products in his coffeehouses in Milan. His son, Davide (1808–1879), decided to abandon using the small bakeries for production, and built the first cookie factory in Lazzaroni. Here, he manufactured not only the family's established product, amaretti, but also cookies made with an egg-enriched mixture, and panettone. The succeeding generation, the brothers Giacinto, Ernesto, and Piero, founded the company of Davide Lazzaroni & C., but overreached themselves with the construction of a new factory. They were obliged to turn to their cousin, Luigi (1847–1933), to save them from bankruptcy. He was at that time already a successful manufacturer of liqueurs and candied fruits in Monza, so had the means to stage a rescue. Under Luigi's management, the company of Lazzaroni grew into a solid presence in the Italian food industry. He even succeeded in beating back competition from British imports, then dominant in the cookie market. He extended the company's product range, and made attempts to expand exports into Europe north of the Alps. He had to battle against setbacks and disasters, including two factory fires (in 1898 and 1911) and the economic crisis of World War I. Following Luigi's death in 1933, he was succeeded by his sons, Paolo and Mario. They too remained faithful to the family philosophy of making sure only the highest quality goods left the factory, and that the cookies must be packed and presented accordingly. This approach led to the introduction of the beautifully designed tins of the 1920s and 1930s, which have become valuable collectors' items.

Pannocchie

Cinfalotti

Pan di Stelle

Gran Cereale

Primi Raggi

Mattutini

Spicchi di Sol

THE GONZAGAS OF MANTUA

The Gonzaga family had already been rulers of Mantua since the early 14th century. It was not a particularly prosperous region, though it provided an adequate living. The family remained self-contained, little concerned with its neighbors, until the cities of the Renaissance began to flourish, and the Gonzagas started to consider how they in their palace at Mantua could raise their standing with the outside world. They were a family of ancient nobility, but had never enjoyed great riches. A "PR strategy" was called for! The court eventually turned its attention to the cultural approach being developed by Lorenzo il Magnifico in the Tuscan city of Florence. There, the ambassadors of foreign courts and influential merchants received their impression of the city's importance through the artistic and architectural splendors that surrounded them. Around 1470, the Gonzagas acquired the services of the universally acclaimed and innovative painter, Andrea Mantegna (1431–1506). This is the first instance in history of an artist being engaged by a prince, and paid a princely salary to work exclusively for the court.

Above: Andrea Mantegna, Ceiling fresco in the *Camera degli Sposi* with heads of women and putti, 1465–1474, Palazzo Ducale, Mantua.

FAREWELL TO THE MIDDLE AGES

Renaissance effects on Italian cooking are closely linked to the names of two men: Maestro Martino of Como and Bartolomeo Sacchi, called Platina, from Piadena which is near Cremona.

Maestro Martino was personal cook to the bishop of Aquileia at the beginning of the 15th century. He wrote a book called *Liber de arte coquinaria* (On the art of cooking). Bartolomeo Sacchi, called Platina, born 1421, began his career at the court of the Gonzagas. He later spent a few years in Florence, before moving on to Rome, where he took up a post as secretary and scribe at the papal court of Pius II. He was promoted to become the first librarian in charge of the Vatican library when Sixtus IV became pope. Platina put together a compendium on the lives of the popes, but also took an interest in texts about less spiritual and more earthly matters. In this way, he came across Maestro Martino's cookbook. He translated and slightly edited it, and prefaced it with a few chapters of his own. The title was *De honesta voluptate et valetudine* (On honest pleasure and health). The book was published in Rome in 1474, and became in effect the very first bestseller in cooking literature. Language was no barrier to its spread, as Latin was a universal language, and it became known as a culinary classic far beyond Italy. Within a hundred years, it had been reprinted over 30 times, and it was freely translated into other languages, including Italian, French, English, and German.

The book's enduring success can be attributed to the fact that it attempts for the first time to present the culinary and gastronomic knowledge of the second half of the 15th century in a comprehensive and systematic way. This is no mere list of practical instructions on kitchen techniques; the book covers all aspects of cuisine. Dietetics and food hygiene feature in it, and there are useful tips about the composition of certain food products, their nutritional value, and their medicinal uses. The book discusses the ethical aspect of nutrition and the joys of the table. This was a book designed for the middle and higher sections of society, with the moral and intellectual capacity to understand such matters. Taken as a whole, it is a plea for a revolution in taste. People should henceforward, in "the unimportant provision of nourishment," aim for the satisfaction of "the pleasure that comes from honest activity." This, it argues, is the satisfaction that leads to happiness, "just as medicine gives the sick man back his health."

The achievements of Maestro Martino and Platina spelled the end of medieval cuisine, and ushered in a new era. The taste of the Middle Ages was for all that was rare and expensive and able to demonstrate the wealth of the host. Costly spices were used in such great quantity that guests could hardly identify the food at all on first tasting it. This may have been no bad thing, as the food itself was chosen for its rarity value. A dinner of tough eagles or venerable bears emphasized the prestige of the host, but the meat had to be precooked for hours before preparation, and swamped in thick sauces afterwards, simply to make it edible. "Modern" cuisine as promoted by Maestro Martino and Platina placed the emphasis on the use of simple, fresh, widely available ingredients, and on bringing out the true flavors by means of short cooking times, not rendering them ineffective with heavy-handed seasoning. These are the principles that guide Italian cuisine to this day.

BARTOLOMEO STEFANI

A native of Bologna, Bartolomeo Stefani was the kitchen chef at the court of the Gonzagas in Mantua in the second half of the 17th century. The exact dates of his birth and death are not known, but the preface of his book, *L'arte di ben cucinare* (The art of good cooking), seems to indicate that he was the nephew and pupil of Giulio Cesare Tirelli, kitchen chef in the services of the Republic of Venice.

L'arte di ben cucinare is firmly rooted in the traditions of Italian cuisine, and keeps the promise stated in its title. It is also the first cookbook to pay attention to the everyday dishes, *vitto ordinario*, eaten by people of the middle classes, rather than to the feasts of the ruling elite. It is an innovative work in other ways, too: Bartolomeo Stefani not only proposes alternatives to the princely banquets, but deals so minutely with the details that he even offers estimates of the cost of ingredients. The first edition of this work appeared in 1662 in Mantua. This was followed by seven further editions, which continued to appear until 1716.

L'ARTE
DI BEN CVCINARE, ET INSTRVIRE
i men periti in questa lodeuole professione.
Doue ance s'insegna à far Pasticci, Sapori, Salse, Gelatine, Torte, & altro
DI BARTOLOMEO STEFANI
Cuoco Bolognese.
All'Ill.mo, & Ecc.mo Sig. Marchese
OTTAVIO GONZAGA
Prencipe del Sacro Romano Imperio, de'Marchesi
di Mantoua, e Signor di Vescouato, &c.

IN MANTOVA, Appresso gli Osanna, Stampatori Ducali. 1663.
Con licenza de' Superiori,

TORTELLI DI ZUCCA
Pasta with pumpkin filling
(Illustration in background)

Serves 6

1 PUMPKIN (ABOUT 5 LB/2 KG IN WEIGHT)
1 1/2 CUPS/150 G CRUSHED AMARETTI
SCANT 1/2 CUP/50 G SWEET AND SOUR PRESERVED APPLES
OR OTHER FRUITS PRESERVED IN MUSTARD (MOSTARDA)
1 CUP/100 G FRESHLY GRATED PARMESAN
1/4 ONION, CHOPPED
GRATED NUTMEG
PASTA DOUGH (SEE PAGE 191)
SALT
2 TBSP BUTTER

Slice the pumpkin, then peel it and remove the center. Bake it for about 20 minutes at 400 °F (200 °C). Transfer to a bowl and crush the cooked pumpkin with a fork. Chop the mustard fruits and add to the pumpkin, with the crushed amaretti, grated Parmesan, chopped onion, and a little grated nutmeg. Stir together using a wooden spoon, and ensure that the mixture is dry. Roll out the pasta dough thinly, and cut into rectangles 1½ inches/4 cm by 3 inches/8 cm. Place a spoonful of filling on each piece, and fold the pasta over in the middle to enclose the filling. Press the edges together firmly. Cook the *tortelli* in plenty of boiling salted water, and serve with melted butter.

FRESHWATER FISH

Lombardy is a land of abundant lakes and rivers. Tourists swarm to Lago d'Iseo, Lago d'Idro, Lago di Varese and Lake Como, but these lakes are also valuable as a source of freshwater fish. Demand exceeds the naturally available supply, so fish farming is now well established. In the province of Brescia, there is a fish farm that breeds not only the usual freshwater fish, such as salmon trout and rainbow trout, but also has tanks for eels. It even farms sturgeon, and produces small quantities of fine caviar. Environmental problems have all but destroyed the northern Italian sturgeon in the wild, although they did once frequent the River Po and its delta.

FILETTI DI LAVARELLO IN CARPIONE
Marinated whitefish
(Illustration left)

2 ONIONS
2 CARROTS
3–4 TBSP EXTRA VIRGIN OLIVE OIL
1 BAY LEAF
1 SPRIG OF PARSLEY
1 GLASS OF WHITE WINE VINEGAR
SALT AND PEPPER
8 WHITEFISH FILLETS, PREPARED

Chop the onions very finely, and thinly slice the carrots. Cook them gently in a little olive oil. Add the bay leaf, parsley, wine vinegar, remaining olive oil, and a glass of water. Season with salt and pepper, and simmer until the liquid has been reduced by half.
Wash the whitefish fillets, season with salt and pepper, and place in a heatproof casserole. Cover with the marinade, and cook for a few minutes. Cool and leave to marinate for at least 12 hours in the refrigerator.
Other fish, such as carp, tench, and common whitefish can be prepared in the same way. It is important to use very high quality vinegar, for flavor and for keeping qualities.

FILETTI DI TROTA IN COTOLETTA
Trout in breadcrumbs

4 TROUT FILLETS
1 CUP/250 ML MILK
SALT
SCANT 1/2 CUP/50 G ALL-PURPOSE FLOUR
1 EGG
BREADCRUMBS
3–4 TBSP EXTRA VIRGIN OLIVE OIL
A FEW SLICES OF LEMON
PARSLEY

Wash and clean the trout fillets, and marinate in salted milk for 1 hour. Pour off the milk, and pat the fish dry. Beat the egg. Coat the fish lightly in flour, then in beaten egg, and finally in the breadcrumbs.
Heat the olive oil in a skillet, and fry the fish until golden. Drain on paper towels. Garnish with lemon slices and parsley to serve.

Trota (Trout)
Rainbow trout, salmon trout, and brook trout all live in the waters of Lombardy. These delicious freshwater fish are much in demand, and farmed in large numbers, though there are few trout left in the wild. Trout are at their best broiled, but are also good marinated or fried in breadcrumbs.

Coregone, lavarello (whitefish)
This small fish – only 12 inches (30 cm) long – is prized for its delicate flesh. It was introduced to northern Italian waters at the end of the 19th century, where it has increased greatly in number, much to the delight of gourmets. Whitefish are versatile, and can be prepared by any method.

Pesce persico (Perch)
Perch are the amateur angler's favorite fish. Every weekend, the lakes of Lombardy attract many such anglers. The fish can be bought in the local stores, ready filleted, by those who prefer not to line the banks with rod and line. The fish is delicious, but has many bones. It can be fried, or served with *antipasto*.

Temolo (grayling)
Grayling are a rare freshwater fish. They mainly frequent very pure, clean waters. Their flesh has a delicate flavor, reminiscent of thyme. Gentle methods of cooking are best for this fish, to preserve the fine flavor.

Storione (sturgeon)
There are no more sturgeon living wild in the upper Italian lakes, though they are being farmed on a small scale. Sturgeon are mainly treasured for their roe, which is used as caviar. The flesh is very oily, but tastes good broiled or fried, or filleted and cooked in breadcrumbs.

VELTELLINA

The meat products of Valtellina, such as *bresaola*, are widely sought after beyond the immediate region, and another local specialty, buckwheat noodles known as *pizzoccheri*, have increased enormously in popularity. Recently, demand has risen to such an extent that an industrial means of production had to be developed. This in turn increased the requirement for buckwheat beyond what could be grown in the valley itself, and made it necessary to import more from Russia and the former Yugoslavia.

Valtellina is one of the last remaining places where this tasty, health-giving cereal still grows – although it is not strictly speaking a "grain" at all in the botanic sense. Buckwheat, or *grano saraceno*, to give it its Italian name, has always had a place in mountain cuisine, where the land is less fertile. The pasta for *pizzoccheri* is made with two thirds buckwheat flour to one third wheat flour. The wheat flour is needed to provide the gluten that holds the pasta together; buckwheat flour lacks gluten. An excellent way to enjoy *pizzoccheri* is in an oven-baked gratin mixture with potatoes, sage, and Savoy cabbage, using a flavorsome Alpine cheese such as *bitto* or *fontina*.

PIZZOCCHERI
Buckwheat noodle bake
(Illustration below)

1 2/3 CUPS/200 G BUCKWHEAT FLOUR
SCANT 1 CUP/100 G ALL-PURPOSE FLOUR
SALT
2–3 TBSP MILK, 2–3 TBSP WATER
1 EGG
SCANT 1/2 LB/200 G POTATOES
1/4 SAVOY CABBAGE
6 1/2 TBSP/100 G BUTTER
1 CLOVE OF GARLIC, FINELY CHOPPED
3 LEAVES OF SAGE, FINELY CHOPPED
1 1/3 CUPS/100 G COARSELY GRATED SEMIHARD CHEESE (BITTO OR FONTINA)
1 CUP/100 G FRESHLY GRATED PARMESAN

Sift the two flours together with a little salt, and mix with about 2–3 tbsp of milk and of water. Knead together with the egg. Roll out the dough and cut into pasta strips. Cover with a cloth.

Peel and slice the potatoes. Wash the cabbage, and cook with the potatoes in plenty of boiling, salted water for 15 minutes. Then add the pasta, and continue cooking until this is al dente. Drain well. Melt the butter in a small saucepan, and add the garlic and sage. Layer the potatoes, cabbage, pasta, the sliced or coarsely grated cheese, the parmesan, and the herb butter in a large casserole dish. Place under the preheated grill for a few minutes. Sprinkle with more parmesan and serve hot.

VALTELLINA WINES

Valtellina used to be the supplier of casked wines for Switzerland, which lies next door. The main grape variety grown in the valley is Nebbiolo, here called Chiavennasca. Small amounts of Pinot nero, Merlot, and local varieties are also used. The Adda valley is so narrow that the sun only reaches its steep vineyard slopes for a few hours a day. This means that grapes grown there do not always achieve maximum ripeness, and it is important to know which precise vineyard produced the wines. The best have achieved DOC recognition. The names of the wines from this region between Sondrio and Montagna are Sassella, Grumello, Inferno, and Valgello. They are sold as Valtellina superiore.

Good Valtellina wines have a fragrance of red fruits and tea leaves, like some Nebbiolo wines from Piedmont. They can be rather hard and unyielding when young, but become round and velvety as they age. The true specialty among Valtellina wines is a *vin de paille* called Sfursat. It is a heavy, dry wine in the style of Amarone, from the Veneto, a wine made by drying the grapes for a time before pressing, in order to increase the concentration of sugar. Only three or four wine growers and wineries produce Sfursat, making it very rare.

Valtellina specialties

Bresaola

Bresaola first entered the list of gastronomic specialties from the small town of Chiavenna over 100 years ago. It is a cured and air-dried beef, originating from Graubünden in Switzerland. As a product, this means it is related to the Swiss *Bündnerfleisch*.

The meat is cut off the leg, and first cured in salt and pepper before being hung for several months to dry. The microclimate of the Chiavenna caves offer ideal conditions for maturation. Occasionally, light smoking is needed in the latter stages.

Bresaola has a delicately aromatic flavor, not too salty. It is nutritious and easy to digest. It is now made industrially, and has gained so much in popularity that it is to be found even in the far south of Italy. Gourmets slice it thinly and serve it with lemon juice, oil, and freshly milled pepper.

Slinzega

Unlike *bresaola*, which is made from beef, *slinzega* can be made from other meats – horse, donkey, or chamois – though it need not be. These meats are used in the province of Sondrio in particular, where *slinzega* is almost never made from beef. The meat is cured in a brine made to an old recipe. Maturation and smoking are carried out as for *bresaola*.

Violino

Violino is made from shoulder or leg of goat or mutton. The process is the same as for ham. The name *violino* comes from the way it is sliced – by holding it up like a violin, and wielding the knife like a bow. The pieces of meat are selected and flavored with garlic and juniper. Sometimes, they are cured in red wine. The maturation process is the same as for *bresaola*.

Bitto

This cheese is named after the River Bitto, a tributary of the Adda. It is made almost exclusively in Sondrio province. The cheese is cylindrical, 3–5 inches (8–12 cm) high, and weighs 33–55 pounds (15–25 kg). The curd is cooked, molded, and salted, and then ripened for three to six months in cool conditions. The ripening time can be a whole year if the cheese is intended for grating. The paste of the young cheese is fine, but becomes denser and more crumbly as it ages, intensifying in flavor. *Bitto* is enjoyed at the end of a meal with a glass of Sassella, Grumello, Inferno, or Valtellina. It is also an essential ingredient of *polenta taragna* and *sciatt*.

Casera

Casera is a cheese made throughout Valtellina from partially skimmed milk. After adding rennet and heating, the curd has to rest. Then the cheeses are molded, and either dry salted straight away or placed in brine. Ripening takes 30 days.

Casera is a cheese with a medium fat content, whitish in color, and with a thin rind. It is also made by dairies in other parts of Lombardy, outside Valtellina.

Sciatt
Cheese flat bread

Serves 6

1 2/3 cups/200 g buckwheat flour
Scant 1 cup/100 g all-purpose flour
Salt
1/4 lb/100 g bitto
2 tsp/10 ml grappa
1 tbsp/15 g butter

Sift the two flours together, and mix in enough lukewarm water to make a moderately stiff dough. Add salt, cover, and leave to rest for about an hour. Slice the cheese thinly, and mix into the dough. Add the grappa. Melt the butter in a non-stick skillet, and cook about a spoonful of the dough at a time, first pressing each portion into a flat cake. Drain on paper towels, and serve hot.

Bresaola condita
Bresaola with egg
(Illustration below)

3/4 lb/350 g bresaola, finely sliced
Extra virgin olive oil
2 egg yolks
Freshly ground pepper
Oregano
Juice of 1 lemon

Arrange wafer-thin slices of the meat on 4 plates, or on a serving platter. Sprinkle with olive oil. Beat the egg yolks, and drizzle over the *bresaola*. Season with pepper and oregano, and leave for a few minutes before sprinkling with lemon juice. Serve with rye bread.

Bresaola mit Parmesan

ITALY'S ANSWER TO CHAMPAGNE

The name Franciacorta belongs to a winegrowing region in the moraine landscape on the southern shores of Lago d'Iseo, the small lake that lies between Bergamo and Brescia. The name may date from Napoleonic times, deriving from the words *corte* (court) and *Francia* (France), as local tradition claims. Alternatively, it may be an older term, from *francae curtes*, meaning free of tax, a status that was conferred on the Benedictines in the Middle Ages. Winegrowing has been carried on here since the time of the Romans, although the only type of wine made here until the mid-20th century was a country red for local consumption.

The career of Franciacorta took off in 1961. A young oenologist from the area was convinced that the region was ideally suited to the production of sparkling wine, and persuaded his employer to begin doing so. In the 1970s, a number of industrialists from nearby Milan invested in the rising Spumante industry, which concentrated on producing its sparkling wine from Pinot and Chardonnay grapes, using the *méthode champenoise*, or bottle fermentation method. Franciacorta is usually made in the Brut style, though there are some excellent products that require no *dosage* of sugar. Today, it is not only the only DOCG sparkling wine produced in Italy, but it can stand alongside the world's best sparkling wines, from Cava to the top German Sekt, and champagne itself, without losing in the comparison.

The region's red and white nonsparkling wines are made from the same grape varieties, and sometimes barrique-aged. Today, they too are often of excellent quality. Since the classification of DOCG was awarded to sparkling Franciacorta, these still wines have been sold under the DOC name of Terre di Franciacorta.

Experienced winemakers are responsible for the sparkling wines of Franciacorta. This was the first Spumante to receive DOCG classification.

The castle of the Scaligeri, Rocca Scaligeri, watches over the small town of Sirmione, on a promontory in the south of Lake Garda. This is the home of Lugana.

The bottles are placed in the racks upside down, so that the yeast sediment can settle in the neck. The bottles are turned every day.

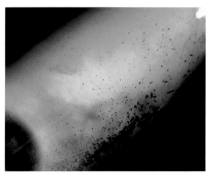

The bottle fermentation method is used to produce Franciacorta. The Spumante remains in contact with the yeast for years. It is eventually removed by disgorging.

WINEGROWING IN LOMBARDY

Think of Lombardy, and the thoughts that spring to mind are of Milan, the opera, fashion, gastronomy, and perhaps the area's trade and industry. Winegrowing is a less obvious association. The region always produced enough wine to supply the giant appetite of Milan, and provided the base wine for the sparkling wine industry of all Italy, but hardly any of its wines, apart from the Spumante of Franciacorta, has so far become at all known outside its borders.

Grapes are, however, grown in almost every part of the region, from the narrow Adda valley in Valtellina down through the western shores of Lake Garda, the Po plain at Mantua, and the hills south of Pavia, to the slopes in the provinces of Bergamo and Brescia. The largest winegrowing region in Lombardy occupies the hills of Oltrepò Pavese in Pavia province. Mainly red varieties are grown here – Barbera and Croatina are the most widely cultivated.

The area's soils suit Pinot Nero, or Pinot Noir. It is also vinified in its own right, resulting in fine, elegant red wines. Careful barrique aging develops its aromas and richness of taste. It is unfortunate that, in recent years, so few of the region's winegrowers have chosen the labor of love that is needed to produce quality wines. All too often still, Pinot Nero is grown here to provide base wine for Italy's sparkling wine production, in conjunction with Chardonnay and Pinot Blanc. It is interesting to note that the base wine provided to these other regions from Oltrepò Pavese is used in the production of some quite famous sparkling wines – in Piedmont or the Trentino, for example – yet its own sparkling wines are hardly known. It has often been the fate of Italian wine-producing regions that the local demand for their products exceeds supply. That fate seems to account for the position of Oltrepò Pavese. It is the area that has traditionally supplied Milan with wine, usually open wines for sale in the city's osterie.

White wines are mainly made around Lake Garda. They are mainly intended for local consumption only. The best known of these is Lugana, and it is probably also the best. The winegrowing region is shared with neighboring Veneto. Another area shared with a neighboring region, this time Emilia-Romagna, is Lambrusco. The quantities of this wine produced here, in the province of Mantua, are very small, though the wine is often better than over the border.

	Valtellina
	Valcalepio
	Franciacorta (DOCG), Terre di Franciacorta
	Cellatica
	Capriano del Colle
◇	Botticino
	Riviera del Garda Bresciano
▭	Tocai di San Martino della Battaglia
◆	Lugana
	Colli Morenici Mantovani del Garda
	Lambrusco Mantovano
	Oltrepo Pavese
	Winegrowing areas in neighboring regions

A visit to the vineyards on the hills of Oltrepò Pavese offers a rewarding panoramic view over the Po plain.

Lambrusco
The Lambrusco from Emilia-Romagna is better known than the wines produced in Lombardy under this name. Lovers of fruity wines with a little body but not too much sweetness may find, however, that the province of Mantua has just such wines to offer.

Terre di Franciacorta
The designation of origin Franciacorta once applied to still red and white wines, as well as sparkling ones. Once the sparkling wines earned their DOCG classification, that

changed. The still wines continue to be produced, but are now called Terre di Franciacorta. The white wines are made from Pinot bianco and Chardonnay, and the best winemakers age them in oak barriques. The reds come from Cabernet, Barbera, Nebbiolo, and Merlot.

Sebino
Sebino is not a DOC classification; it only has the status of a table wine with declaration of origin (Igt). However, some of the most outstanding winemakers of the Franciacorta region bottle their best wines under this label. The white wines are mainly Chardonnay, and the reds a Bordeaux blend. The wines are rich and complex, and can put many Italian DOC offerings in the shade.

Lugana
This white wine is produced on the southern shores of Lake Garda from a local variety of the Trebbiano grape family. The production area lies partly in Lombardy and partly in the Veneto. The aroma of this wine is fairly neutral, but in the mouth, the flavor is soft and harmonious, with little acidity. They are an excellent partner for freshwater fish dishes and also for seafood.

CAMPARI, OF COURSE

The Caffè Campari, opened in 1867 in the Galleria Vittorio Emanuele II in Milan, is a distinguished piece of Italian architecture. Soon after opening, it had attracted a large regular clientele. Behind the bar stood the owner himself, Gaspare Campari, and served his customers a creation of his own, *bitter all'ollandese* – bitters in the style of Holland. This drink, with its marked bitterness and striking red color, was enthusiastically received, and was renamed "bitter Campari." To this day, not a soul – apart, of course, from a few privileged employees in Milan – knows the true secret of Campari's ingredients. It is possible to guess, with a little knowledge of alcoholic liquors, that the bitter flavor must be due to cinchona or bitter orange peel, as it is in other bitter aperitifs, but what else? A dignified silence surrounds the matter. All the company will divulge is that the production of these bitters begins with an infusion of herbs, fruits, and various parts of plants. Then the aromas are extracted with alcohol. This flavor concentrate is topped up with alcohol, water, sugar, and a red coloring. What is this coloring? To answer cryptically: the coloring used to be obtained from the body shell of a small beetle, but it is now synthesized chemically.

Milanese bars like the Camparino, shown here, are inviting places for a quick espresso or Campari orange after an exhausting shopping trip.

DRINKS MIXED USING CAMPARI OR FERNET

All recipes serve 1

CAMPARI ORANGE
(Illustration above)

1 MEASURE OF CAMPARI
2 MEASURES OF ORANGE JUICE

Place ice cubes in a glass. Add Campari, top up with orange juice, and stir gently.

CAMPARI SHAKERATO

MEASURE OF CAMPARI
ICE CUBES

Place the ice cubes and Campari in a cocktail shaker. Shake vigorously, and strain into a chilled glass.

FARMACIA

ICE CUBES
1/2 MEASURE OF FERNET BRANCA
1/2 MEASURE OF SWEET VERMOUTH
1/2 MEASURE OF CRÈME DE MENTHE

Place all the ingredients into a cocktail jug, and stir. Pour into a chilled glass.

FERNET

Imagine the end of a wonderful, but slightly heavy meal. Imagine, too, a highly aromatic and soothing drink, the ease of each sip, the relief even in anticipation. Such is Fernet. And it is not only a fine digestif: it is an example of *ben bere alla milanese* – drinking well, in the style of Milan.

This brew of various top secret herbs and alcohol is traditionally matured in oak casks. The first Fernet bottles, which date back to the 18th century, bore a label stating the health claims of the drink: "Benefits the stomach, promotes digestion, strengthens the body, overcomes cholera, reduces fever, and heals those suffering from nervous weakness, lack of appetite, sickness, or tapeworms; suitable for use as a preventative measure for all who are obliged to reside in damp and infectious conditions. May be taken at any time of day as required, undiluted or mixed with water, soda water, wine, coffee, vermouth, or other beverages."

A few of the indications listed are regarded with a little more doubt today: effective against cholera? One thing, though, has not changed. This eminently drinkable medicine is a magnificent remedy for a full stomach after a copious meal.

The Italian bar

Italian bars, unlike those in some other countries, are open throughout the day. This makes them popular meeting places at any hour: perhaps for a *caffè latte* on the way to work, to be sipped standing at the bar, with a small, sweet brioche or a few cookies – or just the coffee on its own. No importance is attached to breakfast in Italy. Tales of bread rolls and jam, of cold meats, even of the astonishing English breakfast with bacon and eggs, have reached the ears of Italians, but are met with something bordering on disbelief or indifference.

Around ten o'clock, the mid-morning break brings a fresh opportunity to return to the bar for a snack, accompanied by an espresso or even a glass of Spumante.

People often go home for lunch, but any who stay can head for the nearest bar to buy a *tramezzino*. These are elaborately filled sandwiches, sometimes toasted on the outside in a sandwich-maker, especially in the regions of the north.

The next flood of bar customers arrive as the stores and offices close. This time, the espresso is often accompanied by an alcoholic drink. If it is time to take an aperitif in anticipation of the evening meal, then visitors to the bar will order one. Italians tend to prefer bitter appetizers like Campari, Aperol, and various herb-based aperitifs, but dry Spumante is becoming just as popular. After the evening meal, the regulars gather at their favorite bar for a *caffè*

corretto, an espresso whose stimulating caffeine content has been "corrected" by the addition of amaretto, grappa, or sambuca. There will usually be some acquaintance to talk to, whether about plans to buy a new car, the political situation in Italy, or just local chitchat.

Lombardy and its capital, Milan, constitute one of the richest regions of Italy. This former stronghold of the mighty Sforza dynasty is the seat not only of the larger banks, but also of the media and the fashion industry. Any enterprise not actually registered here will still try at least to open a showroom or an elegant boutique in the city. Favorite locations are the Via della Spiga, on the Corso Vittorio Emanuele, and other famous streets in Milan's luxury shopping mile.

VALLE D'AOSTA

How far Italy still is today from having a pan-Italian identity strikes you particularly when you visit the border regions. Often the only evidence that they are politically a part of Italy is the presence of Italian newspapers and television stations, while the dialect, life style, and cuisine appear completely un-Italian. This is also true of the small region of Val d'Aosta. For the inhabitants of the valley, the government in Rome is a long way away, and is seen as a rather too remote figure, since their autonomous status guarantees them a certain political and cultural independence – they speak a Savoy dialect.

In any case, the history of the Aosta Valley belongs in French rather than Italian schoolbooks. After the break-up of the Western Roman Empire, the glacial valley fell to Burgundy in 443, and passed into Frankish hands at the end of the 6th century. In 1025 the Savoyards won control of the area. The new rulers were soon made to realize that the self-willed people of the valley did not like being dictated to, and they changed their strategy accordingly, granting the Valdaostans wide-ranging rights and freedoms. As a result, peace returned to the valley. Even today this policy is still being successfully practiced by Rome.

However, the Valdaostans' striving for independence has nothing to do with any sort of eccentric xenophobia. After all, the valley continued to provide access to important passes, which secured the trade between the boot-shaped peninsula and the economic areas north of the Alps. So travelers today are given the same friendly welcome as they were then, they are fortified before continuing their journey or even encouraged to stay – and above all regaled with delicious specialties. The cuisine of the Aosta Valley is simple and substantial, as befits a mountain region. Hot, wholesome bread soups are just right for snowy winter days, and in pleasant company you can enjoy the *fonduta*, the local version of the cheese fondue so beloved of the Alpine regions. Another time there will be polenta, wholesome rye bread, smoked bacon, tasty sausage specialties, beef and pork, as well as game from the surrounding mountains and forests. Butter and cream are used in stewing, roasting, and braising, since food rich in calories is a tasty and useful weapon against icy temperatures.

Previous double page: Farming the Alpine pastures and the production of cheese play a large part in the Aosta Valley. Young people like Nadir Folget, a budding master cheesemaker in the Casina Folget in Brisogne, see to it that traditions are kept up.

Left: The Aosta Valley is framed by the Valais Alps, the Mont-Blanc massif and the Graian Alps. The castle of Fénis lies between Aosta and St Martin.

RYE BREAD

The traditional rye bread of the Aosta Valley can definitely be described as a specialty. Wonderfully spicy and almost sweet tasting, when lightly spread with butter it makes an excellent accompaniment to the wines of the region.

In the past, even the smallest villages had a communal bakehouse, in which they gathered up to four times a year – mostly in November – to bake bread. To avoid arguments about who owned the bread, each villager cut a distinctive notch in their bread or carved their initials on their loaves. It is true that the bread, which was baked almost exclusively with rye flour, would keep for a whole year, but of course it grew hard with time, so hard that a special tool had to be invented in order to cut it.

BREAD SOUP

As the winters in the Alpine regions are long and cold, a nourishing hot soup is just right for the inhabitants. In the Aosta Valley and its neighboring valleys, bread soup with cheese, cooked slowly in the oven, has always been a favorite food. The simplest version of this dish is *Seupette de Cogne*. It consists only of bread, *fontina*, butter, and stock – all ingredients which could always be found in even the poorest mountain farmhouse kitchen. In comparison, *Zuppa di Valpelline* with its added bacon, Savoy cabbage, and herbs such as marjoram and savory, is almost a luxury version of bread soup.

ZUPPA DI VALPELLINE
Savoy cabbage stew with *fontina* from the Pelline Valley
(Illustrated above)

1 SAVOY CABBAGE
1–2 SLICES/50 G BACON
1 LB/500 G STALE BREAD
SAVORY OR MARJORAM
3 OZ/150 G FONTINA CHEESE, CUT INTO WAFER THIN SLICES
6 TBSP/80 G BUTTER
1 3/4 PINTS/1 LITER MEAT STOCK
SALT AND PEPPER

Wash and roughly chop the cabbage leaves. Dice the bacon very small. Gently simmer the leaves and the bacon in a casserole until the cabbage colors. Slice the bread and toast in the oven.
Cover the base of a casserole with a few slices of toasted bread. Put a layer of cabbage on top, sprinkle with chopped herbs, place a few slices of cheese and a couple of knobs of butter on top. Then add another layer of bread and so on until all the ingredients have been used up, finishing with a top layer of cheese and butter. Finally, pour over the meat stock and put the casserole to simmer in a preheated oven at 320 °F (160 °C) for about an hour.

ZUPPA DI PANE
Bread soup

3 MEDIUM ONIONS/300 G ONIONS
4 TBSP/50 G BUTTER
5 CUPS/1.2 LITERS MEAT STOCK
4 SLICES/200 G STALE BREAD
1 1/4 CUPS/100 G FRESHLY GRATED GRUYÈRE
FRESHLY MILLED BLACK PEPPER

Peel the onions and slice thinly. Melt the butter in a casserole. Add the onions and sauté over a low heat for 20 minutes, without browning. Then pour in the meat stock and boil for about 20 minutes. Meanwhile toast the slices of bread in the oven. Then cover the base of an oven dish with the slices of bread, sprinkle over the grated gruyère and pour in the meat-onion stock. Season the stew with freshly milled black pepper and cook for 20 minutes in a preheated oven at 350 °F (180 °C). Serve very hot!

ZUPPA DI PANE E CAVOLO
Green cabbage soup with bread

1 LB/500 G STALE BREAD
1 CLOVE GARLIC
1 SMALL GREEN CABBAGE
2 TBSP/30 G BUTTER
1 SMALL ONION
1 1/4 CUPS/100 G FRESHLY GRATED GRANA CHEESE
6 CUPS/1.5 LITERS MEAT STOCK
FRESHLY MILLED WHITE PEPPER

First cut the bread in slices and toast lightly in the oven. Then rub the slices of bread with a clove of garlic. Wash the cabbage and simmer the leaves in salt water. Put aside. Peel the onion and chop finely.
Heat the butter in a casserole and gently sauté the onions. Put a layer of cabbage over them and sprinkle with grated cheese. Alternate layers of bread slices, cabbage, and cheese until all the ingredients have been used up. Then pour over the stock, cover, and simmer in a preheated oven for about 2 hours at 320 °F (160 °C). Sprinkle with white pepper and serve hot.

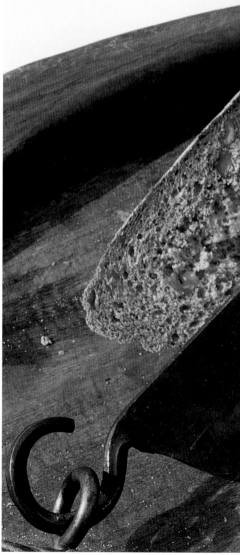

Today the Aosta Valley rye bread is baked with a considerably higher proportion of wheat flour. The round loaves with crosses cut into the tops no longer get as hard as in the old days. On the other hand they do not keep nearly so long, and have to be eaten very quickly.

Typical of the Aosta Valley is the *pane nero* made from rye and wheat flour, which tastes particularly good with the spiced bacon, *lardo*, and the local cheeses.

ALPINE CHEESE

With its lush meadows, the Aosta Valley offers ideal conditions for milk production. No wonder that full-bodied milk, tasty butter, rich cream, and of course the corresponding cheese are right at the top of the Valdaostans' menu. From this point of view, the *fontina*, which is steeped in tradition, is probably the most famous of the valley's cheeses. Its name is derived either from the verb *fondere*, which means to melt, indicating that this cheese is also delicious when melted, or it comes from Alpe Fontin, which is about 15 miles (25 km) from the provincial capital Aosta. Nobody knows for sure. On the other hand, it is a certain fact that the very mild, pale yellow *fontina* is produced from the best, fresh, full-cream milk. The cows which provide this high-quality milk feed exclusively on the grass of the high pastures.

The full-fat *fontina*, which is pale yellow and springy and has a few small holes running through it, has to mature for three to four months at a temperature of 46–53 °F (8–12 ° C). Many cheese factories use special storerooms cut into the rocks for this purpose. Cheeses produced in the summer can be recognized by a particularly buttery consistency and aromatic taste.

While the *fontina* is still young, the locals like to have it on the table for cutting. When it gets a little more mature, it is easy to melt and is therefore also very suitable for cooking. Moreover, the concentrated proteins and fats which it gets from the full-cream milk, make it a valuable part of the daily diet, and the mountain cuisine of the Aosta Valley would be unimaginable without it. It also provides a number of extremely important mineral salts, such as calcium and phosphorus.

In view of all these advantages, it is not surprising that people have tried again and again to copy *fontina*. Probably the best known imitation is *fontal*, which

The protected trademark of the *fontina*.

Like *fontina* and *solignon*, *toma de Gressoney* from the Gressoney Valley is a typical Alpine cheese made from cows' milk.

was created by Danish cheese experts, after they had got to know the merits of the Aosta cheeses during World War II. Production of this industrial version of *fontina* is permitted everywhere, even a long way from Aosta. As a result, the producers of the genuine *fontina* saw the need to protect their product from imitation. First, *fontina* was recognized as a "variety" of cheese. The second step, in 1955, gave it the legally controlled designation of origin DOC. Stamped on the surface of every official, and therefore quality guaranteed, *fontina*, is the trademark of a stylized Matterhorn, and the wording *Consorzio produttori fontina* (Consortium of Fontina Producers).

But the Aosta Valley region has other interesting cheese specialties to offer, for example *solignon*, which comes originally from the Gressoney Valley. *Solignon* consists of a very fatty ricotta, which is mixed with various flavorings: salt, ground paprika, chiles, garlic, juniper, fennel, and caraway seeds. *Solignon* can be eaten fresh or in a smoked version. In the past, the cheeses used to be hung in the chimney flue to dry out. As well as making them keep longer, it gave them a very special individual smoky taste.

Toma de Gressoney, which also comes from the Gressoney Valley, is worth sampling as well. This half-fat cheese is made in the same way as *fontina*. Sometimes it even looks so like it that you could get them mixed up, as the makers use the same shaped molds and also work with the same tools. So if you want a reliable way to distinguish *fontina* from *toma de Gressoney*, only a critical look at the ink stamp will do.

Left: *Fontina* has been produced in the Aosta Valley ever since the Middle Ages.

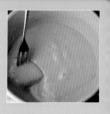

FONDUTA

There is a long tradition of cheese production in the Alpine valleys. Cheese was on the table throughout the day, in all varieties, young or mature, with bread, with porridge, in soups, or as an accompaniment to meat dishes. As leftover bits of cheese could be melted, the classic cheese fondue was not only seen as a nourishing meal, but at the same time fulfilled all the requirements of a thrifty and sensible use of leftovers. Cheese fondue has always been a favorite "stomach-warmer" throughout the Alps. The Aosta Valley is no exception; people here really enjoy their *fonduta*. Whereas in the classic Swiss cheese fondue the cheese, usually a mixture of Emmental and Greyerzer, is melted together with white wine, herbs, and a little lemon juice, the Brillat-Savarin version of the fondue asks for egg yolk as well. *Fonduta* also includes egg yolk and, in addition, calls for the cheese (in this case *fontina*) to be marinated in milk for at least four hours before melting. The ideal pan for *fonduta* should have a rounded base, to make it easier to mix the melting cheese thoroughly with a whisk.

Fonduta, which, incidentally, is a favorite in Piedmont as well, can be served as a starter or as a main course. It is also served as a cheese sauce with rice or tagliatelle, or used to fill ravioli. If you wish to enjoy your *fonduta* in the classic way, you pour the melted cheese into deep terracotta plates and serve with small pieces of toasted bread. In the autumn, the cheese may sometimes be garnished with a light dusting of white truffles.

FONDUTA VALDOSTANA
Fonduta Aosta style

14 OZ/400 G NOT TOO MATURE FONTINA, WITHOUT THE RIND
1 CUP/250 ML FULL-CREAM MILK
2 TBSP/30 G BUTTER
4 EGG YOLKS
1 WHITE TRUFFLE OR A FEW MUSHROOMS
SALT AND WHITE PEPPER
SLICES OF TOASTED BREAD

Cut the *fontina* into thin slices and marinate in milk for at least 4 hours. Put the butter in a fondue pot and place in a bain-marie. Add the cheese slices and 3 tablespoons of the milk in which they were marinated to the butter. Reduce the heat so the water remains just below boiling point. Melt the cheese, stirring continuously, until it can be pulled out in strings. Whisk the egg yolks with the remaining milk and stir in quickly, to give a smooth, thick cream. Season with salt and pepper. Divide the *fonduta* into small bowls, sprinkle thin slices of truffle or mushroom over it, and serve with slices of toast.

Background: Renato Vollget, owner of the Azienda and Trattoria Vollget in Brisogne, checks the maturity of his homemade *fontina*.

The raw material for the specialty cheeses of the Aosta Valley is of course the fresh, aromatic alpine milk of the Valdaostan cows. Natural untreated milk from their own dairies is used in the production of *fontina*.

The fresh untreated milk for the *fontina* is first heated in a big vat and mixed with rennin. When it has curdled the curd is separated from the whey.

Fontina matures for on average three months. During this time the cheesemaker regularly takes samples of the cheese with a curved scoop.

AOSTA VALLEY SPECIALTIES

Tortino di Riso Alla Valdostana
Rice cake with ox tongue

5oz/150 g salted ox tongue
3 1/2 oz/100 g fontina
2 cups/500 ml milk
Salt and pepper
Grated nutmeg
1 3/4 cups/350 g rice (Vialone)
1 small onion
6 tbsp/90 g butter
Freshly grated parmesan
Breadcrumbs

Dice the tongue and the *fontina* and mix together in a bowl. Pour in the milk and season with salt, pepper and nutmeg. Cover and leave to stand in a cool place for 1 hour. Meanwhile, cook the rice until *al dente*, and drain. Chop the onion and sauté gently until transparent in 3 tbsp/50 g butter, add the rice, sprinkle with parmesan, and mix well. Grease a deep ovenproof dish with butter, and then alternate layers of rice and tongue with layers of *fontina*. Scatter breadcrumbs and knobs of butter over it and bake in the oven until golden brown at 400 °F (200 °C).

SWEET CORN AND RICE

Sweet corn did not arrive in the Aosta Valley until around the end of the 18th century. Rice also arrived here relatively late, and first became known through the region's close connections with Piedmont. However, the Valdaostans soon incorporated both these new ingredients into their cuisine. From the sweet corn they prepared polenta, and there is now a long list of traditional polenta dishes. There is *polenta concia* (baked polenta pudding), *polenta condita* (polenta with sauce), *polenta cùnsa* (polenta with cheese) and *polenta alla rascard* (rustic-style polenta, named after the typical valley farmhouse). *Polenta alla rascard* is made with *fontina* and a stew of ground beef, sausages, herbs, and white wine. The corn porridge is allowed to cool, cut in strips, and put in alternate layers with the stew in a deep casserole. Finally the polenta is covered with thin slices of *fontina*.

There is an equally large selection of rice dishes. Particularly tasty ones are *Riso con la fonduta*, rice with *fonduta*, and *Riso con vino di Donnaz*, rice with Donnaz wine. The *Tortino di riso alla valdostana* is not to be despised either. This is a kind of rice cake with *fontina* and salted ox tongue. The *tortino* is most successful if you use a good quality rice variety such as Arborio or Vialone.

POLENTA CÙNSA
Polenta with cheese
(Illustrated below)

10 cups/2.5 liters water
Salt
Scant 2 cups/300 g cornmeal
2 cups/180 g fontina, grated
1 1/4 cups/120 g toma, grated
Scant 2/3 cup/150 g butter
Freshly milled pepper

Bring about 10 cups/2.5 liters water to the boil in a copper pan or a large pot. Salt the water and gradually add the cornmeal, stirring the mixture continuously. Add the grated cheese. Boil for about 50 minutes, stirring continuously with a wooden spoon.
Melt the butter gently. Tip the polenta into a big china bowl, and pour over the butter. Sprinkle with freshly milled pepper and serve hot.

Opposite: *Lepre in civet* – Jugged hare
Below: *Polenta cùnsa* – Polenta with cheese

Jugged hare

Anyone who has no ambitions to hunt or is not sure how to dress a fresh hare, would do best to go for an oven-ready animal. The following recipe is also suitable for chamois meat and pheasant. In the Gran Paradiso, you find a rare but tasty variation using marmot, in which the meat has to marinate for at least 48 hours in a mixture of white wine, carrots, celery, onions, and other herbs, so that it loses its strong, unusual flavor.

Lepre in civet
Jugged hare
(Illustrated in background)

1 OVEN-READY HARE, WITH LIVER AND HEART
2 ONIONS
1 CARROT
2 CLOVES OF GARLIC
1 STICK OF CELERY
1 BAY LEAF
2 BOTTLES/1.5 LITERS RED WINE
3 1/2 TBSP/50 G BUTTER
2–3 SLICES/50 G BACON
SALT AND PEPPER
2–3 TBSP WINE VINEGAR

Preferably have the butcher cut the animal into portions. Place the pieces of hare – without the organ meat – in a bowl. Finely chop 1 onion, the carrot, garlic, and celery, and spread over the meat. Add the bay leaf and pour over the wine. Leave the hare to marinate for 1–2 days. Remove the pieces of hare from the marinade, pat dry with kitchen roll and carefully clean off the remains of skin and sinews. Heat half the butter in a pan and fry the hare on a high heat for about 10 minutes. Remove the meat from the pan, pour off the juices and reserve.
Cut the bacon into small pieces, chop the remaining onion and sauté both in a little butter till the onion is transparent. Put the meat back in the pan, add salt and pepper, and sauté for a further 10 minutes.
Strain the marinade and ladle over the meat. Thicken the liquid over a low heat and continue adding the red wine marinade until the meat is very soft and tender.
Dice the liver and heart finely and sauté briefly in a small casserole with the remaining butter. Add salt and pepper and the wine vinegar. Remove from the heat and stir into the reserved pan juices. Serve the hare with its gravy, and with polenta.

FROM THE KITCHEN AND THE SMOKE-HOUSE

In the past, beef only appeared on the mountain farmers' tables, when an animal had to be destroyed out of necessity. But so that they could live off the stored meat for as long as possible, they salted it to make it keep longer. Even the classic *carbonade* is made from salted beef. Incidentally, stews of this kind are also found in Flemish and Spanish cuisine. The name *carbonade* (from *carbone*, coal) refers to the thick, very dark, almost black, gravy, which forms during the cooking of the meat.

CARBONADE ALL'USO AOSTANO
Beef stew
(Illustrated below)

1 3/4 LBS/800 G BEEF (E.G. SHOULDER)
ALL-PURPOSE FLOUR
3 1/2 TBSP/50 G BUTTER
1 3/4 LBS/800 G ONIONS, CHOPPED
1 BOTTLE/750 ML STRONG RED WINE
SALT AND FRESHLY MILLED PEPPER
FRESHLY GRATED NUTMEG

Cut the beef into pieces, toss in flour, and pan fry in butter over a high heat. Take out the meat and leave on one side. Fry the chopped onions over a high heat, add the meat and simmer gently over a low heat. Gradually pour in the wine. When the meat is ready, (after about 2 hours), season with salt, freshly milled pepper, and grated nutmeg.
In the past *carbonade* was made with salted beef; nowadays they use fresh meat and serve polenta with it.

COSTOLETTA ALLA VALDOSTANA
Veal cutlets with *fontina*

4 VEAL CUTLETS
3 1/2 OZ/100 G FONTINA, SLICED
SALT AND PEPPER
ALL-PURPOSE FLOUR
1 EGG
BREADCRUMBS
1/3 CUP/80 G BUTTER

Without separating them from the bone, cut through the cutlets with a sharp knife to form a pocket. Fill each of these pockets with cheese slices and press the edges together firmly. If necessary, fasten with a toothpick. Salt and pepper them on both sides, then toss them first in flour, then dip in beaten egg and finally coat in breadcrumbs. Fry in the butter until the cutlets are golden brown in color.

Carbonade all'uso aostano – Beef stew

Bacon and sausages

1 Mocetta

Mocetta and bacon from Arnad are among the most important meat specialties of the Aosta Valley. *Mocetta* or *mozzetta* was originally made from the meat of the ibex. As the numbers of these animals living on the Gran Paradiso massif continue to decline, the ibex has been declared a protected species and hunting it is forbidden. So nowadays the *mocetta* is made with chamois or goat meat. The seasoned meat is first placed in brine and compressed with a weight. After 25 days it is taken out and has to dry and mature for three to four months in an airy place. *Mocetta* should be consumed within one year, as after that it becomes too dry and hard. It is cut into thin slices and served as a starter with butter and rye bread spread with honey.

2 Coppa al Ginepro

This neck-end ham from Arnad gets its special flavor from the juniper berries which are rubbed into the surface while it is maturing.

3 Bacon from Arnad

This bacon, which is famous for its keeping qualities and its tangy flavor, is made from the rind of particularly fat pigs. Boned and cut in pieces, the bacon is decorated alternately with salt and herbs (pepper, bay, rosemary, sage, cloves). After it has been left for a few days, the superfluous salt is removed. Then the bacon has to hang for at least three months. Served with rye bread or chopped nuts it makes an appetizing *antipasto*.

4 Bon Bocon

In the soft, mild, and pasty pork filling of the *salamino* "Tasty morsel" from Arnad, you can already taste how close we are to Piedmont.

5 Pancetta steccata

The *pancetta steccata* is a comparatively rare, but nevertheless very tasty specialty of the Aosta Valley. The piece of belly pork with its thick salted rind is sewn together and clamped between two pieces of juniper wood. This presses the superfluous air out of the bacon, helps the maturing process, and in addition the wood adds a hint of aromatic flavor. After about two months, the *pancetta steccata* can be thinly sliced and served with a good, nourishing bread.

Boudin (not pictured)

The *boudin* is a kind of *sanguinato*, a blood sausage, consisting of pig blood and a mixture of boiled potatoes and bacon. It can be eaten fresh or hung, raw or cooked.

Saucisse (not pictured)

The sausage meat for the *saucisse* or *salsiccia* is made from ground beef and pork and is spiced with pepper, nutmeg, cinnamon, and garlic soaked in wine. This sausage tastes best when it has hung for about six months. After that it can also be preserved in oil, to prevent it from getting hard.

The notable specialty of Aosta Valley charcuterie, *pancetta steccata*, is pressed between two pieces of wood.

TERRACES AT DIZZYING HEIGHTS

From the 9th century onward, the smallest region of Italy was part of the Kingdom of Savoy, and since then has lain in the disputed area between France and the Italian region of Piedmont, resulting in a completely bilingual culture and also, of course, giving its wines their special character. The winegrowing area of the region, which does not even amount to 2500 acres (1000 hectares), extends over 56 miles (90 kilometers) of the long, narrow valley of the Dora Baltea, between the town of Morgex near Courmayeur at the foot of Mont Blanc and Donnas on the Piedmont border. Spectacular, narrow terraces are situated on steep rock faces at heights of up to 4300 feet (1300 meters) above sea level – these are the highest vineyards in Europe. The climate of the Alpine valleys is characterized by extreme winters and occasional very hot summers. Big fluctuations between the daytime and nighttime temperatures during the vegetation period give the grapes a strong flavor. While grapes for white wine with a good acid content are grown in many of the higher vineyards, the terraces in the middle part of the valley near Chambave, which face due south and are generally considered to be the very best sites in Aosta, are also suitable for strong, full-bodied red wines.

About three-quarters of the regional wine production comes under the single DOC Valle d'Aosta, which designates 26 different kinds of wine from 22 registered varieties of grapes – no other region of Italy has a greater variety within so small an area. Particularly outstanding among them are the many local varieties, such as Blanc de Morgex, Fumin, Neyret, Petit Rouge, Vien de Nus, and Premetta, but well-known names like Merlot, Pinot Grigio, or Chardonnay are also grown alongside them.

On the middle and lower slopes even the Nebbiolo ripens, a variety which is usually very demanding and produces interesting light rustic wines in the area around Donnas (or Donnaz). Of the other red varieties, the Petit Rouge and the Gamay are the ones to single out in the upper valley, while Blanc de Morges et la Salle and the sweet Moscato di Chambrave stand out among the white wines.

Petit Rouge
Smooth, fruity red wines are made from the Petit Rouge variety, which grows only in the Aosta Valley. The grapes can be pressed as a single variety, but mix well with other varieties – among them Dolcetto, Gamay, and Pinot Noir – to make the red Chambave, Enfer d'Arvier, Novello, Nus Rosso, and Torrette.

Donnaz
The only Nebbiolo wine of the Aosta Valley – Freisa, Neyret, and Vien de Nus can only provide small proportions – is produced close to the Piedmont border and the winegrowing area of Carema. It cannot however be compared with the great Nebbiolo wine of Langa, and at best it can be mellow and fruity, but it never achieves the complexity and lasting quality of Barolo or Barbaresco.

Enfer d'Arvier
This wine comes from the steep vineyards of the Dora-Baltea Valley, which extend up the slopes to a height of 3280 feet (1000 meters). The dry red wine is pressed from Petit Rouge, Dolcetto, Gamay, Neyret, Spätburgunder, and Vien de Nus, and mostly turns out light and low in alcohol.

GROLLA DELL'AMICIZIA

Every family in the Aosta Valley owns a *grolla dell'amicizia*. On important occasions this friendship cup is brought out of the closet to honor a friend or a member of the family. The drinking vessel, carved from a local wood, is round and shallow, closes with a well-fitting lid, and has several spouts coming out of it. People sit together and take turns drinking from the *grolla*. It is traditionally filled with *caffè cognese*; the name doesn't mean a kind of mixed cognac, but refers to the town of Cogne in the Aosta Valley. It's true that every village has a different secret recipe for preparing *caffè cognese*, but it consists mainly of coffee, with a little grappa, sugar, and an orange or a lemon rind. However, the proportions may vary.

Linguists are still arguing over the origin of the term *grolla*. Some maintain that the word goes back to the traditional French *grasal* or *graal*, meaning "dish," and refers to a drinking vessel passed round among the medieval knights. Others think that *grolla* comes directly from the Latin *gradalis*, and is connected with the legend of the Holy Grail, the cup from which Jesus Christ drank at the Last Supper.

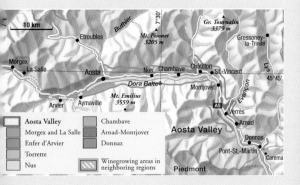

DESSERTS

For the simple but very tasty desserts of the Aosta Valley, only the best basic ingredients from the region are used, and these must be left as close as possible to their natural state. *Pere San Martin al vino rosso* are good evidence for this simple but brilliant philosophy. Although the Aosta Valley is not among the major producers of Italian pears, a very special, aromatic variety is grown here: the small, rosy-cheeked St Martin winter pear. Complete with its stalk, it is covered in red wine and baked in the oven – delicious! *Panna cotta* is also an extremely simple yet – if good cream is used – incredibly delicious dessert. It does not exactly come from the Aosta Valley, but is typical of the whole of northern Italy, because there has always been a milk industry here. Nowadays, however, this "baked cream" is made in almost all parts of the country.

PERE SAN MARTIN AL VINO ROSSO
Winter pears in red wine
(Illustrated right)

1LB/500 G SMALL RED PEARS
GOOD RED WINE
CLOVES
SUPERFINE SUGAR
HEAVY CREAM FOR WHIPPING

Wash the pears and place whole – with the core and stalk – in a deep baking pan. Cover the fruit almost completely with red wine, add a few cloves and sprinkle with sugar. Bake for about 1 hour in a pre-heated medium oven. This will give the liquid a syrupy consistency.
Allow the pears to cool and serve with whipped cream and a spoonful of syrup.

PANNA COTTA
Baked cream
(Illustrated below)

Serves 8

1 OZ/30 G POWDERED GELATIN
4 CUPS/1 LITER LIGHT CREAM
1/3 CUP/80 G SUGAR

Soften the gelatin in a little cold water and squeeze out. Bring the cream to the boil with the sugar, simmer for about 15 minutes. Remove the cream from the heat and completely dissolve the gelatin in it, stirring continuously.
Pour the remainder of the sugar into a pan, caramelize it and pour into ramekins.
Fill up with the cream mixture into ramekins and keep in a cool place for a few hours.
Serve with fruits of the forest or raspberry sauce.

HERBS TO KEEP OUT THE COLD

Genepy is possibly the most famous spirit from the Aosta Valley. It is made according to a strictly guarded recipe, using not only alcohol, sugar, and water, but also a great variety of local herbs, among them gentian and Alpine mugwort. There are strict controls on the collecting of the last of these ingredients, which has the botanical name *artemisia glacialis* and grows under the snow cover in the high mountains, so you need a special permit, and even then you are only allowed to pick very few plants.

Fresh or dried herbs can be used in making Genepy. If the plants are fresh, they give the schnapps a beautiful green color. On the other hand, if dried herbs are used, you get a pale yellow variety. Genepy is around 40 percent proof. It is a favorite tonic, but also does good service as a digestive. What's more, it warms up hordes of frozen skiing enthusiasts every season. A very similar herbal schnapps, which could no doubt do the same job, is Alpinista. It too is made with various herbs from the valley.

Alongside the high-alcohol herbal schnapps, marc brandies are also drunk in the Aosta Valley – and particularly, of course, since they started flavoring the grappa with mountain herbs, fruits of the forest, or honey.

GRAND SAINT BERNARD

Back around the time of the birth of Christ, the Romans extended the Grand Saint Bernard or Gran San Bernardo Pass through the Alps. Since then it has connected the Swiss canton of Valais with the Italian Aosta Valley. Today there is no problem crossing the Alps by train, plane, or automobile, and it is now almost impossible to imagine that the road through this mountain range once represented a dangerous, even foolhardy, undertaking. It meant conquering the pass in a coach – as far as the road allowed – on horseback, on a donkey, or at worst even on foot. You were dependent on local guides, some of whom inspired more confidence than others, who might show you the right path, or lead you into disaster. You had to

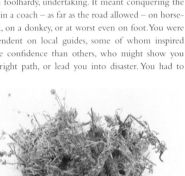

The basic ingredient of Genepy, *Artemisia*, grows at a height of 6500 to 9750 feet/2000 to 3000 meters, and is picked at the end of August.

think carefully about where you could have the animals taken care of and find a place to rest when night fell. Moreover, there were robbers lying in wait in the ravines, who would take the last penny from travelers and pilgrims. Travelers crossing the Alps were often helpless victims of those sudden changes in the weather for which the high mountains are feared, not to mention the constant danger of avalanches. In summer it meant you had to beware of landslides and screes, in winter, you could easily be buried under a blanket of snow.

To provide shelter, food, and emergency help for travelers, in the middle of the 11th century Saint Bernard of Menton, who was then Archdeacon of Aosta, founded a hospice high up on the pass, which was at the time the most important trade and pilgrim route through the Alps. The first written mention of a dog comes from the early 18th century. The monastery chronicle reports that the hospice was open to travelers day and night. All visitors received a free meal of

Above and right: In the distillery of the famous producer of spirits and delicatessen La Valdotaine in St. Marcel, very unusual specialties are produced and, of course, "herbal" grappa. The large selection ranges from raspberry grappa to liquorice grappa and chili grappa.

meat and bread. Big portions of meat were roasted on a spit – an arduous task for the cook. In 1701, the master cook Vincent Canos built a treadmill and put a dog in it, so that it turned the spit as it moved. Around 1750 the *marronniers*, the mountain guides from the hospice, began to take the dogs out on the road with them. The big sturdy St. Bernards had to go ahead of the walkers in order to make a path through the snow with their broad chests. In addition, the dogs proved to have an extraordinary sense of direction, so they could safely guide the *marronnier* and his travelers down to the valley or back to the hospice, even in darkness or fog. The St. Bernards also worked as avalanche dogs. They did not have to be specially trained for this, as it is in their nature to scratch for things they can scent through the snow. The number of buried and frozen travelers did, in fact, fall drastically at that time. The little barrel of brandy, which the St. Bernard supposedly carries on its collar, should be consigned to the realms of legend. Of course, the big dogs did occa-

The dog with the little barrel is part of the Alpine myth, but such a burden would be a hindrance during a rescue, and accident victims should not drink alcohol anyway.

sionally carry loads up to the hospice as well, but their rescue work consisted of tracking missing people, not providing the rescued with alcohol. There is no mention of these mysterious little barrels anywhere in the hospice chronicles.

Today travelers still come to visit the hospice. It is still run by monks, though they no longer see searching for the buried and reviving exhausted travelers as being their most urgent tasks; now they offer their guests a peaceful retreat, away from the hectic rush of the outside world. St. Bernards are no longer employed in mountain rescue either; now there are helicopters and rescue teams equipped with sonar.

The clear herbal schnapps of the Aosta Valley is called Genepy. It is flavored with various herbs and plants, including Alpine mugwort.

PIEMONTE

T he "land at the foot of the mountains," which is how Piedmont translates, is at its most magical in the autumn, when the leaves change color and thick swathes of mist drift over valleys and hills. This is the time to look out for truffles and other delicious fungi in the woods, to collect nuts, gather cardoons, go hunting, or admire the selection of fresh game in the shops. In the evening people sit around the fire, hold long conversations and open a bottle of wine. The Piedmont cuisine may have certain refinements, but it is deeply rooted in a tradition of simple wholesome cooking, which relies on first class, very tasty ingredients. Truffles, garlic, game, and crisp vegetables, together with cheese and rice, are the basis of Piedmont specialties.

Autumn is also the time of the wine harvest. Piedmont has earned a worldwide reputation for a series of outstanding wines. Barolo, Barbaresco, and Barbera are only three of the names, but they all stand for the highest quality. But there are other treasures to be discovered in Piedmontese cellars. Fine sparkling wines, which can compare with the best champagne, are also produced in the region. Of course it is often claimed that Piedmontese cuisine is closely related to the French, but this is a culinary half-truth. You get closer to the facts, if you speak of French influence on Piedmontese cooking – and conversely of Piedmontese influences on French cooking. This flourishing exchange of gastronomic ideas has a history going back some 800 years, as during all that time Piedmont was part of Savoy, a kingdom which included areas that now belong to France, Switzerland, and Italy. The Savoy dialect, which was spoken there, was influenced by French – so many technical terms of French origin are still found in Piedmontese cookbooks today. *Fumèt* means smoked, *civet* means meat stock, and *cocotte* describes a cast iron casserole. But – as we said before – this is a long way from saying that Piedmontese cuisine is a branch of traditional French cookery, since it has completely independent specialties in store: *bagna caoda*, delicious raw Piedmontese vegetables with a tangy anchovy dip, rice dishes such as *risotto alla piemontese*, *paniscia di novara* or world-class cheeses like Gorgonzola or *castelmagno* – these are delights you absolutely must taste.

Previous double page: When it comes to truffle hunting, you don't just need human intelligence, a dog's good sense of smell is even more important.

Left: Lago d'Orta is the most westerly lake on the North Italian side of the Alps. Wooded shores alternate with quiet villages. In the middle of the lake is the island of San Giulio.

CASTELMAGNO

Castelmagno is a Piedmont specialty. This cheese of legally controlled origin (DOC) is produced exclusively in the communities of Castelmagno, Pradleves, and Monterosso Grana in the province of Cuneo. It is easy to recognize the true Castelmagno by its trademark, a little triangle in a stylized letter C on the top side. Like its more famous relative Gorgonzola, Castelmagno can look back on a proud tradition, as the cheese was specifically mentioned in the record of a legal arbitration settlement as long ago as 1277. This paper says that an annual charge was made for the use of a pasture about which the communities of Castelmagno and Celle di Macra were arguing at the time – and it was payable to the Margrave of Saluzzo in the form of Castelmagno cheese. Thanks to the cheesemakers' sense of tradition, today's Castelmagno tastes almost exactly the same as it did in the 13th century. The semisoft cheese has only 34 percent fat in the dry mass. It is usually made only from cow's milk, but may additionally contain small quantities of semiskimmed sheep's or goat's milk. The milk is first allowed to curdle, then hung in a cloth for the whey to drain off. After that the curd stays for a few days in wooden vats before being pressed into molds. The cheeses have to mature for two to five months in well-ventilated caves in the rocks.

A young Castelmagno has a reddish rind and is ivory colored. It tastes slightly salty, with a delicate hint of nuts. Mature Castelmagno has a dark red to gray rind and the blue-green veins of the mold can be clearly seen running through its ocher curd. It tastes strong and tangy. Young or mature, Castelmagno is an outstanding cheese for the table, and is particularly good served with acacia honey and a fortified wine.

After curdling, the cheese curd is emptied into cloths and hung up to allow the remaining whey to drain off.

Castelmagno matures for two to five months, which gives it a full, tangy taste. Cheese-buffs let it get even older.

WHAT DOES THE DOC LABEL MEAN ON A CHEESE?

The abbreviation DOC stands for *Denominazione di origine controllata* and means the origin is legally controlled. In this way high quality cheese varieties – like good wines – are protected from inferior quality imitations. In order to produce a particular cheese, the makers usually join together in a *consorzio di tutela*, a kind of cooperative, to draw up an exact description of the area of origin, the method of production and the finished product. Through a control-system, which they set up themselves, they ensure that these regulations are adhered to. They also apply for the cheese and its area of origin to be officially recognized. If the cheese has received state approval, it can have the letters DOC added to its name from then on, but it must be submitted to regular critical testing by independent experts. Now there are not only DOC standard cheeses in Italy, but also ham, vinegar (Aceto balsamico di Modena DOC), and other specialties, which can boast a protected origin.

GORGONZOLA

Gorgonzola is one of Italy's most famous exports. The little wedges, usually wrapped in silver paper, can be found on cheese boards all over the western world. Like many other kinds of cheese, Gorgonzola is a DOC protected product, but the area in which it is produced is much bigger than, for example, that of Castelmagno. Gorgonzola may come from provinces lying partly in Lombardy and partly in Piedmont, namely Bergamo, Brescia, Como, Cremona, Cuneo, Milan, Novara, Pavia, and Vercelli. Nowadays the

After the whey has been separated, the cheese curd is compressed in molds of 10 to 12 inches (25 to 30 cm) diameter. Then the cheese is allowed to set. Later on, the master cheesemaker will keep taking the cheese out of the mold, in order to salt the surface.

The milk is heated to about 86 °F (30 °C), and rennin is added to make it curdle. Spores of the mold *Penicillium glaucum* are also added.

Gorgonzola is available in various stages of ripeness. The more mature it is, the more piquant the flavor.

majority of Gorgonzola producers are based in Piedmontese Novara.

With its 48 percent fat in dry mass, Gorgonzola is a full-fat cow's milk cheese. It used to be made from unpasteurized milk, but now, for reasons of hygiene, pasteurized milk is used, and the mold *Penicillium glaucum* is added to aid fermentation and produce the blue veins. Gorgonzola matures for two to three months in temperature-controlled conditions in natural caves in the rocks or similar storerooms.

Gorgonzola is an outstanding cheese for the table. It can be served as an appetizer or, with bread and a strong red wine, it can finish off a meal. It also has its uses in the kitchen. Risottos, sauces, fillings, and stuffings will all taste wonderful, if flavored with crumbled Gorgonzola.

Left: To ensure that the mold spreads evenly throughout the cheese, the spores are distributed by boring into the cheese with long stainless steel needles, first from one side, then a week later from the other side.

TRUFFLES

The ancient Romans already had a taste for truffles. In *De re coquinaria* (On the art of cooking), a standard culinary work of antiquity attributed to the Roman epicure Marcus Gavius Apicius, there are a few recipes which include truffles. According to this work, the "noble mushroom" crowned various banquets given by the Roman "in-crowd."

The Romans believed that truffles grew under trees, which Jupiter, the ruler of the forces of nature, had previously struck with one of his lightning bolts. Of course we now know that truffles are fungi which grow underground, living in symbiosis with the root system of oaks, poplars, and also hazel bushes. However, this has not helped us to increase the supply of this most sought-after of all fungi, or even to cultivate them artificially, which we had no problems in doing with ordinary mushrooms, for example. Even if oak roots are prepared with truffle spores, it takes a good ten years for the truffles to mature. So gourmets have to rely on professional truffle hunters, the *trifulau*, as they are known in Piedmont, and will continue to pay a lot of money for this valuable mushroom.

Piedmont, with its abundance of forests, is a classic truffle area. Here you find the white truffle (*Tuber magnatum*), also known as the Alba truffle. It is the most delicious and sought-after truffle in the world. According to historical documents, in 1380, the princes of Acaja made a gift to a certain Princess Bona of some white truffles. During the siege of Alba a few years previously, Charles V had already helped himself to a large portion of this delicacy. In the Langhe, the hilly countryside around Alba, truffle fever still breaks out in October every year, when the first white truffles begin to ripen.

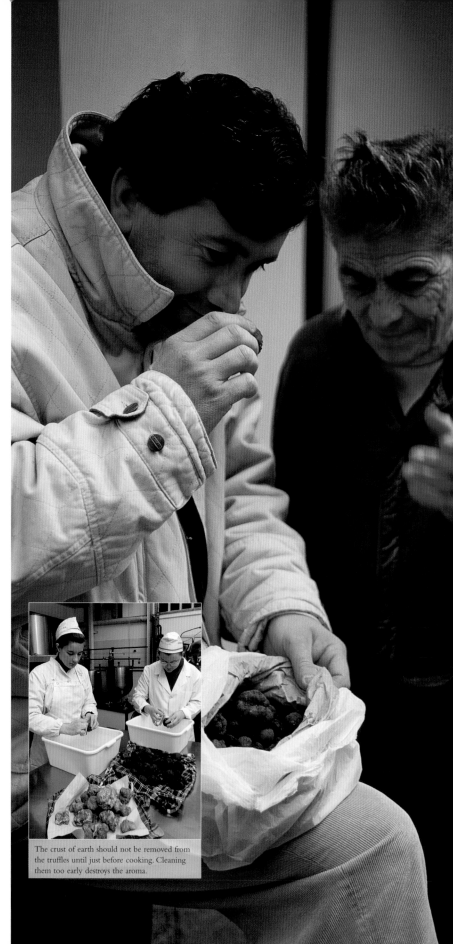

The white Alba truffles grow to any size from a walnut to a fist. Many areas in the Langhe are no longer very productive, so the truffle hunters are moving to Pavia.

The crust of earth should not be removed from the truffles until just before cooking. Cleaning them too early destroys the aroma.

White truffle, Alba truffle (Tuber magnatum)
The white truffle, *tuber magnatum, tartufo bianco*, also known as the Alba truffle, is the most sought-after variety. It has a powerful aroma with a clear echo of garlic and a hint of ripe cheese. It is used raw, grated directly over the dish with a special truffle shaver. It goes well with risotto, eggs, pasta, or raw beef. The white truffle is yellowish, gray, or light ocher in color, and rounded but irregular in shape, and has reddish brown flesh, with characteristic white marbling.

Up to the end of the truffle season on December 31, Alba's already distinguished reputation as a stronghold of wine and special delicacies is crowned by a culinary firework display of excellent truffle dishes.

There are around 50 varieties of truffle, but only a few are edible. As truffles grow underground, they are difficult to collect. But to pinpoint a promising area, you must have a certain feeling for and knowledge of truffles, and these are jealously guarded secrets. So it is not surprising that people have already tried to use magic arts to improve their chances in the truffle hunt, and that many tales, anecdotes, and mysterious rituals connected with truffle hunting have grown up in the Langhe area.

But instead of hoping for help from some mysterious source, most *trifulau* are pragmatists and rely on their trained half-breed dogs, whose keen sense of smell is worth a lot of money. It is also possible to use pigs, of course, but because these animals are not particularly easy to train, it is very difficult to persuade them not to eat their booty on the spot. Of course dogs like truffles too, but they usually accept what their masters offer them instead, and give up the precious mushroom in exchange for one or two biscuits.

When the phase of the moon, or the barometer, or some secret indicator promises favorable conditions, the Piedmontese truffle hunter prefers to go out at dead of night to hunt his fragrant quarry, because that is when the dogs are best able to concentrate on their sense of smell. In the early light of dawn, man and dog return to Alba with the earth-encrusted white truffles, each weighing between 2–4 oz (50–100 grams), and the *trifulau* bargains with the local gourmets, chefs, and gastronomes over the value of the find. Depending on the day's offers, the price can easily reach 350–650 euro for 4 oz (100 grams).

Left: Truffles are a matter of trust, because there are shady dealers here, as there are in every line of business, so most chefs and retailers remain loyal to their regular *trifulau*, and buy only from him.

UOVA ALLA PIEMONTESE CON TARTUFO BIANCO
Eggs with white truffle
(Illustrated above)

8 TBSP /100 G BUTTER
1 HANDFUL PARSLEY, FINELY CHOPPED
1 CLOVE OF GARLIC, FINELY CHOPPED
1 OZ/30 G WHITE TRUFFLE, FINELY CHOPPED
1/2 GLASS DRY MARSALA
4 EGGS
SALT AND PEPPER

Heat 6 tablespoons/70 g of the butter in a casserole, and add the parsley, garlic, and truffle. Sauté for a few minutes over a low heat, and pour over the Marsala. Heat the remaining butter in a pan, fry the eggs, and season with salt and pepper. Arrange the fried eggs on a plate, pour over the truffle sauce, and serve immediately.

CARNE CRUDA ALL'ALBESE
Steak tartare with truffles

2 LBS/1 KG VEAL TOPSIDE
4 ANCHOVY FILLETS
1 CLOVE OF GARLIC
JUICE OF 1 LEMON
1 CUP/250 ML EXTRA VIRGIN OLIVE OIL
SALT AND PEPPER
WHITE TRUFFLE, SHAVED

Cut the meat into small pieces and put it through a food processor. Finely chop the anchovies and garlic and pour into a bowl with the lemon juice. Add the olive oil and a little water, season with salt and pepper, and mix well. Mix the meat and the sauce and leave to stand in the refrigerator for a few hours. Before serving, mix well again and garnish with the shaved truffle.

UOVA AFFOGATE AI TARTUFI
Poached eggs with white truffle

4 CUPS/1 LITER WATER
SALT
1 TBSP VINEGAR
6 EGGS
4 ANCHOVIES
1 OZ/30 G WHITE TRUFFLE, FINELY CHOPPED
1 HANDFUL PARSLEY, FINELY CHOPPED
4 TBSP BUTTER
JUICE OF 1 LEMON

Bring the water to a boil in a casserole. Add the salt and vinegar. Break the eggs and drop them gently into the boiling water. As soon as the whites are firm, remove the eggs with a skimmer and rinse in a bowl of cold water. Remove the boiling water from the heat. Trim the edges of the eggs with a knife, and replace in the water, when it has cooled to lukewarm.
Clean, wash, and fillet the anchovies, and chop finely. Mix the truffle and the parsley in a bowl with half the butter. Heat the remaining butter in a casserole. As soon as it bubbles, add the chopped anchovies and cook over a low heat. Add the truffle and the parsley and stir in the lemon juice. Arrange the poached eggs on plates, pour over the sauce, and serve.

RICE GROWING

There are various theories about how rice came to Italy. While some say that the Romans were already acquainted with rice, others think that it was brought to Sicily by the Arabs about the turn of the first millennium. The preferred version in Venice is that traveling Venetian merchants brought rice back with them from their journeys to the Levant. However, true rice cultivation only started to develop in the 15th century, after plague and famine had devastated vast areas of Europe in the Middle Ages. In Italy, they were also looking for new foods at that time, and they remembered rice. The Cistercian monks of the monastery at Luciedo, near Trino Vercellese, soon discovered that conditions in the well-watered plains of the Po valley were favorable for rice, and that the plants grew very well there. But at first, the inhabitants of the surrounding villages wanted nothing to do with it. They were skeptical about a plant which grew only in water, because they thought that this method of cultivation would encourage the spread of serious diseases like the plague. However, the persuasive skills of the monks, coupled with the need for food, overcame these fears.

In the 19th century, large-scale rice growing began in the Po valley, because it became apparent that the rice trade had significant economic potential for this rather poor region. Great canals were built, such as the Canale Cavour, opened in 1852, and ingenious and efficient irrigation systems were set up, so that increasingly large areas could be opened up for rice growing. Italian rice soon began to enjoy great popularity abroad and exports flourished. Even Thomas Jefferson, the third President of the United States, took a few grains of rice home from his journey through Italy, because the rice grown in the Po valley could withstand the heat better than the rice Jefferson knew from his homeland. So he simply "imported" this firm variety from the Old World, and it quickly gained acceptance in the rice growing areas of the United States.

In the 20th century, rice growing had reached such a stage of perfection that Italy was way ahead of other European producers. But in the fifties, the Po valley was still paying for the presence of the huge rice industry and the prosperity it brought to some people with the immense poverty of the lower strata of the population, who worked in the fields for starvation wages. The fate of the *risaroli*, the seasonal workers, and the *mondine*, the girls who weeded the rice, is recorded in many folksongs and plays, but the most vivid account of the hard labor in the fields is probably that given in the 1949 Italian film *Riso amaro* (Bitter Rice) by the neo-realist director Giuseppe de Santis.

Rice growing today is, of course, largely mechanized – modern machinery has taken over the strenuous work of planting, weeding, and harvesting – but it is still a challenging agricultural occupation, because the fields require a slow but constant flow of water, so they have to slope at a particular angle in order to prevent the water from running away too fast or standing too long, either of which would damage the plants.

The 1949 neo-realistic film *Riso amaro* (Bitter Rice) shows a true-life picture of the conditions suffered by the seasonal workers in the rice fields of the Po valley. Barefoot and stooping, the *mondine* stood day after day for up to 12 hours in the cold water of the rice fields, planting and weeding. Not only were they exposed to the scorching sun, the leeches and the mosquitoes, but often they also suffered tyranny and ill treatment from the foremen.

Rice is harvested in September, by which time the plants are brown and dry.

Big mills separate the grain from the husks, and then the rice is polished.

After sowing in March, the rice fields are flooded and the area between Vercelli, Novara, and Pavia looks almost like one big lake.

VARIETIES OF RICE

The most commonly grown rice variety in Italy is *oryza sativa japonica*, whose grains remain firm when boiled. By contrast, the long-grain rice *Oryza sativa indica*, which cooks quickly and turns to mush, is hardly grown at all. Italian rice is monitored by the National Rice Institute, which regularly checks the quality, purity, and nutritional content of the different varieties. Rice offered for sale is divided into four categories, which must be shown on the packaging: *riso commune* (household rice), *riso semifino* (round grain rice), *riso fino* (medium grain or standard rice), and *riso superfino* (superfine rice).

As rice dishes may call for varieties with different consistencies and cooking qualities, cooks in northern Italy pay particular attention to the selection of rice. Varieties which take a long time to cook, like Razza 77 and Ribe, have big, almost transparent grains, containing little starch. These are suitable for rice salads and boiled or baked rice dishes. Varieties with semisoft grains, like Arborio, Carnaroli, and Vialone, have large grains with a high starch content. They remain moist and juicy, so they are particularly suitable for risotto. Soft varieties, like Maratelli and Balilla, have very small starchy grains, which cook quickly without breaking up. They are particularly suitable for rice soups.

Riso commune (Household rice)
The Balilla, Americano 1600, Elio, Selenio, and Originario varieties belong in this category. *Riso commune* has small, short, round or semicircular grains. It takes 13–14 minutes to cook, gets very soft, and is suitable for desserts, soups, and *timbale*.

Riso semifino (Round grain rice)
This group includes the Maratelli, Vialone nano, Padano, Lido, Argo, Cripto, and Rosa Marchetti varieties. *Riso semifino* has thick, medium length, round or semicircular grains. It takes 15 minutes to cook and is suitable for minestrone and other soups, but also for *timbale* and as a side dish.

Riso fino (Medium grain or standard rice)
This group is subdivided into Fino medio (varieties Europa, Loto, Riva) and Lungo A (varieties Ariete, Cervo, Drago, Ribe, R.B., Rizzotto, Sant'Andrea, Ringo, and Vialone). *Riso fino* has long, spindle-shaped grains (except for Vialone, which has round grains). It takes 16 minutes, cooks evenly, remains firm, and is suitable for risotto, rice salads, soups, and as a side dish.

Riso superfino (Superfine rice)
This group is subdivided into Lungo A (Arborio, Baldo, Roma, Razzo 77, Koral, Volano, and Carnaroli) and Lungo B, which includes Graldo Panda, Pegaso and Thaibonnet. *Riso superfino* has long, thick, half spindle-shaped grains. It takes 18 minutes to cook and is very suitable for risotto. Carnaroli in particular, which is often twice as expensive as other varieties, makes a splendid risotto, and it can also be used for starters – salads, *timbale*, and side dishes.

1 R.B.
2 Riso brillato (polished rice)
3 Riso greggio
4 Roma
5 Riso parboiled
6 Balilla
7 Vialone
8 Arborio

RISOTTO AL BAROLO
Risotto with Barolo
(Illustrated above)

6 TBSP/100 G BUTTER
1 SMALL ONION
2 CUPS/400 G RICE
1 CUP BAROLO (WINE)
ABOUT 4 CUPS/1 LITER MEAT STOCK
2/3 CUP/50 G GRANA CHEESE, GRATED
FRESHLY MILLED BLACK PEPPER
WHITE TRUFFLES, ACCORDING TO TASTE

Heat half the butter in a wide, fairly shallow casserole. Chop the onion finely and sauté in the butter, without browning. Add the rice and sauté briefly, stirring continuously. Then pour over the wine and bring to a boil. Gradually add the preheated stock. Allow to boil gently until the rice has absorbed the liquid and is cooked through.
Remove the casserole from the heat and carefully stir in the remaining butter. Sprinkle with cheese and freshly milled pepper and serve. If desired, the flavor of the risotto may be enhanced with a few shavings of truffle.

Superfine Carnaroli rice makes a splendid risotto. It takes up liquids evenly, but the grains nevertheless remain firm and separate.

Risotto agli spugnole
Risotto with morels

1/2 CUP /120 ML LIGHT CREAM
1 CUP/250 ML WATER
GENEROUS CUP/25 G DRIED MORELS
2 SHALLOTS, CHOPPED
2 TBSP/30 G BUTTER (FOR SAUTÉING)
1 CUP/200 G VIALONE RICE OR OTHER HIGH QUALITY RISOTTO RICE
1 CUP/250 ML WHITE WINE
SALT AND PEPPER
3 CUPS/750 ML HOT CHICKEN STOCK
4 TBSP/60 G BUTTER (FOR THE RISOTTO)
3/4 CUP/60 G FRESHLY GRATED PARMESAN
FINELY CHOPPED PARSLEY

Bring the cream and the water to a boil, pour over the morels, and leave them to soak in the cream and water for about 15 minutes. Pour the liquid into a bowl and reserve. Wash the mushrooms under running water and chop roughly. Sauté the shallots lightly in 2 tablespoons butter. Add the mushrooms and rice, pour over the wine, and season with salt and pepper. Gradually pour in first the reserved liquid, then the chicken stock, until the rice has absorbed all the liquid and is cooked. Then mix in butter, Parmesan, and parsley, and serve hot.

Risotto ai porcini
Risotto with boletus

Serves 4–6

5 1/2 TBSP/85 G BUTTER
1 LARGE ONION, CUT INTO THIN RINGS
3/4 LB/300 G FRESH BOLETUS MUSHROOMS, SLICED
SALT
2 CUPS/400 G CARNAROLI RICE
7 CUPS/1.75 LITERS HOT CHICKEN STOCK
3/4 CUP/60 G FRESHLY GRATED PARMESAN
FRESHLY MILLED PEPPER

Heat half the butter in a pan and sauté the onions and mushrooms until soft. Salt, and add the rice. Gradually pour over the stock, until the rice has absorbed the liquid and is cooked (about 20 minutes). Remove from the heat and add the remaining butter and the parmesan. Season with pepper and serve immediately.

Risotto alla zucca
Pumpkin risotto

6 TBSP/90 G BUTTER
1 ONION, FINELY CHOPPED
3/4 LB/300 G PUMPKIN, DICED
SALT
2 CUPS/400 G ARBORIO RICE
7 CUPS/1.75 LITERS HOT VEGETABLE STOCK
FRESHLY GRATED NUTMEG
PEPPER
3/4 CUP/60 G FRESHLY GRATED PARMESAN

Heat 4 tablespoons of the butter in a pan. Sauté the onion until translucent, add the pumpkin, and cook until tender. Mash with a potato masher and salt. Add the rice and cook for 1 minute, stirring all the time. Gradually pour over the hot stock, until the rice has absorbed the liquid and become white and creamy. Continue to stir. Remove the pan from the heat, and add the remaining butter, nutmeg, pepper, and Parmesan.

Paniscia di Novara
Vegetable soup with rice

1/2 LB/200 G RIPE TOMATOES
2 STICKS CELERY
2 MEDIUM SIZED CARROTS
1 SMALL SAVOY CABBAGE
1/2 LB/300 G FRESH BORLOTTI BEANS
2 OZ/50 G PORK FAT
SALT
1 SMALL SALAMI D'LA DUJA (A SAUSAGE PRESERVED IN OIL)
1 MEDIUM SIZED ONION, CHOPPED
2/3 CUP/50 G BACON, CHOPPED
2 TBSP/30 ML OLIVE OIL
1 2/3 CUPS/300 G ROUND GRAIN RICE
2/3 CUP/150 ML BARBERA (WINE)

Skin the tomatoes and remove the seeds. Clean the celery, peel the carrots and cut both into small pieces. Remove the outer leaves of the cabbage and cut the inner leaves into strips. Shell the beans. Put the vegetables and the pork fat into a large pot, cover with water, and a little salt, and cook for about 2 hours. Skin the salami and cut up small. Fry the onion, bacon, and salami in a casserole in olive oil. Add the rice and stir. Pour over the wine and allow the liquid to boil away. Pour over the vegetable soup and finish cooking over a low heat (about 20 minutes). Allow to stand for a few minutes and serve.

Risotto alla piemontese
Piedmontese-style risotto

1 3/4 CUPS/350 G RISOTTO RICE
4 CUPS/1 LITER HOT MEAT STOCK
4 TBSP BUTTER
1/2 CUP/40 G FRESHLY GRATED PARMESAN
SALT
GRATED NUTMEG
1/4 CUP/40 G GRAVY
TRUFFLE

First boil the rice in the meat stock over a high heat for 15 minutes, stirring occasionally. Remove the pan from the heat, add butter, parmesan, salt, and a little nutmeg. Leave to stand for a few minutes, then pour the rice into a deep, prewarmed bowl. Pour the gravy into the middle of the risotto, garnish with thin slices of truffle, and serve.

MEAT AND POULTRY

Piedmontese cuisine is very varied and sometimes even lavish. For instance, instead of using one or two kinds of meat to make one of the most famous of northern Italy's favorite dishes, *Bollito misto*, the Piedmontese always make it with four or more different meats.

Beef and chicken always go into the pot, but even this simple version of *Bollito* is enriched by adding capon and ox tongue. On the other hand, if you are aiming for a prestigious variant, calf's tongue and leg of veal are also essential ingredients. In addition to the meats already mentioned, genuine *Bollito misto* calls for calf's head, pig trotters, and *cotechino*, a spicy pork sausage. *Bollito* is comparatively easy to prepare. The pieces of meat are put in a pot, either one after the other or, depending on kind and size, all at the same time, and boiled until they are soft and tender. Only the sausages go into a different pot. The pieces of meat are sliced, garnished with the sausages, and the whole thing is served with *Bagnet verd*, a green sauce made from parsley, garlic, anchovies, and oil, or *Bagnet d' tomatiche*, a sweet and sour tomato sauce, or *Mostarda di Cremona*, tart candied fruits in mustard syrup.

However, braised as well as boiled meat dishes are very popular in Piedmont. *Bue brasato* is a typical north Italian dish, consisting of beef slowly braised in strong red wine with vegetables and herbs. Incidentally, this dish owes its name to the method of preparation. *Brasato* comes from the north Italian expression *brasa*, meaning coal, as the pot used to be placed on a coal-fired range and, to ensure the heat is evenly distributed, glowing coals were also placed on the lid of the pot.

MANZO BRASATO AL BAROLO

Braised meat in red wine
(Illustrated below)

For the marinade:
I CARROT
I MEDIUM ONION
I STICK CELERY
2 BAY LEAVES
BLACK PEPPERCORNS
I SMALL PIECE OF CINNAMON STICK
RED WINE (BAROLO)

3 I/2 LBS/I.5 KG BEEF FILLET
6 TBSP/IOO G BUTTER
SALT AND PEPPER
I SMALL GLASS BRANDY

Cut the carrot, onion, and celery into small pieces and put in a large pot with the bay leaves, peppercorns, and a small piece of cinnamon stick. Add the meat, pour over the wine, and leave to marinate for 24 hours in a cool place. Remove the meat from the marinade, drain, and pat dry with kitchen paper.

Heat the butter in a casserole, brown the meat over a high heat, and salt. Strain the marinade and ladle over the meat. Cover and simmer for several hours over a low heat, until the gravy has almost boiled away.

Take out the meat, cut into slices, and arrange on a prewarmed serving-dish. Strain the gravy into a small pan, and continue cooking for a short time over a low heat. Add salt, pepper and the brandy, allow to thicken, and pour over the meat. Serve with mashed potatoes.

BOLLITO MISTO

Mixed stewed meats

Serves 8–10

I SALTED CALF'S TONGUE, WEIGHING ABOUT I I/4 LBS/600 G
SALT
PEPPERCORNS
2 I/4 LBS/I KG BEEF (SHOULDER OR NECK)
I OVEN-READY CHICKEN, WEIGHING ABOUT 3 I/2 LBS/I.5 KG
3 CARROTS
4 STICKS CELERY
I SMALL LEEK
2 ONIONS
I LB/500 G VEAL (TOPSIDE)
I/2 LB/300 G FRESH PORK SAUSAGE, FLAVORED WITH GARLIC

Put the tongue in a pan with just enough water to cover it and bring to the boil. Reduce the heat, and cook the tongue for about 1½ hours until tender.

While it is cooking, boil 12 cups/3 liters water in a large casserole and add the peppercorns and the beef. Reduce the heat and simmer the meat for about 30 minutes. Then add the chicken.

Dice the carrots, celery, leek, and onions, and add them with the veal to the large casserole with the beef and the chicken. Continue to simmer for about 1 hour.

Prick the sausage several times and heat slowly in water. Rinse the tongue, which has now finished cooking, insert a kitchen knife into the tip, and remove the skin. Add the skinned tongue to the casserole with the other meat, and heat.

Cut the various meats into thin slices, divide the chicken and the sausage into portions, and arrange them all on a prewarmed serving dish. Garnish with the vegetables. Serve with *Bagnet verd* (Green sauce, see p. 149).

Serve with *Bagnet verd* (Green sauce, see p. 149).

VEGETABLE FONDUE

The classic Piedmontese dish *Bagna caoda* is a kind of vegetable fondue. Crisp raw or quickly blanched vegetables (cardoons, celery sticks, artichoke hearts, strips of bell pepper, spring vegetables, etc.) are dipped in a hot sauce of garlic and mashed anchovies and eaten with crusty bread.

BAGNA CAODA

Hot sauce

4 TBSP/50 G BUTTER
5 CLOVES OF GARLIC, THINLY SLICED
I CUP/250 ML EXTRA VIRGIN OLIVE OIL
I/4 LB/IOO G ANCHOVY FILLETS

Melt the butter in a pan and sauté the garlic. Gradually pour over the olive oil and stir in the anchovies, until a creamy consistency is obtained. Simmer for about 30 minutes and pour into a terra cotta bowl placed over a spirit burner.

To make the sauce more digestible, it is recommended that the hearts are removed from the garlic cloves, or that the garlic is marinated in milk for a few hours before use.

Vitello tonnato
Veal in tuna fish sauce (Illustrated in background)

1 1/2 lbs/700 g veal (fillet or leg)
Extra virgin olive oil
2 cups/500 ml dry white wine
Salt and pepper
2 bay leaves
2 sticks celery
1 clove garlic
1 scant cup/200 ml olive oil
2 egg yolks
Juice of 1 lemon
6 oz/200 g tuna fish in oil
2 anchovy fillets, finely chopped
2 tbsp capers and paprika

Brown the meat well in a casserole with some oil. Pour over the white wine, and add salt and pepper. Add the bay leaves, celery, and garlic, and braise for about 50 minutes over a medium heat. Allow to cool completely.
Prepare a mayonnaise from the egg yolks, olive oil, and the lemon juice. Rub the mayonnaise, together with the tuna fish, anchovies, and capers through a sieve. Cut the cold meat in thin slices and arrange on flat plates. Cover with the mayonnaise and keep in a cool place for about 2–3 hours. Garnish with capers and paprika, and serve with red wine. This dish is one of the classic starters from Piedmont, and was already famous by the beginning of the 19th century.

The battle and the chicken ragout

There are various and to some extent contradictory theories about the origin of *Polla alla Marengo*. The famous chef Auguste Escoffier (1846–1935) mentions this dish in his book *Le Livre des Menus* (The Book of Menus), and the historian Massimo Alberini, who provided a foreword to this work, gives the following introduction to the recipe: "Marengo is one of the few historical names which are linked to a particular event. On the afternoon or evening of June 14, 1800, the cook of the then First Consul, Napoleon Bonaparte, hastily prepared *Pollo alla Marengo* – probably with hens stolen from a Piedmontese farmer. The cook carved up the birds and braised the pieces in olive oil, white wine, and parsley, while the battle of Marengo raged outside. Escoffier, who was one of the most important chefs of recent times, later made this dish more elaborate by adding tomatoes, freshwater shrimps, bread, and fried eggs, all ingredients which Napoleon, who always remained loyal to 'his' chicken, would never have allowed."

Pollo alla Marengo
Chicken Marengo
(Illustrated left)

1 oven-ready chicken
All-purpose flour
2/3 cup/120 g extra virgin olive oil
Salt and pepper
1 lb/500 g ripe plum tomatoes, with skin and seeds removed
2 cloves garlic, pressed
A few leaves of basil
2 cups/500 ml dry white wine
1/2 lb/200 g fresh mushrooms, sliced
6 freshwater shrimp
6 slices white bread
6 eggs
Juice of 1 lemon
Large handful of parsley, finely chopped

Wash the chicken, cut in pieces, and toss in flour. Heat the olive oil in a pan, brown first the thighs, then the remaining pieces of chicken over a low heat, turning occasionally, and season with salt and pepper. Remove the breast portions from the pan and keep warm. Cut the tomatoes in pieces and add to the pan, together with the garlic and basil. Pour over a glass of white wine, cover, and braise for about 15 minutes over a low heat. Replace the chicken breasts in the pan, add the mushrooms, and braise for a further 20 minutes over a low heat. Heat the remaining wine in a casserole, add the shrimp, and cook for 4–5 minutes. Strain and keep warm. In another pan, fry the bread slices in a little olive oil, so that they remain soft inside. Fry the eggs in the same oil, without allowing them to run together. Drizzle the lemon juice over the chicken, sprinkle with parsley, and salt and pepper. Arrange the chicken pieces with the pan juices in the center of a serving dish. Put a fried egg on each slice of bread and arrange in a circle round the meat, garnish with the shrimp and serve.

Prosciutto baciato

Prosciutto baciato – also known as *Filetto baciato* – is an exquisite Piedmontese specialty. It is made from pork fillet or another lean part of the pig. The piece of meat, which should weigh about 1½–1¾ lbs (700–800 g), is marinated for a week in white wine and herbs. Then a salami paste is made, using plenty of *lardo* (bacon fat), and the fillet is covered with a layer about ⅜–⅝ inch (1–1.5 cm) thick. Then it is all stuffed into natural sausage skins by hand and stored for six months. When cut, the *Prosciutto baciato* looks lovely. The bright red of the fillet contrasts with the pale, almost white, layer surrounding it. Only a very few butchers produce this specialty; annual production is around 20,000.

Bagnet verd
Green sauce

1 small bunch parsley
1 clove garlic
A few capers
2 small pickled gherkins
2 anchovy fillets
1 stale bread roll
3 tbsp wine vinegar
1 hardboiled egg
Extra virgin olive oil
Salt and pepper
1 tsp sugar

Chop the parsley, garlic, and capers finely and cut the gherkins and anchovies in small pieces. Soak the bread roll in vinegar.
Put everything into a mortar and grind. Pass through a sieve and stir in the olive oil. Season with salt, pepper, and sugar. Serve as an accompaniment to beef or *Bollito misto*.

Unlike the standardized factory product, grissini bought from the little bakery on the corner can be as much as 28 inches/70 cm long. If they are to be nice and long and thin and round, you need to know exactly how to pull out the dough.

GRISSINI

In 1860, the House of Savoy ceded its territorial possessions, that is Nice and Savoy, to France, and was awarded royal status in return. Shortly afterward Vittorio Emanuele II was crowned king of Italy. Quite apart from the political upheavals of Italian unification, the king was plagued by worries over his little son. The prince was a poor eater; he was finicky and would not eat bread at all. He consulted his personal physician, who suspected that a digestive disorder might be the cause of the prince's reluctance to eat, and asked the court baker to produce a light, crisp bread without any soft crumb. The court baker thought carefully, and finally came up with a long, thin, easily broken white breadstick, which was particularly easy to digest because of its long baking time. We are not told if the prince overcame his aversion for bread as a result, but the new creation was much imitated by the Turin bakers, who were soon vying with one another as to who could conjure the longest and thinnest sticks out of the oven.

Now grissini have won a permanent place on every Italian table, and they are no longer made exclusively by the bakers of Turin, but are produced by the ton in big factories using high-tech processes. Critics of mass-produced breadsticks in sterile wrappers continually find fault with their insipid taste and prefer to buy their grissini from a traditional bakery of the kind which fortunately still exists in the Turin area.

Grissini are made from wheat flour, water, yeast, and a little salt. To make them really crisp, all the air has to be kneaded out of the dough.

When the grissini leave the oven, they should be thoroughly baked, but must not be too dark.

Handmade grissini are much tastier than packaged breadsticks from the big factories.

DESSERTS

The House of Savoy always loved fine cakes and pastries. *Savoiardi*, delicious sponge fingers, were supposedly baked for the first time in 1348, by a court chef who wished to please his masters. As these long cookies are made not only in Piedmont, but also in other regions which were once part of Savoy, the French city of Yenne also claims them as a specialty.

The origins of Zabaione or Zabaglione are also disputed. Some say it was invented in the 16th century by Bartolomeo Scappi, a pioneering chef of the Renaissance. Others think the name of this creamy dessert comes from Saint Pasquale Bayon, because in Piedmontese dialect, San Pasquale Bayon is easily run together into *Sanbajun*, which, with a little imagination, could sound like *zabagliun*. This saint's feast day is celebrated every year in Turin on May 7, and in 1722 he was even chosen to be the patron saint of the *Associazione cuochi di case e famiglie*, the Association of Home and Family Cooks.

ZABAIONE (ZABAGLIONE)
Zabaglione
(Illustrated above)

12 EGG YOLKS
1/2 CUP/100 G SUGAR
1 PINCH CINNAMON
3/4 CUP/400 ML MARSALA
SMALL GLASS RUM

Whisk the egg yolks and sugar in a bowl until the mixture is almost white. Dissolve the cinnamon in the Marsala and flavor with the rum. Gradually pour the Marsala into the custard, stirring continuously. Place the bowl in a bain-marie and carefully whisk the custard over a low heat. When the custard is smooth and frothy, remove from the heat and pour into dessert bowls.

SAVOIARDI
Savoy biscuits (Ladyfingers)
(Illustrated above)

3 EGGS
1/2 CUP/100 G SUGAR
1/2 CUP/90 G ALL-PURPOSE FLOUR
SALT
2/3 TBSP BUTTER
1/4 CUP/30 G CONFECTIONERS' SUGAR

Separate the eggs. In a bowl, beat the yolks with scant ⅓ cup sugar until frothy. Gradually add scant ⅓ cup flour and a pinch of salt and mix. In another bowl, beat the egg whites until stiff and carefully fold into the egg yolk mixture. Grease a baking sheet with butter, and sprinkle with flour. Fill a piping-bag with a smooth, flat nozzle and an opening about ½ inch/14 mm in diameter with the mixture. Pipe fingers about 4 inches/10 cm long, leaving sufficient room in between.

Mix the confectioners' sugar with the remaining sugar, and sprinkle half over the fingers. Wait about 10 minutes, until the sugar has soaked in, then sprinkle on the remaining sugar mixture and leave to stand for a few minutes more. Bake the fingers until golden yellow in a preheated oven at 300 °F (150 °C). Remove the tray from the oven, carefully transfer the sponge fingers to a wire tray using a spatula, and allow to cool.

BONÉT
Thick dessert cream

2 EGG YOLKS
2/3 CUP/130G SUGAR
2 OZ/50 G AMARETTI
2 TBSP/15 G COCOA POWDER
1 CUP/250 ML MILK
SMALL GLASS RUM

Beat the egg yolks and ½ cup/100 g sugar in a bowl until frothy. Crumble the Amaretti and add to the egg yolks,

CHESTNUTS

Not so very long ago, in mountain regions like Cuneo and Val de Susa sweet chestnuts were still considered a basic foodstuff, and often they even saved the local population from starvation. In Piedmont, many different varieties of chestnut can still be found, but the favorite is certainly the sweet chestnut. Unlike the inedible horse chestnut, which has multiple fruits, this improved variety of sweet chestnut only has single, but exceptionally large and tasty fruits. Chestnuts are not only roasted or boiled, or served as a nibble with wine or as an accompaniment to red meat or game, they are also used for a confection which has become a world-famous specialty, *marrons glacés*. For this, the delicate fruits must be dried by a special process, before being carefully candied and glazed in concentrated sugar syrup. As many are rejected during production (broken chestnuts are immediately sorted out), this confection is relatively expensive. In Piedmont, *marroni canditi*, as they are known in Italian, are eaten at Christmas. They are also a favorite gift.

together with the cocoa powder, milk, and rum, and mix together until smooth and creamy.

Caramelize the remaining sugar, and cover the sides and base of a dessert mold. Fill the mold with the cream and bake in a bain-marie in a preheated oven at 350 °F (180 °C) for about 1 hour, taking care not to let the water boil. Remove the mold from the oven. Leave the cream in the mold for about 15 minutes, then turn out onto a plate. Serve hot or cold.

CONFECTIONERY

Gianduiotto

Since the Conquistadors returned from their journeys of exploration in the West, bringing not only news of a New World, but also cocoa, chocolate fever has been rife. Cortez and his men could not have known, at the beginning of the 16th century, what enthusiasm those unprepossessing beans would arouse. Within a few decades, they had already radically changed European traditions, fashions, and the whole culture of enjoyment. Cocoa had become so widespread in the 17th and 18th centuries, that hot chocolate was obtainable in any inn in Venice or Florence.

At that time, Piedmont and its capital Turin were developing into an important center for chocolate and confectionery. Around 1800 even Swiss confectioners like François Cailler came to the area, eager to learn. We owe the invention of the famous Turin hazelnut praline *gianduiotto* to the best-known Italian confectioners, Peyrano, Streglia, Feletti, Talmone, and Caffarel. It was created during the carnival of 1865 in honor of the traditional theatrical mask Gianduja, a symbol of the city. Genuine *gianduiotto* consists of cocoa, sugar, vanilla, and hazelnuts.

Below: 30–50 whitish seeds, the so-called cocoa beans, are hidden in each of the fruits of the cacao tree (*Theobroma cacao*). Before use, they have to be fermented, roasted, and ground into powdery brown cocoa mass.

How chocolate is produced

The evergreen cacao tree grows up to 25 feet/8 meters high. Its reddish flowers are surprisingly small in relation to the big, cucumber-like red or yellow fruits, which sprout directly from the trunk or the main branches. Cacao trees certainly need warm to hot temperatures, but they cannot tolerate direct sunlight. The shoots in particular are dependent on other plants to give them shade. Cacao trees also demand a high moisture content in the atmosphere. The tree must grow for about ten years before it really bears fruit. The fruits ripen at irregular intervals, so they have to be harvested every 4–6 weeks. Beneath the semihard, ribbed shell is a sugary flesh surrounding the cocoa beans. The freshly picked fruits are broken open, and the 30–50 whitish seeds removed. Then the cocoa beans are put into a tub, where the surrounding flesh begins to ferment. This is when the flavors first begin to develop. Then the beans are dried and the raw cocoa is shipped out. The beans are roasted, peeled, and ground, forming a sort of mushy pulp – the cocoa mass. To extract the oil and produce weak or strong cocoa powder – for drinking or cooking – the mass is pressed until the cocoa butter has separated out, and the pressed cakes are ground. Basic chocolate recipes include cocoa mass, sugar, cocoa butter, milk products such as condensed milk or milk powder, and flavorings such as vanilla or cinnamon. The ingredients are first thoroughly mixed in a melangeur, a kind of crusher. At the same time the mass must ripen for 24 hours at 77–120 °F (25–50 °C), which gives it a doughy consistency. This raw chocolate can be used for basic chocolate products, but for fine chocolate bars, the mass must be put into a machine called a *conche*, where it is compressed by rollers at 140–175 °F (60–80 °C) for several days, so that the flavorings mix and emulsify. Then the pulp is cooled to about 78 °F (28 °C) and poured into bars.

Package design from the first half of the 19th century – the three pretty little girls, in their special aprons, are advertising the three major products of the Caffarel firm: cocoa, chocolate, and pralines.

Ferrero and Nutella

The history of chocolate specialties from Piedmont would be incomplete without the brothers Giovanni and Pietro Ferrero from Farigliano near Cuneo. Born one at the end of the 19th century, the other at the beginning of the 20th, they survived both world wars and the ensuing set-backs. But the family, who owned a little cake store in Alba, were not discouraged. Shortly after the end of World War II, the Ferreros began producing a new kind of nut and cocoa cream, which they christened Nutella and sold at a very favorable price. The appetizing aroma of chocolate and the high quality of Piedmontese hazelnuts soon made this reasonably priced, nutritious spread a success. Lovers of Nutella must have remained loyal to Ferrero, as today the company is Europe's leading confectionery manufacturer and has also been producing other sweet delicacies for a long time.

But Nutella is more than just a chocolate spread – it is a highly addictive passion. On September 27, 1998, a meeting took place in a hotel outside the gates of Alba, where 350 *nutellomani* together indulged a passion, which they share with millions of fellow addicts throughout the world. Alba was, of course, the only possible venue for the celebrations – even the mayor attended, publicly confessing his own passion – because the Ferrero factory, which is still producing several million tonnes of Nutella today, is situated there. The man behind the Nutella party is – coincidentally – called Davide Ferrero, but he is not related to the "genuine" Ferreros. Apart from that, the young lawyer is president of the *Ciococlub*, the umbrella organization for Nutella fans. The club now has its own Internet site, which has been visited by around 10,000 initiates to date. Admission to the Nutella party cost the guests a minimum contribution of the equivalent of about 5 dollars. Part of the proceeds of the party were intended to go to charity, but some of the money was spent on buying 120 pounds/50 kilograms of chocolate spread and the 14 gigantic loaves of bread (each 8 feet/ 2 ½ meters long) consumed by the lucky guests.

Incidentally, the Nutella party and the *Ciococlub* are not advertising or PR stunts, and the president emphasizes that they were not sponsored by Ferrero or any other chocolate firm. The "genuine" Ferrero family had previously made it clear that they wanted nothing to do with the event. But the chocolate-covered enthusiasts didn't give a cocoa bean for that, and it certainly didn't spoil their fun.

Hernando Cortez (1485–1547)
Copper engraving by Isabella Piccini, active around 1665/92, colored after a contemporary portrait.

ALESSI – DESIGN IN THE KITCHEN

In Piedmont there is a tradition of good knives, pots and pans, scissors, and other kitchen equipment. The Strona valley has always offered ideal conditions for the metal-processing industry. Fast-flowing torrents rushing down from the mountains used to provide the necessary water power – an important factor in the days before the invention of our present energy systems. On the north shore of Lake Orta there are still a few manufacturers making household and kitchen wares of stainless steel and other materials. One of these is Alessi. The grandfather of the current company president, Alberto Alessi, from the third generation of the family, founded a small workshop in Omegna in 1921. In 1928, it moved to Crusinallo, where the company still has its headquarters.

Of course Alessi has always been famous for clean, functional design, but in the eighties the company wanted more. In the boardroom, they dreamed of producing kitchenware whose form and function were geared to providing active support for the cook, thereby contributing to the success of the meals. So the creative team, in collaboration with designers, cooks, and historians, developed new products, which not only found their way into Italian kitchens, but soon enjoyed great popularity in the rest of Europe as well. Very few customers are scared off by the relatively high prices, since anyone who knows anything about cooking realizes firstly that good utensils are essential, and secondly that high quality kitchenware is virtually indestructible, and for that reason alone is worth a few lire, dollars pesetas, pounds, drachmas, or marks.

COMPANY HISTORY

Giovanni Alessi

1921
Giovanni Alessi Anghini founds a metal-processing business in Omegna and starts by taking in orders.
1928
The Alessi Company moves to Crusinallo.
1932
Carlo, the founder's eldest son, who had studied industrial design, joins the business. Among the most influential of his designs were the Bombé tea and coffee services.

1955
In the years following the second world war, the company is successfully transformed into a modern industrial undertaking. Carlo moves into management. His brother Ettore begins working with designers like Luigi Massoni, Carlo Mazzeri and Anselmo Vitale.

Alessi Company headquarters in Crusinallo

1970
Alberto, a grandson of the founder with a law degree, joins the firm. His goal is to abolish the distinction between mass production and craftsmanship quality.
1972
Alberto commissions Ettore Sottsass to design some oil and vinegar sets.
1977
Richard Sapper is entrusted with the design of the first *caffettiera*. It is the start of a collaboration, which will produce many classic designs of coffee-maker.
1980
Achille Castiglione works with Alessi and designs Dry, the first Design-Smiths cutlery set. It comes onto the market in 1982.
1983
The Piazza Tea and Coffee Project is brought to life. The idea: famous architects should design a tea and coffee service, without having to consider the limitations of mass production. The result: objects made of high quality materials in limited editions designed by architects like Michael Graves, Hans Hollein, Aldo Rossi, Robert Venturi, and Richard Meier.
1986
Philippe Starck works for Alessi and achieves immediate success with a postmodern classic, the Juicy Salif juice press. It comes onto the market in 1989.
1989
Designers Stefano Giovannoni and Guido Venturini, working as the design duo King Kong, design the amusing Girotondo collection.
1993
Start of the Family Follows Friction Project, a series of utensils by young designers, in shapes inspired by comic figures and toys.
1997
Enzo Mari joins the ranks of famous designers working for Alessi. New designs are produced, but Alessi also reissues some old designs from the sixties, which were produced for Danese.

Right hand page: Juicy Salif juice press Philippe Starck, 1989

Cruet set for oil, vinegar, salt, and pepper
Ettore Sottsass, 1978

La Cupola espresso machine
Aldo Rossi, 1989

9090 cafetière
Richard Sapper, 1979

La Conica coffee pot
Aldo Rossi, 1984

Dry
Achille Castiglioni, 1982

Bread basket
Enzo Mari, 1997

"Singing" kettle
Richard Sapper, 1983

Nonno di Antonio garlic press
Guido Venturini, 1996

Corkscrew Anna G
Alessandro Mendini, 1994

Tea and coffee service Piazza
Hans Hollein, 1983

Bombé tea and coffee service
Carlo Alessi Anghinì, 1945

Toast rack from the Girotondo series
King Kong, 1996

Il Conico kettle
Aldo Rosso, 1986

Sugar bowl
Michael Graves, 1992

VINEGAR

Vinegar is an ancient flavoring. The Romans were already familiar with this form of oxidized wine, in the Middle Ages it was taken as a medicine for the plague, and recently it has made a comeback even in the best kitchens. Vinegar used to be considered a rather coarse ingredient, which would not do for delicately flavored dishes because of its high acidity. Nowadays Italian chefs, in particular, who have gone back to traditional Mediterranean cuisine, no longer think of vinegar as an enemy which destroys flavor, but as a help in the kitchen, adding flavor to a court-bouillon, tenderizing kidneys, brightening up sauces, and making cooked bell peppers easier to digest. It has its place in cold dishes anyway, because a salad dressing made from oil, salt, and garlic would be unimaginable without vinegar. Vinegar is produced by adding acetic acid bacteria (*Acetobacter aceti*) to a low-alcohol white or red wine, and waiting until the bacteria have oxidized the alcohol, converting it into acetic acid. The usual carrier for the bacteria is a "vinegar mother." This gelatinous mass builds up in vessels, which have been repeatedly used for making vinegar. A vinegar mother was once a precious possession because, with its help, it was always

Cesare Giacone is a master vinegar-maker. Here he is carefully checking the color and reflected light of one of his own vinegars.

As the maturing of vinegar must be carefully checked, there is very little difference between the vinegar-maker and the wine-maker.

possible to begin making a new batch of vinegar. Italian law states that good vinegar must be made from wine, and must contain at least 6 percent acetic acid and no more than 1.5 percent residual alcohol. Although today vinegar is usually mass produced, there are still a few companies selling very aromatic white or red wine vinegars produced in the traditional way. In Piedmont, especially, there is determined resistance to the idea that vinegar is simply wine which has "gone off." The firm of Ponti, among others, has its factory here, and though it has a sizeable turnover of 45 million bottles, it is considered in Europe to be one of the famous producers of fine wine vinegar. But alongside Ponti, there are also smaller vinegar enthusiasts like Cesare Giacone of the Restaurant Dei Cacciatori in Alberretto della Torre.

By comparison with other countries in the European Community, the annual vinegar consumption in Italy is very low, only amounting to 0.9 liter (2 U.S. pints) per head, as opposed to an average consumption of 1.4 liters (3 U.S. pints). However, in Central and Southern Italy, vinegar is made at home in the traditional way, and these quantities do not appear in the official sales statistics.

Vinegar can be allowed to get very old. It certainly loses its brilliant color over the years, but its flavor improves as it matures.

Vinegar barrels have a small opening at the top, through which the master vinegar-maker takes samples at regular intervals. As well as testing the taste and smell, it is also tested to see if it still contains alcohol, because the vinegar cannot be judged "ready" until the alcohol has been completely converted.

HONEY VINEGAR

Vinegar does not have to be made from wine. In ancient Egypt, they were already making a honey vinegar, which may very likely be the oldest vinegar in the world. Honey vinegar is still produced today, preferably from fine acacia honey which, when diluted with water, slowly begins to ferment if the temperature and passage of air are carefully controlled. Honey vinegar made in this way is neither pasteurized nor chemically purified, so as not to destroy the healthy enzymes. Its acidity is slightly lower than that of classic wine vinegar, which makes it better for the stomach. It is excellent for salads, because its mineral salts do not clash with the raw vegetables. Sauces and sweet-and-sour dishes also taste good if honey vinegar is used. Diluted with water, it quenches the thirst in summer. It is a popular flavoring for fruit, rice, and cheese salads.

SOTT'ACETI
Vegetables in vinegar

2 LBS/1 KG ASSORTED FRESH VEGETABLES IN SEASON (E.G. SMALL ONIONS, BROCCOLI, CAULIFLOWER, CARROTS, BELL PEPPERS, SMALL CUCUMBERS, ZUCCHINI, EGGPLANT, CELERY, PUMPKIN, ARTICHOKES)
4 CUPS/1 LITER WATER
4 CUPS/1 LITER GOOD WINE VINEGAR
2 TBSP/30 G SALT
1 TBSP/15 G SUGAR
BAY LEAVES IF DESIRED

Prepare the vegetables and cut into small pieces. Mix water, vinegar, salt, and sugar, and bay leaves if desired, in a large saucepan and bring to a boil. As soon as the salt and sugar have dissolved, add the vegetables. Depending on the size of the pieces, boil until they are slightly tender, but still a little crisp.
Pour the vegetables into preserving jars and fill with the liquid. Seal the jars. Either store in a cool place and use quickly or sterilize in the oven at 200 °F (90 °C) for 30 minutes.

FLAVORED VINEGAR

Exotic vinegars, consisting of wine vinegar with added herbal flavorings, have become very popular. However, you should be careful with these preparations, as some of them add a totally different flavor from the usual wine vinegar and may have a very strong effect on a dish, or even make it taste unfamiliar. Fruit vinegars are in a category of their own, as the fruit must first ferment to become fruit wine, before it can be used to make vinegar.
Raspberry, cherry, and fruits of the forest vinegars go well with salads and can make sauces more interesting. Garlic vinegar is suitable for salads, which should take on just a slight flavor of garlic. Tarragon, bay, and rosemary vinegars are especially good with fish, but are also nice in salads.

Raspberry, rosemary, sage, chili, tarragon, and mint vinegar (from left to right)

A Law for wine

There can hardly be another wine law in the world as controversial as the Italian one. When it came into being in 1963, the legislature was above all concerned with protecting the winegrowers from unfair competition. Legally designated origins are important for consumers too, of course, because they guarantee that the wine they have bought really comes from the area shown on the label – which was not necessarily true before. But the wine law does not only define the winegrowing area, but also regulates the varieties of grapes individual wines are made from, and even how they are to be made. In order to classify the different qualities, the legislature created a quality pyramid with four tiers. The majority of wines are sold as simple *vino da tavola*, table wine of no designated origin. Above them are the *vini con indicazione geografica (Igt)*, wines with a simple geographical indication of origin. Quality wines are categorized as DOC, *Denominazione di origine controllata*, controlled designation of origin, and the highest level as DOCG, *Denominazione di origine controllata e garantita*, that is controlled and guaranteed wines. There are in total only 18 designations of origin altogether in this most prestigious category. In practice, the almost 300 labels of designated origin in Italy only rarely guarantee a high quality wine – sadly there are wines of only average quality in many DOC and even DOCG areas, and even whole winegrowing areas which do not actually deserve the title of quality winegrowing area. As a result, many wine-lovers choose their wines exclusively by the name of the producer, not by the legal category, and so it happens that today – paradoxically – even table wines may be among the most expensive and sought-after in Italy.

Map legend:
- Barbera d'Alba
- Nebbiolo d'Alba
- Roero
- Dolcetto d'Alba
- Barbaresco
- Barolo
- Dolcetto di Diano d'Alba
- Asti
- Dolcetto di Dogliani
- Dolcetto delle Langhe Monregalesi
- Winegrowing areas in neighboring regions

5 km

Piedmont

PIEDMONT – KINGDOM OF THE NEBBIOLO

Piedmont lies tucked between the northwestern curve of the Alps and the Apennines, which determine its climate – very hot summers and almost continental cold winters. Wine is grown in almost all parts of the region, but especially in the hilly countryside of the southern half, which is made up of the provinces of Cuneo, Asti, and Alessandria. Of morethan 138,320 acres (56,000 hectares) of grapes, 60 percent is designated for the production of quality wines, which represents a very high proportion for Italy.

The most widely grown grape in Piedmont is – one might almost say of course – red, and is called Barbera. The former mass-grown variety, which was at the center of the country's biggest wine scandal in the eighties, has become something of a star over the last decade. Its wines have achieved a quality which has won the respect of wine-lovers throughout the world. But the region owes its prestige almost exclusively to the Nebbiolo, or more precisely the Nebbiolo wines Barolo and Barbaresco, which are produced on the hills of Langa or Langhe right next to the truffle-capital Alba. In a way, the emergence of the famous Nebbiolo wines in the 19th century marks the birth of modern Italian quality wine production as a whole, as well as that of the Piedmont region as a traditional and dependable producer of fine wines.

"King of wines and wine of kings" – that is what they called Barolo, which is today the most important of the Nebbiolo wines, not least because its "discovery" by the French enologist Oudart in the castle of the Marchesa Giulietta Falletti was actively supported by the House of Savoy. It is an ideal combination of the characteristics of the Nebbiolo grape: strength, elegance, and good keeping quality. As it ages, good Barolo develops hints of truffle, tar, undergrowth, roses, tea, and spices and, when mature, tastes full, round, and velvety in the mouth.

NOT ONLY IN PIEDMONT

Although today Nebbiolo is considered to be one of the best varieties of grape in the world, it has not become widespread, unlike famous French grapes, such as Cabernet Sauvignon or Merlot. In Italy, outside Piedmont, it is cultivated almost exclusively in Lombardy. In the Valtellina valley, where it is the main variety used in the DOC Valtellina, it is known by the name of Chiavennasca, and it makes up a small part of the blend used for the still, red wines of the DOC Terre di Franciacorta, from the Franciacorta area. Apart from that, this variety is occasionally planted in the United States – especially in the Californian winegrowing areas of Sonoma, Paso Robles, Santa Maria, and Santa Barbara – and experimentally in a few Australian vineyards. Most recently, even one German grower has been experimenting with Nebbiolo grapes.

Before Oudart's time, Nebbiolo from Barolo and the surrounding villages was mostly made sweet. Later they allowed the must or the wine to ferment so long on the skins, that, when young, the finished product often seemed harsh and off-putting, with an exaggerated taste of tannin, only developing a certain charm with age. In the eighties, a group of younger Piedmontese winegrowers took it upon themselves to give Barolo a more modern face. They changed the methods of pressing, and allowed the wine to mature in small casks made of new wood, which gave its bouquet an even greater variety, and made it mellower and more attractive when young. As so often in the world when something is revolutionized, in Piedmont, too, modernists and traditionalists argued over who made the genuine, true, and unadulterated Barolo. But basically this argument was unnecessary, since the best adherents of both sides produce outstanding wines which mature well – just in a different style.

From right next to Barolo – on the opposite side of the small town of Alba – comes Barbaresco, a wine which is reputed to be less strong but even more elegant, and to have a certain "femininity." Once the more famous and successful of the two wines, it nevertheless suffered during its time of great commercial success, which led many winegrowers and sellers to produce it in increasing quantities and increasingly dubious quality. It is only in recent years that a handful of growers from Barbaresco and the surrounding area have restored the wine to its former greatness.

Other Nebbiolo wines from the area around Asti, which are no doubt only second rank, but are rising in quality, are Nebbiolo d'Alba, and the red Roero. By contrast, the Nebbiolo wines of Northern Piedmont, Gattinara, and Ghemme – where the grape is known as Spanna – suffered a similar fate to that of Barbaresco, but with far more serious consequences. Even the recently successful application for DOCG status could not breathe new life into them. In Piedmont, Nebbiolo is used in a further 14 DOC wines, which are for the most part (still) fairly unimportant. These include old, traditional, but forgotten names like Boca, Bramaterra, and Fara, as well as the new labels Langhe, Monferrato, and Piemonte, and among them are a series of high-quality former table wines. In some of these, the variety is well supplemented by adding larger or smaller quantities of Barbera.

In summer Nebbiolo needs a lot of light and warmth. The cold Piedmont winters, seen here near Ivrea, provide the optimum conditions for the vines to regenerate.

BARBERA, DOLCETTO, GAVI, AND THE REST

As the main variety used for the simplest mass-produced wines, and the leading character in the biggest Italian wine scandal of the postwar era, Barbera and its DOC wines (Barbera d'Alba, Barbera d'Asti, Barbera del Monferrato) – grape varieties are always female to the Piedmontese – have long enjoyed a more than somewhat dubious reputation. But during the eighties a group of Piedmontese growers, formed around Giacomo Bologna and Angelo Gaja, remembered the quality of this variety and, influenced by their impressions from their travels in France, began a radical overhaul of work in the vineyards and cellar techniques. Barbera, which was traditionally mostly thin and acidic, had its acid content progressively reduced, and was finally stored in small wooden casks, giving it an enriched bouquet and a more refined taste. Because of the much reduced harvests which resulted, they aimed to achieve stronger, more concentrated wines, which would previously have been unthinkable.

The resulting vintages had the strength and the aromatic freshness which distinguish top quality modern wines, and soon took their place among the best red wines of Italy. Made from a single variety, or blended with other grapes – Nebbiolo, Cabernet Sauvignon, and even the difficult Pinot noir are particularly well-suited – the best examples of the DOC labels, Barbera d'Alba, Barbera d'Asti, Langhe, or Piemonte, are today generally considered an ideal accompaniment to regional dishes.

The career of Dolcetto has been just as amazing as that of Barbera. Its wines are not – as its name might suggest – sweet, but dry and slightly fruity. In southern Piedmont, in the Langhe Hills of Cuneo province, Dolcetto used to be thought of as the epitome of everyday wine. Its bouquet is characterized by the scents of cherry and pepper, and it tastes mellow and fruity, though the wine never seems too heavy, even when it has a higher alcohol content. Grignolino, whose wines can be very seductive with their characteristic scents of roses and berries, goes even further in the light and fruity direction. Unfortunately, high-quality wines from Grignolino grapes are rare, and this is also true of the last two red varieties worth mentioning, Bracchetto and Freisa.

Freisa is an old, traditional grape, whose wines can turn out very differently. They are mostly slightly sparkling, sometimes even rather sweet, and are drunk soon after the harvest. But recently, committed winegrowers have proved that full-bodied, almost opulent wines can also be made from Freisa, which even benefit from maturing for some time in the cask. By contrast, Bracchetto wines have a bouquet similar to Moscato

Dolcetto grapes used to be thought of as producing everyday wine, but now top quality wines are made from this variety.

SWEET AND SPARKLING

The grape variety most commonly grown in Piedmont is used not for still but for sparkling wine. This is Muscatel or Moscato, more precisely Moscato di Canelli – not to be confused with Moscato di Alessandria, Moscato giallo, or Moscato rosa, varieties which belong to the same family, but produce very different wines. Varieties in this family are among the very oldest; they were probably being cultivated around the Mediterranean more than three thousand years ago.

The wine made from Muscatel grapes in Piedmont, or to be precise, in the provinces of Asti, Alessandria, and Cuneo, goes by the name of Asti, formerly Asti Spumante. There are actually two varieties of this wine, Moscato d'Asti and Asti. Both are light, sweet sparkling wines, relatively low in alcohol, but they are made by a different process. In the case of traditional Moscato d'Asti, the fermentation of the must is interrupted several times by filtering and started again, until the correct proportions of natural sweetness and the carbonic acid gas which creates the sparkle have been achieved. By contrast, mass produced Asti is made in large fermentation tanks, and becomes *spumante*, which means

sparkling, through a regular second fermentation. It contains much more carbonic acid, so the bottles are under higher pressure than those of Moscato d'Asti. While winegrowing in the Asti area is largely run by the growers, the finished Asti is produced in gigantic tanks in huge factories, most of which are situated in the town of Canelli. These factories built their past success mainly on exports; at times Germany alone took almost half the quantity produced, and became the biggest market for Asti.

In recent years, however, the development curve for Asti has shown a sharp downward trend, which has not been reversed by its promotion from a mass-produced wine to a DOCG label.

Good Moscato d'Asti and good Asti are light, fresh, slightly fruity wines which – when chilled – are particularly good to drink in summer. At other times of the year, their qualities come out best in combination with fresh fruit desserts or light, sweet cakes and pastries.

or Muscatel, which is widespread in Piedmont, and also to Gewürztraminer. However, they are not easy to combine with food.

As for white wines, Chardonnay and Sauvignon Blanc have made inroads into the region in recent years, and the early results have been excellent, but the traditional white grapes of Piedmont are still Arneis and Cortese. In Roero, which lies in the hills next to the Langhe, Ersterer has a DOC area of its own and was, for a time, well on the way to becoming a fashionable variety. However, exorbitant prices and too small quantities soon put an end to that. Cortese grapes are mainly used to make the DOC wine Gavi, the most popular Piedmontese white. This fresh, mellow wine, with its rather neutral aroma, is a good accompaniment to starters and vegetables. The other grape varieties grown in Piedmont, and their wines – Favorita, Bonarda, Erbaluce, Ruché, Pelaverga, Timorasso, and the rest – are of mainly regional importance, but can produce top quality wines in exceptional cases.

Barolo

The king of wines is made from Nebbiolo grapes from the slopes to the southeast of the town of Alba. The three valleys, which extend into the hills of the Langa, give the wine very different characteristics. La Morza produces mellower, slightly fruity wines, whereas Serralunga and Castiglione have a classic hint of tannin. Nowadays the wines are usually made in such a way that they are already very approachable when young, and their tannins no longer act as a deterrent in the way they once did. When they have reached their full maturity, they have a wonderful bouquet, in which one can catch a hint of tealeaves, sweet tobacco, truffles, and leather. They have a full, strong taste, with a mellow, velvety, rounded structure, and are excellent with substantial Piedmontese meat dishes.

Vino da Tavola

Although a number of producers sell their former Vini da Tavola under the Langhe or Piemonte labels, there are still excellent table wines, which helped to found the good reputation of the Italian wine industry during the quality revolution in the eighties. In Piedmont, these wines are often blended from different varieties: Nebbiolo and Barbera, Barbera and Cabernet Sauvignon or Pinot noir, Nebbiolo and Cabernet or Merlot, etc. Usually strong-flavored, elegant, and varied in aroma, they represent the best choice for an elegant dinner with delicately spiced meat dishes.

Barbaresco

This Nebbiolo wine from the slopes to the north of Alba, which until well into the sixties was much more famous than its neighbor Barolo, was then more or less forgotten as a result of a lack of effort from producers become accustomed to success. The fact that Barbaresco usually seemed thinner and weaker was readily interpreted as being due to its basic "femininity." Recently, however, a number of growers have caught the attention with strong, varied Barbaresco wines, which age well. When fully mature, the bouquet harmonizes splendidly with the truffle dishes from the Langhe.

Barbera d'Alba

On the hills of the Barolo and Barbaresco area around the town of Alba, grow the grapes for the strong, tannin-rich Barbera d'Alba. The intense red color, a beautiful, fruity bouquet, and the round, firm body make this wine an ideal accompaniment to wholesome pasta and meat dishes. As many local producers prefer to make the prestigious Barolo or Barbaresco, the quality of the Barbera wines occasionally leaves something to be desired, but the best examples of this label are among the best Barbera wines in the whole of Italy.

Moscato

Moscato d'Asti is the delicately fruity, elegant version of the famous Asti, formerly called Asti Spumante. With their rich, fruity bouquet, in which the aroma of pears may dominate, a pleasant, fruity sweetness and their slight but not aggressive sparkle, these wines are excellent with fruit desserts.

Barbera d'Asti

Formerly too acidic, and produced in too great quantities, today Barbera d'Asti has blossomed into almost the better of the two important Barbera labels. Unlike the Langa, where the best slopes are reserved for Nebbiolo, in the province of Asti, the Barbera grape is considered the best red variety, and is treated as such. It blends excellently with other varieties like Nebbiolo, Spätburgunder or even Cabernet, and gives strong wines, which last well.

Gavi

Gavi, or Gavi di Gavi, was for a long time a fashionable wine in Piedmont, but was unable to achieve any lasting success, mainly on account of its poor value for money. It is made from Cortese grapes in the area around the town of Gavi in the province of Alessandria. The wines have a rather neutral bouquet, and a smooth, mellow taste. They are a very good accompaniment to foods with vegetable side dishes.

Langhe

Of the new DOC wines Piemonte, Montferrato, and Langhe, which each cover a range of red and white wines, DOC Langhe is the most prestigious. This is mainly because many top producers, whose former *vini da tavola* did not fit any of the DOC regulations, because they were made from foreign varieties or were not produced according to the rules, now bottle under this label.

WORMWOOD AND VERMOUTH

The herb-flavored wine vermouth was once scarcely ranked as a valued or prestigious drink. Although it seems to have a long tradition behind it, the name probably goes back to the Old High German word *werimouta*, which describes a kind of vegetable bitters that stimulate the digestion, but which nobody liked drinking. This was to change abruptly in 1786, when Antonio Benedetto Carpano presented the customers in his bar in Turin with his own creation, which he called vermouth.

The new drink was immediately taken up with enthusiasm. Carpano had not only managed to improve local white wine by adding a particularly refined and strictly secret mixture of herbs, he had also succeeded in polishing up the hitherto mediocre image of wormwood and selling it as a luxury wine. Carpano's competitors were also convinced by this concept. Other manufacturers of spirits, particularly Cinzano, began to produce the aromatic fortified wine. Martini & Rossi came on to the market in 1863 with their version of vermouth. Other Piedmontese firms such as Gancia and Cora followed.

Piedmont is still the home of vermouth, and Carpano, Cinzano, and Martini & Rossi are still synonymous with this aromatic drink. The only difference is that now they no longer make it in little witches' kitchens, but with the aid of the most modern technology. The basic ingredient is white wine. While the pioneers of vermouth relied on Moscato d'Asti or Moscato di Canelli, today they use white wines with very little distinctive flavor of their own. They add sugar, alcohol, and a mixture of various herbal extracts, among them mugwort, wormwood leaves, marjoram, nutmeg, thyme, sage, cinnamon, aniseed, fennel, and cloves. The "seasoned" wine is then heated and distilled. Sweet vermouth is colored with caramel. The alcohol content of a dry vermouth must be around 18 percent.

MANHATTAN
(Illustrated left)

1 MEASURE OF CANADIAN WHISKY
1/2 MEASURE OF SWEET VERMOUTH
DASH OF ANGOSTURA BITTERS
ICE
COCKTAIL CHERRIES

Pour the whisky, vermouth, Angostura, and ice into a cocktail shaker, mix, and strain into a chilled cocktail glass. Decorate with cocktail cherries and, if desired, with a twist of lemon peel.

Martini, Carpano, Gancia, Cora, Cinzano – these are the great names of vermouth, which should be found in every well-stocked bar. The two classic Italian cocktails Americano and Negroni both contain vermouth. Negroni apparently owes its name to a certain Count Camillo Negroni, who invented it.

Dry Martini

1 1/4 MEASURES OF GIN
1/4 MEASURE OF VERMOUTH
EXTRA DRY
ICE
1 OLIVE WITH PIT

Pour the gin, vermouth, and ice into a cocktail shaker, mix, and strain into a chilled cocktail glass. Garnish with an olive. Only use olives with pits, never stuffed olives. Olives should not be preserved in oil but in brine. A twist of lemon may be added.

All recipes for 1 drink

Extra Dry Martini

1 1/2 MEASURES OF GIN
DASH OF VERMOUTH EXTRA DRY

Pour the gin and a suggestion of very dry vermouth into a cocktail shaker, mix, and strain into a chilled cocktail glass. Purists insist that the gin should merely be shown the vermouth bottle.

Americano

ICE
3/4 MEASURE OF CAMPARI
3/4 MEASURE OF SWEET
VERMOUTH
SODA WATER
SLICES OF LEMON

Put the ice into a glass. Add Campari and vermouth. Top up with soda water and stir briefly. Garnish with lemon peel.

Negroni

1/2 MEASURE OF CAMPARI
1/2 MEASURE OF SWEET
VERMOUTH
1/2 MEASURE OF GIN
ICE
ORANGE AND LEMON PEEL

Pour the Campari, vermouth, gin, and ice into a cocktail shaker, mix, and strain into a chilled cocktail glass. Garnish with orange and lemon peel.

LIGURIA

Popular tradition accuses the Ligurians of being unreceptive to strangers, feeling happiest at home, and preferring to do everything for themselves. In their cuisine, too, they like to use those trusted products which come from the 220 mile (350 kilometer) long stretch of coastline, with its rough, mountainous hinterland or are fished out of their own waters. The tangy herbs, the crisp vegetables, the sea creatures, the eggs for the *Torta pasqualina* – everything is *nostrano*, that is, local produce, as it says on the notices in the markets. Even the wine, which is grown with great effort on the rough, steeply terraced slopes, and lovingly made into small vintages of the highest quality, seems to have been invented in Liguria, it suits the local food so well. Savory cakes and pies are a Ligurian specialty. As well as *Torta pasqualina*, they still serve the traditional *Torta marinara*, which is not – as the name might lead you to think – a pie filled with fish, but a splendid savory flan. It was made with Swiss chard, ricotta, fresh mushrooms, and parmesan by the seamen's wives, because they knew that husbands on leave after months at sea at the mercy of a ship's cook – who might have been competent if they were lucky, but was usually only capable of serving dried fish and ship's biscuit – always came ashore with a hearty appetite for savory herbs, earthy mushrooms, and fresh cheese. It is not surprising that Ligurian cuisine is nicknamed *cucina del ritorno*, or "homecoming" cooking. A more modest, but no less tasty version of the *Torta salata* or savory cake is Ligurian *focaccia*. In many areas, this thin bread is also filled with cheese, copiously sprinkled with oil, and garnished with onions. The addition of onions was particularly sensible in the harbor towns, because their bactericidal effects and high vitamin C content helped to protect the population against the diseases the men brought back from overseas.

Because the Ligurians like to make everything for themselves, they have also invented a pizza of their own. The focaccia-like specialty, topped with onions and anchovies, comes from Oneglia, now called Imperia, and is known as *Pizza all'Andrea*. It was invented at the end of the 15th or beginning of the 16th century – by the ingenious statesman and naval hero Andrea Doria, at least so the legend goes.

Previous double page: Tasty vegetables such as freshly picked artichokes are a part of the Ligurian cuisine. Here the grower Giampiero Navone is checking his stock.

Left: The steep, inaccessible, terraced vineyards of the Cinqueterre, pictured here near Corniglia, do not permit the use of machinery. The grapes must be tended and harvested by hand.

**Alice (sardelle or anchovy) and sardina
or sarda (sardine)**
With cries such as "Wonderful anchovies for sale, as fresh
and lively as if they had quicksilver in their bodies!" or "I
sell the silver from the sea!"
the fishermen advertise
their freshly caught wares.
Like the sardine, the
sardelle, now better known
as the anchovy, is a
member of the herring
family. They were traditionally caught in the seas
outside the Gulf of Genoa.
But now – probably on
account of their compara-
tively firm flesh – both

Sardelle

Sardine

sardines and anchovies find their way less often into the
cooking pot, which is a real shame, because they taste
very piquant and spicy. Sardines and anchovies are nice
freshly cooked, but can also be tasty when preserved in
oil, salt, or marinade. Sardines, which are good value, are
often sold smoked, if they do not end up in oil, in a can
on the supermarket shelves of the rest of Europe.

Aguglia (garfish)
This valuable fish actually belongs to the cod family, but
is very different in appearance. The garfish has a long,
slender body and grows up to three feet (one meter)
long. Salt water gar can be caught all year round, but the
best time is between September and January. Its fine, firm
flesh is good when braised, and this tasty fish is an essential part of a *fritto misto alla ligure*

Tonno (tuna)
Though the tuna found in Ligurian waters is obviously
smaller than its relatives on other shores, its flesh tastes
just as good, if not better. Fresh tuna can be cut in wafer-
thin slices and served as a *carpaccio*, but it is also a delicacy
when grilled. Tuna preserved in vinegar or oil is good for
savory sauces or as a filling for pasta.

Sgombro (mackerel)
The mackerel, which is related to the tuna, is one of the
commonest fishes throughout the world. Italians are
particularly fond of this tasty, healthy, good value fish.
Mackerel must always be eaten very fresh, because it
quickly goes off.

HUNTING THE BLUE FISH

The seas of the Gulf of Genoa are restless waters. Countless whirlpools, shallows, storms, and other horrors lurk between the Ponente and the Levant, turning the daily tasks of fishermen and sailors into a dangerous adventure. Fishermen in particular always had to struggle to earn a living – and it is still the same today – because the waters are not especially rich in fish. If they are to catch anything at all, they must venture far out to sea, and hope to find the *pesce azzurro*. These fish get their name from the blue-green sheen of their skin and the fact that they live far out in the deep blue waters of the open sea. The "blue fish" group includes herring species like sardines and anchovies, as well as certain others, such as mackerel, tuna, and swordfish.

LIGURIAN FISH DISHES

Stuffed sardines are not really difficult to prepare, but they take a bit of work, because stuffing the tasty mixture into the little bodies is tricky. But it is well worth the effort, as this typical Ligurian specialty tastes absolutely delicious.
Cappon magro, on the other hand, is a rather complicated dish and takes a little time to prepare. The appeal of the "lean capon" lies in the perfect combination of ingredients from the seas with those from the fields and gardens. Originally a simple sailors' dish, its preparation on land has become ever more elaborate, because it had the advantage of fitting neatly into the requirements for fasting. As capons – roosters which have been castrated and fattened up – are very fatty, they were not allowed to be eaten during Lent. So the resourceful Ligurians changed to "lean capon," which – strictly according to Church law – consists of various kinds of fish, but in the cooking can incorporate all kinds of delicious bits of chicken. By contrast, *burrida* is a fairly simple, nutritious fish dish which in former times appeared every day on tables in the fishing villages.

CAPPON MAGRO
Lean capon (Illustrated right)

1 CLEANED AND GUTTED GURNARD
1 SMALL CRAYFISH
12 SCAMPI
ASSORTED SEAFOOD
HERB AND ONION STOCK
OLIVE OIL
JUICE OF ONE LEMON
SALT
1 CAULIFLOWER
1/2 LB/200 G GREEN BEANS
1 LARGE POTATO
1 CELERY HEART
2 CARROTS
1 BUNCH SALSIFY
4 ARTICHOKES
VINEGAR
4–6 SLICES/200–300 G ZWIEBACK
1/2 CLOVE OF GARLIC
6 HARD-BOILED EGGS, QUARTERED
15 GREEN OLIVES
4 OZ/100 G MUSHROOMS IN OIL

For the sauce:
2 STALE ROLLS
VINEGAR
6 SALTED ANCHOVIES
BASIL LEAVES, CHOPPED
1 CLOVE GARLIC, MINCED
1 BUNCH PARSLEY, CHOPPED
1/3 CUP/50 G PINE NUTS
2 TBSP/20 G CAPERS
2 EGG YOLKS
1 CUP OLIVE OIL
1/2 CUP QUALITY VINEGAR

Wash and fillet the gurnard. Clean the crayfish, scampi, and other seafood. Cook them all together in the herb and onion stock. Marinate in oil, lemon juice, and salt.
Boil the prepared cauliflower, beans, potato, celery, and one carrot in a saucepan until tender. Cook the salsify and the quartered artichokes separately. Cut the cooked vegetables into small pieces and dress with oil, vinegar, and salt.
For the sauce, soak the rolls in vinegar. Wash the anchovies and grind in a mortar. Add the basil, garlic, parsley, pine nuts, capers, egg yolks, and rolls, and grind to a fine paste. Sieve the paste into a bowl, and mix well with one glass oil and ½ glass good vinegar. Rub the zwieback slices with garlic and cover the base of a large soup bowl. Drizzle a little oil onto them, and pour over a few spoonfuls of sauce. Arrange vegetables, gurnard, and four hard-boiled eggs in layers. Finally place the crayfish in the middle and arrange the seafood around it. Chop the two remaining hard-boiled eggs and sprinkle over.
Slice the remaining raw carrot and place on small skewers with the shrimp, olives, and mushrooms, and place in the bowl, so that the various colors contrast with one another.

ACCIUGHE RIPIENE AL FORNO
Stuffed anchovies

1 1/4 LB/600 G FRESH ANCHOVIES
1 STALE ROLL
MILK
2 EGGS
1/2 CUP/40 G PARMESAN, GRATED
MARJORAM
1 CLOVE GARLIC, CHOPPED
SALT AND PEPPER
OLIVE OIL
BREADCRUMBS

Left: Steeply rising cliffs are so much characteristic of the Ligurian riviera.

Clean and gut the anchovies, cut off the heads and tails, and allow to drain. Soak the roll in milk, and chop up a few anchovies. For the filling, mix the eggs, cheese, the softened roll, marjoram, garlic, and chopped anchovy in a bowl, and season with salt and pepper. Fill the anchovies with the mixture. Brush a fireproof dish with oil, and sprinkle with breadcrumbs. Place the stuffed anchovies in it, with the filling uppermost, and bake in a preheated oven at 400 °F (200 °C) for 12–15 minutes until the filling is golden brown.

BURRIDA
Fish soup

2 LB/1 KG ONIONS
2 CLOVES GARLIC
5 TBSP OLIVE OIL
1 LB/500 G TOMATOES
SALT
2 LB/1 KG ASSORTED SEA FISH
1 LB/500 G SEAFOOD (SCAMPI, BABY SQUID)
PEPPER
1 BUNCH PARSLEY, CHOPPED
1/2 TSP DRIED OREGANO
1 GLASS DRY WHITE WINE

Cut the onions in thin rings and the garlic in wafer-thin slices. Slowly heat a little olive oil in a pan, and sauté half the onion rings and garlic. Blanch and skin the tomatoes, remove the seeds, and dice small. Add half to the onions and salt.
Gut and clean the fish and seafood. Fillet the fish, peel the scampi, cut the heads off the squid. Add the fish and seafood to the pan, and season with salt and pepper. Cover with the remaining onions, tomatoes, and garlic, and salt and pepper once more. Sprinkle the top with parsley and oregano. Pour over the white wine, and drizzle over the remaining olive oil. Cook over a low heat, until the soup has thickened to a creamy consistency.

COLUMBUS'S GALLEY

In pre-Roman times, Genoa was already an important port, where trade was carried on with the Greeks, the Etruscans, and the Phoenicians. In the 11th century the capital of Liguria developed into a colonial power and ranked alongside Venice, Pisa, and Amalfi as one of the four great maritime republics. Ironically, Genoa lost its strong position on the oceans of the world just after the Genoese Christopher Columbus had discovered America in 1492.

What did the ship's menu actually look like in Columbus's day? How did the crew feed themselves on the week-long, sometimes even months-long voyages to the overseas colonies? A voyage on a galleon or a caravelle was certainly no pleasure cruise, but the ships' cooks did all they could, even during very long crossings, to ensure certain standards of catering were maintained – if only so as not to let the spirits and morale of the crew sink too low, and to keep up their health and strength. But when a voyage lasted longer than planned, or provisions had been wrongly calculated from the start, the cupboard might be absolutely bare and dangerous vitamin deficiency diseases like scurvy might break out.

The crew's staple food was the unavoidable ship's biscuit, because it did not weigh much, was easy to store, and kept for an extremely long time. The seamen ate it soaked in water or oil, or it was supplemented with foods like pork and beans or dried or pickled vegetables. Other sources report that there was even occasionally cheese. According to historians, the men on board 15th-century ships were provided with a daily ration of about 3900 calories, consisting of 70 percent carbohydrates, 15 percent fat, and 15 percent protein, in other words, a suitable diet for keeping the hardworking crew fit. They were not economical with the wine either, quite apart from the fact that its keeping qualities made it the ideal drink on board. A helmsman was given 1 pint (½ liter) of wine, about 1½ pounds (700 grams) of biscuit, 2 ounces (50 grams) of salt pork, and ¼ pound (100 grams) of green or broad beans.

By contrast, passengers in those days had to look after themselves. Their baskets of provisions contained dried or salted meat or salted eel. Opinions differ among historians about whether and how food was cooked on board ship around 1400, but it is generally assumed that the cooks had small portable braziers, which were carried on deck in good weather when the sea was calm – or when the ship was in harbor – whereas in bad weather and heavy seas cold food would be served up to the crew. It seems likely that if conditions were favorable at sea, food would be cooked, as there are indications that the crew caught fresh fish while they were underway, to bring a bit of variety into their diet and eke out the provisions. And as the fish was presumably not eaten raw, there must have been the means to cook it. The distribution of green and broad beans also suggests that simple stews were prepared on board.

The three caravelles, Nina, Pinta, and Santa Maria, in which Columbus sailed on his first voyage of discovery. (Wood engraving, about 1860)

STOCCAFISSO ALLA GENOVESE
Stockfish Genoese style
(Illustrated below left)

2 LB/1 KG PRESOAKED STOCKFISH
1 CARROT
1 ONION
1 STICK CELERY
2 CLOVES GARLIC
EXTRA VIRGIN OLIVE OIL
2 TBSP/20 G PINE NUTS
1 OZ/25 G DRIED MUSHROOMS, SOAKED IN LUKEWARM WATER
1 GLASS DRY WHITE WINE
SALT
1 LB/500 G POTATOES
3–4 TBSP TOMATO SAUCE
1 CUP/150 G BLACK OLIVES

Clean the soaked stockfish and cut in pieces. Peel the carrot, onion, celery, and garlic, cut small, and sauté in olive oil. Add the stockfish, pine nuts, and finely chopped mushrooms. Pour over the white wine, salt, and cook over a low heat for about 30 minutes.

Peel, wash, and chop the potatoes, then add to the stockfish. Mix the tomato sauce with a little lukewarm water, add to the stockfish, and cook for a further 30 minutes.

Shortly before the stockfish and the potatoes are ready, add the olives. Serve hot.

STOCKFISH AND KLIPFISH

Stockfish was very suitable for feeding people at sea. This gutted and dried cod was easily stored in the larder and kept for a long time, without losing any of its nutritional value.

Dried cod comes in two versions: *stoccafisso* and *baccalà*. *Stoccafisso* or stockfish is made by cutting off the cods' heads when they are caught, gutting them, tying them in pairs by the tails, and hanging them up to dry. For *baccalà*, the gutted cod is cut into two halves, its backbone is removed, and the flesh thoroughly salted, before being dried. So the difference is in the salt content. *Stoccafisso* and *baccalà* are currently enjoying a revival in Italian cuisine. Ligurian chefs use almost exclusively

Norwegian cod, which is dried in large quantities on the cliffs above the fjords. It must be beaten before cooking, to break up the fibers so the flesh becomes tender, and it must be soaked in water for at least a day.

Klipfish drying

MODERN SHIPS' KITCHENS

Anyone catching a Mediterranean ferry in Genoa, Livorno, or one of the other ports today, need have no fears about the catering. The ships usually have several restaurants on board, serving everything the land-based catering trade can offer, from a quick self-service meal to a menu of several courses or a lavishly decorated buffet.

Ships' galleys often face greater logistical, organizational, and sometimes purely physical problems than landlubbers' kitchen workplaces. Just loading the supplies and ingredients takes several hours. And because the time in port has to be kept as short as possible, especially for passenger ferries, everything must be standing ready as soon as the ship sails into harbor. While the many vacationers are leaving the ferry via the gangways and ramps, on foot or in their automobiles, and the new passengers are coming on board, the food supplies must be taken to the larders pretty quickly. But space is limited by the fact that you are afloat. Whether in the tiny galley of a small private yacht or the kitchen of a large passenger ferry – everything must be stowed in a suitable place and easy to reach, but with the needs of space saving in mind. After all, the ship owner would obviously rather take a few more fare-paying passengers on board than make unnecessarily large areas available for the ship's services. And then there is the swell, feared equally by both weak-stomached tourists and experienced seagoing cooks. Of course nowadays, big ferries are fitted with very efficient stabilizers to ensure a calm crossing, but particularly in autumn and winter, the normally calm Mediterranean can become extremely rough. To prevent the pots and pans from sliding around on the cooking surfaces and possibly falling off, the hobs are fitted with special devices, which keep things safely in place even when the ship's movement is quite violent. The same goes for the closets and shelves where the appliances and implements are kept.

The restaurants are also equipped for heavy seas, so anyone with a strong enough stomach can enjoy a meal in peace and safety, even with a gale blowing. The table cannot tip over, because it is usually firmly attached to the floor, just as the flower vase is screwed to the tabletop. Anyone who feels the floor tilting on their way to the cold buffet can quickly grab hold of one of the brass rails which are always within easy reach. In any case, sensible cruisers only allow their soup plates to be filled to the brim in harbor, or when the sea is as calm as a millpond, so their own clothing is protected, as well as that of the other guests.

LIGURIAN SURPRISE PACKAGES

As the Gulf of Genoa is not rich in fish, the Ligurians have always had to fall back on other foods. In a barren, stony coastal region, there are limits to the amount of land available for grazing cattle or growing corn. So fruit, herbs, vegetables, and olives are grown in tiny gardens, grapes are planted on steep slopes, but though the fish may be short on quantity, the special quality of the cooking makes up for it. Comparatively simple meals are given "added value" by means of various tricks, such as imaginative fillings. *Cima ripiena* is an impressive dish of breast of veal, stuffed with sweetbreads, brains, vegetables, garlic, marjoram and grated cheese. Pasta also looks a lot more impressive when filled with ricotta, eggs, spinach, or herbs, and *pesto* used to take the place of "foreign" tomatoes.

CIMA RIPIENA
Stuffed breast of veal
(Illustrated left)

1 1/2 LBS/750 G BREAST OF VEAL, WITH A POCKET CUT IN IT READY FOR STUFFING
1 CLOVE GARLIC
8 CUPS/2 LITERS VEGETABLE STOCK
2 BAY LEAVES

For the stuffing:
1/4 LB/100 G FILLET OF VEAL, DICED
1 TBSP/30 G BUTTER
1/4 LB/100 G CALF'S BRAINS, WASHED AND CLEANED
1/4 LB/100 G CALF'S SWEETBREADS, WASHED AND CLEANED
1 GLASS DRY WHITE WINE
1/2 OZ OR 3/4 LOOSELY PACKED CUP/15 G DRIED MUSHROOMS
3/4 CUP/75 G FRESH PEAS
1 TBSP MARJORAM, CHOPPED
2 TBSP/20 G PISTACHIOS
ABOUT 1/2 CUP/30 G FRESHLY GRATED PARMESAN
3 EGGS
SALT
FRESHLY MILLED PEPPER
FRESHLY GRATED NUTMEG

Wash the breast of veal, pat dry, and rub the inside of the pocket with a clove of garlic.
For the stuffing, sauté the diced veal in butter, then add the brains and sweetbreads and sauté gently. Pour over the white wine. Soak the mushrooms in lukewarm water. Grind the meat and the mushrooms in a food processor and pour into a bowl. Add the peas, marjoram, pistachios, parmesan, and the beaten eggs, and mix well. Season with salt, pepper, and grated nutmeg.
Fill the breast of veal two-thirds with the stuffing, sew up, wrap in a kitchen towel, and tie. Place in a pan and cover completely with vegetable stock. Add the bay leaves and simmer in the hot stock for 1 hour without the lid, then for a further hour with the lid on. Pierce the meat wrapping several times with a toothpick or a needle, to prevent it from bursting.
Remove the veal from the cloth, place between two plates with a weight on top, and allow to cool. Slice and serve with a sauce of good olive oil and fresh herbs.

TORTA PASQUALINA
Easter cake

Serves 6–8

For the dough:
2 1/4 CUPS/250 G ALL-PURPOSE FLOUR
2 TBSP EXTRA VIRGIN OLIVE OIL
1 GLASS COLD WATER
SALT

For the filling:
14 OZ/400 G SWISS CHARD
14 OZ/400 G SPINACH
1 BUNCH ARUGULA
EXTRA VIRGIN OLIVE OIL
1 ONION, CHOPPED
2 CLOVES
3 TBSP BREADCRUMBS
1 CUP + 3 1/2 TBSP/300 G GOAT'S CREAM CHEESE
1/2 CUP/50 G CHEESE, GRATED
6 EGGS
SALT
FRESHLY GROUND PEPPER
1 TBSP MARJORAM, CHOPPED

Mix flour, olive oil, water, and a pinch of salt, and knead for about 10 minutes until the dough becomes smooth and flexible. Wrap in a cloth and leave for a few hours.
Wash the Swiss chard, spinach, and arugula, and cut in strips. Heat 2 tbsp olive oil and a little water in a pan, add the chopped onion and the cloves, cover and simmer for about 5 minutes. Remove the cloves, and add the Swiss chard, spinach, and arugula to the pan, stir well and allow to break up. Remove the vegetables from the pan, drain, squeeze out moisture, place in a bowl, and mix with the breadcrumbs, cream cheese, grated cheese, and two eggs. Add salt and pepper to taste, and stir in the marjoram.
Brush the inside of a 7-inch/28-cm diameter springform pan with olive oil. Roll out two-thirds of the dough to ⅛ inch/2–3 mm thick, and cover the base and the sides of the pan. The dough should extend a little over the top edge. Fill the lined pan with three-quarters of the vegetable mixture. Make 4 hollows with a spoon and carefully break an egg into each one. Finally cover with the rest of the filling. Roll out the remaining dough and cover the filling with it. Press the dough that was left at the edge down firmly over the lid. Pierce the dough carefully without scrambling the egg. Brush with oil, and bake in a preheated oven at 350 °F (180 °C) for about 1½ hours. Allow to cool a little before cutting.

OLIVE OIL

After Spain, Italy is now the second largest producer of olive oil in the world. Apart from Lombardy and Piedmont, where the climate is not suited to olive growing, different kinds and sizes of olives grow throughout Italy, and the oils they produce are very varied. Liguria is the home of a particularly fine oil. Unlike the sometimes very tangy and rather bitter Tuscan, or the sharp, fruity oil from Apulia, Ligurian olive oil is very light, with a delicate, aromatic flavor. Unfortunately it is rarely obtainable outside the region, as it is only produced in small quantities. In this mountainous region, with its many steep slopes, it is just as difficult to grow and harvest olives as wine, because the olive trees have to be planted on narrow, and rather inaccessible terraces.

The main varieties grown in Liguria are Taggiasca and Lavagnina, but most of the oil comes from Taggiasca olives. The relatively small fruits are picked in December and January, when they are almost ripe. The whole family is involved in the harvest, as they are forced to pick in the traditional manner here, because the steep, narrow strips of land are unsuitable for the modern machinery that is normally used in flat areas. The team of pickers sets off for the olive grove with big nets and long poles and ladders. First of all, they spread the nets out under the trees, then they carefully strike the branches with the poles, so that the ripe fruits fall. Any that remain are stripped off by hand. This method of harvesting is very labor-intensive, and this is later reflected in the price of the oil. But hand-picked olives have one big advantage. The fruits are not damaged in the gathering, so the oily flesh does not oxidize with the air, which would considerably detract from the taste and quality of the oil later on. Oxidation, an increase in the free oil acid content, and the threat of fermentation are the chief dangers to which the fresh crop is exposed, so the olives must be brought to the oil mill as quickly as possible. To shorten the way to the nearest main road, or even to the provincial capital, which may be very long in those parts of Liguria

which are not highly developed, most villages have installed their own oil mills – known as *gumbi*. These small mills are often found in the cellars of private houses, and were often turned by donkeys. If the village was near a stream or a river, the mill might also be water-powered. Small oil mills are still working in some parts of Liguria today, producing excellent oil in the traditional way.

The olives are first ground to a brownish pulp between massive millstones. Then the oily mass is spread out on round mats, which are piled on top of one another, and the oil is pressed out of this "tower" with constantly increasing pressure from above. The juice which is pressed out contains not only oil, but also water and fruit residue. Formerly – and you can still see some smaller producers using this process today – the emulsion was just left alone, because the oil and fruit juice separate automatically, and the heavier water is left at the bottom of the barrel. But nowadays centrifuges are mostly used to separate the oil and water, as the fruit juices can easily start to ferment. Finally the oil is put into large containers so that the sediment can settle. In Liguria, these traditional containers are called *giare*. Many oil mills even had purpose-built storage tanks lined with ceramic tiles, but now clarification usually takes place in modern stainless steel containers.

Coniglio con olive taggiasche
Rabbit with olives

3 LBS/1.5 KG OVEN-READY RABBIT, WITH ORGAN MEAT (LIVER, HEART, AND KIDNEYS)
1 SMALL ONION
3 CLOVES GARLIC
1 SPRIG ROSEMARY
1 SPRIG THYME
2 BAY LEAVES
1 SMALL PEPERONCINO
EXTRA VIRGIN OLIVE OIL
SALT
3 CUPS/750 ML DRY WHITE WINE
1/2 CUP/70 G BLACK OLIVES IN BRINE

Cut the rabbit in medium pieces, wash, and pat dry. Wash the liver, heart, and kidneys, pat dry, and leave aside. Finely chop the onion, press the garlic, and chop the herbs. Sauté all together with the bay leaves and small peperoncino in olive oil in a casserole. Add the rabbit pieces, and brown on all sides over a high heat. Cut the organ meat into small pieces and add to the casserole. When the meat has colored, add salt, and pour over the wine. Cover, reduce the heat, and allow the wine to boil away slowly. If the meat should get too dry, pour over a little lukewarm water. After about 45 minutes, add the black olives and simmer for about 15 minutes, until the juices have thickened.

The different colors of the freshly picked olives indicate different degrees of ripeness. The darker the fruit, the riper it is.

Geppo antiquo – Extra
virgin olive oil

Gaziello – Extra virgin
olive oil

Trucco – Extra virgin
olive oil

Amoretti Carlo – Extra
virgin olive oil

Ranzo imperia – Extra
virgin olive oil

Podere L'Alpicella –
Extra virgin olive oil

Amoretti Carlo – Extra
virgin olive oil

Trucco – Extra virgin
taggiasca olive oil

The annual basil has leaves of various sizes. The stems grow up to 20 inches (50 cm) high.

PESTO AND OTHER SAUCES

Pesto alla genovese or *Battuto alla genovese* is certainly one of Liguria's most famous specialties. This spicy green paste of basil, olive oil, garlic, pine nuts, and cheese has recently become very popular in the rest of Europe, although there it usually comes straight out of a sterile jar onto the pasta. But it is definitely worth getting to know the flavor of freshly-made pesto.

Whether the traditional Ligurian sauces absolutely must be made in a mortar is arguable – but it is certain that good results can only be obtained by using good ingredients.

Opinions on the ingredients of pesto and theories concerning the only proper way to make it are many and varied. Some insist on the inclusion of pine nuts, while the purists say this is a variation from the district of Savona and has no connection with the original *Pesto alla genovese*. They also argue about whether the basil leaves should be washed, and whether it is permissible to make pesto in a blender, instead of in a marble mortar. All you can say about it is that the metal blades of the blender really can affect the taste of the basil. On the other hand, the machine only takes a short time to produce an even paste, which would have taken a cook, using traditional utensils such as a mortar and a wooden pestle, quite some time to achieve. At any rate, the experts are agreed on two points: the aromatic taste of the pesto is absolutely dependent on the quality of the olive oil and the basil. Only the best Ligurian extra virgin olive oil should be used. Cheap olive oil ruins the pesto, just as surely as limp herbs, which have never seen genuine sunlight in their short life. Even the very strong flavored basil from southern Italy distorts the taste, as it often has a slightly minty aftertaste. Small-leafed Ligurian basil, which has been grown in a tiny herb garden where a strong sea breeze sometimes blows, is undoubtedly the best. Leaves picked while the plant is in flower have the strongest flavor. For anyone unwilling to believe this, a trip to the pesto stronghold of Genoa is recommended. Sampling it here will confirm once and for all that Ligurian pesto simply could not taste as good anywhere else in the world.

The splendid Ligurian pasta creations would also be inconceivable without the delicious local sauces. The pale, creamy *Salsa di noci*, made from walnuts, pine nuts, garlic, butter, and cream, is almost as much of a favorite in Liguria as the green pesto. The combination of nuts and cream or yogurt might suggest that the recipe originated in the Orient. As an important port, Genoa traditionally provided a forum for culinary influences from all over the world. Other Ligurian sauces, too, such as *Sugo di carciofi*, which is made from artichokes, mushrooms, onions, garlic, concentrated tomato paste, and white wine, taste wonderful with *trenette* or *trofie*. Only *Bagnum di acciughe*, a particularly tangy sauce of anchovies and tomatoes, is not used for pasta. Instead, it is spread on slices of toasted white bread.

PESTO ALLA GENOVESE
Genoese pesto (basil sauce)
(Illustrated right)

1 BUNCH BASIL
1 CLOVE GARLIC
2 TBSP/20 G PINE NUTS
COARSE SALT
SCANT 1/3 CUP/25 G NOT TOO STRONG PECORINO, GRATED
SCANT 1/3 CUP/25 G FRESHLY GRATED PARMESAN OR GRANA
2–3 TBSP EXTRA VIRGIN OLIVE OIL

Wash the basil carefully and allow to drain. Chop in a blender, together with the garlic, pine nuts, and a pinch of coarse salt. Gradually add the grated cheese, and work into an even paste. Finally, slowly mix in the olive oil, until a creamy consistency is achieved.
Before pouring over the pasta – *trenette* are the best kind – mix the pesto with a little of the hot water in which the pasta was cooked.

MINESTRONE ALLA GENOVESE
Genoese vegetable soup
(Illustrated pp. 178/179 front left)

1/4 LB/100 G WHITE CABBAGE
SMALL HANDFUL/50 G GREEN BEANS
2 POTATOES
2 CARROTS
2 LEEKS
2 TOMATOES
2 ZUCCHINI
1 ONION
1 CLOVE GARLIC
1 BUNCH PARSLEY
A FEW BORAGE LEAVES
1/4 LB/100 G FRESH OR PRESOAKED RED BEANS
1/2 CUP OLIVE OIL
1 PIECE OF PARMESAN RIND
6 OZ/150 G SHORT NOODLES
1 TBSP PESTO
SALT
FRESHLY GRATED PARMESAN

Clean all vegetables and herbs, and chop in small pieces. In a large pan, bring a good 8 cups/2 liters water to a boil. Add the beans and vegetables, with the exception of the onion, garlic, and herbs and cook until tender in fiercely boiling water. Then add the onion, garlic, and herbs, reduce the heat, cover, and simmer for just under 2 hours, stirring occasionally. After 1 hour, add the oil and the cheese rind, and salt the vegetables. Mash the potatoes and beans with a wooden spoon or a soup ladle, to give the soup a velvety consistency, but do not purée the vegetables. When the vegetables are cooked to a pulp, add the noodles and cook until *al dente*.
Remove the soup from the hob, stir in the pesto, and salt to taste. Pour into soup plates and serve with a dash of olive oil and freshly grated parmesan.

SALSA DI NOCI
Walnut sauce

18 WALNUT KERNELS
1/3 CUP/50 G PINE NUTS
1/2 CLOVE GARLIC
1 BUNCH PARSLEY
1 CUP/250 ML LIGHT CREAM
SALT AND PEPPER
3 TBSP FRESHLY GRATED PARMESAN
1 1/3 TBSP BUTTER

Blanch the walnut kernels and remove the skins. Chop the walnuts, pine nuts, garlic, and parsley finely in a blender, and pour into a bowl. Slowly add the cream, stirring constantly. Season with salt and pepper.
Pour over the pasta, cooked until *al dente* with grated parmesan and melted butter.

BAGNUM DI ACCIUGHE
Anchovies in tomato sauce

1 3/4 LBS/800 G FRESH ANCHOVIES
2 CLOVES GARLIC, FINELY CHOPPED
1 ONION, FINELY CHOPPED
4–5 TBSP OLIVE OIL
3/4 LB/300 G RIPE TOMATOES, SKINNED AND SEEDED
1 GLASS DRY WHITE WINE
1 BUNCH PARSLEY, CHOPPED
SLICES OF WHITE BREAD, TOASTED

Clean and gut the anchovies, and pat dry. Sauté the onion and garlic in olive oil. Dice the tomatoes small, add them to the pan, with salt and pepper, and simmer for 10 minutes. Pour over half the wine, and simmer over a low heat. Place the prepared anchovies in the pan, pour over the remaining wine, cover the anchovies with a little sauce, and sprinkle with parsley, salt, and pepper. Depending on their size, the anchovies will be ready in about 10 minutes. Rub the slices of toast with a little garlic, put them on plates, and arrange the anchovies in their "bagnum" on top.
Bagnum di acciughe was in times gone by the fishermen's breakfast, when they had returned from fishing and were waiting for their nets to dry. There were little cooking stoves on the boats, on which the men could prepare this simple dish for themselves.

PASTA AND FOCACCIA

Nobody is really quite sure today how pasta came to Italy. But the lack of historical evidence is made up for by all kinds of very detailed stories about how it might have arrived.

In Liguria, and especially in Genoa, they naturally have a version in which the proud seaport (*Genova la Superba*, as the Genoese love to call it) and the once flourishing oriental trade play a major role. According to these anecdotes, Genoese seafarers came across noodles on their trading voyages to Mongolia. The nomads even revealed the recipe to their foreign visitors, and told them how the flour and water should be mixed in order to make pasta. This technique for preparing flour was very widespread among the wandering peoples of the Steppes, as the continual migrations did not allow sufficient time to rest for preparations involving the use of yeast to make the dough rise. So they had discovered that dough made only from flour, water, and salt dried quickly in the sun, and was therefore much easier to transport. They were even able to speed up the process by forming the dough into long, thin strings, which hardened even more quickly. The dried strings only had to be cooked in a little water to make them swell up again, then they were ready to eat. Served with a few vegetables or even a little meat, they made a good, solid meal.

The Genoese were impressed, and took the noodle recipe home with them. Back in Liguria, the newfangled dish soon became very popular, especially as noodles turned out to be very nourishing, so that with their help, even a possible gap in the supply of other foods could be bridged. The resourceful Ligurians improved the recipe, invented the most diverse shapes, and created filled pasta. Even today, the Ligurians still claim to have invented ravioli, *pansoti*, *zembi d'arzillo*, and other filled delicacies.

But ravioli, *pansoti*, and the rest are not the only inventions of Ligurian cuisine. As the people of this area have a distinct talent for making a virtue out of necessity, they devised a solution to the local bread problem that was as clever as it was tasty. The sharp, salty air, which dominates the long stretch of coastline, makes it almost impossible to bake good bread, as the yeast does not rise properly in this climate, and the high moisture content in the atmosphere also prevents the crust from hardening, while the crumb remains very moist. The bread goes moldy soon after baking. The Ligurians solved the problem by inventing a thin unleavened loaf, which could be eaten straight from the oven, and focaccia was born. To give it flavor, olive oil was drizzled over it and it was sprinkled with salt. In many areas, people top it with a tasty cheese and garnish it with fennel seeds or, as in San Remo, with chopped onions.

FOCACCIA
Flat bread

1 1/3 CUPS/200 G ALL-PURPOSE FLOUR
SCANT 1/2 CUP/100 ML OLIVE OIL
1/2 TSP SALT
TOPPING OF YOUR CHOICE

Knead the flour and oil into a dough. Work in sufficient cold water to make the dough smooth. Wrap in plastic wrap and leave for 1 hour. Knead thoroughly again and leave to stand for a further 5 minutes. Roll out to a thin dough with a wooden rolling pin. Transfer by hand to a greased baking sheet like a pizza. Bake in a preheated oven at 430 °F (220 °C) for 10 minutes.

PANISSA
Chickpea porridge

1 1/2 CUPS/250 G CHICKPEA FLOUR
EXTRA VIRGIN OLIVE OIL
FRESH SPRING VEGETABLES, CHOPPED
SALT AND FRESHLY GROUND PEPPER

Bring 4 cups/1 liter water to a boil in a pan, gradually add the flour and salt, and mix with a wooden spoon. Sieve the mixture into a casserole and cook for about 1 hour over a low heat.
The *panissa* is ready when the porridge easily comes away from the sides of the casserole. Pour into plates, drizzle with olive oil, and sprinkle with spring vegetables, salt, and pepper. Serve hot or cold. Dry white wine goes very well with it.

PANSOTI
Filled pasta pockets
(Illustrated front right)

Serves 6

For the dough:
3 CUPS/500 G ALL-PURPOSE FLOUR
3 EGGS
SALT

For the filling:
1 LB/500 G SWISS CHARD
1 LB/500 G BORAGE
1/2 LB/250 G CURLY ENDIVE
5 OZ/150 G RICOTTA
2 EGGS
GENEROUS 1/2 CUP 50 G FRESHLY GRATED PARMESAN
SMALL BUNCH MARJORAM
1 CLOVE GARLIC

Knead the flour, eggs, and a little salt into a dough, and add enough water to make it workable. Roll out and cut into triangles the size of the palm of the hand.
Wash the Swiss chard, borage, and endive, and simmer in very little water until they begin to soften. Press out well, blend briefly in a food processor, and mix with the ricotta, eggs, and parmesan. Finely chop the marjoram leaves and garlic, and stir in. Using a teaspoon, take walnut-sized portions of the mixture and place on the triangles. Fold the edges together over the filling to make fat pockets. Cook in salted water for about 10 minutes *al dente*, then take them out. Serve with walnut sauce (see p. 175).

FARINATA AND PANISSA

Chickpeas are mainly grown in the warmth of southern Italy, but are also very popular in Lombardy, Piedmont, and Liguria. They must be carefully soaked before use, and be cooked for around three hours. The dried peas can also be ground into a fine flour, from which tasty cakes like *farinata* or the chickpea porridge *panissa* (not to be confused with the Piedmontese rice dish *paniscia*) can be made. While *panissa* is more of a rustic affair, which is best with a strong white wine, there are some refined variations of *farinata*. In Imperia province, chopped onions are added to the dough, in Savona it is flavored with rosemary, and in other areas they add freshly ground pepper.

For *farinata* dough, chickpea flour is poured slowly into warm water and stirred constantly, to prevent lumps from forming.

Not all *farinata* pans are as big as this one. Ligurian cookshops sell special copper baking forms.

As *farinata* only takes a few minutes to bake at 570 °F (300 °C), the finished product is particularly delicious.

FARINATA
Chickpea cake
(Main illustration left, back)

1 LB/500 G CHICKPEA FLOUR.
SALT
6–8 TBSP EXTRA VIRGIN OLIVE OIL
FRESHLY GRATED BLACK PEPPER

Bring about 6 cups/1.5 liters water to the boil in a large, heavy pan. Gradually pour in the flour, stirring constantly, and add salt. Cook for 1 hour over a low heat, stirring frequently with a wooden spoon. When ready, the mass should be soft and viscous. Brush an ovenproof baking form with oil and spread the mixture evenly in it. Drizzle over a little oil, and bake in a preheated oven at 400 °F (200 °C) for about 30 minutes, until the top is golden brown. Sprinkle with freshly ground pepper and serve immediately.

LIGURIAN PASTA

Corzetti
Corzetti come from the Polcevera valley. They were originally homemade, but now you can buy a mass-produced version of this pasta, which contains a little egg. It

can be served just with melted butter, but also tastes good with meat or mushroom sauces.

Pansoti (Illustration above)
Pansoti are similar to ravioli, but are triangular instead of square. They are filled with a mixture of vegetables called *preboggion*, whose composition varies. *Pansoti* taste good with walnut sauce.

Piccagge
Piccagge is Ligurian for *fettucce*, pasta ribbons. *Piccagge*, which have some egg in them, are best accompanied by artichoke sauce or pesto.

Trenette
Trenette are made from wholewheat flour. They come in long, flat strips and can be bought fresh or dried. They are also served with a sauce made from pesto, boiled beans, and potatoes.

Trofie
Trofie are Ligurian gnocchi. They can be made of wholegrain flour or white wheat flour and, if desired, bran or chestnut flour may be added to the dough. *Trofie* come from the area around Recco and Camogli. The spiral-shaped gnocchi are cooked with beans and potatoes, which are later incorporated into the pesto.

Harvest time in the vegetable covered plains of Albenga in the province of Savona.

VEGETABLES

Vegetable growers in Liguria struggle with the same difficulties as wine and olive growers. Large stretches of level ground suitable for long, flat beds are comparatively rare; in many places, the Ligurians must instead tend and care for small market gardens, split over several terraces. But this does not frighten them off; on the contrary, they love young, crisp vegetables, and they are proud of the regional dishes which they make from them. Artichokes, asparagus, leeks, and tomatoes, as well as olives for the table and dwarf beans, are among their favorite vegetables.

Carciofo, the Italian word for artichoke, probably comes from the Arabic *kharshuf* – an indication that the plant was also grown in the Near East. Today artichokes grow all around the Mediterranean, but very diverse varieties have become naturalized in Italy. In Liguria, the most commonly grown variety is Spinoso di Liguria, which can be harvested in autumn and winter. Artichokes are not only delicious and easily digestible but also healthy. Whether they are sautéd, stuffed, or dipped in sauce a leaf at a time, they contain a lot of mineral salts and roughage, their bitter constituents stimulate the digestive system, they invigorate the liver, detoxify the body, and lower the cholesterol level. Alongside countless recipes for their beloved artichokes, the Ligurians also have in *condijun* a fitting counterpart to the *salade niçoise* of the neighboring French Riviera. And in the winter, *mesciua*, a tasty soup made from dried beans and chickpeas, is a great favorite. According to legend, this specialty was invented in one of the ports. Apparently poor women used to run to the harbor when grain or bean sacks were about to be taken on board or unloaded from the hold of a ship, because some of the sacks would always split while they were being moved, so the women could collect the grain and beans to make soup for their families in the evening.

As well as Spinoso di Liguria, the wonderfully delicate variety Violetto d'Albenga is also grown in Liguria.

SALAD DELIGHTS

In summer on the Riviera, they like crisp salads, smelling of gardens, the sea, and olive oil. Whereas in France you order a *salade niçoise* for lunch, a few miles further east you ask for a Genoese *condiggion*, also known in other areas as *condijun*. Despite the linguistic differences, all these salads are made from fresh vegetables like tomato, cucumber, bell pepper, and onion, dressed with basil, garlic, and a sauce made of vinegar, oil, and salt. This crisp summer salad is garnished with a hard-boiled egg cut into eight and black olives.

CONDIJUN
Colorful salad
(Main illustration, center back)

1 CLOVE GARLIC
4 BEEF TOMATOES, NOT TOO RIPE
2 YELLOW BELL PEPPERS
1 CUCUMBER
2 SPRING ONIONS
1 HANDFUL BLACK OLIVES IN BRINE
2 ANCHOVIES
A FEW BASIL LEAVES
OLIVE OIL
VINEGAR
SALT
1 HARD-BOILED EGG

Rub the inside of a salad bowl with the clove of garlic. Remove the seeds from the tomatoes and peppers. Chop tomatoes, peppers, cucumber, and onions into small pieces. Put everything into the bowl, and add the olives, cleaned anchovies, and basil. Dress with oil, vinegar, and salt. If desired, add a hard-boiled egg cut in eight.
Mix well and allow to stand for about 10 minutes before serving.

Mesciua
Pulse stew

1 1/2 CUPS/300 G CHICKPEAS
1 1/2 CUPS/300 G DRIED WHITE BEANS
1/2 CUP/100 G BUCKWHEAT GRAINS
BAKING SODA
SALT
BLACK PEPPER
OLIVE OIL

The evening before, soak the chickpeas, beans, and buckwheat in plenty of lukewarm water in three separate bowls, to each of which has been added 1 teaspoon of baking soda.
Drain the chickpeas and beans, put in a pan of slightly salted cold water, and boil for about 3 hours. Half an hour before the end of the cooking time, put the buckwheat in a separate pan of slightly salted water and boil for 30 minutes. As soon as they are all ready, pour the buckwheat with its water into the pan with the chickpeas and beans. There should be about 6 cups/1½ liters of liquid in the pan altogether. Salt, and cook for a further 15 minutes.
Pour the stew into a bowl and serve. Have black pepper in a mill and olive oil on the table, for everyone to help themselves.

Fricassea di carciofi
Fricassee of artichokes

12 ARTICHOKES
2 TSP/10 ML LEMON JUICE
3 EGGS
1/3 CUP/30 G GRANA, GRATED
1 CLOVE GARLIC
1 1/2 TBSP/20 ML OLIVE OIL

Clean the artichokes, break off the stalks, and remove the hard outer leaves. Cut in pieces and remove the hairy bits from inside. Place in a bowl of water and lemon juice, and leave aside.
Break the eggs and stir in the cheese. Heat the oil in a pan, and sauté the artichokes with the garlic. Add the egg and cheese mixture to the artichokes in the pan and mix thoroughly. Serve immediately and very hot.

Carciofi ripieni
Stuffed artichokes
(Main illustration, far right)

8 ARTICHOKES
LEMON JUICE
2 CLOVES GARLIC
1 BUNCH PARSLEY
A FEW SPRIGS OF MARJORAM
OLIVE OIL
SALT AND PEPPER
1 TBSP ALL-PURPOSE FLOUR
2 BAY LEAVES

Remove the outer, woody leaves of the artichokes and trim the bases. Bang the ends of the leaves on the chopping board a few times to loosen them. The artichokes should be the shape of a sawn off skittle. Loosen the leaves and remove the hair. Put the artichokes in a bowl with water and lemon juice and leave aside.
Finely chop the hair, garlic, parsley, and marjoram. Mix them all together, then mix in a bowl with oil, salt, and pepper. Fill the artichokes with the mixture, and dust with flour. Heat oil in a deep pan, and fry the artichokes head downward, until the filling is golden brown. Then add hot water, salt, and bay leaves, and turn the artichokes. Cook for a further 30 minutes in an open pan. When the liquid has boiled away, the artichokes are ready. Serve hot.

DESSERTS

When it comes to finding something sweet with which to end a meal, the Ligurians do not rely either on impressive gâteaux or on complicated desserts. They much prefer exquisite little cakes and pastries such as almond cookies, *sciumette* (a carnival time classic), or small, fancy cookies. They are also very fond of candied fruits. *Biscotti del Lagaccio*, Lake Lagaccio cookies, are considered a particular specialty. In 1539, the Ligurian national hero Andrea Doria had this artificial lake made, in order to turn the beautiful Neptune fountain in his garden into something truly magnificent. This apparently vain project was at least useful to the people of the surrounding villages, as the aqueduct bringing the water from the lake into the nobleman's park fed a gunpowder factory and a mill with a bakehouse on its way. The Lagaccio cookies, which were baked there, were taken up enthusiastically and soon sold in great quantities.

BISCOTTI DEL LAGACCIO
Twice-baked cookies

2 OZ COMPRESSED CAKE/50 G FRESH YEAST (IF USING ACTIVE DRY YEAST, FOLLOW MAKER'S INSTRUCTIONS)
3 3/4 CUPS/600 G ALL-PURPOSE FLOUR
1/2 CUP + 2 TBSP/150 G BUTTER
1 CUP/200 G SUGAR
2 1/2 TBSP/20 G FENNEL SEEDS
1 PINCH SALT

Knead the yeast, some lukewarm water, and one quarter of the flour into a soft dough. Leave the dough to rise in a warm place, until it has doubled in volume. Add the remaining flour and knead again. Then work in the butter, which has been melted in a bain-marie, sugar, fennel seeds, and a pinch of salt. If necessary, add a little lukewarm water, to keep the dough soft and workable. Cover with a kitchen towel, and leave to rise in a warm place for 1 hour.
Shape the dough by hand into two long loaves, and leave to rise for a further hour.
Place the loaves on a baking sheet, and bake in a preheated oven for about 30 minutes at 350 °F (180 °C).
Leave until the next day, then cut into ¾ inch (2cm) thick slices and toast them in the oven at a very low heat.

RAVIOLI DOLCI
Sweet ravioli

1/2 LB TUB/200G RICOTTA OR CURD CHEESE
1 WHOLE ORANGE
6 OZ/150 G CANDIED FRUITS, DICED SMALL
10 OZ/300 G READY-MADE PUFF PASTRY (IF FROZEN, BE SURE IT HAS THAWED)
FLOUR FOR ROLLING OUT
OIL FOR FRYING
CONFECTIONERS' SUGAR

Drain the ricotta or curd cheese well. Wash the orange in hot water, dry, and finely grate the peel, add to the diced candied fruits, and mix both into the ricotta.
Roll the pastry out thin on a floured working surface. If using frozen pastry, put the thawed sheets one on top of the other before rolling out. Using a teaspoon, distribute the ricotta and orange mixture over half the dough. Leave about 2 inch (5 cm) gaps between each spoonful. Fold the other half of the dough loosely over the top. Cut round "ravioli" around each spoonful of filling, and press down the edges.

Heat plenty of oil in a deep pan. When little bubbles form around the handle of a wooden spoon, the oil has reached the right temperature. Add the "ravioli" a few at a time, and fry until golden brown.
Drain on kitchen paper, sprinkle with confectioners' sugar, and serve immediately.

SCIUMETTE
Floating islands
(Illustration, back left)

4 EGGS
SCANT 1/2 CUP SUPERFINE SUGAR
4 CUPS/1 LITER MILK
1 TBSP ALL-PURPOSE FLOUR
1/2 TBSP FRESH PISTACHIOS, SHELLED
POWDERED CINNAMON

Separate the egg yolks from the whites. Beat the whites with 1 tbsp of the sugar until stiff. In a casserole, bring the milk to a boil and, using a spoon, very gently add the beaten egg whites, which should set immediately. Cook the resulting "snowballs" very briefly, then lift out with a draining spoon, and leave to drain in a sieve.
Remove the milk from the heat, add the remaining sugar, stir in the flour, and leave to cool.
Crush the pistachios, cook for a few minutes in a little milk, and sieve. Beat the egg yolks, and gradually add to the milk and flour mixture. Finally mix in the pistachio purée. Put the mixture back on the heat in a hot bain-marie, and allow to thicken a little over a low heat. Take care not to let the water boil. Pour the thickened mixture into a bowl, decorate with the "snowballs" and sprinkle with cinnamon.
In Liguria *sciumette* are traditionally made at carnival time.

COBELLETTI
Sweet crust tarts
(Illustration front)

4 1/4 CUPS/500 G ALL-PURPOSE FLOUR
SCANT CUP/200 G SUGAR
1 1/4 CUPS/300 G BUTTER
MILK
1 EGG
1 SMALL GLASS MARSALA
QUINCE JAM

Knead flour, sugar, butter, and a little milk into a dough. Work in the egg and the Marsala. Roll out the dough to about ⅛ inch/3mm thick. Grease small, shallow muffin tins with butter, line with the dough, and put a little jam in the middle of each one. Make lids from the remaining dough, cover, and press the edges together.
Bake in a preheated oven for about 25 minutes at 400 °F (200 °C), until golden yellow.

Above: *Sciumette* – Floating islands
Below: *Cobelletti* – Sweet crust tarts

ROMANENGO'S CONFECTIONERY STORE

If the Duchess of Parma and Giuseppe Verdi were alive today, and strayed into the Via Soziglia in Genoa, they would certainly recognize one store, that of the confectioner Pietro Romanengo, famous for over 200 years for the most exquisite specialties. Pietro's father founded a grocery in the Via Maddalena in 1780, and soon afterward gained a degree in confectionery from the University of Genoa. As his trademark, he chose a dove with an olive twig, in honor of the peace concluded at the end of the Napoleonic wars. To wrap his products, Stefano Romanengo introduced the kind of blue paper which is still used on sugar loaves. Living in the port of Genoa, through which all the oriental goods, such as sugar, fruits, and spices were imported, gave him a special advantage. Stefano's son Pietro was permitted to call himself "premier Confiseur-Chocolatier" and considerably expanded the firm's activities. His major products were conserves, candied fruits, syrup, and liqueurs. He adapted oriental recipes, which the Crusaders had brought home to Genoa in the Middle Ages. Pietro decorated his shop in the Via Soziglia in Parisian style with exotic woods and marble, and produced his wares using French machinery. At the time, the aforementioned Duchess of Parma and the composer Giuseppe Verdi bought exquisite specialties from that very shop in the Via Soziglia. Verdi even mentioned it in his letters.

At the wedding of Prince Umberto and Margherita of Savoy in 1868, the invited guests enjoyed confections from Romanengo's. The written record of this event is to be found in the Genoa community archives and lists: "candied fruits, elegant bonbons, bombonières, and Jordan almonds." These last are still a firm favorite at Italian weddings. They are made with almonds, pistachios, and pine nuts and, according to the book *L'art du confiseur moderne* of 1879, they constitute one of the most difficult tasks for the confectioner. In 1859, the Genoese sugar industry employed 200 workers, producing over 660,000 pounds (300,000 kilograms) of candied fruits per year. The majority was exported to Holland, Germany, Northern Europe, North and South America, and Switzerland.

Today the firm of Romanengo has 24 permanent employees and the same number of seasonal workers, who make all the products by hand according to traditional methods. The factory is sited in Viale Mojon. Here the most delicious conserves, jellies and syrups, and of course the famous candied fruits and Jordan almonds, are made from fresh, ripe fruits, such as bitter oranges, melons, quinces, nuts, and rose petals. In the book *Il negoziante* (1683) by Gian Domenico Pen, conserves and candied fruits from Genoa are described as "the very best in the whole world." For Lent, there were various confectionery articles made without fat. In 1868, the newspaper *Popolo d'Italia* wrote that trade at Romanengo's was very brisk in the days before Easter, because of the great demand for his incomparable Lenten marzipan, which every Catholic was allowed to enjoy without falling prey to the sin of indulgence.

The historic shop in the Via Soziglia, which has remained completely unchanged since it was opened in 1814, is a jewel in the old quarter of Genoa. A collection of old appliances and objects used in the making and packaging of Romanengo's specialties is also on view there.

WINEGROWING IN THE LAND OF THE SEAFARERS

Long ago, the Greeks and the Etruscans brought grapes to this narrowest and most attractive part of the Italian coast, which is tucked in between the peaks of the Apennines and the shores of the Riviera, and stretches from the French border to the white marble cliffs of Carrara. Although grapes have been grown here since ancient times – for instance, the existence of the Dolcetto grape, known as Ormeasco in Liguria, was documented as long ago as the 14th century – viticulture plays a minor role in this land of seafarers, as a branch of the economy which has been supplemented by heavy industry and tourism.

Even the general boom in Italian winegrowing since the end of the sixties is only beginning to have an effect in Liguria. Old, local grape varieties continue to disappear from the scene, because they are no longer being cultivated by the younger generation. Not even five percent of the wine production has quality wine status, and the majority of the wines are still sold directly to tourists and locals. It is probably unfair to suggest that the growers should take better care of their varieties and the diversity of the vineyards, since the work is often so strenuous, and the returns are usually small in relation to the expenditure. Yet it is nonetheless regrettable when a fascinating part of the Italian wine scene continues to waste away or is threatened by progressive urbanization.

The truly recommendable Ligurian wines come from the growing area of Riviera Ligure di Ponente and Rossese di Dolceacqua in the west, Cinque Terre to the north of the port of La Spezia, and Colli di Luni on the border with Tuscany. The last named extends into the neighboring region – which is rare on the Italian wine map.

UNKNOWN GRAPE VARIETIES

Despite the unfavorable conditions, delicious and interesting wines can be found in Liguria, but their names are often almost unknown. One of the best is Rossese di Dolceacqua, from the area round Ventimiglia. The Rossese variety comes originally from France, and produces medium strength red wines, though many growers still make wines from it that are too pale and thin. From the immediate neighborhood comes Ormeasca. It seldom achieves the fullness and intense fruitiness of its various Piedmontese cousins but, especially in the mountains around Pieve di Teco, it can produce lovely round, mellow wines.

The most interesting of Liguria's white wines is made from the variety Pigato. These wines can be really strong, and are perfect with the tangy fish dishes which are served here by the sea. Occasionally they are even stored in wooden casks, which adds even more to their strength and fullness. Finer and fruitier are the wines from the Vermentino grape, which are sold under the DOC labels Riviera Ligure di Ponente and Colli di Luni. But the really famous ones, though not always better than the Vermentino wines, are the whites from Cinque Terre, especially in their sweet version, Schiacchetrà.

FIVE VILLAGES AND A FORGOTTEN SCIACCHETRÀ

Cinque Terre, five villages or five territories, is the name of by far the best-known winegrowing area in Liguria. No bigger in all than a single average Bordeaux establishment, it has one of the most dramatic vineyards in the world. Narrow, almost threatening terraces cover the slopes, which fall steeply down to the sea. Many of these vineyards can only be reached on foot, and cultivating grapes here is an arduous task. If it were not for tourism, which still guarantees a swift trade in the local wines, most would have been given up long ago. However, the small direct sales of wine to uncritical consumers have often prevented the local winemakers from paying enough attention to quality. Sciacchetrà, the most famous specialty of the Cinque Terre, has been almost forgotten. The intense, straw to amber colored, aromatic and balsamic sweet wine, made from the Albarola grape, which may be expected to have a surprisingly spicy taste, is now obtainable in acceptable quality and worthwhile quantities from only a very few winemakers. Let us hope that this ancient monument among Italian wines can be saved, before it dies out completely.

Right: On the narrow terraces of the Cinque Terre, seen here near Levanto, the growers struggle against difficult conditions.

Vermentino Riviera Ligure di Ponente
Like the Vermentino wines from southeastern Liguria, those of the western Riviera Ligure from the slopes of the Apennines between Genoa and Ventimiglia are usually pleasantly fruity. The vintages from the Riviera dei Fiori, Albenga, and Finale are particularly good.

Colli di Luni
The white and red wines with this label originate from the border area between Liguria and Tuscany. The whites are dominated by the fruity Vermentino variety, and the reds by Sangiovese, as are most of the wines from neighboring Tuscany.

Piedmont

Ovada

Mt. Menegosa
1355 m

Mt. Antola
1597 m

Mt. Maggiorasca
1799 m

Fossano

A26

A7

Torriglia

Emilia Romagna

Cuneo

Demonte

Tanaro

Ceva

Millesimo

Arenzano

Genoa

Nervi

Recce

Rapallo

Pontremoli

A15

Borgo
S.Dalmazzo

Mondovì

Varazze

Albisola Marina

S.Margherita
Ligure

Chiavari

Lavagna

Savona

Portofino

Tuscany

Limone
Piemonte

Ormea

Mt. Galero
1708 m

Spotorno

Liguria

Sestri
Levante

A12

Finale Ligure
Pietra Ligure
Loano

Gulf of Genoa

Mt. Saccarello
2200 m

FRANCE

Pieve
di Teco

A10

Levanto

La Spezia

Sarzana

44°N

Albenga

Riomaggiore

Lerici

Alassio

Portovenere

Diano Castello

Dolceacqua
Camporosso

Taggia

Imperia
Porto Maurizio

San Remo

Ventimiglia Bordighera

25 km (15 miles)

Rossese di Dolceacqua

Riviera Ligure di Ponente

Cinqueterre,
Cinqueterre Sciacchetrà

Colli di Luni

Winegrowing areas in
neighboring regions

EMILIA-ROMAGNA

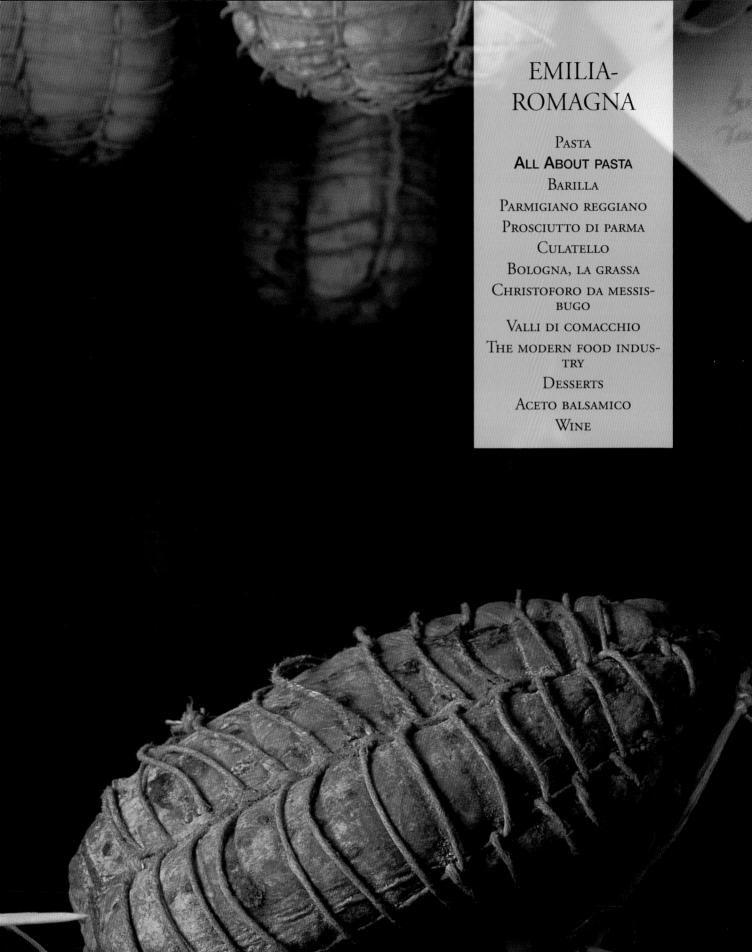

EMILIA-ROMAGNA

The delicatessen stores and cuisine of Emilia-Romagna offer everything the palate could desire: splendid hams and fresh mortadella, tasty parmesan, an endless variety of homemade pasta served with irresistible sauces, sumptuous meat dishes, tangy game, sweet or savory cakes and pastries, delicious desserts, light, sweet wines and, not least, the most splendid vinegar in the world, *aceto balsamico tradizionale*, which is only made by a handful of old-established producers. One reason for the incredible variety of its cuisine is that the region is made up of two different areas: Emilia, the area between the Po valley and northern Tuscany, and Romagna, the mountainous country with the Adriatic coast to the east. The fertile Emilia contributes pasta, dairy produce, and fine meat, while the sometimes rough and inaccessible Romagna offers aromatic herbs, tangy game, and fish dishes from the coast. The menu is completed by specialties from the cities. Parma is proud of its ham and *culatello*, Bologna offers the most exquisite mortadella, the best lasagne, and the most delicious tortellini in the world. Piacenza is the home of tortellini, Reggio Emilia is famous for its braised meat and *erbazzone*, Ferrara is the sausage capital, and in Modena they serve the incomparably tasty *zampone*, or stuffed pig trotters. In Emilia-Romagna they live off good food in two senses. Local specialties end up on their own plates – but have also long been produced for export, thus contributing to the wealth of the region. In the Middle Ages, the rest of the world already held Parma ham and parmesan cheese in high esteem, and no other corner of Italy is so densely packed with small, medium, and large food companies.

Although specialties from Emilia-Romagna are now obtainable all over the world, it is best to get to know them on the spot. Over a glass of Lambrusco and a *piadina*, a traditional dough cake cooked over an open fire, you can have a cozy chat with the Emilians and the Romagnoli about the only disputed subject in the region's cuisine: which is the tastiest pork crackling – the rather dry version from Emilia or the fat, juicy one they prefer in Romagna?

Previous double page: Fernando Cantarelli tests the ripeness of his Culatello ham with the traditional horse bone.

Left: The marshes of the Po delta represent the typical landscape of Emilia, whereas Romagna, which lies to the east, is characterized by its mountains.

PASTA

Emilia-Romagna is a pasta paradise. Apart from the innumerable varieties of *pasta secca* made from durum semolina, homemade *pasta fresca* made from wheat flour and egg is available everywhere for you to try. Connoisseurs maintain that the fresh pasta dough here is smoother and more elastic than in any other region. In the kitchens of Emilia-Romagna, both large and small, *pasta fresca* is made in a huge variety of forms. It can come in strips, diamonds, squares, or rectangles. You can have it filled with meat or cheese, like ravioli, tortellini, tortelli, or steaming lasagne. It can come in the form of *anolini, agnolotti, cappelletti,* or *cappellacci* with *sugo* or with *ragù*. There is no limit to the makers' imagination.

The dough is always prepared according to the same recipe, carefully kneaded, and either pulled out by hand or rolled out thin with a rolling pin. Every *rasdora* – as the housewives were once known in the local dialect – has her own technique and knows the secret regional recipe which affects the "inner life" of the pasta. *Tortelli di primavera*, filled with fine herbs and ricotta, come from around Parma. In other areas they fill the pasta with pumpkin, and in the mountains of Romagna they use chestnuts. Tortellini, for which there are around 110 different recipes, were apparently invented in Bologna. The shape is supposed to symbolize the navel of Venus!

But it is not only tasty varieties of pasta, which can be made from dough, there are also pastry specialties like *torte salate*, savory tarts, and crispy dough cakes like *piadina, tigella,* and *crescentina*. In Reggio Emilia they bake *erbazzone*, a savory cake filled with spinach and Swiss chard, and in Modena they serve *tigella* with pure lard, seasoned with rosemary and garlic.

TORTELLINI ROMAGNOLI
Tortellini filled with turkey
(Illustrated below)

For the dough:
3 1/2 CUPS/400 G ALL-PURPOSE FLOUR
1/2 TSP SALT
4 EGGS

For the filling:
1 TBSP BUTTER
3/4 LB/350 G TURKEY BREAST, CUT SMALL
2 OZ/50 G RICOTTA
2 OZ/50 G BEL PAESE
1/4 CUP/25 G FRSHLY GRATED PARMESAN
Grated rind of 1/2 LEMON
2 EGGS
GRATED NUTMEG
SALT AND FRESHLY MILLED BLACK PEPPER

MELTED BUTTER
FRESHLY GRATED PARMESAN FOR SPRINKLING

For the dough, sieve the flour onto the working surface, and make a well in the middle. Add the salt and eggs and knead to a smooth dough. Shape into a ball, wrap in a damp cloth and leave for 30 minutes.
Melt the butter in a heavy pan, add the turkey meat, and sauté for 15–20 minutes over a low heat. Put the turkey pieces through the food processor and mix with the other ingredients for the filling. Season with nutmeg, salt, and pepper.
Roll the dough out thin and cut circles about 2 inches/5 cm diameter. Put a little filling in the middle of each and fold over into a half moon shape. Wind each one round your finger like a ring and press the ends together.
Cook the tortellini in plenty of vegetable or fish stock until they rise to the surface. This will take about 5 minutes. Take them out, using a draining spoon, and put them in a prewarmed bowl.
Pour over melted butter, and sprinkle with grated parmesan if desired.

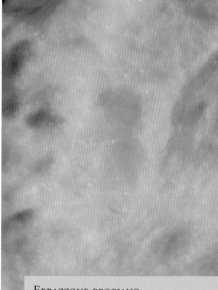

ERBAZZONE REGGIANO
Spinach cake
(Illustrated in background)

Serves 6

For the dough:
2 1/2 CUPS/300 G ALL-PURPOSE FLOUR
1/2 TSP SALT
2 TBSP BUTTER, MELTED
1 TBSP VEGETABLE OIL

For the filling:
2 LBS/1 KG LEAF SPINACH OR SWISS CHARD
4 TBSP OLIVE OIL
2 SLICES/50 G SMOKED HAM, DICED
1 TBSP CHOPPED PARSLEY
1 CLOVE GARLIC, CRUSHED
1 EGG
2/3 CUP/50 G FRESHLY GRATED PARMESAN
SALT
2 TBSP/25 G BUTTER

Sieve flour and salt into a bowl and knead with the melted butter to form a crumbly mixture. Work in the vegetable oil and enough lukewarm water to give a smooth, workable dough. Leave in a cool place.
For the filling, wash the spinach (or Swiss chard), blanch briefly, drain well, and chop fine or puree in the blender. Heat olive oil in a pan, and sauté the diced ham for 2 minutes over a low heat. Stir in the spinach and continue cooking gently for a further 2 minutes. Add the parsley and the crushed garlic, and sauté for a further 2 minutes. Whisk the egg until frothy. Remove the pan from the heat, and stir in the egg and parmesan. Season with salt and leave in a cold place.
Roll two-thirds of the dough out flat, and shape into a thin round. Brush the inside of a 10-inch/25-cm diameter springform pan with a little melted butter, and cover the base and sides with the dough. Fill with the spinach mixture and press down the edges of the dough. Roll out the remaining dough to make a lid, place over the filling, and press the edges down firmly. Prick the lid several times with a fork, and brush with the remaining melted butter. Bake in a preheated oven for 1 hour at most at 400 °F (200 °C). Serve hot or cold.

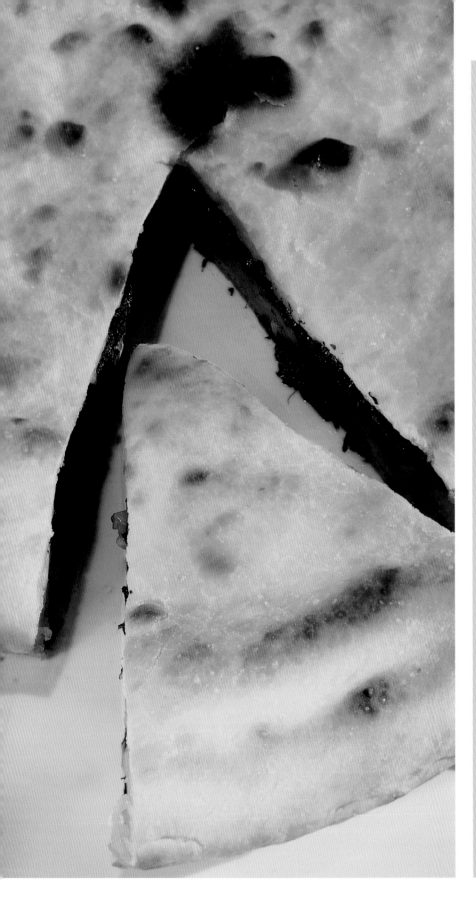

Here *piadina* is being served as a *panino*, a roll or sandwich, filled with tomato and mozarella.

Tigella

Tigella is a traditional bread from the Modena area. It is made by mixing wheat flour, water, and salt to form a soft dough. When the dough has rested for 30 minutes, it is cut into round portions and rolled out. The loaves are baked in special shallow forms. The word *tigella* originally meant the flameproof terra cotta dish it was baked in but, in the course of time, the name was transferred to the bread itself.

Piada or Piadina

In Romagna, instead of being called *tigella*, the round, flat loaf is known as *piada* or *piadina*. The dough consists of wheat flour, water, salt, and a little oil or fat, according to taste. It is rolled out to the size of the round baking dish. These plate-sized baking forms are available in stainless steel or terra cotta, but you can also use a cast iron pan. The *piada* only takes a few minutes to bake, and tastes delicious with Parma ham, cheese, or briefly cooked vegetables.

Crescentina

Crescentina differs from *tigella* and *piada* in the proportion of sour dough it contains. Otherwise the dough is prepared as for the other flat loaves from wheat flour, water, salt, and a little fat. To sour the dough, it must be left to stand for an hour. After that it is cut into small, round slices, and baked on a flat sheet. *Crescentina* can be served instead of bread with any kind of dish, but people mostly like to eat it with ham, cheese, and vegetables.

Gnocco fritto

The dough is made from wheat flour, water, fat, salt, and a pinch of baking powder. It is left to stand in a warm place, then rolled out flat and cut into rounds, which are pierced with a fork. The rounds are deep-fried in oil, and taste best if served very hot.

Erbazzone

Like the Ligurian *torta pasqualina*, *erbazzone reggiano* is a *torta salata*, a piquant, savory tart. But unlike the Ligurian Easter cake, *erbazzone* from Reggio is made not with eggs but with ham or bacon. In many mountain areas it can also be filled with Swiss chard or spinach and boiled rice.

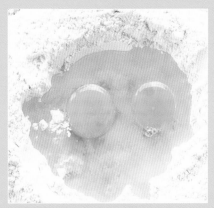

The flour should be as fresh as possible, otherwise annoying holes may form in the dough. As a rule, you can reckon on one egg to ¾ cup/100 grams flour, but this is only a rough indication.

In many parts of Italy, they make pasta with only the egg yolk, or only the white, or sometimes no egg at all, but just wheat flour, water, and a pinch of salt.

First the eggs are mixed with a little flour in a well in the middle. Then the dough is kneaded well and long enough for it to become smooth and workable, so it can be rolled out very thin.

ALL ABOUT PASTA...

Almost all the regions of Italy have their own theory about the origin of pasta. The Ligurians assume that Genoese merchants saw the recipe of the nomadic peoples of Mongolia and brought it back home. The Venetians believe Marco Polo imported noodles from China; they do not care about the suspicion, voiced by certain historians, that in reality the famous traveler never left his native city. In Rome they claim that the ancient emperors and senators ate pasta. The Sicilians insist that pasta arrived on the island with either the ancient Greeks or the medieval Arabs. In Naples, on the other hand, they will have nothing to do with this story, as the Campanians think that the original Greek and Arab pasta consisted of nothing more than rough pieces of dough, and it was the inventive cooks of the Neapolitan macaroni kitchens who made pasta what it is today: a passion all over Italy.

However this may be, it is a fact that today pasta comes in more than 300 varieties, and is one of the favorite courses on the Italian menu. Two different kinds can be distinguished: *Pasta secca* describes pasta made from durum semolina and water, which is sold dried and rarely made at home. *Pasta fresca* or *pasta fatta in casa* means the fresh, homemade pasta, with a dough consisting of wheat flour, egg, and possibly a little water or white wine. There are, however, homemade *pasta fresca* which do not include egg.

Pasta secca is a manufactured product which, because of its impeccable tradition, elegantly overcomes the arguments for and against "ready-made" foodstuffs. Even the most hardworking housewife or the most ambitious chef would leave the making of *pasta secca* to the *pastaio*, that is the pasta-maker, or recently also the pasta factory. *Pasta secca* can be split into two groups: *pasta lunga* and *pasta corta*. *Pasta lunga* includes all varieties over four inches (ten centimeters) long, such as spaghetti, spaghettini, or tagliatelle. Shorter pasta creations, like the splendid penne, medium length farfalle, or the tiny noodles used in soup, fall into the category of *pasta corta*. *Pasta secca* is generally distinguished by its reliable *tenuta di cottura*; this means that the pasta holds together well in the cooking and does not fall to pieces in the bubbling water. Although most manufacturers state the exact cooking time on the packaging of their pasta, a good *tenuta di cottura* also becomes apparent if pasta, which have inadvertently been cooked a little too long, do not become soft or mushy, but still keep their shape and firm consistency, even after a few minutes over the recommended cooking time.

In contrast to most industrially produced *pasta secca*, *pasta fresca* is the personal creation of each individual. There are countless tricks for making the dough particularly smooth and ways of rolling it out especially thin, but the basic recipe is almost always the same. For every ⅞ cup (100 grams) flour, you take an egg and a pinch of salt. *Pasta fresca* comes *a strice*, in strips cut from the smooth dough, or *ripiena*, that is, filled. The fillings are as varied as the shapes of the pasta itself – from pumpkin, via ricotta, to meat and fish, virtually anything finds a place inside little pasta envelopes.

In many parts of Italy, the fresh pasta dough is colored, to make *pasta colorata*. The secret of the *pasta nera* (black pasta) made in coastal regions is cuttlefish ink. Puréed spinach gives *pasta verde* its green color, a spoonful of tomato purée turns the dough light red, and a drop of beetroot juice dyes the pasta a delicate shade of pink. In Sardinia, saffron is used to give *malloreddus* its golden yellow sheen. Nowadays, colored *pasta secca* is also obtainable in the shops. These varieties are colored either with artificial dyes or with the same natural substances that are used for *pasta fresca*. It is just prejudice to say that pasta makes you fat, as 4 oz (100 grams) uncooked *pasta secca* contains only 325 calories, and the same amount of *pasta fresca* around 365 calories. Pasta also provides valuable carbohydrates, contains important mineral salts, and supplies vitamin B1, B2, and niacin. If pasta is not served with a very heavy sauce, it can even appear on a diet sheet.

Tagliatelle are one of the traditional kinds of pasta from Emilia-Romagna, and are made fresh almost every day.

The proper way to cook pasta

Pasta is quick to cook and is always successful, if you follow a couple of basic rules. The pan it is cooked in should be as big and deep as possible. You should reckon on at least 4 cups (1 liter) water to 4 ounces (100 grams) pasta, because the pasta needs room to move, to prevent it from sticking together. For every liter of water, you should add up to ½ teaspoon (10 grams) salt.

Before putting in the pasta, the water must be brought to a rolling boil, and it must keep bubbling throughout the whole cooking time. An occasional stir will ensure the pasta cooks evenly. Filled pasta must be cooked with care, as if the water boils too violently or you stir too roughly, the pasta may be damaged and the filling may leak.

The cooking time is calculated according to the size of the pasta. Very small or thin noodles cook more quickly than the bigger, thicker kinds. Pasta made from fresh dough generally has a shorter cooking time than *pasta secca*. You can only tell if the pasta is ready by trying it. Italian pasta is cooked *al dente*, that is, soft on the outside, but with a firm center. If the pasta is just right, tip the contents of the pan through a strainer.

Basic pasta recipe

Serves 6–8

GENEROUS 4 CUPS/500 G ALL-PURPOSE FLOUR
5 EGGS
1/2 TSP SALT
FLOUR FOR DUSTING

Sieve the flour onto the working surface. Make a well in the middle and add the eggs and salt. Work in the flour around the edges of the well, and form into a coarse dough. Knead for 15 minutes until smooth. Wrap in kitchen foil and leave for 1 hour.
Dust the work surface with flour, and roll out thin, using a floured rolling pin. Keep turning the dough, so that it is spread evenly.

Anyone who does not want to spend time rolling out dough can invest in a pasta machine, which may be hand-cranked or electrically operated. With different attachments, you can produce every imaginable shape.

Long, wide, flat pasta ribbons are usually called tagliatelle. In Parma, they make a version with wheat and chestnut flour.

Know your pasta

Pasta di semola di grano duro secca
This dried pasta made from durum semolina and water keeps for a very long time, if stored correctly.

Pastina or Pasta corta mista
These small noodles made of durum wheat are very good in consommés and soups.

Pasta glutinata
This durum wheat pasta with added gluten is often used for children's meals.

Pasta corta or Pasta tagliata
In this category you find almost all medium-sized durum wheat pasta, which is eaten as *pasta asciutta*, dry pasta, with just a little tomato sauce.

Pasta lunga
Long durum wheat pasta, like spaghetti, is also eaten as *pasta asciutta*.

Pasta di semola fresca
Not dried, but freshly made from durum wheat and water, this kind of pasta is a specialty of the southern regions. Sardinian *malloreddus* is just one example of this kind.

Pasta all'uovo secca
This dried pasta made from durum wheat and egg is often produced in strips. Ready-made, filled ravioli or tortellini also consist of egg dough, but are not as tasty as homemade pasta.

Pasta all'uovo fresca
Homemade pasta of wheat flour (type 00) and egg do not keep long, and should therefore be eaten as soon as possible.

Pasta speciale
This category includes colored pasta, *pasta colorata*, and varieties that have flavorings mixed into the dough (mushrooms, truffle, wine) or contain extra kinds of flour added (wholemeal flour, buckwheat).

Abissina rigate (L 1 ½ in./35mm)

Anelli (Ø 5/16 in./8 mm)

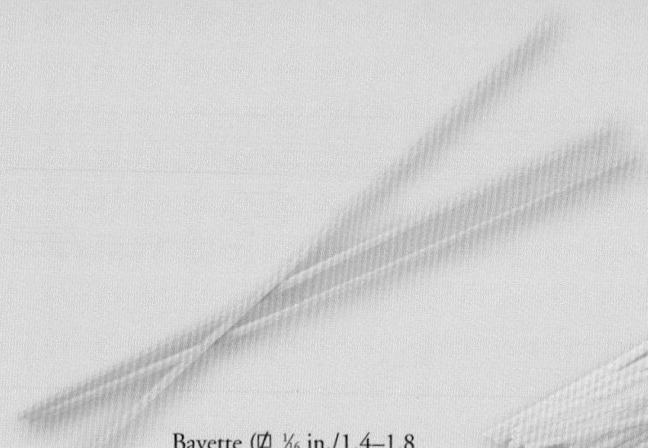

Bavette (⌀ 1/16 in./1.4–1.8 mm

Bucatini (Ø 1/8 in./2.6–2.9 mm)

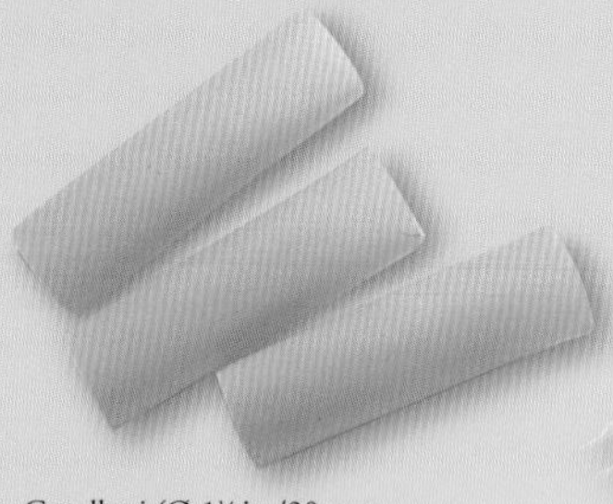

Canelloni (Ø 1¼ in./30 mm, L 4 in./100 mm)

Capellini (Ø 1/16 in./1.2–1.4 mm)

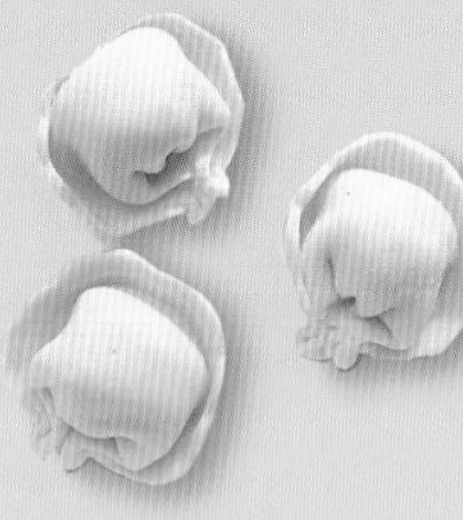

Cappelletti (Ø 1¼–1⅝ in./30–40 mm)

Capunti (L ⅞–1 in./20–25 mm)

Cavatelli (L ⅞ in./20mm)

Cavatelluci (L ⅞ in./20mm)

Chiocciole (L ⅝–⅞ in./15–20 mm)

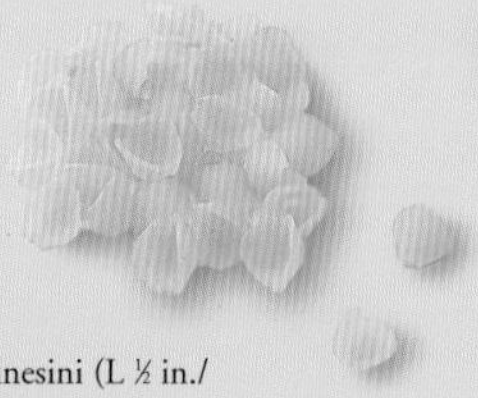

Cinesini (L ½ in./12 mm)

Ciriole (Ø ⅛ in./3mm)

Conchiglie (L 1½ in./35mm)

Ditali rigati (Ø 3/16 in./4mm,

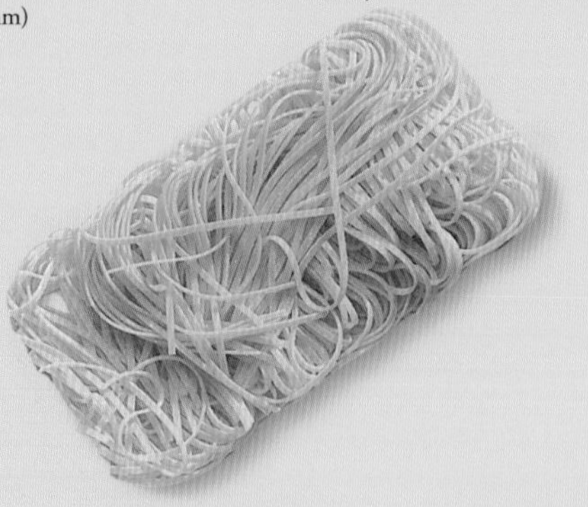

Faresine (⌀ 5/16–7/16 in./8–10 mm)

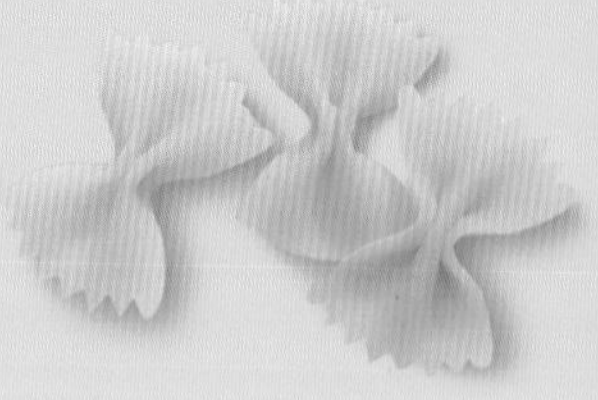

Farfalle (L 1½ in./35mm)

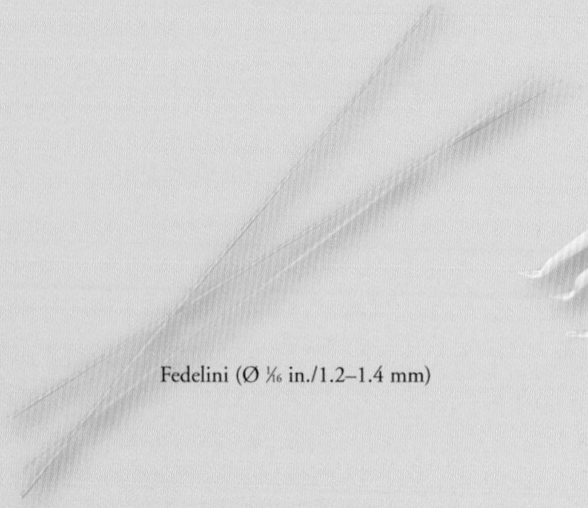

Fedelini (Ø 1/16 in./1.2–1.4 mm)

Fenescècchie (Ø ¼ in./6 mm, L 1⅝ in./40 mm)

Fettuccelle (⌀ ¼–5/16 in./6–7.3 mm)

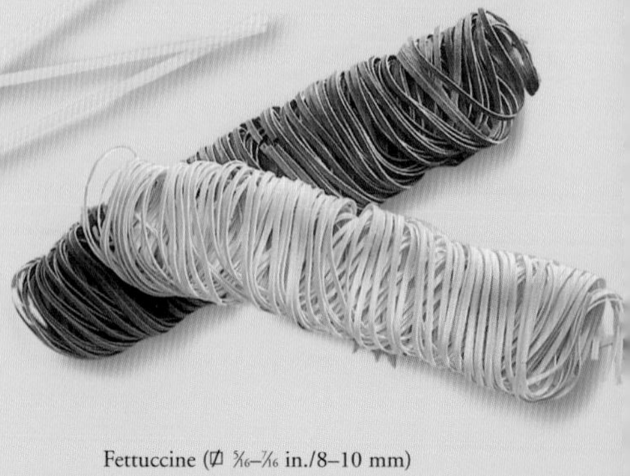

Fettuccine (⌀ 5/16–7/16 in./8–10 mm)

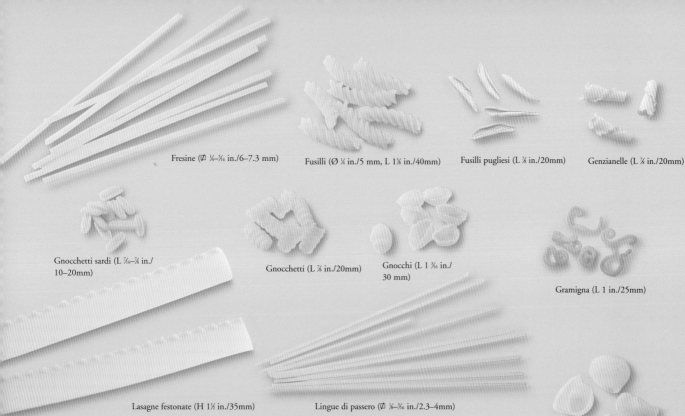

Fresine (Ø ¼–⁹⁄₁₆ in./6–7.3 mm)

Fusilli (Ø ¼ in./5 mm, L 1⅝ in./40mm)

Fusilli pugliesi (L ⅞ in./20mm)

Genzianelle (L ⅞ in./20mm)

Gnocchetti sardi (L ⁷⁄₁₆–¾ in./ 10–20mm)

Gnocchetti (L ⅞ in./20mm)

Gnocchi (L 1 ³⁄₁₆ in./ 30 mm)

Gramigna (L 1 in./25mm)

Lasagne festonate (H 1½ in./35mm)

Lingue di passero (Ø ¹⁄₁₆–³⁄₁₆ in./2.3–4mm)

Lumache rigate grandi (L 1½ in./35mm)

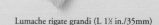

Maccheroni (Ø ³⁄₁₆ in/4mm)

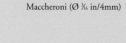

Occhi di pernice (Ø ³⁄₁₆ inch/4 mm)

WHICH SAUCE GOES BEST WITH WHICH PASTA?

The combination of pasta and a tasty sauce is almost a science in itself. Every Italian cook would have his or her personal views on this theme, but there are a few simple rules, which people generally follow.

Filled pasta like ravioli, *pansoti*, *cappelletti*, or tortellini, have so much flavor of their own that they only need to be served with a little sage butter or a very light tomato sauce. In the north, they are often accompanied by a cream sauce.

Thin *pasta fresca*, for instance tagliolini, should not be overwhelmed by a powerful sauce either. A few truffle shavings, a little butter, or a spoonful of grated parmesan, are quite sufficient.

Heavy *pasta fresca* such as tagliatelle, on the other hand, are particularly good, when served with a strong sauce of mushrooms, cheese, cream, ham, or even with fish.

In the case of dried pasta, the choice of possible combinations is wider. Because *pasta secca* does not have a very strong taste, it is all the more dependent on the accompanying sauce. Here the rule of thumb is: the bigger the space inside the pasta, the more sauce it can soak up.

The Campanian pasta-maker Voiello even commissioned the automobile designer Giorgetto Giugiaro to "construct" a kind of pasta, which would take up the maximum amount of sauce. The result is the designer pasta Marilla, which tastes especially good with tomato sauce and parmesan.

Key to the varieties:
in. = inches
mm = millimeters
Ø = diameter
Ø = cross-section
L = length
H = height

SAUCES TO SERVE WITH PASTA – AN OVERVIEW

Aglio e olio
Olive oil and garlic suit long pasta like spaghetti and *linguine*.

Ai frutti di mare
Seafood is only suitable for very thin, long pasta like spaghettini or *capelli d'angelo*.

All'amatriciana
A sauce of tomatoes and bacon suits long, tubular pasta like *bucatini* or macaroni.

Alla napoletana
This classic tomato sauce suits almost all kinds of pasta.

Allo spezzatino
Braised meat is good with pasta strips.

Burro e salvia
Butter and sage improve all kinds of pasta, even those with fillings.

Carbonara
This sauce of bacon, cheese, and egg suits long, thin pasta.

Pesto
The spicy paste of basil, olive oil, pine kernels, pecorino and garlic, suits the strips as well as the long thin kinds, and can even go with filled pasta.

Ragù alla bolognese
Minced meat sauce, which suits all long kinds of pasta, and can be used as a filling for lasagne.

Salsa di noci
This Ligurian walnut sauce suits pasta strips.

Sugo di pesce
Sugo made from tomatoes and fish goes with pasta with big spaces inside, like macaroni or penne.

Orecchiette (Ø ⅞–1 in./20–25mm)

Pansoti (2 x 2 ⅜–3 ¼ in./
50 x 60–80mm)

Panzerotti di magro (2 x 2 ⅜ in./50 x 60mm)

Pappardelle (Ø ½–⅝ in./11–15 mm)

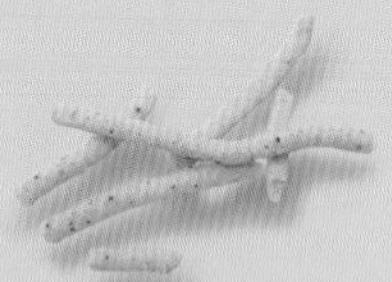
Passatelli (Ø 3/16 in./4mm,
L ⅝–1 ¼ in./15–30mm)

Risoni (L 3/16 in./4mm)

Penne mezzane (Ø 3/16 in./4mm,
L 1 in./25mm)

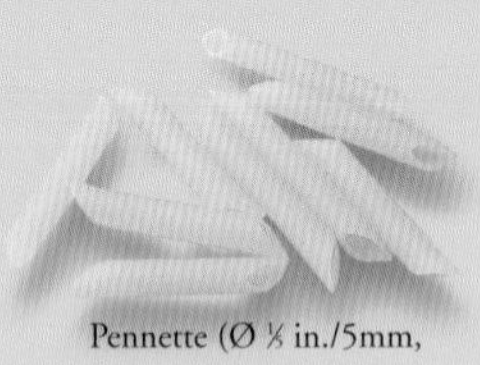
Pennette (Ø ⅕ in./5mm,
L 1 in./25mm)

Mezze penne (Ø ⅕ in./5mm,
L ⅞ in./20mm)

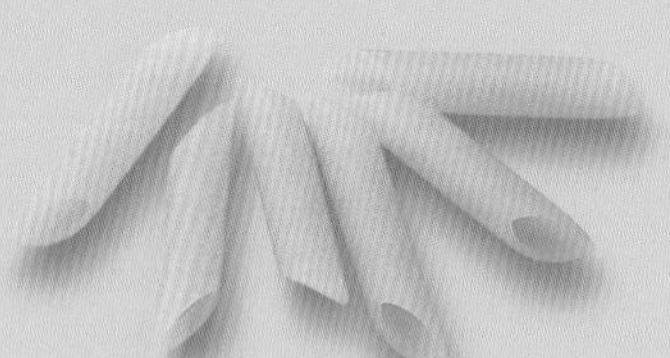
Penne (Ø 5/16 in./8mm, L 1 ⅝ in./40mm)

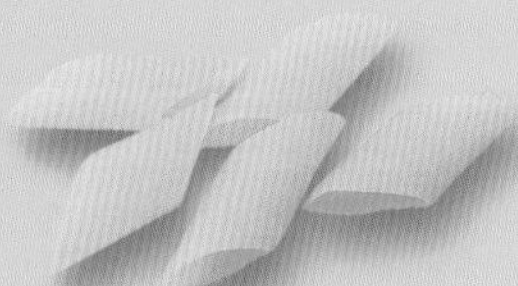
Pennoni rigati (Ø ⅜ in./10mm,
L 1 ½ in. 35mm)

Ravioli (L 1 ⅝–2 in./40–50mm)

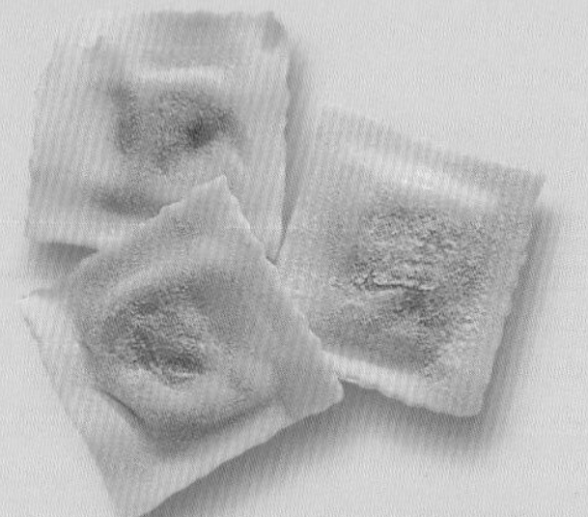
Ravioli alle noci (L 1 ⅝–2 in./40–50mm)

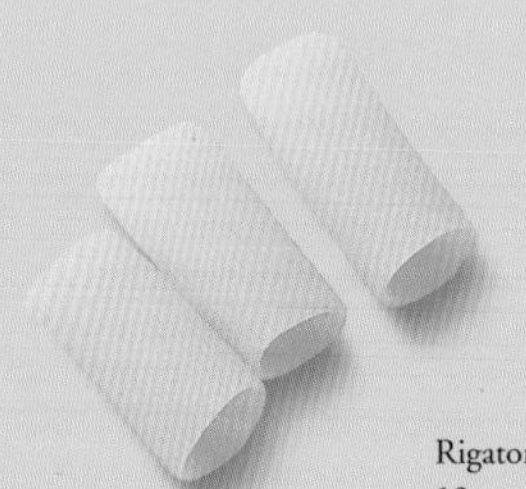
Rigatoni (Ø 7/16 in./
13mm, L 2 ⅜ in./
60mm)

Riscossa (L ⅞–1 in./
20–25mm)

Ruote tricolore (Ø ⅞–1 in./20–24mm)

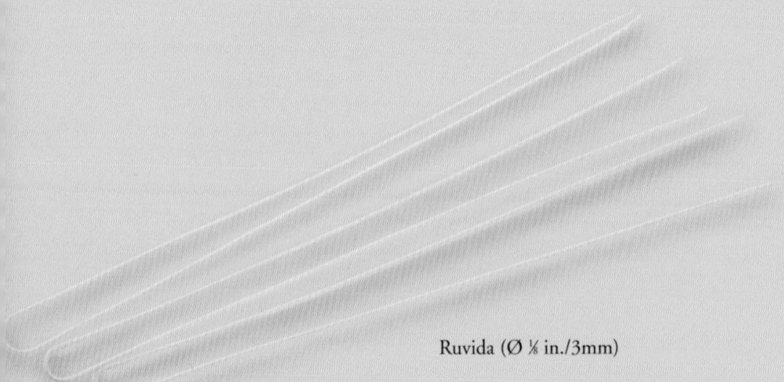
Ruvida (Ø ⅛ in./3mm)

Schiaffoni (Ø ⅜ in./10mm, L 2 3/16 in./55mm)

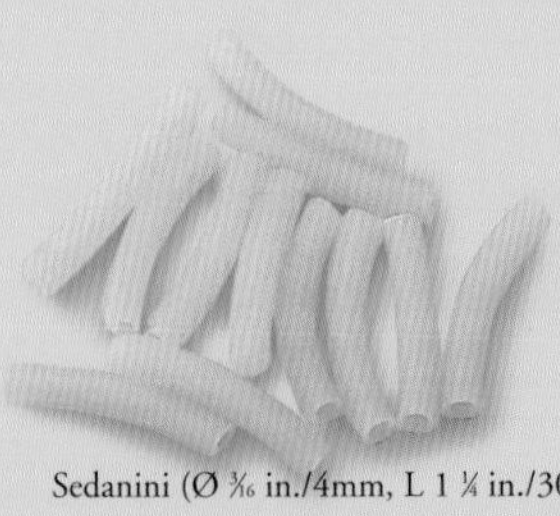
Sedanini (Ø 3/16 in./4mm, L 1 ¼ in./30mm)

Spaghetti (Ø 1/16–1/8 in./1.8–2mm)

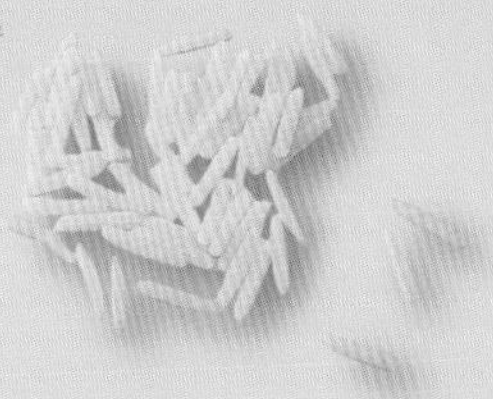
Spiganarda (Ø 1/8 in./3mm, L 5/8 in./15mm)

Spirelli (Ø 1/5 in./5mm, L 15/8 in./40mm)

Strascinati tricolore (L 1 5/8 in./40mm)

Taccheroni (L 1 1/2 in./35mm)

Tagliatelle all'uovo (Ø 3/16–1/4 in./4.3–5.8mm)

Tagliatelle con spinaci (Ø 3/16–1/4 in./4.3–5.8mm)

Taglierini (Ø 1/8 in./3mm)

Tortelli (Ø 2 in./50mm)

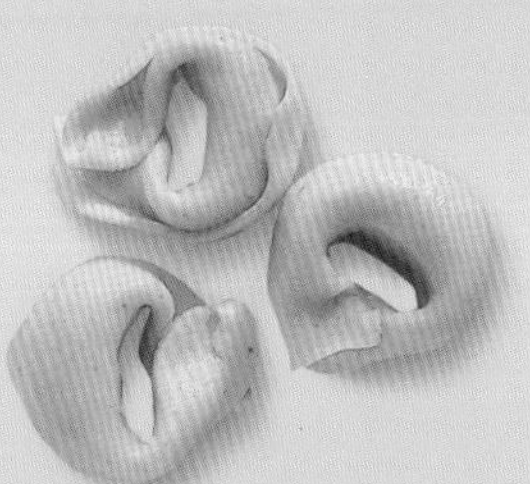
Tortellini (Ø 1 7/8–2 in. /45–50mm)

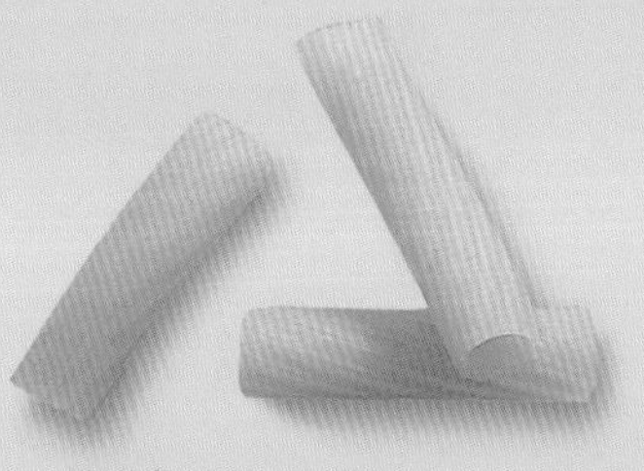
Tortiglioni (Ø 3/8 in./10mm, L 2 in./50mm)

Trenette (Ø 3/16 in./3.5mm)

Triangoli di pasta nera al salmone (2 x 2 3/8–3 1/4 in./50 x 60–80mm)

Trocchi (Ø 3/16 in./4mm)

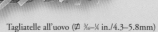

Trofie (Ø 3/16 in./4mm, L 2 in/50mm)

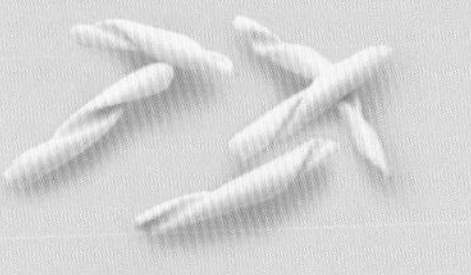
Trucidi pugliesi (Ø 3/16 in./4mm, L 4/5 in./20mm)

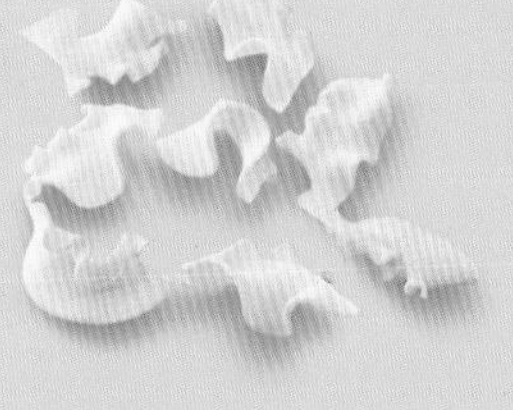
Truciolotti (4/5–1 in./20–25mm)

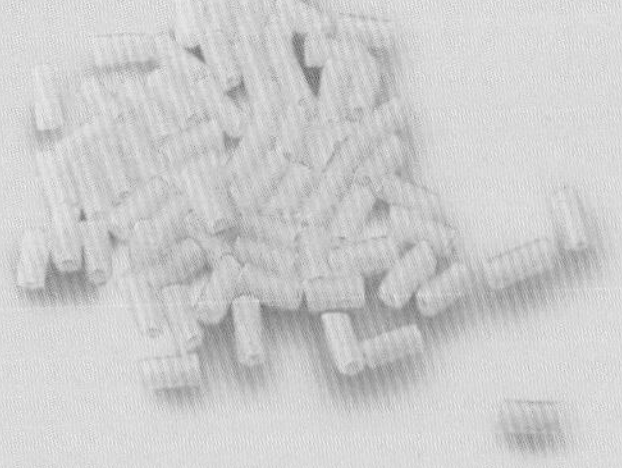
Tubettini (Ø 3/16 in., L 1/4 in./6mm)

BARILLA

"Dove c'è Barilla, c'è casa," (Anywhere there is Barilla, is home) – the slogan sums it up nicely. Few nations draw their identity from their physical well-being to the same extent as the Italians. Their first thought is not of Pisa, but of pasta, more precisely of Barilla, the pasta factory in Parma. *Rigatoni, farfalle* or *bucatini*, in the typical blue cartons with white lettering on a red background, have been around on the supermarket shelves in Moscow and Addis Ababa, Tokyo and Copacabana for a long time. The headquarters of Barilla – the biggest manufacturer of pasta in the world, and the undisputed market leader in Italy –

In the bulk packing area, packets of spaghetti are transported by conveyor belt, and packaged for sending all over the world.

The dried spaghetti must all be cut to the same length, so it fits into the packet.
Right: Long, smooth pasta like spaghetti is hung on a rack to dry before packaging.

form the nucleus of the so-called Italian Food Valley between Parma and Modena, in the Po valley in northern Italy, where a major part of the Italian food industry is concentrated.

In the 19th century, Parma was already the third biggest producer of pasta in Italy – after Naples and Genoa – according to the Leipzig Universal Dictionary of Cookery of 1890. The baker Pietro Barilla also sold pasta – egg noodles and *pasta secca* from durum wheat – in the store he opened in the center of Parma in 1877. He has gone down in company history as the actual founder, because he wanted to make use of the latest technology, and so in 1900 he invested in a new kneading machine and a cast iron dough press, which made a dramatic rise in production possible. New workshops were set up just outside Parma in 1910, and Pietro's sons Gualtiero and Riccardo, bought the most modern bread-ovens, as well as machines for sifting flour, kneading, cutting, folding, and pressing the dough. Soon there were a hundred employees working there, producing 176,000 pounds (80,000 kilograms) of pasta a day. The volume of orders is still rising, They are winning new markets, in other regions of Italy and abroad, especially in America, where those who have emigrated have their pasta sent to them from Italy. Customers always asked for the Pastificio Barilla catalog, whose elegant graphics made good use of the pretty shapes of dozens of different pasta.

From the start, quality has been the most important requirement, and this depends on the quality of the durum wheat flour. Riccardo Barilla used to dust the sleeves of his black suit with flour. If no little specks remained when he brushed it off, the flour was good, that is dry and finely ground. The more elderly citizens of Parma still like to remember Barilla's sunshine yellow carts, laden with fresh bread and pasta, drawn through the early morning streets of Parma by pale carthorses – to cultivate an image which still symbolizes the genuinely nutritious qualities of fresh eggs and wheat.

In the thirties, just 700 workers saw to the production of 176,000 pounds (80,000 kilograms) of pasta and 33,000 pounds (15,000 kilograms) of bread per day. In 1952 – with Pietro's grandson, also a Pietro, now at the helm – they gave up baking bread and concentrated all their forces on achieving the breakthrough to become the national market leader in pasta. With their prize-winning slogan *"Con pasta Barilla è sempre domenica,"* (With Barilla pasta, it's Sunday every day), the brand became an icon for aspiring Italians of the fifties. After an American interlude in the seventies, after which Pietro Barilla bought back the company, today it is the turn of his children, Guido, Paolo, and Luca. In the 30 or so factories, four of which are abroad, they have also started to produce cookies. Under the familiar brand name Mulino Bianco (White Mule), *biscotti* – now an essential on the Italian breakfast table – currently represent half the turnover; a further chapter of success in the Barilla company history.

In 1877 Pietro Barilla opened a store in the center of Parma, where he sold fresh egg pasta and *pasta secca* made from durum wheat.

As early as 1900, Pietro Barilla (1845–1912) invested in modern machinery, which enabled him to increase production dramatically.

CHEESE GRATERS

Many pasta recipes suggest that pasta should be served with grated parmesan, or more commonly in the south, with grated pecorino. But how should these two hard cheeses best be prepared?

The good old household grater gives very satisfactory service, but brings with it a hidden danger of injury, as anyone who has inadvertently grated a fingernail will confirm. Grating cheese in a cheese mill is a lot simpler. The cheese is placed in a drum, with a cylindrical grater inside. The drum is cranked with a handle, and pressed against the cheese. But beware of cheap plastic cheese mills, whose handles can all too easily break off. The final decision on the question of grating methods is a matter of personal preference. The most important thing is that the cheese should always be freshly grated and used immediately. Grated cheese should be kept for as short a time as possible. Ready-grated cheese sold in plastic packs is out of the question!

The best equipment is a flat grater, which will not grate the parmesan too finely.

If you want to grate small pieces of cheese on a rounded kitchen grater, watch out for your fingers.

Cheese mills grate hard cheese quickly, with no danger of injury. Good ones are made from stainless steel.

Cheese mills made from rigid plastic, with good action, provide a colorful alternative.

To make parmesan, milk from the evening and morning milkings are mixed.

The milk is heated and curdled by adding rennin.

The curd is broken up until it is fine and crumbly.

When the curd has been heated again, the young cheese sets.

A linen cloth is pulled under the cheese mass. The first whey drains off.

Two strong men are needed to lift the cheese from the vat.

The cheese is pressed into a mold, so that more whey can drain off.

Young cheese, starting to form a rind, is stored in brine for 3–4 weeks.

PARMIGIANO REGGIANO

Back in the Middle Ages, the big cheeses stored in the dairies of Parma were already considered a tourist attraction. Around 1500, pilgrims and travelers were offered bite-sized pieces of the local specialty cheese as an appetizer. The trademark of Parmigiano Reggiano, which is still valid today, was probably designed in 1612 by a certain Bartolomeo Riva, Treasurer of the Farnese estates under Duke Ranuzzio I. Parmesan – now a DOC product – is still made according to traditional methods, which are just as strictly laid down as the area in which it may be produced. It is only allowed to bear the name Parmigiano Reggiano if it is produced in the provinces of Parma, Reggio Emilia, Modena, Mantua (on the right bank of the Po), and Bologna (but here on the left bank of the Reno). In addition, the milk must come from free-range cows, which have only been fed on green fodder.

In the dairy, the milk is first left to stand overnight, so that the cream can be skimmed off the next morning. Then fresh morning milk is added to the skimmed milk. The mixture is heated in a big copper vat. When it has reached about 86 °F (30 °C), the cheese-master stirs in rennin from calves' stomachs. Fermentation starts immediately, and the milk has curdled within 15 minutes. The curd, the *cagliata*, is then broken up into pieces the size of grains of wheat – which is where the name *grana* (corn) comes from. Then the mass is heated again, at first slowly to 113 °F (45 °C), then finally to 131 °F (55 °C), to separate the cheese from the whey. This curd, weighing up to 132 pounds (60 kilograms), is heaved out of the vat by strong men using a big linen cloth, halved, and pressed into a wooden or metal mold.

Each cheese is stamped by the dairy which produces it.

The man in charge of storing the cheeses tests their condition and aging at regular intervals.

To reach its final maturity, Parmigiano Reggiano must be stored for a long time. The oldest varieties spend three years in the wooden stands.

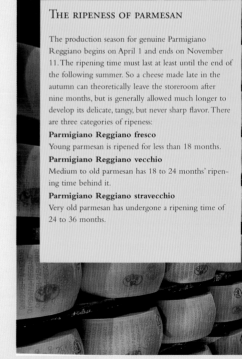

THE RIPENESS OF PARMESAN

The production season for genuine Parmigiano Reggiano begins on April 1 and ends on November 11. The ripening time must last at least until the end of the following summer. So a cheese made late in the autumn can theoretically leave the storeroom after nine months, but is generally allowed much longer to develop its delicate, tangy, but never sharp flavor. There are three categories of ripeness:

Parmigiano Reggiano fresco
Young parmesan is ripened for less than 18 months.

Parmigiano Reggiano vecchio
Medium to old parmesan has 18 to 24 months' ripening time behind it.

Parmigiano Reggiano stravecchio
Very old parmesan has undergone a ripening time of 24 to 36 months.

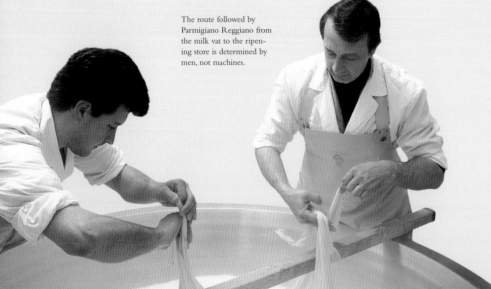

The route followed by Parmigiano Reggiano from the milk vat to the ripening store is determined by men, not machines.

The mold has already been lined with a cloth so that later on the fresh cheese can be safely lifted out. Now the remaining whey is gently pressed out of the soft mass. As soon as the cheese has developed some consistency and started to form a rind, the trademark, consisting of the words "Parmigiano Reggiano" and the date of production picked out in small dots, is stamped on. Then the cheeses have to stand in brine for three to four weeks, after which they dry off for a few days in the sun, to allow the rind to firm and develop further.

Parmesan reaches its final maturity not in the dairy, but in gigantic storerooms, which are maintained by the community or by a sponsor. These so-called "cathedrals" can hold 50,000 to 100,000 cheeses. But the cheese still needs to be looked after while it is ripening. During the first half year, it needs to be turned every four or five days, and in the following months every ten days. At the end of this long process, it must still undergo rigorous testing and — if it passes — be branded with the seal of quality.

Externally, and from the point of view of production technique, genuine parmesan is not very different from the varieties Grana Padano, Grana Vernenga, or Grana Lodigiano. But grana may come from a wide range of areas in northern Italy, and the milk it is made from may come from cows which have been fed on lower quality fodder.

CHIZZE
Filled pasta
(Illustrated above)

For the dough:
3 1/2 CUPS/400 G ALL PURPOSE FLOUR
4 TSP/20 G BUTTER
4 TSP/20 G SHORTENING
4–5 TSP BAKING POWDER
1 PINCH SALT

3 CUPS/200G FINELY GRATED PARMESAN
OIL OR SHORTENING FOR FRYING

Slowly knead the flour, butter, shortening, baking powder, and salt, if necessary adding a little warm water. The dough must not be so moist that it will stick when being rolled out, or so dry that it will break.

Roll the dough on a floured work surface to about ⅛ inch/ 3mm thick, and cut in 3–3½ inch/7–8 cm squares. Sprinkle the squares with parmesan, and fold into triangles. Press the edges firmly together, and fry the *chizze* in hot oil or shortening.

CROSTINI AL PARMIGIANO
Parmesan toasts

2 EGGS
2/3 CUP/150ML MILK
6 CUPS/400G FRESHLY GRATED PARMESAN
PEPPER
GRATED NUTMEG
1 BAGUETTE
1 TBSP/30 G BUTTER
1/3 CUP 100ML RED WINE
Mix the eggs, milk, and cheese, and season with pepper and nutmeg. Slice the bread, and spread each slice with the cheese paste. Heat the butter in a pan, and lightly brown the bread slices. After a few minutes, pour over the wine, and cover the pan. Cook until the cheese has melted.

PORTAFOGLI DI PARMIGIANO
Parmesan wallets

6 THIN SLICES OF VEAL OR PORK
GRATED PARMESAN
6 SLICES PARMA HAM
ALL-PURPOSE FLOUR
2 TBSP/30 G BUTTER
1 GLASS WHITE WINE
3 1/2 TBSP/50 ML LIGHT CREAM
SALT AND PEPPER

Sprinkle each slice of meat with parmesan, cover with a slice of ham, fold in half, and fasten with a toothpick, and toss in flour. Heat the butter in a pan, and brown the meat over a medium heat. Pour over the wine a little at a time, then finally pour over the cream, and cook for a few minutes more. Season with salt and pepper.

PROSCIUTTO DI PARMA

It is not so easy to explain how Parma ham acquires its incomparable taste. Some say it is a result of the particularly favorable climatic conditions in and around Parma; others consider that it is entirely due to the healthy diet of the pigs. Not to mention other important factors, such as using the correct cut from the haunch, expert curing, and allowing sufficient time for it to mature.

"From young pigs which, if possible, should come from the mountains, cured without too much salt, a deliciously fragrant meat" – this description of Parma ham, which sounds almost like an advertisement, was written in the 16th century by Bartolomeo Scappi, Pope Pius V's personal chef. In the past it was quite usual for meat to be salted and dried in order to preserve it. But it was not until the end of the 19th century that there was a real boom in these "preserves." Suddenly everyone was eating this aromatic ham as a starter. Demand rose swiftly, and around 1870 a high quality ham industry quickly grew up in Langhirano, a little village near the provincial capital of Parma.

There are still huge storehouses in Langhirano and the surrounding villages today. Behind their high walls, millions of Parma hams are maturing, and receiving precisely the right amount of air through louvered windows, which are opened or closed according to the weather. Prosciutto di Parma is a DOC controlled product; that means its origin is legally protected and monitored. There is a consortium which supervises adherence to the quality guidelines. Even the pigs, whose hams will later be stamped with the coveted trademark of the crown of Parma, are subject to strict regulations. They must come from inspected pig-houses in northern and central Italy, and during their lifetime must have fed on nothing other than the whey left over from the production of parmesan, forage barley, sweet corn, and fruit. They are slaughtered at the age of ten months, but only if they are nice and fat, and have reached the prescribed minimum weight of 350 pounds (160 kilograms). The fat layer is absolutely necessary, because it will surround the delicate, firm, rosy meat while it is maturing, and protect it from drying out.

In the first production phase, the fresh ham, weighing 22–24 pounds (10–11 kilograms), is continually salted and kept in a cold room at 32–39 °F (0–4 °C). The salt and the cold draw the water out of the meat. From time to time the ham is beaten, so that the salt penetrates right to the innermost fibers. When enough water has been drawn out of the ham, it is washed, and the part of the meat which is not covered by the natural skin and fat is thickly smeared with a fatty paste of lard, rice flour, and pepper, to prevent it from drying out. Then the ham must mature for a few months, to allow the natural biochemical processes to turn the raw, salted meat into an aromatic Parma ham. By the time it has finished maturing, the weight of the ham will have been reduced by about 15 pounds (7 kilograms). A genuine *prosciutto di Parma* takes 10–12 months to mature, but it can be given even longer, to make it taste even more delicate and refined.

Half of all Parma ham goes for export. As people outside Italy prefer their ham off the bone, the hams are carefully boned, and wrapped in foil to seal in the flavor. The other half of the production is eaten by the Italians themselves. *Prosciutto di Parma* may be served as an *antipasto* with just white bread or grissini, but it can also be served with fresh melon or ripe figs. Of course it also goes well with buttered asparagus. However it is presented, it is always important to slice it very thin, otherwise it will not develop its full flavor.

A hollow horse bone can be used to check how the ham is maturing. It works something like an apple-corer.

During the months when the hams are hung in stores under suitable microclimatic conditions (below), the special flavor develops as a result of natural biochemical processes.

Quality ham should be sliced shortly before being served.

A special consortium monitors the quality of Parma ham.

Fernando Cantarelli is not only a master ham-maker, but
also the enthusiastic owner of the Trattoria Cantarelli in
Samboseto. His customers, who include prominent people,
appreciate the quality of his wares.

CULATELLO

Culatello undoubtedly represents the quintessence of
Parma ham. The whole haunch of the pig is not used
to make this kind of ham, only the heart, the precious
center, which consists of soft, tender muscle meat.
When they are slaughtered in autumn, the pigs, which
have been fed on natural foods like whey, bran, sweet
corn, and barley, must be at least 14 months old, and
weigh over 396 pounds (180 kilograms). The haunches
weigh about 33 pounds (15 kilograms), but more than
two-thirds is cut away, so that a *culatello* tips the scales
at a bare 8.8 pounds (4 kilograms).

Culatello comes originally from Zibello, a small town
near Modena. It is still produced here by hand. The
small, pear-shaped, trimmed "hearts" of the haunch are
first treated with brine, and put into a breathable, intes-
tine-like skin. Then the 14-month drying and maturing process begins. *Culatello* is very tender and has a
pleasantly mild taste. A few wafer-thin slices and a little
bread make a simple but very tasty starter. To increase
the enjoyment, remove the skin, and marinate in wine
for 10 days. Experts are still arguing over whether red
or white wine brings out the flavor best.

Background: Genuine *Culatello di Zibello* has been a
protected trademark since 1996.

BOLOGNA, LA GRASSA

Many Italian cities have a nickname of historical origin, or one which characterizes them very accurately. Venice, which is as serene as it is grand, is known as *La Serenissima*, Genoa is *La Superba*, the proud; the Eternal City is called *Roma l'Eterna*, and Bologna is *Bologna la Dotta* – Bologna the Learned – alluding to the fact that this is the home of Europe's oldest university, founded in 1119. But Bologna has a second nickname, *Bologna la Grassa*. The epithet "fat" may perhaps sound a little negative, but it is a fact that the Bolognese have a preference for the ample and sumptuous cuisine of their native city. They cook according to traditional recipes, and often spend a long time in the kitchen. They are skeptical toward innovations, and consider food prepared according to correct dietary principles unpalatable.

The region makes its living largely from food production. Pasta, Parma ham, Parmesan, cattle and pig rearing, balsamic vinegar, milk, and dairy produce – all of these play a part in the local economy. It is not surprising that the cooks here have unlimited culinary resources to draw on, and they all know how to create imaginative combinations of local specialties. Who else would have come up with the idea of a luxury filling for pasta made of loin of pork, raw ham, and mortadella? According to the Bolognese, tortellini really only earn their name when filled with this mixture. They are served with a rich cream sauce. Substantial pies made of pasta dough are also typical of the area. *Pasticcio di maccheroni* is made of pasta, calf's sweetbreads, cheese, ham, meat, and mushrooms, and is baked in the oven until a crisp crust has formed. The favorite in Bologna is perhaps *Pasticcio di tortellini*, but where pasta is concerned, the whole of Emilia-Romagna is agreed: lasagne is absolutely brilliant.

Bologna may be a paradise for sausages and cheese, but there are plenty of fresh fruit and vegetables to be had in the legendary "food streets" – this is the Via Drapperie.

Bologna's stores do not just offer wonderful specialties (below) – anyone who can manage a few more calories is tempted into the *pasticceria* (above).

BOLOGNAS GASTRONOMIC MILL

Good food is the top priority for the Bolognese. In the 22 miles (35 kilometers) of arcades running through the old part of the city, there are countless little stores selling regional specialties. Near the Church of San Petronio, between the Via Drapperie, the Via Caprarie, and the Via Pescherie, there is a real "food district," where the uninitiated visitor simply does not know which window or which colorful display to admire first. Tamburini's traditional delicatessen impressively demonstrates the Bolognese philosophy of consumption. The store is crammed with every imaginable kind of sausage and cheese, and is full of hustle and bustle. They assure you that they only sell handmade produce, meeting the highest standards of quality, because nothing is more likely to ruin a meal for the Bolognese than inferior products.

Tamburini (founded 1932) is not just a delicatessen, delicious food is also served in their bistro.

Bologna is not only the biggest city in Emilia-Romagna, it is also the oldest. The arcades – these are in the Piazza Santo Stefano – invite you to take a stroll.

Tagliatelle al prosciutto
Tagliatelle with ham

For the dough:
2 1/2 cups/300 g all-purpose flour
3 eggs
1 pinch salt
Flour for sifting

6 oz/150 g Parma ham or smoked ham
3 1/2 tbsp/50 g butter
1 small onion, finely chopped
Salt and freshly milled pepper
3/4 cup/50 g freshly grated parmesan

For the dough, knead all the ingredients into an elastic
dough. Cover with a damp cloth and leave for 30
minutes.
Roll the dough out thin on a floured surface, and cut
into long strips, about ¼ inch/6 mm wide and 4
inches/10 cm long. Boil for about 10 minutes in a large
pan in 12 cups/ 3 liters salted water, until *al dente*.
Chop the ham small, separating the fat from the lean
meat. Melt the butter in a large pan, and lightly sauté the
fatty pieces. Add the onion and sauté until transparent,
then add the lean meat, and sauté while stirring.
Add the well-drained pasta to the pan. Mix very well,
season with salt and pepper, and serve with the freshly
grated parmesan.

Lasagne al forno
Oven-baked lasagna
(Illustrated right)

Serves 6

10 oz/300 g fresh pasta dough (see p 191)
Salt
Olive oil
Ragù alla Bolognese (see below)

For the béchamel sauce:
3 tbsp butter
3 tbsp all-purpose flour
Salt and freshly milled pepper
2 cups/500 ml milk

Butter
1 1/2 cups/100 g freshly grated parmesan

Roll out the dough to a thickness of about ⅛ inch/3mm,
and cut into big, even rectangles. Boil these for 5 minutes in
salted water, to which a few drops of oil have been added.
Remove carefully, and drain on kitchen paper.
Prepare *Ragù alla Bolognese* according to the recipe below.
For the Béchamel sauce, melt 3 tbsp butter in a saucepan,
and stir in the flour. Remove from the heat, and add salt
and pepper. Gradually pour over the milk, and mix in. Bring
to a boil, stirring continuously, and simmer for 5 minutes.
Grease the inside of an ovenproof dish with butter. Cover
the base with a layer of lasagne, and cover evenly with
béchamel sauce. Then spread with a layer of *ragù alla Bolognese* and sprinkle with parmesan. Then add another layer of
lasagne, and continue in this way until all the ingredients
have been used, ending with a layer of béchamel sauce,
sprinkled with freshly grated parmesan. Decorate with small
knobs of butter. Bake in a preheated oven for about 20
minutes at 400 °F (200 °C).

Ragù alla Bolognese
Bolognese meat sauce
(Illustrated below)

1 onion
1 small carrot
1 stick celery
4 oz/100 g belly pork
1/2 lb/200 g ground beef
3 tbsp extra virgin olive oil
1 small glass white wine
1 cup/200g tomato purée
2 tbsp tomato paste
Oregano
Salt and pepper
1 cup meat stock

Chop the onion, carrot, and celery, dice the belly pork
small, and fry slowly with the ground beef in the olive oil.
Pour over the white wine and stir well. Add the tomato
purée and tomato paste, and season with oregano, salt, and
pepper. Pour over a little meat stock, and simmer for at least
1 hour over a very low heat.
In Bologna there are almost as many variations on this classic sauce as there are households; for instance,
a favorite addition is chopped chicken
livers. It is important to simmer all
the ingredients for a long time,
because that is what gives
the sauce its strong flavor.

Salama da sugo

This sausage for cooking is a specialty from Ferrara. The meat consists of pig's liver and tongue, wrapped in a coating of ground neck of pork, fat bacon, and pig's head, all stuffed into a pig's bladder. It is seasoned with salt, pepper, cloves, and cinnamon, and sometimes with other herbs as well. Depending on the method of preparation, *salama* may be marinated for a few days in red wine – Sangiovese is best – then it is hung to dry, and takes about a year to mature. Many butchers sprinkle them with ashes, others keep pouring over a marinade of oil and vinegar. *Salama* is cooked before being eaten, so that the delicious juice, the *sugo*, which gives the sausage its name, runs out.

Cappello del prete oder Cappelletto

There is a lot of meat left over from the preparation of *culatella*, the much sought-after little ham from the heart of the pig's haunch, but it is not thrown away; it is chopped and stuffed into the skin from the top of a leg of pork. When this is sewn together, the sausage acquires its characteristic triangular shape, which is reminiscent of a priest's hat, which gives it its name. *Cappello del prete* must be cooked for two hours and, like *cotechino*, it may be served with lentils.

Mortadella

Mortadella, a true child of Bologna, and actually known as *bologna* outside the city, must surely count as one of the most famous Italian specialties. Nowadays it is no longer exclusively produced in the provinces of Parma and Bologna, but also in many other regions.

Mortadella consists of ground pork meat and long strips of fat, which give it the typical mosaic appearance. The pork can be mixed with other kinds of meat, such as beef, veal, donkey, and horse. Sometimes organ meat, pork rind, or sweetbreads are added to the sausage meat. In addition, every butcher has his own secret recipe for the mixture of herbs, which gives mortadella its incomparable taste. Depending on the quality, it may be further refined with wine, garlic, peppercorns, or pistachios. The sausage meat is put into artificial skins, then cooked very slowly and carefully. The sausages may weigh anything between one pound (½ kilogram) and 220 pounds (100 kilograms). Mortadella should be sliced very thin – otherwise the full flavor does not come out – and eaten soon after.

Cotechino

Cotechino is a specialty from Modena. It consists of pork rind (*cotica*), lean pork, other parts of the pig, fat, and seasonings. During cooking, the pork rind turns into a gelatinous mass, which gives the sausage a slightly sticky consistency, but also an incomparable taste. *Cotechino* is not only a favorite in Emilia-Romagna, where it is served with lentils and sauerkraut, it is also an essential ingredient of the Piedmontese *bollito misto*.

Coppa

This delicacy is made from the muscular part of the pig's neck, which is cured in brine for 10–18 days, then stuffed into a cow's intestine. *Coppa* has to mature for about six months, then it is wrapped for storage in a cloth soaked in white wine. *Coppa* should be sliced thin and, with a little bread, it makes a delicious *antipasto*.

Pancetta

Pancetta is the fatty bacon from the belly of the pig (*pancia*). It exists in fresh, smoked, or dried form, and is flavored with seasonings like pepper, cloves, cinnamon, nutmeg, and juniper berries.

Salsiccia

This classic fresh sausage is made from good pork or beef, mixed with bacon from the breast or belly. *Salsiccia* is seasoned in different ways, depending on the region. In Bologna it is flavored with salt, pepper, cinnamon, and a pinch of saltpeter.

Zampone

Stuffed pig trotters are a true specialty of Emilia-Romagna. The stuffing consists of the leg meat, other ground parts of the pig, and various herbs. It is cooked for several hours before serving. It is often served with lentils, but is also good with a *zabaione cotta*.

Bologna is nicknamed *la Grassa*, the fat. A glimpse of the shelves laden with sausages and cheese in one of the specialist shops gives you a clue as to why.

Fave stufate
Beans with mortadella

2 ONIONS
1 OZ/25 G RENDERED FAT BACON OR SHORTENING
2 LBS/1 KG FRESH BROAD BEANS
SALT AND FRESHLY MILLED BLACK PEPPER
2 OZ/50 G MORTADELLA
1 CUP/250 ML CHICKEN STOCK
6 1/2TBSP/100 G BUTTER
4–6 SLICES STALE BREAD

Peel the onions and cut in rings. Heat the bacon or shortening in a casserole, and sauté the onions in it for 5
minutes. Shell the beans, add to the casserole, and season
with salt and pepper.
Dice the mortadella finely and add to the beans. Pour over
the chicken stock, cover, and simmer for about 20 minutes,
until the beans are soft.
Heat the butter in a large pan, and fry the bread slices
golden brown on both sides. Arrange the bread on a
prewarmed plate, and divide the bean mixture among them.

Stufato d'agnello
Lamb stew

1 3/4 LBS/800 G BONED LAMB (SHOULDER OR LEG)
2 TBSP/30 G BUTTER
2 ONIONS, FINELY CHOPPED
4 LARGE POTATOES
3 CARROTS
MEAT STOCK
12 SMALL POTATOES
2 TBSP CHOPPED PARSLEY
BALSAMIC VINEGAR

Carefully clean the lamb, and cut into small pieces. Heat the
butter in a pan, and sauté the onions. Add the meat, and
brown well.
Peel the large potatoes and dice small, slice the carrots, add
both to the meat, and sauté, stirring continuously. Cover the
meat with stock, and allow to boil, then simmer over a low
heat. Wash and peel the smaller potatoes, and add to the pan
after 1 hour.
As soon as they are soft, remove the pan from the heat.
Ladle the lamb stew onto plates, sprinkle with parsley, and
drizzle a little balsamic vinegar over each portion.

Rognoni alla parmigiana
Kidneys Parma style
(Illustrated right)

1 LB/500 G VEAL KIDNEYS
1 TBSP/15 G BUTTER
2 TBSP OLIVE OIL
1 CLOVE GARLIC, FINELY CHOPPED
2 TBSP CHOPPED PARSLEY
SALT
JUICE OF 1 LEMON

Soak the kidneys for several hours, so that they lose their
strong characteristic taste. Drain well, and cut in thin slices.
Heat the butter and oil in a pan, and sauté the garlic with
half the parsley. Add the sliced kidneys, brown well, and add
salt. Remove after 5 minutes, drizzle over the lemon juice,
and sprinkle with parsley. Serve with roasted potatoes.

Cotechino in galera
Stuffed steak

1 1/2 LBS/700 G COTECHINO
1 SLICE BEEF TOPSIDE, WEIGHING ABOUT 1 LB/500 G
2 LARGE SLICES BOILED OR SMOKED HAM
4 TBSP OLIVE OIL
1 ONION, CHOPPED
1 CUP/250 ML RED WINE
1 CUP/250 ML BEEF STOCK
SALT AND FRESHLY MILLED BLACK PEPPER

Prick the sausage several times, wrap in a cloth, cover
completely with water in a large pan, and simmer gently for
1 hour. Remove, drain, remove the cloth, skin the sausage,
and allow to cool. Beat the steak flat, lay the slices of ham
side by side on top of it, and place the *cotechino* in the middle.
Roll it all up, and tie around with plenty of kitchen string.
Heat the oil in a casserole, add the onions, and sauté for
5 minutes. Then add the meat roll, and brown evenly on all
sides. Pour over the wine and meat stock, season with salt
and pepper, cover, and cook until the meat is tender.
Remove the string, and carefully slice the meat. Arrange on
a prewarmed plate, pour over the pan juices, and serve
immediately.

Zampone e lenticchie
Pig trotters with lentils
(Illustrated above)

Serves 4–6

1 PRECOOKED PIG TROTTER, WEIGHING ABOUT 2 LBS/1 KG OR 2
SMALL ONES, ABOUT 1LB/500 G EACH
1 1/2 CUPS/300 G CASTELLUCCIO LENTILS
4–5 SAGE LEAVES
1 SPRIG ROSEMARY
A FEW CELERY LEAVES
2 CLOVES GARLIC, PEELED
2 SUN-DRIED TOMATO HALVES
1 SMALL PEPERONCINO
3 TBSP EXTRA VIRGIN OLIVE OIL
SALT AND PEPPER

Put the precooked pig trotter in a pan of cold water and
bring to a boil, then reduce the heat and simmer for 20
minutes. (Follow the instructions on the packaging if different from the above.) At the same time, put the lentils, herbs,
celery leaves, garlic, tomatoes, and peperoncino in cold
water, bring to a boil, and simmer for 20 minutes until
tender. Remove the herbs and the garlic cloves. Add olive
oil, and season with salt and pepper.
Slice the cooked trotter and mix with the lentils.
A heavy, stuffed fresh pig trotter may be substituted for
the precooked one. A fresh trotter must be simmered for
3–4 hours.

CHRISTOFORO DA MESSISBUGO

Table manners at the end of the Middle Ages were appalling. Everyone ate out of the same pot. Meat was served in one large chunk, from which everyone present cut a piece for themselves. Poultry was not carved up before being put on the table, and people pulled even birds as big as pheasants apart with their hands. In the 16th century, Christoforo da Messisbugo from Ferrara put an end to this unappetizing business. Messisbugo began his career as chief tailor and steward at the court of the d'Este family, who ruled over his native city at the time. If pieces of food were too large, he did not just cut them straight through the middle. During his years of service, he developed such a refined art of carving that in 1533 the emperor Charles V raised him to the rank of Count Palatine, by way of thanks. Before the eyes of the amazed princes and their guests, Messisbugo carved roasts and other foods so expertly that he never touched them with his fingers, but only with the knives and forks that had been provided for that purpose.

As steward, his duties also included running the estates, organizing receptions and banquets, and overseeing an army of servants, whose job it was on such occasions to hand round drinks and towels, bring in and clear away courses, wipe up spilt food discreetly, or watch over the buffet. In addition, he had to see that the table decorations met the esthetic demands of the indulged nobles, and choose the wines and the food.

The d'Este court was the home of the finest manners and exquisite culinary delights. A banquet was no longer what it had been in the Middle Ages, simply a demonstration of power and wealth, but an entertaining work of art which would appeal to more than just the palate. Acrobats, interludes of music and songs, artistic performances, and poetry readings entertained the guests, while the tables, decked with lace, silver, and Florentine porcelain, buckled under the weight of the delicacies. A menu of 120 courses was not unusual in Ferrara.

Christoforo da Messisbugo recorded his knowledge in a book. In "Banquets, Arrangements for Food and Drink, and Organization in General" he gives valuable

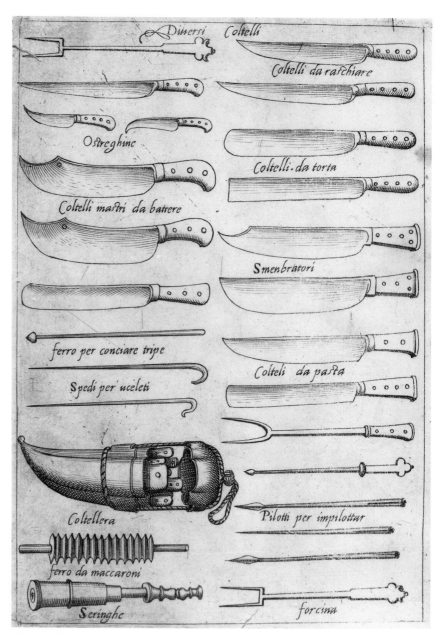

Before the 16th century, eating with knives and forks was not usual. At most, there would be a spoon for the soup.

With the introduction of more refined table manners, the different types of cutlery soon reached the kitchen.

tips about courtly banquets. The section on recipes for pasta, puddings, soups, egg dishes, fish and meat courses includes traditional recipes from the region, but also mentions specialties from Milan, Florence, Naples, Sicily, and Venice, and even from other countries. Published in Ferrara between 1529 and 1548, the work was constantly in print until 1600, and spread the new philosophy of eating as a mental and spiritual pleasure to other European courts.

Jewish cuisine in Ferrara

The fate and history of the city of Ferrara have often been influenced by its large Jewish community, and the same is true of its cuisine. Jewish rules on food handling, and the religious teaching that God should be respected as the sole provider of all food, resulted in the creation of very special dishes, which tasted so good that they were enjoyed not only by the Orthodox Jews of Ferrara, but also by their Christian neighbors. Messisbugo's banquet book also contains evidence of the relevance of Jewish eating customs, as there is a separate section entitled "Jewish Meat Dishes."

Hamim
Brisket of beef with meatballs
(Illustrated in background)

3 LBS/1.5 KG SWISS CHARD
EXTRA VIRGIN OLIVE OIL
3 1/2 CUPS/700 G CANELLINI BEANS
2 LBS/1 KG BRISKET OF BEEF
2 SAUSAGES
2 EGGS
1 CUP/50 G BREADCRUMBS
2 CUPS/500 G LEAN GROUND BEEF
SALT AND PEPPER
2 HARD-BOILED EGGS

Sauté the Swiss chard in a non-stick pan with a little olive oil. Put the beans in a casserole with a little water and some olive oil and simmer over a low heat. After 1 hour, add the Swiss chard, brisket of beef, and sausages, cover and simmer over a very low heat for about 4 hours. Beat the eggs and add, with the breadcrumbs, to the ground beef. Mix well, and season with salt and pepper. Shape the mixture into little balls about the size of a walnut, and boil in water with a little olive oil. As soon as the meatballs are cooked, add to the pan with the Swiss chard. Slice the beef, and decorate with thin slices of hard-boiled egg. Serve with the Swiss chard and meatballs.

Burriche
Filled puff pastries

4 SLICES BREAD
1 CUP MEAT STOCK
10 OZ/300 G CHICKEN
1 ONION
2 TBSP/30 G GOOSE FAT OR EXTRA VIRGIN OLIVE OIL
1 EGG
SALT AND PEPPER
10 OZ/300 G PUFF PASTRY

Soak the bread slices in the meat stock. Cut the chicken meat in small pieces. Chop the onion, and sauté in the goose fat. Add the chicken, salt and pepper, and sauté over a low heat. If necessary, add a little water or stock. Remove the pan from the heat, add the soaked bread and the egg to the chicken, and mix well. Allow to cool, then chop finely or put through a food processor. Season with salt and pepper.
Roll out the puff pastry, not too thin, and cut circles about 4 inches/10 cm diameter. Put a spoonful of filling in the middle, and fold over the dough to form half-moons. Press the edges together firmly. Place in a greased, ovenproof dish, and bake in a preheated oven for about 30 minutes at 300 °F (150 °C).

VALLI DI COMACCHIO

The Valli di Comacchio, one of the biggest lagoons in Italy, once covered an impressive 1550 square miles (400,000 hectares). The draining of the marshes provided fertile agricultural land, but a large part of the even more productive fishing grounds were lost. Fishing still continues in the remaining 50 square miles (13,000 hectares), and the little fishing town of Comacchio has managed to retain some of its charm. A few fishermen actually still live in their *casoni*, the simple fisherman's huts, built in the middle of the lagoon on artificial mounds of earth or quite simply on stilts. Rising out of the water alongside the *casoni* are the primitive looking but actually very efficient constructions of nets and poles with which they catch the fish. The *lavoriero*, which has remained unchanged for hundreds of years, consists of a pointed fish-trap, in which eels are caught in a funnel-shaped basket as they migrate out to sea in the autumn.

Sea-bass, flounders, shrimp, crabs, mullet, and, above all, eels live in the brackish waters of the Valli. Nowhere else, so the fishermen say, can you catch such big eels as here. The long, thin fish, which live in both fresh and salt water, are born in the Sargasso Sea, that part of the Atlantic Ocean which lies between the Antilles and the Azores. They are brought to Europe by the Gulf Stream, and settle in the lakes and estuaries, where they remain for 7, 10, or even 12 years, before they return to their birthplace to spawn – and to die.

The young elvers, which have only just reached European waters, are called "glass eels." They are usually caught out at sea. In Italy, they are known as *cieche*, because they are virtually blind to the fishermen's nets. But not all the young eels are caught immediately. In the Comacchio Lagoon the fishermen wait until the fish have reached the brackish waters, then they close off the eel-ponds with special metal barriers. The eels are not caught until they have put on enough weight.

As eels are a popular food all over Italy, there are many regional recipes. The fish may be grilled, fried, braised, or cooked in sauce. It is not only in Emilia-Romagna that a splendid *capitone*, a yard-long, adult female eel, is considered a classic Christmas fish. They are also prized in the capital Rome, and in the southern regions.

The fishing technique is simple, but is technically controlled. First the net must be brought to the surface of the water.

The fisherman takes his catch from the area of the sea that is fenced off by the frame of the net with a special landing net.

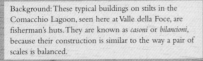
Background: These typical buildings on stilts in the Comacchio Lagoon, seen here at Valle della Foce, are fisherman's huts. They are known as *casoni* or *bilancioni*, because their construction is similar to the way a pair of scales is balanced.

Eels and mullet are often caught in the brackish waters. The freshly caught fish are used to make the regional fish specialties.

A visit to the Valli di Comacchio is not only worthwhile from the culinary point of view. Part of the lagoon has now been declared a nature reserve. Bird-watching enthusiasts can observe over 200 species of birds, including snipe, terns, herons, and storks, which rest here on their way north. Six families of storks and a small flamingo colony seem to like it so much in the Valli that they stay here all year, instead of migrating south with their fellows. The recently opened Museo delle Valli is also worth noting. From spring to autumn it can be visited by boat from the rail station at Foce – 20 minutes from Comacchio by automobile – and has exhibits on the traditional *casoni* and fishing equipment.

Anguilla dei casoni di valle
Eels in wine broth

2 ONIONS, CHOPPED
1 CARROT, DICED
SALT
2 CUPS/500 ML RED WINE
2 EELS, EACH WEIGHING 1 1/4 LB/600 G
3 TOMATOES, SKINNED, SEEDED, AND DICED
1 TBSP WINE VINEGAR
PEPPER
PARSLEY

Bring onions and carrot to the boil in a pan with a pinch of salt, the red wine, and 2 cups/500 ml water. Gut and clean the eels, remove the heads and tails, and cut in pieces about 4 inches/10 cm long. Alternate layers of eel with the cooked vegetables in an ovenproof dish (preferably terra cotta). Add salt and pepper, and pour over the wine/vegetable stock. Bake in a preheated oven for about 45 minutes at 300 °F (150 °C). Shortly before the eels are ready, add the diced tomatoes and wine vinegar, and sprinkle with parsley. Serve with polenta.

ADRIATIC PARADISE

Coastal resorts like Cervia, Cesenatico, Rimini, Riccione, or Catolica make you think of tourists, suntan oil, and too much clubbing at night. Today, the coastal area of Emilia-Romagna is once again enjoying unfailing popularity among swimmers and pleasure-seekers from all countries, now that the algae plague of 1989 has been forgotten. It all began so innocently. When a certain Count Baldini opened a bathing establishment on July 30th 1843 on the beach at Rimini, which at that time still belonged to the austere Vatican State, a cardinal sprinkled six bathing huts with holy water. One hundred and fifty years later, Rimini had become a center for the permissive beach lifestyle. Not many of the visitors knew that Rimini and the surrounding area were also excellent places for good food. All along the Adriatic, they have traditionally served a wide variety of fish dishes. Ravenna and Cervia offer an attractive seaside cuisine, which is quite different from the tradition of heavy, sumptuous cooking typical of other places in Emilia-Romagna. In Rimini you absolutely must try *brodetto*, the delicious fish soup, with which Julius Caesar is supposed to have fortified himself on his march to Rome, after having crossed the Rubicon a little further north, with the oft-quoted words *alea iacta est* (the die is cast).

From spring through to autumn, the coast of Emilia-Romagna with its wide sandy beaches, seen here at Lignano Sabbiadoro, attracts hordes of sunseekers in need of a vacation by the sea.

THE MODERN FOOD INDUSTRY

The food industry has long since begun to make inroads into Italian kitchens, both private and professional. In their hectic everyday lives, Italian housewives are happy to fall back on ready-made products from time to time. The most traditional example of this is *pasta secca*, which is available in all varieties and saves the time and effort spent preparing the pasta dough. Barilla, Buitoni, and other manufacturers answer every need with regard to pasta. *Pomodori pelati*, bright red, peeled, canned tomatoes, are also always used in the north, which is short on sunlight, and therefore also on tomatoes. The time and effort spent stirring polenta can be avoided by using instant polenta, grated cheese can be bought in packs, and the manufacturers even take account of regional tastes. For the Piedmontese and Valdaostans there is a canned cheese mixture for *fonduta*, which only needs to be heated up and never goes lumpy, and in Valtellina they sell *pizzoccheri*, the famous buckwheat noodles, in cardboard boxes.

But in Italy, unlike other European countries, the use of ready-made products has not automatically led to the collapse of culinary traditions. That is because people here still cling firmly to the traditional menu, and ready-made pasta or sauce from a jar is not considered to be the same as homemade sauce, but as a kind of temporary substitute. Whenever possible they will schedule plenty of time for going to the market and for cooking, make fresh pasta instead of *pasta secca*, serve homemade specialties, and they will certainly not be content to round off the meal with a dessert out of the freezer.

The high regard in which Italian cooks, both professional and amateur, hold their food and the value consumers still attach to eating and drinking are responsible for the fact that Italian factory products are on average of better quality and tastier than their European rivals. So there are a number of small and medium-sized businesses, which take great care to manufacture products that are so good they could almost pass for homemade.

Modena, for instance, is the home of the famous firm of Fini AG. From its factory on the outskirts of the city come, among other things, tortelli, tortellini, tortelloni, sausages such as mortadella and *zampone*, a balsamic vinegar which is mass-produced, but extremely tasty, as well as the famous walnut liqueur Nocino, which is hardly ever made by urban families at home any more. Fini AG also runs a chain of freeway restaurants, owns one of the best hotels in town, as well as the famous Restaurant Fini – the place where it all began.

In 1912 Telesforo and Giuditta Fini opened a small restaurant in the back room of a sausage store, with just six old walnut tables. Giuditta created a wonderful pasta dish, *Maltagliati e fagioli*, which turned out to be a winner. The selection was soon enlarged with other dishes such as tortellini, *bollito misto*, braised meat, and inimitable *antipasti*, and the premises were gradually extended. The restaurant acquired such a good reputation, that stars from Hollywood and Cinecittà flocked in, whenever they were staying in Modena.

The firm of Fini offers a wide range of ready-made regional specialties such as *zampone*.

Right: Head waiter Illiano Bulgarelli recommends fresh *bollito misto*, which the customers assemble for themselves.

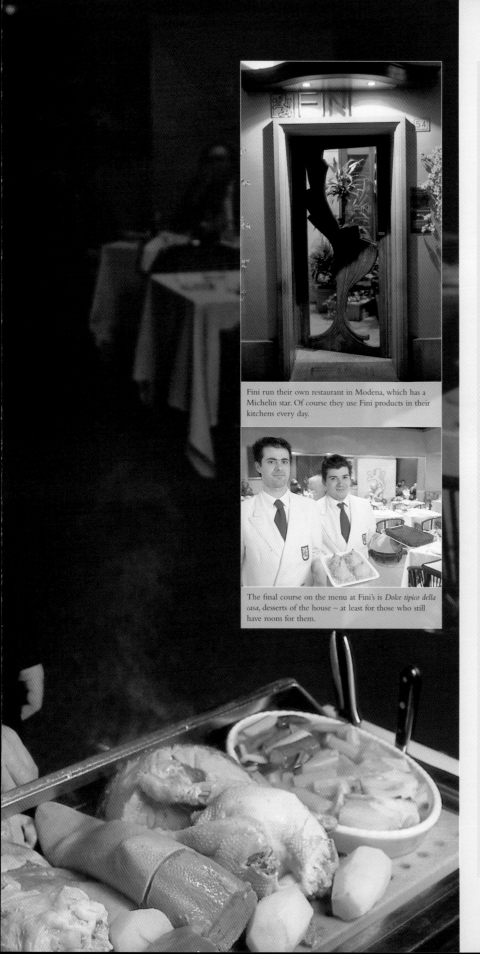

Fini run their own restaurant in Modena, which has a Michelin star. Of course they use Fini products in their kitchens every day.

The final course on the menu at Fini's is *Dolce tipico della casa*, desserts of the house – at least for those who still have room for them.

Nocino

Along with Campania, Emilia-Romagna is the biggest producer of walnuts in Italy. The whole family is involved in gathering the nuts from the trees at harvest time in September and October. But they do not only use the ripe walnuts – the young, green fruits are made into a highly alcoholic specialty, known as Nocino. Nowadays Nocino is made almost all over Italy, and is often mass-produced. In the area around Modena, where this walnut liqueur was apparently invented, the farmers occasionally still make it at home.

The unripe fruits are traditionally gathered around St. John's Day, June 24. The nuts are cleaned and quartered, put into rounded glass bottles with a mixture of alcohol, sugar, cinnamon, and cloves, and finally left to stand for about 40 days in a warm, sunny place. The liquid gradually seeps into the nuts and turns dark brown. Lastly more sugar and spices are added, and – if it has become too strong – the liquid is diluted with a little water. The result is a delicious and highly effective digestif, or so those who drink it would have you believe.

Once a year in Modena a self-appointed commission of private producers of Nocino meets to award a prize to the best liqueur. The committee is made up of housewives, who test each competing product in turn, and choose the Nocino of the year. The fact that it is not taken too seriously might, of course, have something to do with the relatively high alcohol content of the homemade elixir.

DESSERTS

The name *Zuppa inglese* sounds British, but in fact it is a traditional Italian dessert. This sweet was served to the Duke of Correggio in Siena as long ago as 1552. He had been sent to the home of the Palio by Cosimo de' Medici, to negotiate the handing over of the Spaniards, who had been held captive in the fortress by the troops of Enea Piccolomini. *Zuppa inglese* was known at the Medici court in Florence, and was served at important banquets. In the 19th century, this dessert also delighted the palates of the many English people, who lived in what was then the capital of Italy, and that is how it got its name.

Bensone is traditionally served at breakfast. In the Parma area, this cake is known as *bosilan*, around Piacenza it is called *bissolan*, in Reggio Emilia *buccellato*, and in Modena *bensone*.

Zuppa inglese
Trifle
(Illustrated below)

1 1/2 CUPS/350 ML MILK
1/4 TSP VANILLA EXTRACT
4 EGG YOLKS
1/2 CUP/100 G SUGAR
SCANT 1/2 CUP/50 G ALL-PURPOSE FLOUR
SALT
3 1/2 TBSP/50 ML PREFERRED LIQUEUR
24–30/400 G LADYFINGERS
MINT LEAVES

Heat the milk with the vanilla extract and leave for 30 minutes. Stir the sugar into the egg yolks until it has dissolved. Mix the flour with a pinch of salt. Heat the egg mixture and add the milk, a little at a time, stirring continuously, until the custard thickens.
Dilute the liqueur with a little water, and drizzle over the biscuits. In a mold, alternate layers of custard and biscuits. Leave in a cool place for about 2 hours, and decorate with the mint leaves.

Bensone
Breakfast cake

GENEROUS 4 CUPS/500 G ALL-PURPOSE FLOUR
2/3 CUP/150 ML MILK
1 CUP/200 G SUGAR
6 1/2 TBSP/100 G BUTTER
2 EGGS
GRATED RIND OF 1 LEMON
SALT
5 LEVEL TSP BAKING POWDER
VANILLA SUGAR (SUGAR KEPT IN A JAR WITH A VANILLA POD)

Mix the flour with the lukewarm milk, sugar, melted butter, eggs, lemon rind, and a pinch of salt, and work into a dough. Mix in the baking powder, and leave to stand. Place the dough in a baking pan (preferably a ring shaped mold) and bake in a preheated oven for about 50 minutes at 350 °F (175 °C). Sprinkle with vanilla sugar before serving.

Torta Barozzi o Torta nera
Barozzi tart or black tart

For the filling:
1 1/2 CUPS/200 G SHELLED ALMONDS
4 EGGS
GENEROUS 1/2 CUP/120 G SUGAR
7/8 CUP/100 G COCOA POWDER
3 TBSP COFFEE POWDER
GRATED RIND OF 1 LEMON
GENEROUS 1/2 CUP/150 ML SASSOLINO LIQUEUR

For the dough:
1 1/4 CUPS/150 G ALL-PURPOSE FLOUR
10 TBSP/150 G BUTTER
1/3 CUP/70 G SUGAR
1 EGG
SALT

For the filling, toast the almonds and chop finely. Separate the eggs. Beat the egg whites until stiff. Beat the yolks and sugar until frothy. Gradually add cocoa and coffee powder, then the lemon rind and sassolino, and mix well. Fold in the egg whites and leave to stand.
For the dough, knead all the ingredients together and leave for 15 minutes. Cover the base and sides of a greased springform pan with the rolled out pastry. The pastry should come a little above the edge of the mold. Pour in the almond mixture, and fold over the pastry edge onto the filling. Bake in a preheated oven for about 40 minutes at 360 °F (180 °C).

DELICIOUS FRUITS

Emilia-Romagna is a paradise for fruit. Apples, pears, cherries, plums, peaches, apricots, strawberries, and walnuts all grow here, along with many more. In Italy fruit is traditionally served as a refreshing dessert at the end of a substantial meal. The fruits may be served whole or in a fruit salad. *Macedonia di frutta* is made with new combinations of fruit all the time – depending on what is ripe and what the colorful market stalls have to offer on the day.

This fruit salad is extremely simple to prepare. You cut the fruit in bite-size pieces, and drizzle over a dressing made of orange and lemon juice, sugar, and maybe a shot of liqueur – preferably maraschino. In winter, when fresh fruit is less common, a *macedonia* can be made from stewed fruit, such as preserved peaches, fruits of the forest, and pears. In either case it is important to allow the fruit salad to rest for a short while before being served – protected by foil to prevent the fruit from spoiling – so that the flavors of the individual fruits can combine. In any case, it should never be kept for too long, otherwise the fruit will begin to ferment. A *macedonia* should be served chilled, but not frozen. Ideal accompaniments are wafers, cookies, and ice cream. A glass of liqueur or a dessert wine tastes good with it too.

MACEDONIA DI NATALE
Christmas fruit salad
(Illustrated above)

1 LB/500 G MIXED DRIED FRUIT (PEACHES, PLUMS, APRICOTS, PINEAPPLE, FIGS, ETC.)
4/5 CUP/200ML SWEET WHITE WINE
2 CUPS/500 ML WATER
1 1/2 CUPS/300 G SUGAR
PEEL OF 1 LEMON
PEEL OF 1/2 ORANGE
4 CLOVES

Soak the dried fruit in a bowl with the white wine and water for half a day. Remove the fruit from the liquid and keep separate. Pour the liquid into a casserole and add sugar, lemon and orange peel, and cloves. Bring to the boil, stirring slowly. Add the fruit and cook over a medium heat until it is soft. Allow the fruit salad to cool, and remove the cloves, lemon and orange peel. Serve in glass dishes and sprinkle with chopped nuts.

CERAMICS FROM FAENZA

The revolution in table manners at the courts of the Italian renaissance princes inevitably led to an ever-increasing demand for plates, cups, bowls, and dishes. Fortunately, the town of Faenza, to the southeast of Bologna, had been specializing in the production of glazed ceramics since the 15th century, so the courts of Ferrara and Mantua were regularly supplied with the necessary tableware. Luckily it did not have far to travel either, since coach journeys and other means of transport are the natural enemies of delicate china.

Ceramics from Faenza soon became well known outside the region. As a reminder of their origins, they were christened "Faience." Faience is made from white-glazed earthenware, which is then painted. The technique originated in the Near East, where glazed earthenware was already in use in pre-Christian times. Faience was brought to Spain by the Moors in the 14th century, though it was known there as majolica, because Majorca was the main trading center for this colorful pottery produced in the Iberian Peninsula. In Italy they had already become acquainted with Turkish faience through trade with the Levant. Now the craftsmen studied what was produced in Spain as well and perfected the production methods, first in Faenza and later in Florence. Today the International Ceramic Museum reminds us of Faenza's worldwide reputation as the home of glazed earthenware. Faience from Faenza is exhibited alongside other majolica from the Italian renaissance, and an annual art pottery competition is also held each summer.

The decoration of this modern service from Faenza looks back to traditional designs.

SEMIFREDDO
Ice-cold layer cake

Serves 8–10

For the cake base:
2 CUPS/250 G SHELLED ALMONDS
1 1/2 CUPS/150 G CONFECTIONERS' SUGAR
2 EGG WHITES

For the filling:
3 EGGS, AT ROOM TEMPERATURE
1 CUP/200 G BUTTER
1/2 CUP/60 G CONFECTIONERS' SUGAR
GENEROUS TBSP/20 ML BRANDY
1/2 CUP/125 ML STRONG, COLD BLACK COFFEE
6 OZ/150 G DARK CHOCOLATE
3 TBSP FLAKED ALMONDS

For the cake base, grind the shelled almonds very finely, and mix with the confectioners' sugar. Beat the egg whites until stiff, and fold into the almonds. Divide the paste into 3 portions. Roll out each portion thinly between clear plastic film to fit a 9-in. (24-cm) diameter springform pan. Bake the three rounds one after the other on the middle shelf of a preheated oven for 10–15 minutes at 300 °F (150 °C). Allow to cool.

For the filling, separate the eggs, and beat the whites until stiff. Beat the yolks with the butter and confectioners' sugar until frothy. Fold in the whites, a tablespoonful at a time. Mix the brandy with the coffee. Soak one of the cake layers with one third of the coffee and brandy mixture, and spread one third of the filling over the base. Grate the chocolate, and sprinkle half over the filling. Repeat the process with the next layer, finishing with the remainder of the chocolate. Place the third round on the top, pour over the remaining coffee and brandy, and spread with the remaining filling. Cover, and leave to rest in the refrigerator for 4–5 hours. Sprinkle with flaked almonds before serving.

ACETO BALSAMICO

Siroppo acetoso was known as long ago as the Middle Ages. This was syrup which had fermented into vinegar, which at that time was not only sold by grocers as a culinary flavoring, but also by apothecaries as a pharmaceutical product. Noble families like the d'Estes were proud to own their own *acetaia*, a loft where vinegar barrels with their precious contents stood in rows. In the early 17th century, aristocratic circles in Modena were discussing a tincture described as *balsamico*, which was apparently capable of bringing the dead back to life. Of course, this is to be taken with a pinch of salt, but the description is aiming in the right direction. Anyone who has had the pleasure of tasting genuine *aceto balsamico tradizionale* in all its rich harmony of sweetness, sourness, velvety smoothness, and piquancy, can imagine that just a few drops can give fish, salad, meat, and cheese an undreamed of richness of taste, and really "bring them to life."

While white or red wine is the raw material for every other kind of vinegar, the first stage in the production of balsamic vinegar is making must from white Trebbiano grapes from Modena or Reggio Emilia. The must is carefully heated and concentrated, until it turns into a dark brown syrup. This grape juice is then mixed with old wine vinegar to start the fermentation process. Balsamic vinegar is not made in cool, temperature-controlled cellars, but in creaking lofts, which are ice cold in winter, stifling hot in summer, and damp during the spring rains or the autumn mists. Balsamic

Historical representation of a medieval apothecary's shop, selling vinegar syrup. Miniature from the manuscript *Tacuinum Sanitatis*, Italian, end 14th century. Nationalbibliothek, Vienna.

Balsamic vinegar begins its career in a big barrel. Over the years its volume is continually reduced by evaporation. Highly concentrated vinegar is stored in barrels holding 2½–4 gallons (10–15 liters).

vinegar needs these apparently unfavorable climatic conditions to keep reducing its volume (10 gallons of must produce only a couple of pints of the precious vinegar), to mature, and to develop its flavor. It takes about 3 years to complete its two fermentations. First it goes through the alcohol fermentation, where the sugar in the must is turned into alcohol. Only when that has been completed can the vinegar bacteria convert the alcohol to vinegar. But the vinegar is far from being mature, when these three years are up. A good balsamic vinegar takes at least 12 years, but after 30 or even 50 years it is better still! In the vinegar loft, which is known as an *acetaia*, there is always a whole row of different-sized barrels made of various woods. Balsamic vinegar does not mature in a single barrel, but acquires its taste and character from a whole family of vinegars. At the end of the row stands the smallest barrel, which often has a volume of no more than 2½–4 gallons (10–15 liters). The mature balsamic vinegar is drawn off in small portions. The quantity which has been removed is replaced by the same amount of the second oldest vinegar from the second smallest barrel. The second smallest barrel is topped up with vinegar from the third smallest, and so on. The sediment and the vinegar mother found in the barrels, which are sometimes very old, are the most treasured

possessions of the producers of balsamic vinegar, but the wood of the barrels also plays an important part. Ash and oak are used for the smallest barrels, chestnut and cherry for the middle sizes, and the young vinegar matures best in barrels made of mulberry wood. Every producer has his own opinion on the subject, but the ingredients that are added at various stages include cinnamon, cloves, mace, coriander, and liquorice.

Nowadays balsamic vinegar is also made in factories, which sometimes achieve quite acceptable results, which are also much cheaper to buy than the handmade version, with its long maturing time. However, very cheap offers should be avoided, as they are probably nothing more than ordinary wine vinegar which has been done up to look like balsamic vinegar by adding a few spices and a little caramel coloring. Genuine balsamic vinegar can be recognized firstly by its price, secondly by the minute bottles, and thirdly by its official declaration *aceto balsamico tradizionale di Modena* or *aceto balsamico tradizionale di Reggio Emilia*. The consortium in Modena has been in existence since 1987 and has 270 members who are permitted to add the crucial word *tradizionale* to their labels. The description *tradizionale di Reggio Emilia* is also legally protected.

Carpaccio all'aceto balsamico
Carpaccio of beef with balsamic vinegar

BALSAMIC VINEGAR
13 OZ/600 G FILLET OF BEEF, SLICED WAFER THIN
SALT AND FRESHLY MILLED PEPPER
3/4 CUP/100 G SPRING VEGETABLES, CHOPPED
1/4 LB/100 G ARUGULA, CHOPPED
3–4 TBSP EXTRA VIRGIN OLIVE OIL

Brush a large serving dish with balsamic vinegar and arrange the wafer thin slices of beef on it so that they do not overlap. Lightly salt, and sprinkle with pepper, decorate with spring vegetables and arugula, and drizzle over balsamic vinegar. Leave for at least 15 minutes in a cool place. Then drizzle over olive oil, and leave for a further 15 minutes before serving.

Salsa di pomodoro
Tomato sauce

6 FULLY RIPE TOMATOES
4 TBSP EXTRA VIRGIN OLIVE OIL
2 SAGE LEAVES
1 TBSP BALSAMIC VINEGAR
SALT

Blanch and skin the tomatoes. Mash the flesh with a fork, and allow to drain. Then place in a casserole with the olive oil and sage leaves, and simmer for 10–15 minutes. Remove the pan from the heat, remove the sage, mix in balsamic vinegar, and season with salt.
This simple sauce is served with pasta dishes, with a knob of fresh butter and grated parmesan.

Salsa per pesce
Sauce for fish dishes

2 ANCHOVIES
3 HARD-BOILED EGG YOLKS
1 TSP HOT MUSTARD
1 TBSP BALSAMIC VINEGAR
2 RAW EGG YOLKS
EXTRA VIRGIN OLIVE OIL
SALT AND FRESHLY MILLED PEPPER

Bone the anchovies, and mash in a bowl with the hard-boiled egg yolks. Add mustard, balsamic vinegar, and raw egg yolks, and mix well. Stir in enough olive oil to produce a mixture which has the consistency of mayonnaise. Add salt to taste.
Sprinkle with freshly milled pepper and serve with fish dishes.

The Ghirlandina, the 293 ft. (88 m) high bell tower of the archiepiscopal cathedral, is visible from miles around. The Modenese also call it the white cathedral.

The maturity of the vinegar in the various barrels is checked regularly. Or course the master vinegar-maker only takes very small samples, so as not to waste any of the precious vinegar.

WINE

Emilia-Romagna, especially Emilia, the area between Piacenza and Bologna with Parma in the middle, is more renowned for its cuisine than almost any other region of Italy. On the other hand, you cannot say the same for the wines, as only about 10 percent of the production has DOC or DOCG status. This is not because conditions are not favorable for the production of high quality wine; Romagna in particular, whose vineyards are similar to those of neighboring areas, could produce much better wines.

Unlike the fertile plains of the Po valley in Emilia, which produce a sea of mass-market wines like Lambrusco, in Romagna they grow the classic Italian varieties, Sangiovese and Trebbiano, and the slopes on the northern edge of the Apennine mountains conceal many an undiscovered jewel among wines.

The reason why the region lags behind in the matter of modern quality-oriented winegrowing does not lie in the conditions – how else could one explain why in other places Sangiovese and Barbera usually produce only great wines – it is only to be understood against the background of the socio-economic situation. Almost without exception, the winegrowers of the region have always been organized into huge cooperatives, whose mass-oriented marketing policies and concentration on the simpler wine qualities over recent decades determined the direction the wine industry would take. For example, a single one of these gigantic cooperatives processes grapes from an area of over 100 square miles (27,000 hectares).

The region of Emilia-Romagna produces a small number of really interesting wines alongside Lambrusco. Albana di Romagna, the pride of the Romagnoli, which can be made as a dry white or as a sweet wine, is not usually one of them, yet this wine – to the amazement of the critics – was categorized as a DOCG wine in 1987.

However, the red Sangiovese di Romagna and Colli Bolognesi are worth mentioning, and so are one or two other reds, such as Colli Piacentini, made from single variety Chardonnay, Cabernet, or Pinot noir, and Gutturnio from Barbera and Croatina.

All over Italy, a little glass of white wine is a welcome refreshment and a favorite aperitif. People enjoy drinking in their regular local bar, as here in Bologna.

LAMBRUSCO – SOMETIMES BETTER THAN ITS REPUTATION

Somehow they seem to believe in Parma, Modena, Reggio Emilia, and the surrounding area, that only sparkling wines are a fitting match for the local cuisine of an area where generous helpings of specialties made from pork and ham are the rule. Not only the famous, or infamous, Lambrusco, beloved of pizza fans in the seventies and the horror of all lovers of good wine, is here sold as a sparkling wine with varying degrees of fizz. Barbera and a series of other wines are at least *frizzante* here.

Lambrusco, like Prosecco, was originally not a brand name or an origin, but a variety of grape, or rather a whole family of grapes with over 40 different varieties. Traditional Lambrusco has little in common with what was in the millions of bottles that overran the pizzerias of the world during the last few decades. It was usually very dry, coupled with a certain fruitiness, and it was due to the marketing policy of the big cooperatives that it became a sticky-sweet mass-produced drink.

The peak of this development was reached at the end of the eighties, when some of the Lambrusco cooperatives even put it in aluminum cans and tried to sell it on the American market as a competitor to Coca-Cola – an absolute commercial disaster, as can easily be imagined. Its often rather unpleasant sweetness was not always the product of the Lambrusco grapes, but rather of the widespread addition of Ancellotta grapes, whose large-scale use in Lambrusco wines had been allowed by Italian law.

For some time now, people in Emilia have begun to think again about the quality of genuine Lambrusco. Under the DOC labels Lambrusco di Sorbara, Lambrusco di Castelvetro, and Lambrusco Salamino di Santa Croce, small vineyards are again selling wines with the typical note of fruity bitterness, which are relatively dry, and really do suit the local cuisine.

Only a few vineyards in Emilia-Romagna produce such excellent wines as Castelluccio near Modigliano.

TOSCANA

Tuscany

Carrara
Massa
Viareggio   Lucca   Pistoia
Pisa   Arno   Prato   Firenze
Ponte-   San   Arezzo
dera   Miniato
Livorno
San Gimignano   Siena   Cortona
Montepulciano
Piombino   Mte. Amiata
1738 m
Grosseto
Orbetello

W

ell-balanced, simple, rooted in the soil, and yet refined – this describes the cuisine of Tuscany. It creates little fuss, it is straightforward, honest, but full of wit and irony – just like the people who live here. The gently rolling hills, olive groves, and still mountains are filled with the scent of foliage and herbs. The smell of freshly chopped, resinous wood is already in the air before the fire is lit for the broiled or spit-roasted meat and game specialties. Although in the large towns the gastronomic culture proves more luxurious than rural cuisine, sumptuous dishes like those of neighboring Emilia-Romagna are not served here. In Florence, for instance, a luxury consists simply of a particularly good piece of meat, the *Bistecca alla fiorentina* (Florentine beefsteak), or a *Spiedino toscano*, meat on a skewer seasoned with olive oil and rosemary. Otherwise, Florentines also subscribe to Tuscan ideals still held in high esteem, of simplicity, clarity, and naturalness that owe a great deal to the Italian Renaissance. Overly sophisticated dishes are scarcely to be found, and even in the best restaurants the obligatory soup course is served in rustic earthenware bowls. It is in the country, in particular, that cookery without frills comes into its own. Here legumes, bread, cheese, vegetables, and fresh fruit dominate the menu. *Ribollita, Panzanella, Pappa col pomodoro* – these are all dishes that are typical of remote, agricultural Tuscany. The bread, deliberately baked without salt, which tastes just as good as a neutral accompaniment to delicious sausage specialties as it does with strong-flavored pecorino cheese, remains a true staple food here, eaten by Tuscan people throughout the day. Yet in spite of the fact that the ingredients are so modest, no-one would describe Tuscan cuisine as plain, or even boring, for the patience and skill of the cooks are legendary. Preparation of even the most time-consuming specialties is carried out with loving care and always in the traditional manner. Despite being down-to-earth, Tuscan gourmets nevertheless permit themselves one small vanity: they openly claim that Italian ice cream, famous throughout the world, was invented here. The idea is supposed to have occurred to Renaissance architect Bernardo Buontalenti, while he was planning the Forte Belvedere fortifications, as a means of enhancing the banquet. In other parts of Italy, it is believed that the Arabs introduced ice cream to Sicily, from where it spread through the entire peninsula. This theory falls, however, upon deaf ears in Tuscany.

Previous double page: *Panforte senese* is an old and venerated specialty from Siena. The first references to this sweet, spiced bread date back to the 13th century.

Left: The Tuscan landscape is characterized by gently rolling hills, olive trees, and grapevines.

BREAD

Because he was a member of the Ghibelline faction that was loyal to the Holy Roman Emperor, the great 13th-century writer Dante Alighieri was banished from Florence in 1302 by the Guelph faction, loyal to the pope, which had regained power. The exile eventually found refuge in Ravenna, where he remarked upon "the saltiness of other people's bread." If one ignores the possible hidden metaphor in this statement, the student of culinary history will immediately recognize a reference to the difference between Tuscan bread and other central Italian bread. Back in the Middle Ages, the Tuscans were evidently baking their rustic bread, *pane sciocco*, without the addition of any expensive salt. The Tuscan people were no doubt making the point, even then, that there is no need whatsoever to add salt to bread, since its ultimate function is to accompany inherently salty specialties such as sausage, cheese, or meat dishes.

Today, bread remains a staple food in Tuscany. Noodles and rice were once served only on special occasions, and the situation has not changed a great deal. Until recently it was customary in rural areas to heat the large, free-standing ovens once a week to bake bread for the entire village, while families in the towns took their dough to the baker. Payment for this essential service was even fixed by law.

Bread is eaten by Tuscans throughout the day. In the morning, at breakfast time, it is dipped in coffee made with milk, and it serves as an appetizer before lunch in the form of toasted *bruschetta* or daintily garnished *crostino*. Crusty bread with a few drops of the best olive oil makes a wonderful snack. But bread is also used for cooking: it appears as an ingredient in *Cacciucco*, the traditional fish soup; it is found in vegetable dishes; it is crumbled on top of *pinci*, or home-made spaghetti; and it forms a rustic accompaniment to beans and cabbage. At the end of a meal, it tempts one to eat it with a little pecorino cheese, and it also tastes good with dried figs, nuts, and fresh grapes. In the afternoon bread is dipped in wine, spread with butter, or sprinkled with sugar.

The range of different types of bread is correspondingly great. Rustic loaves, whole wheat bread, fine wheat bread, corn bread, and many other specialties are baked using an extremely wide variety of flour blends. Bread appears in the shape of *rondeggiante* (round flat loaves), *bozza* or *pagnotta* (tall, round loaves), or *filone* (long bread sticks). The delicate *semella* is suitable for breakfast or a light snack, the *fiorentina* is a tasty pretzel, and the *schiacciata all'olio* refers to a flat loaf of bread sprinkled with oil. *Bozza* and *filone*, the two most common types, must have a crisp crust and a loose-textured crumb containing lots of holes if they are to be judged a success. In Tuscany there is indeed a saying, *pan bucato e cacio serrato*, "bread needs holes, cheese doesn't."

Pasta secca or *pasta fresca*, which are universal throughout the rest of Italy, play a more subordinate role in Tuscan cuisine. Consequently, *grano-tenero* wheat (soft wheat for the bread that is omnipresent in Tuscany) is the main variety grown in Crete, the granary of the region.

BRUSCHETTA
Toasted bread with tomatoes
(Illustrated below)

4 SLICES TUSCAN BREAD (WHITE BREAD)
2 TOMATOES
1 BUNCH OF BASIL, COARSELY CHOPPED
SALT AND PEPPER
1 CLOVE OF GARLIC
3 TBSP EXTRA VIRGIN OLIVE OIL

Toast the slices of bread in the toaster or under the broiler. Cut the tomatoes into small cubes and mix with the coarsely chopped basil in a dish. Season with salt and pepper. Rub the toasted bread slices with garlic, spread the tomato and basil mixture on the slices of bread, and sprinkle generously with olive oil.

CROSTINO
Toasted bread with chicken livers

1 SMALL ONION
3 TBSP OLIVE OIL
1/2 LB/250 G CHICKEN LIVERS
1 GLASS DRY MARSALA OR VIN SANTO WINE
SALT AND PEPPER
3 1/2 TBSP/50 G ANCHOVY FILLETS
3 1/2 TBSP/50 G CAPERS
3 1/2 TBSP/50 G BUTTER
TUSCAN BREAD (WHITE BREAD), SLICED

Chop the onions finely and sauté gently in the olive oil.
Cut the chicken livers into pieces, add to the onions, and
fry for a few minutes. Pour in the Marsala or Vin Santo and
simmer until the liquid has almost evaporated. Season the
chicken livers with salt and pepper, and sauté for another 5
minutes. Leave to cool slightly, then place in a food
processor with the anchovy fillets, the capers, and the butter,
and blend to a very fine purée. Toast the slices of bread in
the oven and spread thickly with the chicken liver paste.

PANZANELLA
Bread salad

1 LB/500 G STALE TUSCAN BREAD (WHITE BREAD)
SALT
5 RIPE TOMATOES
1 RED ONION
1 CUCUMBER
1 BUNCH OF BASIL
3–4 TBSP EXTRA VIRGIN OLIVE OIL
PEPPER
1–2 TBSP WINE VINEGAR

Cut the bread into small pieces and soak in cold water with
a pinch of salt. When the bread is saturated, squeeze it out
and place in a salad bowl. Dice the tomatoes, cut the onion
and cucumber into small pieces, and add to the bread.
Coarsely chop the basil and stir this into the bread mixture
too. Sprinkle generously with olive oil, season to taste with
salt and pepper, and place in the refrigerator. Before serving,
add the wine vinegar and mix thoroughly again.
This simple, summery dish is very frequently prepared in
the country to use up leftover bread.

PAPPA AL POMODORO
Tomato soup with croutons

4 TBSP OLIVE OIL
1 ONION
3 CLOVES OF GARLIC
1 3/4 LBS/750 G TOMATOES
4 CUPS/1 LITER CHICKEN STOCK
SALT AND FRESHLY GROUND BLACK PEPPER
1/2 LB/250 G STALE TUSCAN BREAD (WHITE BREAD), WITH
CRUSTS REMOVED
A FEW BASIL LEAVES

Heat half the olive oil in a large pan. Peel the onion and
garlic, chop finely, and sauté gently in the hot oil until soft
and transparent. Blanch the tomatoes, skin, and cut into
cubes. Add the tomatoes to the onion and garlic mixture in
the pan and sauté for 5 minutes. Then add the stock
gradually. Season with salt and pepper and cook for
30 minutes.
Heat the remaining oil in a shallow pan, cut the bread into
small cubes, and brown in the hot fat. Chop the basil leaves.
Pour the soup into soup dishes and sprinkle with the
croutons and the basil leaves. Serve immediately.

Pan di granturco
Pan di granturco like *ciaccia* from the Maremma, is made
from maize flour.

Pane classico integrale
Unsalted *classico integrale*, made
from semolina, has a very crisp
crust

Schiacciatina
Schiacciatina, like *spolettina*, is made from salt
dough, and, like *treccina*, it is made from fine flour,
yeast, and olive oil. It is a small, flat loaf.

Filone
Filone is the classic Tuscan
unsalted loaf.

Pan di ramerino
Pan di ramerino, rosemary bread, used to be baked during
Holy Week. The loaves were decorated with a cross and
sold in church porches by the *semellai*, the traveling bread
sellers. The dough is enhanced by the addition of sugar,
raisins, and chopped rosemary leaves. As this bread is very
nourishing, it soon began to be eaten throughout the year,
rather than exclusively at Easter. It remains very popular
throughout Tuscany today.

Pane con i grassetti
This bread is typical of the Garfagnana area. The dough has
pork crackling mixed into it.

Pane con l'uva
In Lombardia, *pane con l'uva* is the term used to describe small loaves
or rolls that are eaten mainly at Easter. In Tuscany, by contrast, this
grape bread is made by rolling out the dough on a baking sheet in
the manner of a classic *schiacciata*, adding a generous layer of red
grapes, and sprinkling it with sugar. This bread is typically eaten here
in the autumn. At harvest time it is often served instead of desserts.
In many areas, Tuscans eat it as an accompaniment to fresh figs.

TUSCAN BREAD

Tuscan enthusiasm for bread and bread
specialties is quite inexhaustible. In addition
to the varieties already mentioned, there is
pane pazzo, or "mad" bread, containing
pepper; *pane di Radicofani*, with grapes,
honey, and pepper; *pan co santi*, the bread of
the saints, containing nuts, raisins, almonds,
honey, pepper, and oil; *pane dicembrino*, or
December bread, with raisins, nuts, honey,
and pumpkin; *ciambella di quaresima* or
quaresimali, a pretzel for fasting periods, as
well as various cookies and *panforte*.

Carsenta lunigianese
This bread, from Lunigiana, is baked in a
pan on a layer of chestnut leaves. It is
served on Good Friday.

Ciaccia
This bread, from the Maremma, is made
from maize flour.

Donzelle
In order to make *donzelle*, the dough is
rolled out with a rolling pin, then cut into
diamond shapes, and finally fried in olive
oil. In the area around Prato these small
loaves are known as *ficattole*, and in the
Lunigiana area they are sold as *sgabei*.

Fiandolone
Fiandolone was the bread eaten by the
forest workers and miners of Mount
Amiata. The dough is made with sweet
chestnut flour and is baked in the oven,
strewn with finely chopped rosemary
leaves.

Pan maroko
Pan maroko contains equal parts of wheat
and maize flour. The dough is made with
oil, water, and yeast, and has raisins and
pine nuts added to it.

Panigaccio
Panigaccio is a specialty of the *Lunigiana*
area. The dough, made from flour, water,
and salt, is baked in glowing red-hot
crucibles, and is served with grated cheese
and a hint of oil.

Panina gialla aretina
This yellow bread from the Arezzo area is
eaten at Easter time, like *panina unta* with its
very high fat content. It is often enhanced
by the addition of raisins, saffron, and spices,
and is served with eggs that have been
consecrated in church beforehand.

Panini di San Antonio
These sweet rolls are eaten in the country
on January 17, the feast day of St. Antony,
although not until they have received a
blessing, alongside the livestock and the
fields, in church that morning.

Schiacciata
Schiacciata is made from bread dough that is
rolled out on a baking sheet, brushed with
olive oil, and generously salted. Imaginative
variations on this loaf include added pork
crackling, herbs, potatoes, and tomatoes.

OIL
MYTHOLOGY

According to legend, Athena and Poseidon were unable to agree which of them was to rule Attica. Zeus, the father of the gods, was summoned to arbitrate. He told the squabbling pair that he would declare as the victor whichever of them could show him the most beneficial discovery for mankind. Athena immediately commanded Mother Earth to grow a new and unusual tree, and the olive tree was created. Zeus was very pleased with this, and announced that the goddess had won.

The olive tree originally came from the region between Pamir and Turkestan. It spread from there throughout the entire Mediterranean region 5000 years ago, and made its mark on more than the culinary habits of the native peoples, for in many regions the olive tree was also revered in religious culture. Its branches and fruit, as well as its oil, were all regarded as symbols of life, fertility, and light. The tree had particularly high status in Greece. Legend has it that the marriage bed of Odysseus and Penelope was in the hollowed-out trunk of an olive tree, and the statues of the gods – from Zeus to Athena – were rubbed with the precious oil to retain the spirits of the deities in their likenesses. Greek athletes anointed themselves with olive oil, and the victors of the Olympic Games were crowned with olive branches. The Spartans laid the dead to their final rest on beds of olive leaves.

A major industry grew up around the olive in imperial Rome. Olive oil even acquired its own commodity market, the *arca olearia*, to control the flourishing trade. Pliny tells us that no fewer than 15 varieties were available for purchase.

The religious and economic significance of the olive tree was so great that the Christian Church was unable to disregard it either. The olive branch became a symbol of peace, and the oil itself was used in religious rites such as Extreme Unction.

The Greek doctor Hippocrates had already recommended the use of fresh olive oil for various illnesses. Following the decline of the Roman Empire, when the olive groves stood for the most part neglected, experiments continued in the monasteries. The oil was used to make skin care products; it was a reliable palliative for the itchy rash caused by stinging nettles; it helped alleviate headaches, stomach pains, and ear infections; and if necessary it was used against the "evil eye." Chewing an olive leaf regularly strengthened the gums and kept the teeth white. Today, the health-giving properties of olive oil have been scientifically proven. It is easily digested, is good for the stomach and gut, affords protection against diseases of the heart and circulatory system, and – by contrast with animal fats and other vegetable fats – is not broken down into harmful substances, even when heated for frying food.

Right: a genuine olive tree (*Olea europaea*) can grow to a height of 30 to 50 feet (10 to 16 meters) and can live for over 1000 years. The white blossom opens in spring.

TUSCAN OLIVE OIL

Florentine merchants were being supplied with olive oil from Apulia and Campagna as early as the 4th century. They either sold it directly in their native city or processed it to make a special soap for the wool industry. As a result of high oil prices and the difficulties of obtaining adequate supplies on the European markets, they eventually realized that it would make more sense to produce their own oil in Tuscany. Measures were even introduced by the state to increase the numbers of olive trees, which until that time had been sparse. Olive grove owners were required to augment their plantations by two or four olive trees a year, depending on the size of the grove. The Medicis, in particular, went to great lengths to promote the cultivation of olives. It is thanks to their rural planning and economic initiatives that, even today, Tuscany remains a significant oil producer as well as a magnificent stretch of countryside. The Medici family's most effective initiative was to encourage transferred ownership of hilly, wooded parcels of land to the local authorities, so that the latter could lease them to the peasants at an attractive price, on condition that cultivation was confined to grapes and olive trees.

This agricultural policy proved extremely successful, with the result that Tuscan oil was even being exported to other regions in the early 16th century. Since then olive growing has steadily increased. The great olive groves of the Maremma and the Val di Chiana, for example, were planted in the second half of the 19th century. However, most plantations are still found in the hill ranges around Florence, extending from Siena and Arezzo as far as the lowlands of Pistoia and the countryside surrounding Lucca and Carmignano. After the frost of 1985, in particular, the farmers took the opportunity of replacing their frosted olive trees with varieties that were more suitable and considered more "modern" in the light of agricultural findings. Mixed cultivation of grapevines and olive trees, as practiced initially, was also gradually abandoned, and monoculture is now the preferred option of growers in this area.

The varieties predominantly grown in Tuscany are Frantoio, Leccino, Moraiolo, and Pendolino. Each region has its own methods and traditions of planting the groves and ensuring a good harvest, for oil production requires, above all, a conscientious approach and experience. The properties of the finished olive oil depend primarily on the climate and the time of harvesting. An oil from mild climatic zones, mostly by the sea, such as the area around Lucca or Grossetto, has a softer, rounder taste, and the typically earthy flavor is not as prominent. In the hilly areas, on the other hand, and in the foothills of the Apennines, where temperatures are lower, the olives do not ripen as much. They produce a spicy, fruity oil with a slightly bitter flavor, which is nevertheless well-balanced and full-bodied. The greener oil varieties are obtained from olives "that have not darkened yet," as they say here – in other words, olives harvested while they are still relatively unripe.

The quality of an olive oil is determined by its free oleic acid content. The acid content of an *Olio d'oliva extra vergine* must not exceed one percent. However, the best oils have an even lower content, namely between 0.2 and 0.5 percent. They are transparent, of a luminous golden-green color, and have a full, pronounced flavor. Occasionally they may have a delicate almond flavor, or a very slight scent of apple, artichoke, or paprika. Price is a good indicator of quality. The best olive oils are always the most expensive.

Moraiolo
Moraiolo is one of the most important varieties of olive. It is native to Tuscany, but has established itself throughout central Italy, especially in the area around Spoleto, in Umbria. Moraiolo produces a typically fruity oil with an intense flavor, and leaves a slightly bitter and sharp after-taste on the tongue.

Frantoio
Frantoio is a variety of olive that produces a very fruity oil. It tastes very strongly of olives, but not aggressively so, nor does it have a bitter or sharp after-taste. If Moraiolo and Leccino are blended with the emerald-green oil that is produced from this variety of olive, it will certainly keep even better.

Leccino
An extremely mild, golden-yellow oil with a delicate almond flavor is produced from the variety of olive known as Leccino. However, this olive oil does not have an especially strong character, with the result that it soon fades. For this reason it is often blended with Moraiolo oil, which retains its flavor for longer. Conversely, Moraiolo oils benefit from the addition of Leccino oil, which renders them a great deal milder without any loss of their outstanding qualities.

Pendolino
The variety Pendolino has been adopted, especially in the province of Florence, to supplement the olive groves, and serves as a pollinator. It produces an oil that closely resembles Leccino, but has less body. It is added in small quantities to blends of other varieties, either to tone down or emphasize their respective properties, as it has a harmonizing effect. The high art of oil production, therefore, includes deciding upon the correct blend to produce a balanced oil that will serve for a number of uses.

HARVESTING OLIVES

The fruit of the olive tree is harvested during the weeks between the beginning of November and the middle of December. The exact time of the harvest must be carefully chosen, for the olives must neither be too unripe, nor completely ripe. Harvesting is still frequently done by hand, even today. The olives, which are picked or carefully "combed off" with a special rake, fall on to nylon sheets laid out beneath the trees before harvesting begins. Many olive growers, however, rely on technology rather than manual work, and use a machine that shakes off the olive crop. An articulated arm grasps the olive tree, shakes it, and catches the fruit in a container shaped like an inverted umbrella, from which the olives are extracted and the stalks and leaves removed. This method of harvesting can only be used in specially adapted olive groves, however. Regardless of whether the harvest is mechanical or manual, olives must be gathered as quickly as possible and taken to the oil mill, since oxidation and uncontrolled fermentation are a threat, as they are in white wine production. In the oil mill the stalks and leaves are removed from the fruit,

which is then washed. It is then crushed by the rolling motion of heavy granite millstones. Although far more modern equipment exists, Tuscan growers are attached to these stone monsters, since they make light work of even the hardest olive stones, thus guaranteeing a very uniform olive pulp. After milling, the pulp is "kneaded," in other words stirred slowly and carefully. After this, the oil miller spreads it in layers, just under an inch (two to three centimeters) thick, on the waiting press mats, which are then stacked in a suitable frame. A hydraulic press now begins the pressing operation. The mixture of oil and water emerges from the sides of the mats, and is collected. The water is separated out in a centrifuge. The fresh oil is poured into terra cotta jugs or, in the case of modern mills, into steel tanks, and then takes between 30 and 40 days to clear, protected from the effects of light and temperature fluctuations, after which it is again filtered.

Some oil mills nowadays do not operate entirely in accordance with the traditional system. Although, in such a modified production system, the olives are also crushed first, the pulp is not then placed in the traditional press, but is instead spun at high speeds. Processing of the resulting mixture of oil and water then continues in a centrifuge, until the pure oil is separated out.

The young olives ripen through summer and fall on the tree. Harvesting does not begin until winter.

Huge granite millstones crush even the hard stones.

Below: Although harvesting by hand is tedious, it has the advantage that the fruit is not damaged.

LEVELS OF QUALITY

Olio d'oliva extra vergine
Extra virgin olive oil from the first pressing, of the best quality.

Olio d'oliva vergine
Virgin olive oil from the second and third pressings, still of very good quality.

Olio d'oliva
Olive oil (also pure olive oil), blended from native and refined oil.

Olio di sansa d'oliva
Olive pomace oil, obtained almost exclusively from the pomace residues left after pressing, extracted with the aid of solvents.

Next the olive pulp is spread on circular mats and the stack of mats is compressed. The oil emerges as soon as the press exerts force on the stacked mats.

Many types of olive are grown in the Marche region. The well-balanced oil is among the best in Italy.

The sharp, fruity oil from Apulia is obtained from olives that are fully ripe, and therefore is extremely acidic.

Tuscan oils — depending on their place of origin — taste spicy, nutty, or sometimes peppery.

Sicilian olive oil, like that from Apulia, has a strong and sharp, yet fruity flavor.

The fine olive oil from Umbria has a delicate scent of herbs and a pronounced green color.

The olive oil from Molise is greenish in color, with yellow accents. It has a mild flavor.

The emerald-green olive oil from Abruzzi has a fruity aroma and a strong flavor.

Florence c. 1480, copy of the Carta della Catena (detail), Museo di Firenze com'era, Florence

THE CUISINE OF THE RENAISSANCE

The culinary Renaissance in Italy also has its roots in the rediscovery of antiquity. In the kitchens of monasteries and aristocrats' palaces, where by that time a measure of affluence had been attained, attention was given to the products of Greek and Roman culinary arts, and the author Apicius, in particular, was frequently studied. Cooks and banquet organizers now attempted to apply the ideals espoused by the Renaissance – of order, proportion, harmony, and balance – to culinary matters as well. Influences from the Levant, an area with which trade was flourishing, as well as from the Arabian-occupied Sicily, were welcomed and assimilated without prejudice. Whereas, in the Middle Ages, people still retained a marked preference for prestigious dishes that were first boiled, then roasted, and finally submerged under a sauce containing the largest possible amount of expensive spices, Renaissance cooks were at pains to develop straightforward recipes and gentler cooking methods intended to emphasize, rather than grossly alter, the taste of the ingredients themselves. Opulent mixtures of spices and food that had been skillfully changed beyond all recognition gradually fell out of fashion, therefore, and instead any gourmet could for the first time identify, without too much guesswork, what was on his plate.

Although Italians henceforth strove to achieve simple and noble dishes, only very sparing use was made of regional peasant cookery. Cooks preferred to adapt new dishes from distant foreign countries. Tuscan peasant dishes such as polenta (porridge made from grain) or vegetable purée with hot onions or sharp-flavored garlic were considered unrefined – and were to remain so for a long time to come, for the cookery revolution passed the less privileged by, leaving practically no trace in their cooking pots.

The Renaissance is also the period in which a connection was first made between pathology and day-to-day nutrition. What had previously been considered self-evident was suddenly discussed, commented upon, analyzed, and ultimately viewed from a completely new angle by doctors and physiologists: namely, that food can bring health, but can also precipitate illnesses or exacerbate existing complaints. So, in the same way that man, who had become the focus of interest, was classified as choleric, melancholic, phlegmatic, or sanguine, depending on whether his bodily humors were hot or cold, sweet or sour, thick or thin, green, black, or yellow, scholars now examined the special properties of foodstuffs and ingredients using similar criteria, in order to recommend strongly that certain groups of people eat a particular dish or ingredient, or alternatively advise them against doing so if at all possible.

CATHERINE'S COOKS

In September 1533, when Catherine de' Medici boarded the ship in Portovenere that was to take her to her marriage to Henry II of France, she clearly had more than an overnight case with her. For reasons of security, Catherine, a native of Florence, took numerous containers full of provisions as well as her chests of clothes and jewel boxes. Her royal entourage included, in addition to those who repeatedly came under suspicion of preparing poison, cooks' apprentices, cup bearers, bakers, confectioners, and some very capable chefs.

Catherine's skepticism regarding French cuisine was nevertheless quite justified, for gastronomic culture on the banks of the Seine was in a sorry state at the beginning of the 16th century. The French court clung to the medieval precepts of Lucullus, according to which a meal was supposed to reflect the wealth of the household, an ingredient which was exotic by virtue of its cost was held in higher esteem than a fresh local product, the foodstuffs were subjected to the most tortuous preparation methods and veritable orgies of seasoning, and the meal would conclude with a guessing game as to what ingredients the dishes might have contained. Although the seminal work on Italian gastronomic and culinary matters, Bartolomeo Sacchi's revised version of the *Liber de Arte coquinaria* by Maestro Martino, had been translated into French a few years previously, and although the humanist, who was also known by the name Platina, was, moreover, genuinely at pains in his treatise *De honesta voluptate et valetudine* to explain the rules that were fundamental to good food, the French seemed to have great difficulty in grasping them. This state of affairs changed abruptly as Catherine entered the political and culinary arena. Her marriage to the French king, cleverly engineered by the diplomatic skill of Pope Clement VII, finally brought a lighter touch to the gloomy sauces of the French chefs. Catherine, who was herself fond of eating, and whose reforms were far removed from asceticism, abolished the bad habit of serving sweet and sour, or piquant and salty dishes at the same time, and instead arranged for dishes to be served that really went well together. Inelegant, structureless, and gluttonous feasts became a thing of the past thereafter, and banquets became ceremonial, characterized by fine dishes, elegance, and refined table manners. Heavy goblets gave way to elegant glassware from Venice, and glazed earthenware, known as faience, was imported from Faenza in Italy. Catherine even introduced the use of the fork, but was more successful in this respect with her son, Henry III, than with her husband, whose table manners continued to leave much to be desired.

Furthermore, Catherine improved the reputation of "cheap" staple foods such as oil or beans, and favored dishes and specialties such as guinea fowl with sweet chestnuts, fricassée, pot-roasts, pies, sorbets, and a liqueur that was prepared from the recipe of the monastery at Murate. She made spinach cooked in the Florentine style fashionable, ordered vast amounts of artichokes to be prepared for her husband, and, if various claims are to be believed, was even responsible for introducing the Trebbiano grape. Other sources, by contrast, claim that the daughter of the house of Medici smuggled the Cabernet grape into Tuscany from France.

In short, any aspiring Parisian was at pains to adopt Catherine's precepts and to dine *à la mode de la Reine Catherine*. Centuries later, she was still being given credit for the new initiatives in culinary techniques. No lesser a figure than Antoine Carême (1784–1833), gifted chef of both the emperor Napoleon and Talleyrand, held the opinion that French chefs had first to learn the arts of cooking and baking from Catherine's Italian cooks before they could develop them into great French *cuisine*.

Santi di Tito (1536–1603), *Portrait of Catherine de' Medici, Queen of France*, 1585/86, oil on wood, 56 x 46½ inches (142 x 118 cm), The Uffizi, Florence

Torta di zucca
Pumpkin tart
(Illustrated in the background)

1 LB/500 G PUMPKIN
SCANT 2 1/2 CUPS/600 ML MILK
1/2 CUP/100 G SUGAR
1/8 TSP GINGER
1/8 TSP CINNAMON
3 EGGS
1 PINCH SAFFRON
BUTTER
1 LB/500 G PUFF PASTRY
1 TBSP ROSEWATER

Peel the pumpkin. Cut the flesh into pieces, grate finely, and cook for 15 minutes in 2 cups (500 ml) milk. Drain, pressing the pumpkin to remove excess liquid, and mix with the sugar, ginger, cinnamon, eggs, saffron, 3½ tablespoons (50 g) butter, and the remaining milk. Roll out the puff pastry into two thin circles and place one of them on a baking sheet greased with butter. Spread the filling over and cover with the second pastry circle. Bake at 350 °F (180 °C) for about 50 minutes. When the filling has risen, sprinkle with rosewater and serve.

Pesce impanato
Fish in batter
(Illustrated below)

For the batter:
1 3/4 CUPS/200 G ALL-PURPOSE FLOUR
1 TSP SALT
1 CUP/250 ML FLAT BEER
2 TBSP OLIVE OIL
3 EGG WHITES

2 LB 5 OZ/600 G FISH FILLETS (E.G. SOLE, PLAICE,
HADDOCK, ETC.)
SALT AND PEPPER
2 TBSP LEMON JUICE
OIL FOR DEEP FRYING

To make the batter, mix together the flour and salt, and stir in the beer. Then incorporate the olive oil and leave the batter to stand for 30 minutes. Next beat the egg whites until stiff and carefully fold into the batter.
Wash the fish fillets, cut in half, season with salt and pepper, and sprinkle with lemon juice. Coat the fillets in the batter and fry in hot oil for about 5 minutes until they are crisp.

Tortellini rinascimentali
Tortellini with pork filling

For the dough:
5 CUPS/600 G ALL-PURPOSE FLOUR
6 EGGS
1/2 TSP SALT

For the filling:
2 TBSP/50 G SALT PORK, CHOPPED FINELY
1 1/2 CUPS/300 G GROUND PORK
3/4 CUP/50 G PARMESAN, GRATED
1/2 CUP/50 G PROVENTURA CHEESE, SLICED
1/2 TSP CINNAMON
1/8 TSP PEPPER
1/8 TSP GROUND CLOVES
1/8 TSP GRATED NUTMEG
1 PINCH SAFFRON
1 TBSP RAISINS
1 TBSP PARSLEY, FINELY CHOPPED
2 EGGS
8 CUPS/2 LITERS MEAT STOCK
PARMESAN
SUGAR AND CINNAMON

To make the dough, place the flour in a heap on the work surface and make a hollow in the center. Pour the eggs into this and knead slowly into a dough. Dissolve the salt in 3 tablespoons lukewarm water and add gradually, a drop at a time. Cover the dough and leave to stand for about 1 hour. To make the filling, mix the chopped salt pork with the ground pork, parmesan and *proventura* (a type of smoked Mozzarella) and fry for a few minutes. Add the spices, raisins, parsley, and eggs, mix well, and leave to cool slightly. Roll out the dough on a floured work surface and stamp out small circles. Heap some of the filling on each circle, lay another circle on top, and press the edges together tightly.

Cook in the stock, which should be boiling but not bubbling fiercely, for approximately 10 minutes. Remove with a skimming spoon and serve hot.
Serve grated parmesan, sugar, and cinnamon separately, to sprinkle on according to taste.

Zuppa di funghi
Mushroom soup

1/2 LB/200 G FRESH GOOD-QUALITY MUSHROOMS (PREFERABLY
WILD)
2 CUPS/500 ML SWEET WHITE WINE
1/2 TSP PEPPER
SCANT 1/2 CUP/100 ML OLIVE OIL
1/3 CUP/80 ML UNFERMENTED SOUR FRUIT JUICE OR CIDER
SALT
SUGAR
4 SLICES OF WHITE BREAD, TOASTED
1 CUP ORANGE JUICE
1/2 TBSP CINNAMON
5 CLOVES

Remove the stalks from the mushrooms, place in cold water and wash several times. Bring the mushrooms to the boil with 1 cup (250 ml) wine and the pepper, drain, and cut into bite-sized pieces. Pour the oil into a shallow pan, add the mushrooms and braise slowly. Add the unfermented fruit juice or cider and simmer for at least 15 minutes. Season with salt, and a little sugar if desired. Place the mushrooms in bowls with a generous helping of stock.
Place the toasted slices of bread in a pan with 1 cup (250 ml) of wine, the orange juice, cinnamon, cloves, and 5 teaspoons sugar, and bring to a boil. Carefully remove the soaked slices of bread and lay on top of the mushrooms. Serve hot.

HERBS

Even in ancient times it was known which herbs were suitable for eating and which had healing powers. The Greek doctor Hippocrates bequeathed for posterity descriptions of the precise botanical and medicinal properties of the relevant plants, and the Roman scholar Pliny evidently knew a great deal about the herb garden too. In the Middle Ages, cultivation of herbs was confined to a few small monastery gardens, but in the Renaissance, with its enthusiasm for antiquity, the full spectrum of herbs, together with their culinary and physical importance, was rediscovered. In the 15th century, when Pisa and Padua took the lead in establishing herb gardens, Florence was determined not to be left behind, and Cosimo de' Medici immediately gave instructions for the creation of the *Giardini dei semplice*. Lucca and Siena followed this example. Aromatic greenery soon became a cult phenomenon, for ultimately these unlikely little plants were most beneficial, both for body and soul.

Parsley was considered a tonic, alleviated kidney complaints, and, as Pliny claims, even cured fish if was chopped and scattered in the fishpond. Basil alleviated stomachache and nausea. Sage had antiseptic properties, and thyme was a remedy for headache caused by drunkenness. Rosemary was a tonic for the nerves, while peppermint was a stimulant. Tarragon supposedly assisted recovery from snake bites. Borage brought comfort for the soul, gave courage, and relieved pain from pulled muscles. Fennel soothed children (and so on, and so forth). Quite under-standably, everyone wished to profit from the healing power of herbs.

Today, no excessive claims are made about the healing powers of culinary herbs, but it has become quite impossible to imagine cooking without them. Tuscany, in particular, is a paradise of herbs, for many species grow wild here, and those who live in towns insist on growing, at the very least, basil, sage, and rosemary in window boxes or tiny earthenware pots, even on the smallest balcony, so they can have the aromatic leaves and stems constantly available to use when cooking.

Right: Herbs play an important role in Tuscan cuisine. There is always a comprehensive range of fresh herbs for sale on the market stalls.

Fennel
In southern Italy, fennel (*finocchio*) grows wild by the roadside. The stems, leaves, and seeds can be used for cooking, as well as the bulbous roots. Fennel goes well with pork, and is used to flavor the Tuscan dish *finocchiona*.

Parsley

In Italy, someone who never misses a party or social occasion is described as *come il prezzemolo*, like parsley, since parsley is found everywhere. Affection for this ubiquitous herb is not confined to Tuscany. Parsley goes well with fish, salad, vegetables, and mushrooms, and is also used to flavor soups and organ meat.

Mint

The variety of mint most frequently used in Tuscany is the small-leafed peppermint, *Mentha nepetella*, a member of the labiate plant family. Its leaves are added to mushrooms and tasty braised dishes. This aromatic herb is also an essential ingredient in many salads, vegetable dishes, and various herb liqueurs.

Basil

Basil (*basilico*) is indispensable to Mediterranean cookery. The moment one touches it or pulls off its leaves, its characteristic fragrance pours forth. Basil goes well with salad, tomato sauce, and the typically Tuscan *bruschetta*, which are crisply toasted slices of bread.

Tarragon

Chicken and fish taste especially good with tarragon (*estragone, serpentaria*, or *dragoncello*). This herb is frequently used to flavor vinegar. However, the leaves can also be dipped in thin batter and fried in oil until crispy. According to legend, tarragon was first cultivated by the French in St. Antimo near Montalcino in around 744.

Rosemary

Rosemary (*rosmarino* or *ramerino*), a member of the labiate plant family, grows wild in Italy. The narrow leaves of this herb go equally well with roast meat and fish as with many sweet dishes, such as *castagnaccio*, the delicious chestnut tart from the Maremma region.

Thyme

Thyme (*timo*) is used for flavoring meat dishes and is especially well suited to pork, lamb, and game. It grows almost everywhere and is easily gathered, without having to search. Thyme is also used to flavor sauces and is used as an ingredient in many herb liqueurs.

Sage

Sage (*salvia*) is used to accompany all roast dishes, whether meat or fish, and to flavor marinades for many game dishes. Roasted sage leaves also taste very good.

Borage

The flowers of borage (*boragine* or *borrana*, as the Tuscans call it) are used to enhance salads. Borage leaves can be prepared in the same way as spinach, or can be roasted.

PINZIMONIO

Anything that is fragrant and is crisp and fresh when it arrives on the table is a favorite in Tuscan cookery, so it is no wonder that vegetables of all kinds are very popular, as well as aromatic herbs. Artichokes, tomatoes, celery, salad onions and scallions, asparagus, carrots, and peppers are all used to make tasty dishes, or appear raw as essential ingredients in the typically Tuscan platter of crudités known as *Pinzimonio*. Strips of young vegetables are just dipped in a sauce made from the best olive oil, salt, and pepper – and they taste simply delicious. Obviously, though, enjoyment can be guaranteed only if the vegetables are really young and fresh. In unpretentious restaurants, *Pinzimonio* is often served as a starter. It is not unknown for people to eat so much of it that they then have trouble managing the more substantial courses that follow.

Raw vegetables with a cold dip or hot sauce are also served in other regions of Italy. In Piedmont, strips of raw or briefly blanched vegetables are dipped in a hot mixture of crushed anchovies and garlic – a vegetable fondue which is known as *bagna caoda*, while natives of Lazio and Rome, like Tuscans, prefer a simple cold sauce and have christened the dish *Cazzimperio*.

Pinzimonio
Crudités with dip
(Illustrated in the background)

Celery sticks
Carrots
Fennel
Scallions
Radishes
Endives
Peppers
Extra virgin olive oil
Salt and pepper

Wash the vegetables, cut into strips, and arrange on a large platter, which is placed in the center of the table. Serve a small dish of olive oil, salt, and pepper for each guest. Dip the vegetables in the olive oil and eat raw. Serve accompanied by fresh white Tuscan bread.

VEGETABLE SPECIALTIES

Vegetables play an important role in Tuscan cuisine. The dish known as *Ribollita*, which means cooked for a second time or reheated, is well named, for like most stews it does not taste really good until the second day. In households in the Tuscan countryside it was once the custom to keep a pan of this soup on the stove all the time. While bacon and ham bones are added to *Ribollita*, *Acquacotta maremmana* is a strictly vegetarian variant of this vegetable soup. Its name, meaning "boiled water," is perhaps a reference to the fact that it is thin, or to the absence of meat.

The Florentines are also great vegetable fans. Their *Crespelle* are filled with Swiss chard or spinach, accompanied by ricotta and parmesan, and their famous tripe specialty, *Trippa alla fiorentina*, is cooked with vegetables. Tripe comes from the stomachs – the first and second stomach and the omasum – of ruminants, either of calves or beef cattle. It is best to buy tripe from a reputable butcher, cleaned and ready to cook in whichever way you choose.

FAGIOLI ALL'UCCELLETTO
Cooked beans

STEAMED BEANS
3 CUPS/600 G DRIED CANNELLINI BEANS
3/4 LB/300 G TOMATOES
5 TBSP EXTRA VIRGIN OLIVE OIL
3 CLOVES OF GARLIC
4 SAGE LEAVES
1 CHILI PEPPER
SALT AND PEPPER

Soak the beans in cold water the night before. Next day, drain them and cook in plenty of water for about 2 hours until tender. Blanch the tomatoes, remove the skins, and dice. Heat the olive oil and gently sauté the unpeeled garlic cloves, sage, and chili pepper. Add the tomatoes and remove the chili pepper. Simmer for at least 10 minutes, then add the beans. Season to taste with salt and pepper, and simmer for a further 15–20 minutes.

CRESPELLE ALLA FIORENTINA
Pancakes Florentine-style

For the filling:
3/4 LB/300 G SPINACH
1/2 LB/200 G RICOTTA
3/4 CUP/50 G PARMESAN, GRATED
2 EGGS
SALT AND PEPPER
GRATED NUTMEG

For the batter:
1/2 CUP/60 G ALL-PURPOSE FLOUR
2 EGGS
4 TSP BUTTER
1/2 CUP/125 ML MILK

For the béchamel sauce:
3 1/2 TBSP/50 G BUTTER
SCANT 1/2 CUP/50 G ALL-PURPOSE FLOUR
2 CUPS/500 ML MILK
SALT AND PEPPER

GRATED NUTMEG
BUTTER
1 CUP/250 ML TOMATO SAUCE

To make the filling, wash the spinach and steam without adding extra water. Squeeze out the liquid and chop the spinach coarsely with a knife. Combine briefly with the ricotta through a food processor or mix as well as possible by hand. Add the parmesan, eggs, salt, pepper, and a little nutmeg, and mix well.
To make the batter, mix the flour with the eggs, a pinch of salt, the melted butter, and the milk, and leave to stand in the refrigerator for at least 30 minutes.
Melt a little butter in a non-stick shallow pan and make thin pancakes with the batter. Spread the pancakes evenly with the spinach and ricotta filling, roll them up, and cut into pieces approximately 1½ inches (4 cm) long. Grease a soufflé dish and lay the pieces of pancake in it.
To make the sauce, melt the butter, stir in the flour, and cook for 1 minute. Then pour in the milk and bring to a boil, stirring constantly until the sauce has thickened. Season to taste with salt, pepper, and a pinch of nutmeg. Pour the sauce over the *crespelle* and bake in a preheated oven at 300 °F/150 °C for just 15 minutes. Before serving, pour a little tomato sauce over.

RIBOLLITA
Reheated vegetable soup

Serves 6

1 1/4 CUPS/250 G DRIED WHITE BEANS
3 TBSP OLIVE OIL
1 CUP/100 G BACON, CUT INTO SMALL PIECES
1 SMALL LEEK, SLICED THINLY
2 CARROTS, DICED
2 STICKS CELERY, SLICED THINLY
1 ONION, DICED
2 CLOVES OF GARLIC, CHOPPED FINELY
8 CUPS/2 LITERS MEAT STOCK OR MEAT JUICES
1–2 SPRIGS OF FRESH THYME
1 HAM BONE
1 LB/400 G SAVOY CABBAGE, CUT INTO STRIPS
SALT AND FRESHLY MILLED PEPPER
ABOUT 8 SLICES/300 G STALE WHITE BREAD

Soak the beans in plenty of water the night before. Next day, bring the beans to a boil in the water in which they have been soaked, and cook over a low heat for 1½ hours. Heat the olive oil and sauté the bacon, leek, carrots, celery, onion, and garlic. Pour in the meat stock and add the sprigs of thyme and the ham bone. Cover and cook over a low heat for 30 minutes. Add the strips of Savoy cabbage and cook for a further 30 minutes.
Purée half the cooked beans. Add to the whole beans in the pan and simmer for another 15 minutes. Remove the bone and season the soup with salt and pepper. Slice the bread and layer with the soup in a large dish. Chill overnight and bring to a boil again before serving. Sprinkle with oil and season with thyme, salt, and pepper.

AQUACOTTA MAREMMANA
"Boiled water"

1 ONION
1 STICK CELERY
1 CARROT
2 CLOVES OF GARLIC
OLIVE OIL
5–6 SWISS CHARD LEAVES, CUT INTO SMALL PIECES
4 RIPE TOMATOES, DICED
1 CHILI PEPPER
4 EGG YOLKS
4 SLICES STALE WHITE BREAD
1 CUP/100 G PECORINO, GRATED

Cut the onion, celery, carrot, and garlic into small pieces and sauté in a little olive oil. Add the Swiss chard, tomatoes, and chili pepper. Pour in 4 cups (1 liter) water and cook for approximately 20 minutes. Just before serving, whisk the egg yolks and add to the soup, but do not boil. Toast the slices of bread, rub with garlic if desired, place in deep bowls, and pour the soup over. Sprinkle with grated cheese.

TRIPPA ALLA FIORENTINA
Tripe Florentine-style
(Illustrated below)

1 ONION
2 CARROTS
2 STICKS CELERY
6–7 TBSP EXTRA VIRGIN OLIVE OIL
1 3/4 LB/800 G PRECOOKED VEAL TRIPE, CUT INTO STRIPS
1 LB/400 G SKINNED, SIEVED TOMATOES
SALT AND PEPPER
1 1/2 CUPS/100 G PARMESAN, GRATED

Cut the onions, carrots, and celery into small pieces. Heat the olive oil and sauté the vegetables over a low heat for approximately 30 minutes. Add the tripe and cook for 10 minutes, turning frequently. Add the tomatoes, season with salt and pepper, and mix well. Cover with a lid and simmer over a low heat for a further 20 minutes. Stir in a little parmesan and leave to stand for a few minutes for the flavors to develop. Serve hot, with extra parmesan sprinkled over the tripe.

MUSHROOMS

The people of Central Italy are passionate about mushrooms. In Umbria, in Marche, in Lazio, and also in Tuscany and the Maremma, mushroom pickers zealously comb the wooded areas from late summer to the end of autumn. The popular *porcino* mushroom, or *boletus edulis*, is just one of the many varieties that find their way into the baskets of mushroom fanciers every year. Chanterelles, morels, saffron milk cap, honey agaric, and numerous other kinds can be found beneath trees and in the meadows. In some areas the enthusiasm for gathering autumn mushrooms reached such a pitch that the authorities were obliged to place an official restriction on the amount that could be collected per person per day of six and a half pounds (three kilograms).

CHEESE

When one thinks of pecorino, one associates it first with the southernmost regions of Italy, but this aromatic ewe's milk cheese is just as typical of central Italy and Tuscany, where no larder is without *cacio*, as it is known here. It used to be regarded as a coarse peasant's specialty, often eaten as a snack with a chunk of bread and strong Tuscan wine, but now it is once more to be found in the finest kitchens. The best known varieties of pecorino toscano are produced in the heart of the region, in Chianti, near Cortona and Casentino, Pietrasanta and Lucardo, near Siena, and in the Maremma. Pecorino is available in varying degrees of ripeness. Very new pecorino is on sale after two to four weeks, while medium mature pecorino is ripened for two months. Mature pecorino, which is used instead of parmesan for grating, takes six months to ripen, but is often stored for longer.

Tuscans claim that the fragrant herbs for which the region is famous impart an incomparable flavor to this ewe's milk cheese. For this reason, the cheesemakers make sure that the animals can graze undisturbed on extensive pastures. Pecorino is produced from December to August. First, rennet is added to full-fat ewe's milk. After half an hour the coagulation process is complete, and the curd can be pressed. The resulting mass, which resembles quark, can now be left to stand in a warm place before being put in molds. The new cheese has to be carefully salted and turned by hand every day so that it can develop a rind. In many areas the rind is treated with tomato concentrate, so that it assumes an orange appearance. Other procedures involve using edible charcoal to impart a gray color, or placing the cheese on walnut leaves while it ripens to turn the rind a brownish color. *Marzolino*, a small egg-shaped pecorino, which is made from the first milk in spring (usually in March, hence its name – is a particularly remarkable specialty. It tastes best when it is still quite new.

There are so many different types of pecorino that Tuscan cuisine hardly needs any other kind of cheese. Occasionally, however, *raveggiolo*, a fine, mild cheese, is served, quite new and preferably with a little olive oil. To make savory tarts and robust fillings of all kinds, as well as sweet dishes and desserts, Tuscan cooks (like their counterparts elsewhere in Italy) use ricotta, which is made from whey and resembles cream cheese.

PECORINO CON I BACCELLI
Pecorino with broad bean pods
(Illustrated above)

BOILED BROAD BEANS IN THE POD
FRESH PECORINO

This dish can be served as a snack in the afternoon, or to follow the second course. Boil the beans in their pods in lightly salted water, then drain off the water. Arrange in an attractive wicker basket, put the cheese on a wooden board, and place in the center of the table. The beans are shelled, the skins are removed, and then they are dipped in salt and eaten with a small piece of pecorino, accompanied by homemade bread and a glass of Chianti.

A modern alternative is to shell the cooked beans, cut the pecorino into small cubes, and place in a ceramic dish. A sauce is prepared using sparkling white wine, salt, olive oil, and freshly milled pepper, in which the cheese and beans are marinated. This is a delicious starter for a wholesome country meal.

FUNGHI MISTI
Mushroom ragout

2 LBS/1 KG MIXED FRESH WOODLAND MUSHROOMS
1 SMALL BUNCH OF PARSLEY
2 CLOVES OF GARLIC
5 TBSP OLIVE OIL
3 TBSP WHITE WINE

Clean the mushrooms, wash and chop the parsley, peel and quarter the garlic cloves. Heat the olive oil in a heavy pan, add the garlic, and sauté for a few minutes. Add the mushrooms and fry briefly. Reduce the heat and pour in the white wine. Braise the mushrooms until they are soft. Serve sprinkled with parsley.

Porcino mushrooms
(Illustrated in the background)

The porcino mushroom (edible *boletus*) is by far the favorite Italian mushroom. Its large, round caps are stuffed, thinly sliced to accompany meat dishes, or finely chopped and added to sauces. The porcino mushroom can even be pickled in vinegar or preserved in other ways without losing much of its natural flavor.

THE WHITE TRUFFLES OF SAN MINIATO

Anthelme Brillat-Savarin, the great French gourmet and author of *The Physiology of Taste*, published in 1825, described the truffle as the "diamond of cuisine," a view that is willingly shared in many regions of Italy. The aroma of this noble mushroom, therefore, is just as well-loved in Tuscany as the scent of forests, meadows, and herbs. Truffle lovers make their pilgrimage to San Miniato every year. The white truffles from this region were once sold in various Tuscan markets, or even disappeared via dubious channels, only to re-emerge in Alba in the Piedmont, where they were sold at top prices as coveted Alba truffles. In order to combat this, the truffle hunters of San Miniato, Montopoli, and Pontedera banded together. In October and November they organize their own market, for which the romantic alleyways of San Miniato, bathed in gentle autumn sunlight, provide the ideal backdrop. Compared with those from other regions, the white truffles of San Miniato are relatively large, and have a very intense flavor. In the kitchen they are grated raw over the top of dishes, or used as an aromatic filling for specialties such as *Fagiano tartufato*, pheasant with truffles.

San Miniato is the Tuscan fortress that is the home of the white truffle. A truffle market is held here in October and November.

Honey agaric
The honey agaric mushroom (*chiodino* or *famigliola buona*) must always be cooked, because, like other members of its family, it is poisonous when raw. If properly prepared, however, it is a mushroom that is full of flavor and very versatile. The honey agaric mushroom has a wonderfully sweet taste, and is perfect for making mushroom risotto.

Field mushrooms
The field mushroom (*prataiolo*) has far more flavor than the white button mushroom, which is artificially cultivated and has a lonely upbringing in a dark cellar or grotto. Mushrooms should never be peeled, but should be cleaned by careful brushing, which is the only way in which they retain their delicate flavor.

Imperial mushrooms
The imperial mushroom (*fungo imperiale* or *amanita cesarea*) is one of the most sought-after mushrooms in Italy. In a warm climate it thrives particularly well. Caution is nevertheless advisable for private collectors, for this family of mushrooms also includes some poisonous specimens such as the notorious deadly amanita.

Morel mushrooms
The morel mushroom (*spugnola* or *eleta*) is an extremely interesting mushroom, which is also frequently used in cookery when dried. The delicate, spongy cap is especially prized by gourmets. It is advisable not to gather morels oneself, however, as it is extremely easy to confuse them with their poisonous relatives.

Chanterelle mushroom
The chanterelle mushroom (*cantarello* or *finferlo*) is one of the most popular and most common mushrooms worldwide. It has a delicate flavor, an appetizing fragrance, a good texture, an attractive appearance, and is a perfect accompaniment to rice or light meat dishes. It is also wonderful on its own, especially with parsley, mild onions, and a butter sauce.

Saffron milk cap
The saffron milk cap (*agarico delizioso*) is gathered on account of its nutty flavor. Caution is advisable, however, for it must not be confused with its poisonous relative, the sharp agaric. It is also susceptible to attack by pests, so it should be carefully inspected before purchase or thoroughly cleaned before preparation.

Oyster mushroom
Although the popular oyster mushroom (*gelone, fungo ostrica* or *pleuroto*) is grown commercially on a large scale, it does not then taste nearly as good as specimens allowed to grow on the stumps of fallen trees. It is very good fried or broiled, and, when finely sliced, can even be used raw as an ingredient in a cold salad.

BEEF FROM THE CHIANA VALLEY

Some scholars are of the opinion that Chiana cattle are descended from *bos primigenius*, the cattle that can be seen in prehistoric cave paintings. These cattle were held in high esteem by Etruscans and Romans, not only because of their meat, but also on account of their porcelain-colored white hide, and consequently these beautiful animals were often shown in carnival processions and then sacrificed to the gods.

Today, the Chianina breed is one of the most sought-after and valuable in Italy. Given optimal conditions, such as those in the Chiana valley, the cattle grow rapidly, attaining a comparatively large size. They can be recognized by the pale coloring, the light, short-horned head, and the elongated rump with broad back and loin sections. Meat from the Chiana valley is low in fat without being dry, and is particularly spicy and flavorsome as a result of the natural grazing available to the animals. Tuscans say it has a salty taste. The young animals, which reach weights of up to 1540 pounds (700 kilograms), provide large cuts of meat, including the huge T-bone steaks for *Bistecca alla fiorentina*. The meat is so tender that it needs only to be laid on a charcoal grill for a few minutes, and can almost be eaten raw. The writer Aldo Santini calls *Bistecca alla fiorentina* the "Giotto of good cooking." The word *bistecca* comes from the English *beefsteak*. Legend has it that in 1565, during a feast in the Piazza San Lorenzo in Florence, spit-roasted beef was served to the populace. The guests included some Englishmen, who, when they caught sight of the juicy meat, began chanting "Beefsteak, beefsteak" to emphasize their desire for a piece of meat. The Florentines immediately translated the cry into "bistecca." Before this feast, steaks had been called *carbonate*, literally carbon steaks, since they were broiled on charcoal, but the new name soon replaced this. This method of preparation was known even in ancient times: the Etruscans were already cooking T-bone steaks.

BISTECCA ALLA FIORENTINA
Florentine T-bone steak
(Illustrated below)

Serves 3–4

1 BEEFSTEAK ON THE BONE, TWO FINGERS THICK, AT LEAST
1 LB 12 OZ/800 G IN WEIGHT
SALT
FRESHLY MILLED PEPPER

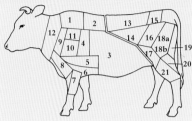

In Italy a bewildering array of expressions and names is currently in use for the various parts of cattle. Although state guidelines exist regarding the correct terminology, hardly anybody takes any notice of them. Since both the butchers and their customers prefer to keep using the names to which they are accustomed, which are often in dialect, the terms listed below serve merely as a guide.

Quarto anteriore (forequarter)
1. *Costata:* cutlet, chine
2. *Sottospalla:* forerib
3. *Pancia:* thin flank
4. *Fesone di spalla:* thin rib
5. *Reale:* thick rib
6. *Petto:* skirt
7. *Muscolo anteriore:* shank
8. *Polpa di spalla:* brisket
9. *Girello di spalla:* shoulder
10. *Copertina:* chuck
11. *Copertina di sotto:* blade
12. *Collo:* neck

Quarto posteriore (hindquarter)
13. *Lombata:* sirloin
14. *Filetto:* fillet
15. *Scamone:* top rump
16. *Fianchetto:* piece of loin from head of bone
17. *Noce:* tender cut from lower head of bone and thick flank
18a *Fesa:* tender cut of topside
18b *Sottofesa:* tender cut of silverside
19. *Girello:* round
20. *Campanello:* shank
21. *Muscolo posteriore:* hind shank

Classification of animals:
Vitello: veal, very pale meat, also
Vitello di latte: milk veal.
Vitellone: young animal, one to two years old; heifers must not have calved.
Manzo: three-year old animal; bulls have been castrated, heifers have not yet calved.
Bue: castrated bull (bullock), four years old or more.
Toro: fully grown bull.
Vacca: fully grown cow that has calved.

The meat should be at room temperature before broiling. Lay the steak on a grid and broil over red-hot charcoal, glowing but without flames, until a good crust has formed. This takes approximately 5 minutes. Then turn, without piercing the meat with the fork. Season the side that has already been broiled with salt. Broil the other side for a similar length of time until a crust has formed. The meat inside should still be red. Remove from the heat, season with salt and pepper, and serve immediately. White beans or lamb's lettuce are a suitable accompaniment.

OSSIBUCHI ALLA TOSCANA
Osso buco, sliced veal shank, Tuscan-style

4 SLICES OF VEAL SHANK, WITH MARROWBONE
ALL-PURPOSE FLOUR
4 TSP/20 G BUTTER
3–4 TBSP EXTRA VIRGIN OLIVE OIL
1 ONION
2 STICKS CELERY
1 CARROT
1 GLASS RED WINE
1/2 LB/200 G SIEVED TOMATOES
SALT AND PEPPER
MEAT STOCK IF REQUIRED

Coat the pieces of shank in flour and then fry in butter and olive oil until they are browned evenly on all sides. Remove from the pan and set aside in a warm place. Cut the onion, celery, and carrot into small pieces and sauté in the same pan. Add the red wine and stir in the tomatoes. Lay the pieces of meat in this sauce, adding enough water to cover them completely. Cover with a lid and braise for about 1 hour. Turn the pieces of veal after 30 minutes and season with salt and pepper. If the sauce thickens too much, add a little stock.

Above: Tuscan meat has an outstanding reputation. In order to safeguard it, the Chiana and Maremma cattle breeders have formed a consortium for their protection, watching carefully to ensure that the breeds retain their characteristics and are kept in the traditional way, roaming freely in their natural environment. This results in healthy, well-bred animals that provide lean, tasty, juicy meat. These top-quality products are sold in selected butchers' shops. Look for the mark of the consortium, stamped in ink or branded on the meat, then you will surely have the best.

BEEF FROM THE MAREMMA

The conclusion can be drawn from the archaeological finds at Cere and the bull's head in the museum at Vetulonia that cattle were already being bred in the Maremma in Etruscan times. They are descended from the so-called wild oxen mentioned by Pliny. Maremma cattle are strong, robust animals that were used by farmers for working in the fields before the advent of agricultural machinery.

Today, the gray cattle with their prominent horns – those of the bulls are half-moon-shaped and can grow to a length of three feet (one meter), while those of the females are curved like a lyre – are bred almost exclusively for their tender, tasty meat. In order to refine the species further, they have been cross-bred with Chiana and French Charolais cattle.

237

PORK

Pig-rearing has been an important economic factor in Italy since the time of the Langobardi in the 7th century. The medieval custom of measuring the size and value of a forest, not by the acre or hectare, but instead by the number of pigs it could sustain, shows how important this source of meat and fat must have been. Indeed, a family could live off a pig for a whole year, and the undemanding creature had the advantage of being easy to keep, since it could be fed on kitchen scraps and other waste. In addition to this, every part of the pig could be used: the meat either came directly to the table, or was made into robust sausages and ham; the lard and fat were important sources of energy; the skin could be tanned; and the bristles were used to make brushes.

Tuscans traditionally enjoy eating pork. Cold cuts and a *crostino* are rated equally highly as an *antipasto* or as a light snack between meals. And in rural areas, as recently as a few years ago, a plate of sausage was served in between the main course and the dessert as the high point of the meal and as a mark of esteem. Two different groups of products result from the processing of pork. On one hand there are the specialties consisting of "whole" meat, such as ham, shoulder cuts, belly, bacon, chuck, neck, and loin, and on the other hand there are the sausage products that are made from ground meat with the addition of salt, preservatives, and spices, such as *salsiccia* (sausage), *soppressata* (brawn), *buristo* (blood sausage), *salame* (salami), *finocchiona* and the crumbly *sbricciolona* (two typically Tuscan fennel sausages). Between Pisa and Arezzo, Prato, and Grosseto, there are still many small family businesses where pigs are slaughtered in the traditional manner, and where the meat is processed to make high-quality products. A number have specialized in maturing sausages carefully in order to develop their own characteristic flavors. And because Tuscany is a vast region with the most diverse climatic conditions, there is a correspondingly wide variety of local specialties. Furthermore, every butcher here is the proud possessor and guardian of his own secret recipe, often inherited from his grandfather, according to which he seasons the sausagemeat or smokes the ham.

Tuscan pork is of especially high quality, and bears no resemblance to the watery cutlets that shrink in the frying pan to half their original volume, which are on sale all too frequently at the meat counter in supermarkets north of the Alps. The indigenous breeds, which once populated the gently rolling Tuscan hills, feeding on acorns, beechnuts, and the fruits and berries in the undergrowth, are nevertheless under threat of extinction. One of these endangered species is the Cinta senese, which was originally a native of the heavily forested areas around Siena. These animals cannot be kept in pigsties, since they would put on too much fat too quickly, and water would be stored in their tissues. It is too expensive for the breeders to keep them under free-range conditions. In recent years, however, the demand for meat from free-range animals has risen.

A number of Tuscan breeders have now joined together to form an association, the *Compagnia della Cinta senese*. They all breed pigs in the proper manner, rearing the piglets quite naturally without the use of any fattening feed. The breeders know that at present they are offering a niche product, but experience has

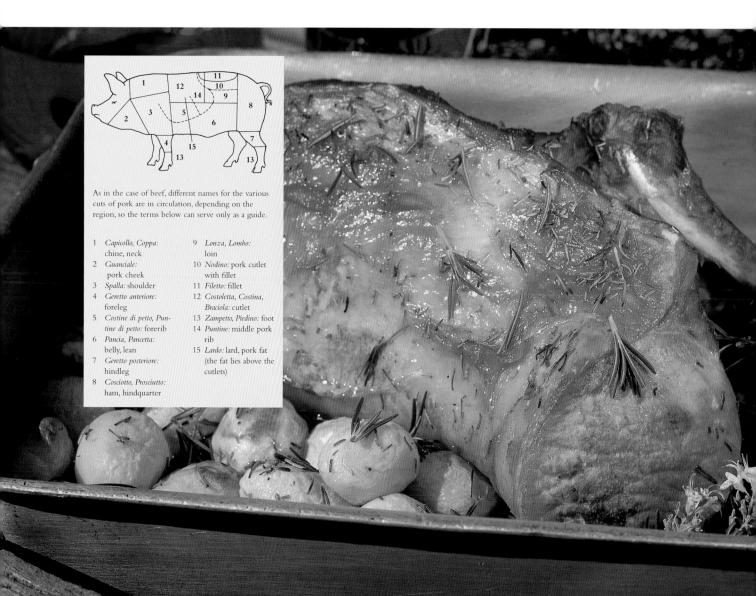

As in the case of beef, different names for the various cuts of pork are in circulation, depending on the region, so the terms below can serve only as a guide.

1 *Capicollo, Coppa:* chine, neck
2 *Guanciale:* pork cheek
3 *Spalla:* shoulder
4 *Geretto anteriore:* foreleg
5 *Costine di petto, Puntine di petto:* forerib
6 *Pancia, Pancetta:* belly, lean
7 *Geretto posteriore:* hindleg
8 *Cosciotto, Prosciutto:* ham, hindquarter
9 *Lonza, Lombo:* loin
10 *Nodino:* pork cutlet with fillet
11 *Filetto:* fillet
12 *Costoletta, Costina, Braciola:* cutlet
13 *Zampetto, Piedino:* foot
14 *Puntine:* middle pork rib
15 *Lardo:* lard, pork fat (the fat lies above the cutlets)

also taught them that customers appreciate the special flavor of products from free-range pigs, and are quite prepared to reach a little deeper into their pockets to buy it. The best example of the legendary Tuscan concern for quality is provided by the Chini family, which not only runs a butchery but also rears its own pigs in a forest near Gaiole, in Chianti. The father, Vincenzo Chini, for the most part concentrates on slaughtering pigs and preparing sausages, while his son Lorenzo is responsible for rearing the pigs. For centuries, since 1682 to be precise, the Chini family have adhered steadfastly to the traditional production methods for regional sausage specialties – and as a consequence have been repeatedly rewarded with numerous medals and prizes.

TONNO DEL CHIANTI

Tonno del Chianti, Chianti tuna fish, is made with the meat from suckling pigs. The *lattonzoli* (the Tuscan name for a suckling pig) weigh between 88 and 110 pounds (40–50 kilograms). In Tuscany, superfluous young animals, which the farmers had been unable to feed, were traditionally slaughtered during June and July. Because of the intense summer heat, however, it was impossible to salt the meat to preserve it, and so it was cooked in Vin Brusco. To a certain extent, Vin Brusco can be described as a "by-product" obtained from pressing Chianti: it is the wine made from the remaining white Trebbiano and Malvasia grapes.
Afterwards the meat was stored in olive oil. For some reason, this method of preparation imparted a flavor of tuna fish to the meat, and the Tuscans, who used not to catch tuna fish, thereby discovered an extremely tasty substitute.
For years, production of *Tonno del Chianti* was completely neglected. Today, thanks to Dario Cecchini of Panzano in Chianti, there is once again a single butcher's shop in Chianti – and worldwide – where *Tonno* is produced.

ARISTA ALLA FIORENTINA
Florentine roast pork
(Illustrated below left)

Serves 6

3–3 1/2 LB/1.5 KG PORK ROASTING JOINT, WITH BONE
2 CLOVES OF GARLIC
1 SPRIG OF ROSEMARY
SALT AND PEPPER
OLIVE OIL
2 LB/1 KG POTATOES

Loosen the meat from the bone. Finely chop the garlic and rosemary and mix with salt and pepper. Spread half the mixture on the bone. Replace the meat on the bone, and rub the other half of the herb mixture into the meat, using the hands. Sprinkle with oil and braise in a preheated oven at 350 °F (180 °C) for approximately 1 hour 20 minutes, basting repeatedly with the juices from the meat. Peel the potatoes and cut into large pieces. Add to the roast after 30 minutes.
Leave the roast to stand for at least 10 minutes after it comes out of the oven. Remove the bone, cut the meat into pieces and serve.

CREMA PARADISO
Tuscan creamed bacon

2 LB/1 KG FIRM BACK BACON
2 TBSP/20 G SEA SALT
BLACK PEPPERCORNS, CRUSHED
WINE VINEGAR
5–6 CLOVES OF GARLIC, CRUSHED
A FEW SPRIGS OF FRESH ROSEMARY, CHOPPED

Grind the bacon in a food processor. Add the salt, peppercorns, a few drops of wine vinegar, the garlic, and the rosemary. Knead the bacon on a marble slab until a light, delicate cream is formed. Spread on hot toast and serve with Chianti.

LUMACHE AFFUMICIATE CON CAPICOLLO LARDELLATO
Smoked snails with bacon and pork chine

24 SNAILS
1 STICK CELERY, COARSELY CHOPPED
1 SHALLOT, COARSELY CHOPPED
1 SMALL CARROT, COARSELY CHOPPED
3/4 CUP/200 ML WHITE WINE
SALT AND PEPPER

For the filling:

6 1/2 TBSP/100 G BUTTER
1 SLICE BROILED PORK CHINE, 1/4 LB/100 G IN WEIGHT
2/3 CUP/50 G BACON, COARSELY CHOPPED
2 OZ/50 G SMOKED SCARMORZA CHEESE, COARSELY CHOPPED
1 CLOVE OF GARLIC
SALT AND PEPPER

Wash and clean the snails and place in a pan with the celery, shallot, carrot, wine, and plenty of cold water. Boil for about 4–5 hours, occasionally adding a little water if necessary; do not season with salt and pepper until the end of the cooking time.
To make the filling, put the butter, pork chine, bacon, cheese, and garlic in the food processor and process until smooth. Season to taste with salt and pepper. Leave the snails to cool in the cooking liquid, drain, and prepare as follows: first place some of the filling in a dish, lay the snails on top, then cover with filling, but not to the top of the dish. Cook in the oven at 400 °F (200 °C) until the top is brown, and serve very hot.

FEGATELLI DI MAIALE
Pig's liver in a pig's stomach

1 LB/500 G PIG'S LIVER
1/2 LB/200 G LEAN PORK
1 CLOVE OF GARLIC
SALT AND PEPPER
1/2 LB/200 G PIG'S STOMACH
5–6 BAY LEAVES
2–3 TBSP EXTRA VIRGIN OLIVE OIL
RED WINE OR MEAT STOCK

To make the filling, cut the liver, pork, and garlic cloves into small pieces, and season with salt and pepper. Place the pig's stomach in boiling water for a few minutes, drain, and pat dry. Cut into pieces big enough to hold a portion of filling about the size of a fist. Stuff the pieces of pig's stomach with the filling, place a bay leaf in each, and secure with a cocktail stick.
Cook in olive oil in the oven for approximately 20 minutes, adding a little red wine or meat stock if necessary.

FILETTO DI MAIALE GRATINATO
Pork fillet au gratin with herbs

1 CUP MIXED/100 G THYME, ROSEMARY, MARJORAM, AND SAGE
2 1/2 CUPS/300 G BREADCRUMBS
1 CUP/100 G PECORINO, GRATED
3 1/2 TBSP/50 ML EXTRA VIRGIN OLIVE OIL
1 PORK FILLET, ABOUT 1 1/2–1 3/4 LB/700–800 G IN WEIGHT
SALT AND PEPPER
2 EGGS
SCANT 1/2 CUP/100 ML SUNFLOWER OIL

Finely chop all the herbs. Add the breadcrumbs, cheese, and a little olive oil, and mix. Season the pork fillet with salt and pepper. Beat the eggs, then dip the fillet in the egg and turn to coat it. Spread with the herb mixture. Fry in sunflower oil in a preheated pan for approximately 3 minutes on each side. Cook in the oven at 320 °F (160 °C) for about 10 minutes. Cut the fillet into thin slices, and serve with Savoy cabbage and smoked bacon.

FEGATELLI DI MAIALE AGLI AROMI
Pig's liver in herb stock

Serves 6

1 LB/500 G PIG'S LIVER
8 SAGE LEAVES
1/2 LB/200 G PIG'S STOMACH
1 CUP/100 G BACON, FINELY DICED
1 ONION, CUT INTO RINGS
8 ROSEMARY LEAVES
LARGE HANDFUL FRESH PARSLEY
SALT AND PEPPER
3/4 CUP/200 ML DRY WHITE WINE

Cut the liver into 8 evenly sized pieces and wrap individually with a sage leaf in pieces of pig's stomach. Fry the bacon with the onion rings, rosemary, and coarsely chopped parsley in a shallow pan for several minutes. Add the liver and cook for at least 20 minutes over a low heat, adding the salt, pepper, and wine.
Arrange the liver on a toasted slice of polenta, and serve with braised beans.

Sausages

Sbricciolona

Sbricciolona, like *finocchiona*, is made from lean meat, but the proportion of added fat is greater and the ripening time is essentially shorter. Consequently, *sbricciolona* has a rather soft consistency and crumbles when it is cut – hence its name, which means "crumbly sausage." It is eaten cold.

Soppressata

Soppressata, also known as *capocchia* or *coppa di testa*, is a pressed sausage. It consists of tongue, pork belly, the pig's head, stomach, and unused pieces of meat from which the bones are removed. The meat is then chopped into small pieces, cooked with spices, and finally used to fill a jute bag. In Italy there are many different varieties of *soppressata*, but the most famous pressed sausage is probably that from Siena. It is prepared using the same flavorings as *panforte*, namely cloves, coriander, black pepper, nutmeg, and cinnamon. The sausage known as *soppressata in cuffia* is also popular. To make this, the bones are removed from a pig's head, which is then stuffed with sausage meat.

Buristo

Buristo is a blood sausage containing small pieces of fat left over from the production of other types of sausage. This specialty, which is seasoned with herbs, has a strong, lingering flavor, and will keep for eight to ten days when raw, a little longer if cooked. It is sliced, fried briefly, and then boiled in wine for a few minutes before being eaten. A pig's stomach is stuffed with the blood sausage filling to make *buristo in cuffia*.

Migliacci

Fresh pig's blood can be made into a tasty, round loaf on the day the pig is slaughtered. Four cups (1 liter) of blood is mixed with a scant ½ cup (50 grams) of flour and seasoned with what are known as "blood herbs," a sprig of rosemary and a little fennel. A few tablespoons of oil are heated in a non-stick pan, the mixture is ladled in, and cooked in the same way as a pancake. When it is ready, the loaf is seasoned with salt, sprinkled generously with grated pecorino cheese, and served hot. In many regions *migliacci* are also served sweet, with the addition of sugar.

Salame

Salame is a long-life sausage and is made from the best lean pork and a spicy mixture, accounting for between 25 and 40 percent by volume, of diced bacon, salt, peppercorns, and red wine. The filling is put into natural pig's gut and carefully bound by hand. It ripens over a period of between three and six months.

Salsiccia fresca and Salsiccia secca

Salsiccia secca is an air-dried sausage made using meat from domestic pigs or wild boar. *Salsiccia fresca*, on the other hand, is a spicy fresh sausage that is probably the original prototype for all sausages. Made from fresh meat with small pieces of belly, neck, and shoulder, the sausages dangle invitingly in long rows above the counters in butchers' shops. They are eaten cold on bread, but can also be pan-fried or broiled. At harvest time, farmers' wives often used to serve a stew made from beans, grapes, and *salsiccia*. If the sausages are to be fried, it is a good idea to prick the skins beforehand with a needle or cocktail stick so they do not burst in the hot pan and retain their shape. In the area around Siena the sausagemeat is flavored with ginger or chili pepper.

Finocchiona

Finocchiona comes from the rural area around Florence. This coarse salami, made from good, lean meat and bacon or pig's cheek, derives its unmistakable flavor from the addition of wild fennel seeds. The sausage meat is used to fill thick, firm gut and left to hang for about a year before it is sold. Wafer-thin slices of *finocchiona* are an essential feature of Tuscan plates of *antipasto*.

Ham and other pork products

Prosciutto (ham)

The hind leg of the pig is made into ham. In Tuscany, the piece of meat cut from the leg is often seasoned with garlic, cloves, and pepper, before being stored for six weeks in salt, after which the maturing process begins. After about six months the meat begins to dry out, so from that point onward it needs a protective layer of lard. After a further six months of constant ventilation and tender care, the ham is ready and can be served in wafer-thin slices with a stout loaf of bread. Ham from Casentino is especially popular; after the salting process, the surface is rubbed with garlic a second time.

Spalla (pork shoulder)

Although it is treated with the same seasonings as ham, pork shoulder matures for only three to four months. The sliced meat has a strong flavor, but does not quite achieve the same quality as ham.

Pancetta (belly bacon)

Bacon from the belly of the pig is salted for a week and can be cut into delicate slices and served with wholesome bread after maturing for only 14 days. In Tuscany *rigatino*, thinly sliced belly bacon streaked with fat, is especially popular.

Capicollo (pork neck)

Pork neck is seasoned with various herbs, salt, and pepper, and, like *coppa* from Piacenza, needs to ripen for about three to six months before being eaten. It tastes good as an *antipasto*.

Lonza (loin)

Loin of pork is marinated for 48 hours in red wine, salt, garlic, cloves, pepper, rosemary, or other herbs and spices. Then it is used to fill a fine skin of natural pig's gut and left to hang for one to two months.

Lardo (bacon fat)

Bacon fat used to be regarded as poor man's fare. The poorer sector of the population included workers in the marble quarries in the Apuan Alps, who have been producing their own, extremely delicious varieties of bacon fat since time immemorial. On the day the pig was slaughtered, the cooled bacon fat was immediately put into a marble dish and rubbed with salt, pepper, garlic, rosemary, cloves, coriander, juniper, and nutmeg, and covered with a stone slab. The container was stored in the cellar, and after six months the bacon fat could be cut into thin slices. It was soft, delicate, white, and thoroughly wholesome. Today, this method of bacon fat production is hardly ever practiced, but there are some enterprises run by craftsmen that still produce very good bacon fat. *Bruschetta*, crisply toasted white bread, is excellent when served with bacon fat.

Grassetti, ciccioli (pork scratchings)

Pork scratchings are cooked left-over bacon rind, small irregularly shaped pieces of dark meat. Their flavor is so strong that it makes connoisseurs' mouths water, and it is precisely for this reason that they are often served as an appetizer before meals in the country. They provide a wholesome snack when served with some hearty rustic bread and a glass of country wine.

Wild boar and small game

The Maremma is a bleak, inaccessible area, largely undiscovered by the tourist industry, where mushrooms can spring up and wild boar can live undisturbed. Yet here too, as in many mountainous regions, people like the spicy flavor of game, with the result that the animals have to be on their guard against native huntsmen.

Wild boar meat, in addition to providing very flavorsome hams, is also used to make small huntsmen's sausages and tasty salami. Sausages made from wild boar generally have a more intense, characteristic flavor than products made from the domestic pig. The sausages can be eaten raw, but are also air-dried and then preserved in oil or lard. In the Maremma, however, there is also a passion for hunting hare and other small game, which are then prepared in extremely varied ways.

Pappardelle alla lepre
Noodles with hare ragout

1 HALF PORTION OF WILD HARE
1 ONION
1 CARROT
1 STICK CELERY
1 PARSLEY ROOT
3 TBSP EXTRA VIRGIN OLIVE OIL
3 1/2 TBSP/50 G BUTTER
SALT AND FRESHLY MILLED PEPPER
1 BAY LEAF
A FEW JUNIPER BERRIES, CRUSHED
1 GLASS OF RED WINE
MEAT STOCK
ABOUT 1 LB/400 G PAPPARDELLE
3/4 CUP/50 G PARMESAN, GRATED

Wash the meat, trim, and cut into large pieces. Cut the onion, carrot, celery, and parsley root into small pieces and sauté gently in oil and butter. Add the meat and fry on all sides, seasoning with salt and pepper.

Add the bay leaf, crushed juniper berries, and wine, cover with a lid and braise. When the meat is tender, remove the bones and cut the meat into small pieces. Strain the sauce and bring to a boil with a little stock, then replace the meat.

Cook the *pappardelle* until *al dente*, drain, and place in a warmed dish. Pour over the hare ragout, sprinkle generously with grated parmesan, and serve.

In Tuscany, wild boar meat is not only eaten fresh but is also made into robust salami sausages.

First the meat is passed through the meat grinder. It is ground coarsely or finely, depending on the type of sausage.

After the butcher has seasoned the sausage meat according to his own special recipe, he uses the mixture to fill lengths of gut.

The sausages are securely tied with the aid of a special machine. Wild boar salami sausages are usually small and not very long.

Cinghiale alla cacciatora
Wild boar, huntsman-style
(Illustrated in the background)

Serves 6–8

2 ONIONS
2 CARROTS
2 STICKS OF CELERY
EXTRA VIRGIN OLIVE OIL
4 LB/1.8 KG LEG OF PORK, PREFERABLY FROM A YOUNG
WILD BOAR
1 SPRIG OF ROSEMARY
2 1/2 CUPS/625 ML RED WINE
1 SMALL ONION, CHOPPED
1 CLOVE OF GARLIC, CRUSHED
1 CHILI PEPPER
1/2 LB/200 G SKINNED AND SIEVED TOMATOES
SALT AND PEPPER
MEAT STOCK

Cut the onions, carrots, and celery into small pieces and sauté in olive oil. Place the meat in a covered terrine, adding the sautéed vegetables and the rosemary, and pour over 2 cups (500 ml) of red wine. Leave the meat to stand in a cool place for at least 12 hours to absorb the flavors of the marinade. Pour off the marinade, Remove the bone from the joint, trim the meat, cut into cubes, and sauté in a pan with 2 tablespoons olive oil until the juices, with their aroma of game, begin to run.

Sauté the onion, garlic, and chili pepper in a little olive oil in a roasting pan. Add the meat cubes and fry, stirring constantly. Pour in ½ cup (125 ml) red wine and boil to reduce a little. Add the tomatoes, season with salt and pepper, and braise for approximately 2 hours over a low heat, adding a little meat stock if necessary. Serve the wild boar ragout with the tomato sauce and rice or pasta.

STILL LIFE

The painter Jacopo Chimenti (1551–1640) had a reputation as a gourmet, even as a glutton, with the result that his friends occasionally called him by the name Empilo – meaning "fill him up" – in a play on words on his nickname, Empoli. However, it was not necessarily his liking for good food and drink that led him to paint still lifes. Although the *natura morta* was in great demand in the 17th century because of its decorative value, as a subject for painting it was ranked so far beneath the altarpieces, historical paintings, landscapes, and portraits that it was extremely badly paid. Only a few artists relied upon this genre. The ten still-life paintings attributed to Chimenti tend to be regarded as minor works, proof of the fact that the artist was primarily concerned with specifically artistic aims. His flat arrangement of natural produce and kitchen objects, in which the background is suppressed, harks back to earlier examples from northern Italy, but may also have been inspired by Spanish painters. In the foreground, a multitude of goods is on display, such as could undoubtedly be seen in the flourishing urban markets at that time. Reproducing the material differences between the individual objects was such an enormous challenge to the painter's artistic capabilities that the construction of a pleasing, decorative composition receded into the background. The artist achieved his painterly aim solely with the aid of the oblique lighting that falls upon the hanging poultry, the sausages and

Jacopo Chimenti, called d'Empoli (1551(1640), *The Larder, c.* 1620–30, oil on canvas, 47 x 60 inches (119 x 152 cm), Palazzo Pitti, Galleria Palatina, Florence
Chimenti distinguishes between prepared food on the table and raw ingredients hanging from a beam. As can be seen from the rustic vessels that are lined up in a slightly disorderly fashion, we are probably looking at the well-stocked larder of a country house.

Michelangelo Merisi, called Caravaggio (1571–1609), *Basket of fruit*, 1595/96, oil on canvas, 12¼ x 18½ inches (31 x 47 cm), Pinacoteca Ambrosiana, Milan
Caravaggio often supplemented his paintings of figures with skillful still-life depictions of fruit. The reason why he painted his one unique still life remains a mystery. The detail in the reproduction is evident, even to the extent of the wormholes in the apples and pears, which can perhaps be construed as a reference to the transience of nature.

the meat, the vessels, and the prepared food lying on the table. The dark wall in the background intensifies the effect of the light in such a way that it is possible to imagine one can almost feel the different textures of the raw and cooked food that is depicted, and even the hardness of the fired earthenware and the coldness of the metal.

The principle underlying all still-life painting is the reproduction of natural appearances that transcends the visible, a deception of the human eye.

Giovanni Battista Recco (1615– *c.* 1660), *Still life with fish and mussels*, 1653, oil on canvas, 39 x 50 inches (100 x 126 cm), National Museum, Stockholm
The Neapolitan painter Recco often painted the rich pickings of native fishermen. Using only a few colors in his palette, but with highly differentiated nuances, he gave volume and life to the shimmering forms of the fish that are depicted.

The means at the disposal of the artist are a sure mastery of perspective and skilled use of lighting, as demonstrated in 1595 by Michelangelo Merisi, known as Caravaggio, in his *Basket of fruit*, the only purely still-life painting he executed. Painted from a viewpoint slightly lower than the subject, the foreshortening of the perspective emphasizes the plasticity and volume of each individual fruit, stalk, and leaf, while the fine gradations of reflected light serve to differentiate the various surfaces. This masterpiece inspired numerous imitators in subsequent decades. The artists of Lombardy, however, countered Caravaggio's refined painting with paintings devoted to ordinary rural subjects. Influenced by the Flemish still-life paintings of kitchens and market stalls, painters such as Vincenzo Campi (1535/40–1591) created still lifes peopled with figures, in which bustling, earthy everyday life and the sumptuous wares on offer in rural markets complement one another. However, the religious, moralizing undercurrent that was so typical of Dutch still-life painting was suppressed in Italy, where the tradition of the religious image remained unbroken, in favor of a pronounced, detailed realism in both approach and execution. A preoccupation with earthly life remained a distinguishing feature of Italian still-life painting.

Against this background, many local schools emerged during the 17th century, in whose pictures regional specialties loom large. Typical of these are the paintings of the Neapolitan artists Giovanni Battista (1615–*c.* 1660) and Giuseppe Recco (1634–1695), brothers who specialized in still-life paintings with fish, and developed enormous virtuosity in painting their shimmering forms.

Perception and reproduction, aimed at deceiving the eye, of differentiations in the superficial and material properties of plants and animals became a central concern for painters. The sumptuous arrangements of fruit, as seen, for instance, in the work of Giovanni Paolo Castelli, called Spadino (1659–*c.* 1730), were especially attractive to many artists, particularly in the schools of Rome, Milan, and Bologna. It is the artistic skill of the painter that endows peaches with an almost unearthly velvet quality and gives grapes a gleaming skin, while citrus fruits in contrast are distinguished by their exaggeratedly rough, wrinkled peel, and bursting figs, pomegranates, or ripe melons are found lying next to noble vessels with smooth, gleaming bodies – with the result that the eye loses itself in details. For other painters, the scales clothing the fish, the plumage of the birds, and the furs on the game are the springboard from which the highest artistic achievements are attained. Prepared food, well known from Dutch still-life paintings of tables, is included only in isolated instances here, mostly in the form of sweet pastries, as in the work of Cristoforo Munari (1667–1720). Eventually, with the introduction of calculated disorder and a gradual opening-out of the space depicted, even to the extent of including landscape, the representational methods of still-life painting evolved to accommodate the taste of the 18th century, which was defined by aristocratic ideals. Not until the end of the century did this genre of painting find new, forward-looking subjects and forms.

THE UFFIZI

Attention in the princely courts of the Renaissance was not confined to ruling; efforts were also made with regard to public relations. In one of the first cultural political initiatives in history, the Medici family in Florence engaged the architect Vasari to erect a splendid building, which from the very beginning was intended solely to demonstrate the family's wealth, impress foreign visitors, and display the artistic treasures in its possession in appropriate surroundings. The gallery was founded by Francesco I in 1581, and it was only ten years later that a certain writer called Bocchi, compiling the first guide to Florence, praised the Uffizi as "so magnificent, so regal." Art-loving travelers in those early days were happy to follow Bocchi's recommendation, for visitors were admitted from 1591 onward. The Medici family made their mark as extraordinary patrons. They administered the contents of their museum with care, acquired new

collections, assimilated artistic legacies – and the expense account of Lorenzo the Magnificent was severely stretched in the antique markets of Rome, for ancient Roman and Greek objects were very popular acquisitions during the Renaissance.

Cristoforo Munari (1667–1720), *Ice bucket, majolica jug and biscotti, c.* 1710, oil on canvas, 28 x 23 inches (70.5 x 58.5 cm), in the Molinari Pradelli collection, Castenaso. Pastries frequently feature in the paintings of Munari and are arranged in a decorative ensemble together with vessels, glasses, and occasionally also musical instruments. The light shadow in the room and the fragility of the objects are suggestive of the transitory nature of existence.

THE PALIO DI SIENA

On July 2, *Palio della Madonna di Provenzano*, and on August 16, *Palio dell'Assunta*, the whole of Siena is out and about, for it is on these days that the famous horse races are held. Lots are drawn in these riding festivals to decide which ten districts, out of a total of 17 autonomous districts into which the city of Siena has been divided since the Middle Ages, will be the contenders. The racecourse is built on the Piazza del Campo, and each participating *contrada* and its riders is feverish with excitement. The natives of Siena feel such an affinity with the district in which they were born that, in earlier times, rivalries of epic proportions between the *contrade* were not unknown.

Today, all the *contrade* still have their own symbolic colors, coats of arms, and heraldic beasts: eagles, snails, wave with dolphin, panther, forest with rhinoceros, turtle, owl, unicorn, mussel, tower with elephant, ram, caterpillar, dragon, giraffe, porcupine, wolf, and goose.

The race course at the Piazza del Campo is very small. Falls and injuries to riders and horses are not uncommon. The Palio is also dangerous for spectators.

Formerly, each *contrada* used to prepare its own dishes for the spectacle. Since the slaughterhouses were located in the *Oca* district, the *contrada* of the goose, meat dishes were cooked there. Pork butchers' businesses were found in the *Tòrre*, the *contrada* of the tower, and so they produced pork specialties. In the *Aquila*, the *contrada* of the eagle, risotto with black truffles was served.

The kitchens of Siena do not stand idle on the two main days on which the races are held. Families fortunate enough to live directly next to the Piazza del Campo, with a window, or even a balcony, from which to watch the big event, invite their friends. Typical traditional Sienese dishes are then eaten, such as *Panzanella* (bread salad), *Crocchette di formaggio* (cheese croquettes), *Timballo di riso con piccioni in salmì* (timbale of rice with pigeon salmi), *Crostini rossi alla milza* (red crostini with spleen), *Brasato al Brunello* (pot roast in red Brunello wine), and for dessert *Babà allo zabaglione* (zabaglione baba). All this is accompanied by the good local wine.

As soon as the Palio is over, the victorious *contrade* launch themselves into preparations for the *cena della vittoria*, the culinary victory feast. At the table of honor are seated not only the leaders and riders of the winning *contrade*, but also civic dignitaries from the relevant districts of the city. The winning horses are also given their own special meal after the race. During these festivities, which can continue for a whole week in gratitude for their performance, countless banquets and feasts are organized, which all citizens can attend.

Even the winning horses share the festive mood, for they are given their own special feast-day meal.

Background: The Palio di Siena is not merely a competitive riding event, but also a culinary festival lasting an entire week. All the citizens of Siena and their guests can attend the banquets.

PANFORTE

Siena's most famous confectionery is indisputably *panforte* (which literally means strong bread), or perhaps even *panpepato* (peppered bread). The Sienese love it so much that they even assigned it a patron saint, since when St. Laurence, whose feast day falls on August 10, has been associated with this specialty.

Sweet bread made with flour and honey is mentioned as early as the 1st century A.D., in a collection of Latin recipes. Sienese *panforte*, however, appears to have developed, not from this honey bread, but from the native *melatello*. This simple sweetmeat was made of flour, dried fruits, and water in which apples had previously been washed, but had the disadvantage that it quickly turned moldy and sour, and hence *fortis*.

The first written evidence that *panforte* or *panpepato* was traditionally made in the Siena region is found in a document dating from the year 1205, which originates from the monastery of Montecelso. This document mentions that the peasants were obliged to pay a tax to the nuns in the form of a considerable number of pepper cakes or loaves of honey bread. If the traditional story is to be believed, this monastery did in fact play an important role in the history of the famous spiced bread. Legend has it that Nicoló de Salimbeni, a young man from one of the best families in Siena, was afflicted by wild extravagance, and was failing to live by Christian principles. One day, however, he realized the error of his ways, embraced his faith once more, and gave away what remained of his wealth and possessions: a small bag of spices, which at that time were so precious that they were also used as currency, and the recipe for a sumptuous sweetmeat, in which generous use was made of these spices. The recipient was a certain Sister Berta, who lived a virtuous life as a nun in the monastery of Montecelso. Although Sister Berta tried out the recipe, she came to the conclusion that the sensual pleasure afforded by such a sweetmeat was not the proper thing for a nunnery, and gave it to the episcopal court. As a result the recipe for the spiced bread was passed from bishop to bishop until it reached the hands of Ubaldino, brother of Cardinal Ottaviano della Pila, who was such an excellent cook that he was immortalized by Dante in "Purgatory" in the *Divine Comedy*. Ubaldino improved the dish further by adding almonds, hazelnuts, candied fruits, and only the most aromatic and delicious spices.

Panforte from Siena soon became a branded product and a top export. The spiced bread was also being eaten in Venice on ceremonial occasions as early as 1370. Because of the large quantity of spices contained in it, the widely acclaimed foodstuff was considered an aphrodisiac. Several centuries later, Enrico Righi, the proprietor at that time of the Panforte Parenti spiced cake enterprise, created the *panforte Margherita* on the occasion of the visit of Queen Margherita of Savoy. This "white panforte" was distinguished from traditional types by the new method used to make the candied fruits, as well as by the addition of marzipan, which made it softer, more succulent, and also paler in color. Another sweet specialty, beloved and highly

Panforte senese is a nourishing sweatmeat made from nuts, candied lemon and orange peel, flour, sugar, and honey.

prized throughout Tuscany, comes, not from Siena, but from Prato. *Biscotti di Prato*, which elsewhere are also called *cantucci*, *cantuccini*, or *giottini*, consist of flour, eggs, sugar, and almonds, flavored with lemon. They are baked twice and must be really hard, like rusks. These crisp cookies are eaten dipped in Vin Santo for dessert.

PANFORTE SENESE
Pepper cakes, Siena-style
(Illustrated above)

1/2 CUP/75 G HAZELNUTS
1/2 CUP/75 G ALMONDS
1 CUP/175 G CANDIED LEMON AND ORANGE PEEL
SCANT 1/2 CUP/50 G ALL-PURPOSE FLOUR
1/4 CUP/25 G COCOA
1/2 TSP CINNAMON
1/2 TSP GINGER SPICE
1/2 CUP/100 G SUGAR
3 TBSP/100 G HONEY
2 TBSP CONFECTIONERS' SUGAR
1 TSP CINNAMON

Spread the hazelnuts on a baking sheet and roast in a preheated oven at 375 °F (190 °C) for 5–10 minutes. Then rub off the skins using a clean cloth, and chop coarsely. Blanch the almonds briefly, hold between thumb and forefinger to squeeze them out of their brown skin, then chop them coarsely.

Finely chop the lemon and orange peel, place in a bowl with the flour, cocoa, hazelnuts, almonds, and spices, and mix all the ingredients well. Put the sugar and honey in a pan and heat gently until both have dissolved. Then boil until the mixture has reached a temperature of approximately 240 °F (115 °C). If you do not have a sugar thermometer, test as follows: Drop a little of the mixture into a cup of cold water, if it forms a ball, the right

temperature has been reached. Remove from the stove immediately and stir into the nut mixture. Put the dough in a flat springform pan, 8 inches (20 cm) in diameter, lined with waxed paper, and spread until level. The dough should be less than half an inch thick. Bake the cake in a preheated oven at 300 °F (150 °C) for approximately 30 minutes, then turn out onto a cake rack, remove the waxed paper, and leave to cool. Sprinkle with cinnamon and confectioners' sugar and serve in wedges.

BISCOTTI DI PRATO OR CANTUCCINI
Prato *biscotti*

2 CUPS/300 G ALMONDS, SKINNED AND ROASTED
4 1/4 CUPS/500 G ALL-PURPOSE FLOUR
1 1/2 CUPS/300 G SUGAR
4 EGGS
SALT
GRATED RIND OF 1 LEMON
1 TBSP ANISEED
BUTTER
1 EGG

Crush the almonds coarsely and mix with the flour, sugar, eggs, and a pinch of salt in a mixing bowl. Add the lemon zest and aniseed to taste. Make the dough into rolls, about 1 inch (2.5 cm) in diameter, and place on a greased baking sheet. Whisk the egg with a little sugar and brush the rolls with it. Place in a preheated oven and bake, or rather dry, at 250 °F (120 °C) for no more than 30 minutes. Cut the rolls into ½-inch (1-cm) slices diagonally, and bake these for about another 15 minutes.

WINEGROWING IN ITALY

The history of winegrowing in Italy begins in about 800 B.C., when Greeks planted vines they had brought with them when they colonized Sicily. For a long time, southern Italy remained the Greeks' most important winegrowing center. In the year A.D. 79, however, the wine world was shaken by a catastrophe: the masses of lava from Vesuvius not only buried Pompeii, but, by destroying the most important port in the empire, also destroyed the foundations of the trade in wine with other countries in the Mediterranean region. From that point onward, winegrowing advanced farther and farther north, at first into the hills near Rome, and later, especially during the reign of the emperor Probus (276–82), even reached the most remote provinces beyond the Alps. The foundations for the present-day winegrowing regions of Bordeaux, Moselle, and Wachau had been laid. With the eventual fall of the Roman empire in the 4th century A.D., Italian viticulture also went into decline. It was not until Renaissance times, when Tuscan merchants began to take an interest in the wine trade, that cultivation of vines regained its economic importance. Grape juice was a perfectly natural product and was at that time seldom considered a luxury as had been the case in ancient Rome. In the second half of the 19th century, the country experienced a genuine winegrowing revolution. Under the influence of the modernists, the followers of Garibaldi and founders of the Republic, winegrowing and cellar techniques were significantly improved, and wines were created that have remained popular to this day: Chianti and Barolo, Valpolicella and Brunello. However, the first half of the 20th century saw a setback. Until well after World War II, many producers laid more emphasis on large-scale production than on growths that were superior in quality. This state of affairs did not change until the 1970s and 1980s, since when the quality of Italian wines has improved so much that the best products can be compared on equal terms with the great names in international winegrowing.

TUSCAN ARISTOCRACY SUPPLIES THE WORLD

While the central European winegrowing areas of Rheingau, Moselle, Burgundy, and Bordeaux were blossoming for the first time in the Middle Ages, winegrowing in Italy was descending into a deep crisis. It was not until the 13th and 14th centuries that it began to recover a little. In Tuscany, aristocratic families such as those of the Marchesi Antinori and Marchesi Frescobaldi – families that today still number among the leading Tuscan winegrowers – began to devote themselves to the wine trade in addition to their various banking and commercial activities. The extent of their influence is demonstrated by the fact that, from time to time, the Frescobaldi family financed the English court, and acted as a tax collector for the Vatican.

In winter, when the vines are in their resting phase, the foundations for the next season are already being laid. This is when the shoots are pruned and the soil is ploughed.

Harvesting takes place in September and October. The grapes should be picked as quickly as possible.

FROM DIONYSUS TO THE BACCHANALIA

Like the Greeks, the Romans also had a god of wine. In ancient Athens, Dionysus was the god of fertility, wine, and ecstasy. Because such things were definitely regarded as "women's matters" in ancient times, it was mainly the women who commemorated "their" god every winter by means of long, relaxed feasts, during the course of which wine and all kinds of intoxicants imaginable were consumed in great quantities. These rites continued in the Roman Empire as bacchanalia, feasts in honor of Bacchus, the god of wine. The excesses were sometimes so great that the feasts were forbidden due to fears for public order. It was not until Christianity was established as the official state religion in the 7th century in our calendar that the bacchanalia came to an end.

Background: At the end of May the flowering stems can be seen in all their glory. They are growing especially quickly at this point. In order to ensure optimal conditions for the grapes later on, the new shoots are again tied in.

The buds break in March and April. The vintner ties the quickly growing shoots to a framework of wires that has been erected previously.

It is still difficult to tell whether this is a white or a red grape variety, since most grapes look much the same until they ripen in July.

Quality control in the vineyard is achieved by means of the refractometer, an optical device used to ascertain the specific gravity of the must.

Now there is no time to lose, for uncontrolled fermentation or decay jeopardize quality.

After the fresh must has been clarified and any cloudiness removed, fermentation is started.

Racking, transferring the wine to another container, is necessary to separate the new wine from the yeast.

When maturing quality red wines in wooden casks, both large barrels and small barrique-type containers are used.

The vintner checks at regular intervals to ensure that the wine is maturing in the barrels according to plan.

Unlabeled bottles are temporarily stored in the cellar.

After labeling, the bottles are ready for sale.

CHIANTI – A SUPERSTAR

Tuscany ranks alongside Piedmont as the most famous winegrowing region in Italy. Though it provides a contrast with Piedmont, where the wine industry is characterized on one hand by rural production methods that are still quite antiquated, and on the other hand by the very elitist image of its top wines, Tuscany also enjoys great popularity. Wines with names such as Chianti, Brunello, Nobile di Montepulciano, Vernaccia di San Gimignano, Galestro, or Sassicaia are famous throughout the world, and every wine-lover knows what to expect from them. Tuscany can also be considered the perfect embodiment of the unity between wine and culture, and there have been few great artists in the past who have not sung the praises of its wine in one form or another to hand down to succeeding generations. The history of Tuscan winegrowing has always been determined by the interplay of the major landowners – especially the clergy and the nobility – and the

mezzadri, or sharecroppers, tenant farmers allowed to live on the land and cultivate it in return for half the crop. When the big estates were broken up after World War II, and many of the *mezzadri* migrated to the towns, there was a danger that winegrowing in the region would be forgotten. Many of the neglected properties were acquired at that time by businessmen and migrants from the rich cities of northern Italy and from abroad, who invested heavily in their restoration. In order to process the grapes they had harvested, they were obliged to rely on the help of learned oenologists. If the wines were to be sold, they had to meet the more exacting standards of wine connoisseurs all over the world. Experiments were conducted with new pressing methods, with the maturing process, in other words storing the wine in small barrels made from new wood, with French grape varieties, and with unusual combinations of varieties. Modern Italian wine had been born, and bore a Tuscan name.

Unfortunately, these revolutionary wines often failed to comply with the regulations, some of which were very rigid, of the system governing designation of origin, and as a result the region, which was one of the first in history to use protected designations of origin – Carmignano is one of the oldest ever – was obliged to sell its top wines as mere table wines. However, even this anomaly could not halt the trend to high-quality products. The Sangiovese grape variety in particular, which is suited to the almost universally hilly landscape of the region, and which needs both the intensive sunshine of the terraced vineyards and the pronounced fluctuations between day and night temperatures that occur at altitude, became an absolute superstar here.

The Sangiovese grape was not only responsible for the famous Brunello di Montalcino wine, but also accounted for an increasingly large proportion of the blend of grapes used to make Chianti, which today, following a corresponding change in the law in the 1990s, may now be pressed exclusively from the Sangiovese grape. It guaranteed the quality of Nobile di Montepulciano and Morellino di Scansano, of Carmignano and some of the great table wines, known as the *Super-Tuscans*, according to the apt name coined for them by the Anglo-Saxon world. Among the other red grape varieties, which continue to deliver outstanding results here, the varieties of French provenance – Cabernet Sauvignon, Merlot, and to a lesser extent also Shiraz and Pinot Noir – are particularly noteworthy.

Tuscany's white wines, however, are less compelling. Although Galestro was a successful, fresh, uncomplicated branded wine made from Trebbiano grapes in the 1980s, although Vernaccia di San Gimignano and white Montecarlo wine enjoy a very good reputation, and despite the fact that the occasional interesting Chardonnay can now be found in the very heart of the Chianti region, white Tuscan wines have never approached the prestige and class that has been achieved by the reds.

Wines from the Chianti-Rufina area have an astonishing capacity for aging.

In the center of Tuscany, nestling between Chianti, Brunello, and Nobile, lies the spectacular countryside of Crete Senesi.

Right: The Castello di Brolio near Gaiole in the Chianti region dates back to the year 1141. It was here that Baron Ricasoli "discovered" modern Chianti in the 19th century.

VIN SANTO

Vin Santo, or holy wine, is a soft, medium-dry to sweet, straw-colored dessert wine, containing 15 to 16 percent alcohol by volume. In the autumn, the freshly harvested grapes are hung up to dry and pressed only when they are almost completely transformed into raisins. The resulting must has a correspondingly high concentration and sugar content. After fermentation, small oak or chestnut barrels are half-filled with the wine and then hermetically sealed. Because of the residual yeast from previous vintages, a secondary fermentation starts in the barrels. These are stored beneath the roof, so that the wine develops in the summer heat and the winter cold, which accounts for its rich flavors of nuts, apricots, honey, spices, and blossom. It takes two to six years for the wine to mature. After a meal, Tuscans like to dip hard almond cookies, *Biscotti di Prato* or *cantuccini*, in small glasses of this wine. However, a good, old Vin Santo wine is also exceedingly suitable as a "meditation wine," as the Italians call it, in other words a wine for moments of reflection between mealtimes.

CHIANTI – ITALY'S MOST POPULAR WINE

Chianti, in addition to being one of the oldest wines, is above all one of the quality wines that Italy produces in the greatest quantity – by far outstripping Asti, Soave, Prosecco, or Valpolicella. In years when the yield is good, almost 26.42 million U.S. gallons (1.3 million hectoliters) of Chianti are bottled and exported all over the world. However, Chianti does not describe one single product: it is a generic term, encompassing very different wines produced in various parts of Tuscany. At the heart of the Chianti region is the most famous area, Chianti Classico, recently singled out by a separate law of designated origin – the historic central area of Tuscany between Florence in the north and Siena in the south. It was here, over 150 years ago, that Baron Ricasoli developed his recipe for Chianti at Castello di Brolio. He specified that the wine should

consist of a blend of 70 percent Sangiovese, 15 percent Canaiolo nero, 10 percent white Trebbiano Toscano and Malvasia del Chianti grapes, and 5 percent of other grape varieties. The purpose of this blend was to give the Sangiovese grape a more intense color and more flavor, and to make it more accessible, even while still new, by adding other grape varieties.

Only as a result of the winegrowing revolution of the past 30 years has Ricasoli's recipe become obsolete. Talented winemakers have managed to crystallize all the desired properties from the Sangiovese grape, without needing to compromise its unmistakable character by adding other varieties of inferior quality. As a result, more and more vintners are pressing their Chianti exclusively from Sangiovese grapes, while others are dispensing with the majority of the traditional blending varieties, and, especially as regards the white grapes, are instead substituting small quantities of finer, imported varieties

such as Cabernet, Shiraz, or Merlot. Modern, well-made Chianti Classico is characterized by the marriage of great finesse and elegance with good strength and aging properties. It not only goes extremely well with most Tuscan dishes, but also successfully complements the cuisine of other countries. Although the name and the grape varieties used are identical, the wines produced from the legally defined zones of the Chianti region are sometimes very different. The most famous of them is Chianti Rufina, from a small winegrowing area east of Florence. When new, these wines have more pronounced acidity than the Classico, but they have better aging properties. Wines produced in the Chianti zones of Colli Fiorentini (near Florence), Colli Aretini (near Arezzo), Colli Senesi (a huge area south of Siena), Colline Pisane (near Pisa), Montalbano (the area west of Florence, in which Carmignano is also produced), and Montespertoli (a new part of the region, near the town of the same name) are lighter and less complex in character than those of the Classico and Rufina areas.

249

BRUNELLO AND OTHER WINES

If Chianti is regarded as the most popular Italian wine, then Brunello is surely one of the most renowned. By contrast with Chianti, it is pressed exclusively from the Sangiovese grape. Feruccio Biondi-Santi is credited with the creation of this wine. Not only did he fill the first bottle, officially called Brunello di Montalcino, in 1888, but had also carefully selected especially suitable vines for his production beforehand. For a long time it was thought that the grape, referred to by the vintners of Montalcino as Sangiovese Grosso, was a special variety of Sangiovese, but the grapes chosen by Biondi-Santi were probably just the best specimens of the vines that were normally grown in the Chianti region.

Good Brunello is immensely strong, characterized by strong tannins when new, and after a long maturing process develops a wonderfully aromatic bouquet reminiscent of spices, game, hide, and sweet tobacco. For a long time, unfortunately, the DOC regulations forced the vintners to mature the wine for four or even five years in huge wooden barrels, which was simply too long for weaker vintages – after this period maturing in the wood they seemed thinner and more drained than before, and during the course

of the aging process they quickly lost their luster and charm. Today, a shorter period of storage in the cask and the use of small barrique-type barrels have given even Brunello a more modern appearance. The wine of secondary quality, which is drunk when newer, from this wine-producing area is sold under the name Rosso di Montalcino. Last but not least, the wine Moscadello di Montalcino is pressed here from Muscat grapes.

A NOBLE WINE

Prugnolo gentile is the name given to the Sangiovese grape in the area around the small town of Montepulciano, where the main wine produced is the Vino Nobile di Montepulciano. This small medieval town stands in solitary splendor high above the Chiana valley – famous for its cattle – and above the Lago Trasimeno. Stronger than the second-quality wine of the region, the Rosso di Montepulciano, it nevertheless has a flowery bouquet and leaves a firm, substantial impression on the palate that falls somewhere between Chianti and Brunello. It is, of course, best when drunk with a good Chiana beef steak.

THE OLDEST DESIGNATION OF ORIGIN IN THE WORLD

Carmignano is grown on the hills to the west of Florence, protected as long ago as 1716 by Cosimo III by means of a statutory designation of origin – possibly the first DOC wine in Italy, and perhaps even the first *appellation* in the world. It was also the first Tuscan wine in which the French grape variety Cabernet Sauvignon was officially permitted. In terms of strength and substance, the wine is

comparable with the Nobile di Montepulciano. Wines from good vintages made by top producers can be aged for several decades. In the Carmignano area there is also a wine of secondary quality with DOC status, the Barco Reale di Carmignano, which contains no Cabernet, but only Sangiovese and Canaiolo grapes.

A SECOND TUSCAN REVOLUTION

For a long time the Tuscan coast between Livorno and Grosseto was a no-man's land in terms of winegrowing. There was practically only one DOC wine, the rosé wine from Bolgheri.

Since the 1970s, however, great advances have been made by a table wine from this area, Sassicaia. This was destined to become the most famous Italian wine

San Gimignano, with its famous towers, is the birthplace of the first Italian DOC white wine.

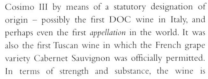

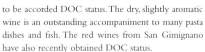

Cypresses, vines, meandering roads, and typical farmhouses – this is the image of Tuscany that is known and loved the world over.

produced from a single grape variety, and was pressed entirely from the Cabernet grapes from vines imported directly from the Bordeaux region by Count Incisa della Rochetta.

In due course, Sassicaia was much imitated, and the resulting wines included Sassicaia's neighbor Ornellaia, for which Cabernet Sauvignon, Cabernet franc and Merlot grapes were blended, and Grattamacco, which contained a large proportion of Sangiovese grapes. In

the meantime, however, the designations of origin of the region have been changed, with the effect that these famous table wines can also be labeled as DOC wines, thus acquiring a recognized seal of quality. They are enjoyed at their best with red meat dishes, such as *Osso Buco*.

WHITE WINE AND THE TOWERS OF SAN GIMIGNANO

The most famous white wine from Tuscany comes from San Gimignano, the city famous for its many towers rising high into the sky. Vernaccia grapes have been cultivated in this area since the 13th century, and Vernaccia was the first Italian white wine to be accorded DOC status. The dry, slightly aromatic wine is an outstanding accompaniment to many pasta dishes and fish. The red wines from San Gimignano have also recently obtained DOC status.

SMALLER DESIGNATED REGIONS

Currently the most dynamic winegrowing area in Tuscany is the southern province of Grosseto. Until recently only the Morellino di Scansano, a fruitier

Sangiovese wine and the more neutral, lighter Bianco di Pitigliano were produced. Since the 1990s however, the area has been experiencing an upsurge.

Hundreds of hectares were replanted and the red Merlot has been expanding alongside the established Sangiovese, which can produce excellent results.

Finally the white wine region of Montecarlo from the province of Lucca in northern Tuscany and the Pomino region in the mountains above Chianti Rufina deserve a mention. Excellent reds are pressed here from Sangiovese, Cabernet, and Merlot grapes, and a modern white wine is created from white Burgundy, Chardonnay, and Trebbiano grapes, which goes exceedingly well with the fresh, aromatic specialties of the region.

UMBRIA

U mbria – the very name is redolent of shady forests and still lakes. The landscape appears overlaid with gold, especially in the fall. Echoes of long-forgotten fairy tales can be heard in enchanted groves, and, in the still retreats and monasteries, the visitor can understand what may have inspired St. Francis of Assisi to compose his ode to the sun. Umbrians have had a mystic, and at the same time very respectful, relationship with nature since time immemorial. The simple "Franciscan" dishes of Umbrian cuisine also appear natural, or left in their natural state. Complicated fillings, pies, or stuffings are just as difficult to find here as heavy cream sauces. Food here is boiled, roasted, flavored, and embellished using the local light olive oil, with its delicate scent of herbs, that is one of the best in Italy and is sometimes as green as Umbria itself.

The food served is whatever happens to be in season. Vegetable dishes predominate in spring and summer, while in the autumn and winter the focus is on the spoils of the hunting season and the famous black truffles from Norcia. This picturesque little medieval town is justifiably regarded as a culinary stronghold in the region. It is worth a visit, not just in late autumn, when the "black gold" is in season, for the art of butchery and sausage-making has been perfected here to the extent that the butchers have been closely identified with their native town. As a result, the word *norcino* signifies not only an inhabitant of Norcia, but also – and this applies throughout Italy – a pork butcher and sausage producer.

In Umbria the manner in which expensive ingredients, specialties, and delicacies are handled is refreshingly casual. It is taken completely for granted that the best natural ingredients should be used in this simple, down-to-earth cuisine. Nutritious soups, spit-roasted meat, home-made noodles – all are prepared with a great deal of love and care. And this relaxed approach even applies to the famous truffles. Umbrian chefs dice them, pound them in a pestle and mortar with anchovies and garlic, use them to add a lingering flavor to a meat sauce for pasta, beat generous quantities into the eggs used to make omelets, and even use these noble mushrooms in their *Torta di pasqua*. The Umbrian philosophy is that things have always been done this way, and anyway the results taste good.

Previous double page: The Norcineria Ansuini in Norcia is famous for its handmade sausage and ham production.

Left: The quiet town of Assisi lies on the slopes of Mount Subasio. It was here that St. Francis founded his order at the beginning of the 13th century.

NORCINERIA

The outstanding reputation enjoyed by Umbrian pork and wild boar meat can be attributed both to the healthy, natural diet of the animals – which are fed on acorns, maize, and cereals – and to the master butchers of Norcia, who are regarded throughout Italy as the best in their profession. The very word *norcino* is a synonym, signifying a butcher as well as an inhabitant of Norcia. Nowhere else is the art of expertly slaughtering and butchering a pig and producing delicious fresh or air-dried sausages or delicately cured ham from the cuts of meat better understood, and so, for many connoisseurs from the surrounding area, Norcia is the destination and high point of culinary expeditions on the weekend. As well as buying the robust specialties in the *norcineria*, the store belonging to the *norcino* or butcher, one can also sample them, prepared in various ways, in many restaurants.

The Norcineria Ansuini is one of these very traditional family businesses. Four generations have now stood behind the butcher's block and served behind the counter – and the fifth generation is already working in the business. At Ansuini's one can, of course, buy sausages and ham, including wild boar ham, but the best Umbrian olive oils, some types of cheese, and other delicacies are also available. Customers from outside the local area, in particular, appreciate the opportunity to become acquainted with other regional specialties to take home when they buy their meat, sausage, and ham.

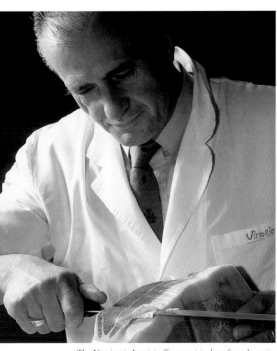

The Norcineria Ansuini offers exquisite ham from domestic pigs and from wild boar. It is important that the ham is freshly cut in wafer-thin slices.

Barbozzo
Barbozzo is a cured, matured pig's cheek.

Mazzafegati
These sausages, made out of piquant spiced pig's liver, are also available in a sweet version containing raisins, orange peel, and sugar, the recipe for which is said to date back to the Renaissance.

Budellacci
Budellacci are smoked, spiced lengths of intestine, which can either be eaten raw, spit-roasted, or broiled.

Capocollo
In some regions *capocollo*, pork collar, is also called *lonza*. It is generously seasoned with garlic and pepper.

Coppa
Coppa is the Umbrian name for sausage made from meat from the pig's head and has nothing to do with *coppa di Piacenza*.

Prosciutto di Norcia
Ham from Norcia or Spoleto is especially tasty since the *norcini* only use haunches of pigs that have been fed a wholesome diet of acorns. It is seasoned only with a little salt, pepper, and garlic. A *prosciutto di Norcia* ham weighs between 17 and 22 pounds (eight to ten kilograms) after being matured for one year.

Two brothers and their sons work in the Ansuini family business. Butchery and production of sausage and ham are all carried out here according to old, traditional methods. Potential customers are attracted to Ansuini's, not just by the mouth-watering spicy aromas floating out of the store, but also by the window displays featuring the heads of animals.

BLACK GOLD FROM NORCIA

The natives of Piedmont have Alba, the Tuscans have San Miniato, and the Umbrians travel to Norcia to buy truffles. Whereas white truffles predominate in Piedmont and Tuscany, Umbria is known for its black truffles, although light-colored varieties are also found here. The dispute among chefs and truffle lovers as to which type is tastier will probably never be settled. All that is certain is that the black truffle is more versatile than its white sister, for it can be eaten raw and is also a suitable ingredient or addition for flavoring sauces, pies, and pasta, without losing its aroma when it is heated. The Umbrian truffle areas extend along the rivers Nera, Corno, and Sordo, as far as the Monti Martani and the mountains near Trevi and Subasio. The knobby black mushroom is gathered mainly in the area around Norcia and Spoleto, white varieties are found around Gubbio, and one comes across black winter truffles, as well as both black and white summer truffles, throughout Umbria.

Above and in the background: The black Norcia truffle (*tuber melanosporum*, also known as the Périgord truffle) can be eaten raw, but is also used to flavor other food.

TIPS FOR COOKING TRUFFLES

- White truffles should always be prepared and eaten raw.
- Never boil black truffles, but heat them gently.
- It is not always necessary to combine truffles with cheese.
- Salt and the best extra virgin olive oil are essential.
- Only use truffles for dishes that do not have their own strong characteristic flavor.
- Before preparing truffles, remove any remaining soil using a soft brush, and then soak them for a few minutes in lukewarm water. The outer skin of the truffle is edible as well as the flesh.

BLACK TRUFFLE VARIETIES

Black Norcia truffles

The black Norcia truffle (*tuber melanosporum*) is gathered mainly in the area around Norcia and Spoleto. It thrives at altitude on hills and mountains, and prefers the company of oaks, holm oaks, and walnut trees, among which it forms circular, smooth areas devoid of grass, known as *pianelli*. The Norcia truffle has a black skin covered with small, slightly indented wart-like bumps. Its flesh is a purplish black with distinct white veining. It has a delicate, pleasant scent. Hunting for this delicacy is permitted only during the period between December 1 and March 15.

Black winter truffles

The black winter truffle (*tuber brumale Vitt.*) (illustrated below) grows in various regions and is not particularly demanding as regards its habitat. Its skin is dark and has wart-like protuberances, but these are not prickly when touched. Its gray flesh has sharply contrasting white veins, and its aroma is strong and pervasive. The season for winter truffles lasts from December 1 to March 15.

Black Muscat truffles

The black Muscat truffle (*tuber brumale Vitt. Var. Moscatum, De Ferry*) is a close relative of the black winter truffle. It also has a black wart-covered skin, but its flesh is blackish with broad white veins. In addition, the Muscat truffle appears to have practically no scent. It is gathered between December 1 and March 15.

Black Bagnoli truffles

The black Bagnoli truffle (*tuber masentericum Vitt.*) is a variety of Norcia truffle, found mainly in Campania. However, it also thrives in the mountains and beech groves of other regions. It has a black, wart-covered outer skin, and its flesh is gray with white veins. This truffle is not to everyone's taste, as it has a rather unpleasant smell of tar or carbolic acid, but its devotees gather it between November 1 and March 15.

- Do not remove the soil immediately, as this acts as a protective shield against microorganisms and prevents loss of flavor.
- Wrap each individual truffle in waxed paper and store in a sealed container in the vegetable compartment of the refrigerator or other cool place.
- Change the paper every day.
- Truffles can be fried in oil and then made into a sauce that will keep for over a month in the refrigerator. They can also be thinly sliced or cut into small pieces, however, and blended with softened butter and a little salt to form a smooth paste that keeps equally well in the refrigerator.

Right: The olive oil is heated in a heavy cast iron pan and the mixture of egg, cream, and truffles is poured in.

The eggs are beaten with the cream and seasoned with salt and pepper. The diced truffles are then added.

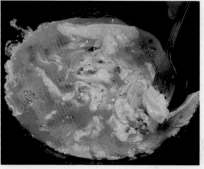

When the *frittata* begins to set, it is loosened from the sides and bottom of the pan with a fork.

FRITTATA AI TARTUFI
Truffle omelet
(Illustrated above)

1 MEDIUM-SIZED BLACK TRUFFLE FROM NORCIA
6 EGGS
4 TBSP CREAM
SALT AND PEPPER
1–2 TBSP OLIVE OIL
JUICE OF 1 LEMON

Brush any earth off the truffles, clean with paper towels, and cut into thin slices. Reserve the two best slices and dice the remainder. Beat the eggs, cream, salt, pepper, and add the truffles. Heat the olive oil in a cast iron pan, add the egg mixture, and allow it to set. Turn over carefully and cook on the other side until it turns golden brown. Slide the *frittata* on to a plate, sprinkle with lemon juice, decorate with the two truffle slices, and serve immediately.

SPAGHETTI ALLA NORCINA
Spaghetti Norcia-style

14 OZ/400 G SPAGHETTI
4–5 TBSP EXTRA VIRGIN OLIVE OIL
2 CLOVES OF GARLIC
3 ANCHOVY FILLETS, CUT INTO SMALL PIECES

5 OZ/150 G BLACK TRUFFLES, THINLY SLICED
SALT AND PEPPER

Boil the spaghetti in plenty of salted water until it is *al dente*. Heat the olive oil in a small pan and sauté the cloves of garlic. Remove the garlic, add the anchovy fillets to the oil, and allow them to disintegrate slowly over a low heat. Remove the pan from the stove and mix most of the thinly sliced truffles into the anchovy paste. Season with salt and pepper, then spread over the spaghetti. Garnish with the remaining truffle slices.

CROSTINI UMBRI
Toasted bread with truffle paste

1/4 LB/100 G BLACK TRUFFLES FROM NORCIA
2 ANCHOVY FILLETS
4–5 TBSP EXTRA VIRGIN OLIVE OIL
SALT
4 SLICES WHITE OR BROWN BREAD

Brush the truffles well under running water, pat dry, and grate finely. Crush the anchovy fillets and mix with the olive oil to form a smooth paste. Stir in the truffles and add a very small amount of salt. Spread the paste on the freshly toasted slices of bread.

LENTILS FROM CASTELLUCCIO

Lentils are a very ancient cultivated plant that reached the Mediterranean region from the Orient. Although cultivation of lentils is not common in Umbria, the few plants that are grown are of extraordinarily high quality. The famous lenticchie di *Castelluccio*, the most sought-after lentils in Italy, grow on the high plain of Castelluccio, at an altitude of 4600 feet (1400 meters). They are small and green, and very healthy, due to the large amount of proteins and mineral salts they contain – and at the same time so tender that they do not need soaking and are tender after cooking for only 20 to 30 minutes. Unfortunately, only very limited quantities appear on the market. Only a few tens of thousands of pounds can be produced on the high plain, and the Annifio and Colfiorito plantations contribute approximately another 20,000 pounds. Those who have the opportunity to try these legumes, now protected by a designation of origin, should jump at the chance.

Beans, onions, and celery

Tender lentils are not the only field-grown specialty that Umbria has to offer. A great deal of time, patience, and care has always been devoted to the cultivation of vegetables in general here.

Cave belongs to the Foligno district and lies in the center of the "fruit garden" on the banks of the river Topino. Beans flourish here on the alluvial soil, which is extremely fertile and rich in minerals, and the ideal soil conditions enable them to be grown completely organically. Two large and 15 smaller agricultural businesses produce the two main varieties. Both the green and yellow beans have a soft shell and a very delicate flavor. They are suitable for soups and starters, but also taste good steamed, embellished only with a little delicate Umbrian olive oil.

The "onion growers' country," as it is called here, is near Cannara. Onions have always been an indispensable feature of Umbrian cooking. Historical documents show that they were served in the 17th century with beet, leeks, cabbage, and beans. The summer and autumn varieties grown in the region today can be eaten raw, but can also be steamed, oven-baked, eaten cold in salads, as an accompaniment to deep-fried food, or in soups and sauces. Those cooks who are sensitive to onions should slice them and leave them to stand in cold water for a few hours before handling them further. As a result, Umbrian onion soup, or *cipollata*, becomes an unadulterated pleasure.

Black celery has been cultivated in Trevi since the middle of the 18th century. This vegetable could be found in all the markets until it was largely ousted by the American celery that was imported increasingly often after World War II. In Trevi, though, there are still a few indomitable growers who cling to "their" celery. Genuine Trevi celery, with its strong aroma, has no unpalatable tough fibers, is very tall, dark green on the outside, and consists of a single bulbous heart from which the leaf-shaped sticks grow. An attempt to make *Parmigiana alla Trevi*, the oven-baked celery soufflé with a cheese topping, using a different variety of celery may be successful, but will never taste as good as the original.

Furthermore, celery is extremely healthy – it is a valuable source of minerals, and also provides a great deal of Vitamin B and Provitamin A.

Lenticchie di Castelluccio
con salsicce
Lentil stew with sausages
(Illustrated left)

1 1/2 cups/300 g Castelluccio lentils
Salt
4 strips/80 g bacon
2 tbsp extra virgin olive oil
1 tbsp butter
1 onion
1 stick celery
2/3 cup/150 g sieved tomatoes
4 cups/1 liter meat stock
4–8 fresh salsicce
Pepper

Soak the lentils the night before in lightly salted lukewarm water. Cut the bacon across into pieces and fry gently in a pan with 1 tablespoon olive oil and 1 tablespoon butter. Chop the onion and celery finely and fry gently for a few minutes. Add the well-drained lentils and the sieved tomatoes and pour in the hot meat stock. Cover the pan and cook the lentils for 1 hour over a low heat. Fry the *salsicce* in a pan with 1 tbsp olive oil. When they are nearly cooked, season the lentils with salt and pepper and add the *salsicce*. Serve on soup plates.

SPELT

Spelt was used long ago by the ancient Romans as an ingredient in their *puls latina*, a dish comprising a mixture of cereal and legumes cooked in water. Every family possessed a special mill to separate the grain from the hard, bearded husks.

Botanically speaking, Umbrian spelt belongs to the variety *Triticum durum dicoccum*, and is cultivated primarily in the region around Monteleone and Spoleto. Following the introduction of wheat, which was easier to process, the importance of spelt, which has to undergo a special process to remove the husk after threshing, declined rapidly. This undemanding cereal plant continued to be grown only in regions where nothing else would grow. In recent years, however, spelt has been rediscovered – not least because of its dietary and nutritional value – and consumption is steadily increasing.

Spelt contains more essential amino acids, in other words the protein building blocks necessary for life, than many types of wheat. It also provides more vitamins and trace elements. Since spelt also contains a considerable amount of silicic acid, it not only ensures a good complexion and shining hair, but is also reputed to stimulate the mental faculties. As a rule, spelt needs soaking for between 12 and 48 hours, and then requires several hours' cooking. Nowadays, cooking time can be halved with the aid of the pressure cooker. If the grain is coarsely ground before it is prepared, soaking can be eliminated entirely. The time required for cooking is then only 20 to 30 minutes, as long as is necessary to swell the spelt over

Above: Unlike other cereals, in which the grain and husk are separated by threshing, spelt grain has to be released using special mills. The spelt grain accounts for one-third of the total weight of the harvest.

a low heat. *Minestra di farro*, spelt soup, is one of the most traditional spelt dishes, which is also familiar in Lazio. The popular and wholesome *imbrecciata* is a stew made from various types of cereal and legumes.

IMBRECCIATA
Legume and cereal stew
(Illustrated right)

1/4 CUP/50 G EACH OF PEARL BARLEY, WHEAT, AND SPELT
1/3 CUP/50 G PINTO BEANS AND LENTILS
1/2 CUP/50 G EACH OF CORN, GARBANZO BEANS, AND FAVA BEANS
5 TBSP EXTRA VIRGIN OLIVE OIL
1/4 LB/100 G BACON, CUT INTO STRIPS
2 ONIONS, CHOPPED
1 BUNCH OF MARJORAM, COARSELY CHOPPED
2/3 CUP/150 G TOMATO PASTE
SALT AND PEPPER
4 CUPS/1 LITER WATER OR STOCK

Soak the cereal and legumes separately overnight. Next day, drain off the water and cook each variety separately, noting the difference in cooking times.
Heat the olive oil in a large pan and sauté the bacon strips and the chopped onions. Add the coarsely chopped marjoram and the tomato paste, and simmer over a low heat for about 15 minutes. Add the legumes and the cereal, and mix together thoroughly.
Add the water or stock, and simmer for a few minutes longer.

MINESTRA DI FARRO
Spelt soup

1 HAM BONE WITH A LITTLE MEAT, COARSELY CHOPPED
1 BUNCH OF SOUP VEGETABLES (2 CARROTS, 1 LEEK, 2 CELERY STALKS, PARSLEY)
1/4 LB/100 G SMOKED HAM, DICED
3/4 CUP/150 G SPELT, COARSELY GROUND
SALT AND PEPPER
1/4 LB/100 G PECORINO, GRATED

Boil the ham bone in plenty of water for about 15 minutes. Remove the bone and discard the water. Clean the soup vegetables and cut into small pieces. Boil with the diced ham and the bone for about 2 hours in 12 cups (3 liters) water. Add the spelt, season with salt and pepper, and allow to swell over a low heat for about 15 to 20 minutes. The spelt grains should not be completely soft, but should retain a little of their bite. Season to taste with salt and pepper. Serve with grated pecorino.

FRESHWATER FISH

Although Umbria has no sea coast, this does not mean fish is absent from the menu here. This stretch of countryside has numerous lakes and rivers running through it, the most important of which is Lake Trasimeno, which lies half an hour's drive west of Perugia. Covering nearly 50 square miles (128 square kilometers) in area, Lake Trasimeno is one of Italy's largest inland lakes.

The sparse population of Umbria and the largely unspoiled natural environment guarantee clean fishing grounds, in which enthusiastic anglers have free choice. There are roach, eels, freshwater perch, trout, grayling, barbel, whitefish, tench – and, it is claimed, the fattest carp south of the Alps. The catch is broiled, baked in the oven, or made into a splendid freshwater fish soup, which is more than equal to any saltwater versions from the coast.

REGINA IN PORCHETTA
Carp in fennel sauce
(Illustrated below)

1 CARP, APPROX. 2 1/2 LBS/1.2 KG IN WEIGHT
1/4 LB/100 G SMOKED HAM OR BACON
2 SPRIGS OF FRESH ROSEMARY
1 TBSP FENNEL SEEDS
4 CLOVES OF GARLIC
JUICE OF 1/2 LEMON
1/2 GLASS OLIVE OIL
SALT AND PEPPER
1 LEMON

Gut the fish, remove the scales, and wash. Pull the rosemary leaves off the stems. Combine the ham, fennel seeds, garlic cloves, and rosemary in a food processor. Stuff the carp with this mixture and place in a flameproof dish. If there is any stuffing left over, this can be spread on top of the fish. Cook in a preheated oven at 400 °F (200 °C) for approximately 30 minutes. Beat the lemon juice with the olive oil and baste the carp with this mixture occasionally. Finally, season with salt and pepper. Decorate with slices of lemon and serve.

Right: Lake Trasimeno, with its abundance of fish, attracts many fishermen, especially on weekends.

Carpa (carp)
Anglers claim that the largest carp in Italy are found in Umbrian waters. They are often oven-baked.

Lasca (roach)
This fish tastes rather like pike, but its flesh is not quite so firm and it has slightly less flavor.

Trota (trout)
This popular little fish is very frequently served in Umbria as *Trota al tartufo*, trout with truffles.

Pesce persico (freshwater perch)
The firm, tasty flesh of freshwater perch can be deep-fried, but it is also suitable for pickling.

Temolo (grayling)
The tender, aromatic flesh of the grayling has a delicate flavor of thyme, and seasoning should therefore be used sparingly.

Anguilla (eel)
Freshwater eels grow much fatter than their marine counterparts; Umbrians grill them or serve them in sauce.

Barbo (barbel)
Barbel must never be eaten raw, since their uncooked flesh is poisonous. They taste very good boiled or fried.

Alborella (whitefish)
This outstanding fish tastes sweet and is extremely suitable for almost all methods of cooking.

Tinca (tench)
The tender, sweet flesh of this fish, a relative of carp, tastes very good fried or else baked.

FISHING

Those who consider that fishing is a typical northern European pastime should just take a walk in an Italian town or along an Italian lakeside. In the towns the keen observer will find many specialist shops for this relaxing sport, selling rubber boots and fly boxes, while on the weekend thousands of fishing enthusiasts drive to the inland waterways, prepare their bait, and wait patiently for a fish – the size of which is almost always irrelevant – to bite.

Artificial lakes have already been constructed in many regions, and are stocked at regular intervals with freshwater fish to make weekend expeditions worthwhile. In Umbria, however, such measures are unnecessary, since the lakes of the region contain fish in extraordinary abundance. In particular, many anglers drive to Lake Trasimeno, for it is here – as is proudly claimed on the shores of the lake – that the fattest carp in Italy are landed. However, the other types of fish offered by the lake are also well worth waiting for.

School of Giotto, fresco in the upper church of the Basilica of San Francesco, Assisi, *c.* 1290–99. This detail from the fresco shows St. Francis being received by the Count of Celano. The latter, however, died before the meal. In the Christian faith, this in itself very sad event symbolizes the invitation to the wedding feast of eternal life. Immediately on entering the upper church of the Basilica the visitor is reminded by the image to prepare himself for this.

SPIRITUAL AND PHYSICAL WELLBEING

Umbria is a region of saints. In around 480, St. Benedict, founder of western monasticism, was born in Norcia. St. Francis came into the world almost exactly 700 years later in Assisi, where he founded the Order of the Lesser Brethren, recognized by Pope Honorius III in 1223. St. Clare, whose order of Poor Clares was affiliated to the Franciscans, was also a native of Umbria. According to the *Legenda Aurea*, a medieval collection of legends about the saints, St. Francis is said to have "picked up worms from the street, so they would not be trodden underfoot by passersby. He provided the bees with good honey and wine, so they should not perish during the cold winter. And he called all animals his brothers." Respect for nature has, it seems, always been a typically Umbrian characteristic. However, as well as an atmosphere tending sometimes toward the spiritual, Umbria also has a predilection for colorful festivals, during which lavish quantities of food and plenty of strong country wine are consumed. Every year, during the first few days of May, the quiet town of Assisi is transformed into the site for merry festivities, in which historic costumes, the loud noise of drums and fanfares, and festive torchlight in the evenings recreate the medieval aspect of the town. Suckling pig and other freshly roasted meat is sold at the stalls and grill stands. Wild spit-roasted pigeon are also a popular delicacy. Those wishing to eat in more comfortable surroundings look out for an empty table in one of the picturesque alleys, where substantial specialties, prepared using recipes from ancient manuscripts, are served: bean soup with spelt, roast wild boar, pepper cake, and many others.

PALOMBACCE ALLA GHIOTTA
Roast pigeon
(Illustrated below left)

4 OVEN-READY PIGEONS, WITH GIBLETS
1 SPRIG OF ROSEMARY
4–5 SAGE LEAVES
1 ONION
2 CLOVES OF GARLIC
3–4 TBSP EXTRA VIRGIN OLIVE OIL
1/4 LB/100 G STALE WHITE BREAD
1/2 BOTTLE DRY WHITE WINE
1/2 BOTTLE DRY RED WINE
SALT AND PEPPER
JUICE AND GRATED RIND OF 1 LEMON
2–3 TBSP PITTED BLACK OLIVES

To make the sauce, cut the tips of the wings, necks, and heads from the pigeons, remove as much meat from these as possible, and chop into small pieces. Dice the giblets finely. Pull the rosemary leaves off the stem and chop finely with the sage leaves. Finely chop the onion and garlic. Heat a little olive oil in a casserole and sauté the prepared ingredients in this for 10 minutes, stirring constantly. Break the bread into pieces and fry with the other ingredients. Reserve 1 glass of white wine, then pour the remainder with the red wine into the pan, and leave to simmer over a low heat until the liquid is reduced by a third.
Grease a roasting pot with oil. Season the pigeons with salt and pepper, and brown them in the pot. Pour on the remaining white wine, cover, and braise the pigeons until they are nearly cooked. After about 45 minutes, remove the pigeons from the roasting pot and set aside. Strain the sauce containing the giblets through a sieve and pour into a large braising pan.

Stir in the meat juices, together with the lemon juice and grated lemon rind. Cut the pigeons into bite-sized pieces and add to the sauce. Halve the olives and stir into the sauce. Season to taste and cook the pigeon for a further 20 minutes. Divide into portions and serve with white bread.

Salsa ghiotta
Chicken liver sauce

1/4 LB/100 G CHICKEN LIVERS
7–10 SAGE LEAVES
1 TBSP CAPERS
3 CLOVES OF GARLIC, FINELY CHOPPED
3 ANCHOVY FILLETS
1 SPRIG OF ROSEMARY
2–3 JUNIPER BERRIES
SALT AND PEPPERCORNS
4–5 TBSP EXTRA VIRGIN OLIVE OIL
2 GLASSES DRY RED WINE

Clean the chicken livers and chop finely. Crush the sage, capers, garlic, anchovy fillets, the leaves from the sprig of rosemary, juniper berries, salt, and peppercorns coarsely in a dish or pestle and mortar. Heat half the olive oil in a pan and fry the chicken livers in it for a few minutes. Add the crushed ingredients and fry until golden yellow.
Pour in the red wine. Boil to reduce the sauce by half, and mix with the remaining olive oil in a dish.

Piccioni allo spiedo
Spit-roasted pigeons

2 LARGE OVEN-READY PIGEONS, WITH GIBLETS
3 TBSP OLIVE OIL
SALT AND PEPPER
1 TBSP WINE VINEGAR
1 GLASS DRY RED WINE
5 BLACK OLIVES
1 LEMON
4–5 SAGE LEAVES
4 SLICES WHITE BREAD

Remove the giblets from the pigeons and wash them inside and outside. Clean the heart, liver, and stomach, and replace inside the pigeons. Place the pigeons on a spit, brush with olive oil, season with salt and pepper, and broil in the oven very slowly at a very low temperature.
Pour the vinegar and wine into the bottom of the broiler. Chop the olives into small pieces, peel the lemon and cut into thin slices, and place with the sage leaves in the bottom of the broiler. Brush this mixture over the pigeons occasionally while they are broiling. When they are cooked, remove the giblets and set the pigeons aside in a warm place while you make the sauce.
Chop the giblets very finely and stir into the juices in the broiler with a wooden spoon. Halve the pigeons, place on a serving dish, and pour over the sauce. Serve with toasted slices of white bread.

Barbecuing

This method of cooking meat over an open fire is without doubt one of man's first culinary achievements. In the early days of the barbecue, swords and lances were probably misappropriated to hold the meat in the flames. Yet it is clear that the results were not always satisfactory. The problem was solved by the invention of the manually operated rotary spit. This simple, but ingenious, construction consisted of a sharp metal stake, fitted at one end with a rotating handle. This stake was held in the vertical position by two supports, while the meat was turned with the aid of the handle and was able to cook evenly, without risk either to the cook or the meat. However, since inattentive chefs were continually burning parts of the meat, Leonardo da Vinci gave the problem his attention in the 15th century. He constructed a spit that turned by itself, driven by the heat of the fire. It is remarkable that this invention was ignored, and that people continued to burn their fingers on red-hot spit handles. Today, a range of equipment is available, designed to make the convivial barbecuing of meat an even simpler matter. However, problems arise, not usually as a result of unsuitable equipment, but because, in the age of the microwave and electric oven, only a very few people still know how to light a fire, how to use the heat from the glowing charcoal properly, and how to prepare the meat.

Faraona ripiena
Stuffed guinea fowl
(Illustrated in the background)

1 OVEN-READY GUINEA FOWL
2–3 SALSICCE
5 SAGE LEAVES
A LITTLE ROSEMARY
3 CLOVES OF GARLIC
1 TSP JUNIPER BERRIES
SALT AND PEPPER
4 TBSP OLIVE OIL
1–2 GLASSES DRY WHITE WINE
SLICED LEMON

Clean and wash the guinea fowl and dry well. Skin the sausages and combine in a food processor with the herbs and garlic. Mix in the juniper berries. Season the mixture with salt and pepper, and stuff the guinea fowl with half of it. Brush the guinea fowl with olive oil, sprinkle the outside with salt and pepper, and place in a casserole with the remaining sausage mixture. Braise in a preheated oven at 400 °F (200 °C). Pour in the wine after 15 minutes, then continue roasting until the bird is crisp.
Garnish the guinea fowl with lemon slices and serve with the juices from the roasting pan.

Serpentone delle monache
Snake cake
(Illustrated right)

3 PRUNES
3 DRIED FIGS
1/2 CUP/50 G RAISINS
1/2 CUP/100 G ALMONDS, COARSELY CHOPPED
1/2 CUP/50 G WALNUTS, COARSELY CHOPPED
1/3 CUP/50 G PINE NUTS, COARSELY CHOPPED
3/4 CUP/150 G SUGAR
2 CUPS EXTRA VIRGIN OLIVE OIL
2 TBSP VIN SANTO WINE
3 1/2 CUPS/400 G ALL-PURPOSE FLOUR
1 CUP WATER
2 APPLES
1–2 EGG YOLKS
A LITTLE CRYSTALLIZED SUGAR

Cut the prunes and figs into small pieces. Mix with the
raisins, almonds, walnuts, pine nuts, half of the sugar,
half of the olive oil, and the Vin Santo, and leave to stand for a while.
Prepare a dough using the remaining sugar, the remaining oil,
and the flour, and leave to rest for a while. Peel the apples and
cut into thin slices. Roll out the dough thinly into a
rectangle, spread the apple slices and nut mixture on top,
and roll up the dough to form a snake. Brush with egg yolk
and sprinkle with sugar crystals. Bake in a preheated oven at
350 °F (180 °C) for approximately 45 minutes.

Ciaramicola
Ring cake

4 1/4 CUPS/500 G ALL-PURPOSE FLOUR
1/2 CUP/100 G LARD OR BUTTER
3/4 CUP/150 G SUGAR
3 EGGS
GRATED RIND OF 1/2 LEMON
1 OZ/25 G FRESH YEAST (IF USING ACTIVE DRY YEAST, FOLLOW
THE MAKER'S INSTRUCTIONS)
2 EGG WHITES
SCANT 1 CUP/100 G CONFECTIONERS' SUGAR
SUGAR CRYSTALS

Mix together the flour, lard, sugar, eggs, lemon rind, and yeast
to make a dough. Cover the mixture and let it rise for 30
minutes. Grease a baking sheet and shape the main portion of
dough into a large ring. Make two rolls out of the remaining
dough and place them on top of the ring, forming a cross.
Bake in the center of a preheated oven at 400 °F (200 °C) for
approximately 30 minutes. Beat the egg whites until stiff, and
mix in the confectioners' sugar. When the cake is cooked,
brush it with this mixture and decorate with sugar crystals.

Pinoccate
Pine nut cookies

2 1/2 CUPS/500 G SUGAR
2–3 CUPS WATER
2 1/3 CUPS/400 G PINE NUTS
GRATED RIND OF 1 LEMON
1/4 LB/100 G CHOCOLATE, GRATED
20 WAFERS

Heat the sugar slowly in the water. When it has dissolved,
add the pine nuts, grated lemon rind, and chocolate, and
mix well. Using a spoon, place a small heap of the mixture
on each wafer, then chill.
The mixture can also be placed on a damp marble slab,
spread out smoothly with a knife, cut into pieces while still
warm, and wrapped in brightly colored paper like candy.

Zuccotto
Sponge bombe filled with ice cream
(Illustrated below left)

1 SPONGE BASE, MEASURING APPROX. 10 X 15 INCHES/
25 X 39 CM
1/3 CUP/80 ML CHERRY LIQUEUR
3 TBSP COINTREAU
1/3 CUP/80 ML RUM, COGNAC, GRAND MARNIER,
OR MARASCHINO
2 CUPS/500 ML HEAVY (DOUBLE) CREAM
3 OZ/90 G BAKER'S SEMI-SWEET ALMOND CHOCOLATE, FINELY
CHOPPED
3/4 CUP/165 G CANDIED FRUITS, FINELY CHOPPED
1/4 LB/100 G BAKER'S SEMI-SWEET CHOCOLATE, MELTED
3/4 CUP/70 G ROASTED HAZELNUTS, CHOPPED
COCOA POWDER AND CONFECTIONERS' SUGAR
FOR DECORATION

Line a 2½ pint/1.5 liter pudding mold with a damp cloth.
Cut the sponge base into 12 pointed strips using a sharp
knife. Mix the liqueurs together and use half of this mixture
to brush the sponge strips, one at a time. Then arrange them
loosely in the mold, with the narrow ends meeting in the
middle. Brush the sponge with the remaining liqueur
mixture and chill.
Beat the cream until it forms stiff peaks. Divide in half,
stirring the almond chocolate and candied fruits into one
half. Spread this mixture evenly over the sponge.
Mix the remaining cream with the cooled melted chocolate
and the hazelnuts, pour into the center of the mold, and
spread. Smooth the surface, then cover and chill overnight
in the freezer.
Turn the *Zuccotto* out onto a serving plate and dust
generously with cocoa powder and confectioners' sugar. A
cardboard template can be used to keep the cocoa and
confectioners' sugar separate from one another and create
decorative patterns. However, another person is needed to
hold the template.
Serve the *Zuccotto* immediately, since the cream mixture
softens quickly.

PERUGIA – CITY OF CHOCOLATE

Perugia already enjoys the reputation of a city that has housed the finest confectionery since time immemorial, but between October 17 and 25 a veritable chocolate fever breaks out in the Umbrian capital. Throughout these nine days, the city makes available all its public places, amenities, hotels, and restaurants, so it can welcome chocolate connoisseurs from all over the world and provide them with their favorite confectionery, the "food of the gods." The name of this spectacular event is Eurochocolate; it was held for the eleventh time in 2004, and will no doubt continue in future, since on each occasion the number of guests arriving from Italy, from the rest of Europe, and even from as far afield as Japan and the USA, has been overwhelming.

Chocolate can be nibbled everywhere during this time, an unforgettable experience for any true chocoholic. White chocolate, dark chocolate, bitter chocolate, drinking chocolate, pralines by the hundred, works of art made of chocolate – all these can be tasted or admired, throughout the city. Eurochocolate is the largest event of its kind in Europe, as testified by the 60,000-plus official program guides, printed not on ordinary card, but on very special paper perfumed with the scent of cocoa. Those with a mania for chocolate do not stay in ordinary hotels during the fair, but book a room well in advance at Perugia's Etruscan Choco-hotel (three stars) in the Via Campo di Marte, where the entire establishment revolves around the cultivation of cocoa, the manufacture of chocolate, and of course the sweet temptation itself. In some of the rooms, for example, there are *cioccoscriavanie*, small desks with glass tops, beneath which the keen guest can admire historic examples of cups that were designed for drinking chocolate.

Eurochocolate is not Perugia's only initiative to promote chocolate, however. The Compagnia del Cioccolato, a company registered in the city, is a non-profit-making organization committed to lobbying bodies such as the European Commission to ensure that this extremely popular product is always manufactured in accordance with specified standards, and that its quality is not compromised by contamination with palm oil or other additives. In 1998, the Compagnia del Cioccolato already had 900 members – the youngest of whom was just a few months old when he joined. The association offers different classes of membership with different membership fees, so that each chocolate connoisseur can participate in accordance with his means. Seminars and lectures about chocolate, cookery courses, gastronomic weekends revolving around chocolate, and regular meetings of chocolate-lovers are arranged, both in Italy and elsewhere. The *Inno al cioccolato*, or hymn extolling chocolate, is an extremely impressive exposition of the shared beliefs of the members:

SURPRISE EGGS

Surprise eggs are extremely popular in Italy. They are produced by craftsmen in small businesses as well as in the large factories of the confectionery industry. Most are wrapped in very brightly colored paper, and they come in all conceivable sizes. Candy is hidden inside, or even small gifts and toys for children.

Chocolate Easter eggs are actually a French idea, or to be more precise the invention of the highly specialized confectioner at the court of Louis XIV, the Sun King, at Versailles. The idea of hiding a surprise, of greater or lesser value, in an egg made either of chocolate or some other material – Fabergé's precious eggs come to mind – is also attributable to the French. However, this in no way dampens Italian enthusiasm for this exciting Easter gift.

"Chocolate is one of the great pleasures of life. And, for true friends of chocolate, who honor the 'food of the gods' in a manner resembling a religious cult, this is enough to lead them to reject decisively all accusations of a dietary nature. Calories, skin problems, enlargement of the liver, release of histamines – these are nothing but silly rumors. In reality, chocolate has numerous advantages, and is very versatile. Chocolate consoles the victim of misfortunes, betrayal, injustices suffered during the course of a lifetime, sadness over a lost love, or a love never experienced, and helps to overcome all of these. It restores good cheer to the heart, and momentarily relieves the oppressed of their burden. Yet chocolate is also a stimulant. Very few people are aware that it has the same properties as coffee. It refreshes the mind, the soul, and even the muscles, and encourages strokes of genius and helpful insights. It is cocaine for the wise, an amphetamine for those who love life. And – unlike coffee – chocolate can also have a sedative effect. It relaxes the nerves, bringing the sleep of the just when things have occasionally gone wrong during the course of the day. Only simple souls take camomile tea. Chocolate, therefore, is mother, lover, and father to everyone, in the perfect combination. Always by our side, when it is needed, yet far away, when it is not. And it is also – what loving parents sometimes find difficult to achieve – genuinely complicit."

Hand-made pastries and pralines (above) are sold in the Pasticceria Sandri (background), founded in 1860, on the Corso Vannucci in Perugia.

THE TORGIANO WINE MUSEUM

This wine museum, opened in 1974 on the estate of the Lungarotti family, lies at the heart of Umbria, to be more accurate in Torgiano. Situated close to the Umbrian capital of Perugia, this quiet, medieval village with its defending walls and towers has just the right atmosphere for tasting a few good wines and touring the museum to glean information about the history of winegrowing. The museum owes its existence to the doyen of winegrowing in the region, Giorgio Lungarotti, and his wife, Maria Grazia, a couple who were also responsible for arranging the rooms of the Palazzo Graziani Baglioni, an old 17th-century nobleman's residence.

The rooms of the museum, which are also of architectural interest, and which originally belonged to the *pars agricola*, the part of the estate used for agricultural purposes, invite the visitor to travel in time

through the world of wine. One wanders through the Middle East, where the first vines were cultivated 2500 years ago, follows the land and sea trade routes, via which the grape spread through the Mediterranean region, and discovers what methods were used to make wine at the time of the birth of Christ.

The wine culture of Umbria is worthy of special attention, and, in addition to early examples of wine produced in the region, the museum also houses an impressive collection of antique and modern wine containers. These are a reminder of the pottery industry that flourished well into the 18th century in many central Italian towns. In one of the adjacent rooms there is an old Umbrian wood-fired kiln, which is still occasionally heated so that visitors can fire their own wine goblets. Emerging from this fine little museum, one feels that one understands why there is more to wine than a glass of fermented grape juice – it is a culture that makes changes and leaves a lasting impression, not only on its native countryside, but also on people.

Above: The Lungarotti family has made Torgiano wine famous.

Below: In the Torgiano wine museum, which is run by the Lungarotti foundation, one can learn about historic methods of making wine.

FROM ORVIETO TO MONTEFALCO

Although Umbria is commonly called the green heart of Italy, in winegrowing terms it has long stood in the shadow of neighboring Tuscany. Despite this, wines such as Orvieto were well known, despite a less than outstanding reputation for quality.

The region first began attracting the attention of wine connoisseurs throughout the world when Giorgio Lungarotti from Torgiano instituted his annual wine competition, the Banco d'Assaggio, which has been highly regarded for some time. Admittedly, Torgiano wine, which was recognized with a controlled designation of origin, or DOC, and in the case of Torgiano Riserva even a DOCG, a controlled and guaranteed designation of origin, did not enjoy any particular international success, which was probably due to the fact that Lungarotti remained its only producer. From that time on, however, nothing was to stand in the way of the development of quality wine production in the region. The best known wine in the region prior to this, the white Orvieto, which still accounts for two thirds of the region's DOC wine production, led the field, and was transformed from a generally unprepossessing, thin white wine, even drunk as a sweet wine by the natives, into a bold, dry wine, suitable for serving even with robustly-flavored dishes. Although most of the wine is produced by no more than three large cooperatives, a handful of smaller and medium-sized vintners have been able to make their mark with surprising experiments and strikingly good wines. During the course of these experiments, which focused primarily on Orvieto Classico, the geographical heart of the winegrowing area, some excellent table wines emerged, the producers of which had pulled out all the stops in terms of modern Italian

In front of the impressive silhouette of the Orvieto Cathedral grow the grapes for the city's favorite white wine.

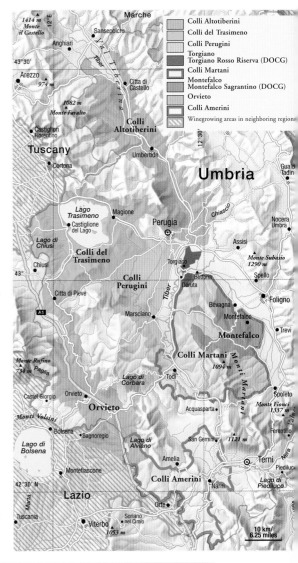

winemaking – for example, using international grape varieties, storing the wine in small, new wooden barrels, regulating fermentation temperature, and employing the most up-to-date cellar technology. Most other parts of the region now have their own designations of origin too, including wines of a quality ranging from good to very good. The most famous of these come from the region around the Umbrian capital, Perugia, and from the borders with Tuscany. Bottles labeled Colli del Trasimeno and Colli Perugini contain fresh white and red wines, which are pressed from the same grape varieties as many famous Tuscan wines: Sangiovese, Merlot, and Cabernet among the reds, Trebbiano, Grechetto, and Chardonnay among the whites.

The wines of Montefalco, in the north of the region, have also made an impressive leap in quality, especially in the case of the reds, which are made from Sangiovese and the indigenous Sagrantino grapes. Sagrantino di Montefalco, the wine made from a single grape variety that has been elevated to DOCG status, has great strength and fullness, combined with an intense bouquet of fruit and spices, and is comparable with the really great wines of Italy. Passito, the sweet version of Sagrantino di Montefalco, is sumptuous, fruity, and full-bodied – a genuine Umbrian specialty.

Torgiano Riserva
Umbria's most famous wine is Torgiano Riserva, made from Sangiovese and other indigenous grape varieties. This elegant wine is not excessively strong or alcoholic, is an excellent accompaniment to red meat, and can age very well, but unfortunately it is offered by only one top producer.

Colli Martani
Colli Altotiberini, Colli Amerini, Colli del Trasimeno, Colli Martani, and Colli Perugini are Umbrian designations of origin from the northern part of the region. The white wines are mostly pressed from Trebbiano toscano grapes, while the reds

are pressed from Sangiovese, blended with Montepulciano, Merlot, or other varieties. These wines are largely unassuming and rather light, and are not particularly prestigious.

Sagrantino di Montefalco
Sagrantino is a variant of the red Montefalco, pressed exclusively from grapes of the same name. These are mostly processed when they have dried slightly, producing a very strong red wine with a high alcohol content.

Orvieto
Alongside Soave and Frascati, this white wine, which is for the most part produced in Umbria – except for a corner that extends into Lazio – ranks among the most popular wines in Italy. The best growths come from the Classico zone, and their pleasant, mild fruit is balanced by a little harmonious acidity.
These white wines, which are produced around the city with the famous cathedral, are occasionally also fermented and matured in small wooden barrels, or barriques. However, this method of maturing the wine is successful only if the strength and concentration of the grapes used are well above average.

MARCH

The sea, dense forests containing oak trees that are hundreds of years old, churches, monasteries, and fortresses rising up from the medieval towns perched high up in the delightful ranges of hills, and hospitable people, who love their native land more than anything – all these are typical of Marche, a region still largely undiscovered by the tourist industry. From a culinary point of view, too, the character of this region is quite unique. Whereas the cuisine in neighboring Umbria is for the most part simple, even spartan, the people of Marche have expensive and sophisticated tastes, though they do not indulge these to excess. Even the most sumptuous stuffing for suckling pig is invariably rooted in the traditions of robust, country cooking.

Even in Gioacchino Rossini's time, cooking and eating well were considered important. It is no wonder that the composer devoted at least as much attention to questions of the *buona tavola* as to his virtuoso music. Not without good reason is the aristocratic tag *alla Rossini* still attached to the names of numerous dishes of variable authenticity. Above all, the cuisine of Marche is one of great variety that unfolds as one progresses from the Adriatic to the Apennines. On the coast, fish and seafood are transformed into fantastic dishes. They may be grilled on a spit, or made into the traditional *brodetto*, a creamy-textured fish soup consisting of no fewer than 13 types of fish. In the hills and mountains inland, gourmets swear by the wild and domestic pigs, the succulent haunches of which are transformed by dedicated butchers and sausage-makers into products such as tasty ham, which, by contrast with other parts of Italy, is served not in thin slices, but cut into bite-sized chunks. The natives of Marche claim to have invented roast suckling pig, and if one watches the men sitting by the fire, turning the spit reflectively, and indulging in technical talk about cooking times, one might almost believe them. Meanwhile, the women can be found in the kitchen, preparing silky smooth tagliatelle. This delicious pasta, made from eggs, flour, and a little semolina, is either served with a thick, reduced sauce, or alternatively filled with a robust meat sauce, for the natives of Marche have a real passion for fillings. Suckling pig, chicken, and fish are almost always stuffed, and if one takes the trouble to pit it properly, there is room for stuffing in even the smallest olive.

Previous double page: The delicious stuffed olives from Ascoli Piceno are known as *olive ascolane*. Although time-consuming to produce, they are well worth the effort.

Left: Many festivals are held on the Piazza del Popolo in Pesaro, whose focal point is the magnificent fountain with its seahorses and tritons.

FISH SOUPS AND OTHER DELIGHTS

The fish caught off the coast of Marche cover ten percent of Italy's requirement for fish and seafood. On board the cutters that dock every day in the ports of San Benedetto del Tronto, Fano, Porto San Giorgio, and Civitanove Marche are sardines, large and small octopus, turbot, squid, and scorpion fish. Crustaceans such as lobster, crayfish, mantis shrimp, and spider crabs are also caught in the rich fishing grounds of the Adriatic. In addition, cockles, mussels, sea dates, and razor fish can also be found in the frequently rocky coastal waters.

Originally, the dish known as *brodetto* was born of necessity. Because every fishing boat always has its complement of fish and seafood that cannot be sold due to poor quality or inadequate size, the fishermen of Marche invented a creamy-textured fish soup, a delicious way to use up all the "B class" produce. This simple dish could also be prepared straight away on board ship, using a little seawater, vinegar, and olive oil. In due course, landlubbers also came to appreciate *brodetto*, and transformed the simple fishermen's fare into a delicacy by adding a careful blend of spices and by choosing superior quality fish. *Brodetto* always tastes different, depending on the season and what fish the catch yields – and this fish stew is a constant challenge for every cook, for the ingredients must always be combined in an imaginative way, as well as being appropriate for the season.

Almost every town and every settlement on the coast has its own basic recipe for *Brodetto*, and the inhabitants all believe their particular recipe to be the best in the whole region. However – if one disregards the many variations – it is possible to identify two approaches to the art of making *Brodetto*. On one hand there is *Brodetto all'anconitana*, which comes from the area between Pesaro, Monte Conero, and Ancona, while the other school is represented by *Brodetto portorecanatese*, which is cooked between Porto Recanati and San Benedetto del Tronto, in the south of Marche. *Brodetto all'anconitana* is regarded as the original and the most traditional version. Between nine and 13 different varieties of fish and seafood are used to make it, and it is flavored with tomatoes, onions, parsley, garlic, vinegar, and oil.

However, there are also recipes that specifically exclude vinegar, and in Ancona itself a pure, very aristocratic *Brodetto* made from sole is often served. *Brodetto portorecanatese* is *giallo dorato*, golden yellow, as it is colored with saffron. Porto San Giorgio *Brodetto*, on the other hand, contains chili pepper, turning it into a really fiery soup for palates that are not accustomed to it. These are just a few examples – it would be quite impossible to give all the recipes here. Nevertheless, the natives of Marche are so proud of their classic fish soup that they have founded an association specifically for the purpose of preserving it: the *Accademia del Brodetto*.

Salinge are a very unusual specialty, found only in this region. They are crustaceans, particularly well known in the area around Ancona. In Marotta they are called *garagoj*, and in the local dialect they are called *murici*. These gastropods were known in antiquity, for reasons other than their culinary qualities. They secrete a substance that was used as a dye in ancient times and from which the crimson dye industry originates. Today, these shellfish, which are usually cooked with bacon in restaurants, are just eaten as a choice seafood, and a festival devoted to them is held annually in the town of Marotta.

BRODETTO ALL'ANCONITANA
Fish stew, Ancona-style
(Illustrated right)

Serves 6

3 1/2 LBS/1.5 KG PREPARED MIXED SALTWATER FISH AND SHELLFISH
3–5 TBSP EXTRA VIRGIN OLIVE OIL
ALL-PURPOSE FLOUR
3 CLOVES OF GARLIC
1 ONION, CHOPPED
2 BAY LEAVES
1 PIECE PICKLED CHILI PEPPER
1 LB/500 G TOMATOES
1 TBSP CHOPPED PARSLEY
SALT AND FRESHLY MILLED BLACK PEPPER
2 TBSP WINE VINEGAR
6 SLICES WHITE BREAD

Place the shellfish with 2 tablespoons olive oil in a pan and sauté until the shells have opened: discard any that haven't. Remove the meat from the shells and set aside. Clean the fish, cut into small pieces, and coat in flour. Heat the remaining olive oil in a casserole and add the peeled garlic cloves, the chopped onion, the bay leaves, and the chili pepper. Sauté for 10 minutes, then remove the garlic cloves. Skin the tomatoes, dice and add with the parsley to the casserole. Season to taste with salt and pepper, and simmer for 20 minutes. Strain the sauce through a sieve, return to the casserole, and add the pieces of fish. Cover with a lid and simmer gently for 15 minutes until the fish is tender. Add the shellfish and vinegar and simmer for 5 minutes. Place a slice of bread in each bowl and pour the soup over.

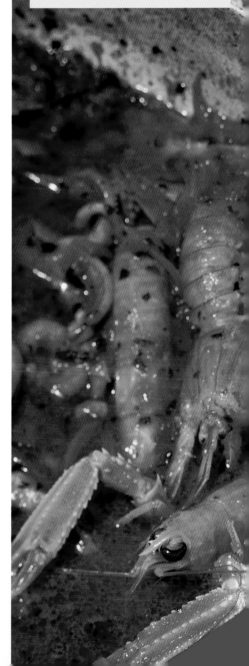

The fishing port of San Benedetto del Tronto also supplies markets inland, such as that of Ascoli Piceno.

Calamari ripieni in teglia
Stuffed squid
(Illustrated left)

Serves 6

4 CLOVES OF GARLIC
1 BUNCH OF PARSLEY
A FEW MINT LEAVES
3/4 LB/300 G LEAN VEAL
2 TBSP BREADCRUMBS
EXTRA VIRGIN OLIVE OIL
SALT AND PEPPER
1 3/4 LBS/800 G PREPARED SQUID
2 TBSP TOMATO PASTE
JUICE OF 1/2 A LEMON

Heat a pan of salted water with 3 garlic cloves, half of the
parsley, and the mint leaves, add the veal and cook for
approximately 40 minutes until tender. Grind the meat in a
food processor with the breadcrumbs, add a little oil, and
season with salt and pepper. Wash the squid, season with salt
and pepper, stuff with the ground meat mixture, and secure
with a cocktail stick or thread. Chop the remaining clove of
garlic and sauté briefly with the rest of the parsley in a large
pan. Add the tomato paste, and season to taste with salt,
pepper, and lemon juice. Place the stuffed squid in the pan,
cover with the tomato sauce, cover with a lid, and cook
over a low heat for approximately 15 minutes until tender.
Serve hot.

Brodetto di San Benedetto del Tronto
Fish stew, San Benedetto del Tronto-style

Serves 8

1 3/4 LBS/1.5 KG PREPARED ASSORTED FISH AND SEAFOOD (IF
POSSIBLE SQUID, CALAMARI, SCORPION FISH, MONKFISH, RED
MULLET, GRAY MULLET, JOHN DORY, COCKLES, AND MUSSELS)
OLIVE OIL
1 ONION, CHOPPED
1 SMALL PIECE CHILI PEPPER
1 1/2 LBS/700 G TOMATOES
1 PINCH SALT
FISH STOCK (MADE USING FISH HEADS, FISH BONES, AND
VEGETABLES)
1 GLASS WHITE WINE
8 SLICES TOASTED CRUSTY BREAD

Clean the fish and seafood. Heat some olive oil in a pan and
sauté the onions gently. Add the chili pepper, tomatoes, salt,
fish stock, squid, and calamari, and cook for 15 minutes.
In another pan, layer first the scorpion fish, then the
monkfish, followed by the red mullet, gray mullet, and John
Dory. Pour some of the stock containing the seafood over
each layer. Add the cockles and mussels, pour in the wine,
and cook in a covered pan for approximately 25 minutes.
Serve on toasted slices of bread.

Left: *Brodetto all'anconitana* – fish stew, Ancona-style (in the
foreground) and *Calamari ripieni in teglia* – stuffed squid
(to the rear).

BEATRICE'S FAVORITE DISHES

Beatrice Sforza (1475–1497), daughter of the house of Este, Duchess of Urbino, and wife of Duke Ludovico il Moro, in addition to her patronage of artists such as Bramante and Leonardo da Vinci and her involvement in building the castle at Milan and the Charterhouse at Pavia, also had a penchant for gastronomic pleasures, and was even reputed to be a good cook herself. However, the dishes bearing her name today are not necessarily the result of the ingenuity and culinary skill of the duchess, having instead been created by various cooks in accordance with her tastes. The dish dedicated to her, for example, mixed vegetables "à la Beatrice," was invented by a French cook, who liked to serve his creation, consisting of morel mushrooms, glazed carrots, artichoke hearts, and new potatoes, as an accompaniment to roast meat.

The snail-shaped pasta stew enriched with chicken livers, known as *Lumachelle all'urbinate*, is also called

Giovanni Ambrogio de Predis (1455–1508), *Portrait of Beatrice d'Este*, second half of the 15th century, Pinacoteca Ambrosiana, Milan.

Piatto alla Beatrice Sforza Duchessa d'Urbino, and apparently has its origins in the dukedom of Urbino in its heyday. It is now suspected, however, that the dish owes its name to the simple fact that only the rich and powerful could afford this specialty, rather than to Beatrice herself.

LUMACHELLE ALL'URBINATE
Vegetable soup with pasta
(Illustrated below)

2 MEDIUM-SIZED CARROTS
1/4 WHITE CABBAGE
2 SALSICCE
2 CHICKEN LIVERS
1/4 CUP/60 G BUTTER
3/4 LB/300 G TOMATOES, SKINNED AND DICED
4 CUPS/1 LITER MEAT STOCK
SALT AND PEPPER
3/4 LB/300 G SMALL PASTA SNAILS (*lumachelle*)
1 1/2 CUPS/100 G PARMESAN, FRESHLY GRATED

Dice the carrots finely, and cut the cabbage into strips. Squeeze the *salsicce* out of their skins and chop coarsely, and cut the chicken livers into small pieces. Sauté all these ingredients in butter, then add the diced tomatoes and leave to simmer over a low heat until the sauce has thickened. Add the meat stock, and season to taste with salt and pepper. Add the pasta to the soup and cook until *al dente*. Sprinkle with grated parmesan before serving.

URBINO

After Urbino was declared a dukedom in the middle of the 15th century, the city swiftly developed to become the center of a dynamic and flourishing state. By contrast with the princely courts of Tuscany or Emilia-Romagna, however, splendid banquets seem to have been held only on rare occasions in the Palazzo Ducale, one of the most beautiful architectural works of the Italian Renaissance. The ducal influence on the culinary traditions of the region was therefore correspondingly slight, and only a few dishes were named in honor of the court. The natives of Marche were again to demonstrate their continuing immunity to external influence later, when even the opulence of the 18th century passed them by, leaving no trace. Nevertheless, there is one specialty with a "grand" history. *Vincisgrassi*, a sumptuous dish of baked pasta with a spicy meat filling, similar to lasagne, was originally eaten only by rich noblemen. At that time it was called *Princisgrassi*, a reference to the corpulence of those who could afford to consume this expensive dish. In 1849, when Austrian troops marched into Marche, their general, Prince Windischgraetz, enthused so much about the sheets of pasta with their meat sauce filling that the inhabitants of Marche, who naturally felt honored, promptly decided to change the name of the dish to "Windischgraetz." Unfortunately, however, since scarcely anyone could pronounce the prince's name properly, the name *Vincisgrassi* seems to have been coined instead.

The Palazzo Ducale in Urbino was probably built as a result of the marriage of Federigo da Montefeltro and Battista Sforza in 1460. It was constructed by Luciano da Laurana, and with its magnificent façade and superb interior decoration it is among the most artistically important architectural works in Italy.

VINCISGRASSI
Lasagne with meat sauce

Serves 6

For the sauce:
3–4 TBSP OLIVE OIL
3 1/2 TBSP/50 G BUTTER
1 ONION, CHOPPED
3/4 LB/350 G GROUND BEEF
1 CUP/100 G RAW HAM OR BACON, FINELY CHOPPED
4 TBSP WHITE WINE
4 TOMATOES, SKINNED AND DICED
GRATED NUTMEG
SALT AND FRESHLY MILLED BLACK PEPPER
3/4 LB/350 G VEAL SWEETBREADS

For the pasta:
3 1/2 CUPS/400 G ALL-PURPOSE FLOUR
1 PINCH SALT
1 CUP/150 G SEMOLINA
4 EGGS
3 1/2 TBSP/50 G SHORTENING
3–4 TBSP WHITE WINE

BUTTER
1 1/2 CUPS/100 G PARMESAN, FRESHLY GRATED
2 1/2 OZ/75 G MOZZARELLA

To make the sauce, heat the oil and butter in a pan and fry the chopped onions until they are soft and transparent. Add the ground beef and the finely chopped ham, and continue to fry for 10 minutes over a low heat. Pour in the wine, add the tomatoes, season with nutmeg, salt, and pepper, and cook for approximately 1 hour over a low heat. Boil the veal sweetbreads in water for 10 minutes, then remove the outer skin and cut the sweetbreads into small cubes. Add these to the meat sauce and braise for 5 minutes.

To make the pasta, sift the flour on to a work surface, sprinkle the salt and semolina on top, and make a hollow in the center. Add the eggs, shortening, and wine, and knead into a smooth dough. Roll into a ball, wrap in a damp cloth, and leave to stand for 30 minutes. Roll the dough out thinly and cut into wide strips, approximately 4 inches (10 cm) long. Boil the lasagne in plenty of salted water until it is just tender and drain well.

Grease a flameproof dish with butter, and arrange a layer of lasagne in the bottom. Pour over some of the meat sauce, sprinkle with grated parmesan, and place a few slices of mozzarella on top. Cover with another layer of lasagne. Repeat the process until all the ingredients have been used, finishing with a layer of cheese. Melt 3½ tablespoons (50 g) butter and drizzle over the top. Bake the lasagne in a preheated oven at 400 °F (200 °C) for approximately 40 minutes.

POLLO IN POTACCHIO
Roast chicken with onions and chili pepper

3–4 TBSP EXTRA VIRGIN OLIVE OIL
1 SMALL ONION, CUT IN RINGS
2 CLOVES OF GARLIC, CRUSHED
1 OVEN-READY CHICKEN
1 SMALL CHILI PEPPER
SALT AND FRESHLY MILLED BLACK PEPPER
1 TBSP TOMATO PASTE
1 GLASS DRY WHITE WINE
A FEW SPRIGS OF ROSEMARY
6–8 TBSP CHICKEN STOCK

Heat the oil in a casserole and sauté the onion rings and the crushed garlic for 5 minutes. Cut the chicken into pieces and add, followed by the finely chopped chili pepper. Season to taste with salt and pepper, and brown the chicken on all sides over a moderate heat.

Mix the tomato paste with a little warm water and add to the chicken, together with the wine. Reduce the temperature, cover with a lid, and braise the chicken for approximately 30 minutes. Finely chop a sprig of rosemary and sprinkle over the pieces of meat. Braise the chicken for a further 30 minutes until tender, occasionally adding a little stock. Scatter over the remaining sprigs of rosemary as a garnish and serve.

PASSATELLI ALL'URBINATE
Spinach and meat dumplings

SCANT 1/2 LB/200 G SPINACH
10 1/2 OZ/300 G FILLET OF VEAL
1 OZ/30 G BEEF BONE MARROW
2 TBSP/30 G BUTTER
2 3/4 OZ/80 G FRESH BREADCRUMBS
4 EGGS
GRATED NUTMEG
SALT
1 1/2 CUPS/100 G PARMESAN, FRESHLY GRATED
6 CUPS/1.5 LITERS STOCK

Wash the spinach, tear into small pieces, and heat for a few minutes without adding any water. Cut the veal fillet into small pieces, grind finely in a food processor, and purée with the beef bone marrow, spinach, and butter in a pestle and mortar. Place this mixture in a dish. Add the breadcrumbs, eggs, a pinch of nutmeg, salt, and at least half of the grated parmesan, and mix well. The meat mixture should be quite firm. Form into short, fat dumplings (*passatelli*), and cook these in the stock until they float to the surface. Serve in a soup tureen with the stock, and sprinkle with the remaining parmesan.

GIOACCHINO ROSSINI

In 1829, Gioacchino Rossini wrote his last major opera, "William Tell." After this, at the height of his popularity, the 37-year-old composer and maestro of Italian opera buffa went into voluntary retirement, in order to have sufficient time and leisure in the next 39 years to devote to his hobby, the *buona tavola*. When Rossini died in Paris in 1868, he left several recipes he had invented himself. Furthermore, many cooks had dedicated their own creations to him, with the result that today there are more than a hundred dishes with names bearing the tag *alla Rossini*.

Rossini was born on February 29, 1792 in Pesaro, a port in the north of Marche, but – owing to his profession – spent most of his life in Paris, where he assembled menus consisting not just of French delicacies, but of a combination of these with Italian specialties that he arranged to have despatched to his residence from his homeland on a regular basis. It seems that he had a particular weakness for Marsala, but supplies of risotto rice, truffles, and sun-ripened tomatoes were also received for the maestro himself to combine with the specialties available locally.

One of the composer's original recipes is for *Maccheroni siringati*, piped macaroni. This owes its name to the laborious method of preparation, which involves introducing a stuffing made of foie gras, creamed York ham, and truffles into cooked pasta tubes using a tiny silver syringe. Today, there is a slightly modernized version of this recipe known by the name *Maccheroni alla pesarese*.

There are countless anecdotes concerning Rossini the gourmet. For example, in a letter to the soprano Maria Colbran, following the scintillating première of the "Barber of Seville," instead of enthusing about his

Above: The hand-written notation is from Gioacchino Rossini's "The Barber of Seville" ("Il Barbiere di Siviglia"). The first performance of this opera buffa was given in Rome in 1816.

successful opera buffa, he wrote about a new recipe for truffles that he had discovered: "Take oil from Provence, English mustard, French vinegar, a little lemon juice, pepper, and salt, mix everything together well, and add a few truffles cut into small pieces, the wonderful smell of which will transport the connoisseur into a state of ecstasy." It appears that Maria Colbran liked it – she later became Rossini's wife. And the apostolic secretary, a cardinal whose acquaintance Rossini had just made, insisted on blessing this recipe for sensual pleasure.

Cannelloni alla pesarese
Cannelloni Pesaro-style

1/4 LB/150 G COOKED HAM, NOT TOO LEAN
I SMALL ONION
1/4 LB/100 G LEAN VEAL
6 1/2 TBSP/100 G BUTTER
I CUP MEAT STOCK
SALT AND FRESHLY MILLED BLACK PEPPER
1/4 LB/100 G CHICKEN LIVERS
I BLACK TRUFFLE
I CUP FRESH CREAM
10 OZ/300 G CANNELLONI
1 1/2 CUPS/100 G PARMESAN, FRESHLY GRATED

Chop the ham, onion, and veal very finely and fry for a few minutes in 8 teaspoons (40 g) butter over a low heat. Pour in the meat stock, season with salt and pepper, and simmer over a low heat for approximately 30 minutes.
Pass the chicken livers and finely chopped truffle through a sieve, stir with a wooden spoon, and season to taste with salt and pepper. Gradually fold in two-thirds of the cream. The stuffing should be smooth, but not too soft.
Half cook the cannelloni in salted water. Rinse with cold water, drain, and lay on a cloth to dry.
Grease the base of a wide, flameproof dish with butter. Put the stuffing in a piping bag and fill the cannelloni with it.

The port of Pesaro, birthplace of the composer Gioacchino Rossini, is in northern Marche.

Place half the pasta in the dish. Cover with some of the veal and onion sauce and sprinkle with parmesan. Then place a second layer on top, cover with the remaining sauce, and sprinkle with the rest of the parmesan. Pour over the remaining cream, and dot the rest of the butter over the top. Bake in a preheated oven at 400 °F (200 °C) for approximately 15–20 minutes, until golden brown and crisp on top.

Filetto alla Rossini
Fillet of beef Rossini-style
(Illustrated below)

2 TBSP EXTRA VIRGIN OLIVE OIL
8 TSP/40 G BUTTER
4 FILLET STEAKS
I TBSP ALL-PURPOSE FLOUR
1/2 GLASS MARSALA
SALT AND PEPPER
4 SLICES GRUYÈRE
4 SLICES RAW HAM
1/2 CUP BÉCHAMEL SAUCE
4 SLICES WHITE BREAD
WHITE TRUFFLES

Heat the olive oil and butter in a heavy pan and fry the fillet steaks. When the meat starts to brown, dust with flour, sprinkle with the Marsala, and boil until the sauce thickens. Season on both sides with salt and pepper. Braise the meat until it has absorbed the liquid, then remove and place in a flameproof dish. Lay the slices of cheese and ham on top, pour over the béchamel sauce, and bake for a few minutes in a preheated oven at 400 °F (200 °C) until the top is brown. Fry the slices of bread in butter, arrange the fillet steaks on them, and top with wafer-thin slices of truffle.

Vincenzo Camuccini (1773–1844), *The composer Gioacchino Rossini*, first half of the 19th century, Museo Teatrale alla Scala, Milan.

CHEESE

Pecorino, a ewe's milk cheese, is produced in Marche as well as throughout the rest of central and southern Italy, but as well as eating it, the natives of Marche also used it for the purpose of sport. Today, the *gioco della ruzzola* event is held in only a few communities, and a wooden replica is used instead of a cheese. Originally, the idea was to roll a large, well-matured pecorino cheese along the street, usually with teams from neighboring villages competing against one another. Each cheese roller had three attempts, and the team that rolled the pecorino the furthest was the winner. This sporting competition was reminiscent of the legend of the devil's bridge at Tolentino.

After the river bridge at Tolentino had collapsed for the umpteenth time, because of the simple fact that it was unable to stand firm in the silt of the river bed, the builder, one Mastro Bentivegna, made a pact with the devil in desperation. In return for building a stable bridge, the devil was promised the soul of the first person to cross it. The devil agreed and built the bridge in a single night. When St. Nicholas arrived on the scene to bless the new structure, accompanied by a little dog, he suddenly removed a small pecorino cheese from his habit and rolled it across the bridge. The dog chased eagerly after the cheese, and was therefore the first to cross the bridge. The devil was left with nothing.

Below: Antonio Budano runs a cheese business in the port of Ancona. This store is famous for its specialties, and is a veritable treasure trove for lovers of cheese. Antonio Budano is one of the few dealers who are concerned with preserving and marketing regional cheese specialties that have now become rare.

CHEESE

1 Casciotta d'Urbino

As early as 1545, *casciotta* is mentioned in a document concerning the statutes of the duchies of Urbino and Solone di Campiello. The Renaissance painter Michelangelo Buonarroti is said to have been so fond of the mild, buttery cheese that he bought estates in this region. *Casciotta* consists of between 70 and 80 percent ewe's milk, and the color of the porous cheese varies from whitish to straw yellow. In the area around Castel Durante and Urbino, where there were traditionally many potteries, new cheese was pressed in special ceramic containers, while presses made from maple or beech wood were used elsewhere.

2 Ricotta

Ricotta is not a type of curd cheese, as is frequently supposed, but a cheese made from whey. It can be made using cow's or ewe's milk, and has a mild or sharp flavor depending on the degree of ripeness.

3 Cagiolo

Cagiolo is now produced in only a few cheese-producing dairies in the Osimo area. It is a cross between a hard cheese and a firm ricotta. Children, in particular, used to eat it with their fingers, as a snack between meals.

4 Slattato

Slattato resembles *crescenza* from Lombardia and *squacquarone* from Romagna. It is a soft cheese made from full-cream milk, which is stored in dark, warm rooms.

5 Pecorino in Fossa

Pecorino in fossa can be translated roughly as "trench pecorino". First, a ewe's milk cheese with the greatest possible fat content must be produced in spring, and air-dried until the summer. In the middle of August the "trenches" are prepared. Only the districts of Talamello and Sogliano have the tuff, a type of volcanic rock, that is suitable for storing the cheese. A deep shaft is dug in the ground, the trench walls are scorched with a torch, and the floor is covered with straw. Then the cheeses,

SAUSAGE AND HAM SPECIALTIES

Ham

Ham has always been produced with particular care and attention by craftsmen in Marche. Before food technologists and experts on smoking techniques were available to dispense advice, people relied on their experience, and to a certain extent this is still true today. Farmers in the area around Porto Recanati, who smoke ham over their fires for their own consumption, are convinced that a glow-worm in the house is a bad omen for the ham, and will spoil it.

The trade in ham and pecorino dates back to medieval times. The annual market at Pistia, on the border between Marche and Umbria, was not just the scene of lively trading: it also attracted many minstrels, who serenaded courting couples with verses that were supposed to bring good luck.

Ciauscolo

Ciauscolo is made from the belly and shoulder of the pig. The meat is supplemented with half its weight in fat and is flavored with salt, pepper, garlic, fennel, and orange peel. The mixture is then passed through the meat grinder until a very fine-grained mass is obtained. The meat is used to fill lengths of intestine, the sausages are dried in a smoking chamber, and then hung up to mature for a period of about three weeks. *Ciauscolo* tastes good spread on bread, but can also be used whole as a substitute for a *cotechino*.

Coppa

In the area around Ascoli Piceno the term *coppa* is used to describe a boiling sausage made using meat from the head, bacon, pepper, nutmeg, and orange peel. Sometimes pine nuts or almonds are also added. The meat is used to fill lengths of thick intestine, and the sausages can be eaten the next day. *Coppa* should not be kept for more than 30 days, or it loses its flavor.

Salame del Montefeltro

Salame del Montefeltro is a piquant-flavored sausage made from the leg and loin meat of free-range black pigs. It is produced with the addition of generous quantities of ground pepper and whole peppercorns.

Salame lardellato

The sausage meat of *salame lardellato* consists of lean pork shoulder or leg meat, diced bacon, salt, pepper, and whole peppercorns. The sausage meat is used to stuff the pig's large intestine and is initially dried for a day and a half, followed by three or four days in a warm room with an open fire, then two days in a cold room, and finally two months in a well-ventilated storage area.

Salame da Fabriano

Salame da Fabriano is made in the same way as *salame lardellato*, except that the sausage meat consists exclusively of leg of pork, seasoned with salt and pepper.

Fegatino

Fegatino is a liver sausage. Like *ciauscolo*, it consists of pork belly and shoulder, but liver is added instead of fat.

Soppressata da Fabriano

Soppressata da Fabriano consists of a mixture of meat, passed through the meat grinder several times, flavored with diced bacon, salt, and pepper. The sausage meat is used to stuff skins made from natural intestines, and the sausages are smoked before maturing.

Mazzafegato da Fabriano

Mazzafegato da Fabriano is a mortadella made from fat and lean pork, to which organ meat (liver and lungs) is added. The fine-grained sausage meat is seasoned to taste with salt and pepper, stuffed into intestines, and smoked. *Mazzafegato* is typically eaten at carnival time.

Prosciutto di Montefeltro

The spicy, pear-shaped *prosciutto di Montefeltro* ham is made from the meat of free-range, black pigs. Before it is hung in the smoking chamber, it is washed with vinegar and rubbed with ground pepper.

---

wrapped in walnut leaves and cotton sacks, are laid in the trench. In order for the maturing process to begin, the trench must have an airtight seal. After a minimum of three months, the *pecorino in fossa* is brought to the surface, like buried treasure.

6 Biagiotto or pecorino nostrano
This is a soft cheese resembling Casciotta d'Urbino that is very common in Marche. It is also known as *Pecorino di Senigallia*, after the area in which it is made. It can consist either of a mixture of cow's and ewe's milk, or purely of ewe's milk, like the example illustrated. It tastes best after it has matured for two months.

7 Barzotto di Grotta
Barzotto di grotta is a soft cheese made from ewe's milk or from a mixture of cow's and ewe's milk. The qualification *di grotta* is a reference to the fact that this cheese is ripened in a ventilated cave.

8 Pecorino tartufato
Black and white truffles are ground and mixed into this ewe's milk cheese when it is new, before it is matured for two to three months.

9 Ricotta secca
A lot of salt is added to this cheese, made from the whey of ewe's or cow's milk, to help it mature. It is then left to drain and dry out, and hardens after four to five months. It can either be crumbled over fresh summer salads or, when it has hardened and thus acquired a sharper flavor, grated over hot pasta dishes.

10 Pecorino alle Vinacce
After maturing for seven to eight months in a cave, this ewe's milk cheese is sealed for a further three months in a bed of dried marc in old, obsolete red wine barrels. The temperature rises, and the cheese begins to ferment again. At the end of the process it has a violet-colored rind and a spicy flavor, slightly reminiscent of wine must.

STUFFED OLIVES – HOW IT'S DONE

The pit of the olive is removed using a sharp, pointed knife. Only the large varieties with small stones, such as tenera ascolana, are suitable for stuffing.

As far as possible, it is important that the flesh of the olive should remain undamaged and intact when it is pitted.

The filling consists of beef and pork, tomato paste, chicken livers, egg, parmesan, and breadcrumbs.

The fine-textured mixture, which has been passed through a meat grinder, is carefully stuffed into the cavity, and the olive is pressed back into shape.

STUFFED OLIVES FROM ASCOLI PICENO

Olives are the culinary emblem of Ascoli Piceno. The ancient Roman writer Martial describes how olives from Ascoli were served at every banquet, as an appetizer at the beginning and to clear the palate at the end. Pliny considered this variety of olive to be the best in Italy, and the satirist Petronius describes Trimalchio gossiping about a banquet at which Nero and his entourage were apparently offered the olives in question as a first course. In the 18th century, the resourceful cooks from this small town in southern Marche hit upon the idea of stuffing the olives and then deep-frying them. A delicacy was born.

This costly specialty can really only be prepared using olives of the variety tenera ascolana, which grow all around Ascoli in very chalky soil on a small plantation of just under 250 acres (100 hectares). The harvest is comparatively modest, but because tenera ascolana olives have particularly soft, mild-tasting flesh and an extremely small pit, they are especially suitable for stuffing. Those who have sufficient patience, however, can also try using larger-pitted varieties.

Whether or not they are stuffed, the olives must ferment for about ten days under controlled conditions. They are then marinated in brine (3½ tablespoons (70 grams) of salt to 4 cups (1 liter) of water), enhanced by the addition of fennel. This is what gives them their mild, yet delicate flavor, and at the same time makes them suitable for keeping.

Left: In the Villa Cicchi, on the Azienda Agraria Conca D'Oro near Ascoli Piceno, the stuffed olives are served very fresh and very hot, for this is when they taste best.

Below: The olives must be deep-fried in plenty of hot olive oil. They are then drained briefly on kitchen towels.

Olive all'ascolana
Stuffed olives
(Illustrated above and below)

Serves 6

Breadcrumbs
1 CUP STOCK
1/4 LB/100 G BACON, FINELY CHOPPED
2 TBSP OLIVE OIL
1/4 LB/100 G PORK
ABOUT 6 OZ/150 G BEEF
1 TBSP TOMATO PASTE
3–4/50 G CHICKEN LIVERS
1 EGG
3/4 CUP/50 G PARMESAN, FRESHLY GRATED
CINNAMON
GRATED NUTMEG
SALT AND PEPPER
APPROXIMATELY 50 LARGE, GREEN OLIVES IN BRINE
2 TBSP ALL-PURPOSE FLOUR
2 EGGS
OIL FOR DEEP FRYING

Soak 3 tablespoons of breadcrumbs in stock. Fry the bacon in olive oil, add the pork and beef, and fry these as well. Dilute the tomato paste with lukewarm water and add to the meat. When the meat is tender, add the chicken livers and fry for a further 5 minutes. Then grind all these ingredients in a food processor. Add the egg, parmesan, and the soaked breadcrumbs to the meat and mix well. Season to taste with cinnamon, nutmeg, salt, and pepper. Pit the olives and stuff with the mixture. Coat in flour, beaten egg, and breadcrumbs, and deep-fry in plenty of hot olive oil until crisp. Drain on kitchen towels and serve hot.

SWEET DISHES

Like their neighbors in Umbria, the natives of Marche also like to bake rich, sweet cakes such as *Bostrengo*, a substantial rice cake, containing raisins, dried figs, cocoa powder, cornstarch, rum, coffee, sugar, or honey, as well as fresh fruit. *Ciambellone*, on the other hand, is a ring-shaped cake that is included – naturally with variations, according to regional preferences – in the dessert repertoire in many parts of Italy.

CIAMBELLONE
Ring cake

5 EGGS, BEATEN
2 CUPS/400 G SUGAR
SCANT CUP/200 G BUTTER, MELTED IN A BASIN OVER HOT WATER
1 GLASS MILK
8 3/4 CUPS/1 KG ALL-PURPOSE FLOUR
5 LEVEL TSP BAKING POWDER
1 SMALL GLASS MISTRÀ
1 PINCH BAKING SODA
1/2 CUP/50 G RAISINS
JUICE AND GRATED RIND OF 2 LEMONS
BUTTER AND FLOUR FOR THE CAKE PAN
2 EGG WHITES
SUGAR
JUICE OF 1/2 LEMON
COLORFUL SUGAR STRANDS AND SILVER BALLS FOR DECORATION

Mix the eggs, sugar, butter, and milk together. Stir the baking powder into the flour, and gradually incorporate in the mixture, stirring constantly. Then add the Mistrà, followed by the baking soda, raisins, lemon rind, and lemon juice, and mix everything together quickly, as the dough should not be handled for too long.

Grease a ring-shaped cake pan with butter and dust with flour. Place the dough in the pan and bake in a preheated oven at 340 °F (170 °C) for 1 hour.

After the cake has cooled, brush with a glaze made from beaten egg white, sugar, and lemon juice, and decorate with sugar strands and decorative balls.

BOSTRENGO
Sweet rice cake
(Illustrated right)

1 LB/500 G RICE
4 CUPS/1 LITER MILK
1 1/4 CUPS/300 G SUGAR OR 10 TBSP HONEY
3 EGGS
GRATED RIND OF 1 ORANGE AND 1 LEMON
5 CUPS/300 G BREADCRUMBS
2 CUPS/200 G RAISINS
3 SMALL GLASSES RUM
6 CUPS ESPRESSO COFFEE
1 1/2 CUPS/150 G DRIED FIGS, FINELY CHOPPED
1 1/4 CUPS/150 G CORNSTARCH
1 3/4 CUPS/200 G COCOA POWDER
2 TBSP EXTRA VIRGIN OLIVE OIL
2 LBS/1 KG APPLES AND PEARS, DICED OR SLICED
CONFECTIONERS' SUGAR

Cook the rice in salted water or in milk until just tender. Put all the other ingredients, except for the confectioners' sugar, in a large pan and cook for a few minutes, stirring constantly. Then stir in the cooked rice. If it is too dry, add a little lukewarm milk. Place the mixture in a large, greased springform pan and bake in a preheated oven at a low heat for approximately 1 hour. Sprinkle with confectioners' sugar before serving.

ANISEED SPIRIT AND ANISEED LIQUEUR

Long ago, the ancient Egyptians and Babylonians were familiar with aniseed. This aromatic umbelliferous plant was said by doctors such as Hippocrates, Celsus, and Galenus to have healing powers. Pliny claimed that it aided digestion, and aniseed juice was used in Arabia to treat rheumatic complaints. Even Charles the Great was a self-confessed aniseed lover, and cultivated the plant in his gardens. Aniseed spread throughout the Italian peninsula after the Arabs had brought it to Sicily. The first liqueurs were – like many other intellectually stimulating drinks – first brewed in the monasteries. In the 19th century *anice* became extremely fashionable.

In Italy today there is a huge variety of aniseed liqueurs that are especially popular in central and southern Italy. Anicione, Sassolino, Sambuca, which is probably the best known Italian aniseed liqueur, Anisetta, and Mistrà are regarded with the same reverence here that northern Italians accord to their *grappa*.

Aniseed liqueur is distilled from the fruit of the green aniseed plant and other aromatic ingredients. It can be clear, milky white, or straw yellow, and has a not altogether innocuous alcohol content – 40 to 60, and in exceptional cases even 80 percent by volume. It is drunk either diluted with water or neat, on ice or at room temperature. Aniseed liqueur is also a traditional *ammazzacaffè*, a "coffee killer," which is either poured directly into espresso or drunk after strong coffee to get rid of the bitter aftertaste. Ice cream with aniseed liqueur is simply irresistible.

1 Although Sassolino actually comes from Emilia-Romagna, more precisely from Sassuolo near Modena, it is also very popular in Marche.

2 Anisetta is an aromatic liqueur made from star aniseed, green aniseed, fennel, sassafras, lemon peel, and orange peel. Depending on the brand, its alcohol content varies between 40 and 80 percent by volume.

3 Sambuca obtains its unmistakable flavor from ethereal dill oils, anethole, star aniseed, and an infusion of elderflowers. Two kinds are available: Sambuca Bianca, flavored with coffee, and Sambuca Nigra, which is enhanced by the addition of chocolate.

4 Mistrà from the Vernelli distillery, which has been produced since the middle of the 19th century, is one of the favorite aniseed liqueurs in central Italy. It owes its dry flavor to the special method of preparing the green aniseed. Mistrà tastes good in coffee (*caffè corretto*), as a liqueur (*liscio*), or, diluted with water, as a milky thirst-quencher.

DRIED FIG BREAD – OR SAUSAGE

Figs are among the oldest fruit known to man – and today they are still a welcome sight on our plates for dessert, or we take them with us as a light snack on outings to the countryside, or we pick them – more or less surreptitiously – straight from the trees when we are on summer vacation, to enjoy them at their freshest when they are ripe. There are various different types of fig grown in Italy.

In Marche, the varieties with black, green, and yellow skins predominate. The area around Recanati is particularly famous for its *fichi cori*, heart-shaped figs, which are green on the outside and a luminous red inside, and which are said to have been praised by Pope Innocent XIII in person back in the early part of the 18th century.

Given the popularity of the fig, resourceful housewives have long been keen to ensure the availability of the sought-after fruit in the winter months as well. The old custom of dusting the figs with flour, threading them on string or sticks, and leaving them to dry in the sun so that they will keep, still survives in Marche. A very special delicacy made with the dried fruit is *panetti di fichi secchi*, also known as *salame di fichi*. The name of this confection is taken from its shape, which resembles a loaf or a sausage. Even the writer Giacomo Leopardi, who suffered throughout his life from lack of appetite, is said to have been practically addicted to this specialty, which seems to have originated in the Monsampolo district.

Panetti di fichi secchi is made using dried figs with the skins removed to make them taste sweeter. The base and sides of a rectangular or oval pan are covered with the fruit. Layers of chopped roasted almonds, pistachios, chocolate flakes, candied citrus fruits, vanilla and mint extract are then alternated with layers of figs. The top layer should consist of figs. The mixture is then firmly pressed down once again, and the pan is covered with a tight-fitting lid. The fig bread or fig sausage has to dry out for several days, after which the dessert – which is admittedly not exactly low in calories – can be removed from the pan and wrapped in silver foil so it stays fresh. This keeps the *panetti di fichi secchi* soft and crumbly.

Emilia-Romagna
Rimini
Riccione
13°E   25 km/15 miles   44°N
Cattolica
SAN MARINO
San Marino
A14   Pesaro
Fano
Maròcchia   Adriatic Sea
Montefeltro   Foglia
Colli Pesaresi   Mondolfo
Tuscany   Urbino   Fossombrone   Senigallia
1454 m   Falconara
Mt. dei Frati   Urbania   Marittima   Ancona
Sansepolcro   Chiaravalle
Pergola   Barbara   Jesi   Marche
Città   Mt. Catria   Osimo   Castelfidardo
di Castello   1701 m   Sassoferrato   Cupramontana
Fabriano   Recanati   Loreto
Cingoli
Matelica   San Severino   Civitanova
Esino   Macerata   Marche
Gualdo   Marche   Tolentino
Tadino   Porto
Nocera   San Giorgio
Umbra   1571 m   Camerino   Maceratesi Hills   43°
Monte
Pennino   Grottammare
Falerio dei
Amandola   Colli Ascolani
Mt. Sibilla   San Benedetto
2176 m   del Tronto
Ascoli   Martinsicuro
Umbria   Piceno
A14
Spoleto
Norcia   Mt. Piselli
1676 m   Abruzzi
Teramo

Colli Pesaresi
Bianchello del Metauro
Verdicchio dei
Castelli di Jesi
Lacrima di Morro d'Alba
Rosso Piceno
Esino
Rosso Conero
Colli Maceratesi
Verdicchio di Matelica
Vernaccia di Matelica
Vernaccia di Serrapetrona
Falerio dei Colli Ascolani
Winegrowing areas in
neighboring regions

ADRIATIC WINES FROM NORTH TO SOUTH

Marche constitutes a kind of natural, southern extension of Romagna, or, viewed from a different angle, the northern continuation of Abruzzi. Its wine shares a whole range of features with that of its neighbors, including Umbria and Tuscany, from the best grape varieties to the various types of soil and the climate. Situated only a few miles from the tourist beaches of Rimini, the region has long enjoyed the privilege of straightforward, lucrative marketing. However, this has not necessarily helped the region to achieve labor-intensive and capital-intensive quality wine production.

Vineyards cover large areas of the hills inland from the long Adriatic beaches, and occasionally extend right down to the sea, for instance around the rocky outcrops of Ancona. Because of the sea, it is noticeably mild here, in stark contrast with the cooler, harsher climate of the Apennine or Abruzzi valleys penetrating deep inland, which brings out particular characteristics in the wine. For a long time, the most famous wine from Marche was white Verdicchio, sold since the

1950s in a green bottle, shaped like an amphora that is its trademark. The fact that this bottle is not actually a traditional one, but was invented by a marketing specialist in Milan, has not detracted from its commercial success. In recent decades, however, there has been a definite shift in the quality spectrum from white to red wines, based on the Montepulciano and Sangiovese grape varieties – one of the greatest and most famous of Italian red wines is produced in Tuscany from Sangiovese grapes.

RED WINE FROM ANCONA

The best-known, and perhaps also the best, red wine from Marche is Rosso Conero. It should only be made using Montepulciano grapes, but a little Sangiovese probably finds its way into some wines. It originates from the coastal area around the city of Ancona, and

has developed over the past two decades into a really good product, which can, moreover, still be obtained very cheaply – an advantage

Left: Every year, approximately 9,504,000 US gallons (360,000 hectoliters) of DOC wine, such as white Verdicchio and red Rosso Conero, are produced from vineyards in Marche.

that, unfortunately, has often been lost by most renowned wines from other regions of Italy.

Rosso Piceno, on the other hand, its counterpart from the south of the region, is officially a blend of Sangiovese and Montepulciano grapes, although there

are vintners and wine-making experts who maintain that the Montepulciano grape is simply a variety of the Sangiovese. It is said that in wines made from a blend of both types, the Sangiovese grapes are responsible for the finesse and complexity, while the Montepulciano grapes give body and fullness.

CHANGE OF STYLE FOR VERDICCHIO

As far as the white wines of Marche are concerned, Verdicchio wine from the two DOC regions of Castelli di Jesi and Matelica is really the only wine with a role to play. Until very recently, Verdicchio was a decidedly rustic, strong white wine, frequently lacking the elegance, fruitiness, and freshness needed to satisfy the wine connoisseurs of Italy and the world. However, since the vintners of Marche stopped the practice of leaving the must to stand on the crushed grape skins and instead started pressing it straight away, and since they dispensed with the old Governo procedure, in which dried grapes were added to the finished wine to restart fermentation, Verdicchio has become a pleasantly fruity white wine of light to medium strength, a real pleasure when drunk as an

accompaniment to an excellent fish dish.

Last but not least, it should also be mentioned that the most famous winemakers of Marche turned their backs on their homeland several decades ago: the winemakers in question, the Mondavi family, have been producing wine in the Napa valley in California since the 1960s, and are now among the best-known names in wine production worldwide.

LAZIO
ROMA

Rome and Lazio constitute a vast region. The flavor of their cuisine is impossible to sum up in a couple of words – the culinary traditions of Rome, the Eternal City, and its rural surroundings are far too diverse. Hospitality, such as was practiced in ancient times, is considered very important here, as is the cuisine, which relies heavily upon the butcher, and features robust organ meat dishes. Refined Jewish specialties share equal status with simple dishes that originate from the Sabine mountains.

Rome, the capital of Christendom, has always had many guests to accommodate. In the inns and taverns, pilgrims and travelers were served nourishing meals, consisting of pasta, broccoli, beans, rocket, and ewe's milk cheese, accompanied by strong country wine. *Bavette alla carrettiera, spaghetti alla puttanesca*, and *spaghetti alla carbonara* are still found on the menus of the unspoiled eating houses. Specialties obtained from what is known as the "fifth quarter" of the animal are produced in the great slaughterhouses in the heart of the city. When the enticing aroma of *coda alla vaccinara* or *rigatoni alla paiata* streams forth from the kitchen, one would not think that these were the less popular, mostly cheaper cuts of beef or pork. The dishes of modern Roman haute cuisine, on the other hand, are derived from a completely different tradition: residents in the Jewish quarter have long since ceased cooking just for themselves, but instead prepare *pizza ebraica d'erbe* or endives with anchovies for visitors from other parts of the city as well. Rome is also a city of bars, cafés and restaurants. Even the morning cappuccino is drunk in a local bar, and Romans go out to eat with family or friends whenever they can. There may well be historical reasons underlying the lack of enthusiasm for cooking in the private kitchens of Rome: owing to the dense population of the city and the fear of a catastrophic fire, people living in the rented apartments of ancient Rome were not permitted to light a fire for the purpose of cooking. As a result, the average Roman was already eating cold food at home over 2000 years ago – and, if he felt like something hot, he had recourse to one of the numerous hot food stalls. Even in affluent households with their own fireplaces, people preferred to leave the preparation of everyday meals, as well as the creation of opulent banquets, to experts engaged for the purpose. It would appear that modern caterers and party organizers may well have originated from ancient Rome.

Previous double page: The large coffee machine, dispensing espresso and cappucino, is an indispensable feature of every Italian bar.

Left: There are magnificent views of the landscape from the autoroute between Terni and Rome, like this one near Magliano Sabina, in the border region between Umbria and Lazio.

ANCIENT ROMAN CUISINE

Before Rome became a world power, people living on the banks of the Tiber were accustomed to a relatively modest gastronomic culture. *Puls*, a cereal dish resembling modern polenta, was served either as a thick gruel or as a loaf baked in oil. Vegetables were also frequently cooked to a pulp, and flavored with onions and garlic. Eggs, cheese, pork, and chicken were among the culinary highlights in more affluent households. Although the Roman Empire was unable to remedy the social divisions in Rome – a third of the citizens in the empire were so poor that they relied on the public purse to prevent them starving – an astonishing transformation began to take place on the tables of the well-to-do and *nouveaux riches*. Not only were the Roman legions conquering new provinces: they were also continually bringing back local specialties from their campaigns, as well as cooks who could prepare them. In Sicily, which was at that time a colony of Greece, the Romans, who were inclined to be boorish, on one hand became acquainted with fine Mediterranean cuisine, and on the other, as far as feasts were concerned, began imitating modern Greek culture, in which the primary purpose of a banquet was the edification of the soul through conversation and artistic performances. As a consequence, it became fashionable in Rome to engage a Greek cook and to invite guests to enjoy civilized pleasures. The fact that most of these gatherings nevertheless ended in a terrible orgy may have resulted from the Romans'

refusal to follow the Greek custom of diluting their wine with water to make it more digestible.

Greece, Carthage and Egypt provided new luxuries, and ensured – albeit at the expense of their own people – continuity of supply as regards the gigantic quantities of food consumed on a daily basis in Rome. It soon became good form to serve foodstuffs and ingredients from the remotest possible sources, which were correspondingly expensive, and therefore demonstrated the wealth of the host. Turtles were imported from Arabia, ham from Gaul, and it was essential to have salmon from the Rhine. The merchants and hauliers were constantly inventing new ways of ensuring that the goods arrived in the city in as fresh a condition as possible.

One imagines that the "international" cuisine of Rome, which benefited enormously from the culinary arts of even the remotest provinces, must have been extremely palatable. There was a marked awareness of high-quality, and above all fresh, produce. Roman agronomists were remarkably successful at growing fruit and vegetables in the surrounding Latin countryside, and in the covered markets there were even well-chilled live oysters. The prelude to a meal was almost inevitably an egg dish. There followed meat, game, or poultry, served with vegetables, and the meal was concluded with a sweet dessert, or a platter of fruit. Even a typical day in the culinary life of the average Roman has similarities with modern Mediterranean customs. For breakfast he would have eaten a little white bread, dipped in wine, and at midday there would be cheese, onions, eggs, and perhaps some cold meat. Those who were so inclined could go to one of the many hot food stalls offering hot dishes to take away. For reasons of safety, it was not

This floor mosaic, showing food left over after a banquet, is an example of what is called an asaroton motif (from the Greek, *asarotos oikos*, an unswept house). The mosaic, which is in the Museo Gregoriano Profano in the Vatican, dates from the first century AD, and its creator is identified as a certain Heraclitus.

permitted to light fires for cooking in rented apartments, so cold food was the norm at home. The most important meal of the day was taken in the evening, when one went to dine with friends or invited guests to one's own home.

The only weakness of ancient Roman cuisine lay in its preoccupation with prestige. The price of the ingredients often determined the menu, instead of whether the obscenely expensive pickled vegetables from Spain actually went well with the Indian ginger and the Illyrian hazelwort. Complicated methods of preparing food similarly enjoyed enormous popularity, for these too made an excellent impression on the guests. High society in Rome became increasingly enslaved by the deluded notion of turning the table into a stage and the meal into a spectacle. "Mock" dishes – trompe-l'oeil for the tastebuds – appeared on the menu. The best reputation was enjoyed by cooks who could prepare veal in such a way that it tasted like carp, and could ostensibly serve salt cod without actually doing so. This predilection for expensive, ostentatious dishes and sophisticated culinary skill, which found expression in the Roman saying "nobody will ever guess what is in this dish," was to persist for several more centuries at the tables of European princes and kings. It was not until the Renaissance that certain outstanding gastronomic reformers began propounding the idea that less expensive foodstuffs, prepared in natural ways, could also taste exceptionally good, despite their simplicity.

Roman cuisine also had its own protagonists, however. In the first century after the birth of Christ, Marcus Gavius Apicius made his entrance on the culinary stage of Rome. Apicius, a rake who was a contemporary of the emperors Augustus and Tiberius, repeatedly found himself on the receiving end of the scorn and malice of philosophers counseling moderation: Clement of Alexandria, Pliny, and Seneca, who advanced the criticism that modern youth was no longer interested in learning rhetoric and wisdom, preferring instead to hang around in Apicius' kitchens. Apicius, however, remained impervious to attacks of an ascetic nature. He discovered a way of making pig's liver even tastier ("feed the animals with figs and sweet must"), devised various recipes for snails ("feed the creatures with milk"), and finally gathered together his accumulated culinary knowledge in a book. Today, unfortunately, we no longer have an original copy of this Latin cookery classic, for Apicius' work has been repeatedly copied, edited, supplemented, and revised over the course of the centuries, and the – mainly monastic – publishers have not always distinguished themselves by their knowledge of the subject. Nevertheless, Apicius' work conveys an impression of what was likely to have been on the tables and sideboards when the Romans reclined to eat a meal.

The light menu featured here would probably have been very much in Apicius' style. It follows the rule for the sequence of dishes, *ex ovo usque ad malum*, from the egg to the apple, where "apple" indicates any kind of dessert fruit. The main course, chicken salad à la Apicius, could well have been created by the master himself.

Sala cattabia Apiciana
Chicken salad à la Apicius

1/4 LB/100 G VEAL SWEETBREADS
VINEGAR
SALT
1 TSP LEMON JUICE
1 TBSP/15 G BUTTER
1 LARGE/200 G CHICKEN BREAST
1 TBSP/15 G BUTTER FOR FRYING
SCANT 1/2 CUP/100 ML MILK
1/4 TSP HONEY
4 SLICES GRAHAM BREAD OR WHOLE WHEAT TOAST
FLOUR
1/4 LB/100 G PECORINO, DICED
2 TBSP PINE NUTS
1 CUCUMBER, FINELY SLICED
1 ONION, CHOPPED

For the sauce:
1 TSP FINELY CHOPPED CELERY LEAVES
1 TSP FINELY CHOPPED LEMON BALM
1 TSP FINELY CHOPPED MINT
1 TSP FINELY CHOPPED CORIANDER
1/2 TSP FINELY CHOPPED ROOT GINGER
2 TBSP GOLDEN RAISINS
2 TBSP RUNNY HONEY
4 TBSP WINE VINEGAR
4 TBSP SAFFLOWER OIL

Soak the sweetbreads in cold water for about 2 hours, then lay them in 2 cups (500 ml) water containing ½ tablespoon vinegar for 1 hour. Remove and cook at just below boiling point in 4 cups (1 liter) water with 1 tablespoon salt and 1 teaspoon lemon juice for about 15 minutes. Leave to cool in the cooking liquor, then carefully remove the outer skin. Cut the sweetbreads into bite-sized pieces and sauté in hot butter. Season sparingly with pepper.

Skin and cut the chicken meat into bite-sized pieces and fry thoroughly in the butter. Season with salt and pepper. Mix together all the ingredients for the sauce.
Dip the bread in a mixture of milk and honey, and lay a slice of bread on each plate. Arrange the cold sweetbreads and chicken with the pecorino cubes, pine nuts, cucumber slices, and chopped onion on top of the bread. Pour over the sauce and serve.

Patina de piris
Pear patina

ABOUT 2 LBS/1 KG PEARS
SALT AND FRESHLY MILLED PEPPER
FRESHLY GROUND CARAWAY SEEDS
2 TBSP HONEY
1 TBSP SAFFLOWER OIL
3 EGGS, BEATEN
1 TSP CORNSTARCH
3 TBSP MARSALA
1 TBSP/15 G BUTTER

Peel and core the pears and cook for at least 15 minutes in a little water. Drain well and purée with a hand blender. Mix in 1 pinch each of salt, pepper, and caraway, as well as the honey, oil, and beaten eggs.
Blend the cornstarch with a little of the Marsala, then add the rest. Add the pear purée, stir thoroughly once again, and pour into a soufflé dish greased with butter.
Bake in a preheated oven at 350 °F (180 °C) for about 25 minutes until brown on top.

In ovis hapalis
Sauce for boiled eggs
(Illustrated in the background)

1/3 CUP/50 G PINE NUTS, SOAKED
SALT AND PEPPER
1 TSP FINELY CHOPPED LOVAGE
1/4 TSP HONEY
4 EGGS
VINEGAR

Crush the soaked pine nuts and mix with 1 pinch each of salt and pepper, and the lovage and honey. Heat 4 cups (1 liter) water with 1 teaspoon salt and 2 tablespoons vinegar. Break the eggs into boiling water and cook for 4 minutes, or, as an alternative, use hard-boiled eggs. Pour the sauce over the eggs.

ROMAN HOSPITALITY

Rome is a hospitable city. Christian pilgrims, worldly businessmen, Church officials, commercial travelers, art-loving tourists, artists, literary folk, and pleasure-seekers of whatever kind – the Eternal City has been positively overrun by such visitors since time immemorial. Even in ancient times, life on the seven hills attracted curious people from all the Roman provinces. It was when Christendom emerged as a world power that Rome, the navel of the world, became a really popular travel destination. In 1300, when Pope Boniface VIII invited guests to a gigantic millennial celebration, around two million pilgrims streamed into the city. This huge volume of visitors presented a major challenge, both for the Roman infrastructure and the hotel and innkeeping business. Where were all these people to be accommodated? Which staging posts and courtyards would they be able to use to change horses, and by which routes would they enter the city? What was to be offered to the guests by way of food and drink, and where would the necessary quantities of food be obtained? In the early days of tourism, as travel became more common, monasteries and convents assumed responsibility for the spiritual and physical well-being of travelers, and, in most parts of the Christian world, weary travelers or those who had been caught unawares by bad weather, illness, or injury, could always count on the help and hospitality of monks and nuns in the monastic orders. In Rome, however, the number of visitors far

Historic painting of pilgrims in a tavern, a miniature from the manuscript *Tacuinum Sanitatis*, Italy, late 14th century, Nationalbibliothek, Vienna.

exceeded the capacity of ecclesiastical shelters. Private hotels and inns sprang up out of the ground like mushrooms, for business with the foreigners was profitable. Bars and taverns flourished, and, during the period between 1500 and 1800, Rome was the city with the best and cheapest gastronomy.

In the middle of the 19th century there were over 200 restaurants, 200 cafés, and around 100 inns and lodging houses. In those days, of course, one could not speak of these as "hotels" as we know them today. Single rooms in guest houses were very rare, and the more affluent

travelers spent the night in crowded dormitories, while the servants were obliged to bed down in the stables with the horses. The catering, too, was extremely simple. The owner's wife often did the cooking, serving robust traditional Roman or Latin fare with a tankard of table wine.

In order to ensure a continuous supply of drink for the thirsty guests, the coachmen usually broke their journey in the *castelli* during the night, and delivered new wine barrels on a daily basis to the innkeepers at the crack of dawn.

In order to put a damper on the competition between landlords, various corporate bodies of innkeepers and hoteliers were formed. These enforced the ban on sending employees to intercept approaching pilgrims or commercial travelers outside the city gates, in order to direct them to their own particular establishments. Since the majority of the potential guests was illiterate, entrepreneurs were obliged to advertise with the aid of striking signs or attractive pictures on the doors and walls of their premises. As a result there were inns called "The Bear," "The Crossed Swords," "The Twin Towers," and also the "Osteria del Gallinaccio," which means giant cockerel (near what is now the Via del Tritone), which was famous for its roast turkey. In order to convey the message that drink was also available, bars and taverns were decorated with vine leaves or branches. This foliage, or *frasche*, gave the name *frasca* or *fraschetta* to the genuine Roman restaurant. Today, however, these charming establishments must take care that they are not ousted by the increasing numbers of fast-food chains, for competition to attract the paying guest is just as fierce now, at the beginning of the third millennium after the birth of Christ, as it was in olden times.

Abbacchio al forno con patate
Lamb with potatoes

Serves 6

4 1/2 LBS/2 KG SHOULDER OR LEG OF LAMB
3 CLOVES OF GARLIC
2 SPRIGS OF ROSEMARY
4 TSP/20 G BUTTER
1 1/2 LBS/700 G POTATOES, CUT INTO CUBES
SALT AND FRESHLY MILLED BLACK PEPPER
3–4 TBSP EXTRA VIRGIN OLIVE OIL

Rinse the lamb under running water, pat dry, and spike with the cloves of garlic, halved lengthways, and the sprigs of rosemary. Brush the butter over the meat and place in a casserole with the potato cubes. Season with salt and pepper, sprinkle with the olive oil, and bake in a preheated moderate oven for at least 45 minutes, occasionally basting the lamb with the meat juices.

Saltimbocca alla romana
Veal cutlet, Roman-style
(Illustrated on facing page, below)

8 SMALL VEAL CUTLETS
8 SLICES RAW HAM
8–12 SAGE LEAVES
3 1/2 TBSP/50 G BUTTER
7 TBSP DRY WHITE WINE OR MARSALA
SALT AND FRESHLY MILLED BLACK PEPPER

Place a slice of ham on each veal cutlet, with the sage leaves on top, securing with a wooden cocktail stick. Heat the butter in a wide pan and fry the cutlets gently on both sides. Pour in the wine, season to taste with salt and pepper, and simmer for 6–8 minutes, until the meat is tender. Arrange the cutlets on a warmed plate, and remove the cocktail sticks. Add 1 tablespoon water to the meat juices, stir, and pour over the meat.

Coda alla vaccinara
Oxtail ragout

Serves 8

4 1/2 LBS/2 KG OXTAIL
SALT
1 LEEK
2 STICKS CELERY
1 CARROT
1 BAY LEAF
1 SPRIG OF THYME
GENEROUS 1/4 LB/150 G RAW HAM
1 ONION
1 SPRIG OF MARJORAM
3 TBSP EXTRA VIRGIN OLIVE OIL
1 GLASS DRY WHITE WINE
2 LBS/1 KG SIEVED TOMATOES
PEPPER
1 OZ/30 G SEMISWEET CHOCOLATE
GROUND CINNAMON
NUTMEG
1 TBSP RAISINS
1 TBSP PINE NUTS

Cut the oxtail into pieces, pour boiling salted water over them, and leave to stand for 10 minutes. Place the pieces of meat in a casserole, cover with cold water, add some salt, and bring to the boil. Chop the leek, 1 stick of celery, and the carrot. Add with the bay leaf and the sprig of thyme to the meat, and simmer for about 2½ hours.
Finely chop the ham, onion, and marjoram, and fry in olive

The genuine *osteria* is threatened with extinction today. Only a few of these traditional bars, like this one at Frascati, are able to survive.

Nowadays, *osteria* often means a restaurant with a wine cellar. The old, traditional bars, however, had no kitchens or cooks and only served drinks. The guests had to bring their own food, such as bread, pizza, or cheese. Nevertheless, the *osteria* was an ideal place for a convivial gathering of friends and workmates.

oil. Remove the oxtail pieces from the stock, drain well, and add to the ham. Pour in the white wine and boil rapidly to reduce. Add the sieved tomatoes, season with salt and pepper, mix well, and simmer for 1 hour.
Remove a little of the sauce from the frying pan, mix with the grated chocolate, and stir back into the sauce in the pan to thicken it.
Cut the remaining celery into pieces, blanch in salted water, and add to the oxtail. Season to taste with a small pinch of cinnamon and grated nutmeg. Add the raisins and pine nuts, and remove the pan from the stove. Serve the oxtail ragout hot with the celery.

Capitone marinato
Marinated eel

2 LBS/1 KG EEL
OIL FOR FRYING
2 CUPS/500 ML RED WINE VINEGAR
1 CLOVE OF GARLIC
1 BAY LEAF
A FEW BLACK PEPPERCORNS
SALT

Cut the eel into pieces and fry, with the skin on, in hot oil. Heat the wine vinegar in a casserole with the peeled and finely chopped clove of garlic, the bay leaf, and the whole peppercorns.
Lay the fried pieces of eel in a ceramic dish and pour over the hot marinade.
Leave the eel to stand in the marinade to absorb the flavors for some time, preferably 2 weeks.

ANTIPASTI

In Italy, a distinction is drawn between hot and cold starters. If a hot starter is served – usually a pasta specialty – cold canapés of one kind or another are served beforehand. To draw up a complete list of cold *antipasti* would be just as hopeless a task as compiling a list of all the Spanish *tapas*. The choice is simply too great, reflecting the imagination of the cooks, housewives, and restaurateurs, who try to put their guests in the right mood for the forthcoming meal with some novelty or other to tickle the palate. Whereas one would perhaps just serve a few slices of Parma ham with some white bread at home, most restaurants have large glass cabinets from which the guest can assemble his own very personal selection of *antipasti*. In some restaurants the waiter even brings a trolley bearing an appetizing arrangement of these little delicacies to the table, so that one has only to point to one's choice of individual specialties.

Cold *antipasti* can be roughly divided into seven groups: *sott'aceto*, *sott'olio*, *sotto sale*, *a base di carne*, *a base di pesce*, *a base di formaggio*, and *a base di pane*. The *sott'aceto* group of starters includes vegetables pickled in vinegar, such as pickled onions, gherkins, sour pickled olives, or artichoke hearts. An *antipasto sott'olio* also usually consists of vegetables, this time preserved in oil. *Sotto sale* means salted starters, such as salted olives, dried and salted tomatoes, or other raw or cooked vegetables preserved in salt. *Antipasti a base di carne* consist of ham, sausage, or meat products – a few slices of air-dried salami, fresh mortadella, or exquisite ham, for instance. *Antipasti a base di pesce* are cold starters based on fish. The best-known example of this sort is without doubt seafood salad. *Antipasti a base di formaggio* are rare, since cheese is usually served at the end of the meal. Despite this, mozzarella with olive oil or a little Parmesan taste very good as a starter. *Antipasti a base di pane* include all the starters that are based on bread.

Prosciutto di Parma (Parma ham)
Parma ham is cut into wafer-thin slices, for it is then that its sweet flavor develops and it positively melts in the mouth.

Cipollini sott'aceto (pickled onions)
These small, white onions are boiled in water and vinegar, or alternatively prepared in sweet and sour fashion with sugar, flour, water, and vinegar, and then served either hot or cold.

Olive sott'aceto (olives in vinegar)
These olives acquire a special tang from being marinated in vinegar.

Olive ripiene (stuffed olives)
These olives stuffed with almonds and peppers are available throughout Italy as *antipasti*. *Olive ascolante* are stuffed and deep-fried olives from Ascoli.

Melanzane sott'olio (eggplant slices in oil)
The eggplants are covered in salt for a few hours, dried, broiled, and finally flavored with chili pepper, oregano, vinegar, and plenty of olive oil.

Zucchini sott'olio (zucchini slices in oil)
The zucchini are deep-fried in oil, then flavored with peppermint, a few drops of balsamic vinegar, salt, and pepper, and served cold.

Funghi misti sott'olio (mixed mushroom salad in oil)
Boletus edulis, chanterelle, and field mushrooms are cooked in white vinegar, put in glass jars, flavored with herbs such as garlic, bay, and cloves, and covered with plenty of oil.

Prataioli ripieni (stuffed field mushrooms)
The mushrooms can be stuffed with ground meat, ewe's milk cheese, or anchovies with breadcrumbs, garlic, and parsley.

Pomodori secchi sott'olio (sun-dried tomatoes in oil)
The dried tomatoes are flavored with basil and preserved in oil. They can also be ground and served spread on *crostini*.

Peperoni sott'olio (broiled bell peppers in oil)
Bell peppers are broiled, the skins are removed, and then they are cut into small strips and flavored with oil, garlic, and parsley.

Crostini di tartufi (toasted slices of bread with truffles)
The truffles are briefly fried in oil with a little anchovy fillet, garlic, and the juice of a lemon.

Salame (salami)
Regional salami specialties such as *salame di Milano* or *salame del Montefeltro* are used for this *antipasto*.

Mortadella
Mortadella, which comes from Bologna, is the best-known fresh sausage in Italy. It is often eaten in a hot *pizza bianca* as a classic "builder's breakfast."

Insalata frutti di mare (seafood salad)
Seafood salad consists of cooked gambas, shrimp, mussels, calamari, squid, and chopped olives.

Bottarga (dried tuna roe)
On the island of Sardinia, *bottarga* is served thinly sliced as a starter, seasoned with olive oil, lemon juice, salt, and pepper.

Ostriche (oysters)
Oysters are served on a plate with crushed ice. They are the perfect *antipasto* for a meal in which fish is the main course.

Mozzarella con olio d'oliva (Mozzarella with olive oil)
Genuine buffalo mozzarella has a pure taste, and served with a few drops of olive oil it is a true gastronomic experience.

Cozze in marinata (marinated mussels)
Mussels are cooked in a sauce made from wine, tomatoes, salt, pepper, finely chopped onion, garlic, bay, thyme, and parsley, and served in their shells.

Parmigiano Reggiano (Parmesan)
Cut into pieces, Parmesan accompanies salads such as *rughetta*, but also goes very well with carpaccio or *bresaola*. Served on its own, it is also rated very highly as a dessert.

Focaccia (flat bread with garlic, oil, and herbs)
Flat bread from Liguria must be warm and crusty for the flavor of the herbs, such as sage or rosemary, to develop.

Carciofini in marinata (pickled artichoke hearts)
Cooked artichoke hearts are flavored with pennyroyal, garlic, and a few drops of vinegar, and preserved in vinegar and oil.

Ricotta salata (salted ricotta)
This ricotta is often eaten as a starter on Sardinia. It tastes excellent when combined with the rare arbutus honey, *miele di corbezzolo*.

Frisella con pomodori e basilico (hard bread, softened in water, with tomatoes and basil)
This specialty is from Apulia, and is common throughout southern Italy today.

Fagioli bianchi in aceto sott'olio (white beans in vinegar and oil)
Fresh beans are browned with garlic and flavored with a sauce made from breadcrumbs, vinegar, ewe's milk cheese, and peppermint.

Taralli
Taralli, from Apulia, are dipped in a marinade of oil, vinegar, salt, and pepper.

Crostini di capperi (toasted slices of bread with capers)
These delicious *crostini* have a topping of capers, raisins, and pine nuts.

COFFEE

Good espresso always comes from a professional machine, because this is the only way that the high pressure and constant temperatures required can be generated.

It is possible that we owe coffee to Abyssinian or Arabian goats, which, to the great astonishment of the goatherds, became unusually lively as soon as they nibbled the leaves and berries of a shrub known as *kif* or *koffe*. It was suspected that the animals' energy was derived from this plant with its luminous red fruit. The shrub spread from the high plains of Ethiopia as far as Sudan and the Yemen, where experiments with the red capsules began. The Arabs finally developed a process to harness the stimulant effect in a form that was palatable. They released the seeds from the seed pods, roasted them – in the same way that nuts were treated – ground them in a mill, and finally poured boiling water on the powder. The very first cup of coffee was ready. Although the Koran forbade the consumption of alcohol, it made no mention of coffee, and so it was impossible to halt the victory march of this new, bitter, but highly stimulating drink through the Arabian world. In Mecca it was guaranteed to put even the most exhausted pilgrim back on his feet. Soon, coffee plants were flourishing in various regions of Arabia, the first cafés opened in Damascus and Constantinople, and craftsmen in Cairo and Syria produced dainty glasses and cups in which the drink, an acquired taste, was served. In Turkey the cafés were rapidly transformed into important centers of communication, where men discussed the questions of life, both great and small, over one or several cups of mocha, and could watch the belly-dancers when there was a pause in the conversation.

The name "mocha" is a reference to the Yemeni port of Moka. Large quantities of the yellowish-green seeds were shipped from here, not just to Muslim countries, but, beginning in the early 15th century, to Christian areas as well. Merchants in northern Italy were quick to recognize the commercial possibilities of the coffee bean, and unloaded huge consignments at Riva degli Schiavoni, in Venice, and in the port of Trieste. They were right to do so, for in no time at all the brown infusion had conquered Europe. In Venice there were some stores that had long dealt in imported goods, such as expensive wines from Cyprus and Candia; they immediately included the new product in their range, and thereafter began calling themselves *caffè*. Toward the end of the 17th century, the Venetian authorities were forced to limit the total number of cafés in Venice to 206, since ten such establishments had opened in quick succession in the Piazza San Marco under the Procuratie Vecchie, and 15 more under the Procuratie Nuove. However, Venice and Trieste were not the only ports in which coffee played a role. From 1632 onward, good profits were also made in Livorno and Genoa, thanks to the Neapolitan trade routes. Moral and religious justification for

Espresso is the favorite coffee of the Italians. It is drunk throughout the day, from breakfast time to the last *digestif* of the evening.

enjoying coffee in the West was provided by the papacy. At the end of the 16th century, the oriental drink, which at first was impossible to regard unreservedly as "politically correct," was declared a Christian refreshment without further ado by Pope Clement VIII, and Prospero Lambertini, who sat on the apostolic throne from 1740 to 1758 as Benedict XIV, even had a coffee house in the English style built in the garden of his residence on the Quirinale, so that he could recover there from the exertions imposed by his high office.

1 Caffè con panna

Caffè con panna signifies a diluted espresso with a topping of whipped, unsweetened cream, with cocoa powder sprinkled on top.

2 Caffè e latte (caffellatte)

Caffè e latte is milky coffee. It consists of equal parts of "long," in other words diluted, espresso and hot full-cream milk.

3 Caffè corretto

In *caffè corretto*, the stimulant effect of the caffeine is "corrected" by the addition of alcohol, which is either added to the coffee itself or drunk separately. Grappa is preferred in the north, whereas aniseed liqueurs are particularly popular drunk with coffee in central and southern Italy.

4 Caffè shakerato

Caffè shakerato is shaken with sugar and ice cubes and is a very popular drink throughout Italy in the summertime, but especially in the southern regions.

5 Caffè macchiato

Caffè macchiato literally means flecked coffee, since a small white fleck is the only trace left by the dash of milk that is often frothed, as for a cappuccino, and then added to the espresso.

6 Caffè lungo

To make *caffè lungo*, the hot water is left to run through the filter for a few seconds longer than in the case of normal espresso coffee. This is a minor self-deception, since although the coffee tastes thinner and more watery, it is not, as might have been hoped, any less strong. On the contrary, more bitter substances are extracted in the longer time that is taken for the water to run through the coffee grounds. *Caffè lungo* nevertheless remains very popular.

7 Cappuccino

Cappuccino was so named because its nut-brown color, resulting from the mixture of frothy milk with espresso, was considered to be reminiscent of the habits of Capuchin friars. It is drunk at breakfast time, to accompany a croissant, or something else from the selection of pastries on offer at the coffee bar.

Caffè ristretto (not illustrated)

Caffè ristretto is double strength, correspondingly strong, and rather sharp. The small cup is drained bravely by the drinker in a single draught.

Caffè doppio (not illustrated)

A double espresso, served in a large cup.

Espresso

In Italy, espresso is just called *caffè*. Starting at breakfast time, it is drunk throughout the day. People even drink it late in the evening, as a *digestif* after a sumptuous meal. A good espresso should be drunk really hot from a cup that has been warmed, usually with a lot of sugar. The delicate *crema*, the light brown foamy layer that floats on top of the dark, black liquid, is a sign that the espresso machine is working at the correct temperature and pressure and offers a good espresso.

GELATO AL CAFFÈ

Coffee ice
(Illustrated in the background)

Serves 6

8 3/4 OZ/250 G EGG YOLKS (ABOUT 10–12)
1 CUP/200 G SUGAR
1/2 CUP/125 ML ESPRESSO

Mix all the ingredients together well using a balloon whisk, then chill for 30 minutes. Pour into an ice cream maker and leave until the mixture is frozen. Alternatively, chill for 30 minutes, then place in the freezer for 2 hours, stirring thoroughly with a balloon whisk every 10–15 minutes or so.

THE ESPRESSO MACHINE

In around 1937, after some initial experiments, Achille Gaggia succeeded in producing a machine using piston technology that functioned in accordance with a combined pump and pressure principle. Thanks to this process, espresso coffee henceforth acquired its characteristic *crema*. Series production of this machine began after World War II.

The large espresso machines found in every Italian bar and restaurant from the Alps to the toe of Sicily basically operate on the same principle as the *moka per il caffè*, in which water is also forced through coffee grounds under high pressure. From a purely technical point of view, the process can be described as follows: water at a temperature of 194–203°F (90–95°C) is forced through a few grams of powder under pressure of 9 bars in 25 to 30 seconds, resulting in 25 milliliters (less than two tablespoons) of coffee. However, this utterly fails to describe the essence of espresso coffee. It should be deep black, and the foam, or *crema*, on its surface must be a delicate, shimmering light brown. It is then that the coffee is at its best, refreshing the mind,

cheering the spirit, and disposing the drinker both to dream and to reflect.

Italian coffee – and espresso in particular – is commonly held to be exceptionally strong. The opposite is the case, however. In reality, the beans for the Italian market are just more heavily roasted than the varieties destined for sale in northern European countries. In Italy, as in other countries, the coffee varieties are blended. Up to seven varieties are used in coffee bars, of which arabica is the finest. Although the special roasting process in Italy enhances the aromatic substances, the process simultaneously removes most of the caffeine from the beans. Italian *caffè*, provided it is drunk in moderation, is therefore perfectly suitable even for people suffering from circulatory disorders.

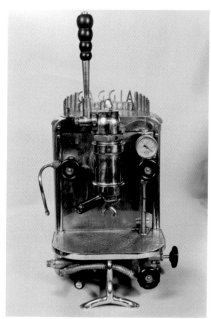

Right: Gaggia's historic levered machine was made in 1948. Achille Gaggia had attempted to develop a new type of coffee machine as long ago as 1937. Series production of his machine, which uses piston technology and employs a combined pump and pressure process, began after the end of World War II.

THE DOMESTIC ESPRESSO MACHINE

Espresso machines for domestic use work in accordance with the same principle as the large machines in restaurants and bars. They also produce coffee under pressure, and most of them also have a nozzle to make frothy milk for cappuccino. In domestic machines it is important – whether or not they are in constant use – that the nozzle for the milk is continually cleaned, otherwise milk residues might turn sour or even block the nozzle. In addition, care should be taken to ensure that the equipment does not become furred with limescale. If the mains water supply is very hard, it is advisable to use still mineral water to make coffee. The manufacturer's instructions should be followed to descale the espresso machine, should this become necessary at any time.

Although machines without a brand name are an attractive proposition due to their low prices, and though most of them function for a time, the consumer would be better advised to buy a branded product. Interestingly, and perhaps significantly, domestic espresso machines have never met with as much success south of the Alps as in the north. This may be connected with the dense concentration in the south of bars and cafés, in which espresso of outstanding quality is available.

PREPARING ESPRESSO

Coffee is prepared using three different methods in Italian households: on kitchen stoves the *napoletana* or *moka per il caffè* methods are used, while in rather more modern kitchens the task is performed by a small espresso machine of modest dimensions, designed for domestic use. In the numerous bars and cafés, by contrast, there is always a large, powerful machine made by a reputable firm such as Gaggia, for this is the only way in which to meet the enormous demand for this popular black drink.

The coffee grounds, preferably freshly milled, are loosely packed in the filter, without pressing down hard.

Milk can be made frothy with the aid of the steam nozzle if the espresso is to be turned into a cappuccino.

The metal filter is suspended in the espresso machine and screwed tightly into the thread.

The espresso machine (left) and its working parts

1 Steam nozzles, on the left, for heating and frothing milk; on the right, for heating water for tea
2 Pressure regulator
3 Knob for regulating the overflow valve (6)
4 Steam outlet to keep the cups on the machine warm
5 Filter holder
6 Overflow valve
7 Lever for regulating the flow of water
8 Manometer above measures water temperature; manometer below measures pressure for water pump
9 Twin spouts for two cups
10 Single spout for one cup
11 Water level indicator
12 Water inlet
13 Additional tap for connecting alternative water supply (for descaling)
14 Circulation of water for cleaning (e.g. for descaling)

A BRIEF LESSON ON COFFEE

The two varieties of coffee that are important on the global market are arabica and robusta. Arabica (mountain coffee, or *Coffea arabica*) is of higher quality and is now cultivated primarily in Brazil. Whereas arabica requires altitudes of between 1300 and 4250 feet (400 and 1300 meters) and requires particular soil conditions, the second most important variety, robusta (Congo coffee, *Coffea canephora*), though less temperamental, produces coffee of lesser quality. Robusta is cultivated in West Africa, Indonesia, and India. A coffee tree can grow to a height of 13 to 20 feet (4 to 6 meters), but on the coffee plantations it is grown only as a low bush so that the ripe coffee cherries can be harvested easily. To obtain the coffee beans, the cherries are dried and the flesh is peeled away mechanically. The beans are then fermented, washed, and dried. It is the wholesaler who assumes responsibility for roasting the beans. Lightly roasted coffee is pale, with hardly any bitterness. It is, however, more acidic, and also has a proper coffee flavor. At the same time, it is high in caffeine. Although the more heavily roasted beans are darker, they are less acidic and less flavorsome, and contain a smaller proportion of caffeine.

La Napoletana

The *caffetiera napoletana* consists of four parts: the kettle, the filter section, the holder for the coffee grounds inside the filter, and the can with its small spout that screws on top. The holder inside the filter is filled with loosely packed coffee grounds and the kettle is filled with water. As soon as the water begins to boil, the *napoletana* is removed from the stove and inverted. Assisted by gravity, the bubbling hot water then passes through the coffee grounds, dripping into the can as espresso coffee.

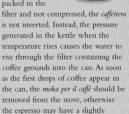

Moka per il caffè

The mocha machine works according to a rather different principle. Although the coffee grounds must be loosely packed in the filter and not compressed, the *caffetiera* is not inverted. Instead, the pressure generated in the kettle when the temperature rises causes the water to rise through the filter containing the coffee grounds into the can. As soon as the first drops of coffee appear in the can, the *moka per il caffè* should be removed from the stove, otherwise the espresso may have a slightly "scorched" flavor.

Left: It would be hard to imagine Roman cuisine without artichokes. Large-headed varieties can be stuffed, or they can be boiled and eaten one leaf at a time.

ARTICHOKES

Artichokes are popular all over Italy. The Romans, however, positively adore them. Nearly all the varieties from this region and from other parts of the country are found on the vegetable stalls in the market: the large, conical, thornless Romanesco artichoke, the Catanese variety, which is also thornless, the Violetto, which is grown in Tuscany and also in the Palermo region, the widely grown Spinosa sarda and the slightly less common Masedu from Sardinia, the Veneto from Chioggia, and finally the small Ligurian artichokes.

The ancient Romans called the artichoke *cynara*, because an old tale relates how a girl with this name was once turned into the highly prized plant. Later, as the tasty composite flower, a member of the thistle family, became more widely cultivated, the Italians began calling it *carciofo*, from the Arabic name *kharshuf*. During the Renaissance, therapeutic powers were attributed to artichokes, including purification of the blood. They were sold in herb and vegetable stores at correspondingly high prices, and only the very prosperous were able to afford them. Today we are no longer absolutely sure about their medicinal properties (although many are still convinced that the plant protects the liver), but artichokes are nevertheless now grown throughout Italy, and are within everybody's means.

All the famous chefs have adopted the artichoke and have used it to create delicious specialties. Back in the 16th century, Bartolomeo Scappi, the personal chef of Pope Pius V, recommended stuffing the plant with a mixture of lean veal, ham, cheese, eggs, spices, garlic, and herbs.

Those who are confronted for the first time with an artichoke that has been cooked and served whole might perhaps feel a little unsure, particularly on a formal occasion, of the proper etiquette surrounding the consumption of this sometimes prickly vegetable. Eating artichokes is, however, perfectly straightforward. Knife and fork can be dispensed with: the leaves are simply pulled off with the fingers. The tender end is then dipped in the accompanying sauce, and the flesh is scraped from the leaf with the teeth. What remains of the leaves is then deposited either on one's own plate, or on a plate specially provided for the purpose. When all the leaves have been plucked off, the hairy "choke" can be seen. It is inedible (except in very small and tender varieties) and is carefully removed using a fork. Now the real delicacy is visible – the artichoke heart. Sprinkled with a little vinaigrette, and eaten with a knife and fork, it is a simple, but immensely subtle, delicacy.

ANGELO VALIANI AND HIS SON CARCIOFINO

With nostalgia, Rome occasionally commemorates Angelo Valiani, a character who made his name at the end of the 19th century as a master of the cold buffet, first at the station of his native town Orbetello, later in Grosseto, and finally also in Rome. His specialty was *Carciofini sott'olio* – small, juicy, and very tender artichoke heads in oil, which had a mild, slightly bitter flavor and positively melted in the mouth. Valiani possessed several artichoke fields and personally supervised the planting, harvesting, and processing. He sold the large heads, plucked the outer leaves from the small ones, removed the "choke," boiled them in a stock of water, vinegar, baking soda, and salt, then dried them and layered them carefully with peppercorns and bay leaves in glass jars, covering them with the best extra virgin olive oil as a final crowning touch. Day after day the Romans crowded into his station buffet, for everyone wanted to eat these delicious artichokes. Valiani's specialty brought him fame and honor, and made him prosperous. When his son was born, Valiani decided to call him – for obvious reasons – Carciofino. However, when the baby was to be baptized in the cathedral at Orbetello, the priest refused, for he did not consider it proper that a child should go through life with the name of a plant. The master chef, however, had his answer ready, and replied laconically, "Father, if our Pope, Leo XIII, bears the name of a wild beast, then surely my child can be named after a plant." The priest could not argue with this, and finally acceded to his unusual request.

The purple **Violetto di Toscana** is medium-sized and very tender.

Romanesco artichokes have large, round heads, and are thornless.

The **Catanese** variety is elongated in shape and thornless.

PUNTARELLE AND OTHER VEGETABLES

The Roman vegetable dish par excellence – if for no other reason than that it is only found in Rome – is *puntarelle*, the shoots of a particular kind of chicory, called *catalogna*. Preparing *puntarelle* is extremely time-consuming, and it is only in Rome that they can be bought ready-prepared at greengrocery stores. The shoots are cut into narrow, longish strips and soaked in ice-cold water so that they roll up into rings. *Puntarelle* are made into a salad using a recipe that dates back to ancient Roman times. A pesto sauce is made in a pestle and mortar with one or more garlic cloves, washed anchovy fillets, a little vinegar, plenty of olive oil, and some salt and pepper. If speed is of the essence, slight changes can be made to the traditional method of preparation. The sauce can be made in no time at all using anchovy paste, crushed garlic, vinegar, and a good olive oil from Sabina. The results are equally delicious. In addition to *puntarelle*, chicory is eaten in Rome prepared in many other ways. Firstly, there is *cicorietta di campo selvatica*, the wild field chicory, which is often found on Roman market stalls and has a slightly bitter taste. It is boiled for a few minutes, drained, and then tossed in a pan with olive oil, garlic, and chili pepper. Common chicory is found all year round; it is prepared in just the same way as field chicory. *Cicorione*, on the other hand, the autumn dandelion, with its large, bright green leaves, is eaten raw in spring as a salad vegetable, while in winter it is steamed and prepared with oil and lemon.

A few chicory leaves are also included in *misticanza*, the famous Roman salad. *Misticanza* can be traced back to the Capuchin friars, who at one time used to show their appreciation by presenting their benefactors with a bunch of colorful herbs from the monastery garden. Ready mixed *misticanza* can still be bought today in the markets of Rome, consisting of eleven different herbs and salad vegetables, ranging from pimpernel, lamb's lettuce, rocket, and chervil to borage and sorrel. The salad should be prepared according to an old Roman saying: *Pe' condì bene l'insalata ce vonno quattro persone: un sapiente pe mettece er sale, un avaro l'aceto, uno sprecone l'ojo e un matto che la mischi e la smucini*, which means: four people are needed to make a good salad – a wise man to add the salt, a miser for the vinegar, a spendthrift for the oil, and a madman to mix it all together.

There are more Roman vegetable specialties than these, however. The Eternal City offers a special variety of broccoli, called broccolo romanesco, which looks more like a green cauliflower, but which is pointed at the top end, rather like a pine tree. This broccoli is cooked in a frying pan – without first being boiled – with plenty of garlic and chili pepper, and is also the main ingredient in *minestra*, a dish most commonly found in Rome, which is made with broccoli, pasta, and both lean and fat ham. Roman zucchini with their strong, slightly bitter, flavor are among the best flavored zucchini varieties. They are easily recognized by their pale coloring and their "edges" – in cross-section they are hexagonal rather than round. The best zucchini recipes, and indeed the best Roman vegetable recipes altogether, are derived from Jewish cookery – a Jewish minority has lived in Rome since the time of the emperor Nero. Deep-fried zucchini flowers stuffed with mozzarella and anchovies, as well as zucchini cut lengthwise and stuffed with ground meat, for instance, are rooted in the Jewish tradition.

PUNTARELLE IN SALSA DI ALICI
Chicory with anchovies

1 3/4 LBS/800 G CHICORY
1 CLOVE OF GARLIC
8 ANCHOVY FILLETS IN OIL
1–2 TBSP WINE VINEGAR
4–5 TBSP EXTRA VIRGIN OLIVE OIL
SALT AND PEPPER

Clean the chicory. Cut the leaves into two, three, or four strips, depending on size. Wash the strips and soak in cold water for about 30 minutes, so that they curl up. Drain them well.

Crush the garlic and the anchovies with vinegar and olive oil in a pestle and mortar or a blender to make a thick sauce. Season to taste with salt and pepper.

Place the chicory in a dish, pour over the sauce, and allow to stand in a cool place for about 1 hour to absorb the flavors. Sprinkle with freshly milled pepper before serving.

CARCIOFI ALLA ROMANA
Artichokes Roman-style
(Illustrated in the background)

8 ARTICHOKES
1 LEMON
FRESH MINT, CHOPPED
1 CLOVE OF GARLIC, CHOPPED
1 CUP/50 G BREADCRUMBS
SALT AND FRESHLY MILLED PEPPER
4–5 TBSP EXTRA VIRGIN OLIVE OIL

Remove the outer, woody leaves from the artichokes. Cut off the top leaves that have no flesh on them, trim the inner leaves with a sharp knife, and cut the bottoms level. Trim the stem to a length of 1½–2 inches (4–5 centimeters) and rub the cut surfaces immediately with lemon to prevent discoloration.

Mix the mint, garlic, breadcrumbs, salt, pepper, and a little oil. Spread out the artichoke leaves with the fingers and fill the cavity with the mixture. Rearrange the leaves so no stuffing escapes. Arrange the artichokes with the heads facing upwards in an ovenproof dish. Pour over a ladle of water, cover the dish with greased baking parchment, and cover with a lid. Bake in a preheated oven at 350 °F (180 °C) for about 1 hour. Serve hot as a side dish, or cold as a starter.

A PASSION FOR PASTA

In Rome there is a passion for pasta that seems to break all records. Even such icons of the Italian film industry as Gina Lollobrigida and Sophia Loren have always publicly acknowledged their love of pasta, and have provided the most compelling evidence that noodles do not make one at all fat or ugly. Sophia Loren's husband, film producer Carlo Ponti, is said to have told his wife quite categorically to eat as much pasta as often as she wished, since the occasional periods of abstinence from pasta that the *grande dame* of Italian cinema had imposed on herself resulted only in bad temper and domestic strife.

Rome – at least according to the Romans – is the birthplace of world-famous creations such as *spaghetti alla carbonara* (spaghetti, with bacon, egg, and Parmesan), *bavette alla carrettiera* (bavette with pork, tuna, and mushrooms), *spaghetti all'amatriciana* (spaghetti with bacon, tomatoes, and chili pepper), and *spaghetti alla puttanesca* (spaghetti with anchovies and olives). Rome is a city full of contrasts, in which rich and poor sometimes live no more than a stone's throw away from one another. Although all Romans are united by their love of pasta, for the less well-to-do it provides a cheap, satisfying, healthy, and tasty meal.

MEALS FOR FAST DAYS

Much as the Romans enjoy the high life, and despite the fact that they can never have enough of their specialties, many citizens still observe the culinary rules laid down by the Church when a period of fasting begins. Many meat-free dishes have been invented in Roman cuisine for fasts, for ultimately even periods of fasting should not be completely devoid of pleasure. Most of these *piatti da magro*, or "lean" vegetarian dishes (for the Catholic Church forbids consumption of meat and meat products at such times) were therefore usually served as fast day meals or as traditional fare for Good Friday.

On Good Friday, when, as is well known, the most stringent fasting rules apply, Romans first visit their family graves and then attend mass. As soon as darkness begins to fall, housewives hurry into their kitchens and begin making preparations for the classic Good Friday evening meal: there is a choice of the famous *zuppa del Venerdì santo* (Good Friday soup), the sumptuous *luccio brodettato* (pike cooked in stock), nourishing *zuppa di aragosta* (lobster soup), or *pasta e broccoli in brodo di arzilla* (pasta and broccoli in ray stock).

PASTA E BROCCOLI IN BRODO DI ARZILLA
Pasta and broccoli in ray stock

2 CLOVES OF GARLIC
1 SMALL ONION
1 BUNCH OF PARSLEY, COARSELY CHOPPED
SALT
2 LBS/1 KG FRESH RAY, READY TO COOK
1 SALTED ANCHOVY
2 TBSP/30 ML OLIVE OIL
SCANT 1/3 CUP/75 ML DRY WHITE WINE
1 SMALL PIECE HOT CHILI PEPPER
1/2 LB/200 G TOMATO FLESH
GENEROUS 1/2 LB/300 G BROCCOLI FLORETS
7 OZ/200 G SPAGHETTI

Place 6 cups (1.5 liters) water with 1 clove of garlic, the onion, half of the chopped parsley, and a little salt in a pan large enough to hold the ray, and boil for about 10 minutes.

Clean the ray, add to the pan, and boil for a further 20 minutes. Remove the fish from the water, bone the fish, and set aside the fillets. Add the rest of the fish to the stock and boil for another 20 minutes. Strain the stock through a sieve into a pan.

Wash the salt off the anchovy and remove the bones. Fry in olive oil in a casserole with 1 clove of garlic and the remaining parsley. Pour in the wine and allow to evaporate. Then add the chili pepper, the tomato, and a little salt, and simmer for 20 minutes.

Wash the broccoli florets, add to the casserole, and pour in the stock. Simmer for 5 minutes.

Break the spaghetti in pieces and cook in the stock *al dente* – until it is just tender.

Finally, cut the fish fillets into pieces, add to the stock, and serve the stew very hot.

SPAGHETTI ALLA CARBONARA
Spaghetti with bacon, egg, and Parmesan
(Illustrated in the background)

2 TBSP/30 G BUTTER
1/4 LB/100 G BACON
1 CLOVE OF GARLIC
14 OZ/400 G SPAGHETTI
SALT AND PEPPER
2 EGGS, BEATEN
SCANT 1/2 CUP/40 G PECORINO, GRATED
SCANT 1/2 CUP/40 G PARMESAN, GRATED

Heat the butter in a heavy pan, add the diced bacon and the garlic, and fry until they turn brown. Remove the garlic.

Cook the spaghetti *al dente* in plenty of salted water, pour off the water and drain well. Add the spaghetti to the fried bacon in the pan and mix thoroughly.

Remove from the stove and stir in a little pepper, the beaten eggs, and half of the grated cheese, until the eggs begin to set. Mix in the remaining cheese and serve immediately.

Spaghetti all'amatriciana
Spaghetti with bacon, tomatoes, and chili pepper
(Illustrated in the background)

1 TBSP OLIVE OIL
1/4 LB/100 G LEAN BACON
3/4 LB/350 G TOMATOES, SKINNED AND DICED
1 CHILI PEPPER
14 OZ/400 G SPAGHETTI
SALT
1/2 CUP/50 G PECORINO OR PARMESAN, GRATED

Heat the olive oil in a pan and fry the diced bacon
well for 5 minutes. Add the skinned, diced tomatoes
and the chili pepper, and sauté for a further 10
minutes, stirring occasionally with a wooden spoon.
Cook the spaghetti *al dente* in plenty of salted water,
pour away the water and drain well.
Remove the chili pepper from the sauce. Place the
spaghetti in a warmed dish, pour the sauce over the
top, and sprinkle with cheese.

Gnocchi di semolino alla romana
Semolina dumplings, Roman-style

4 CUPS/1 LITER MILK
SCANT 1 1/2 CUPS/200 G HARD WHEAT SEMOLINA
2 EGG YOLKS
6 1/2 TBSP/100 G BUTTER
SCANT CUP/80 G PARMESAN, GRATED

Bring the milk to the boil in a pan and gradually sprinkle in
the semolina, stirring constantly with a wooden spoon.
Cook the semolina for 15–20 minutes, then remove from
the stove. Beat the egg yolks in a basin with a few spoonfuls
of milk. Before the semolina cools, stir in half of the butter
and the beaten egg yolk, stirring constantly to prevent the
eggs curdling in the hot semolina. Pour the semolina on to
a wet plate and spread out to form a layer just under 1/2 inch
(1 centimeter) thick. Leave for several hours until
completely cold.
Turn the semolina on to a work surface and cut out small
circles using a thin-rimmed glass. Arrange the dumplings
alongside one another in a soufflé dish greased with butter.
Sprinkle with melted butter and bake in a preheated oven at
350 °F (180 °C) for 20–25 minutes, until golden brown.
Sprinkle with grated Parmesan and serve.

Bavette alla carrettiera
Bavette with pork, tuna, and mushrooms

2 OZ/50 G PORK CHEEK OR BACON
2 OZ/50 G TUNA FISH IN OIL
1/2 LB/200 G FRESH BOLETUS EDULIS MUSHROOMS
4 TBSP OLIVE OIL
1 CLOVE OF GARLIC, CHOPPED
SALT AND FRESHLY MILLED PEPPER
A LITTLE MEAT STOCK
14 OZ/400 G BAVETTE
1/2 CUP/50 G PARMESAN, GRATED

Cut the pork cheek or bacon into thin strips. Flake the tuna
fish. Clean the mushrooms thoroughly and cut into thin
slices. Fry the garlic and strips of pork cheek with the olive
oil in a pan until the pieces of meat become transparent.
Add the mushrooms, season with salt and pepper, and sauté
over a low heat for about 10 minutes. Pour in a few
spoonfuls of meat stock and stir in the pieces of tuna fish.
Cook the pasta *al dente* in plenty of salted water, pour off
the water, drain well, and mix with the sauce in a serving
dish. Sprinkle with grated parmesan.

Spaghetti alla puttanesca
Spaghetti with anchovies and olives
(Illustrated right)

4 SALTED ANCHOVY FILLETS
2 CLOVES OF GARLIC
3–4 TBSP EXTRA VIRGIN OLIVE OIL
2 TBSP/30 G BUTTER
1 CUP/150 G PITTED BLACK OLIVES
1 TBSP SALTED CAPERS
5 RIPE TOMATOES
SALT
14 OZ/400 G SPAGHETTI
1 TBSP CHOPPED PARSLEY

Wash the salt off the anchovies, cut the fillets into small
pieces, and fry gently with the garlic in the olive oil and
butter over a low heat. Skin and dice the tomatoes and add
to the anchovies with the olives and capers. Season with salt
and simmer for approximately 20 minutes over a low heat.
Cook the spaghetti *al dente* in plenty of salted water, pour
off the water, drain and place in a warmed dish. Pour over
the hot sauce, mix thoroughly, and sprinkle with parsley.
Serve hot.

PAPAL CUISINE

In general, the supreme authorities in the Catholic Church have not been conspicuously hostile to sensual pleasure, or even ascetic in their culinary habits. Whereas, at the beginning of the 13th century, Pope Innocent III was still advocating spartan living, and insisting that only one main dish was served at his table, toward the end of that century Martin IV was showing a marked predilection for eel, particularly when it came from Bolsena. The pontiff is said to have procured live eels and stored them in special containers, so that he could eat them soaked in Vernaccia and broiled. About a hundred years later, Pietro Tomacelli was elected pope. Although his official name was Boniface IX, it was rumored that *tomaselle*, the liver dumplings enjoyed by His Holiness throughout his life, were named after him. Eugenius IV reintroduced a more economical culinary era, and even assembled independent observers around his meager table in order to demonstrate his moderation. As the 15th century drew to a close, Alexander VI had his daughter Lucrezia Borgia to cook for him, for nobody knew better than she which sweet delicacies her father loved best. In the years from 1513 to 1521, when Leo X was in office, dining in the Vatican accurately reflected Florentine cuisine. The festivities and exquisite banquets of the Medici popes were soon the talk of the entire city.

Any Roman who had aspirations began to take an interest in elevated gourmet cuisine. At papal banquets it now became the custom, not just to eat and drink a great deal, but to feast on noble, refined luxuries and to enjoy the tightrope walkers, musicians, and other artists who provided the program of entertainment. Neither was Leo X averse to a little joke from time to time. It is reported that once he arranged for a hemp rope to be served as eel, which a few unfortunate guests actually consumed, to the great delight of their table companions.

In the mid-16th century, Julius III reigned in the Vatican. He loved stuffed roast peacock and onions from Gaeta. After his successor, Marcellus II, had been on the apostolic throne for a short time, Paul IV became pontiff. It is known that he would sit at the table for up to three hours without interruption, and usually partook of up to 20 courses. Pius V, who was later canonized, engaged the most expensive chef of his times. This culinary genius was none other than Bartolomeo Scappi, author of *Opera dell'arte del cucinare*

THE CONCLAVE

The high life at the Vatican was punctuated by the repeated need to hold conclaves for the purpose of electing a new Holy Father. The procedure followed in the conclave was always subject to strict regulations. The members of the conclave were not allowed any contact with the outside world, and, in order to prevent secret information being passed to them, specially appointed inspectors had to examine all the food before the servants were allowed to place it before their ecclesiastical masters. Baked dishes that were browned on top, inside which a note might have been concealed, were forbidden, as was the use of silver cutlery on which messages might have been etched.

In the event of the election taking more than eight days, the dignitaries were to be served a meager diet consisting

Frontispiece from the *Opera dell'arte del cucinare* by Bartolomeo Scappi, printed in Venice in 1610. During a conclave, servants in procession are carrying baskets of cold appetizing morsels from the larder, hot dishes from the kitchen, and noble beverages from the cellar. Each basket bears the insignia of a cardinal.

of only bread and water – at least this is what is written in the canonical code – probably with the hidden motive of accelerating the procedure. In around 1700, officials nevertheless formed the opinion that such a regulation was unworthy, and subsequently installed an extremely well-appointed kitchen in the apostolic chambers, in which cooks, masters of ceremonies, cup bearers, and cellarers went about their business with alacrity.

and reformer of Western cuisine. In his standard culinary work of 1570, Scappi also recorded some favorite papal dishes, including fish from Lake Garda or Liguria, and caviar from Alexandria in Egypt. In the 19th century, too, high living was the order of the day in Rome. Gregory XVI was without doubt an accomplished gourmet, and we even know the favorite sequence of dishes of Pius IX: risotto, various items from the bakery, roast meat with vegetables and fruit, all accompanied by Bordeaux wines. The meal was always rounded off with a tart or pie and coffee. This, however, marked the end of the great era of kitchens

in the apostolic chambers. The plain meals of modern popes are prepared outside the hallowed walls of the Vatican. It is said that some degree of consideration is given only to certain regional preferences – depending on the geographical origins of the head of the Church.

Pope Martin IV
(pontificate: 1281–1285)

Pope Boniface IX
(pontificate: 1389–1404)

Pope Alexander VI
(pontificate: 1492–1503)

Pope Leo X (pontificate: 1513–1521)

Pope Julius III (pontificate: 1550–1555)

Pope Pius V (pontificate: 1566–1572)

BARTOLOMEO SCAPPI

Alongside Maestro Martino and the humanist Platina, Bartolomeo Scappi ranks as one of the most important innovators in Italian cuisine. Born in Veneto around 1500, by his mid-thirties he was in the service of Cardinal Campeggio, for whom he had to organize the festive banquet for the emperor Charles V. In 1549 – by which time Scappi was working for Cardinal Carpi – the conclave gathered to elect a new Holy Father following the death of Paul III. Scappi's catering for the committee of electors was so outstanding that it took over two months to reach the announcement *habemus Papam*. The new pope, Julius III, appointed Scappi as his *cuoco secreto*, his personal chef, a position held by this eminent cook throughout the reign of the next six heads of the Church.

In accordance with the spirit of the Renaissance, Scappi strove above all for harmony and balance in his creations. Expensive spices, which would disguise rather than emphasize the character of the food, receded into the background. Attention was directed toward conservative, "high-precision" cooking techniques, which admittedly presented a much greater challenge for the chef. In 1570 the book *Opera di Bartolomeo Scappi, maestro dell'arte del cucinare, cuoco secreto di Papa Pio Quinto divisa in sei libri* appeared in Venice. This work, published in six volumes with the blessing of the pope, became a culinary standard for both courtly and prosperous bourgeois cuisine. In it, Scappi not only divulges technical tips and tricks, but also lists numerous recipes for braised, roasted, poached, deep-fried, sour, robust, piquant, and sweet fare, many of which can be found in our modern cookery books today.

ANATRA ALLA SCAPPI
Duck à la Bartolomeo Scappi
(Illustrated below)

2 OVEN-READY WILD DUCKS WITH GIBLETS,
EXCEPT FOR THE LIVER
1/2 LB/250 G COOKED HAM, CUT INTO SMALL PIECES
1 BOTTLE RED WINE
SCANT 1/2 CUP/100 ML RED WINE VINEGAR
2 1/2 TBSP/30 G SUGAR
SCANT 1/2 LB/150 G PITTED PLUMS
1/2 TSP FRESHLY MILLED WHITE PEPPER
4 CLOVES, GROUND
A LITTLE GROUND CINNAMON
GROUND NUTMEG
GROUND GINGER
GENEROUS CUP/120 G RAISINS, SOAKED IN LUKEWARM WATER
SALT

Clean the ducks and place in a casserole with all the ingredients except the salt. Cover with a lid and bring to a boil on top of the stove. Then transfer the casserole to a preheated oven and cook at 300 °F (150 °C) for about 1 hour. Depending on the size and age of the ducks, the cooking time can be extended. Then arrange the ducks on a plate with the plums and set aside in a warm place. Reduce the sauce on top of the stove and season with salt. Serve the sauce separately from the meat.

JEWISH CUISINE IN ROME

Before the birth of Christ a Jewish community was in existence in Rome, which even had a synagogue in Ostia. From the 10th century onward, the preferred place of residence of Jewish merchants and craftsmen was near the Ponte Fabricio, which was later renamed the Pons Judeorum. The quarter expanded rapidly during the Middle Ages, finally extending as far as the Regola and Sant'Angelo districts. In the mid-16th century, however, Pope Paul IV put an end to the flourishing Jewish way of life by creating a ghetto near the Teatro di Marcello. Roman Jews were forbidden by decree to move freely outside this area, and in addition the gates were locked at night. It was not until 1870 that the ghetto was dissolved.

Today, some hundred or so Jewish families live in the quarter, which has a somewhat dilapidated appearance. They cook, as they have always done, in accordance with the strict precepts of their faith: the flesh of animals that are not ruminants may not be eaten, nor may fish that have neither fins nor scales. Pigs, rabbits, hare, and marine mollusks are thus regarded as unclean. The animals that are permitted must be slaughtered using traditional methods, inflicting as little pain as possible, and must be bled completely dry before consumption.

Although Jewish cookery is simple, it always appears novel and interesting thanks to its oriental influences. The plain ingredients are frequently prepared with raisins, pine nuts, cinnamon, and cloves. Nowadays an increasing number of non-Jews are coming into the former ghetto to buy high-quality meats, stock up with delicious confectionery at the bakery, or to dine in one of the kosher restaurants.

PIZZA EBRAICA D'ERBE
Vegetable pizza

Serves 8

GENEROUS 3/4 LB/400 G SPINACH
3 ARTICHOKES
JUICE OF 1 LEMON
2 1/2 LBS/1.2 KG FRESH PEAS
1 ONION
1 BUNCH OF PARSLEY
3–4 TBSP EXTRA VIRGIN OLIVE OIL
2 EGGS
SALT AND PEPPER
1 LB/450 G SAVORY PLAIN CRUST PASTRY

Wash the spinach, drain well, and cut into strips. Remove the outer, hard leaves from the artichokes, and break off the stems. Cut the artichokes into thin slices and place in water containing lemon juice to prevent them discoloring. Shell the peas, and finely chop the onion and parsley. Heat the olive oil in a casserole and cook all the vegetables in it. Leave to cool, transfer to a dish, and mix with the eggs. Season to taste with salt and pepper.

Roll the pastry dough out to form two circles, one a little larger than the other. Use the larger circle to line the base and sides of a springform pan, fill with the vegetable mixture, and cover with the smaller pastry circle. Press the edges firmly together and prick the top several times with a fork.

Bake in a preheated oven at 350 °F (180 °C) for about 45 minutes.

THE CAMPO DE' FIORI

Tourists arriving in Rome who wish to see more than the doubtless interesting, but extremely crowded, St. Peter's Square or Sistine Chapel, should treat themselves to a rewarding walk through the most beautiful market in Rome, the market at the Campo de' fiori. However, the visitor will not understand much, even if his knowledge of Italian is good, for on many of the stalls the Roman dialect continues to be used for haggling, dealing, chatting with neighbors, and discussing the general political situation of the city and the country as a whole. This really is an unadulterated slice of Roman life, seen, as it were, in the flesh. The range of fresh fruit and vegetables on sale is also exceptionally good. Much of the produce is locally grown, which means it is not harvested until fully ripe. The best bargains are to be had toward the end of the day in the market, for it is then that the stallholders try to dispose of their remaining produce, sometimes at rock-bottom prices. It is not kept from one day to the next. On the next market day, a small farm truck will draw up again to deliver produce that has ripened to the peak of perfection. In addition to all the colorful varieties of fruit and vegetables, a huge range of herbs and spices is available, depending on the season. It is unlikely that any visitor will forget in a hurry the tremendously intense fragrance of these exotic wares.

Batavia is a variant of the iceberg lettuce that is common throughout northern Europe. It has wavy, curled leaves.

Lollo bianca, Lollo bionda or Lollo verde has very crinkly, wavy leaves with light green to yellow tips.

Lollo Rossa has the same shaped leaf as its paler relative, but has a nutty flavor and is sufficiently robust for a strong dressing.

Radicchio (red chicory, red endive) has a pleasantly bitter taste. There are many different varieties in Italy.

Lattuga (round lettuce, green salad) is grown in many different varieties all the year round throughout Italy.

Romana (romaine lettuce, summer endive, Romana) has fibrous, rather hard outer leaves, but its heart is tender.

Indivia belga (chicory, Belgian endive, blanched chicory) is forced in the dark so that the leaves stay pale in color.

Foglia di quercia (oakleaf lettuce) has reddish tips to the leaves, which resemble oak leaves, and a nutty flavor.

Dente di leone (dandelion) like *catalogna* or *puntarelle*, is a type of chicory, available in the spring.

Indivia (frisée chicory, curly endive) has curly leaves with pronounced indentations. It is aromatic and has a delicate flavor.

Scarola (escarole, smooth endive, winter endive) is equally suitable as a salad and as a cooked vegetable.

Rucola, Rughetta (arugula, rocket) has longish, often rather sharp and nutty-flavored leaves, which are used in salads.

Vegetables such as eggplants, tomatoes, zucchini, potatoes, leeks, onions, garlic, carrots, spinach, artichokes, and broccoli continue to play a significant role in Italian cookery, despite the influence of fast food, and are ultimately the reason why Italian food is so healthy and easily digested.

Alloro (bay) is added to fish and meat dishes, as well as to soups.

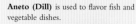

Aneto (Dill) is used to flavor fish and vegetable dishes.

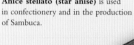

Anice (aniseed) is an ingredient in pastries, confectionery, and liqueurs.

Anice stellato (star anise) is used in confectionery and in the production of Sambuca.

Aromi (bouquet garni) can be used in almost all dishes.

Basilico genovese (Genovese basil) has small leaves and a delicate flavor. It is suitable for pesto.

As well as the Campo de' fiori market, which is a popular subject for the tourists' cameras, the Romans like to go to the large Mercato Trionfale and the Mercato Testaccio.

Camomilla (chamomile) is used to make herbal and medicinal teas.

Basilico napoletano (Neapolitan basil) has large leaves and an intense flavor. It is suitable for pizza and salads

Borragine (borage) is included in the Ligurian mixture of herbs known as *preboggion*.

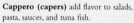

Cacao (cocoa powder) is used in desserts, cakes, and confectionery.

Cannella (cinnamon) can be used to flavor savory as well as sweet dishes.

Cappero (capers) add flavor to salads, pasta, sauces, and tuna fish.

Cardamomo (cardamom) adds spice to liqueurs, confectionery, and panforte.

Cerfoglio (chervil) is used in vegetable dishes, soups, and egg dishes.

Chiodi di garofano (cloves) go well with dark meat and pick

Coriandolo (coriander) is used to flavor sausage products (mortadella), as well as confectionery and liqueurs.

Cren, Rafano (horseradish) is found in northern Italian dishes, which are influenced by Austrian cuisine.

Crescione (cress) tastes particularly good in robust-flavored soups and salads.

Cumino (caraway) is used in northern Italian food such as bread and sauerkraut.

Estragone (tarragon) can be used in almost all dishes.

Erba cipollina (chives) goes well with egg dishes and soft varieties of cheese.

Maggiorana (marjoram) can be used in any savory dish.

Ginepro (juniper) is added in marinades for fish and game.

Noce moscata (nutmeg) is added to roast and braised dishes.

Pepe (pepper) is used for *panpepato*, pork dishes, and sauces.

Menta (mint) is used to flavor sweet dishes, but also roast meat and poultry.

Origano (Oregano) is used throughout Italian cuisine.

Salvia (sage) goes well with light meat, such as pork, and calf's liver.

Prezzemolo (parsley) is used for *salsa verde* and much else besides.

Rosmarino (rosemary) flavors marinades and broiled meat.

Peperoncino (chili pepper) is used to flavor anything that should be hot and spicy.

Vaniglia (vanilla) is an ingredient in *panna cotta* and is used in desserts and all types of confectionery.

Zenzero (ginger) is indispensable when preparing *panpepato* and panforte.

Timo (thyme) is added to most meat dishes and also to many liqueurs.

Zafferano (saffron) is used in *risotto alla milanese* and to color other dishes yellow.

LA DOLCE VITA

In earlier times, desserts, sweet pastries, and confectionery were an expensive luxury, and were therefore associated with special occasions. Fortunately, however, there were always enough feast days in the capital city of Christendom and its surrounding provinces to justify self-indulgence. In the early days of the confectioner's art, people contented themselves with crumbly cookies made with flour, honey, and dried fruits. Plain crust pastry, cakes baked with shortening, and sweet pretzels made their appearance around 1300. Furthermore, the fact that sugar was becoming increasingly widespread resulted in the invention of jellied and candied dried fruits, as well as fruit preserved in syrup. Alongside the new sweet fare, exotic spices from distant lands were also becoming popular. Pepper, cinnamon, and ginger were introduced to the bakeries, and *panpepato*, the pepper or spice cake specialty, became especially popular. Around 1500, the feast day tables of Rome were overrun by marzipan and crisp, flaky puff pastry, which was costly to prepare and could have either a sweet or savory filling. However, fruit, which was brought to the capital every day from provincial Lazio, indisputably played the principal role in the preparation of confectionery and sweet dishes. A century later, yeast dough, which the Romans used when baking such delicacies as *maritozzi*, sweet raisin buns with pine nuts, became established.

At first, confectionery was either made at home or bought in the tavern. As coffee and cocoa became increasingly fashionable, the newly opened cafés also started selling sweet pastries. Housewives were also able to turn with confidence to the nunneries, where the finest sweet specialties were traditionally made for Church festivals.

In Italy, bars are also cake shops – and the other way round. The Roman Caffè Faggiani in the Via G.B. Ferrari is well known for homemade cakes.

BUDINO DI RICOTTA
Ricotta pudding
(Illustrated below left)

3 TBSP SEMOLINA
14 OZ/400 G RICOTTA
4 TBSP CONFECTIONERS' SUGAR
4 EGGS
2 OZ/50 G CANDIED FRUITS, FINELY CHOPPED
1 TBSP RAISINS, SOAKED IN RUM
1 PINCH OF GROUND CINNAMON
GRATED RIND OF 1/2 LEMON
BUTTER AND FLOUR FOR THE PAN
VANILLA SUGAR

Bring 1 glass of water to a boil in a pan. Sprinkle in the semolina, stir well, and remove from the stove after a few minutes. Place the semolina on a wet plate, smooth with a knife, and leave to cool. Mix the ricotta with the confectioners' sugar, a whole egg, 3 egg yolks, the candied fruits, the raisins, cinnamon, and lemon rind. Beat one egg white until stiff and stir into the ricotta mixture with the semolina. Grease with butter a pudding dish with a capacity of 6 cups (1.5 liters) and pour in the batter. Bake in a preheated oven at 350 °F (180 °C) for approximately 1 hour. Turn out of the dish and sprinkle with vanilla sugar.

MARITOZZI
Raisin buns

4 CUPS/500 G ALL-PURPOSE FLOUR
1 CAKE YEAST (IF USING ACTIVE DRY YEAST, FOLLOW THE MAKER'S INSTRUCTIONS)
1 CUP/250 ML MILK
3 TBSP SUGAR
1/2 CUP/50 G RAISINS
3 TBSP/30 G PINE NUTS
2 OZ/50 G CANDIED FRUITS, FINELY CHOPPED
2 TBSP EXTRA VIRGIN OLIVE OIL
SALT
BUTTER TO GREASE THE PAN

Place the flour in a bowl and make a hollow in the center. Dissolve the yeast in the lukewarm milk and pour into the hollow, adding a pinch of sugar. Cover with a little flour from around the edge and leave the dough to rise in a warm, draft-free place for about 30 minutes.
Then mix the dough and knead it, either by hand or in a food processor, and roll into a ball. Place in a bowl, cover, set aside in a warm place, and leave until it has doubled in size and is puffy.
Knead the dough thoroughly and gradually incorporate all the remaining ingredients, together with 3 tablespoons sugar and a pinch of salt. Form into elongated rolls and place on a baking sheet greased with butter. Leave to rise for 1 hour in a warm, draft-free place. Then bake in a preheated oven at 400 °F (200 °C) until golden brown. Serve hot or cold with a glass of liqueur.

MASCARPONE AND RICOTTA

Mascarpone is a very creamy, soft new cheese with a delicate flavor. It is produced using the cream from cow's milk, and in some southern areas it is also made using the cream from buffalo milk. The cream is heated to a temperature of 170–200 °F (75–90 °C) and lemon juice or white wine vinegar is added to start the coagulation process. Mascarpone is intended to be consumed promptly, as it soon spoils. With a fat content of more than 50 percent, it is frequently used for making desserts. Mascarpone is also encountered outside Italy, as an ingredient in the bittersweet *Tiramisù. Torta di Gorgonzola*, on the other hand, is a savory dish made with mascarpone, in which Gorgonzola is cut horizontally into thin slices with layers of mascarpone in between.
Ricotta is often confused with curd cheese. However, curd cheese is produced at an entirely different stage of dairy processing. First, milk is heated and mixed with rennin in a tub, so that it coagulates and the casein is precipitated. The result of this procedure is a very new cheese – curd cheese. To make ricotta, the whey that has separated out is heated once again (*ri-cotta* means cooked again) and sometimes mixed with a coagulating agent, producing a frothy mixture on the surface, known as whey cheese. Ricotta can be made with the whey from either cow's or ewe's milk. Both mild and piquant-tasting varieties are available. Very new, mild ricotta must be used quite quickly, as a filling for ravioli and other types of pasta or as an ingredient in desserts. Stronger-flavored ricotta can be stored for longer, since the mixture is formed into loaves that are salted and left to mature for about two months. In central and southern Italy, matured ricotta is sprinkled over pasta and other savory dishes instead of parmesan.

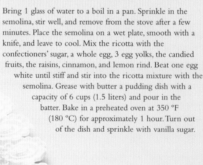

Pick me up

Tiramisù, which, literally translated, means "pick me up," enjoys cult status as a dessert throughout Italy, and many regions claim to have invented it. The natives of Piedmont point to the sponge fingers ("ladyfingers"), known as *savoiardi*, believing that these Savoy cookies are proof enough of the origins of the dish. The natives of Lombardia argue that mascarpone ultimately originates from their country, and therefore that the honor should go to Lombardia. Venetians and Tuscans are just as keen to take the credit for its invention. And the Romans, as genuine metropolitans, regard the dessert as typically Italian – and therefore Roman. Accordingly, a wide variety of recipes abounds for this cold, fresh cream cheese dessert. The major differences of opinion relate to the spirits to be used: all kinds are possible, from cognac, Marsala, Amaretto, whisky, and rum to coffee liqueur.

Tiramisù
(Illustrated bottom right)

3/4 CUP/200 ML HEAVY CREAM
5 TBSP SUGAR
4 EGG YOLKS
1 LB/500 G MASCARPONE
ABOUT 24 LADYFINGERS
4 TBSP STRONG ESPRESSO COFFEE
4 TBSP AMARETTO
COCOA POWDER

Beat the cream with 1 tablespoon sugar until stiff. Whisk the egg yolks with the remaining sugar until creamy, using a hand-held whisk on maximum speed. Stir in the mascarpone one spoonful at a time, and then, at a slower speed, stir in the cream.
Line a flat dish with ladyfingers. Mix the espresso and Amaretto and sprinkle over the ladyfingers, but do not soak. Spread a layer of cream on top and cover this with a layer of ladyfingers, sprinkle with the espresso and Amaretto mixture, and spread the remaining cream on top. Sprinkle with cocoa powder and chill for at least 1 hour in the refrigerator.

Gelato di ricotta alla romana
Ricotta ice cream

1 LB/500 G VERY FRESH RICOTTA
1/2 CUP/125 ML COLD, VERY STRONG ESPRESSO COFFEE
1/2 CUP/100 G SUGAR
4 EGG YOLKS
3 TBSP HEAVY CREAM
1 TSP VANILLA SUGAR (OR ESSENCE)
4 TBSP WHITE RUM
3 TBSP CHOPPED UNSALTED PISTACHIO NUTS

Pass the ricotta through a fine sieve and then mix with the espresso. Mix the sugar and egg yolks together until the mixture is pale and creamy. Beat the cream with the vanilla sugar until it is stiff, then add the rum. Mix the ricotta and espresso with the egg yolk mixture and carefully fold in the cream.
Line a rectangular dish with a capacity of about 4 cups (1 liter) with plastic wrap. Pour the cream into the dish, cover with plastic wrap, and freeze for about 3 hours in the deep freeze. Cut the ricotta ice cream into slices and garnish with the chopped pistachio nuts.

How to make tiramisù

The success of a good Tiramisù depends on the quality of the ingredients. Beat the cream with one tablespoon sugar.

Mix the egg yolks with sugar until they are creamy, then stir in the mascarpone and the cream, one spoonful at a time.

Line a rectangular dish with sponge fingers and sprinkle these with the Amaretto mixture.

Fill the dish with alternate layers of sponge fingers and mascarpone cream, finishing with a mascarpone layer.

THE LEGACY OF FALERNO

In ancient times, Lazio served not only as a larder for Rome, but also as its cellar. It was here that a grape variety called Aminea was used to produce the ultimate Roman house wine *par excellence*, Falerno. Apparently the Volsci people, the original inhabitants of the region in pre-Roman times, had pressed this wine and named it after the town of Falernum, situated in the center of the area where the vines were cultivated. According to Horace, Virgil, Propertius, and Martial, both red and white Falerno wine was available. Pliny the Elder nominated it as the best growth of his time, and recorded that it could be made sweet and light, but strong as well.

The modern DOC wine, Falerno del Massico, bears little resemblance to its historic forerunner. The grape variety disappeared from the range grown in Italy centuries ago, and, furthermore, the wine is no longer pressed in Lazio, but in neighboring Campagna. The full-bodied red Falerno in particular, which is made from Aglianico and Piedirosso grapes, can develop into a powerful wine that is full of character, but it is scarcely known beyond the borders of the region, and Romans nowadays do not drink it at all.

Modern Lazio, with its almost 118,560 acres (48,000 hectares) of vineyards, where at least 30 percent of the wine produced is DOC wine, is one of the most important winegrowing regions in Italy. Its reputation is mainly due to its white wines, the overwhelming majority of which are pressed using different varieties of the Malvasia and Trebbiano grape. At least as popular as Orvieto, the vineyards of which actually extend a little way into Lazio, and the northern Italian Soave, is Frascati, a white wine produced on the slopes south of Rome that stretch up to the Alban mountains, which should be drunk chilled when it is young. For centuries it was extremely popular with the Roman clergy, but in those days, unlike today, it was drunk mostly as a medium dry or even sweet wine – a fructose-laden variety known here as Cannellino.

DOC wines with characteristics similar to those of Frascati include Colli Albani, Colli Lanuvini, Marino, and Zagarola, as well as the white wines of Castelli Romani, Cerveteri, Cori and Velletri, of which there are also red versions. In the various vineyards of Lazio it is possible to find vintners experimenting here and there with imported grape varieties, including Chardonnay, Sauvignon blanc, Cabernet, Merlot, and, most recently, even Shiraz – and some of the wines pressed from these can be quite complex and suitable for aging. A few of these varieties of French origin had already been introduced at the beginning of the 20th century by Venetian settlers in the marshland of Lazio, which had at that time just been drained for the first time, making it suitable for winegrowing.

Unfortunately, the indigenous red variety, Cesanese, is seldom impressive, and could have even more of a struggle in future. Good vintners are already reducing the proportion of Cesanese grapes in their wines wherever the regulations for DOC wines permit this – usually in favor of the Sangiovese, which is also used in many red wines here, but also in favor of the imported grape varieties mentioned.

The winegrowing estates of Lazio cover about 150,000 acres (60,000 hectares) of vineyards in total, and account for the production of about 13,600,000 US gallons (515,000 hectoliters) of DOC wine.

Montefiascone lies in the province of Viterbo, near the Lago di Bolsena. Est! Est!! Est!!! di Montefiascone is produced here.

Autumn in the Montefiascone vineyards. The winegrowing regions of Lazio are among the most traditional in the whole of Italy. Wine has been pressed here since ancient times.

Halt! Good wine here!

Est! Est!! Est!!! di Montefiascone, one of Lazio's many wines, which is made mainly from Malvasia and Trebbiano grapes, comes from the province of Viterbo, and owes its unusual name to an anonymous German bishop. Legend has it that this bishop's prelate, while on his way to Rome, was under orders to look out for good wines. Whenever he found any, he was supposed to write the word "Est!" on the door of the cellar or bar in question. This would mark out the best places to drink for the benefit of dignitaries who made the journey later.

In Montefiascone the German taster was so enchanted with the local wines that he did not write the arranged code word on the wooden doors just once, but, in order to emphasize the outstanding quality of the wine, chose instead to repeat it twice. The legend goes on to say that the prelate liked Est! Est!! Est!!! di Montefiascone so much that he was indulging in this wine when he eventually breathed his last.

Today, Est! Est!! Est!!! di Montefiascone is a wine of a clear, pale appearance, which can taste dry and well-balanced. Unfortunately, its great success with later travelers to Rome of all nations has not been very beneficial, at least as far as quality is concerned. And so, for various reasons, one is obliged to conclude that neighboring Orvieto, the vineyards of which extend along the shores of the Lago di Bolsena into Lazio, is often the better choice.

Frascati

The most popular wine from the Eternal City originates from the slopes of the Colli Albani, situated to the south of Rome. For a long time the white wines produced here were the favorite wines of Romans and tourists visiting the Vatican, and were often drunk as medium dry rather than dry wines. Only with the advent of modern methods in the cellars has Frascati become a fruity, soft, harmonious white wine, which is a good accompaniment to fish.

Marino

Marino is one of the vine-growing areas that extends partly into Rome. The white wine is pressed mainly from the grape variety Malvasia bianca di Candia. There are just a small handful of very good producers, who sometimes mature their wine in large wooden barrels.

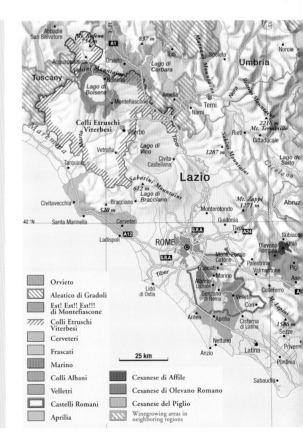

Orvieto
Aleatico di Gradoli
Est! Est!! Est!!! di Montefiascone
Colli Etruschi Viterbesi
Cerveteri
Frascati
Marino
Colli Albani
Velletri
Castelli Romani
Aprilia
Cesanese di Affile
Cesanese di Olevano Romano
Cesanese del Piglio
Winegrowing areas in neighboring regions

25 km

ABRUZZO
MOLISE

ABRUZZO · MOLISE

Sheep and goats

Chitarra, ceppa, and
rontrocilo

Saffron

Meat and milk products

Candy, sugarcoated
candy, and
confectionery

Brightly colored works
of art

Linking north and
south

A ttractive to look at, stimulating to the senses, and decidedly fiery on the tongue – that's the red chili pepper or *peperoncino*, known affectionately by the people of Abruzzi and Molise as *diavolino*, little devil. Caution is advised when tasting the specialties of this region, because the cuisine here is hearty, cheering, and often devilishly spicy. With the exception of their desserts, everything seems to be flavored with chili powder. According to the hardened inhabitants of this harsh mountain region, you need fire to survive the frosty winter days. And by fire they mean three different sources of heat: the spicy preparations on their plates, the open fireplaces in their cozy kitchens, and the centerba: a strong, spicy herbal liqueur made from around a hundred herbs.

Livestock production and arable farming are the typical occupations of this region. Culinary traditions are thus also firmly rooted in the soil. Pasta, vegetables, and meat are the staples of Abruzzi cuisine. For many centuries, the ability of the chefs in this region to conjure up the tastiest dishes from these few ingredients has been unsurpassed. The Val di Sangro, a mountain valley in the Chieti province, has produced whole dynasties of chefs, and many large restaurants, hotels, and cruise lines continue to benefit from their ability to turn simple and sophisticated, nutritious and light, exotic and local ingredients into appetizing creations. These culinary conjurers have learned their trade not only from the shepherds but also from the farmers' wives. Many exquisite lamb dishes and aromatic cheeses owe their creation to pasture farming and the changeable everyday life of the shepherds, while in the kitchens of the resident farmers homemade pastas were prepared using a *chitarra*, a dough cutting frame stretched over with fine strings. A steaming plate of *Maccheroni alla chitarra con ragù d'agnello,* macaroni with lamb sauce, combines the two traditions in a simple but ingenious way.

But despite its earthy and modest roots, the cuisine of the Abruzzi and Molise regions is also perfectly capable of excesses. Weddings are traditionally celebrated in great style. Traditionally, guests bring magnificent baskets, which they then take home with them after the celebrations filled with anything they could not manage to eat up during the banquet. The more the guests take away with them after the celebrations, the greater the compliment to the chef.

Previous double page: People with a sweet tooth are in capable hands at the shop of Fratelli Nurzia in L'Aquila. One of the delicacies they can buy here is the famous *torrone* (nougat).

Left: L'Aquila lies at the foot of the Gran Sasso. Now the capital town of Abruzzi, it was founded in the middle of the 13th century by Emperor Frederick II.

SHEEP AND GOATS

Arable farming is not the only feature of the regions of Abruzzi and Molise. They are also famous for livestock production. Many shepherds – although their number is constantly declining – continue even today to keep their livestock using the traditional, albeit work intensive, transhumance farming method: in the warm season the herds are left to graze on flower-covered alpine meadows, being driven down to the lowlands to overwinter when autumn comes. Because this way of keeping livestock is more natural for the animals than being reared in a barn, the milk they produce is more aromatic and their meat better. This tradition does, however, require the shepherds to spend months living away from their families.

Sheep play a significant role in the cultural history of the Mediterranean region. Not without reason was the lamb one of the most important sacrificial animals both in the ancient mythologies and in early Christian rituals. In the Christian tradition, the Lamb of God is the New Testament symbol for Jesus.

Even in earlier times, sheep breeding was a worthwhile occupation, primarily because the animals provided the wool that was so important for people's survival in winter, and which they used to make warm blankets, clothes, and other textiles. They were able to use the milk to make tasty cheeses. Even when slaughtered, sheep and lambs were of considerable value, as practically all parts could be used, including the innards. Practically all southern countries have dishes that use lamb or mutton. In some regions, lamb and particularly mutton, perhaps because of their sometimes-strong smell, used to be thought of as food fit only for the poor who could afford nothing better. However, this idea changed long ago, and you now need a bulging wallet to buy a milk lamb. Despite this, no Italian, Spanish, Turkish, or Greek gourmets would want to go without their favorite tasty lamb or mutton dishes, whether they be *Arrosto di agnello di latte* (roast milk lamb), *Piernas de cordero con alcachofas* (leg of lamb with artichokes), *Koyun pirzolas* (baked mutton chops), or *Arní kléftiko* (a dish of lamb with vegetables cooked in paper parcels).

Below: The meat of sheep, castrated rams and lambs plays a particularly important role in the cuisine of central and southern Italy

1. *Collo*: Neck
2. *Spalla*: Shoulder
3. *Pancia, Petto*: Breast
4. *Costine, Puntine*: Rib
5. *Cosciotto accorciato*: Leg
6. *Sella*: Saddle of lamb
7. *Costolette lombari con filetto*: Lamb cutlets with filet
8. *Costolette primarie*: Saddle of lamb chops
9. *Costolette secondarie*: Lamb shoulder chops
10. *Piedino*: Shank

Costolette scoperte (Lamb cutlets) from 4, 8, 9

Agnello all'uovo e limone
Lamb with egg and lemon

1 CUP CHOPPED ONION
4 OZ/100 G RAW HAM
2 TBSP/20 G BUTTER
SALT AND PEPPER
NUTMEG
2 1/4 LBS/1 KG LAMB
ALL-PURPOSE FLOUR
1 CUP/250 ML MEAT STOCK
1 CUP/250 ML DRY WHITE WINE
2 EGG YOLKS
JUICE OF 1 LEMON

Cut the ham into strips and sauté in butter with the onion.
Season and add grated nutmeg.
Cut the lamb into pieces, toss in flour, add to the onions,
and brown quickly. Pour over the meat stock, and gradually
allow to thicken. Add the white wine, season again, and
cook over a low heat for about 2 hours. When cooked,
remove the lamb from the pan and keep warm.
Beat the egg yolk with the lemon juice and stir into the
meat juices. Return the pan to the heat and continue beating over a very low heat until the sauce is frothy. Pour over
the lamb and serve immediately.

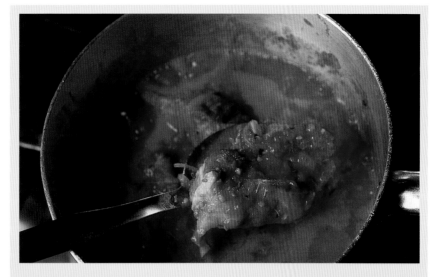

Goats

In central and southern Italy, goats are kept mainly for
their milk. It is the inhabitants of the poorest areas who
particularly like to keep the odd goat as well as the odd
pig, because, even more so than the pig, a goat provides a
little financial security. If things are bad, they can sell the
goat, exchange it as a material asset for other farm
produce, or slaughter it themselves and live off the meat
for a while. If, on the other hand, things are not so bad,
the goat provides milk for aromatic cheese, which can
either be enjoyed by the family or converted into cash at
the local market, thus ensuring a modest, but steady
supplementary income.

Goat meat rarely appears on the menu in central and
northern Europe. People have now got used to lamb, but
a tasty goat roast is still a rather rare delicacy. Although
such skepticism is unfounded, it is true that goat meat
does present the gourmet with an interesting culinary
experience. Contrary to what many people expect, goat
meat is not strong-flavored or tough, but has a quite
distinctive, delicate, gamy taste, especially when it comes
from a young animal. In Italy, goat meat is used quite
often, particularly in the central and southern regions,
and in many areas a tender young kid is the classic Easter
dish. Particularly in spring, when they are still young,
goats produce very fragrant and tender meat – true to the
saying often cited in Abruzzi: *marz'e aprile, agnell' e caprette
ggendile*, in March and April the lambs and kids are at
their most tender.

Capra alla molisana
Molise-style goat stew
(Illustrated above)

Serves 6

2 1/4 LBS/1 KG GOAT MEAT
1 1/4 PINTS/1 LITER RED WINE
2 BAY LEAVES
2 SAGE LEAVES
2 SPRIGS OF ROSEMARY
1 PEPERONCINO
5–6 TBSP EXTRA VIRGIN OLIVE OIL
1 CUP FINELY CHOPPED ONION
SALT
1 LB/500 G RIPE TOMATOES

Wash the goat meat, pat dry, and cut into small pieces.
Put in a bowl and add the red wine, bay leaves, sage, rosemary, and peperoncino. Leave the meat to marinate
overnight in a cool place. Heat the olive oil in a shallow
saucepan, add the onion, and soften. Add the meat and
brown quickly. Gradually add some wine from the marinade. When the wine has reduced, season with salt, and
add the roughly chopped, skinned, and seeded tomatoes.
Cover and continue to cook in the pan, occasionally
adding slightly salted boiling water. Cook over a low heat
until the meat is tender and the sauce quite thick.

Goats are kept mainly for their milk, from which an
aromatic cheese can be made.

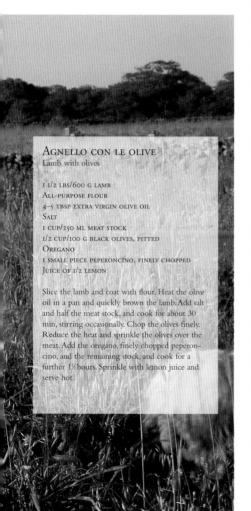

Agnello con le olive
Lamb with olives

1 1/2 LBS/600 G LAMB
ALL-PURPOSE FLOUR
4–5 TBSP EXTRA VIRGIN OLIVE OIL
SALT
1 CUP/250 ML MEAT STOCK
1/2 CUP/100 G BLACK OLIVES, PITTED
OREGANO
1 SMALL PIECE PEPERONCINO, FINELY CHOPPED
JUICE OF 1/2 LEMON

Slice the lamb and coat with flour. Heat the olive
oil in a pan and quickly brown the lamb. Add salt
and half the meat stock, and cook for about 30
min, stirring occasionally. Chop the olives finely.
Reduce the heat and sprinkle the olives over the
meat. Add the oregano, finely chopped peperoncino, and the remaining stock, and cook for a
further 1½ hours. Sprinkle with lemon juice and
serve hot.

CHITARRA, CEPPA, AND RONTROCILO

No one knows who invented the *chitarra*. If anybody did know, however, the inventor of this very simple, but ingenious macaroni machine would definitely be a celebrity in Abruzzi and Molise. The *chitarra* comprises a rectangular beech-wood frame, over which fine metal strings are stretched at millimeter intervals. A special key comes with it to tighten the strings if they become loose over time, as well as a collecting tray, into which the cut pasta falls. To make *Maccheroni alla chitarra*, the thinly-rolled dough is laid over the strings, rolled over with a rolling-pin, and so cut into uniformly fine, long pasta. Of course, as with all home-made pasta, the dough must be of good quality if *Maccheroni alla chitarra* to be a success. To serve six, allow 1 pound 2 ounces (500 grams) durum wheat semolina, five eggs, and a pinch of salt. Place the flour on the worktop. Make a well in the middle. Add the eggs and salt. It is important to knead the dough by hand for at least 20 minutes, as the dough must be compact and well-worked if the pasta is to cook *al dente*, and if the flavors of the egg and durum wheat are to come to the fore. When the dough is the correct consistency, leave it to rest for 15 minutes before rolling it out thinly using a rolling pin or the pasta machine so popular nowadays. It should be no thicker than the distance between two strings of the *chitarra*. *Maccheroni alla chitarra* tastes particularly good served with lamb, tomato, and peperoncino sauces, an *all'amatriciana* sauce, or simply with chopped bacon fried in butter. Pasta is always served with plenty of freshly grated pecorino cheese.

In Abruzzi and Molise, in addition to *Maccheroni alla chitarra*, they also serve *Maccheroni al rintrocilo* and *Maccheroni alla ceppa*. *Maccheroni al rintrocilo* is a specialty of Chieti, particularly the region around Lanciano. It owes its name to the special appliance used to make it. The *rintrocilo* is a grooved rolling pin that produces rectangular strips of pasta when rolled hard over the dough. *Maccheroni al rintrocilo* is not as thin as *Maccheroni alla chitarra*, as the dough is not rolled out so thinly before cutting. To make *Maccheroni alla ceppa*, small pieces of dough are rolled round a knitting needle sized wooden stick, the *ceppa*. In Molise, this long, slightly "permed" looking pasta is also called *fusilli*. There it is served with a spicy lamb and peperoncino sauce and garnished with plenty of freshly grated pecorino cheese before being sent to table.

Tomato sauces or ragouts made from chicken giblets and veal also go well with *Maccheroni al rintrocilo* and *Maccheroni alla ceppa*.

Fresh pasta is served daily at Luisa Pavia's Restaurant Italia in Sulmona. Here she is preparing the dough for *Maccheroni alla chitarra*.

To make the *chitarra* scissors, clippers, wire, and screw clamps are needed.

Gabriele Colasante of San Buceto near Pescara, one of only two *chitarra* makers, adds the strings.

The strings are tightened in the same way as on a guitar. You can buy a *chitarra* from Sulmona market.

Generally, macaroni, spaghetti, and other long pasta are made by extruding the dough at high pressure through small holes. But there are other ways: you can lay the dough over a *chitarra* and then roll over it with a rolling pin, so that the metal wires act like small knives and divide the dough into thin pasta, on the same principle as an egg slice. *Pasta alla chitarra* thus has a square-shaped cross-section, whereas that of conventional long pasta is round.

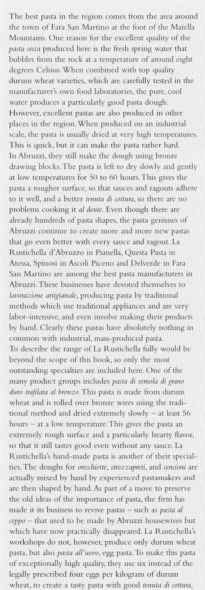

Traditional pasta making in Abruzzi

The best pasta in the region comes from the area around the town of Fara San Martino at the foot of the Maiella Mountains. One reason for the excellent quality of the *pasta secca* produced here is the fresh spring water that bubbles from the rock at a temperature of around eight degrees Celsius. When combined with top quality durum wheat varieties, which are carefully tested in the manufacturer's own food laboratories, the pure, cool water produces a particularly good pasta dough. However, excellent pastas are also produced in other places in the region. When produced on an industrial scale, the pasta is usually dried at very high temperatures. This is quick, but it can make the pasta rather hard. In Abruzzi, they still make the dough using bronze drawing blocks. The pasta is left to dry slowly and gently at low temperatures for 50 to 60 hours. This gives the pasta a rougher surface, so that sauces and ragouts adhere to it well, and a better *tenuta di cottura*, so there are no problems cooking it *al dente*. Even though there are already hundreds of pasta shapes, the pasta geniuses of Abruzzi continue to create more and more new pastas that go even better with every sauce and ragout. La Rustichella d'Abruzzo in Pianella, Questa Pasta in Atessa, Spinosi in Ascoli Piceno and Delverde in Fara San Martino are among the best pasta manufacturers in Abruzzi. These businesses have devoted themselves to *lavorazione artigianale*, producing pasta by traditional methods which use traditional appliances and are very labor-intensive, and even involve making their products by hand. Clearly these pastas have absolutely nothing in common with industrial, mass-produced pasta.

To describe the range of La Rustichella fully would be beyond the scope of this book, so only the most outstanding specialties are included here. One of the many product groups includes *pasta di semola di grano duro trafilata al bronzo*. This pasta is made from durum wheat and is rolled over bronze wires using the traditional method and dried extremely slowly – at least 56 hours – at a low temperature. This gives the pasta an extremely rough surface and a particularly hearty flavor, so that it still tastes good even without any sauce. La Rustichella's hand-made pasta is another of their specialties. The doughs for *orecchiette*, *strozzapreti*, and *cencioni* are actually mixed by hand by experienced pastamakers and are then shaped by hand. As part of a move to preserve the old ideas of the importance of pasta, the firm has made it its business to revive pastas – such as *pasta al ceppo* – that used to be made by Abruzzi housewives but which have now practically disappeared. La Rustichella's workshops do not, however, produce only durum wheat pasta, but also *pasta all'uovo*, egg pasta. To make this pasta of exceptionally high quality, they use six instead of the legally prescribed four eggs per kilogram of durum wheat, to create a tasty pasta with good *tenuta di cottura*,

so that the pasta does not disintegrate during cooking. The flavorsome narrow strip egg pasta that comes in saffron, salmon, chives and truffle flavors among others is particularly sought after in gastronomic circles as it takes only three to five minutes to cook. But the range of the "pasta-smiths" is still not complete. In the past few years, as demand for highly nutritious foods has become ever greater in Italy too, the company has also created pasta made from whole-wheat/durum wheat flours or even emmer wheat. This pasta is particularly rich in vitamins and fiber and is best eaten with a simple sauce.

It goes without saying that the firm of Questa Pasta in Atessa, which mainly produces durum wheat semolina pasta, and the manufacturer of the brand name of La Pasta di Vicenzo Spinosi I Ascoli Piceno, whose products, as they themselves state, are made with durum wheat semolina, eggs, experience and a passion for tradition, are no less demanding in terms of quality than La Rustichella.

Nor is Delverde in Fara San Martino any less demanding. This pasta factory, which is one of the largest in the region, combines handicraft skills with modern production methods, without exposing the pasta to rapid drying or other processes that can have a detrimental effect on the quality of the end product. The factory produces about 30 long tons (300,000 kilograms) of pasta every day. The firm's 260 employees ensure that the 170 pasta varieties offered for sale by Delverde do actually come off the conveyor belt each day. However, noodles are not the only things on offer from this monument to pasta, which has also come out strongly in support of protecting its local environment, and which sticks rigidly to its strict, self-imposed ecological standards. There is now also an oil mill that produces the purest olive oil exclusively from Abruzzi olives. Delverde also sells rice, fresh pasta, flour, semolina, ready-made pasta sauces in jars, various tomato products, pesto, and *sott'aceti* (pickles). The firm is well on the way to gaining a foothold in markets beyond Italy. Even now, a good 30 percent of its total pasta sales are exported. Look out for the excellent products from Abruzzi next time you go to your local Italian delicatessen!

MACCHERONI ALLA CHITARRA
Narrow strip pasta with sauce
(Illustrated, right, front)

1 2/3 CUPS/300 G FINE DURUM WHEAT SEMOLINA
4 EGGS
SALT

For the sauce:
3 TABLESPOONS BUTTER
2–3 SLICES/60 G BACON, CUT INTO THIN STRIPS
4 RIPE TOMATOES, SKINNED AND SEEDED
SCANT 1/2 CUP/50 G PECORINO CHEESE, GRATED
FRESHLY MILLED PEPPER

Knead the semolina, eggs, and a pinch of salt together to
form a very elastic and smooth dough. It should be
smoother than the usual pasta dough. Knead the dough
thoroughly and then roll it out not too thinly. It should be
just as thick as the gap between the *chitarra* strings. Cut the
dough into rectangles to fit the *chitarra*. Lay one rectangle
over the *chitarra* and roll over with a rolling pin. Repeat for
the remaining rectangles, pressing the dough through the
wires to form "square-shaped spaghetti". You can use a pasta
machine instead of the special wooden frame with its thin
wires. In this case, roll the dough out quite thick and pass it
through the machine set as for tagliatelle. Boil the pasta in a
large pan of water until it is cooked *al dente*, then pour off
the water and drain.
To make the sauce, fry the bacon in the butter in a pan.
Squeeze the tomatoes to a pulp and add to the pan. Allow
the sauce to thicken slightly, pour over the pasta, and sprinkle with grated pecorino cheese and freshly milled pepper.

FUSILLI ALLA MOLISANA
Molise-style fusilli

14 OZ/400 G FUSILLI
1/4 LB/100 G LEAN, RAW HAM
1 SCANT CUP/200 G RICOTTA CHEESE
SALT AND PEPPER
2–3 TBSP EXTRA VIRGIN OLIVE OIL
GENEROUS 1/2 CUP/70 G PECORINO CHEESE, GRATED

Cook the pasta until *al dente*, pour off the water, and leave
to drain. Dice the ham and mix well with the ricotta
cheese. Season with salt and pepper.
Heat the olive oil in a skillet, add the ricotta/ham mixture
and heat gently. Add the pasta and mix thoroughly. Sprinkle
with grated pecorino cheese.

SUGO DI CASTRATO
Mutton sauce

1 CUP CHOPPED ONION
1 SPRIG ROSEMARY
2 SLICES/50 G BACON
1/2 LB/250 G MUTTON
1 GLASS DRY WHITE WINE
SALT AND PEPPER
3/4 LB/350 G RIPE TOMATOES, SKINNED AND CHOPPED

Finely chop the rosemary and bacon. Cut the mutton into
small pieces. Sauté everything in a pan with the onion.
When the meat has browned, pour in the wine, and season
with salt and pepper. Cook for about 15 minutes over a
medium heat.
Then add the chopped tomatoes. Cover and cook for at
least 1 hour over a low heat. This sauce is a good accompaniment to pasta dishes.

OLIO SANTO

Olio Santo, holy oil, is extremely spicy because it is
flavored with the brilliant red chili peppers so popular
throughout Abruzzi and Molise and known there as
peperoncini. This fiery member of the *Capsicum* family
has made a name for itself not only as a spicy ingredient, but also for the curative properties attributed to it
for centuries. Rheumatism, hair loss, slow-healing
wounds, high cholesterol level: all can be remedied,
either allegedly or in actual fact, with the aid of these
peppery pods so rich in vitamin C and alkaloids. What
is more, because it has the effect of increasing the
blood supply, peperoncino is also reputed to stimulate
the libido, an unusual property for a "holy" oil.

Front: *Maccheroni alla chitarra* – narrow strip pasta
with sauce
Back: *Spaghetti aglio, olio e peperoncino* – spaghetti with
garlic, oil and peperoncino

Cavetelli 'ncatenati
Mini-dumplings with bacon and eggs

For the dumplings:
2 GENEROUS CUPS/400 G DURUM WHEAT SEMOLINA
HAND-HOT WATER
SALT

For the sauce:
5 EGGS
4 OZ/100 G BACON
OLIVE OIL
SALT AND FRESHLY MILLED PEPPER

Sift the semolina on to the table and sprinkle with a pinch of salt. Gradually add some hand-hot water and slowly work with the semolina to form a soft, elastic dough. The dough is ready when it no longer sticks to the hands. Leave to rest. Then, using the ball of the thumb, roll small quantities of dough on the work surface to make pencil-thick rolls. Cut them into ¾-in./2-cm long pieces. Using the thumb, create a slight groove in the middle of each dumpling. Boil in salted boiling water until *al dente* and then drain. Beat the eggs thoroughly. Dice the bacon and brown slightly in the olive oil in a skillet. Mix in the dumplings, then add the beaten eggs and season with salt and pepper. Finally, mix thoroughly and serve immediately.

Ragù d'agnello
Pasta sauce with lamb

1/2 LB/200 G LEAN LAMB
SALT AND PEPPER
2 CLOVES GARLIC
2 BAY LEAVES
3–4 TBSP EXTRA VIRGIN OLIVE OIL
1 GLASS DRY WHITE WINE
2 RIPE TOMATOES, FINELY CHOPPED
2 RED PEPPERS, CUT INTO STRIPS

Cut the meat into small pieces, season well with salt and pepper, and leave to stand for 1 hour. Sauté the garlic cloves and bay leaves in the oil over a low heat. Remove the garlic as soon as it starts to brown. Add the lamb to the pan and brown on all sides. Add the wine and leave to reduce. Add the tomatoes and red peppers to the meat. Add salt, cover, and braise for around 1½ hours over a low heat, stirring occasionally, and adding hot stock if necessary.

Spaghetti aglio, olio e peperoncino
Spaghetti with garlic, oil, and peperoncino
(Illustrated bottom left)

14 OZ/400 G SPAGHETTI
3–4 TBSP OLIVE OIL
2 CLOVES GARLIC
1 PEPERONCINO CHILI PEPPER
1 TBSP CHOPPED PARSLEY

Heat the oil in a skillet, then add the peeled cloves of garlic and the chopped peperoncino chili pepper. Brown the garlic. Boil the spaghetti in copious salted water until *al dente*, then pour off the water, drain well, and arrange on a warmed plate. Remove the garlic and pieces of peperoncino chili pepper from the oil. Pour the oil over the spaghetti, sprinkle with parsley, and mix carefully. Serve immediately.

SAFFRON

Considering the tiny portions in which saffron is sold and the few recipes that still require its use today, it is hard to imagine that the flower pistils of *Crocus sativus* were once one of the most sought-after items of merchandise in the West.

As long ago as in classical times, the Greeks and Romans loved saffron, even sprinkling it in the theaters to create a pleasant atmosphere for the performance. They also used the orange-red threads to dye precious silk fabrics or sewed it into pillows, as it was reputed to have a soporific effect. It was not until the Middle Ages that saffron became a status symbol. Throughout Europe, great importance was attached to making a meal look as good as possible, for the table decked with food was intended to display power and wealth. As a result, every meat dish, whether boiled or broiled on a spit, was "gilded," in other words covered with a brilliant yellow preparation made from saffron. However, the fragrant luxury spice was subject to high rates of tax, so even in those days gourmets had to dig deep into their pockets to pay for the quantities they required. A document written in English around 1400 states that a pound in weight (500 grams) of saffron was equal in value to one horse.

In the Abruzzi town of L'Aquila, which from the late 13th century had a flourishing trade with Venice, Milan, and Marseilles, tempted by the high profit margins, they began to grow crocuses themselves. The crocus growers' hopes were not disappointed, because L'Aquila came to be a major exporter. Particularly in Germany, there was such a high demand for the expensive commodity that the penalty for adulterating or falsifying Abruzzi saffron was death. It was not until 300 years later, when the nascent chemical industry made synthetic dyes and flavorings available, that the era of the yellow powder gradually came to an end.

There are, however, still some traditional dishes that from both a flavor and color point of view cannot do without genuine saffron. *Risotto alla Milanese* would be unthinkable without its beautiful, rich yellow, and the Spanish paella would also be a rather pale imitation without saffron.

Before use, saffron threads should be crushed with a pestle and mortar and left to infuse in a little warm water to release the flavor. The danger with the saffron powder frequently sold in shops is that it could contain undesirable additives.

Opposite and above: The saffron crocus (*Crocus sativus*) grows naturally only on the poorest of soils. Its pistils have long been valued for their dyeing and medicinal properties.

Opposite and below: At least 200,000 flower heads are required to obtain two and a quarter pounds (one kilogram) of saffron threads, making it correspondingly expensive.

Crocus blossoms are harvested in October. They have to be picked as quickly as possible, as the plants are in flower for only two weeks.

Saffron is usually sold in tiny jars or even as individual threads, because it takes a great deal of skilled handiwork to produce.

MOZZARELLINE ALLO ZAFFERANO
Mini-mozzarella cheeses with saffron
(Illustrated above)

A FEW THREADS OF SAFFRON
SALT
1 GENEROUS CUP/150 G WHEAT FLOUR
12 SMALL MOZZARELLA CHEESES
BREADCRUMBS
VEGETABLE OIL FOR FRYING

Infuse the saffron in 4 tablespoons salted water. Gradually stir in the flour and enough water to produce a thick batter. Coat the mozzarella cheeses in the batter and then roll them in the breadcrumbs. Heat the oil in a deep skillet, and fry the cheeses until golden yellow. Serve hot.

FRITTATINE DI PATATE E ZAFFERANO
Saffron potato cakes

Serves 6

1 1/2 LBS/600 G POTATOES
A PINCH OF SAFFRON
EXTRA VIRGIN OLIVE OIL
3 EGGS
2 TBSP CHOPPED PARSLEY
ALL-PURPOSE FLOUR AS REQUIRED
SALT AND PEPPER

Boil and peel the potatoes, then pass them through a potato ricer. Soak the saffron in 3 tablespoons olive oil.
Put the potatoes, eggs, parsley, and saffron oil in a bowl and knead gently to form a dough. Add more olive oil or a little flour as necessary. Season with salt and pepper. The potato mixture should be soft and light. Spoon the mixture into a lightly greased skillet, press smooth, and fry over a low heat.

327

1 Ventricina di Montenero di Bisaccia

This heartily seasoned spreading sausage from the area of Campobasso in Molise is made from lean pork leg meat. When stored in a cool place, it will keep for up to one and a half years.

2 Guanciale

The pig's cheek is soaked in wine, seasoned with salt and pepper, and then left to rest for 30 to 40 days in a stone tub. It is served cut into thin slices on bruschetta bread.

3/7 Mortadella amatriciana (Mortadella di Campotosto)

This sausage (illustrated right) from the Amatrice and Campotosto region on the Gran Sasso is also called *coglione del mulo*. Contrary to the image conjured up by this name, it is not made from donkeys' testicles, but from ham, with a whole piece of fatty bacon being placed in the center of the sausage mixture. When it has cured for ten days at a constant temperature in well-ventilated rooms, Mortadella di Campotosto, which is made from pork shoulder, loin, and bacon, will keep for about four months if stored in a cool place.

4 Ventricina di Guilmi

Made from filet, loin, and lean leftovers from ham production, this specialty is smoked for between 10 and 15 days, and will keep for up to six months if stored in a cool place.

5 Fegatazzo di Ortona

This sausage, another specialty of Ortona, is made from liver, lights, spleen, streaky bacon and pig's cheek generously seasoned with salt, peperoncino, orange peel, and, of course, garlic.

6 Salsicciotto di Guilmi

The sausage from Guilmi (Province of Chieti) mainly consists of pigs' loin, seasoned with salt and pepper and stuffed into a sausage skin. It has to mature for 20 days and can then be preserved in lard or oil.

8 Ventricina di Crognaleto

This real paprika sausage is made from both fatty and lean pork, generously seasoned with paprika and some peperoncino, and stuffed into a casing made from a pig's stomach. It keeps for a long time and is therefore a useful item to have in the store cupboard.

Not illustrated:

Annoia di Ortona

This sausage made from pork tripe, salt, peperoncino, and fennel seed, is made throughout Abruzzi. The best place to taste it is said to be Ortona in Chieti.

Fegato dolce

This "sweet" sausage from the L'Aquila region is made from pork liver and meat loaf, flavored with salt, pepper, a lot of honey, candied fruits, pine nuts, and pistachio nuts.

Saggicciotto

Made from lean meat and streaky bacon, this sausage is smoked for a week and will keep for up to four months if stored in a cool place.

Soppressata di Rionero Sannitico

Made from loin, head, neck, and two percent bacon, this specialty from Molise is stored for around ten days in well-ventilated rooms and can then be kept for up to five months in a cool place.

Salsicce di fegato di Rionero Sannitico

These sausages are made from lean meat, liver, heart, lights, and bacon, and stored in warm, airy rooms for five days. They keep for 20 to 30 days and can then be preserved in pork fat.

Sanguinaccio

This sausage made from pig's blood, nuts, pine kernels, raisins, orange peel, cocoa, precooked spelt, and streaky bacon is cooked for one hour and should then be eaten immediately.

MEAT AND MILK PRODUCTS

Abruzzi and Molise are not the richest regions in the Italian peninsula. The barren mountain ranges and comparatively cold winters in the mountains have long made life hard for the farmers and herdsmen. Families were often large with many children, whereas arable land and livestock were in contrast in rather short supply. The little that they had was needed on the one hand as a source of income, and on the other to feed the many hungry mouths. It was such a close run thing that the housewives never had anything left over. When a pig or sheep was slaughtered, they kept a close eye on the butcher and sausage-maker to ensure that they really did carefully process and make use of every single part. Under no circumstance should anything be wasted or thrown away.

The typical thriftiness of poor areas is also reflected in the specialty sausages of the region. The *ventricina di Guilmi* provides a good illustration of this, as it is a tasty sausage made from the leftovers after making ham. The *salsiccia di fegato* is another "leftover sausage." Its ingredients include pork liver, heart, and lights. Even the blood from slaughtering the animal is not poured away immediately, but used instead to make *sanguinaccio*. As its name suggests, this specialty blood sausage is made from pig's blood. For central European palates, this sausage has a decidedly "Christmassy flavor," because its ingredients are padded out with nuts, pine kernels, spelt, cocoa, and orange peel.

Today, Abruzzi and Molise, together with the other regions of southern Italy (Campania, Apulia, Basilicata, Calabria, and the two islands of Sardinia and Sicily), account for more than a quarter of the total national demand for sausage and ham specialties. Products from Abruzzi and Molise also have a particularly good reputation, because increasingly large numbers of small animal breeders here are now returning to letting their pigs roam free rather than keeping them in a sty. This type of animal husbandry improves the flavor of the meat considerably, because the animals find themselves food such as acorns and chestnuts in the wild, instead of being fed merely on the family's kitchen waste. There is also a move back to traditional methods of slaughtering and sausage making. Many town dwellers, who can obviously not keep their own pig, have now discovered their own private, country butcher, from whom they procure naturally-raised and first-class produce that is not available in the super-market.

Central and southern Italy produces mainly varieties of sheep's milk cheeses and types of *pasta-filata* made from cow's milk. Occasionally goat's milk is also used, but the cheesemaker frequently mixes this with cow's and/or sheep's milk. The only cheese to be made of buffalo milk is the famous *mozzarella di bufala*, a specialty of the south. Abruzzi and Molise mainly produce pecorino, the famous hard cheese made from full fat sheep's milk. However, three *pasta-filata* cheeses are also made in the region: *scamorza, caciocavallo di agnone* and *fior di latte*. The name *pasta-filata* refers to the special treatment applied in the cheesemaking process. The curds are cured in warm whey and are then scalded with hot water and kneaded thoroughly to produce a cohesive and elastic mass.

Burrino, or *butirro* as it is known in the far south of the country, is another specialty. It is a ball of butter surrounded by a layer of cheese. The production process is simple: You make a hollow *pasta-filata* cheese, into which you put the butterball. The cheese is then carefully sealed and can subsequently be enjoyed young, ripe or smoked. This way, the butter remains fresh, an advantage that was particularly appreciated in central and southern Italy in the days when modern refrigeration facilities were to be found only in very wealthy homes.

1 Fior di latte
From the outside, *fior di latte* may look like mozzarella, but it is made from cow's milk, not buffalo milk. The balls of cheese are white to grayish-white and are compact in texture, often with whey remaining in the holes. Although this *pasta-filata* cheese is produced throughout the year, it tastes best in spring and summer.

2 Pecorino di Castel del Monte
Made from sheep's milk, this log-shaped cheese has to ripen for between 40 days and two years. It has a nut-brown rind, while inside the cheese itself is pale yellow, with an intensive aroma and piquant flavor. A good 100 long tons (100,000 kilograms) are produced between Easter and August.

3 Fior di monte
The milk of this young pecorino cheese, which ripens for up to 70 days, comes from sheep that graze on the Camp Imperatore plateau on the Gran Sasso.

4 Caciocavallo di Agnone
After maturing for between three months and up to three years at a constant room temperature and with steady venti-lation, this pear-shaped *pasta-filata* cheese made from cow's milk has a hard, nut-brown rind and has a compact texture inside. Its aroma is intensive and when eaten young it has a sweet and creamy taste, which becomes more piquant the longer it matures.

5 Scamorza
Scamorza is a pear-shaped fresh cheese made from cow's milk. It should be eaten within one week. It is made using the *pasta-filata* method. The cheese is whitish and has a sweet-sour taste. Although it is made throughout the year, it is mainly produced during July and August. Like mozzarella, it can also be smoked.

Caciofiore (not illustrated)
Caciofiore is a typical fresh cheese from central Italy. The special key to its production is that a vegetable setting agent made from artichokes is used instead of the customary rennet. In Abruzzi, this soft cheese is sometimes colored with saffron. After maturing for about two weeks, it is ready to be eaten or cooked.

Burrino (not illustrated)
Burrino cheese is a decidedly ingenious invention. Inside it is hidden a heart of butter, which in the hot summers of central and southern Italy would otherwise not keep for more than a couple of days. The cheese layer, however, reliably prevents the butter from going off. *Burrino* can be eaten fresh, but can also be enjoyed cured or smoked.

CANDY, SUGAR-COATED CANDY, AND CONFECTIONERY

Even in ancient times, people enjoyed confectionery: The Chinese, the Egyptians, and later the Romans coated fruits, flower blossom, nuts, and seeds in honey. With the increasing popularity of sugar in the years after it was introduced from Persia, it was first added to the honey coating, but subsequently replaced the

Below: Since the Renaissance, confectionery has been made into flowers and other shapes in Sulmona. The tradition originated in the Santa Chiara monastery.

honey altogether, candy then being made solely with sugar coatings.

Italians differentiate between hard and soft confectionery by whether these sugarcoated candies have a hard or a liquid or creamy center. Soft confectionery is filled with liqueurs, almond paste, or flavored creams. Sometimes jellied or candied fruits are also added. Hard confectionery on the other hand has centers made from shelled or roasted almonds, pistachios, or hazelnuts. A *bassina* is used to coat the center. This hemispherical, slightly warmed copper vessel always hung from a chain and was moved by hand. In 1850, a clever inventor designed the first *bassina* with electric beaters. The nuts were first treated with syrup or gum Arabic so that they would retain the sugar layers. They were then coated in the *bassina*. At first, the syrup is fluid, but for the final few layers it needs to be stickier. When the coatings have dried, the confectionery is whitened and polished.

In the case of soft confectionery, the liquid filling has to be poured into the inside of the sweet morsel. Only

when this is done is it polished to a high gloss using a mixture of cocoa butter and a binding agent (gum arabic).

Since the Renaissance, Sulmona has been the confectionery-manufacturing center of Abruzzi. It is here that the greatest variety of dragées or Jordan almonds and other candies is created and then transformed using silk, plastic, colored paper, wire, and other accessories into flowers, blossom, ears of wheat, exotic fruits, and many other things. Even the color of the confectionery is important, as it has symbolic meaning. At the celebrations for weddings or 25th or 50th wedding anniversaries, there are white, silver, or golden dragées or Jordan almonds. When new arrivals are baptized, the candy is pale blue or pink in color depending on the sex of the child. Red is the color for academic success (the candies are put in a little fabric bag the color of the coat of arms of the faculty in question). Finally, confectionery is yellow for second marriages. However, the latter is not in widespread use in this part of Italy!

Sulmona is the confectionery capital. Six factories and numerous dealers are involved in producing the candy specialties and selling them to the customer in wonderfully attractive shops.

BRIGHTLY COLORED WORKS OF ART

The confectioners of Abruzzi are not only among the best in the world, but also certainly some of the most creative. For the celebration to mark the 500th anniversary of the discovery of America, the firm of Confetti D'Alessandro created a caravel, a 15th-century Spanish or Portuguese small, fast, light ship, entirely from candy. It can now be found in the New York Columbus Foundation museum. This workshop also produced a baseball bat, created to mark the visit of Joe di Maggio to Italy, and a table decoration for the G-7 summit in Naples. Among the particular specialties of Alessandro are the *panelle*, in which brightly colored confectionery is arranged like a mosaic.

U DULCIT

The 360-square-yard (300-square-meter) *Parco nazionale d'Abruzzo*, one of the four nature reserves in Abruzzi, has its own candy specialty. In addition to the chamois, wolves, golden eagles, otters, and lynx that roam Italy's oldest national park, there is also the rare Apennine brown bear, which inspired the baker Antonio from Civitella Alfedena to create his bear cake. This chocolate-coated cake is sold to its many fans under the name *U Dulcit – Il dolce del Parco* (Park candy).

This *panella* (mosaic made out of confectionery) by Confetti D'Alessandro shows an advertisement for the Post Office.

Confetti D'Alessandro also made this *panella* to help world food aid.

Decorated with sparkling stars and sporting festive red and green, this bouquet would make a wonderful Christmas gift.

It goes without saying that wedding confectionery like this pretty "bouquet of flowers" has got to be white.

TORRONE BY NURZIA

Sometime between the end of the 18th and the beginning of the 19th centuries, Gennaro Nurzia, a specialist in distilled liqueurs by trade, moved from the small mountain village of Arischia in Abruzzi to the capital, L'Aquila. Here he opened a store and soon broadened his range of commercial activities to include the production of confectionery, especially *torrone*. One of his descendents, Ulisse, created the *torrone Nurzia tenero al cioccolato*, an astonishing creation for the time, in that it neither melted in the heat nor became too hard in the cold. The secret lies in an old, closely-guarded recipe, and in the exact proportion of the ingredients.

Another *torrone* specialty, made with dried figs, comes from the province of Chieti. The people of Abruzzi particularly enjoy eating this full-flavored and calorific candy on cold winter days. Nowadays, there are even firms who import it from Italy.

LINKING
NORTH AND
SOUTH

While the Marches belong geographically to central Italy and, as far as their wine is concerned, represent the transition between northern and southern Italy, Abruzzi can definitely be thought of as belonging to the South, even if this is not always to the liking of the people of Abruzzi. The landscape of the Adriatic region is very similar to that of the Marches and from a winegrowing point of view the two regions have a certain amount in common in the form of the Montepulciano grape.

Typically, the Abruzzi winegrowing area is hilly and not many grape varieties are grown. The foothills of the mighty Gran Sasso d'Italia, the highest elevation in the central Italian mountain range that starts in the north as the Apennines and continues here as Abruzzi, are covered in vines to a height of almost 2000 feet (600 meters). This creates a good balance between the warming sun and the finesse-giving coolness, which, when combined with the right soil and above all the right grape varieties, produces big wines.

With regard to the grape varieties, the region of Abruzzi is dominated by a quasi-monopoly in both red and white wines. A variety of the Trebbiano family forms the basic ingredient for the Trebbiano d'Abruzzi mark of origin. Its wines are mainly light and neutral in quality, but some characterful representatives can produce very striking bouquets that are not always to everyone's taste.

The red variety, Montepulciano d'Abruzzo – which is not to be confused with the Tuscan marks of origin: Rosso di Montepulciano and Vino Nobile di Montepulciano, which are made primarily from Sangiovese grapes – covers the majority of the winegrowing area in Abruzzi. It can produce robust wines with a low acid content and strong tannins. The risk of confusing Abruzzo Montepulciano with Vino Nobile from the town of Montepulciano is further increased when you discover that some researchers now believe that the Montepulciano grape variety is nothing but a variety of the Sangiovese grape.

Robust, full-bodied Montepulciano wines often surprise the wine-drinker with nuances of animal aromas, which go particularly well with game dishes. Nowadays, however, the wines are mainly kept with fruity overtones. They are made to be easy-drinking and full-flavored, rather than overemphasizing their tannin structure. The rosé variety of Montepulciano, sold under the name of Cerasuolo, has a particularly

pleasant fruity flavor. The new, independent mark of origin, Controguerra, an area that used to belong to the DOC Montepulciano d'Abruzzo, also produces some single grape variety wines from grapes that were

not originally indigenous to this region. Although the wine production of neighboring Molise is 600 times that of the Aosta valley, it produces only about 53 U.S. gallons (a couple of hectoliters) more quality wine than the alpine region. There are decidedly few DOC wines here. As in Abruzzi, Montepulciano and Trebbiano are the two main types of grape used, although a little Aglianico and Sangiovese may also be included in the two separate marks of origin of Biferno and Pentro di Isernia. However, the positive developments in Abruzzi

will probably also extend to Molise in the next few years, for even now one or two producers are coming out in favor of rediscovering and cultivating old grape varieties while using new production techniques.

Opposite: Lined up in ranks, the vines rise upward on the slopes in the shadow of the Gran Sasso.

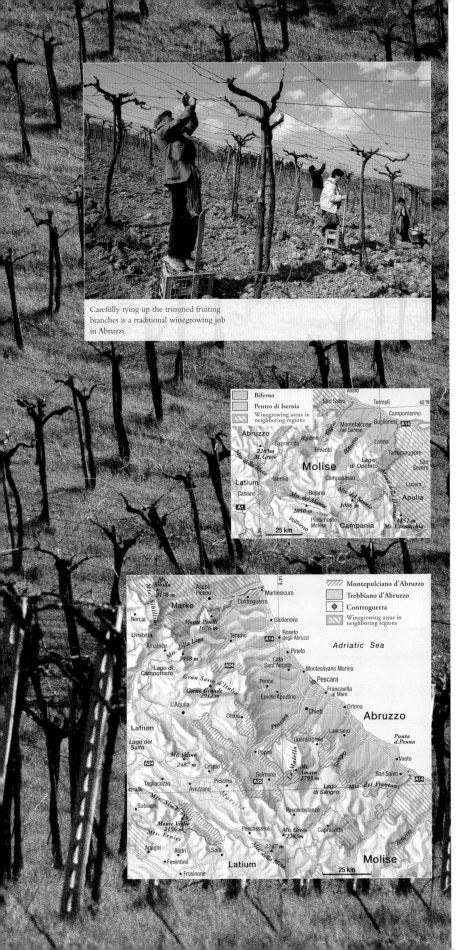

Carefully tying up the trimmed fruiting branches is a traditional winegrowing job in Abruzzi.

Ofena is one of the typical, small winegrowing towns in the Abruzzi hinterland.

Grapes are still grown even at quite high altitudes in Abruzzi.

CENTERBA

Centerba is distilled from various plants indigenous to the alpine region of Abruzzi. We shall never know whether, as its name suggests, a hundred herbs really are required to produce this greenish concoction, for the manufacturer will keep the exact proportion of the ingredients a closely-guarded secret for ever. True to the Abruzzi motto "the spicier the better," centerba produces such a powerful burning sensation in the throat that you could almost believe it was spiced with peperoncino..

CAMPANIA

Naples immediately brings to mind the liveliness of Italy – bustling, noisy, shimmering in the summer heat, and full of unrestrained *joie de vivre*, even fearlessly defying the volcanic threat. Neapolitans are said to have an exuberant temperament and an inexhaustible supply of good humor that enables them to overcome the vicissitudes of their far from simple lives with stoic calm. Whether or not this gross generalization is true, one thing is certain: there is nothing bland about Neapolitan cuisine. Here people like to see tasty results as quickly as possible. Life in Naples is hectic, so people do not want to wait long for their food. It therefore comes as no surprise that the cuisine of Campania has become famous for its delightfully simple specialties. The farm produce – tomatoes, capsicums, spring onions, potatoes, artichokes, fennel, lemons, or oranges – ripened on the fertile volcanic soils at the foot of Vesuvius under the generous warmth of the southern sun, is all so good, that no expensive refinements are necessary. Fish and seafood can be brought fresh each day from the Gulf of Naples or other coastal waters. The durum wheat needed to produce the world-famous Neapolitan pasta is either grown in Campania itself or imported from neighboring Apulia. Livestock production provides meat for the obligatory pasta meat sauce, and even buffalo milk, used to make the extremely aromatic mozzarella cheese of Campania. These are the only ingredients the Neapolitan kitchen conjurers require to serve up the *pièces de résistance* of their culinary tradition: vegetable dishes, omelets, spicy fish soups, stir-fries, and, of course, the two staples of Campanian cuisine: pasta and pizza.

Naples has experienced life under the ruling houses of the Normans, Hohenstaufens, Bourbons, Aragon, Anjou, and Savoy, but not one of these foreign powers was able to leave any lasting mark on the region's cuisine. The only exception is, perhaps, the influence of the French language dating from 1786, and the introduction of French etiquette at court, broadening their vocabulary with culinary terms such as *ragù* (meat sauce), *gattò* (cake), and *crocchè* (croquette). The excellent dishes typical of the people of Campania, however, such as *Maccheroni alla napoletana*, *Pizza margherita*, *Insalata caprese*, *Mozzarella in carrozza* or *Costoletta alla pizzaiola*, do not need any such embellishment.

Previous double page: Genuine mozzarella, as produced here at the Vannulo cheese-dairy, is made from buffalo, not cow's milk.

Left: View over the Bay of Naples. The island of Capri can be seen in the distance. Each year it attracts a small but sophisticated flock of visitors.

MACARONI AND SPAGHETTI

Contrary to the claims of many Neapolitans, delicious Italian pasta was not invented at the foot ofVesuvius. It was not until toward the end of the 18th century that Naples adopted pasta, successfully devising ways to make it increasingly popular. Exactly who invented pasta dough is still debatable. Some consider the Chinese to be the true inventors, others the Romans. According to classical sources, a dough mixture made from water and flour, called *langanum*, was common in Rome. Its successor, *langanella*, is a dry dough with no egg, and is still known even today in Campania. But Sardinia and Sicily also have early types of pasta. Although, in his 14th-century *Decameron*, the writer and scholar Giovanni Boccaccio does speak of pasta, it is regrettable that he does not provide any precise description of the product.

Definite references to macaroni or spaghetti as we think of them now can be found in a source dating from the beginning of the 17th century. This source describes a primitive but effective device used to stretch the dough into long, thin pasta. It was not until the beginning of the 19th century that anything like a pasta industry became established in Naples and the surrounding area. It was during this period that the traveling pasta-sellers roamed through the streets offering their wares to passersby. In 1833, Ferdinand II, himself a great pizza and pasta fan, attended the opening of the first factory able to produce pasta on an industrial scale. This laid the foundation stone not only for the region's remarkable economic upturn, but also for the ideological differences of opinion that still persist today between the devotees of homemade pasta on the one hand and the advocates of mass-produced pasta on the other. The 19th century was also the period in which the burgeoning Naples attracted painters, writers, and travelers from all parts of Europe. One of them, Alexandre Dumas the Elder, wrote a portrayal of manners describing Neapolitan life. It was not altogether flattering, but all the more interesting for that in terms of culinary history. Pasta plays the main role, being constantly gobbled up by greedy citizens, as described by the novelist.

Cesare Spadaccini, the pasta factory that opened at that time, was not to remain the only example of its kind. Production methods quickly improved and more and more new firms began to produce pasta in the area around Vesuvius. The towns of Gragnano, Torre Annunziata, and Torre del Greco were pioneers in *pasta secca*. And so it was from this region of Campania, that pasta set out to conquer the world. It developed into a modern form of nutrition that other parts of Europe were justifiably happy to emulate, and no one has been able to beat it yet.

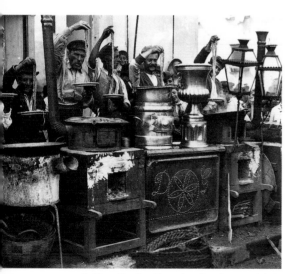

Peddlers selling the widest variety of goods were typical of 19th-century Neapolitan street life. Even spaghetti was sold in this way.

A word about terminology

The term *macaroni* means different things to different people, depending on where they are. In southern Italy it is used to describe pasta of any shape, so that the long, thick *ziti* are just as likely to come under this category as spaghetti, penne, and *linguine*. In central and northern Italy, however, *macaroni* is used to describe only the thick hollow pasta, whether long or short, grooved or not. Outside Italy, the word is sometimes used as a rather uncomplimentary name for the inhabitants of the Italian peninsula.

Pasta cacio e pepe

Pasta with cheese and pepper
(Illustrated opposite, above left)

14 oz/400 g spaghetti (or any other pasta)
1 cup/100 g caciocavallo cheese, grated
Freshly milled black pepper

Boil the spaghetti until *al dente*, then drain, retaining a few tablespoons of the cooking liquid. Put the pasta in a bowl and sprinkle generously with the cheese and pepper. Add sufficient hot pasta-cooking water to make the cheese melt and become slightly creamy. Mix thoroughly and serve hot.

Spaghetti con le vongole

Spaghetti with clams
(Illustrated opposite, above right)

2 1/4 lbs/1 kg fresh clams
4–5 tbsp extra virgin olive oil
3 cloves of garlic, chopped
1 cup/200 g ripe tomatoes, skinned and crushed
14 oz/400 g spaghetti
Salt and freshly milled black pepper
2 tbsp chopped parsley

Brush the clams and cook in a little water until their shells open. Discard any unopened clams. Remove the clam flesh, then strain the cooking liquid through a fine sieve, and reserve. Quickly sauté the garlic in olive oil in a skillet, and then remove. Add the tomatoes and clam cooking liquid, stir, and cook for 20 minutes. Boil the spaghetti in copious salted water until *al dente*, then drain. Combine the clams, pepper, and parsley with the tomato sauce. Pour the sauce over the spaghetti and serve.

Maccheroni alla napoletana

Macaroni with Neapolitan sauce
(Illustrated opposite, bottom right)

Serves 6–8

2 1/4 lbs/1 kg braising beef
6 tbsp olive oil
1 carrot, sliced
1/2 cup sliced green celery
2 onions, sliced
2 cloves of garlic, finely chopped
Salt and pepper
2 cups/500 ml dry white wine
4 tbsp tomato paste
1 lb/500 g macaroni
3/4 lb/300 g caciocavallo cheese (or mozzarella if not available), cut in slices
1 bunch of fresh basil
2 tbsp butter

Tie the beef in shape using kitchen string. Heat half the olive oil in a flameproof baking pan and brown the meat all over. Add the carrot, celery, onions, and garlic, and cook until soft, stirring occasionally. Season well. Gradually add some of the wine. Boil until reduced by half, then add the remaining wine. Stir in the tomato paste and about 2 cups/500 ml water, enough to just cover the meat. Cover partially, and cook the meat over a low heat for at least 3 hours. The juices should bubble only occasionally. Remove the meat; it can be served as the main course. Bring the sauce to a boil and season to taste with salt and pepper – it should be dark, creamy, and full of flavor. Crush the vegetables in the sauce using a fork. Break the macaroni into pieces about 2 in. (5 cm) long, and cook in copious water until *al dente*. Drain and mix with 2 tablespoons oil. Brush a large, flameproof baking dish with one tablespoon oil, and add a layer of pasta. Cover with a generous layer of meat sauce, and top with the cheese slices and basil leaves. Cover with another layer of macaroni, and proceed in the same way until all the ingredients have been used up. Reserve a few basil leaves. Finish with a layer of sauce, topped with knobs of butter. Bake in a preheated oven at 400 °F (200 °C) for about 10 minutes. Sprinkle with the reserved basil leaves, and serve immediately.

Pasta al pomodoro crudo

Pasta with raw tomatoes
(Illustrated opposite, bottom left)

14 oz/400 g cherry tomatoes
1 clove of garlic, chopped
1 tbsp chopped basil
Extra virgin olive oil
Salt and pepper
14 oz/400 g spaghetti or rigatoni
Oregano
1 tbsp chopped parsley

Mix the tomatoes, garlic, and basil together in a bowl. Add a generous amount of olive oil and season to taste with salt and pepper. Cook the pasta until *al dente*, drain, and add to the tomatoes. Sprinkle with the oregano and parsley, mix thoroughly, and serve immediately.

Southern Italy does not just provide tomatoes for its own people in the northern regions, but also exports them throughout the world. The tomato is an important commodity in the economy, and investments made by the major food companies go some way to helping to improve the chronically-strained economic situation in the south.

TOMATOES

The tomato has to be the Italians' favorite vegetable. They are served at mealtimes practically every day, no matter what the season, and in many guises: in pasta sauce, as a salad or accompaniment, or stuffed or stewed – Italian cooks are always coming up with something new. There are now around 5000 varieties of this typical Mediterranean fruit worldwide, and, particularly in the United States, breeders and biologists are in the process of developing new hybrids that are reported to be even more disease-resistant, quick-growing, and healthy.

Although the tomato had already reached Europe from the New World by the middle of the 16th century, it was not welcomed into the kitchen until 200 years later. Even in the kingdom of Naples, the red fruits were sometimes thought to be poisonous, and the plant was grown in ornamental gardens as an exotic novelty. The plants did not make it to the vegetable garden until about 1750 – well after people had discovered that the tasty *pomo d'oro*, the golden apple, fitted in extremely well with culinary traditions around Vesuvius. A carnival song from about this time even mentions the new delicacy.

Although the tomato was being cultivated in Campania by the middle of the 18th century, it had to wait a while longer to become the undisputed leader and hence the essential ingredient of southern Italian cuisine that it is today. However, vegetable growers gradually much improved the tomato through breeding, and cooks began to discover the versatility of this garden produce. From then on, there was no stopping people's enthusiasm for the tomato. Even the nickname for the people of Naples changed to take into account their new eating habits: until then, they had been called *mangiafoglie*, leaf eaters, but this changed to *mangiamaccheroni*, because now, instead of salad and vegetables, people ate mainly pasta served with tomato sauce.

Tomatoes can be harvested from summer to late autumn. However, Neapolitans did not want to be without them during the rest of the year either, so processes to preserve them began to develop. During the 19th century, Italian scientists wrote learned tracts earnestly debating the question of how to ensure a supply of tomatoes throughout the year.

It was not until the 20th century that a whole sector of industry grew up around the city at the foot of Vesuvius, specializing in the cultivation and processing of this member of the nightshade family. The region's best varieties were developed by optimum selection and breeding to produce high yields of top-quality tomatoes. The best-known tomato from Campania has to be the San Marzano. This brilliant red variety produces small, plum-shaped, juicy, fleshy fruits with thin skins and not many seeds. They are suitable both for industrial processing and all domestic uses.

Tomato concentrate or tomato paste (*concentrato di pomodoro*) provides extra tomato flavor.

Canned chopped tomatoes, *polpa di pomodoro*, are a basic ingredient for quick and easy tomato sauces.

Peeled tomatoes (*pomodori pelati*) usually need to be seeded and chopped before use.

Sieved tomatoes (*passata di pomodori*) are a thick tomato juice ready for use in the kitchen.

ITALIAN VARIETIES OF TOMATO

San Marzano
The elongated or oval fruits of the San Marzano variety are used for canning and drying or to make freshly prepared pasta sauces. Its flesh is sweet and firm.

Sorrento
This variety of the well-known San Marzano tomato is softer and is therefore used only to produce tomato preserves for export.

Casalino
Casalino is a small, sweet-flavored tomato that grows in clusters. It used to be stored in cellars, hanging from the ceiling, and kept throughout the winter.

Pomodoro di Cerignola
The Pomodoro di Cerignola belongs to the large group of cherry or cocktail tomatoes. It has a sweetish flavor, and can be eaten raw in salads, or cooked quickly in sauces.

Marena
Like other tomatoes from the south, the Marena variety is also wonderfully ripe, red, and sweet. However, it is very demanding in terms of growing conditions, and, in addition to a lot of sunshine, it also requires potash-rich soil.

Roma
The Roma variety also needs potash-rich soil, so it is typical of the tomatoes grown in southern Italy. It is very good for preserving, whether canned or dried.

Pachino
The Italian cocktail tomatoes, also called *ciliegini*, are named for the Sicilian town of Pachino, where the best tomatoes of this type are grown. The Pachino tomato has an intense and slightly sour flavor.

Perino
With its firm skin and flesh, the elongated Perino tomato is used in the food industry, and usually ends up in a can as *pomodoro pelato*, peeled tomatoes.

Sardo
This variety can be used in any dish, pan, or salad bowl. It ripens in winter, and is particularly good eaten raw. At present, attempts are being made to breed yellow tomatoes.

Ramato
This tomato got its name because it grows on *rami*, strong branches, with several glowing red fruits hanging from each one. The tomatoes can weigh up to five ounces (130 g) each. They are easy to peel and very versatile in the kitchen.

Napoli
This variety needs potash-rich soils as found in the volcanic soil around Vesuvius. It is somewhat smaller and rounder than the San Marzano tomato.

Palla di Fuoco
The Palla di Fuoco, fireball, is also a popular variety in the north. It makes a particularly good tomato salad or *Insalata mista* or mixed salad.

Cuore di Bue
A Cuore di Bue (ox heart) tomato can weigh over eight ounces (250 g). This variety is very fleshy, but has very few seeds. Cuore di Bue is an excellent salad tomato, and is only eaten raw. In northern Italy, it is also eaten while still green, when it contains more acid than when ripe. "Ox heart" tomatoes are delicious served with a little oil, salt, and pepper.

Homemade tomato preserves

There are so many top-quality products available through-out Italy that it is no longer really necessary to make tomato preserves *alla casalinga* (at home). However, in many regions of southern Italy, people often do still make them themselves. As tomatoes are used everyday in the kitchen, you need to have a correspondingly large supply if you want to survive the winter and spring without any seasonal shortages. Bottling the tasty red fruits and producing tomato paste are also very labor-intensive preserving methods. To cope with the glut of tomatoes in late summer, friends and neighbors all help each other make preserves for the winter. Afterwards, when the work is over, they have a cozy evening meal, where the latest local gossip and news are exchanged.

Preserving

Food preserved at home is not really sterilized, as it is in food factories at high pressure and high temperature, but only gently pasteurized by means of heat. To do this, the filled jars are stood "up to their necks" in water – in other words the water level must be higher than the level of the tomatoes inside the container, as this is the only way to ensure that the heat is distributed evenly. The water can also be salted to raise the boiling point and to pasteurize the tomatoes even more effectively. Wrap the jars in cloths or strips of newspaper to prevent them from knocking against each other and shattering. Cook over a medium heat for about 40 minutes, longer if the containers are very large. Once pasteurized, leave the jars in the water to cool. Make sure that all lids are firmly on and are airtight, then store the preserves in a cool, dry place.

Pomodori pelati – peeled tomatoes

Washing, skinning, and preserving freshly picked tomatoes can easily be a full day's work. As well as energetic support, you will also need a lot of water to wash the fruits before processing them further, a great many clean, dry glass jars with close-fitting lids, some large slotted spoons, and big pots and pans for sterilizing the preserves.
First blanch the tomatoes for about ten seconds in boiling water, then refresh under cold water to loosen the skin from

the flesh. Put the skinned tomatoes in the prepared glass jars in tightly-packed layers to prevent air bubbles forming. Add some basil leaves to make the preserved tomatoes delight-fully fragrant. Place the filled jars in the pans of hot water.

Passata di pomodoro – homemade tomato paste

To make a good stock of homemade tomato paste, it is important to select the best and juiciest fruits. Dice them coarsely, and boil fiercely over a low heat in a large pan with basil and salt to produce a thick sauce. Fortunately, you need no longer pass the steaming mass through a sieve, but can use a turn-handle food mill, which retains the skins, seeds and stalks just as quickly and effectively. Fill the prepared jars to the brim with the paste and seal well. Then pasteurize in the same way as for *pomodori pelati*.

Pasta al pomodoro cotto
Pasta with tomato sauce

7 TBSP OLIVE OIL
I CUP CHOPPED ONION
I 3/4 LBS/750 G TOMATOES, SKINNED
I TBSP CHOPPED BASIL
SALT AND FRESHLY MILLED BLACK PEPPER
I4 OZ/400 G SPAGHETTI
GRATED PARMESAN OR PECORINO CHEESE

Heat the olive oil in a heavy skillet and fry the chopped onion until translucent. Add the chopped tomatoes and basil. Season to taste with salt and pepper. Cook over a low heat for 30 minutes.
Boil the spaghetti in copious salted water until *al dente*, then drain. Arrange the pasta on plates, pour over the tomato sauce, and sprinkle with cheese.

Zuppa di pomodoro
Tomato soup

2 I/4 LBS/I KG FRESH RIPE TOMATOES
3–4 TBSP OLIVE OIL
2 CUPS CHOPPED ONION
3 CLOVES OF GARLIC
I BOUQUET GARNI (A FEW SPRIGS OF PARSLEY, ROSEMARY, MARJORAM, BASIL, THYME, AND SAGE TIED TOGETHER WITH KITCHEN STRING)
I I/4 CUPS/I/4 LITER MEAT OR VEGETABLE STOCK
SALT
FRESHLY MILLED PEPPER
4 TBSP CREAM (OPTIONAL)

Blanch, skin, seed, and dice the tomatoes. Heat the olive oil in a heavy-bottomed pan and fry the onions until translucent. Add the garlic and fry briefly. Add the tomatoes and bouquet garni, and simmer gently for 30–45 minutes. Remove the bouquet garni and pass the resultant tomato pulp through a sieve. Add the meat stock, and bring the soup to the boil. Season to taste with salt and freshly milled pepper. Beat the cream until stiff, and garnish each bowl of soup with a spoonful (optional).

In this age of factory-produced canned food, home-preserved vegetables are a luxury that is easy to make and tastes delicious.

Cleanliness is the most important requirement. Boil the preserving jar and the sealing ring in bubbling water.

Cut a cross in the top of the tomatoes using a small, sharp cooking knife.

Carefully place the tomatoes in very hot, but not boiling water using a large perforated spoon.

Remove the tomatoes from the water as soon as the skins start to peel back and become detached from the flesh.

Now carefully peel the tomatoes. The less the damage to the flesh, the more appetizing the result.

Place the skinned tomatoes in layers in the preserving jar. To give flavor, add some basil or bay leaves (optional).

Fill the jars with water or a mixture of vinegar and water. It is important to cover the tomatoes completely.

Above: Cook the tomatoes in boiling water to preserve them.

Below: Homemade *pomodori pelati* will actually keep for a few months, but, as with other homemade preserved foods, they must be stored in a cool, dry place, and checked regularly in order to ensure that they are still in perfect condition.

TOMATOES FOR WINTER

To have a supply of fresh whole tomatoes even in winter, people hang small, round bush tomatoes, picked when still green, to ripen and then dry in a well-ventilated place protected from the rain. In winter, nearly all balconies and windows in Campania are adorned with red garlands of tomatoes. With their intense flavor, these dried fruits can be used to make tomato sauces or to enrich soups.

Pomodori secchi – sun-dried tomatoes

Unlike *pomodori pelati* and *passata di pomodoro*, *pomodori secchi* are relatively quick to prepare. Halve the very ripe fruits, which should not be too big, season lightly with salt, place on a wire rack, and leave them to their own devices in a sunny spot. After only a few days, the juicy fruits will have shriveled up, and can then be put in good-quality olive oil or in a spice mixture of your own to preserve their concentrated flavor. If you do not have enough space or do not want to dry them yourself for any other reason, you can buy the ready-dried items on the market – for dried tomatoes preserved using *mamma's* or *nonna's* recipe are an essential part of winter in Campania.

Below: Sun-dried tomatoes can be preserved in oil with garlic and herbs. They make a tasty morsel in winter, bringing a taste of summer back to your taste buds. Drain slightly before serving with very fresh bread.

PIZZA

The origins of pizza can be traced back to the Romans, when they baked a type of focaccia bread known as *picea*. At the end of the first millennium and the beginning of the second, the name *piza* had already become accepted, although the flat, round thing produced from the early medieval oven still looked very like an ordinary flat cake. It was a long time before the genuine Neapolitan pizza with tomato sauce, anchovies, capers, and mozzarella came into being. In his book, *Usi e costumi di Napoli e contorni* (Manners and customs of Naples and the surrounding area), published in 1858, Emanuele Rocco describes something much more like the culinary bestseller we know today. Rocco's pizza recipe states tersely that you could cover a piece of dough rolled out into a flat, round shape using a rolling pin or the hands, with "anything that came into your head," add oil or lard, and then bake in the oven. He then lists the various ingredients – chopped garlic, grated cheese, a few basil leaves, thin slices of fish, and a few slices of mozzarella cheese – and goes on to mention that the covered dough could be folded over in half to make what we would now call pizza calzone.

This 19th-century text also mentions the pizza bakeries that traditionally exuded such a seductive aroma that even Naples' crowned heads could not resist it. To find out what was so good about this new specialty, contrary to all the rules of protocol, the Bourbon king Ferdinand I went to see the bakery of a certain Antonio Testa, and immediately acquired the taste. As the queen was anything but enthusiastic about her husband's passion for pizza, the king was forced to disguise himself as an ordinary citizen to sneak into the city's pizzerias. The circular delicacy did not become acceptable in the salons until the rule of the next

LEAVING HOME – OUT OF NECESSITY

It is generally known that even today southern Italy is still one of the poorer regions of Italy, but toward the end of the 19th century there was regular starvation. Farmland produced very little and, because of the weak industrial infrastructure, jobs were few and far between. It therefore comes as no surprise that between 1899 and 1910 about two million people from southern Italy could no longer see any alternative but to leave their homeland and try their luck on the other side of the Atlantic – in the United States of America.

About 500,000 new arrivals stayed in New York and gradually created a quarter there that soon became known as Little Italy. The Italian families, feeling very homesick, stuck closely together and made great efforts to keep their old traditions alive. One of these was the culinary art that the people brought with them from Naples, Bari, and Sicily. The Italian immigrants then tried their hand – with

In 1923, 2447 Italian emigrants reach New York by ship.

great success – at importing sausage, cheese, and ham from their homeland. Others pushed handcarts through the streets of New York, selling excellent fruit and vegetables. In 1930, the then mayor, Fiorello La Guardia, banned the sale of food in the open air, but this did not stop the Italian dealers from their activities. Many had now saved up enough money to buy a small store. However, the trade in imported goods was not to remain the sole area of business in which the Italians emerged. In 1905, Gennaro Lombardi opened the first pizzeria in New York. The flat cake of dough, with its delicious toppings, became an overnight success, and many other *pizzaioli* followed Lombardi's example.

Pizza dough is made from flour, yeast, water, and salt. It is important to give it enough time to rise.

Divide the dough, which should be beautifully elastic and not too firm, into equal, pizza-sized portions.

Press the portions of dough flat using the palms of the hands or alternatively a rolling pin.

Any combination of toppings is possible. Here, diced tomato and peppers are first arranged on the dough…

… followed by cubes of mozzarella. Other cheeses can also be used, such as ricotta or parmesan.

Drizzle a little olive oil over the finished pizza before placing it in the oven.

Bourbon monarch. When Ferdinand II commissioned Don Domenico Testa, another famous *pizzaiolo* (pizza-maker), to practice his art in honor of the ladies of the court in the garden of the magnificent Capodimonte estate, he could be sure of the full support of his wife. Don Domenico's pizza sent the king into such raptures that he granted the pizzamaker the title *monzù*. In 18th-century Naples, this honorable title, a corruption of the French word *monsieur*, was actually reserved for the French *chefs de cuisine* who worked in the rich households. Ferdinand II is said to have been so fond of the dishes from Campania – especially pizza – that he had special pizza ovens built right by the palace, so that he could treat himself and his guests to this delicacy whenever he wanted.

After the Bourbons, the House of Savoy gained the ascendancy in 1861. Italy was on the way toward national unification and, when they visited the city at the foot of Vesuvius in 1889, Umberto I and his wife Margherita were received with great honor. When the queen asked for a pizza, the pizzamaker Raffaele Esposito baked a creation using green basil, white mozzarella, and red tomatoes, these being the national colors of the emerging state, and called the result Pizza Margherita in her honor.

Surprisingly, for a long time pizza remained a regional specialty. Other products from Campania spread slowly but surely to the north. The dough base with its delicious toppings that people bought as they passed the street pizzamakers and ate as a little snack between meals, first made a detour via New York, for it was there that the first Neapolitan pizzeria was opened in 1905. The little store was destined to achieve great success. By the 1960s, pizza had become established not only in the United States, but was also eagerly devoured in northern Europe. It was only in Italy – with the exception of Naples – that pizza was still unknown. This nutritious snack did not make its entrance into Rome and the northern parts of Italy until the 1970s and 1980s. Now, however, pizza is even mentioned in the Guinness Book of Records. The pizzamakers' guild regularly organizes competitions in which the most talented *pizzaioli* are rewarded not only for unusual creations but also for their sometimes acrobatic skills when throwing the thin, flat cakes of dough into the air and catching them again.

Today, pizza is eaten throughout the world, and has perhaps even overtaken spaghetti as being a foreigner's idea of "genuine Italian" food. Even in the most remote European small towns, there is at least one pizzeria, and in the large cities a whole army of lively pizza couriers advertises for custom with brightly-colored flyers. In the United States, whole chains specialize in this round delicacy from the Old World – even if they are sometimes very fanciful and not always orthodox Italian creations. The supermarkets sell all types of frozen pizza in a wide price range. And if you want to try out your own skills at being a *pizzaiolo*, your local market is sure to sell the necessary ingredients, such as flour, yeast, water, salt, tomatoes, mozzarella, capers, salted anchovies, and possibly oregano and basil.

Pizza dough

1 3/4 CAKES/30 G COMPRESSED YEAST (IF USING ACTIVE DRY YEAST, FOLLOW THE MAKER'S INSTRUCTIONS)
1/2 CUP/125 ML HAND-HOT WATER
4 CUPS/500 G ALL-PURPOSE FLOUR
1/2 TSP SALT
FLOUR FOR ROLLING OUT
OLIVE OIL

Dissolve the yeast in a little hand-hot water in a small bowl. Add 2–3 tablespoons flour and mix to a smooth paste. Cover with a cloth and leave in a warm place for 30 minutes.
Preheat the oven to about 475 °F (250 °C).
Sift the remaining flour on to the worktop, and combine with the paste. Add a little salt, and knead thoroughly to form a firm but soft dough. Continue to knead the dough for 10 minutes until it becomes very elastic, gradually adding hand-hot water. Divide the dough into 4 equal pieces, dredge with flour, cover and leave to rise in a warm place for about 2 hours. Roll out the pieces, and press out on a floured surface either by hand or using a rolling pin to form ¼-in. (0.5-cm) thick bases. Grease a baking sheet with oil, place the pizza bases on top, and add toppings of your choice. Bake for 15–20 minutes.

Left: Pizza tastes best when baked in a wood-fired stone oven, because only then will the necessary temperature of about 750 °F (400 °C) be achieved. The pizza is ready for serving when the base is crisp and crusty, and the cheese has melted thoroughly.

PIZZA ALLA NAPOLETANA
Neapolitan pizza

3–4/160 G VERY RIPE TOMATOES
8 SALTED ANCHOVIES
4 OZ/120 G MOZZARELLA
1 TBSP OREGANO
4 TBSP EXTRA VIRGIN OLIVE OIL

Skin, seed, and dice the tomatoes. Rinse the anchovies, and remove any bones. Dice the mozzarella. Arrange the ingredients on the pizza base (see p. 345), sprinkle with oregano, and drizzle with olive oil.

PIZZA ALLE CIPOLLE
Onion pizza

2–3/100 G VERY RIPE TOMATOES
2 ONIONS
12 ANCHOVY FILETS
16 BLACK OLIVES, PITTED
16 CAPERS
8 BASIL LEAVES
4 TBSP EXTRA VIRGIN OLIVE OIL

Skin, seed, and dice the tomatoes. Slice the onions into rings and sauté in a little olive oil in a skillet. Add the remaining ingredients, except for the basil leaves. Spread the mixture over the pizza base (see p. 345), and sprinkle over the basil leaves.

PIZZA MARGHERITA
Pizza with tomatoes, mozzarella, and basil

6 OZ/150 G MOZZARELLA
2–3/100 G VERY RIPE TOMATOES
12 BASIL LEAVES
3 TBSP EXTRA VIRGIN OLIVE OIL
SALT AND PEPPER

Dice the mozzarella. Skin, seed, and dice the tomatoes. Arrange the mozzarella and tomatoes on the pizza base (see p. 345), drizzle with olive oil, and season with salt and pepper.

PIZZA AGLIO, OLIO E PEPERONCINO
Pizza with garlic, oil, and peperoncini

4 TBSP GARLIC, SLICED
1 TBSP OREGANO
2 PEPERONCINI, FINELY CHOPPED
3 TBSP EXTRA VIRGIN OLIVE OIL

Arrange the garlic, oregano, and peperoncini on the pizza base (see p. 345). Drizzle with olive oil.

PIZZA AL PROSCIUTTO
Pizza with ham

2–3/100 G VERY RIPE TOMATOES
6 OZ/150 G RICOTTA CHEESE
3–4 SLICES/150 G BOILED HAM
2 TBSP EXTRA VIRGIN OLIVE OIL

Skin, seed, and dice the tomatoes. Crumble the ricotta, and chop the ham into small pieces. Arrange on the pizza base (see p. 345), and drizzle with olive oil.

PIZZA ALLA PARMIGIANA
Parmesan pizza

2–3/100 G VERY RIPE TOMATOES
3 OZ/80 G PARMESAN
6 OZ/150 G RICOTTA CHEESE
3 TBSP EXTRA VIRGIN OLIVE OIL
SALT

Skin, seed, and dice the tomatoes. Slice the parmesan, and crumble the ricotta. Arrange the ingredients on the pizza base (see p. 345). Drizzle with olive oil, and season lightly with salt.

PIZZA AI FORMAGGI
Four-cheese pizza

2 OZ/60 G PROVOLONE CHEESE
2 OZ/60 G PARMESAN
2 OZ/60 G GRUYÈRE CHEESE
2 OZ/60 G PECORINO CHEESE
2–3/100 G VERY RIPE TOMATOES
4 TBSP EXTRA VIRGIN OLIVE OIL
SALT

Slice the cheeses. Skin, seed, and dice the tomatoes. Arrange the ingredients on the pizza base (see p. 345). Drizzle with olive oil, and season with salt.

PIZZA ALLA RUCOLA
Pizza with arugula

2–3/100 G VERY RIPE TOMATOES
SMALL BUNCH/80 G ARUGULA
4 OZ/100 G SMOKED SCAMORZA CHEESE
2–3 SLICES/80 G SMOKED BACON
3 TBSP EXTRA VIRGIN OLIVE OIL

Skin, seed, and dice the tomatoes. Rinse the arugula, and thinly slice the scamorza and bacon. Arrange all the ingredients on the pizza base (see p. 345), and drizzle with olive oil.

Tasty tomatoes for pizzas

Traditional pizza recipes often specify fresh, very ripe tomatoes. In central and northern Europe, however, these can often be hard to come by in winter. *Pomodori pelati*, peeled tomatoes in a can, provide a good and time-saving alternative if drained before use. Alternatively, you can also make a sauce using fried onions, chopped tomatoes, tomato paste, and oregano.

Pizza alla salsiccia
Pizza with pork sausage

2–3/100 G VERY RIPE TOMATOES
8 OZ/200 G MOZZARELLA, DICED
4 OZ/100 G SALSICCIA SAUSAGE, FINELY SLICED
2 OZ/40 G PECORINO CHEESE, DICED
3 TBSP EXTRA VIRGIN OLIVE OIL

Skin, seed, and dice the tomatoes. Dice the mozzarella, cut the sausage into thin slices and mince the pecorino. Arrange the ingredients on the pizza base (see p. 345), and drizzle with olive oil.

Calzone ripieno al forno
Folded pizza

2–3/100 G VERY RIPE TOMATOES
8 OZ/200 G RICOTTA CHEESE
6 OZ/150 G MOZZARELLA
4 OZ/100 G SALAMI, IN A PIECE
3–4 TBSP CHOPPED BASIL
3 TBSP OLIVE OIL
SALT AND PEPPER
1/2 CUP/50 G PARMESAN CHEESE, GRATED

Skin, seed, and dice the tomatoes, then arrange them on the pizza base (see p. 345). Crumble the ricotta, finely dice the mozzarella and salami, and combine with the ricotta and basil. Add the olive oil and beat until smooth. Season with salt and pepper. Arrange the mixture on the pizza base and sprinkle with grated parmesan. Fold the pizza over to form a semicircle and press together well at the edges.

Pizza alle vongole
Pizza with clams

2–3/100 G VERY RIPE TOMATOES
1 LB/500 G CLAMS
4 TBSP EXTRA VIRGIN OLIVE OIL
1 CLOVE OF GARLIC, CHOPPED
1 SMALL BUNCH OF PARSLEY, CHOPPED
1 TSP OREGANO
FRESHLY MILLED PEPPER

Skin, seed, and dice the tomatoes, and arrange them on the pizza base (see p. 345). Bake the pizza. Scrub the clams carefully and cook with 3 tablespoons olive oil, garlic, and parsley in a pan with no water for about 5 minutes, until the shells open. Discard any shells that do not open. Remove the clam flesh and keep warm in the juices.
Arrange the clams over the baked pizza, and sprinkle with oregano and pepper.

Pizza alle cozze
Pizza with mussels
(Illustrated below)

1 LB/500 G MUSSELS
1/2 CUP/80 G POTATOES, PEELED AND DICED
2–3/100 G VERY RIPE TOMATOES
8 OZ/200 G RICOTTA CHEESE
3 TBSP EXTRA VIRGIN OLIVE OIL
SALT AND FRESHLY MILLED BLACK PEPPER

Scrub the mussels carefully and cook for about 5 minutes, without adding any water, until the shells have opened fully. Discard any unopened mussels. Remove the mussel flesh and keep warm in the juices. Boil the diced potatoes in salted water. Skin, seed, and dice the tomatoes. Arrange the tomatoes, ricotta, potatoes, and mussels on the pizza base (see p. 345), drizzle with olive oil, and season with salt and pepper.

Throughout southern Italy you can still see foldaway mobile stalls. However, their numbers are dwindling as new supermarkets open.

MUSSELS AND OTHER SEAFOOD

Typically Neapolitan oyster stalls used to be a common sight near trattorias and restaurants or at other strategic points in the city. The brightly-colored wooden constructions were usually decorated with picturesque illustrations of the Gulf of Naples or Vesuvius, and bore the inscription *ostricaro fisico*, strong oyster seller. We have to look back to Ferdinand II to find an explanation of this odd title. On seeing a well-built Neapolitan man when visiting the fishing village of Santa Lucia, the Bourbon king is said to have exclaimed, "tu si nu fisico" ("You have the body of an athlete"). Flattered, the oyster seller rushed to write the title granted him by the king on his store sign. Naturally, his colleagues did not want to miss out, and they have all been "muscular" or "athletic" oyster sellers, thus *ostricari fisici*, ever since.

Although many restaurants have once again made oysters their specialty, fishmongers now sell not only oysters, but also other shellfish such as mussels, sea truffles, clams, and sea urchins. All seafood is extremely good for most people's health as, in addition to valuable protein, it contains iodine and other minerals, trace elements, and unsaturated fatty acids. To enjoy seafood without any unpleasant repercussions, it must be top-quality and absolutely fresh. Crustaceans and shellfish must come from perfectly clean waters, particularly if they are to be eaten raw. If you are not happy about this, just choose recipes where they need to be cooked.

It would be hard to imagine Neapolitan cuisine without *cozze*, but mussels should be bought from a reliable supplier and cleaned meticulously before they are cooked. They are sold in plastic nets that should clearly display the obligatory certificate of health and proof of having been cleaned already. Even so, you should still rinse them thoroughly in cold water when you get them home. You then remove the beard, *bisso* in Italian, which has held the creature underwater on the mussel bed. Use a small, sharp knife for this, taking care not to injure the mussel. You can also use this little knife to scrape off any deposits on the mussel shell. When you have completed this process, wash the mussels again. The mussels can make it to the pan only when the rinsing water stays really clear. Cleaning the mussels may sound time-consuming, but it is actually quite quick, now that breeders and dealers have modern brushing equipment with which to pre-clean the mussels thoroughly.

Like the other beautiful bays in Campania, the Gulf of Naples also has quite a few tasty fish to offer in addition to mussels and other seafood. The surprisingly fleshy, lively little anchovy that darts about in these waters is said to be the only one that can be served *au gratin* in a ramekin dish, or even just simply fried with green pepper in olive oil. Moreover, fish from Neapolitan waters have their own natural "seal of freshness." Before rigor mortis sets in, the fishermen arrange the red fish and sea bass they have caught into a curve before placing them in the fishmongers' baskets. This way the customer can tell that they are absolutely freshly caught, because in older fish, rigor mortis would already have set in and the body would have returned to its natural position.

Even the Romans preferred fish from the gulf, and Lucullus, the proven culinary pioneer, even had his own fish-breeding business in Naples. When Emperor Tiberius stayed on Capri, he ordered the fishermen to bring him their best catches. There were rumors of giant barbs that were literally worth their weight in gold. The Neapolitans also remember the Romans' deplorably cruel, if as yet historically unproven custom of keeping morays in sea-water basins and allegedly feeding them on the flesh of pitiful slaves.

Fritto misto di mare
Fried mixed seafood
(Illustrated below and left)

1 LB/500 G SMALL FRESH SQUID
4 SMALL RED MULLET, 4 OZ/100 G EACH
SALT
1 LB/500 G FRESH ANCHOVIES OR VERY SMALL SARDINES
ABOUT 1/2 LB/250 G JUMBO SHRIMP
OLIVE OIL FOR FRYING
2 CLOVES OF GARLIC
FLOUR TO COAT
2–3 LEMONS

To remove the ink sack, insides, head, and triangular "fin"
inside the body of the squid, pull off the membranes, pull
the tentacles and the insides out of the body, and cut off just
behind the head. Wash and pat dry. If the squid are quite
large, cut the body into rings.
Scale and gut the red mullet, then cut off the heads and fins.
Rinse under running water and pat dry using paper towels.
Season with salt.
Carefully scale and gut the anchovies (or sardines), then
remove all fins apart from the tail fin. If the fish are very
small, they can be eaten with their heads on. Wash and pat
dry using paper towels. Season with salt.
Pull off the heads of the shrimp, and remove the intestines.
Leave the scales and tail on. Alternatively, you can remove
the skins completely, toss the shrimp in some flour, and
then sauté.
Heat a generous quantity of olive oil in a deep skillet or
french-fry pan. Add the garlic. Test the temperature of the
oil by dipping in the handle of a wooden spoon. The oil has
reached the correct temperature when small bubbles begin
to rise. Remove the garlic before frying.
Lightly coat the squid with flour, and deep fry in portions
until crispy. Drain on paper towels, and keep warm in a
preheated oven at 300 °F (150 °C).
Lightly coat the fish in flour. Add to the hot oil a few at a
time, and sauté until crispy. The red mullet will need about
3–4 minutes, the anchovies 2 minutes. Remove the fried
fish using a slotted spoon, and leave to drain on paper
towels. Keep them warm in the oven.
Unshelled shrimp do not need to be tossed in flour before
deep-frying. Toss peeled shrimp in flour, and then sauté.
Drain well on paper towels.
Cover a large serving platter with thick white paper
napkins. Arrange the fish and seafood on top, and sprinkle
with salt. Cut the lemons into wedges, arrange on the plate,
and serve immediately.

Impepata di cozze
Mussels in their juice
(Illustrated right and behind)

2 1/4 LBS/1 KG MUSSELS
1 PEPERONCINO, DICED
2 TBSP CHOPPED PARSLEY
1 LEMON
8 SLICES OF WHITE BREAD, TOASTED

Scrub and wash the mussels, then cook them in a pan in a
little water with the peperoncino until their shells open.
Discard any unopened mussels. Remove the mussel flesh
from the shells, and strain the mussel juice through a fine
sieve. Return the mussels to the juice, and cook for a
further 3 minutes. Sprinkle with parsley and lemon juice
(optional). Serve with toasted white bread.

Acciughe all'origano
Sardines with oregano
(Illustrated below, front right)

1 3/4 LBS/800 G SARDINES
5–6 TBSP EXTRA VIRGIN OLIVE OIL
1 TBSP WHITE WINE VINEGAR
2 TBSP CHOPPED PARSLEY
1 TBSP OREGANO
2 CLOVES OF GARLIC, CHOPPED
SALT AND PEPPER

Bone and thoroughly clean the fish. Remove the heads.
Place the sardines in layers in a flameproof ceramic baking
dish greased with a little olive oil. Mix together the olive
oil, white wine vinegar, parsley, oregano, and garlic. Season
with salt and pepper, and pour over the sardines. Bake in a
preheated oven at 340 °F (170°C) for about 15 minutes.
Serve the sardines warm or cold.

Front and right: *Acciughe all'origano* – Sardines with oregano
Front and left: *Fritto misto di mare* – Fried mixed seafood
Behind: *Impepata di cozze* – Mussels in their juice

Polpi di scoglio alla luciana
Santa Lucia octopus

2 READY-PREPARED OCTOPUS, 14 OZ/400 G EACH
1 CLOVE OF GARLIC, CHOPPED
3–4 TABLESPOONS EXTRA VIRGIN OLIVE OIL
1–2 RIPE TOMATOES
1/2 PEPERONCINO
1 TABLESPOON CHOPPED PARSLEY
SALT AND PEPPER
JUICE OF 1 LEMON
CHOPPED PARSLEY TO FINISH

Thoroughly clean and tenderize the octopus. Sauté the
garlic in a pan with the olive oil, then add the octopus.
Blanch, skin, and dice the tomatoes. Add to the octopus
with the peperoncino and parsley. Season with salt and
pepper. Cover with a close-fitting lid, so that no steam can
escape. Simmer over a low heat for about 2 hours, shaking
the pan occasionally to prevent the octopus from sticking.
Serve the octopus hot, warm, or cold sprinkled with lemon
juice and chopped parsley.

Smoked mozzarella

Ricotta

Fresh ricotta

Mozzarella in brine

There are many different varieties of mozzarella and ricotta fresh soft cheeses. Mozzarella is usually sold as a snow-white ball, but it is also sometimes gently smoked. You can get ricotta as a young, mild cheese, but it can also be cured and pressed, and then bought at different stages of maturity.

Genuine mozzarella is made from the milk of the black water buffalo. It is left to stand for about 20 minutes before the fresh curds are cut.

To attain mozzarella's characteristic consistency, nearly-boiling water is poured over the crumbled curds, which are then kneaded by hand.

The mixture must be sufficiently elastic for threads to be pulled without ripping. Mozzarella can also be described as a *pasta-filata* cheese because of its paste-like consistency.

The cheesemaker divides the mixture into equal portions. This process is known as *mozzatura* and gave the tasty fresh soft cheese its name.

The portions of mixture are shaped quickly and skillfully into large or small balls or made into braids. You can also find other mozzarella shapes in certain specialist dairy produce stores.

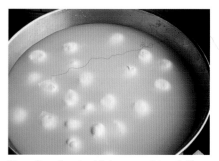

Mozzarella can be enjoyed fresh as soon as it is made. If you wish to keep the balls of cheese, you should lay them in whey brine, but even then they will keep for only a few days at most.

MOZZARELLA

Fresh mozzarella is extremely perishable. It is at its best when eaten *di giornata*, on the day it was made. If kept in whey at a suitably cool temperature, it will keep for a few days. If you need to keep it for longer, or want to transport it even just to northern Italy, never mind farther afield, the only solution is to seal the small, white balls in brine-filled plastic bags. Until modern food technology made such processes possible, mozzarella was really only a regional pleasure for gourmets in Campania and Apulia. It is not surprising that the milky cheese has given some national dishes from this region their distinctive character. It would be hard to imagine Neapolitan pizza without deliciously soft, melted mozzarella. The same is true for Capri's very Italian-looking combination of green basil, white cheese, and red tomatoes.

As with any other cheese, mozzarella is produced by first separating the milk using rennet. The curds this produces are then roughly chopped into pieces, and heated to between 180 and 190 °F (80 and 90 °C). The cheesemaker now stirs and kneads the steaming mass until it forms an elastic paste from which he can draw out long threads. The paste is then divided into equal-sized portions. This process is called *mozzatura* (cutting or chopping off), and gave the cheese its name. The individual portions of paste are formed into balls, braids, or other shapes.

As a result of the great demand for this fresh soft cheese, it is now also made from cow's milk. Strictly speaking, in this case it should not be called mozzarella, but *fior di latte* or *fiordellatte* (milk flower). The genuine, traditional variety, on the other hand, is made from the milk of the black water buffalo, which is kept in large herds mainly on the fertile plain of the Volturno river northwest of Naples and in the triangle between Salerno, Eboli, and Paestum. In 1993, the *mozzarella di bufala campana* mark of origin gained official recognition, and was given a DOC rating. It is produced not only in Campania, but also in provinces in Lazio, and the Foggia region in Apulia. Authentic mozzarella cheese can be recognized by the protection consortium's quality mark.

Mozzarella is also known as a *pasta-filata* cheese, because of its thread-producing properties. Specialties such as *provolo* and *caciocavallo*, which are made in the same way, also come under this category. *Provola* is made from the mozzarella mixture, which is then smoked and left to mature for a while. *Caciocavallo* is a cow's milk cheese that can be eaten when relatively fresh or left for up to a year. In southern Italy, people like to grate the older cheese and use it instead of pecorino romano or parmesan.

MOZZARELLA IN A CARRIAGE

Mozzarella in carrozza, mozzarella in a carriage, is really one of the most traditional dishes of Campania. However, the specialty can now be found on pizzeria menus throughout Italy, where *mozzarella in carrozza* is usually made with white sliced bread and *fior di latte*, a cow's milk mozzarella. But that is not really how it should be. The original recipe from Campania specifies stale bread from the local bakery and genuine buffalo milk mozzarella. The difference between these two methods could not be greater. Buffalo milk mozzarella has a higher fat content and is less watery, with the result that it stays between the slices of bread when fried, and does not leak out, making the whole dish look rather unappetizing, as often happens with *fior di latte*.

MOZZARELLA IN CARROZZA
Fried mozzarella sandwiches
(Illustrated above)

3 EGGS
SALT
MILK
1 LB/500 G STALE BREAD
1 1/2 LBS/700 G MOZZARELLA
ALL-PURPOSE FLOUR
OIL FOR DEEP-FRYING

Beat the eggs in a bowl together with some salt and a little milk. Cut the bread into 24 slices, each about ½ in. (1 cm) thick. Cut the mozzarella into 12 equal pieces. Place one piece of mozzarella between two slices of bread to make 12 sandwiches. Coat each sandwich in flour, and soak in the egg mixture until it has absorbed as much liquid as possible. Sauté in very hot oil until golden brown, and serve hot.

The Vannulo cheese dairy in Capaccio near Salerno has its own buffalo herd. Of almost 250 animals, only seven are bulls. The Vannulo cheese dairy produces genuine *mozzarella di bufala* by traditional methods. The mozzarella you get from the supermarket, on the other hand, is made from cow's milk and should really be called *fior di latte* (milk flower).

CAPRI

Capri has long been a top tourist attraction. Even Homer sang the praises of the island, giving it the name Antheomoessa (land of blossom). The Greek colonialists called it Capros (wild boar, as suggested by its shape). The Romans named it Capraea (rough, rocky island) or Insula Sirenussae (island of the sirens), and for Emperor Tiberius it was simply the Apragopolis, a land of sweet, carefree idleness. All these attributes reflect the contrasts that make up the unparalleled attraction of the sometimes rugged, sometimes gentle island of Capri. Even now, these icons of the superior Italy tourist trade have lost none of their charm and splendor. In the *alta stagione*, the high season in August, well-to-do Capri lovers meet year after year for a fashionable vacation, and the informal meetings of the rich and beautiful are just as important a part of the plan as the calorific sins that they will commit. There is nothing meager about the start of the day on Capri. You can choose from fragrant brioche buns, so big that they could have been used as props in any Fellini film, succulent croissants or the *babà*, a rich yeast bun specialty served with rum, cream, or cherries. Champagne, carpano with orange juice, peppermint tea, or bay leaf, myrtle, or lemon liqueurs ring in a night on Capri. The hours in between are filled with equally tempting culinary delights. At midday, people prefer trattorias, which promise a breath of fresh air and relaxation combined with good, solid cooking. Here, chefs serve *bombolotti*, little pasta parcels oozing cheese and tomatoes, baked mussels and sea dates, or fish cooked in seawater or *acqua pazza*, crazy water, as they say in Capri. Around the swimming pool, visitors nibble croquettes, artichokes, and totano-calmare with potatoes. Alternatively, they sample the typical pasta dishes of the island: *spaghetti aumm aumm* (with basil, mozzarella, and eggplant) and *spaghetti sciuè sciuè* (served with the delicious cocktail tomatoes grown on Capri, fried with some garlic and red peperoncini). After a sun-drenched day on the beach, you can relax with a cup of tea under the large, white shades, quench your thirst with a freshly squeezed orange juice, or treat yourself to an exquisite *granita* at one of the many refreshment kiosks. In the evening, high-flying tourists prefer to go to an "in" restaurant – not just to eat, but also to see and be seen. Here the rich and beautiful like to dine out on *ravioli capresi*, undisputedly the national dish of this romantic island. So many gourmets and cooks have now fallen in love with this dish, that the various recipes in circulation are all convincingly declared to be the original. Of course, how to prepare it is a matter of individual taste, but to make genuine *ravioli capresi*, you need to follow two basic principles: The pasta dough must always be made without egg (the egg goes with the cheese), and the filling is always based on fresh *caciotta*. Purists insist that it must be *caciotta* from Capri. Other cooks prefer a mixture of *caciotta caprese*, *caciotta romana*, and parmesan.

Above: The *Grotta Azzura*, the Blue Grotto, owes its name to the blue reflected light on the rock walls. Two Germans, August Kopisch and Ernst Fries, explored the cave in 1826. When they returned home, they told people how beautiful it was, and Capri became a dream destination.

Ravioli capresi
Ravioli from Capri
(Illustrated opposite, bottom left)

8 CUPS/1 KG ALL-PURPOSE FLOUR
2/3 CUP/150 ML OLIVE OIL

For the filling:
4 CACIOTTE CAPRESI (SOFT CHEESE FROM CAPRI)
1/2 CACIOTTA ROMANA (SOFT CHEESE FROM ROME)
1/2 CUP/50 G GRATED PARMESAN
1 EGG
PEPPER
MARJORAM

Knead the flour with sufficient boiling water to produce a smooth dough. Gradually incorporate the olive oil. Wrap the dough in a damp cloth and set aside. To make the filling, cut the soft cheese into small pieces. Combine with the parmesan cheese, egg, pepper, and marjoram. Roll the dough out thinly into a rectangle. Cut in half. Place small dollops of filling on one half, roughly 2 in. (5 cm) apart. Cover with the remaining half, and press down lightly around the mounds. Cut out small squares using a pasta cutter. Cook for about 5 minutes in lots of salted water. Serve with tomato sauce.

Insalata caprese
Tomatoes, mozzarella, and basil
(Illustrated behind)

4 LARGE TOMATOES
9 OZ/250 G BUFFALO MILK MOZZARELLA
BASIL OR OREGANO
FRESHLY MILLED BLACK PEPPER
EXTRA VIRGIN OLIVE OIL.

Slice the tomatoes and mozzarella, and arrange alternately on plates or a serving dish, so that they overlap slightly. Arrange small fresh basil leaves or oregano on top, and sprinkle with pepper. Drizzle with plenty of olive oil, and serve with white bread.

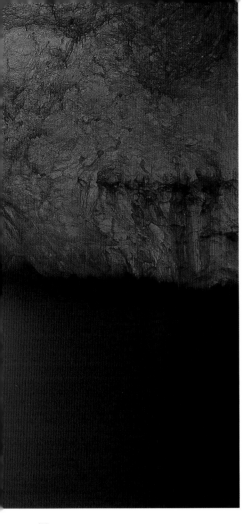

Torta caprese
Capri cake

2 cups/300 g almonds, skins on
8 oz/200 g cooking chocolate
3/4 cup + 1 tbsp/200 g butter
1 cup/200 g sugar
6 eggs
2 1/2 level tsp baking powder
2 tbsp flavored liqueur (e.g. cocoa, *strega*)
Confectioners' sugar

Chop the almonds and chocolate very finely. Beat the butter with the sugar in a bowl until creamy. Beat the eggs thoroughly in a separate bowl, and add to the butter cream mixture. Add the almonds and chocolate, then stir in the baking powder and liqueur.
Place the mixture in an 11-in. (28-cm) diameter springform cake pan greased with butter or lined with silicon paper. Bake in a preheated oven at 350 °F (180 °C) for about 50 minutes.
Turn the cake out on to a wire rack to cool, then dredge with confectioners' sugar.

Ischia

The island of Ischia, which is barely 20 square miles (50 square kilometers) in area, is well known for two reasons: curative thermal springs and good wine. Wealthy Romans used both and let the spa doctors of that time get them into good physical condition for their exertions on their estates in Campania or running the Roman Empire. Ischia's thermal springs are between 130 and 145 °F (54 to 62 °C) in temperature, and still help people with gout even today. They offer bath cures, fango cures, and sweat cures, and year after year they entice patients from all over the world to this island in the Gulf of Naples.
Like the cures in the thermal springs, the fertile soils on which the Ischia Bianco grows, amongst other things, are also of volcanic origin. If you have had enough of the cure, you can find a small trattoria and enjoy a glass of good wine, while sampling the specialty *coniglio all'ischitana*, a tasty fried rabbit, or the fresh fish dishes.

Coniglio all'ischitana
Rabbit with tomatoes and herbs
(Illustrated below)

1 medium, ready-prepared rabbit
Vinegar
3 1/2 tbsp/50 ml olive oil
2 cloves of garlic
2/3 cup/150 ml dry white wine
1 lb/500 g small tomatoes, cut into pieces
1 peperoncino, finely chopped
Salt and pepper
Mixed herbs: basil, thyme, marjoram, rosemary

Joint the rabbit, wash in water and vinegar, and pat dry. Gently brown the garlic in the oil in a broad skillet. Remove the garlic, increase the heat, and brown the rabbit portions all over. Pour in the white wine, bring to a boil and leave to reduce. Add the tomatoes and peperoncino, season with salt and pepper. Chop the herbs finely and stir in. Simmer for about 30 minutes.
Serve warm.

NUTS FROM IRPINIA

Naples, pizza, Vesuvius, pasta, Capri, or mozzarella spring to mind when you think of Campania. But not many visitors know, that, tucked away inland, it is totally different. Far away from the coast lie tranquil regions with strange-sounding names such as Irpinia and Benevento. Irpinia and its provincial capital, Avellino, were sadly the focus of media attention for a few weeks in 1980, when the major earthquake that shook large parts of Campania had particularly serious consequences here. The final toll was 5000 dead and half a million homeless. Although they have still not quite got over the shock of the catastrophe, the people of Irpinia are making brave efforts to gradually improve their situation. A feature of the reconstruction is the Irpinian motto: "work here, don't emigrate."

Traditionally, a small brown fruit with a hard shell has always made an important contribution to the region's economic survival: Even in the pre-Christian era, people knew of the *avellana*, the tasty filbert from Avella, a small town near the provincial capital. Now Campania's remote mountainous provinces provide about half the total Italian filbert crop. These little energy and nutrient providers are protected by a thin, but very hard shell. However, like all nuts, filberts should still be stored in a cool, dry place, to prevent them spoiling.

The warmth-loving hazelnut plant *(Corylus avellana)* which grows up to five meters comes originally from Turkey. It also feels at home now in Irpinia.

RUM BABÀ AND PASTIERA

One of Campania's sweet specialties is known locally as *babà napoletano*, although it actually comes from Poland. Legend has it that it dates back to the 18th century and to King Stanislaus. The monarch allegedly liked to dunk little pieces of German *gugelhupf* cake in rum before eating them. To reduce the length of time it took to perform this ritual, the court baker developed a recipe that involved soaking the cake in the alcoholic liquid while still in the bakery. Apparently the king was so impressed with it, that he named his new favorite dessert after Ali Baba from the "Arabian Nights." When Stanislaus lost the Polish throne and came to France, the ingenious cake became part of French cuisine and from there, together with French court etiquette, to the Kingdom of Naples. If you find this anecdote hard to believe, you may well be right, as a rum cake called *babà* probably actually predates the cake-fan king. As well as the sumptuous *babà*, Neapolitans are also partial to another sweet confection, *pastiera napoletana*. This really is a ritual calorific bomb, made mainly at Easter. It is made out of durum wheat and wheat flour, ricotta, loads of raisins, and lots of candied fruits. Of course, every family in Campania has its own secret recipe, and the guests make a game of judging the result of this year's culinary efforts, claiming that they can remember quite precisely the qualities of last year's *pastiera*.

BABÀ ALLA NAPOLETANA
Neapolitan rum baba
(Illustrated opposite, top)

Serves 6

For the dough:
2 1/3 CAKES/40 G COMPRESSED YEAST (IF USING ACTIVE DRY YEAST, FOLLOW THE MAKER'S INSTRUCTIONS)
2/3 CUP/150 ML MILK
3 CUPS/350 G ALL-PURPOSE FLOUR
6 EGGS, SEPARATED
3/4 CUP + 1 TBSP/200 G BUTTER, SOFTENED
2 TBSP/20 G SUGAR
A PINCH OF SALT

For the syrup:
2 1/2 CUPS/500 G SUGAR
4 CUPS/1 LITER WATER
THE RIND OF 1 LEMON, GRATED
2 1/2 TBSP/40 ML RUM

Dissolve the yeast in a little hand-hot milk, and gradually incorporate the flour. Leave the dough to rise in a warm place for about 30 minutes, until it has doubled in volume. Put the egg yolks, softened butter, and sugar into a bowl, and beat using an electric mixer at medium speed until the mixture becomes slightly frothy. Beat the egg whites with the salt until stiff. Gradually incorporate the yeast dough into the egg-yolk mixture. If the dough becomes too stiff, add a few spoonfuls of beaten egg white. Pour the mixture into a 10½-in. (26-cm) diameter brioche pan, and leave to rise once more, until it has doubled in volume. Bake in a preheated oven at 350 °F (180 °C) for about 40 minutes.

To make the syrup, dissolve the sugar in the water over a low heat, and simmer gently for about 10 minutes. Leave to cool slightly, and then stir in the lemon rind and rum. Leave the cake to cool, then turn it out on to a plate. Spoon the syrup over the cake, including any juice that collects on the plate.
Serve the cake with sour cherry jam, whipped cream, strawberries, or zabaglione.

PASTIERA NAPOLETANA
Neapolitan ricotta cake

Serves 12

For the filling:
1 CUP/200 G DURUM WHEAT GRAINS, SOAKED FOR 3 DAYS
2 CUPS/500 ML SKIMMED MILK
THE RIND OF 1 LEMON, GRATED
2 1/4 TBSP/10 G CINNAMON
1 CUP/200 G SUGAR
1 LB/500 G RICOTTA
4 EGGS, SEPARATED
2 1/2 TBSP/40 ML ORANGE FLOWER WATER
1 CUP/150 G CANDIED CITRUS AND TROPICAL FRUITS AND RAISINS
1/4 CUP/30 G CONFECTIONERS' SUGAR

For the dough:
2 1/2 CUPS/300 G FLOUR
3/4 CUP/150 G SUGAR
2/3 CUP/150 G BUTTER
3 EGG YOLKS
BUTTER FOR GREASING
CONFECTIONERS' SUGAR

To make the filling, soak the durum wheat grains in water for 3 days, changing the water daily.
Drain and boil the grains in fresh water for 15 minutes. Drain, put the grains in a pan with the hot milk, half the lemon rind, a pinch of cinnamon, and 1 tablespoon sugar, and cook over a medium heat until the milk has been totally absorbed.
Beat the ricotta in a bowl until creamy. Stir the egg yolks, orange flower water, candied fruits, raisins, the remaining cinnamon, sugar, and lemon rind, and finally the wheat grain mixture into the ricotta. Leave to rest in a refrigerator. When ready to bake, beat the egg whites until stiff, and then fold into the filling.
To make the dough, place the flour on the work surface, mix in the sugar, butter, and egg yolks, and work to form a dough. Leave to rest in a refrigerator for 1 hour.
Grease an 11½-in. (30-cm) diameter springform cake pan with butter. Roll out three-quarters of the dough into a 1-in. (3-cm) thick circle, and place in the pan, covering the base and sides. Pour the filling into the cake pan, and cover with strips of dough to make a trellis pattern. Bake in a preheated oven at 350 °F (180 °C) for about 1 hour. The cake is ready when it is a beautiful golden color. Leave to cool on a wire rack, and dredge with confectioners' sugar.

Babà alla napoletana –
Neapolitan rum babà

Nut brittle

In southern Italy, homemade nut brittle is made mainly at Christmas time, and traditionally eaten on Christmas Eve. As soon as it has cooled slightly, skilled hands shape the nut brittle mixture into beautiful bowls or baskets, and fill them with candied fruits. Decorated with brightly colored little bows or gauze fabric, *croccante* is a popular winter gift for the family, neighbors, and close friends.

Croccante
Nut brittle nest

250 ALMONDS
1 1/4 CUPS/250 G SUGAR
CANDIED FRUITS AND COOKIES OF YOUR CHOICE

Blanch the almonds, then, holding between the thumb and forefinger, squeeze out of the brown skin, and chop finely. Dry in an oven at a low heat for about 10 minutes, turning occasionally. Pour the sugar into a non-galvanized copper pan, and brown gently over a low heat, stirring constantly with a wooden spoon. Add the almonds and roast for a few minutes over a very low heat, stirring constantly. Turn the mixture out onto a buttered baking sheet, and roll out using a greased rolling pin (preferably made of marble). As soon as the mixture has cooled sufficiently for you to work it with your hands, shape it into a basket with a handle. When cool, fill with candied fruits and cookies.

Benevento

Benevento is another part of that "other Campania." The people who live here are quiet and serious and do not have much in common with the Mediterranean people of the Gulf of Naples. They prefer to consider themselves as descendants of the Samnites, a proud race who long ago fought with the Romans for supremacy in the Old World. Although the Samnites lost the battle, the Langobards did manage to settle in the region in the 6th century, and even today, the people here are still proud of that fact.

To preserve their cultural inheritance, the Samnites, as the people of Benevento call themselves, would like to set up their own state, Sannio. As far as cooking is concerned at least, they have already almost succeeded, because the agricultural products from the province of Benevento are systematically marketed under the historical name of the area. Around the capital town of Benevento, fruit and olives are grown and marketed. *Torrone* and other confectionery is made by small, but top-quality firms, and DOC wine, such as the red Solopaca, is produced in cellars.

However, the best-known label in Benevento has to be *strega*, a herbal liqueur produced to a closely-guarded secret recipe by the Alberti family for almost 140 years.

The famous literary prize founded by the firm in 1947 to promote contemporary Italian literature is also called after this "witch's brew." One of the top award winners of the *Premio Strega* is Umberto Eco, who was chosen for his bestselling novel, *The Name of the Rose.*

IN THE SHADOW OF VESUVIUS

Campania was one of the favorite wine-growing regions of Ancient Rome. The words Sorrentino, Calenio, Massico were just as familiar to the inhabitants of the Eternal City as Valpolicella, Barolo, or Chianti are to Italian wine connoisseurs today. Wine production was of strategic importance not only to the

region itself. The port of Pompeii meant that it also possessed the largest wine-trading center in the classical world. The eruption of Vesuvius in A.D. 79 signified a far-reaching turning point in its development. The harbor was destroyed, cutting off the flow of wine from Greece and Asia Minor, and the obliteration of large vineyards in the region also robbed the Romans of some of their very favorite wines. As a result of this disaster, they began to develop winegrowing systematically in all parts of their empire. This development policy continued until, as for example in Lazio, practically all cultivatable agricultural land had been turned over to winegrowing, thus threatening the capital town with food shortages.

As history took its course, Campania's years of glory slipped way. The lava flows from the erupting Vesuvius gave the region ideal winegrowing soils, they had a better climate for viticulture – sheltered and warm, with long and hot summers – than anywhere else in Italy, and the Aglianico, Greco, and other indigenous grape varieties produced good and very good wines; but the social and political climate has unfortunately not really produced a flourishing economy since the Middle Ages. This is also true for winegrowing. Some producers, however, are aware of the significance of the region to the history of viticulture, and want to make Campania into an important Italian winegrowing area once again.

Wall paintings such as these from Herculaneum depicting a couple at a banquet, 50–20 B.C., now in the National Museum in Naples, adorned the houses of affluent Romans.

THE VOLCANO'S RARE GEMS

Even though the Ancient Romans knew Campania had ideal conditions for winegrowing, the region's role in modern Italian viticulture is barely noticeable. The impoverishment of the region, which strikes any visitor as soon as they leave the tourist centers of Amalfi, Naples, Ischia, or Capri, has not spared its viticulture. Campania may be able to boast 27 DOC, DOCG or Igt wines as its own, but you gain a real sense of its significance once you know that in total they account for only five percent of wine production in this region.

In actual fact, some of the marks of origin produce only between 13,000 and 16,000 U.S. gallons (500 or 600 hectoliters) per year, Capri only 6340 U.S. gallons (240 hl), which in other places would barely be enough to fill a single, large steel container. So it should come as no surprise that names such as Campi Flegrei, Cilento, Falerno, Galuccio, Guardiolo, Sannio, or even Solopaca, are hardly known outside the region. There

are, however, a few exceptions in this regard, Taurasi, for example. Campania's only DOCG wine, pressed from the same Aglianico grape variety that gives the wines of neighboring Basilicata their class, comes from the slopes of the province of Avellino. Good wine producers can make it into a fascinating vintage with an intense bouquet and flavor.

Aglianico grapes are also used in the cultivation areas of Campi Flegrei, Cilento, Costa d'Amalfi, Falerno, Sannio, Sant'Agata de' Goti, and Solopaca, but rarely with such excellent results as in the Taurasi area. The same province of Avellino, home of the latter, also produces Campania's two most interesting white wines, Greco di Tufo and Fiano d'Avellino. The Greco from the area around the village of Tufo is made from the grape of the same name, usually blended with the Falanghina and Biancolella varieties, a direct descendant of a Greek variety that has both red and white grapes. Whereas the Calabrian Greco di Bianco is an excellent sweet wine, the dry Greco di Tufo proves itself by its characterful fruity and almond bouquet.

Like Greco wine, Fiano from the province of Avellino has more character than most other Italian white wines. This variety is also Greek in origin, and the Romans already knew

it by the name *Vitis Apianae*, bee wine. The best representatives of this mark of origin are fresh and robust, with peach and nut bouquets, well balanced, and complex. If you wanted to make a similar claim for Campania's coastal and island white wines, you would probably be accused of being grossly dishonest. The islands of Capri and Ischia do, however, produce pleasant, fruity summer wines, albeit in very small quantities, that can be delicious when visiting the sunny islands.

There are, of course, also interesting single-grape wines in some of the other DOC areas. Aglianico del Taburno is pressed from the same variety as the Taurasi. Falerno blends Aglianico and Piedirosso to produce the red wine, whereas the white is made from Falanghina grapes. The various red and white wines from the Sannio region (where surprisingly there are also single-grape representatives of the northern and central Italian Barbera, Sangiovese, and Trebbiano toscano grape varieties), and the Sant'Agata de' Goti (white wines from Greco and Galanghina grapes, red wines from Aglianico and Piedirosso). The DOC names such as Costa d'Amalfi, Penisola Sorrentina and Vesuvio, on the other hand, which have until now struck everyone as being popular, remain less convincing.

LIMONCELLO

Limoncello, or *limunciel*, as it is called in Campania, is a liqueur flavored with the lemons for which the Amalfi coast is famous. It is just as essential an end to a Campanian meal as grappa or anise liqueur is in other regions. Like the liqueurs of northern and central Italy, the lemon liqueur is said to be good for the digestion. However that may be, with its intense citrus fragrance, limoncello is a perfect end to a pleasant evening spent with family or friends.

As early as the 7th century, the fruit farmers in Minori, a small village near Amalfi, were beginning to establish large-scale lemon groves. Their proximity to the sea and the favorable soil and climate conditions meant that the trees flourished. People improved their yields further by developing more and more new cultivation and irrigation techniques.

They also experimented with different citrus species, until they succeeded in breeding a very special species of lemon, for which the region has now become famous throughout Italy and beyond.

The people of Campania speculate that the golden apple tree that the gods ordered the three beautiful Hesperides, Islands of the Blessed, to protect, was not in fact an apple tree but a lemon tree. Even a few centuries ago, the Renaissance writer, Giambattista della Porta shared this suspicion when, convinced he had traced the mythical garden of the Hesperides, he sang the praises of the exquisite flavor of the *limon amalfitanus*.

Although about 90 percent of Italian lemons now come from Sicily, and Campania's contribution to the total crop is only very small, the indigenous Nostrano variety is still considered to be Italy's best variety of lemon. It goes without saying that it also provides the flavor for genuine limoncello.

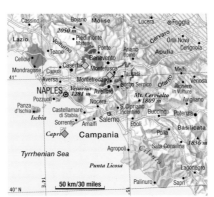

357

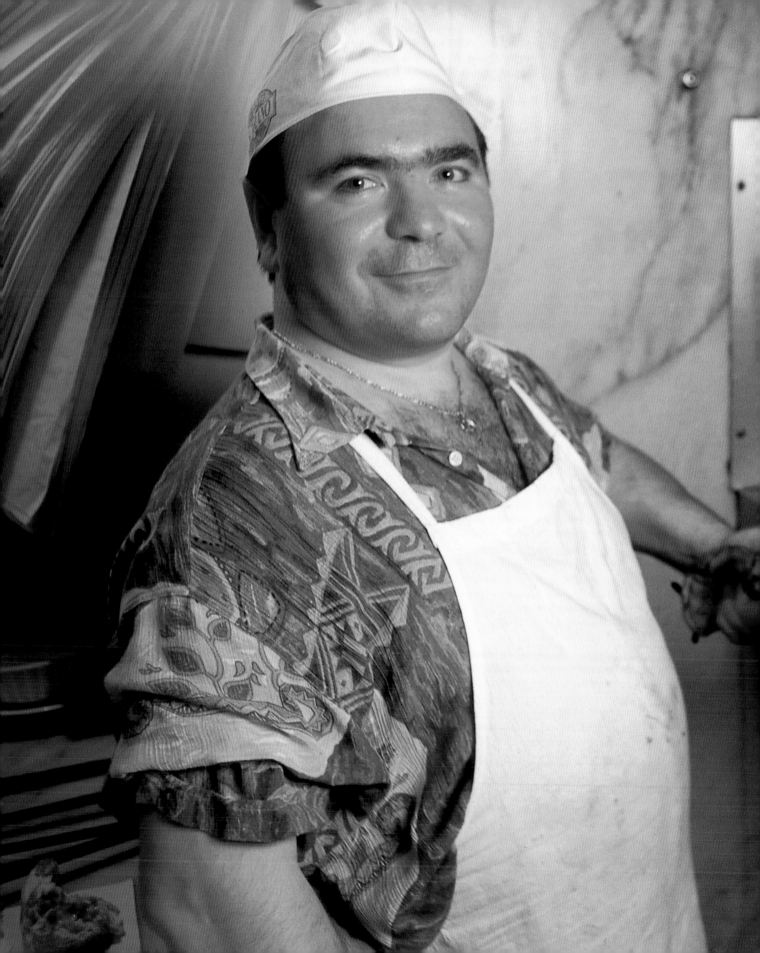

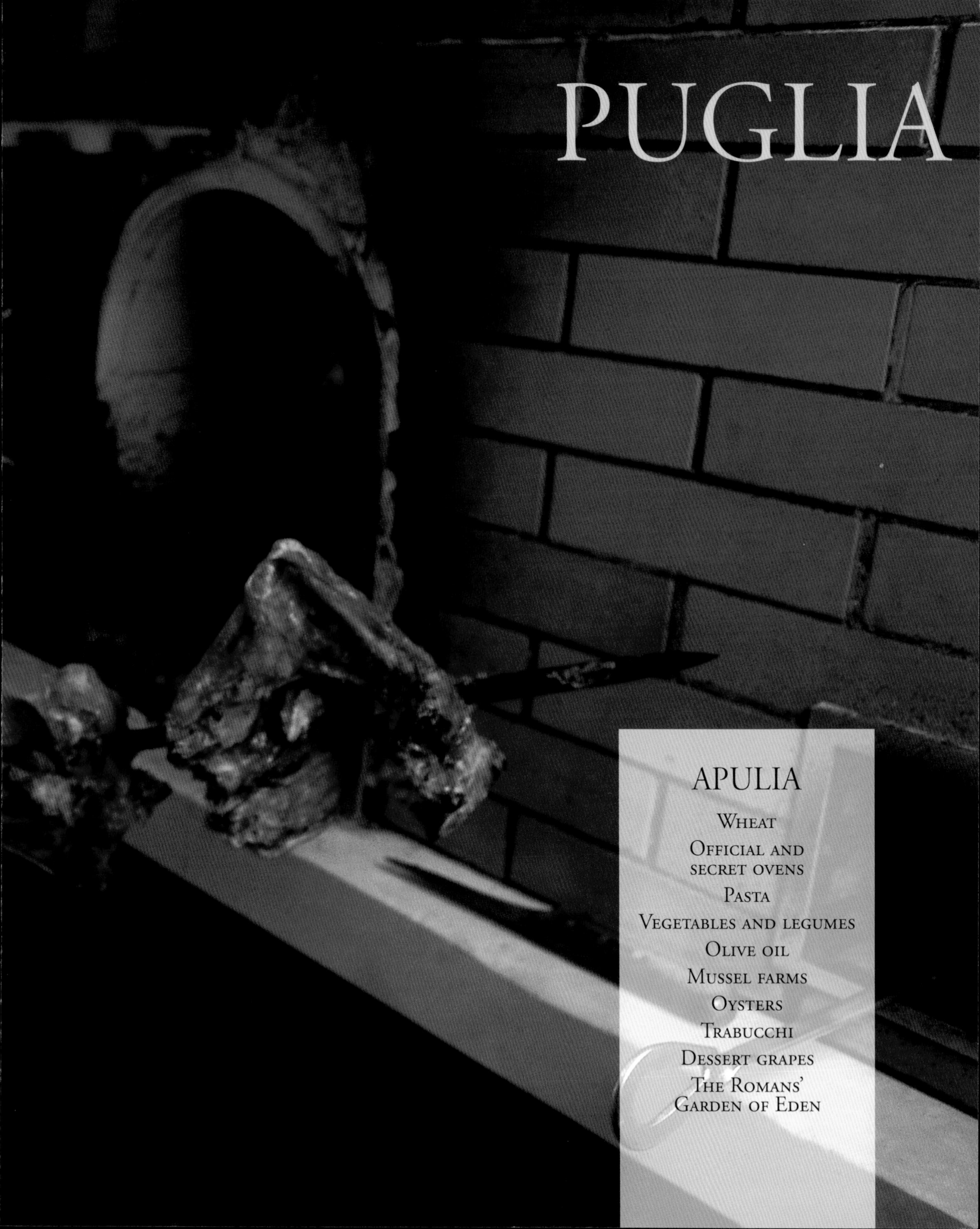

PUGLIA

APULIA

Wheat

Official and
secret ovens

Pasta

Vegetables and legumes

Olive oil

Mussel farms

Oysters

Trabucchi

Dessert grapes

The Romans'
Garden of Eden

Bright, cheerful, and noisy – that is life not only on Campania's Tyrrhenian coast, but also on Apulia's Adriatic coast. This elongated region, *Puglia* in Italian, extends from the spur that reaches 44 miles (70 kilometers) into the sea right to the tip of Italy's heel. Even though Apulia has experienced hard times in economic terms, its people love their region and are proud of their local, rural traditions. Apulian cuisine is also simple, rustic, and cheerful, with a clear North-South divide in culinary terms. In northern Apulia, people cook with a lot of garlic, the "central" Apulians like onions as well as garlic, and in the far south, they have a clear preference for the onion.

Apart from these subtle differences in flavoring, there is some common ground in the cuisine throughout Apulia. Apulia is Italy's breadbasket, so the region supplies most of the durum wheat used throughout Italy to make *pasta secca*. It is therefore not surprising that pasta, whether homemade or bought, and bread play an important role here. In the carefully irrigated plains of Apulia, they grow tomatoes, zucchini, broccoli, bell peppers, potatoes, spinach, eggplants, cauliflower, fennel, Belgian endive, and legumes such as chickpeas, lentils, and beans. So vegetables can thus be said to be the second pillar of Apulian cuisine. The third is olive oil. Apulia is Italy's largest oil producer, and not only stocks the shelves of northern Italy with its spicy, fruity, acidic oil made from fully ripe olives, but also exports its "green gold" to the rest of Europe. The fourth pillar of Apulian cuisine is the sea. With their complicated-looking catching machines, *trabucchi*, the fishermen pull their haul from the Adriatic Sea, and in the Mar Piccolo, the "Little Sea" in the Gulf of Taranto, the seafood farms have specialized in mussels and oysters.

Apulia's simple cuisine therefore uses a wide variety of quality ingredients. Its people also inherited Epicurean philosophy from the Greeks over 2500 years ago, when Apulia belonged to Magna Graecia. Even today, Apulian feast days are a sensational event: extremely cheerful, with crispy lamb or goat roasts, warm hospitality, spicy cheese, good wine, and incredibly sweet *dolci* (desserts). A real banquet, in fact.

Previous double page: In the old town of Martina Franca, the Ricci brothers run a very traditional butcher's store and sausage grill. Here, Nino Ricci places various meats and sausages on a skewer ready for grilling.

Opposite: Extensive olive groves are a defining feature of the Apulian landscape.

Types of bread

1 Pane di Altamura
This sourdough durum wheat bread, compact and full of holes, keeps well, and is now popular throughout Italy. In Apulia, the tasty, round, flat loaves can weigh up to 44 pounds (20 kilograms).

2 Pane casareccio
Not so very long ago, every family used to bake their own *pane casareccio*, Apulia's classic loaf made from durum wheat flour, salt, water, and yeast. Now the loaves you can buy from the baker as just as tasty and satisfying.

3 Puccia di pane
When baked, this small, soft, nutritious round loaf, enriched with olives, is tossed in white flour to remind people of the purity of the Virgin Mary. The province of Lecce is the main place for this bread, although it can also be found in Brindisi and Ostuni.

4 Puddica
The basic ingredients, ordinary bread dough and mashed potato, are kneaded to form a smooth dough, which is then rolled out into flat cakes. These are then covered with halved tomatoes, seasoned with salt, and pepper, drizzled with olive oil, and baked in the oven.

5 Focaccia ripiena
This parcel of bread dough is filled with mozzarella, tomatoes, ham, and onion or leek, baked in the oven, then cut into slices, and eaten.

6 Taralli
Wheat flour, lard, olive oil, brewer's yeast, fennel seeds, ground red pepper or freshly milled pepper, and a little salt are the main ingredients for these crispy bread rings. They are a popular aperitif in southern Italy.

7 Crostini
Slices of white bread roasted in the oven are drizzled with fresh olive oil and sprinkled with oregano. They can also be served with olive, anchovy, or tuna paste.

8 Friselle
These small, round, golden-brown loaves made of barley flour and durum wheat flour are baked twice, first in a hot oven, and then in a moderate oven. If an audible crack is produced when the loaf is broken open, it is a sure sign that it is really crusty and good. *Friselle* keep for a very long time, if kept in an airtight container.

If you want to discover Apulia's many different types of bread, you can do no better than to visit the Angelini bakery in Martina Franca, where they bake *taralli, friselle, focaccia,* and all the other tasty specialties in an authentic atmosphere full of Apulian cheer.

Taralli
Bread rings
(Illustrated below, no. 6)

4 CUPS/500 G FLOUR
SALT AND PEPPER
1/2 CUP/125 G LARD
2 OZ/55 G BREWER'S YEAST
FENNEL SEEDS (OPTIONAL)
WATER
OLIVE OIL

Combine the flour with a little salt and pepper, then knead together with the lard, brewer's yeast, and fennel seeds, if using. Add sufficient water to produce a smooth dough. Cut off small pieces of dough and shape into rings. Drizzle with a little oil, place on a greased baking sheet, and leave to rise for 1 hour. Then bake in a preheated oven at 300 °F (150 °C) for 1 hour.

WHEAT

There are more than 360 varieties of wheat throughout the world. Wheat can be roughly divided up into three groups: durum wheat provides heavy corn with lots of grits. It is not very strong. Soft wheat forms within white grains, from which white flour can be milled. The properties of semihard varieties are somewhere between these two groups. They are often used because they provide white flour, and it is easy to separate the bran. In Apulia, they cultivate mainly durum wheat (*triticum durum*), but sometimes also other varieties of wheat. The advantage of durum

wheat is that it thrives in the dry, hot climate of this region. Seed wheat is very demanding in terms of the mineral content of the soil and moisture, which is why it was preferable to grow durum wheat.

For centuries, life in Apulia has focused on arable farming and has been governed by the harvest calendar, so it is not surprising that they have taken equal care when processing field crops. Fresh, homemade pasta still features prominently on Apulian menus, but the various types of bread also have an established place. Throughout Italy, bread from Apulia is considered to be particularly good. They knead a great variety of pasta in their kitchens, and bake many different types of bread in their bakeries. Baked to varying degrees of crustiness, whether best enjoyed fresh, or suitable for the store cupboard, hearty, or delicate and sweet, the imagination knows no bounds. The quality of a loaf depends on various factors. Which flour or flour mixture does the baker use? Bread made from durum wheat may not be such a beautiful, radiant white, but it keeps very well, and does not go stale so quickly. How was the corn harvested, and how was it milled? Does the baker add yeast or other raising agents? What baking pans does he use? And finally, how does he bake them, and in what sort of oven? The bakers of Apulia are experts in all these questions. However, their various kinds of bread all have one thing in common: they taste fabulous.

Below: *Grano duro*, durum wheat (*triticum durum*), is primarily grown in southern Italy, because this variety tolerates the dry, hot climate. Milled durum wheat, known as semolina or *semolino* in Italian, is an essential ingredient in the cuisine of the Italian peninsula, because it is the basic ingredient for pasta.

Customers stand in line at the Ricci brothers' grill to buy their genuine, traditional delicacies.

Gnumerelli are made by hand. Here the intestinal casings are being filled with ground meat.

It is vital to ensure that the *bombette*, cheese-filled pork rolls, do not burst when being placed on the skewer.

Of course, cooking times vary for each specialty, but that is no cause for alarm for the professional.

Amongst other things, the Fratelli Ricci butcher's store and sausage grill in Martina Franca is famous for its *gnumerelli*. These are small pieces of lamb organ meat wrapped in intestinal casings. Sadly, they have now become a rare delicacy in Italy.

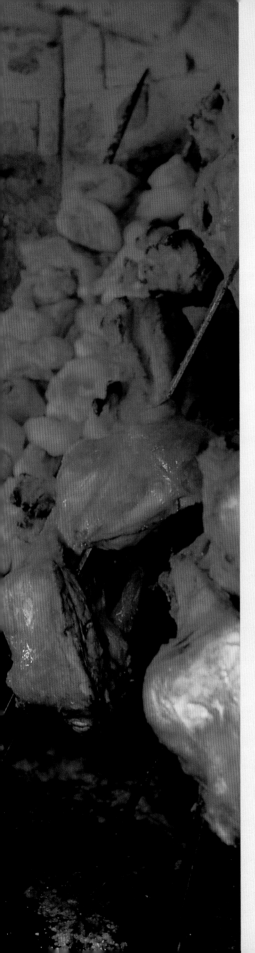

OFFICIAL AND SECRET OVENS

The oven is essential to the rustic cuisine of Apulia, and is also used for meat dishes. It did not use to be so simple to get your bread and cooking baked, as they would say in current parlance. The old town regulations made it illegal to have ovens in private houses. This was the authorities' way of dealing with the dreaded fire risk, and also ensured a firm source of income, as they forced the population to use the communal ovens under official control. The duty of overseeing the ovens often fell to the universities, such as those of Bisceglie and Terlizzi.

To escape the heavy tax on baking, the Apulians built small, unobtrusive stone ovens in the countryside, where they did their baking secretly, but for free. If a baking official appeared, they would quickly pull down the primitive construction, and could claim, with a clear conscience, that it was a pile of rubble, not an oven. The tax-dodging ovens became the focus of Apulian cuisine, and are still obligatory today. People use them to cook sweet or savory dishes in a *tiella*, an earthenware pot with a tin lid, and to bake a wide variety of breads. They are also used to bake *focaccia*, *calzuni* (a short pastry topped with onions, tomatoes, pitted olives, and salted anchovy fillets), and *panzerotti*, (short pastry parcels filled with tomatoes, mozzarella, anchovies, and onions). But the good, old, wood-fired oven is also essential for the preparation of Apulian meat specialties.

TIELLA ALLA BARESE
Bari-style bake
(Illustrated above)

1 CUP/200 G RICE
1 1/2 LBS/700 G MUSSELS
1 CLOVE OF GARLIC
ABOUT 1 LB/400 G POTATOES
EXTRA VIRGIN OLIVE OIL
1 LARGE ONION, FINELY SLICED
1/2 CUP/70 G PECORINO CHEESE, GRATED
CHOPPED PARSLEY
FRESHLY MILLED PEPPER

Cook the rice in water.
Scrub the mussels, rinse under cold water, put in a pan with the clove of garlic, and cook for a few minutes. When the shells have opened, strain the juice through a fine sieve or cloth and reserve. Discard any unopened mussel shells. Remove the mussel flesh from the shells and set aside. Peel, wash, and finely slice the potatoes.
Grease a pudding dish with olive oil and add a layer of potatoes. Then add layers of rice, onion rings, pecorino cheese, parsley, and mussels. Repeat the process until all the ingredients have been used up. The final layer should be potato. Season with pepper, drizzle with olive oil, pour over the mussel juice, and bake in a preheated oven at 350 °F (180 °C) for about 45 minutes.

PIZZA DI PATATE
Potato pizza

Serves 6

1 3/4 LBS/750 G POTATOES
2 TBSP OLIVE OIL
SALT
4 TBSP/50 G ALL-PURPOSE FLOUR

Boil the potatoes, then put through a potato ricer or mash until smooth. Add the olive oil and salt, then set aside.
As soon as the potato mixture has cooled, add the flour and knead. The mixture should not be too sticky. Add more flour if necessary. Roll the mixture out onto an 11-in. (28-cm) diameter, round baking sheet.
Cover with any of your favorite pizza toppings, and bake in a preheated oven at 390 °F (200 °C) for about 40 minutes.

Opposite: Nearly everything is baked in an oven in Apulia – bread, sweet or savory dishes, sausages or even whole pieces of meat.

PASTA

In Apulia, one wheat field follows on from another. To be more precise, it is durum wheat, the raw material for Italian *pasta secca*. In the breadbasket between the spur and toe of the Italian boot, this abundance is processed not only in their own factories, but is also used by pasta manufacturers throughout Italy.

Even though there is a very good range of mass-produced pasta, in Apulia they have never lost their preference for traditional, homemade pastas. So each area steadfastly cultivates its own taste for *pasta fresca*: in Bari, there are the smaller *chianciarelle* and the somewhat bigger *paciocche*, known by the rest of the world as *orecchiette*. Foggia is the home of *troccoli*, similar to the *maccheroni alla chitarra* for which Abruzzi is famed. Brindisi is known for its lasagne, called *staggiotta*, and *turcinelli* come from Lecce. An almost inexhaustible choice of vegetable-, pork- or lamb-based sauces, often spicy-hot, being seasoned with red peperoncini, provide for variety.

In Bari in 1647, there was even an uprising in the name of pasta. The town's inhabitants rose up against the Spanish rulers, who were demanding they pay a recently introduced flour tax, and were even sending tax inspectors into people's homes to check their flour consumption. Such was the rage of the people of Bari, who were extremely proud of the burgeoning pasta and bread production in their town, that the Spaniards gave up after eight days and withdrew the tax.

Strascinati con la mollica –
Pasta with breadcrumbs

CAVOLFIORE E PASTA
Cauliflower with pasta
(Illustrated opposite right)

8 SALTED ANCHOVIES
2 1/4 LBS/1 KG CAULIFLOWER
SALT
2 CLOVES OF GARLIC
2 TBSP EXTRA VIRGIN OLIVE OIL
12 OZ/300 G FRESH, HOMEMADE PASTA
1/4 CUP/30 G PECORINO CHEESE, GRATED
PEPPER

Scale and wash the anchovies, then cut in pieces. Wash the cauliflower, divide it into florets, and put into boiling, salted water. Sauté the cloves of garlic in a skillet with olive oil until they start to color. Using a slotted spoon, remove the cauliflower from the water when almost cooked. Add the pasta to the cauliflower water and cook until *al dente*. Remove the skillet from the heat, and add the cheese and anchovies. Peel the cloves of garlic and crush them, together with the anchovies, using a wooden spoon.
Drain the pasta and cauliflower in a sieve, then add to the other ingredients in the skillet, and mix thoroughly. Season with salt and pepper, add a little more olive oil if necessary, and serve hot.

TIELLA DI VERDURE
Vegetable bake
(Illustrated below, middle)

3/4 LB/300 G TOMATOES
2 YELLOW BELL PEPPERS
2 EGGPLANTS
1 LB/500 G POTATOES
EXTRA VIRGIN OLIVE OIL
8 OZ/250 G MOZZARELLA CHEESE
SALT AND PEPPER
1 BUNCH OF BASIL, CHOPPED
BREADCRUMBS
FRESH OREGANO, CHOPPED

Clean and finely slice the vegetables. Grease a casserole dish (preferably earthenware) with olive oil, and fill with layers of vegetables and mozzarella, until they have all been used up. Season each layer with salt and pepper and sprinkle with basil. Combine the breadcrumbs with oregano, salt, and pepper, and sprinkle over the vegetables and cheese. Drizzle with olive oil, and bake in a preheated oven at 390 °F (200 °C) for about 1 hour.

TIELLA DI VERDURE

Tiella di verdure is said to be of Spanish origin, as its name, which sounds odd to Apulian ears, is similar to the Spanish word, paella. The original recipe, with rice and mussels, is also very similar to the Iberian specialty. The word *tiella* was later used to describe all dishes made in a pot of a particular shape. The *tiella di verdure*, prepared with mixed vegetables, is a common *primo* (first course) in Apulia, and is served as an alternative to pasta.

STRASCINATI CON LA MOLLICA

Pasta with breadcrumbs
(Illustrated opposite left)

2 SALTED ANCHOVIES
4–5 TBSP EXTRA VIRGIN OLIVE OIL
2 1/2 CUPS/150 G BREADCRUMBS
FRESHLY MILLED PEPPER
14 OZ/400 G STRASCINATI OR ORECCHIETTE PASTA

Scale and wash the anchovies, then cut into pieces. Heat the olive oil in a skillet and add the anchovies and breadcrumbs. Add the pepper and stir well with a wooden spoon. Cook the pasta in copious salted water until *al dente*, pour through a colander, drain, and add to the breadcrumbs in the skillet. Mix carefully and serve hot.

Tiella di verdure –
Vegetable bake

Chianciarelle

Chianciarelle are a slightly smaller version of the classic *orecchiette*.

Fenescecchie

Fenescecchie are made by shaping the pasta dough into long strips, which are then wound round a knitting needle to give them their distinctive spiral effect.

Mignuicchie

Mignuicchie are small dumplings made of durum wheat semolina.

Orecchiette

These little pasta ear-shapes are one of southern Italy's best-known pastas. They are also eaten in northern Italy, and can also be bought factory-made. You need to be fairly skilled to make them yourself.

Paciocche

Paciocche are *orecchiette* that turned out a bit too big!

Strascinati

Strascinati are pasta squares rolled over a grooved pasta board, so that they have a smooth and a rough side. Their name refers to the Italian word for the process, *strascinare*, to drag over.

Troccoli

Troccoli are similar to Abruzzi *maccheroni alla chitarra*, and are a specialty of the province of Foggia. Their name is derived from the device used to shape them, a rolling pin with circular blades that cuts the dough while rolling it out. It is related to the *ferro da maccheroni* (macaroni iron) used in the 16th century.

Cavolfiore e pasta –
Cauliflower with pasta

VEGETABLES AND LEGUMES

Crispy vegetables and tender, fresh legumes are essential ingredients in Apulian cuisine. As early as 1171, a legal document mentioned the intensive cultivation of the allotment gardens, *ortaggi*, in Italian cities. No matter how small the garden, every family had their own olive and almond trees, and grew legumes for their own consumption throughout the year. Until the end of the 19th century, they grew mainly broad beans (or horse beans), followed by chickpeas and lentils. Peas and climbing beans, which are now equally popular, did not arrive on the scene until later.

Broad beans go very well with the numerous varieties of chicory that sources prove were gathered and included in the menu as early as the 17th century. In addition to the usual chicory varieties, dandelion and *catalogna* are now cultivated. The *catalogna* variety (the autumn dandelion) is a cultivated relative of wild chicory (*cichorium intybus*, succory), which basically looks like the dandelion, but can grow up to one and a half feet (half a meter) tall. The *Catalogna puntarelle* variety has a particularly bushy habit. Chicory has a refreshing taste and is a popular choice in Apulia to make classic southern Italian dishes such as *Catalogna racante*, for example.

However, Apulia has even more vegetables to offer. Tomatoes, zucchini, bell peppers, potatoes, spinach, eggplants, and fennel are grown not just for Apulian consumption, but are also exported to northern Italy and the rest of Europe, so garden produce is an important factor in the Apulian economy. Brassica cultivation has been particularly successful, because broccoli, sprouts, turnip tops, and cauliflower find the soil conditions here absolutely perfect. Since scientists have acknowledged that these plants may even protect against cancer, sales of excellent varieties of broccoli, tasty *cime di rapa* (turnip tops) from Fasano, and cauliflower have risen even higher. Another sales hit of this narrow region on Italy's heel are the exquisitely tender, sweet, and smooth artichokes, such as the *locale di Mola*, and the bulbs of wild hyacinths, called *lampascioni*, which taste slightly more bitter than shallots and are becoming increasingly popular.

Chicory varieties such as *catalogna* or *puntarelle* are often used in Italian cooking. They occur as wild plants (*Cicoria selvatica*) and as salad or vegetable plants cultivated from wild plants.

PUREA DI FAVE
Broad bean purée

2 LARGE POTATOES
3/4 LB/300 G BROAD BEANS
SALT
7–8 TBSP EXTRA VIRGIN OLIVE OIL

Peel, wash, and dice the potatoes. Shell the beans and place in a pan with the potatoes. Cover with water, cover the pan, and simmer for about 20 minutes. Pour off the water, cover the potatoes and beans with fresh water, season lightly with salt, and cook for a further 30 minutes. Pass the potato/bean mixture through a sieve and return to the pan. Stir with a wooden spoon, gradually adding the olive oil, until the puree achieves the correct consistency. Serve as a fresh vegetable.

MUERSI
Country bread with broccoli and peas

2 1/4 LBS/1 KG BROCCOLI
SALT
1 1/2 CUPS/200 G PEAS
8 OZ/200 G WHITE BREAD, SLICED
4–5 TBSP EXTRA VIRGIN OLIVE OIL
1 PEPERONCINO

Blanch the broccoli in lightly-salted water, drain, and set aside. Cook the peas in salted water for about 10 minutes. Heat the olive oil with the peperoncino in a pot (preferably earthenware), and sauté the slices of bread. When the bread is golden-brown, add the peas and broccoli, chopped into small pieces. Mix well and cook for 10 minutes. Serve hot.

CATALOGNE RACANATE
Autumn dandelion crumble
(Illustrated left)

2 CLOVES OF GARLIC
1 TOMATO
SALT
2 3/4 LBS/1.3 KG AUTUMN DANDELION LEAVES
CAPERS
BREADCRUMBS
OLIVE OIL

Finely slice the garlic and tomato. Cook in a little salted water until soft.
Wash the dandelion leaves and put in a casserole dish, then arrange the garlic, tomato, and capers on top. Sprinkle generously with breadcrumbs and drizzle with olive oil. Bake in a preheated oven at 390 °F (200 °C) until the breadcrumbs are crispy.

OLIVE OIL

With its intense flavor, the fruity and very acidic olive oil of Apulia is just as essential to cooking as it is to the region's economy. No other agricultural product has had such a profound effect on the nature and life of the people in the southernmost tip of Italy as this fragrant oil. The lime soils and the dry climate offered – and continue to offer – ideal conditions for successful olive growing. Table olives used to be served as an energy-rich accompaniment to bread, and oil-bearing olives provided a raw material that people could use not only for cooking, but also as fuel for domestic lamps.

Even today, olive-oil production is the most important economic factor in the region of Apulia. The olive oil and table olives produced here account for 40 percent of Italian and 15 percent of global production. The cultivation areas extend over three strips of land: the province of Foggia, the province of Bari, and the Salento peninsula, to which the provinces of Lecce, Brindisi, and Taranto belong. However, this division says nothing about which varieties of olive are grown in which province, because the soil and micro-climatic differences within the three zones are too diverse.

In Apulia, you can now gaze in amazement not only at beautiful works of art and historic buildings, but also at *trappeti*, the ancestor of modern oil mills. In the subterranean pressing cellars, the temperature was constant. The caves wrought from the limestone rock also had only one entrance to the south, to protect against the damaging north wind. Another advantage of the *trappeto* was that it did not cost much to build. The naturally thick walls of the vault cut out of the rock were sufficiently strong to withstand the tremors caused by the extremely heavy millstones, without the need for any additional fortification or complex building work. Feeding the presses was also easier than with other types of mill, as the olives were simply shaken down through the purpose-built shafts. Any waste ran off along the natural fissures in the hollowed-out limestone bedrock. There are about 35 such mills in the area around Gallipoli.

Southern Italy has a long tradition of growing olives. The extensive groves provide almost half of Italy's total olive production.

There may be many varieties, but the olives grown in the south usually produce golden yellow oils that are robust, with a slightly nutty aroma.

Left: The Masseria Serra dell'Isola in Mola di Bari still has an old oil mill.

MUSSEL FARMING

Between the heel and sole of the Italian boot lies the Gulf of Taranto. The inhabitants of the port call the waters around their coast "Mar Piccolo." The "Little Sea," which has relatively warm water temperatures from spring to autumn, is good for breeding both oysters and mussels. These marine-dwellers, *cozze* in Italian, are harvested practically throughout the year. The mussels are bred on boats or platforms firmly anchored to the seabed. From these floating breeding stations hang nets or long nylon ropes, each bearing 200 to 400 pounds (100 to 200 kilograms) of mussels. While growing, the creatures hold on to the ropes with byssus filaments, which cooks call a beard. They must be carefully removed before cooking. The sea swills minerals and algae around, on which the mussels feed. When, after 12 to 14 months, they have reached the correct size, the ropes are heaved out the water and the mussels are removed.

At this stage, the mussels are covered in algal and chalk deposits, so must first be taken to a purification plant. At the same time, they are inspected by the Italian supervisory authorities to ensure that the produce is perfect in terms of hygiene – a control measure that is absolutely sensible in view of the environmental pressure on these coastlines. When the blue-black crustaceans have been precleaned at the factory, they are packed in various weights in plastic nets and sent to the market, where customers are already waiting, because *cozze* are extremely popular in southern Italy and on the islands.

ZUPPA DI COZZE ALLA TARANTINA
Tarento-style mussels

Hors d'oeuvre

2 1/2 LBS/1.2 KG MUSSELS
1/4 PEPERONCINO
1 CLOVE OF GARLIC, WHOLE
2 TBSP EXTRA VIRGIN OLIVE OIL
3/4 LB/300 G RIPE TOMATOES, SKINNED AND SEEDED
1 GLASS DRY WHITE WINE
1 CLOVE OF GARLIC, CHOPPED
SALT AND PEPPER
SLICES OF WHITE BREAD, TOASTED

Scrub the mussels and wash under running water. Sauté the peperoncino and garlic in olive oil. As soon as the garlic starts to brown, remove the garlic and peperoncino from the skillet and add the tomatoes, finely chopped. Simmer for 10 minutes, then add the mussels. Increase the heat and boil until the shells open, shaking occasionally. (Discard any unopened shells.) Add the wine and reduce. Finally add the chopped clove of garlic. Season with salt and pepper. Serve hot with slices of toast.

COZZE RIPIENE
Stuffed mussels

Hors d'oeuvre

2 1/2 LBS/1.2 KG MUSSELS
SCANT 1/2 CUP/100 ML OLIVE OIL
1 CLOVE OF GARLIC
3/4 LB/400 G TOMATOES, SIEVED
4 EGGS
GENEROUS 3 CUPS/200 G FRESH BREADCRUMBS
3/4 CUP/100 G PECORINO CHEESE, GRATED
CHOPPED PARSLEY
SALT AND PEPPER

Scrub the mussels and wash under running water. Cook for about 5 minutes, until they open. Discard any unopened mussels. Heat the olive oil in a large skillet and sauté the clove of garlic until golden brown. Add the sieved tomatoes and cook over a low heat for about 10 minutes.
Beat the eggs in a bowl, then mix in the breadcrumbs, cheese, and parsley. The mixture should be creamy, but not runny. Fill the mussels with the mixture, and close the shells. Carefully add the mussels to the skillet containing the tomatoes and bake in a preheated oven at 390 °F (200 °C) for about 15 minutes.

COZZE GRATINATE
Mussels gratiné
(Illustrated left)

Hors d'oeuvre

2 1/2 LBS/1.2 KG MUSSELS
CHOPPED GARLIC
CHOPPED PARSLEY
BREADCRUMBS
OLIVE OIL

Scrub the mussels and wash under running water. Cook for about 5 minutes, until they open. Discard any unopened mussels. Remove the upper shell and arrange the lower shells containing the mussel flesh in a flameproof dish. Sprinkle with garlic, parsley, and breadcrumbs, and drizzle with a little olive oil.
Bake in a preheated oven at 390 °F (200 °C) for a few minutes.

In this typical mussel farm, the mussels are suspended in tubular nets over platforms anchored to the seabed.

Warm, shallow waters provide the best growing conditions for mussels. They must be very clean, as otherwise the mussels absorb harmful substances.

The mussels are collected and sorted. The larger ones are sold, while the smaller ones are returned to the nets to continue growing.

The Mar Piccolo ("Little Sea") at Taranto (above and background) provides ideal conditions for breeding top-quality mussels.

Rock shells belong to the sea snail family. They have striking, thick-walled, and sometimes even spiny shells.

Tyrian purple from Taranto

Tyrian purple was the most precious dye of ancient times. Obtained from the hypobranchial gland of the rock shell (*Murex brandaris*), it was initially used only to dye the robes of the Roman emperor. Later, rich patricians and high-ranking state officials were also allowed to drape themselves in purple robes. In A.D. 314, the Church discovered purple: Sylvester I was the first pope to incorporate the noble color in his ceremonial vestments.

The ridiculously high price the dye reached on the ancient world market can be explained by the fact that it is extremely difficult to obtain. It took a good 10,000 rock shells to produce just 0.035 ounces (1.2 grams). The Phoenician city of Tyre and the Apulian town of Taranto were long-standing rivals for dominance in the purple dye industry, but in the end the products of Italian provenance were victorious. They were distinctive for their brilliant color, which ranged from bright violet to deep, glowing wine red. Horace described Tyrian purple from Taranto as the definitive imitation of the color of violets.

OYSTERS

The Mar Piccolo at Taranto is a bastion of southern Italian mussel farming. In addition to mussels, they also farm oysters, as they find conditions here ideal. The sea is calm, and in summer the water temperature is always over 71 °F (22 °C). Even Pliny enthused about the mussel beds here, and extolled the oysters from Taranto, the majority of which ended up on the overflowing plates of the Roman upper classes.

Under the emperor Trajan, the city on the gulf became the official farming center and oyster supplier to the capital. However, with the fall of the Roman Empire, interest in the luxury seafood dwindled. It was not until 1784 that the Bourbon king Ferdinand IV, later to become King of Two Sicilies, got the neglected farming beds back into working order, so that his court kitchen could have a constant supply of oysters and mussels.

Mollusks of the very best quality are still farmed here even today. The scientific name of the Taranto oyster is *Lamellosa tarentina*. The very fragile, soft lamellae around the rim are a distinctive feature of its very jagged, wavy, and green-colored shell, while inside, the mussel shells gleam pearly-white. Two-year-old oysters can be called *stragrossa*, extra large. They have a particularly intense flavor and should be enjoyed raw, and well-chilled. Taranto oysters may not be quite so well-known or have quite the reputation of the famous French varieties from Marenne or Arcachon, but they can easily stand comparison with them.

To open an oyster, you will need to wear protective gloves. Place the oyster in the palm of your hand, with the concave shell facing downward to avoid spilling the tasty natural juices contained in the shell together with the much-sought after mollusk. Then run a suitable sharp knife between the shells, and lever them open. When the sphincter muscle has been severed, the oyster can be opened. If it is not going to be eaten immediately, it should be stored temporarily on a bed of ice. It is easy to loosen the creature from its shell

using an oyster fork, which has a sharp blade on one side. Now swallow the oyster and its juices down in one gulp straight from the shell. If you like, you can add a squeeze of lemon juice or a sprinkle of pepper before eating. Slices of white or rye bread, spread with chilled butter, are a good accompaniment to oysters. It is best to refrain from any other extras, as they drown the distinctive, subtle flavor of this delicate creature. There are also more complicated oyster recipes.

To avoid spilling the precious juice, place the oyster in the palm with the more concave shell facing downward.

Holding the knife horizontally, insert it between the two halves of the shell, and then lever the oyster open.

Lift off the top shell. The oyster flesh is in the lower shell, but is still firmly attached.

With a single cut, sever the muscle, so that the oyster and its juice can be easily gulped down straight from the shell.

OSTRICHE ARROSTO
Broiled oysters
(Illustrated opposite)

6 OYSTERS PER PERSON
CHOPPED PARSLEY
2 CLOVES OF GARLIC PER PERSON, CHOPPED
BREADCRUMBS
OREGANO
LEMON JUICE
OLIVE OIL
SALT AND PEPPER

Open the oysters, remove the upper shells, and place the lower halves containing the oyster flesh on a wire rack. Sprinkle the parsley and garlic evenly over the oysters, followed by the breadcrumbs and oregano, and then drizzle with 2–3 drops of lemon juice and a little olive oil. Season with salt and pepper, and broil for 15 minutes.

Opposite: Oysters are less sensitive than you think: A journey of three or four days makes no difference to them.

ZUPPA DI PESCE DI GALLIPOLI
Gallipoli fish soup

2 1/4 LBS/2 KG MIXED FISH AND SEAFOOD (E.G. SEA BASS,
BRACE, SCORPION FISH, SQUID, SCAMPI, MUSSELS, SURMULLET)
1/2 CUP/120 ML OLIVE OIL
I ONION, FINELY SLICED
I 1/4 LBS/600 G TOMATOES, SEEDED AND CUT INTO STRIPS
2 TBSP WHITE WINE VINEGAR
SALT AND PEPPER
SLICES OF TOAST

Gut, wash, and scale the fish. Remove the innards and cut
the squid into rings. Scrub and wash the mussels. Discard
opened mussels
Heat the oil in a large pan, and sauté the onion until soft.
Add the tomatoes, a pinch of salt, and a little pepper, and
cook for 10 minutes.
First add the larger fish and seafood, and bring to a boil.
Then add the smaller fish and seafood, so that everything
will be cooked at the same time. Simmer over a low heat
for 20–30 minutes. Do not stir. Season to taste with salt,
pepper, and vinegar, and serve with the toast.

Above: *Ombrine al sale* – Corb in a salt crust
Bottom right: *Triglie al cartoccio* – Rock mullet cooked in foil parcels

TRABUCCHI

Apulians catch fish in two ways: either they sail far out
to sea and fish using lines and nets, or they stay near
the shore and make the work easier by using a *trabucco*.
On the Gargano coast on the spur of the Italian boot,
they prefer the second option.

The word *trabucco* is probably derived from the
Provençale-Majorcan word *trabajar*, to work. Later the
term became established as a synonym for a high-
masted fishing boat with large sails. If, due to old age
or damage, the ship's hull was no longer usable, the
fishermen dismantled the strong masts and used them
to make *trabucchi*, the fishing devices that made it
possible to fish near the shore. The coasts along the
spur of the Italian boot are the best place to go if you
want to gaze in wonder at numerous *trabucchi*, which,
according to historians, date back to the Saracens.

Fishing with the *trabucco* still requires just as much
patient and attentive sea-gazing by a *rais*, who watches
out for shoals of fish from the top of a beam "floating"
horizontally on the sea. As soon as the prey is directly
over the nets laid out on the sea bed, the *rais* gives the
command to quickly draw up the nets. This is done by
means of a winch, the cables of which run over a
powerful winding drum. These bizarre-looking fishing
devices with their many vertical and horizontal masts
and poles have even been captured by some Italian
artists, who were fascinated by them.

The fish caught using the *trabucco* are prepared in the
tastiest ways. The fishermen's wives cook the fish in a
salt crust, making it wonderfully moist and spicy, or
broil or sauté it. Alternatively, they make the famous
Zuppa di pesce di Gallipoli, a fish soup made in the area
around Gallipoli.

Incidentally, people are passionate about fish soup
throughout Italy, so that it has become a dish found in
virtually all parts of this large, regionally diverse,

culinary landscape. Italy is, after all, the land of the long
coasts, quite apart from the two large and numerous
small islands whose shores are also lapped by the sea.
Only five of Italy's 19 regions, namely Piedmont, the
Aosta valley, Trentino and South Tyrol, Lombardy, and
finally Umbria, have no direct access to the sea. The
rest of the country prides itself on delicious fish or
seafood dishes, and each region makes its own fish
soup. In Liguria and on the Tuscan coast, you can
sample *cacciucco* or *burrida*, in Emilia-Romagna you can
try *brodetto* from Rimini. On the coast of the Marches,
the ports compete to make the best fish soup, and they
have even set up an *Accademia del Brodetto*. The
Neapolitans love hot fish dishes, Sardinia has its own
recipe, Apulia makes *Zuppa di pesce di Gallipoli*, and
Umbria has a freshwater fish dish.

SEPPIE RIPIENE CON PISELLI
Squid stuffed with peas

I 3/4 LBS/800 G READY-PREPARED SQUID
3/4 CUP/40 G BREADCRUMBS
MILK
1/2 CUP/50 G GRATED PECORINO CHEESE
I EGG
2 CLOVES OF GARLIC, CHOPPED
2 TBSP CHOPPED PARSLEY
SALT AND PEPPER
3–4 TBSP EXTRA VIRGIN OLIVE OIL
I CUP CHOPPED ONION
2 3/4 CUPS/400 G PEAS

Wash the squid thoroughly and leave to drain. Moisten the
breadcrumbs with a little milk, combine well with the
cheese, egg, garlic, and parsley, and season to taste with salt
and pepper.
Fill the squid with the mixture, seal with cooking thread,
and place in a pan with the olive oil and onions. Sauté over
a low heat, and then add the shelled peas and a little water.
Season with salt and pepper and cook over a low heat for
about 45 minutes.

Triglie al cartoccio
Rock mullet cooked in foil parcels
(Illustrated below)

Serves two

4 MEDIUM-SIZED READY-PREPARED ROCK MULLET
2 CLOVES OF GARLIC, CRUSHED
THE JUICE OF 1/2 LEMON
OLIVE OIL
3 BAY LEAVES
1/2 TSP PEPPERCORNS
SALT AND PEPPER
3–4 TBSP BLACK OLIVES, PITTED
KITCHEN FOIL (ALTERNATIVELY 4 LARGE SHEETS OF WAXED
PAPER OR ROASTING BAGS)

Scale and wash the fish, then place in a bowl. Combine the
garlic with the lemon juice and 4 tablespoons olive oil.
Crush the bay leaves and peppercorns, and add to the lemon
juice and olive oil mixture. Drizzle the marinade over the
fish, and leave in a refrigerator for at least 2 hours, turning
the fish once.
Preheat the oven to 400 °F (200°C). Brush the kitchen foil
with 1 tablespoon oil. Transfer the fish from the marinade to
the foil, season with salt and pepper, and drizzle with the
marinade. Finely dice the olives and sprinkle over the fish.

Wrap the fish in the foil, crimping the edges of the foil to
seal the "parcel".
Bake in the oven for about 8 minutes. Serve hot in the
kitchen foil.

Ombrine al sale
Corb in a salt crust
(Illustrated opposite, top)

2 CORB (OR SEA BASS), ABOUT 1 LB/500 G EACH
2 1/4 LBS/1 KG COARSE-GRAINED SALT
FRESHLY MILLED PEPPER

Gut the fish and wash well, but do not scale. Put half the
salt in a baking pan, place the fish on top, and cover with
the remaining salt. Cover the pan with a lid, and cook in a
preheated oven at 400 °F (200 °C) for about 30 minutes.
Break open the salt crust, remove the skin, and sprinkle
freshly ground pepper over the fish.

Sogliola gratinata
Sole gratiné

4 READY-PREPARED SOLE, SKINNED, FINS TRIMMED
SALT AND PEPPER
8 TBSP BREADCRUMBS

1 CLOVE OF GARLIC, VERY FINELY CHOPPED
4 TBSP FINELY CHOPPED PARSLEY
6 TBSP GRATED PECORINO CHEESE
6 TBSP OLIVE OIL

Preheat the oven to 430 °F (220 °C). Make an incision in
the fish along the middle as far as the main bone, sprinkle
with pepper, and place on a baking sheet. Combine the
breadcrumbs, garlic, and parsley and spread over both sides
of the incisions. Sprinkle the cheese in the incisions, and
drizzle olive oil over the fish. Then bake for about
15 minutes. Serve immediately.

There is often a dessert buffet at Apulian weddings

A gateau made from ladyfingers, fruit, meringue, and cream

A waiter serves the guests with portions of gateau.

Vito Colucci is the current owner of the Caffè Tripoli, founded in 1911, in Martina Franca. His homemade *crostate* are worth a trip. The café's ice-cream specialties are still made by traditional methods. Vito Colucci uses no colorings or other artificial additives in his cookies and gateaux, which are always freshly made.

CONFECTIONERY

Despite having a busy confectionery trade, Apulian confectionery is practically unknown outside the region. Even so, as early as the Middle Ages, the nuns and professional confectioners had their work cut out for them making sufficient quantities of sweet delicacies for feast days. The confectionery masters, initially known as *pistores* and subsequently as *speziali manuali*, made a decisive contribution to the development of the Apulian sweet tooth. However, the candies were often expensive and therefore kept for special occasions, such as Christmas and Easter, saints' days, a wedding or even a funeral, where friends and relatives gave the bereaved family a *consolo*, a candy consolation.

Unlike other southern Italian confectionery traditions, the Apulians did not initially rely solely on raisins, figs, lemons, and cinnamon, but primarily used two typical products of the region, namely ricotta and almonds. They now use all types of ingredients, however, and in Apulia, they round off a meal with a dessert at least once a week. Fortunately, there are enough saints and other excuses to justify this luxury. *Zeppole*, which are fried in hot oil and flavored with sugar and cinnamon, used to be reserved for St. Joseph's day. Nowadays, the delicious rings are also made on other days, and are baked in the oven to that they are not quite so heavy or fattening.

At Christmas, there are *cartellate*, a star-shaped cookie specialty, laced with white wine and lots of honey or must syrup. The thick, sticky must syrup, *mostocotto*, is also used to make the small, very tasty, jam or marzipan-filled *panzerotti*.

CARTELLATE
Christmas cookies

4 1/4 CUPS/500 G ALL-PURPOSE FLOUR
4–5 TBSP EXTRA VIRGIN OLIVE OIL
1 GLASS OF DRY WHITE WINE
OIL FOR DEEP-FRYING
SCANT 1 CUP/300 G BOILED MUST, SYRUP OR HONEY
CINNAMON

Combine the flour, olive oil, and white wine to make a light, smooth dough. Leave to rest for 1 hour. Roll out the dough very thinly to form a rectangle, and cut into 6-in. (15-cm) long, 1¼-in. (3-cm) wide strips. Roll the strips of dough into snail shapes, and leave to dry overnight. Heat the olive oil, deep-fry the dough snails, and leave to drain on paper towels.

Carefully, immerse the snails totally in the heated boiled must or honey. Transfer to a plate using a slotted spoon, and sprinkle with cinnamon.

SYRUP

Wine must reduced to a syrup has various names in central and southern Italy. The sweet, sticky product obtained when fresh must is reduced to half its original volume or less, is known as *mostocotto*, *sapa*, *saba*, or *vincotto*. *Vincotto*, or boiled wine, is rather a misleading description, because it is not the alcoholic wine that is reduced, but the unfermented must. Even the ancient Romans knew this sort of syrup and enjoyed it mixed with snow to make a classical sorbet. In the Middle Ages, the master chefs left it to rest for a month in airtight conditions, before using it in their confectionery recipes.

As usual with popular confections, every Apulian village has its own recipe for *mostocotto*, but the basic principle is always the same: fresh, ripe wine grapes are pressed through a very fine sieve placed over a non-galvanized copper pan. The sieved mixture is slowly brought to a boil on the top of the stove, any scum being removed with a slotted spoon. The syrup is ready when the grape juice has been reduced to half its original volume. The syrup is then poured into glazed ceramic containers or glass bottles, which must be carefully sealed to prevent the *mostocotto* from spoiling. Traditionally, menstruating women or women who do not belong to the family may not be present when the syrup is being prepared, as otherwise the must is bound to separate into two layers, sugar on the bottom, and an aqueous solution on the top.

The Apulians used to make sweet syrups not only from wine must, but also from figs. Of course, every village had its own secret recipe, but we can divulge the basic process: In the second half of August, the peasants harvested the ripe figs, and cooked them, preferably over a wood fire, for a few hours, until the fruit mixture had reduced by half. A fabric bag was then filled with the concentrated contents of the pot, and then hung for at least 24 hours outside in the fresh air or in a suitable place indoors, to allow the fig juice to drip out. The juice was collected in a pot, and then cooked again over a low heat for about 3 hours, until it had become a dense syrup. Like *mostocotto*, *cotto di fichi* also has to be kept in hermetically sealed containers to keep out bacteria.

The **Chasselas dorata** has medium-sized clusters, on which hang medium-sized, oval grapes. They have a delicate flavor, reminiscent of nutmeg .

The **Italia** is the leading variety of the Italian peninsula. It produces clusters of tear-shaped grapes, and is harvested in mid-September.

DESSERT GRAPES

Italy is a land of grapes. They not only grow wine grapes for winemaking, but also excellent dessert grapes. Apulia provides more than half of the Italian consumption of *uva di tavola*. The varieties cultivated here are particularly sweet and juicy because of the fertile soils and the warm climate. The Chasselas dorata, Italia, Regina, and Baresana varieties are now also exported to the rest of Europe. Throughout Italy, grapes are often served with other fruits for dessert. The green or golden grapes are also used in *macedonia di frutta*, fruit salad, and to decorate the tops of cakes.

Mostocotto
Reduced grape must

Grape must from white or red grapes
Sugar to taste
or
2 cups/500 ml strong red or white country wine
2 cups/200 g sugar

Either reduce the grape must, adding sugar to taste, to form a thick syrup, or try the following variation:

Heat the wine and sugar in a heavy pan until the sugar has dissolved. Reduce the mixture by at least a half, preferable two-thirds. Leave to cool, pour into a bottle, and store in a refrigerator.

Grano al mostocotto
Wheat with boiled must
(Illustrated below)

1 1/2 cups/300 g wheat grains
Salt
2 oz/50 g chocolate almond clusters
1/3 cup/50 g chopped hazelnuts
4 oz/100 g chocolate, grated
4 oz/100 g candied citrus peel, finely diced
1 tsp ground cloves
1 tsp cinnamon
2 cups/200 g ripe pomegranate seeds
Boiled must

Soak the wheat grains in water for 3 days, changing the water daily. Then boil the grains in copious salted water until soft, drain, leave to cool, and transfer to a pan. Add all the remaining ingredients, and mix thoroughly. Divide into portions, and serve with boiled must.

The **regina** grape is also ready for harvesting in mid-September. The splendid clusters of large, sweet, shimmering-golden grapes taste very sweet.

Grano al mostocotto – Wheat with boiled must.

CASTEL DEL MONTE

Castel del Monte lies south of Andria in the heart of
Apulia, and forms a perfect octagon. The odd-looking
fortress, which was built by Frederick II between 1240
and 1250, has an octagonal ground plan, is reinforced
with eight octagonal towers, and has eight rooms per
story. Even historians do not know exactly what the
Hohenstaufen emperor wanted to achieve by this
remarkable construction. Subsequent generations used
the castel as a prison, a bastion against the plague, or a
place of refuge in case of danger. Since the 19th
century, the Castel del Monte has been repeatedly
restored, and is now open to visitors. The name of the
fortress has now been given to a group of DOC wines
that are made from various grape varieties (Aglianico,
Uva di Troia, Pinot nero, Chardonnay, Pinot bianco,
and Sauvignon). These are northern Apulia's top
quality wines.

Background: Castel del Monte (1240–1250) rises
impressively from a hill that dominates the landscape.

THE ROMANS' GARDEN OF EDEN

The Romans thought Apulia was a real Garden of Eden, or, more prosaically, a major supplier of excellent agricultural produce and wines. Particularly in the south of the region, the influence of Greek culture is unmistakable, and in their everyday dialect, the inhabitants still even use some ancient Greek words. In addition to wine grapes, large quantities of dessert grapes are also cultivated here, and the area devoted to growing these two types of grape is almost twice as large as all German vineyards put together.

Apulia is Italy's grape factory. Yields are higher here than anywhere else in Italy, and in some vineyards, up to 16 tons of grapes are harvested per acre (40 tons of grapes per hectare) – four times the amount usually considered to be the upper limit for good wines. In addition to the high yields, which are obtained mainly in the huge, mechanically-worked grape fields of the wide Apulian plains, Apulia's winegrowing is remarkable for a second reason. Although less than two percent of Italy's entire wine production has DOC status, in other words is viewed, at least in the eyes of the law, as a quality wine, Apulia has a practically infinite number of DOC labels. Almost every village,

Brilliant white *trulli*, small, skittle-shaped buildings, are a feature of the landscape around Locorotondo in central Apulia.

Salento

Salento is a very recent denomination for a table wine with a geographic mark of origin (Igt). This was partly created to reintegrate some of the best wines of Apulia, which did not comply with the DOC stipulations in style or varietal composition, into the origin system. A myriad of varieties and types of wine is now sold under the name of Salento. Many of the appellations are used for both white and red wines, even for rosé, dessert, liqueur, and sparkling wines, which makes it no easier for the consumer to get accurate information.

Castel del Monte

This most northern of top-quality wines from Apulia is produced in the area around the Hohenstaufen castle of the same name in central Apulia. The red wines are pressed from Montepulciano d'Abruzzo and Uva di Troia, and can be very elegant and complex. They are a good accompaniment to an entire meal of sumptuous Apulian cooking.

Salice Salentino

The Salice Salentino is one of the oldest DOC wines of Apulia and should not be confused with the Igt Salento. The single-village appellation from the place of the same name and its direct surrounding area exists in a great number of different varieties, including not only red, white, and rosé wines, but also the sweet Aleatico wine.

Primitivo di Manduria

The only mark of origin in Apulia to designate a single-varietal wine from the Primitivo (Zinfandel) grape, it has recently produced a range of attractive and interesting wines. It is used for wines from numerous areas in the provinces of Taranto and Bari. The wines are dry and have a soft, fruity flavor.

Copertino

This red wine from the province of Lecce in the extreme south comes from one of the numerous single-village appellations. It is made primarily from Negroamaro grapes, and is sometimes even a single-varietal Negroamaro wine, although Malvasia, Montepulciano, and Sangiovese can also be used.

Locorotondo

The only, slightly better-known, white DOC wine from Apulia comes from the center of the region. It is mainly produced using the Verdeca and Bianco d'Alessano varieties, and is light in style and quality. Sometimes it can also be pleasantly fruity. However, very few producers sell really good products.

Brindisi

This is another Negroamaro red wine named after its province of origin, and here too the variety can be enriched in flavor by adding various other varieties. There is also a Riserva quality of the red Brindisi wine, which has to be matured for longer in the barrel and has to have a higher alcohol content.

San Severo, Alezio & Co.

Of the numerous DOC and Igt wines, the following should be mentioned: San Severo (white, red, and rosé wines) from the northernmost parts of the region: Alezio (red and rosé wine made from Negroamaro grapes); the sweet Aleatico di Puglia, the Gioia del Colle, which also includes Primitivo in its range of varieties; the Leverano (a neighbor and relative of the Salice Salentino); and finally the wine with the unpronounceable name of Cacc'e Mmite di Lucera (which is a red wine made from various varieties).

especially in the provinces of Brindisi and Lecce, seems to make its own DOC wine, and often wines of this label are bottled by only one or two winegrowers. The majority of the grapes and wines serves only as raw material for the large vermouth factories in the north or to produce grape must concentrate, which is used in Italy instead of beet sugar to increase the alcohol content of more feeble wines.

Apulia thus definitely has talents that it could turn to good account. But unfortunately only a few winegrowers and viniculturists in the region use and exploit this potential. In this southern region, not only is the climate ideal for winegrowing, but there is also a whole range of characteristic, independent grape varieties that give its wines a distinctive character. The most common is the red Negroamaro, used in many

DOC wines, such as Brindisi, Alezio, Leverano, or Salice Salentino, but also in the sweet Aleatico wine. Its wines are usually dark in color and have a robust flavor, occasionally even slightly rough and rustic.

Primitivo, which is also red, originated from the Croatian grape Crljenak kastelanski, from which the original Californian Zinfandel variety and the Croatian Plavac mali developed. All three therefore, have very similar qualities, although for a long time only the Californian Zinfandel produced really superior, interesting wines. The Zinfandel was long thought to have originated from the Primitivo, but the Italian variety did not appear until Zinfandel had already become firmly established in California. Nowadays it is believed that Primitivo and Zinfandel developed from the Crljenak kastelanski independent of each other.

As far as the Montepulciano d'Abruzzo is concerned, which is particularly popular in the Abruzzi and in the Marches, it is used in many Apulian wines together with Negroamaro, and gives the wines a pleasantly rounded, harmonious flavor. The red Uva di Troia, a component of Castel del Monte wine, and the white Bombino are also worth mentioning. The most interesting white wines of Apulia are, however, made from the internationally popular French Chardonnay or Sauvignon varieties.

BASILICATA

BASILICATA

Peperoncino
Lucanica sausages
Happy pigs
Bread
Confectionery
Homemade pasta
Lamb
Honey
Hellenic wine

Basilicata is a tranquil, secluded region. Visitors rarely stray into this sun-drenched, inaccessible but nonetheless fascinating region between the heel and the sole of the Italian boot, and travelers who come only for the cuisine are even rarer, even though Basilicata definitely has a few specialties to offer. Even in ancient times, when this stretch of land was still called Lucania, Roman writers such as Cicero, Martial, and Horace praised the local sausages. And the Epicurean Apicius went so far as to provide the first description of the *lucanica*, a tasty, fresh pork sausage, served by Lucanian slaves to their Roman masters. Even today, pork continues to play an important role in the cuisine of Basilicata. Almost every family rears its own pig, and they throw a big party when the pig is slaughtered. If the meat is not being made into the excellent, traditional sausages, such as *lucanica*, *pezzenta*, and *cotechinata*, it is roasted on a spit. This is also their preferred way of cooking mutton and lamb.

Pasta is another mainstay of the regional cuisine. As in the neighboring southern regions, in Basilicata homemade pasta is made from durum wheat and water. Delicious vegetable or meat sauces transform this simple but nutritious dish into a distinctive culinary experience. On feast days, kitchens are filled with the aroma of *Ragù della mamma*, made to a recipe that has remained so secret that all we know is that it is made from large chunks of meat.

However, the most distinguishing feature of Basilicata's cuisine is the peperoncino. These bright red, devilishly hot chili peppers are used in almost every dish. Every market sells them, tied into pretty braids, and in this region, even the mild varieties have long been considered a healthy staple food. Pork, sausage, pasta, and peperoncini – that sounds like good, solid cooking, but hardly suitable ingredients for dessert. However, Basilicata is surprisingly good for desserts. Here, they finish a meal either with a spicy cheese, preferably a *provolone*, which should be ripened over your own fireplace, or a delicious dessert, either baked or that has been mixed with lots of honey.

After a sumptuous Lucanian feast, people like to take a time-tested digestive, the bitter Amaro Lucano, which is now enjoyed throughout Italy.

Previous double page: Wine is prepared for transport at the vineyards of Armando Martino in Rionero Vulture (province of Potenza).

Left: Rivello, situated beneath Monte Sirino, is one of Basilicata's most beautiful small towns.

PEPERONCINO

People cook with fiery passion in Basilicata. Just as in Abruzzi, peperoncini, also known as chili peppers in English, can be found in all sorts of shapes and sizes at the local market. But whether they are small and round, or somewhat larger and more elongated, these peppers have one thing in common: their glowing red color and their fiery piquancy, which can leave you gasping for breath and hastily reaching for the nearest glass of water if you do not eat them with the caution that is necessary.

Alongside pork, these breath-taking peperoncini, which come from the same family as the bell pepper, are the distinctive culinary emblem of Basilicata. In strict botanical terminology, the varieties represented here, called *Capsicum abbreviatum*, *Capsicum acuminatum*, and *Capsicum fasciculatum*, belong to *Capsicum annuum*. These are just three representatives of the hundreds of varieties that exist throughout the world, some of which display extremely different shapes, sizes, aromas, and degrees of piquancy. Our paprika, for example, is made from a less spicy variety, whereas Tabasco owes its fiery effect to an extremely piquant variety.

However, in Basilicata, they do not bother with the botanical subtleties and strings of names. Affectionately known here as *frangisella*, *cersella*, *pupon*, or *diavulicciu*, the peppery, sun-drenched fruit is primarily used to flavor the region's meat and sausage specialties, as well as the delicious pasta meat sauce, the recipe for which is known only to *mamma* and *nonna*. Lucanian kitchens are old-fashioned but cozy places, with strings of peperoncini hanging from the ceiling, so they are always to hand, even on the busiest cooking days, such as a wedding or a religious festival. It is no coincidence that Basilicata has the highest per capita consumption of the little red devils.

No one knows exactly how the peperoncino came to Europe. Some think it found its way to the major sea ports of the Mediterranean from the East – first chopped into pieces as merchandise, then also as a complete plant, because the spice made from the red fruits used to be known as *Indian Pepper*. Others, however, believe that this description should not be taken literally in geographical terms, as *Indian* was often synonymous with *West Indian*, so that peperoncino therefore must have come from America. Christopher Columbus is alleged to have brought the plant back from his second journey to the New World. The discoverer's boats thus transported not only maize, potatoes, and tomatoes to the ports of his home country, Spain, but also the chili pepper plant. In support of this theory, it is true that the new spice first spread through Spain, and only moved on from there to conquer the rest of Europe. The undemanding plants found the conditions in the Mediterranean favorable and had no difficulty becoming established in vegetable gardens.

Kitchens also welcomed the spicy pods, because peperoncini not only lent a stimulating spiciness to the foods it was used to flavor, but were also a good way of preserving meat dishes, fish, and sauces. And what is more, the little bundles of flavor also proved to be extremely good for medicinal purposes. Their extremely high vitamin C content, which they share with their milder bell pepper relatives, helped protect poor farmers against the dreaded deficiency diseases of scurvy and tooth loss. They also proved to be an effective antiseptic, good for the digestion, and helpful in cases of impotence. Used externally, they also relieved muscular tension and sciatica.

Peperoncini play an important role in the cuisine of Basilicata. The Enoteca La Farmacia dei Sani in Maratea sells peppery spiced oils as well as wine.

The little condiment even found its way into literature. In a cookery book he published, Alexandre Dumas the Older cites the peperoncino as an essential ingredient in his favorite salad, and his Italian colleague Gabriele D'Annunzio describes the peppers as being "crazy, bright red devil's teeth." Filippo Tommaso Marinetti's futurists even considered the spice plant to be an "impromptu hors d'oeuvres, a fiery little horn that should be nibbled straight from the hand."

You should, however, handle the little devil with caution. If you want to make the peperoncini slightly less piquant, remove the seeds and the white membranes. It is essential to wash your hands thoroughly after preparing peperoncini, to avoid getting capsaicin, the ingredient responsible for their spiciness, in the eyes. When cooking with peperoncini, always remember that the little pods have a direct link to hell. This will prevent any mishaps.

PENNE ALL'ARRABBIATA
Penne served with a spicy sauce
(Illustrated opposite and below)

2 1/4 CUPS/500 G TOMATOES, SKINNED, SEEDED, AND FINELY DICED
2 TBSP BUTTER
1/4 LB/100 G BACON, DICED
I CUP FINELY CHOPPED ONION
2 CLOVES OF GARLIC, SLICED
2 DRIED PEPERONCINI, CRUSHED
SALT AND PEPPER
I LB/500 G PENNE
A BUNCH OF FLAT-LEAFED PARSLEY, FINELY CHOPPED
1/2 CUP/50 G FRESHLY GRATED PECORINO CHEESE

Pass the chopped tomato through a sieve. Melt the butter in a skillet. Add the bacon and onion and sauté over a low heat, stirring occasionally. Mix in the garlic, sieved tomato, and peperoncini. Season with salt and pepper, then simmer. Meanwhile, boil the penne until *al dente*, then mix with the sauce. Add the parsley and serve with a sprinkling of grated pecorino on top.

PATATE E SEDANO
Potatoes with celery

OLIVE OIL
2 CLOVES OF GARLIC, CHOPPED
2–3 TBSP CHOPPED PARSLEY
A GENEROUS POUND/500 G TOMATOES, SKINNED
SALT
I DRIED PEPERONCINO, CRUSHED
2 LBS/1 KG BLANCHED CELERY, CUT INTO SMALL PIECES
2 LBS/1 KG POTATOES, PEELED AND CUT INTO PIECES
SLICES OF TOAST

Heat the olive oil, add the garlic, parsley, and tomatoes, together with a little water if necessary, and then season with salt and peperoncino. When the sauce begins to boil, add the celery and cook for about 15 minutes. Then add the

Peperoncini, also known as chili peppers, paprika, or Spanish peppers, come in various sizes. The narrow, tapered varieties are between 1¼ and 6 inches (3–15 centimeters) long. They are also found in round and square forms.

In Basilicata, the small peppers are considered to be the hottest and are therefore known as *diavolicci*, little devils. However, the long, thin types, called *sigarette*, are also extremely piquant, and you have to be accustomed to very spicy food already to appreciate fully the truly authentic cuisine of Basilicata. When experimenting with the spice at home, you should proceed with caution, using too little rather than too much, as the spiciness increases when cooked. Storing the spicy peppers presents no problem. String them together and hang the cord up in the autumn sunshine for a few days or weeks. They lose nothing of their aroma or piquancy when dried. Due to water loss, they become hard and light as a feather. Before using, crush them in a mortar or chop them with a heavy knife.

potatoes and continue to cook until soft. Arrange the slices of toast on deep plates, pour over the stewed vegetables, and serve immediately.

POLLO ALLA POTENTINA
Potenza-style chicken
(Illustrated left)

I CHICKEN, 2 3/4 LB/1.2 KG IN WEIGHT
6–8/300 G RIPE TOMATOES
2 TBSP/30 G BUTTER
2 TBSP/30 ML OLIVE OIL
I ONION, SLICED
2/3 CUP/150 ML DRY WHITE WINE
I PEPERONCINO, CRUSHED
I TBSP CHOPPED BASIL
I TBSP CHOPPED PARSLEY
1/2 CUP/50 G PECORINO CHEESE, CRUMBLED
SALT

Wash and joint the chicken. Skin, seed, and divide each tomato into eight. Heat the butter and oil in a skillet, add the onions, and then brown the chicken pieces on all sides. Add the white wine and sprinkle with the peperoncino. As soon as the wine has reduced, add the tomato pieces, basil, parsley, and pecorino. Cover and leave to cook over a low heat for about 1 hour, adding water occasionally if necessary. Serve with sauté potatoes.

LUCANICA SAUSAGES

The *salsicce lucane*, the pork sausages from Lucania, come in several varieties. The most sought-after are made using only top quality meat, filet or leg, with every trace of fat or gristle removed. The meat mixture is either seasoned with salt, pepper, and fennel seeds, or with rendered pork fat, pepper, salt, peperoncino, and fennel seeds. When made, the sausages are left to dry for 20 to 30 days.

The long, thin *salsiccia* is popular throughout Italy, and the regions therefore squabble over where it originated. The fact that the delicious little pork sausages are also called *lucanica* makes it more likely that they originated from southern Italy. The people of Lombardy, however, want nothing to do with this theory and cite their own tradition, according to which Theodolinde, the queen of the Langobards, invented this special sausage in the 7th century. Legend has it that she subsequently not only gave the tribe the famous iron crown, now kept in Monza cathedral, but also the recipe for this culinary creation. With the inhabitants of Veneto, this story produces only a weary smile, because they are firmly convinced that the pork

Above: Resonsible breeders make an effort to look after wild pigs such as the Cinta senese.

sausage was born in their territory. All central Italians are of the same opinion.

The sausages were also extremely popular in ancient Rome. Varro, a contemporary of Cicero, expressed a firm opinion on the origin of the little sausage: *Lucanica a Lucanis populis a quibus romani milites primum didicerunt*. (When staying with the people of Lucania, the Roman soldiers discovered a sausage by the name of Lucanica.) This would seem to decide the dispute over the origin of the Lucanica in Basilicata's favor, but who knows if Varro was telling the truth…

Lucanica - Pork sausage

HAPPY PIGS

Pork is a staple food in Basilicata, and the popular saying *crisc' lu purch'ca t'ung' lu muss* (a pig gives you a full belly) is a culinary doctrine. However, the animals are not often bred commercially. It is more a case of each family rearing its own pig, looking after it with tender, loving care, and then celebrating its slaughter with a big party.

Most of the meat is used to make tasty sausage products, which serve as a store for the family. In hard times, the marketable meat is also sold to prosperous towns. Thus in this region, the pig is not only a bristly member of the household, but also has a real economic value. And in the poorest region of Italy, where yields from agriculture are comparatively low, that is of great reassurance to the farmers.

Even today, pigs reared in Basilicata are still fed almost entirely on natural foodstuffs, such as broad beans, maize, and acorns, which enhance the flavor of the meat. The methods used to preserve the meat are also natural. Sausages are preserved under a layer of rendered pork fat. This has two advantages: Food additives are rendered superfluous, and the fat does not penetrate the sausage, so does not affect its composition or flavor.

BRUSCHETTA ALLA PANCETTA
Country bread with bacon

1 LEEK
2 SLICES/50 G SMOKED BACON, DICED
1 CUP/150 G SIEVED TOMATOES
6 BLACK OLIVES, PITTED AND FINELY CHOPPED
SALT
1 DRIED PEPERONCINO, CRUSHED
A FEW SLICES OF WHITE BREAD, TOASTED
A FEW SLICES OF CACIOCAVALLO CHEESE

Cut the leek into small pieces and fry in a skillet with the diced bacon. Add the sieved tomatoes and olives, and season with salt and peperoncino.
Arrange the cheese slices on the hot toast and serve with the tomato sauce.

SPEZZATINO DI MAIALE
Pork goulash
(Illustrated below)

1 1/4 LB/600 G LEAN PORK
1 SPRIG OF ROSEMARY
5 CLOVES OF GARLIC
2–3 TBSP EXTRA VIRGIN OLIVE OIL
SALT AND PEPPER
1 PEPERONCINO
1 1/2 CUPS/300 G RIPE TOMATOES, SEEDED AND CHOPPED

Cut the meat into pieces and sauté in olive oil with the rosemary and garlic until brown. Season with salt and pepper and add the peperoncino and tomato. Braise for about 1 hour, adding a little hand-hot water if necessary.

Casertana
Towards the end of the 19th century, the Casertana breed could be found in almost all provinces of Campania, from Lazio to Molise, and in other regions of southern Italy. Now the creatures have practically died out and are kept only in a few breeding farms in Benevento.

Mora romagnola
Only a very few Mora romagnola pigs remain. Mario Lazzari, a pigbreeder in Faenza, has devoted himself to keeping the breed for several years now. Originally these free-roaming pigs could be found throughout the provinces of Forlì and Ravenna.

Siciliana
The Siciliana breed probably developed from the Casertana. Until the end of the 19th century, these pigs could be found throughout Sicily. Now, only a few continue to live in the quiet, inaccessible areas such as Madonia and Nebrodi.

Large white italiano
The Large White breed, which comes from Great Britain, is the most common in the world. The typically pink-colored animals can adapt to any environment, are also well-suited to life in a sty, and fatten quickly. Crossbreeding with Italian breeds means that we can now talk of a large white italiano.

At the Arena bakery (Trecchina, province of Potenza), the dough is prepared in the traditional way (above) and baked in a wood oven (background).

BREAD

Nn nghè mangiat r're cchiù sapurit'r rippan is an old Lucanian proverb, meaning, "There's no dish more regal than bread." No saying could be more fitting for the basic idea behind the culinary art in Basilicata: how, with a lot of love, you can conjure up a tasty dish from a few plain, simple ingredients. Cheap and simple bread products assume an important position. In many parts of the region, housewives still bake the traditional bread, *panella*, themselves. The dough is made from wheat flour, yeast, and cooked potatoes. Each of these very substantial loaves is the size of a car wheel and will provide a family with enough bread for a week.

PANCOTTO
Bread soup
(Illustrated above right)

4–6/200 G TOMATOES
5–6 TBSP EXTRA VIRGIN OLIVE OIL
1 BUNCH OF PARSLEY
2 BAY LEAVES
1 CLOVE OF GARLIC
1 STICK OF CELERY
4 POTATOES
VEGETABLES OF THE SEASON,
EG. CAVOLONERO OR SAVOY CABBAGE
SALT AND FRESHLY MILLED PEPPER

1 LB/500 G STALE BREAD, SLICED AND TOASTED
GRATED PECORINO CHEESE.

Dice the tomatoes and put in a pan together with the olive oil, parsley, bay leaves, garlic, and chopped celery. Put the peeled and diced potatoes and the finely chopped vegetables in the pan. Add a generous 4 cups (1 liter) water, season with salt and pepper. Cut the bread slices in half and cook in the soup for ca. 30 minutes. Serve with freshly grated pecorino.

ACQUASALE
"Salted water"
(Illustrated right and below)

1 ONION, FINELY SLICED
3–4 TBSP EXTRA VIRGIN OLIVE OIL
1 CLOVE OF GARLIC
2 TBSP CHOPPED PARSLEY
1 DRIED PEPERONCINO, CRUSHED
SALT
3 TOMATOES
4 SLICES OF STALE BREAD
FRESHLY MILLED PEPPER

Sauté the onion in olive oil. Add the garlic, parsley, and a little peperoncino, and season lightly with salt. Blanch, skin, seed, and coarsely dice the tomatoes. As soon as the onion starts to brown, add the tomatoes and a little boiling water. Bring to a boil. Arrange the slices of bread on plates, pour the tomato-onion mixture on top, and sprinkle with freshly milled pepper.

CONFECTIONERY

The very traditional confectionery of Basilicata differs from the sugary temptations of the neighboring regions of Campania, Apulia, Calabria, and indeed Sicily, in that it is quite down-to-earth. Of course, on feast days Basilicata can come up with all kinds of sweet and sticky confectionery, but the desserts served on a "normal" Sunday are perhaps a bit less sweet than you would expect in the south of Italy. Also, the obvious poverty of their region has long forced the Lucanian confectioners to conjure up a little delicacy from the simplest of ingredients. Admittedly, such delicacies can still not compete with a sumptuous cake from Sicily, but they definitely have a particular charm of their own and taste wonderful.

COPETE
Almond drops
(Illustrated above right)

1 CUP/120 G ALMONDS
2 EGG WHITES
CINNAMON
3 CUPS/380 G CONFECTIONERS' SUGAR

Pour boiling water over the almonds, then peel, roast in the oven, and chop finely. Beat the egg whites in a bowl until stiff. Add the almonds, a little cinnamon, and 2¾ cups confectioners' sugar. Mix well. Using a spoon, shape into approximately 30 droplets, arranging them on a baking sheet lined with baking parchment.
Dredge with the remaining sugar and bake in a preheated oven at 400 °F (200 °C) for about 15 minutes. Leave to cool and then serve.

UOVA RIPIENE AL CIOCCOLATO
Chocolate-filled eggs

4 EGGS
1/2 CUP/50 G CONFECTIONERS' SUGAR
3 TBSP/30 G COCOA POWDER
5 TSP VANILLA SUGAR
1 1/2 OZ/40 G DARK CHOCOLATE, GRATED
1 SMALL GLASS HERB LIQUEUR (STREGA)
1 EGG WHITE
1/4 CUP/30 G ALL-PURPOSE FLOUR
EXTRA VIRGIN OLIVE OIL

Hard-boil the eggs, cut in half lengthwise, remove the egg yolks and place in a bowl. Crumble the egg yolks and mix together with half the confectioners' sugar, the cocoa powder, a little vanilla sugar (sugar kept in a jar with a vanilla bean), the dark chocolate, and the herb liqueur to form a smooth paste. Beat the egg white until it is stiff.
Fill the cavities in the halved eggs with the mixture, coat with flour, dip in the egg white and deep-fry in copious olive oil. Remove the eggs using a slotted spoon, leave to drain on paper towels, dredge with the remaining confectioners' sugar, and serve warm.

WE'RE NO CHRISTIANS

The doctor, author, and painter Carlo Levi (1902–1975) was exiled to Lucania, in other words Basilicata, in 1935/36 for his antifascist activities. The educated native of Turin described his experiences there in his autobiographical work *Christ stopped at Eboli*. In the 1930s, the picture presented to the onlooker by the southern half of a totally exhausted Italy was particularly terrible. At that time, in the mountains behind Salerno a different world began, and not only for Carlo Levi, a world of abject poverty, terminal illness, relentless misery, and primeval superstition. But the educated man from the "civilized" north was not the only one to recognize the grayness of life. The long-suffering people to whom this backward region was home were also aware of it. Lucanian cooking during the fascist era also became meager. Carlo Levi reports that the poor ate nothing but bread all year round, not the tasty bread of the south of Italy that today's travelers can enjoy, but rather coarse, country bread.

In 1979, Carlo Levi's novel *Cristo si è fermato a Eboli* was filmed by Francesco Rosi. Like the book, the film is concerned with the living conditions in Lucania in the fascist period. One of the lead roles in the film is played by Irene Papas.

HOMEMADE PASTA

The cuisine of Basilicata may be simple, but it is by no means unimaginative. Quite the opposite, in fact, for even the simplest ingredients are treated here with patience and love. The basic pasta dough, which is still often made at home, consists almost solely of durum wheat and water. The addition of eggs is practically unheard of. The fact that, despite this, the simple, but very nutritious food has become a culinary highlight is due to the wealth of imaginative ideas of the Lucanian cooks. They have invented not only spicy sauces and stews, but also an infinite variety of pasta shapes, sometimes made using very simple devices.

Take the *cavarola*, for example. It is a small, grooved wooden chopping board usually handcrafted by shepherds. The pasta dough is rolled over the board to make *strascinati*, literally meaning dragged pasta shapes. The *maccarunara* is another special pasta board used to make *tagliolini*, which are similar to *maccheroni alla chitarra*. To make *triid*, on the other hand, all you need

Strascinati, literally meaning dragged pasta shapes, are made by rolling small portions of dough over the *cavarola*. This gives the pasta its characteristic pattern.

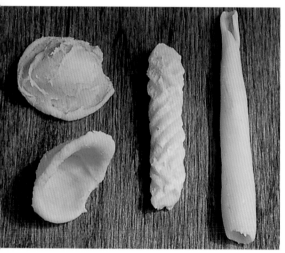

From left to right: *Orecchiette, strascinati* and *ferrettini*.

Above: In the Antica Osteria Marconi restaurant in Potenza, traditional Lucanian pasta is made by hand.

is nimble fingers. This very traditional pasta is said to be derived from the Sicilian *trie* and was brought to the southern Italian mainland in the early 12th century by the Norman prince Roger II. To make these long pasta strips, which in other regions are called *vermicelli* or *spaghettini*, a hole is pressed into the center of a ball of dough weighing approximately three-quarters of a pound (300 grams). The ring of dough is then rolled using jerky hand movements to form an increasingly long strip, which is then wound up like wool. The soft strips should not tear, nor should they stick together.

You need a lot of pasta-making experience in order to make *triid*. A single "cord of dough" has to be produced from a ring of dough.

The "cord of dough" is then drawn out further until it is a "string of dough." The great skill is to avoid breaking the dough.

The *rasola* is a sharp-edged wooden or metal spatula that is used to cut equal-sized portions from a strip of dough.

Orecchiette are made by pinching the precut portions of dough between the thumb and index finger to form an ear shape.

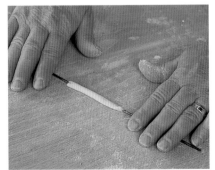

A *ferretta*, a special metal rod, is used to make *ferretti* or *ferrettini*.

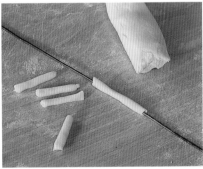

The thinly-rolled dough is first wrapped around the *ferretta*. The dough is then cut and the pasta shapes carefully twisted off the rod.

STRASCINATI ALLA MENTA
Strascinati with mint

14 OZ/400 G STRASCINATI (OR ANY OTHER HOMEMADE PASTA)
1 SLICE/30 G BACON, FINELY DICED
1 CLOVE OF GARLIC, CHOPPED
1 PEPERONCINO, CHOPPED
3–4 TBSP EXTRA VIRGIN OLIVE OIL
A FEW LEAVES OF MINT

Boil the pasta in copious salted water until *al dente*.
Meanwhile fry the diced bacon, garlic, and peperoncino in the olive oil. When the pasta is almost cooked, add the mint leaves to the bacon.
Drain the pasta, arrange on plates, and pour over the sauce.

CHEESE

The range of cheeses in Basilicata is typical of southern Italy. Ricotta is sold as a fresh product or used as a cured and matured hard cheese. Mozzarella, *scamorza*, and *provolone* play a major role, as does *butirro*. This is a mozzarella cheese with

Cacciocavallo

a knob of unsalted butter in the center. The cheese will keep for about two months and prevents the enveloped butter from spoiling. This meant that people could still enjoy butter in the hot summer months even before the invention of the refrigerator.

As well as *pasta-filata* cheeses, there are also many types of sheep's cheeses: *Caciocavalla* and pecorino come in various stages of ripeness. The mild varieties are a popular table cheese, while the older types are grated and used in cooking. Pecorino from Moliterno is a specialty. In some areas the rustic cheesemakers use special cheese molds to decorate *caciocavallo* cheese with the shapes of knights and ladies.

AGNELLO SOTT'ACETO
Lamb marinated in vinegar

2 CUPS/500 ML WATER
2 CUPS/500 ML WHITE WINE VINEGAR
2 LBS/1 KG LAMB, CUT INTO PIECES
SALT
1 DRIED PEPERONCINO, CRUSHED

Pour the water and vinegar into a pan and cook the lamb in it. Transfer the lamb to a glass bowl with a lid and add enough of the hot water/vinegar cooking liquid to cover the meat completely. Season with salt and peperoncino and cover. The lamb will then keep for about a week.

LAMB

Even just a few decades ago, lamb was still a real delicacy in Basilicata, the best present you could give a friend. Shepherds were too poor to be able to afford to eat the lambs they themselves had reared. In times of poverty and hunger, the delicate, lean meat was considered to be an unfailing remedy: If a relative was seriously ill, the family would exchange its belongings for a lamb. Even today, the meat is still much sought-after. Particularly at high feast days such as Easter or Christmas, people try to get hold of a corn-fed lamb. That is no simple matter, however, because many farms in Basilicata are now managed by Apulian farmers, who prefer to sell their animals to Apulia.

The meat of the adult sheep is also popular in this region. Often, a single adult sheep is cooked to make a communal meal for 10 to 20 people. When the grapes or olives have been successfully harvested, people all sit down together and eat *pecora*. The Lucanians leave the meat to simmer with tomatoes, potatoes, onions, and celery in an earthenware pot for hours until it is sufficiently tender, and the heavy aroma of *pecora* hangs in the air for days after.

Even the poor people of Lucania treat themselves at Christmas. Traditionally, 13 different dishes were served up, from chicory soup to salt cod with paprika to roast lamb, which, as the *piatto forte*, was the centerpiece of this comparatively opulent feast.

In the cuisine of central and southern Italy, sheep are important not only for their meat, but also for their milk, which is used to make specialty cheeses such as pecorino and *caciocavallo*.

Agnello alla pastora
Lamb with potatoes
(Illustrated left)

Scant 2 lbs/800 g lamb
1 lb/500 g potatoes
6–8/300 g ripe tomatoes, skinned, seeded, and finely chopped
3–4 tbsp extra virgin olive oil
2 tbsp chopped parsley
1 sprig of rosemary
1 tsp oregano
1 onion, finely sliced
1 clove of garlic, chopped
Salt and pepper
1/2 cup/50 g grated pecorino cheese

Cut the lamb into pieces. Peel, wash, and coarsely dice the potatoes and place together with the lamb in a deep, flameproof baking pan. Put the tomatoes in a bowl and combine with the olive oil, herbs, onion, and garlic. Season with salt and pepper and add to the lamb. Sprinkle with the grated pecorino cheese.
Cover the tin with kitchen foil and bake the lamb in a preheated oven at 340 °F (170 °C) for about 2 hours.

Pignata di pecora
Lamb stew

Serves 6

2 lbs/1 kg lamb
1 clove of garlic, chopped
Olive oil
1/4 lb/100 g ham
2 1/2 cups/300 g finely chopped onions
1 stick of celery, finely chopped
4–5/200 g tomatoes, skinned, seeded, and coarsely diced
2 1/2 cups/300 g potatoes, peeled and diced
Salt and freshly milled pepper
1/2 cup/50 g grated pecorino cheese

Coarsely dice the meat, chop the garlic, and sauté together in the olive oil. Finely chop the ham and add to the lamb, together with the vegetables. Season with salt and pepper and pour in 1 glass of water. Cover and braise the lamb over a medium heat for about 1½ hours.
Sprinkle with grated pecorino cheese and serve hot.

HONEY

Honey was the classic Mediterranean sweetener. In the Middle Ages this much sought-after product of hardworking colonies of bees was used not only in the workshops of the confectioner and the liqueur distiller, but also as a medicament, for the sticky substance was said to have medicinal properties. After all, honey shimmered like amber and glistened like gold – and these substances were also thought to be good for your health and able to prevent harm. However, in the 17th century, when raw cane sugar, then considered to be very prestigious, reached Europe, honey's popularity began to wane. With the introduction of white refined sugar in the 20th century, honey was finally written off as old-fashioned. It was not until the 1980s, when more emphasis was placed on cooking with healthy and natural ingredients, that honey began to be appreciated once more. It is now becoming increasingly popular.

Honey is made from flower nectar, which the bees enrich in their pollen sacks with glandular secretions that contain enzymes and leave in the beehive to mature as it dries out and ferments. The sweet end product, which presents people with a sticky problem when it comes to being harvested, does actually have an energizing and anti-inflammatory effect.

In Italy, there are now around 85,000 beekeepers, whose colonies of bees produce about 11,000 tons of honey each year. Multifloral honeys are made from the converted nectar of different flowers, whereas monofloral ones are made primarily from the nectar of a single species of plant. The latter may be more expensive, but often taste better and allow the characteristics of the flower to shine through. The best products from the Italian peninsula bear the seal *Miele Italiano* (Italian honey). Some beekeepers have joined together under this quality mark, and voluntarily comply with the high quality requirements of the consortium. Their honeys, which are usually single-varietal, come from strictly controlled areas. They are particularly fresh, of a thick consistency, form fine, even crystals, and are sold only in jars.

In Italy, there is a honey to suit every taste, from the clear, light sorts such as citrus and acacia honey to the heavy, dark, and very aromatic specialties such as pine, strawberry tree (*Arbutus unedo*), and thyme honeys. The delicious sweetener is produced in every region. The different flowers found in different areas mean that the honeys produced in the mountainous north (Piedmont and Lombardy are the largest producers in numerical terms) do not taste the same as those produced in the hills of Tuscany or even the maquis of the hot south. However, the regions of the lower part of the Italian boot produce particularly exotic honeys almost unheard of outside Italy: citrus honey, eucalyptus honey, and cockscomb honey are definitely worth a try.

PUNCH AL MIELE
Honey punch

6 EGGS
1/3 CUP/125 G HONEY
4 CUPS/1 LITER MILK
FRESHLY GRATED NUTMEG

Beat the eggs thoroughly using an electric beater, then gradually add the honey, continuing to beat until the mixture is frothy. Then gradually pour in the hot milk, so that the eggs do not collapse.
Sprinkle with nutmeg and serve hot. A perfect drink for a cold winter's evening!

HONEY AND RICOTTA

Honey and fresh ricotta – a magic combination of flavors – is an age-old dessert, either on its own or as an ingredient in other desserts, which even tickled the taste buds of the Ancient Romans. The dessert *suavillum*, mentioned by Cato, was made from these two ingredients. The origins of our present delicacies such as cassata, the filling for Sicilian *cannoli*, the Sardinian *sebadas*, and finally even the Anglo-Saxon cheesecake go back to this ancient Roman temptation.

MIELE E RICOTTA
Honey with ricotta
(Background illustration)

A GENEROUS POUND/500 G RICOTTA
2 EGGS
3 EGG YOLKS
SCANT 1/2 CUP/100 ML LIQUID HONEY
A PINCH OF CINNAMON
1/3 CUP/50 G CHOPPED CANDIED FRUITS
1 TBSP GRATED LEMON RIND
3 EGG WHITES
2 TSP MARSALA

Pass the ricotta through a sieve into a bowl. Add the whole eggs, egg yolks, honey, cinnamon, candied fruits, and grated lemon rind, and mix thoroughly. Beat the egg whites until stiff and carefully fold in the Marsala.
Transfer to a greased, flameproof baking pan and bake in a preheated oven at 300 °F (150 °C) for about 30 minutes.

The flower nectar that is gathered by the worker bees is made into honey in the hive by being restructured, dried out, and fermented.

About 11,000 tons of honey are produced each year in Italy, including Miele di nettare di Arancio (left) and Miele millefiori (middle and right).

Miele d'abete (Pine honey)

This very dark, almost black pine honey comes from the Alpine regions or the Apennine ranges in Tuscany and Romagna. It smells slightly resinous, with a hint of burned wood and caramelized sugar. Pine honey tastes less sweet than nectar honey and has malty overtones.

Miele di agrumi (Citrus honey)

This very light and white crystallizing citrus honey is produced in southern Italy and on the islands of Sardinia and Sicily. It has an intensive orange fragrance, and its very aromatic flavor alternates between flowers and fruits.

Miele di castagno (Chestnut honey)

Chestnut honey, which can be anything from amber-colored to almost black depending on where it was produced, is made in all the hilly regions of Italy. This pervasively fragrant specialty tastes hot on the tongue initially and then releases a relatively bitter aftertaste.

Miele di corbezzolo (Strawberry tree honey)

Amber-colored, slightly gray-green shimmering strawberry tree honey is produced mainly in the Mediterranean maquis of Sardinia and in central Italy. Its fragrance brings to mind coffee grounds and it has a bitter taste.

Miele di lavanda (Lavender honey)

Pale to amber-colored lavender honey comes from Liguria. It smells strongly of lavender, and is reminiscent of passion fruit in flavor.

Miele di robinia (Acacia honey)

Very light acacia honey comes primarily from the Alpine foothills of Lombardy, but is also produced in many other hilly regions in Italy. It has a delicate fragrance of the tree blossom and a soft vanilla flavor.

Miele di rododendro (Rhododendron honey)

Very light and white crystallizing rhododendron honey is produced solely in the mountains. It smells soft and tastes of wild berries.

Miele di erica (Heather honey)

Amber-colored, orange glowing heather honey is produced in the vernal maquis from Liguria to Calabria. It smells and tastes of caramel.

Miele di eucalipto (Eucalyptus honey)

Rich amber-colored eucalyptus honey with its gray crystals comes from central and southern Italy. Oddly, it hardly smells of eucalyptus at all, and its intense flavor tastes is more reminiscent of liquorice.

Miele di girasole (Sunflower honey)

Pale yellow sunflower honey is produced wherever sunflowers are cultivated. It has a delicate smell of straw and wax, and has slight herbal overtones in flavor.

Miele di tiglio (Linden tree honey)

This honey from the wild linden tree, which ranges in color from very pale to very dark depending on where it has come from, is produced on the Alpine slopes. It is often sold blended with chestnut honey. It smells of menthol and has a slightly medicinal aftertaste.

Miele di timo (Thyme honey)

Italy has many varieties of thyme, and thyme honey is also found in many blended honeys. In the mountainous hinterland of Sicily, on the other hand, a pure thyme honey is made, rich amber in color, with a pervasive fragrance and intense flavor.

HELLENIC WINE

Basilicata may have almost as many vineyards as the famous north Italian combined region of Trentino-South Tyrol, but its quality wine accounts for barely ten percent of its DOC production. The decidedly mountainous region, which goes down to sea level only in the southeast, is one of the poorest in Italy. It

has only one mark of origin, which in terms of quality has no need to hide its light under a bushel, that of the red Aglianico del Vulture. Most of the wine produced, however, is sold as anonymous bulk wine and is used to no small extent to enrich many a reputable table wine from the more northern regions of the Italian peninsula.

On the slopes of Monte Vulture, an extinct volcano in the north of Basilicata, at a height of between 1500 and 2000 feet (450–600 meters), grow the famous Aglianico grapes. These are said to have originated from the Ancient Greeks – Aglianico is only a derivation of *ellenico*, the Italian word for Greek – and form the basis of probably the most well-known and most important DOC wine of

The winegrowers have dug their cellars in the high loessial cliffs of the valleys around Monte Vulture.

southern Italy. With their dark color, powerful bouquet and full body, and provided they receive the correct viticultural attention and careful cellar management, the best wines from Aglianico have nothing to fear even from the Sangiovese and Nebbiolo wines. They can even be stored in oak casks, and a few concerns have been using this method of production with great success for more than ten years now.

An unusual feature of the rugged landscape around the towns of Barile (Italian for barrel or cask) and Rionero are the earth cellars that have been dug into the loessial cliffs of the small river valleys. Another typical feature of winegrowing in this region is the way the vines are

grown on old, almost pyramidal poles. These can still be seen in most of the vineyards today and many wine-

growers believe this method is considerably better for high quality Aglianico grapes than the modern, productive, and easy-to-work wire frames.

Beyond Basilicata, the Aglianico grape plays a significant role only in Campania and Apulia, where the famous Taurasi and the Castel del Monte wines are pressed from its grapes, whether as single varietals or as a blend with other varieties. Italy's other DOC wines that contain Aglianico grapes, such as Taburno, Cilento, Sant'Agata de' Goti, or Lacryma Christi, play a very subordinate role in the world's wine markets.

Above: Basilicata's annual production may be an impressive 12,400,000 U.S. gallons (470,000 hectoliters), but almost 90 percent are sold as blended wines in other regions.

Opposite and below: The popular bitters from Basilicata is called Amaro Lucano. Its fans attribute remarkable properties to the tincture.

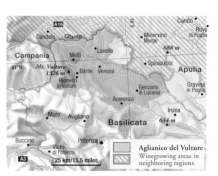

LIQUEUR

Many families in Basilicata still make liqueurs themselves (background), the most popular being Nocino, Amarello, and Rosolio. Nocino is actually a specialty from Emilia-Romagna, but is also very popular in the south. It is made from green walnuts steeped until soft in high-proof alcohol. After about 40 days, the mixture has transformed into a brownish and very effective digestive.

Rosolio gets its name from the rose petals that are steeped together with wild berries or other flavorings in sweetened alcohol. Citrus fruits are a favorite in Basilicata. Amaro Lucano is manufactured in the small Lucanian town of Pisticci. You will find this famous bitters in any well-stocked bar in the cities of Milan, Venice, Rome, or Naples.

CALABRIA

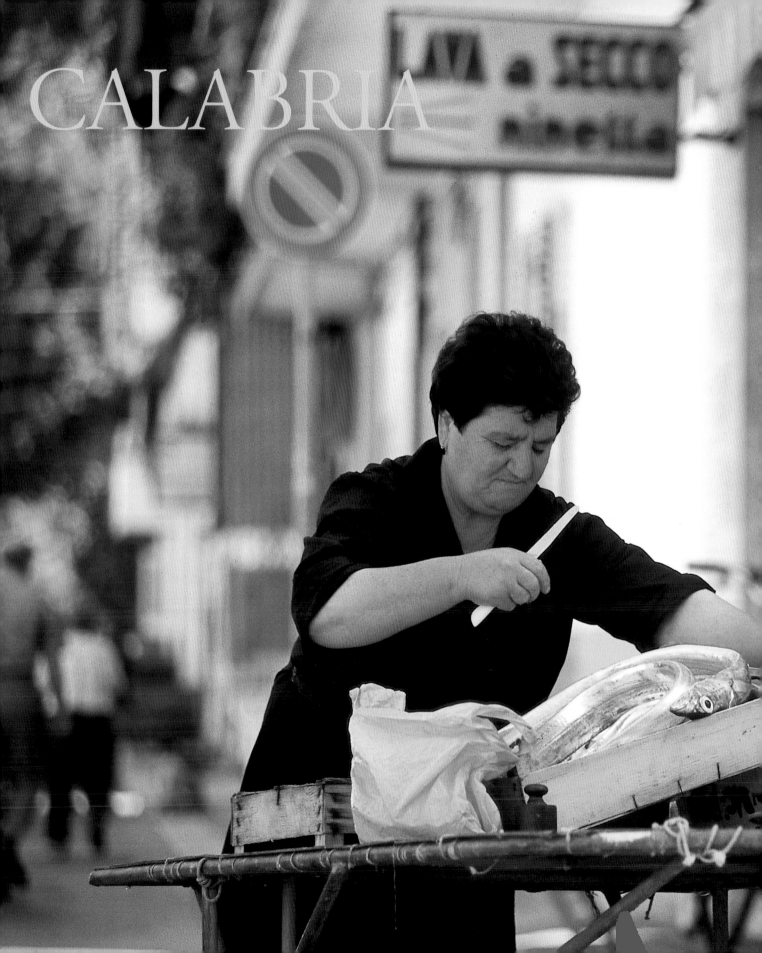

C

alabria's strategically favorable position providing direct access both to the Tyrrhenian and Ionian Seas has attracted the attentions of foreign rulers since time immemorial. During the 8th century B.C., this region was ruled by the Greeks after they had absorbed the area comprising the sole, instep, and toe of the Italian boot into their large colony to the West. The Calabrians not only profited from the culinary know-how of these occupying nations but also took over their traditions and customs, some of which continue to this day. Whenever a pig is slaughtered – an occasion for celebration in itself – it is a not-to-be-missed opportunity for a family to have its future read or have the sex of an expected baby predicted from the entrails.

Around 500 years after the Greeks, Calabria was occupied by the Romans who derived great pleasure from the viniculture which their predecessors had introduced into the region. After the collapse of the Roman Empire, there followed a continuous stream of Teutons, Goths, Lombards, Franks, Sicilians, Saracens, French, and Spaniards one after the other. Naturally enough, all of them left their imprint on Calabrian cuisine. The Arabs brought oranges, lemons, raisins, artichokes, and aubergines – all of which remain to this day important ingredients in the traditional dishes of the region. The Cistercian monks, who held large estates in the Sibari region, introduced new agricultural methods and the art of dairying, which at that time constituted a major advance in farming. During the rule of the House of Anjou and, later, Napoleon, French influences were assimilated and the Spaniards likewise left their mark. The word for cake, *gatò*, derives from the French *gateau* and the delicious meat paté *murseddu* or *mursiellu* has its origins in the Spanish word *almuerzo* (breakfast, meal).

Despite all these foreign influences, Calabrian cuisine has an identity very much its own. All too often, the inhabitants of the toe of Italy were forced to flee from invaders into the mountains where they continued to cook their traditional dishes based on simple produce coaxed from the poor soil and some livestock farming. Although they may sometimes have been slow to absorb foreign tastes, once Calabrians finally do take to something, then they do so in a big way. Just as a visitor will eventually be welcomed with great hospitality after some initial wariness, the eggplant likewise has been embraced wholeheartedly by the people of the region.

Previous double page: The fishwives of Bagnara Calabra, the so-called *bagnarote*, displaying their wares in the morning.

Left: A swordfish boat – known as *luntru* in Calabrian dialect – entering Bagnara harbor.

EGGPLANTS

Melanzane alla parmigiana sounds like a specialty from Parma. However, this popular vegetable dish, in which slices of eggplant are liberally sprinkled with Parmesan cheese and baked in the oven, stems not from the Emilia-Romagna region, but was invented in Calabria. Before there is a rush of protest from all the Campanians, Sicilians, Sardinians, and Apulians, let us just say that this is a dish that is entirely typical of the Italian south, the *mezzogiorno*.

This tasty concoction owes its name not to its geographical origins but solely to the fact that it is made with the hard cheese from this part of northern Italy. In their search for new specialties, the gourmets of southern Italy must at some time have discovered a preference for Parmigiano Reggiano, whereas northern Italian bon vivants prefer to use the mature pecorino cheese from the toe of Italy for grating. The Calabrians, in any case, have ample ingenuity to think up other delicious dishes involving eggplants: eggplant purée, for example. Naturally enough, the cooks of Calabria claim to have invented this dish themselves, but, in actual fact, it is a feature of the so-called *mèzzes*, the hors d'oeuvres, served in Greek, Turkish, and Egyptian restaurants – in other words, a typical delicacy of Mediterranean cuisine. Another dish definitely worth trying is *Melanzane al pomodoro,* an irresistible combination of eggplants and tomatoes, enhanced with grated cheese.

The exchange of specialties between Italian regions was not always smooth a process as the "cheese swapping" practise mentioned earlier. Right up until the late 19th century, the eggplant was viewed in central and northern Italy with great suspicion, as it was reputed to cause feeblemindedness and other mental disorders. In the south, however, this plant of the Solanaceae family was becoming increasingly popular and could be prepared in so many appetizing ways that scarcely anyone could understand how people in Turin or Milan could accuse it of having a bland taste. It could be that this was simply due to the fact that eggplants grown in the cool, less sunny north tended not to have a particularly strong flavor. The Calabrians, however, are crazy about their eggplants. Calabria provides the perfect growing conditions for this fruit, which is said to have originated in China or India and which was introduced into Italy toward the end of the 16th century by the Arabs, who called it *badigian*. Although the dry climate, silicon-rich, almost chalk-free soil and the high temperatures serve to restrict growth, these factors at the same time prevent a build-up of bitter juices in the flesh and help to produce a concentrated flavor. In order to remove any bitter juices still remaining, the sliced eggplant is placed in salt water before preparation.

Eggplants are harvested between June and October. The color and shape of the fruit vary according to the variety. The flesh, which is soft and peppered with numerous small, white seeds, can be whitish, beige or greenish in color. The long, larger varieties have a strong flavor, while the smaller, rounder types have a milder taste. The most well-known and common varieties include Violetta di Firenze, Belezza nera, Violetta lunga di Napoli and Larga morada.

Far right: Melanzane alla menta (eggplants with mint) are best eaten around three hours after being prepared. This gives the herbs adequate time to combine with the oil-vinegar mixture.

The eggplant, a member of the Solanaceae family. It can reach over three feet (one meter) in height, originated in India and now thrives all over the Mediterranean region.

Eggplants are harvested from June to October. The flesh must still be firm when picked, but the skins should be an even color.

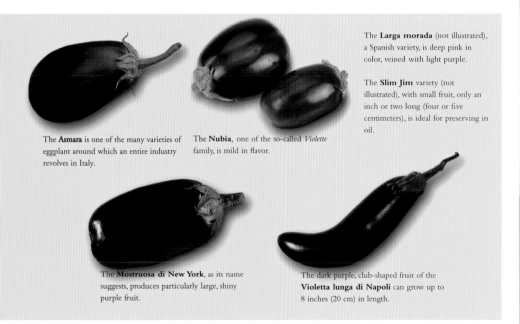

The **Asmara** is one of the many varieties of eggplant around which an entire industry revolves in Italy.

The **Nubia**, one of the so-called *Violette* family, is mild in flavor.

The **Larga morada** (not illustrated), a Spanish variety, is deep pink in color, veined with light purple.

The **Slim Jim** variety (not illustrated), with small fruit, only an inch or two long (four or five centimeters), is ideal for preserving in oil.

The **Mostruosa di New York**, as its name suggests, produces particularly large, shiny purple fruit.

The dark purple, club-shaped fruit of the **Violetta lunga di Napoli** can grow up to 8 inches (20 cm) in length.

Melanzane alla menta

Eggplants with mint
(Background illustration)

5 LONG EGGPLANTS
OIL FOR FRYING
SALT
3–4 TBSP EXTRA VIRGIN OLIVE OIL
2 CLOVES OF GARLIC, CRUSHED
10 LEAVES OF FRESH MINT, CHOPPED
VINEGAR
4 TBSP BREADCRUMBS

Wash the eggplants, divide into quarters lengthwise, remove a little of the flesh, and cut into slices, just under ½ inch (1 cm) thick. Fry the eggplants in plenty of oil, allow to drain, and season with a little salt.

Mix the olive oil with the garlic and fresh mint in a shallow dish. Add the eggplants after a few minutes, sprinkle with a little vinegar and mix together well. Add the breadcrumbs and allow to stand for several hours. Serve cold.

Melanzane al pomodoro

Eggplants with tomatoes

2 LBS/1 KG LONG EGGPLANTS
OIL FOR FRYING
3/4 LB/400 G PLUM TOMATOES

1 CLOVE OF GARLIC
2 TBSP/30 ML OLIVE OIL
1 BUNCH OF FRESH BASIL
GRATED PARMESAN OR PECORINO CHEESE

Wash and slice the eggplants, then fry in oil. Lay the fried eggplant slices on paper towel to remove excess oil. Skin the tomatoes, press lightly, and cut into slices. Cook with the eggplants, garlic and olive oil for 15 minutes over a high heat.

Set aside a few leaves of fresh basil and add the rest to the eggplants. Season with salt and cook for a further 5 minutes. Remove the pan from the heat and stir in the cheese. Garnish with the remaining fresh basil leaves and serve.

Parmigiana di melanzane alla calabrese

Baked eggplants

ABOUT 4 LBS/2 KG EGGPLANTS
2 TBSP FLOUR
OIL FOR FRYING
ABOUT 1 LB/500 G TOMATOES, SKINNED
6–7 TBSP EXTRA VIRGIN OLIVE OIL
10 LEAVES OF FRESH BASIL
1/2 LB/200 G GROUND BEEF
5 EGGS
3 TBSP BREADCRUMBS

2 TBSP CHOPPED PARSLEY
SALT AND PEPPER
1/2 LB/200 G CACIOCAVALLO
1/2 LB/200 G SALSICCIA
1 CUP/100 G GRATED PARMESAN

Wash the eggplants, cut into thin slices and sprinkle with a little salt in order to draw out the rather bitter juices. Place in a colander and allow to drain. Sprinkle with flour and fry in plenty of oil. Place on paper towel to remove excess oil and set aside. Pass the skinned tomatoes through a sieve and place in a saucepan, together with the olive oil and fresh basil, season with a little salt, and cook over a low heat until the tomatoes have formed a thick sauce. Put the ground beef in a mixing bowl along with 3 eggs, the breadcrumbs, and the chopped parsley and mix well. Season with salt and pepper. Shape small amounts of the ground beef mixture into croquettes and sauté in oil. Boil the two remaining eggs until hard and cut into thin slices. Thinly slice the *caciocavallo* and *salsiccia*.

Spread some of the tomato sauce over the bottom of an ovenproof dish, cover with a layer of eggplant slices and sprinkle with some of the Parmesan cheese. Then, add a layer of croquettes and the slices of egg, sausage, and cheese and pour over some of the tomato sauce. Cover with the remaining slices of eggplant, sprinkle with Parmesan cheese and pour over the rest of the tomato sauce. Bake in a pre-heated oven at 400 °F (200 °C) for about 30 minutes and serve hot.

Pitta arriganata con l'origano
Pitta bread with sardines and oregano
(Illustrated above)

Serves 6

Generous 1 lb/500 g pitta dough
8 salted sardine fillets
Crushed black peppercorns
2 tbsp/30 g capers, in vinegar
Extra virgin olive oil
Oregano

Roll out the dough into a flat round and place on an oiled baking tray. Arrange the sardines, peppercorns, and capers on top and sprinkle with a few drops of olive oil and oregano. Bake in a preheated oven at 430 °F (220 °C) for about 20–30 minutes.

Pitta secca can likewise be served with a colorful topping.

Pitta
(Basic recipe for pitta dough)

1 3/4 cakes/30 g fresh yeast (if using active dry yeast, follow maker's instructions)
5 cups/600 g bread flour
3 tbsp extra virgin olive oil
Salt
Water

Dissolve the yeast in some lukewarm water. Sieve the flour onto a work surface and add the yeast, olive oil, a pinch of salt, and enough water to enable the mixture to be kneaded into a smooth dough. Shape the dough into a ball and allow to stand for about 1 hour at room temperature until the dough has doubled in size. Place the dough in an oiled bowl and leave to rise a second time.

Pitta coi pomodori
Pitta bread with tomatoes

Serves 6

3/4 lb/300 g ripe tomatoes
2 green bell peppers
6 leaves of fresh basil
Extra virgin olive oil
Generous 1 lb/500 g pitta dough
10 black olives
2 tbsp capers
Grated pecorino cheese

Core the tomatoes, deseed the peppers, dice and sauté lightly with the basil leaves in olive oil. Roll out the dough into a round and place on an oiled baking sheet. Spread with the tomato and pepper mixture, the olives, and capers and top with pecorino cheese. Sprinkle with a little olive oil and bake for about 20–30 minutes in a preheated oven at 430 °F (220 °C).

Right: Rodolfo and his colleague from the Fornaio Albino Mandera in Rende with freshly baked *pitta fresca* (left) and *pitta secca* (right).

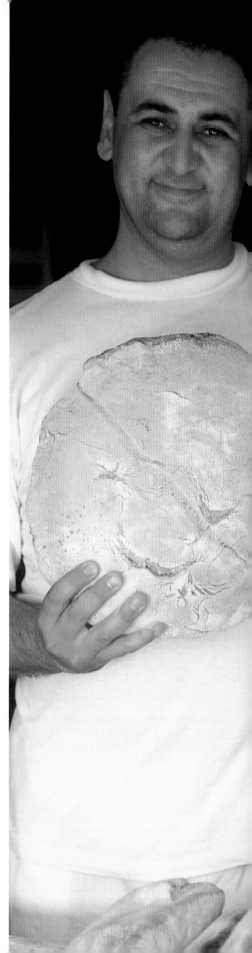

THE RITUAL OF BAKING BREAD

The barren region of Calabria is not exactly bountiful toward its inhabitants. A great deal of patience is required in order to wrest any sort of return from the soil. The fruits of the field are therefore very precious and are treated accordingly with great respect. Once upon a time, an entire family's well-being could often depend on whether or not the bread was correctly prepared as virtually no-one could afford to spoil the dough or end up with inedible bread. Obviously, the baker entrusted with baking the bread, if a family did not have its own oven, had to be someone who was utterly reliable.

Even today, in some remote districts, bread baking is still a social occasion, but nevertheless one that is taken very seriously. Preparations get underway during the afternoon of the day before when the women reactivate the yeast dough kept back from the previous batch of baking by mixing it with fresh flour and lukewarm water. On baking day itself, the fire is lit in the oven at the crack of dawn to ensure that the stacked-up wood can burn slowly to leave glowing ash. Once the oven is heated through, it is thoroughly cleaned with iron scrapers, scrubbing brushes and damp cloths. In the meantime, more women arrive at the house to take charge of the yeast dough since this is a job which can only be entrusted to experts. These women see to the correct mixing of yeast, flour, and water, knead the dough and place it in wooden containers where it is covered with fresh linen cloths and left to prove.

While they are waiting, the women mutter secret imprecations and make special signs, combining pagan rites and Christian rituals with a fair amount of superstition. These rites are supposed to ward off evil and ensure that the bread turns out well. Anyone entering the room must ask for St. Martin's blessing and magic words are intoned once more when the linen cloths are removed. Three crosses are then made in the freshly risen dough. Once the first loaves have been shaped out of the dough, they are placed in the oven and the oven door is finally closed to the echo of further words in praise of San Martino and fervent prayers for good bread and a full oven.

The ancient Romans used to put small rounds of dough in the oven along with the bread when it was being baked. These *pictae*, which were similar to focaccia, were offered up to the gods in thanks. This custom is still practiced in Calabria, although these small by-products from the baking session are nowadays offered not to the gods but to neighbors. It is not only regular loaves that emerge from the oven, therefore, but delicious-smelling bread rings which are eaten straight from the oven, either salted, brushed with olive oil or filled with ricotta cheese. The flat, round pitta bread, typical of Calabria, is another common by-product of baking day.

People used to make pittas when a pig was slaughtered. The dripping was placed on the fresh pitta and melted on the warm dough.

Friselle keep for a fortnight or more. To soften them they are briefly immersed in water and then covered with fresh tomatoes.

IN PRAISE OF A HEARTY BREAKFAST

When you consider the sort of breakfast that most Italians eat, it seems strange that Calabrians, should consider breakfast to be the most important meal of the day. Generally speaking, breakfast for the people in this part of the world consists of no more than milky coffee in which they might dunk some white bread or a pastry. In Calabria, however, the people will have no truck with such minimalism and this region in the extreme south of Italy is probably the only one in the country that could take to the idea of an English "cooked breakfast." People here firmly believe in the merits of a good, solid meal to start the day and there is an old saying *chi mangia de bon'ura ccu nu pugno scascia nu muru* which means "if you have a good meal to start the day, you'll be able to break through walls with one blow of your fist."

The favorite breakfast dish, which enables Calabrians to muster the necessary strength to get through the day, is called *murseddu*, *marsieddu*, or *mursiellu*. The name is clearly Spanish in origin and derives from the word *almuerzo*, meaning breakfast. This is a nourishing meat paté consisting of finely ground pork and/or pig meat. The ground meat is cooked slowly in its own fat over a low heat, after which tomatoes and herbs are added. In order to wake up even the sleepiest of sleepyheads, the whole dish is spiced up with a liberal amount of *pipazzu* or *pipazellu*, the bright red, devilishly hot peperoncini (chili pepper). Once it is ready, this ragù can be used as a filling in pitta bread. The Calabrians like to partake of their *murseddu* in the company of friends and relatives at a nearby inn.

The *nduja* is a soft, coarse sausage from the Tropea region. It consists of ground meat from the poorer cuts of pork, which are left over after the production of ham, salami and *salsicce*. This is a hot speciality containing ground peperoncino and can be spread on bread, used to enrich sauces for pasta, or as an ingredient in *murseddu*.

MURSEDDU
Meat pâté

For the dough:
2/3 CAKE/10 G FRESH YEAST (IF USING ACTIVE DRY YEAST, FOLLOW MAKER'S INSTRUCTIONS)
2 CUPS/250 G ALL-PURPOSE FLOUR
FLOUR FOR ROLLING OUT
SALT

For the filling:
5 OZ/150 G PIG'S LIVER
5 OZ/150 G CALF'S LIVER
1/2 LB/250 G NECK OF PORK
1 ONION
2 CLOVES OF GARLIC
2 TBSP LARD
1 PEPERONCINO
1 TSP OREGANO
SALT AND FRESHLY GROUND PEPPER
4 TBSP TOMATO PASTE

Miscellaneous:
OLIVE OIL
1 TSP OREGANO

To make the dough, mix the yeast and 2 tablespoons of flour into a paste with 2 tablespoons of lukewarm water. Put the remaining flour into a mixing bowl, make a hollow in the middle and add a pinch of salt and the yeast paste. Cover with a cloth and leave for 30 minutes in a warm place to prove. Then, add about half a cup of lukewarm water and knead into a smooth, elastic dough. Cover once more and leave to stand for about 1 hour until the dough has doubled in size.
Meanwhile, dice the pig's and calf's liver and neck of pork into small cubes to make the filling. Finely chop the onion and garlic cloves. Heat the lard in a large pan and quickly sauté the diced liver before removing it from the pan. Add the onion, garlic, and peperoncino to the hot fat and let it cook for a few minutes, stirring occasionally. Turn up the heat and sauté the diced neck of pork well, seasoning it with oregano, salt, and pepper. Mix the tomato paste with 4 tablespoons of water until smooth and pour over the meat. Cover and cook for 10 minutes. Add the diced liver and cook for a further 10 minutes. Remove the lid and allow to simmer. Remove the peperoncino and add salt and pepper to taste. Grease a 10 ½-inch/26-cm springform pan with olive oil. Using two thirds of the dough, roll out to about ¼ inch (1 cm) thickness on a lightly floured surface. Line the springform pan with the dough, leaving an overlap around the sides. Pour the meat sauce onto the dough and fold the overlapping flaps of dough in toward the middle. Roll out the remaining dough to make a lid to cover the filling. Press down the edges firmly, then pierce the pie lid a few times with fork. Brush with olive oil and sprinkle with oregano, if desired. Bake in a preheated oven at 350 °F (180 °C) for about 50 minutes.

BEANS

Lima beans and white beans are important elements of Calabrian dishes designed for those cold winter days. Down here, these tasty pulses are not combined, as they usually are in the north of Italy, with sausage, bacon, pig trotters, strong spices, or other similar ingredients which tend to outflavor the beans themselves, but are allowed to develop their full flavor alongside milder accompaniments such as tomatoes, celeriac, *catalogna* and lots of olive oil.

Whereas some varieties of bean, such as the cannellino and white kidney bean, originally enjoyed more popularity in the north, before eventually finding favor in the south, the lima bean, fava, found its way into northern Italian cuisine a long time ago. However, it is and will always be grown primarily in the warm south. Spring, when the roughly three foot (1 m) high plants produce their tender fruit, is the time for using fresh beans in cooking. Throughout the rest of the year, people have to fall back on dried beans. These have to be left to soak in water for at least 24 hours and then require a further two hours of cooking before they are ready for use.

MACCO DI FAVE
Bean stew

GENEROUS 1 LB/500 G DRIED LIMA BEANS
SALT
BASIL LEAVES
1 HOT, RED PEPERONCINO
1 TBSP TOMATO PASTE
OLIVE OIL
GRATED PECORINO CHEESE
TOASTED BREAD

Soak the beans overnight in lukewarm water. Pour off the water and bring the beans to the boil in plenty of fresh salted water, to which the chopped basil, peperoncino, and tomato paste have been added. Cook until the beans are pulpy. Add some olive oil and the grated pecorino. Serve on slices of toast, preferably made from home-baked bread.

MINESTRONE DI FAGIOLI, CAVOLO E PATATE
Minestrone made from beans, cabbage, and potatoes

1/2 LB/200 G DRIED BEANS
1/2 MEDIUM-SIZED CABBAGE
3/4 LB/400 G POTATOES
10 OZ/300 G PIECE OF BACON
1 TBSP LARD OR BUTTER
1 PEPERONCINO
SALT

Soak the beans overnight in water. Pour off the water and cook the beans in fresh water until soft. Clean and wash the cabbage and cut into strips. Peel, wash, and dice the potatoes. Cook the potatoes and cabbage in salted water and then add the beans. By this time only very little liquid should be left in the saucepan.
Dice the bacon and fry out the fat in lard or butter, then add it to the mixture in the saucepan. Season with salt and garnish with chopped peperoncino just before serving.

Luntru is the Calabrian name for the typical boat used for catching swordfish. It has a 65-foot (20-m) mast and an almost equally long platform jutting out from the bow.

A sailor keeps a look-out for the swordfish from the crow's nest at the top of the mast. As soon as he is heard to shout *U'pisci spada!*, the pursuit gets underway.

One of the fishermen stations himself on the platform and attacks the swordfish with a multipronged harpoon until it succumbs.

FISHING FOR SWORDFISH

Calabria's fishermen have the choice of the Tyrrhenian Sea stretching along the region's western coast and the Ionian Sea to the east. Thanks to modern transport methods, even the remotest of villages can be supplied with fresh fish and you no longer have to live on the coast to enjoy fish dishes. May and June are the traditional months for catching tuna fish in the Gulf of Sant'Eufemia between Pizzo and Tropea. Throughout the summer, the fishermen venture forth on pitch-black, moonless nights in search of garfish. In the Ionian Sea, they lay nets for sardines and anchovies, which the women of the region turn into a dish called *mustica*, a name derived from Arabic, so possibly of North African origin.

The Calabrian fishermen's particular favorite, however, is the swordfish, whose upper jaw is compressed and elongated. These fish, which can grow 12 to 13 feet (4 meters) in length, are fished from March to September all along the coast between Cannitello, Scilla, Bagnara, and Palmi. Each July, Bagnara stages a big festival including a procession of boats in honor of the *pesce spada*.

The tradition of fishing for swordfish in the Straits of Messina goes back a long way. Since time immemorial, this coveted prize has been hunted not just by Calabrian fishermen, but by their Sicilian counterparts as well. Back in the 18th century, Antonio Mongitore, a Sicilian historian, described the procedure in his "Biblioteca Sicula" as follows: "The fishermen prepare their boat, the so-called *luntre*, very thoroughly – this peculiar name probably comes from the Latin word *linter*, meaning a small light boat. This special boat measures 22 spans in length, 8 spans in breadth, 5 spans in height and can accommodate a large number of people. At the front end of the boat, which is broader than the stern, there is a mast, 20 spans in height, with climbing rungs enabling access to the crow's nest on top from which one of the crew keeps a look-out for the fish. Two powerful harpoons, each armed with several iron prongs, are attached to a 120-foot cable. In order to spot the shoal of fish at the earliest opportunity and be able to alert the crew on the *luntre* in good time, two other boats accompany it, each with a man keeping watch from their respective perch at the top of the mast. Once the crew on the *luntre* have been alerted to the approaching swordfish and know the direction they are taking, they race toward them in pursuit. It is now up to the daring fisherman on the long platform jutting out from the bow to judge the right moment for launching the harpoon, a decision which requires great skill and courage. The fish, wounded by the harpoon, tries to escape and the cable, locally known as the *calom* unwinds to its full length, until the fish, exhausted by the struggle, finally gives up and is heaved on board. Sometimes the wounded creature does not try to get away, but … attacks the *luntre* in its rage and desperation."

This passion for swordfish, which both eastern Sicily and western Calabria – separated from each other only by the Straits of Medina – have in common, was also shared by Byzantine Constantinople. You will find almost identical swordfish dishes being prepared in kitchens throughout all three of these regions. Fishing for swordfish around the Golden Horn hardly differs at all from the methods used in the Straits of Messina. The Italian *intinneri*, who is the first to spot the fish from his look-out, still uses Byzantine expressions to warn of the approaching prey. It is likely that Genoan and Sicilian seafarers, who frequented Byzantium in the late Middle Ages, brought these terms back with them to Italy.

To this day, little has changed with regard to the methods used for catching the swordfish, except that the look-out mast is higher and the platform from which the fisherman fires his harpoon is now longer. This method of harpoon-fishing only targets adult fish, whereas the kind of dragnet fishing sometimes employed by Japanese fleets very often nets young swordfish. Since swordfish usually swim in pairs, the fishermen try to hit the female first, knowing that the male will not leave her side and therefore offers an easy second target. The singer Domenico Modugno immortalized the faithfulness of the swordfish to his wounded mate in a song that has become popular – the fishermen in the Straits of Messina all know the poignant *Canzone del pesce spada*.

Once the tasty swordfish has given up the struggle and is dead, the fishermen bring it back in a rowing boat.

The swordfish is prepared for sale. It is then brought into the harbor in the *luntre*, the main fishing boat.

Processing and cutting up the swordfish begin out at sea. The best bit, the fin, is eaten straight away.

BAGNARA CALABRA

At the beginning of July – in other words, at the end of the swordfish season – Bagnara Calabra celebrates a swordfish festival. On this special day, none of the eight or so traditional fishing boats still in use dare return to harbor empty-handed. This is just as well since a great many visitors from the surrounding area, as well as from Sicily across the Straits of Messina, come on purpose to try swordfish specialities of every conceivable variety. Visitors patiently wait in line at the swordfish buffet and happily pay a few extra lire for the delicacies on offer. An absolute must is pasta with swordfish (*della scozzetta*, in other words with the delicious neck meat), as well as *Filetti di pesce spada alla griglia* and, of course, the famous *Involtini di pesce spada* or swordfish rolls. Once the worst of their hunger has been satisfied, the visitors are then sufficiently fortified to give their full attention to the spectacular climax of the festival: a big firework display held over the sea at midnight, an unforgettable sight. Even today, 2000 of Bagnara's 11,000-strong population are fishermen and the main square, known as the Piazza Marconi, symbolizes the importance of the swordfish in this region. The men of the town have erected a monument here to their womenfolk, the *bagnarote*. It was the *bagnarote* who once traveled all over Calabria, selling the fish caught by their menfolk or else trading it for oil, wine, meat, and cloth. To this day, the *bagnarote* remain proud of their reputation for being the best traveling fish-sellers anywhere.

Background illustration: The freshly caught swordfish is unloaded and taken ashore to be weighed. Often, there is already a buyer for it, who has, if necessary, already spent several hours at the harbor waiting for the precious cargo finally to arrive.

CULINARY FESTIVALS

The whole of southern Italy is home to a wealth of culinary celebrations. Although the Church tolerates these festivals, all of which openly flaunt their pagan origins to a greater or lesser degree, they are not always liked. This does not deter the gourmets, however, who gather at specific times of the year to indulge in some particular delicacy or other. In July, for example, Bagnara in Calabria celebrates its swordfish festival, at which the landed catch is not only duly admired but also enjoyed in a variety of dishes. These festivals, which even ancient Roman writers such as Ovid and Makrobius mentioned in their writings, date from a time – almost inconceivable to us nowadays – when the rhythm of life was determined by people's work on the land or the needs of their livestock. In the spring, people celebrated the seed sowing and looked forward to the newborn lambs, while summer was the season to enjoy the blessing of the ripe fruits. Autumn was the time to give thanks for a good harvest and in the depths of winter, all kinds of magic ceremonies were performed to banish the cold weather and keep people's spirits up.

Today, more and more communities are remembering their old customs, consulting the chronicles and lovingly trying to revive these traditional festivals. Not only does this delight the tourists, who feel they are experiencing a real authentic piece of Italy, but, above all, it helps the villages, towns, or communities to revive a part of their culture and preserve their country's diversity from the uniformity that is the legacy of supermarkets.

Anyone who is keen to experience a typical *fiera* or *sagra* on a trip to Italy should note down some dates. The following have, of course, merely been selected as samples. It is not true, by the way, that it is only southern Italy that celebrates such "food festivals." It is just that they are somewhat jollier, more colorful, and certainly more boisterous down here than they are in the more reserved north. In July, Casalfiumanese holds its apricot festival and in April the orange has pride of place in Ribera near Agrigento. A visit to San Damiano d'Asti in September is a must for anyone with a passion for *bollito misto*. In autumn, the sweet chestnut is center-stage in Marradi near Florence while gnocchi can be sampled in Castel del Rio near Bologna in June. Figure-conscious visitors can have a field day at the salad festival in Treviso in December while August is the month for celebrating the famous Castelluccio lentils in Norcia and mozzarella cheese in Eboli. Anyone with any room left can visit the pizza festival in Albanella, in the Campanian province of Salerno, also in August. Torrone (nougat) can be sampled in Cremona or Faenza in October and November and if you find yourself in Sardinia in August, you can enjoy the tomato festival (Zeddiani, Oristano province) or the Vernaccia grape festival (Nurachi, also in the Oristano province) at which Sardinian traditional costumes are worn.

Background: Strings of colored lights light up Bagnara which plays host to the swordfish festival. This spectacular event attracts crowds of visitors to this small village from all over the region as well as from neighboring Sicily.

INVOLTINI DI PESCE SPADA
Swordfish rolls

Serves 6

ABOUT 1 1/2 LBS/600 G FRESH SWORDFISH, CUT INTO
THIN RECTANGULAR SLICES ABOUT 2 1/2 INCHES BY
4 INCHES (6.5 X 10 CM)
4 OZ/100 G STEAMED SWORDFISH MEAT
1/2 CUP/50 G CACIOVALLO, FRESHLY GRATED
1 CUP/60 G FRESH BREADCRUMBS
12 STONED BLACK OLIVES, CHOPPED
ONION RINGS
BAY LEAVES

Salsa salmoriglio:
1/3 CUP/100 ML OLIVE OIL
1 HANDFUL OF CHOPPED PARSLEY
2 GARLIC CLOVES, MINCED
CHOPPED CAPERS, AS REQUIRED
1 TSP OREGANO
SALT AND PEPPER

Lay the swordfish steaks on a marble board and
tenderize with a rolling-pin, taking care not to split
them. Dice the steamed swordfish meat and mix with
the *caciovallo*, the breadcrumbs, and the olives. Spread
this mixture over the slices of fish, then roll them up.
Put the rolls on a skewer, alternating them with the
onion rings and bay leaves, then cook over a charcoal
grill, brushing them with the *Salsa salmoriglio* marinade.
To make the *Salsa salmoriglio*, mix the olive oil with 4
tablespoons of hot water, adding parsley, garlic, capers,
oregano, and salt and pepper to taste.

PESCE SPADA ALLA GHIOTTA
Swordfish rolls in tomato sauce
(Illustration below, foreground)

1/2 LB/200 G TOMATOES, PASSED THROUGH A SIEVE
4 BASIL LEAVES
SALT
4–5 CUPS/250 G FRESH BREADCRUMBS
4 OZ/100 G STONED BLACK OLIVES, CHOPPED
3 TBSP CAPERS
1 SMALL BUNCH OF PARSLEY, CHOPPED
1 PEPERONCINO, CHOPPED
GENEROUS 2 LBS/1 KG SWORDFISH, CUT INTO THIN SLICES
3–4 TBSP OLIVE OIL

Cook the tomatoes in a saucepan with the basil until the
mixture forms a sauce. Season with salt and set aside. In a
bowl, mix together the breadcrumbs, olives, capers, parsley,
and peperoncino, adding a little water and salt. Spread the
paste onto the slices of swordfish and then roll up, securing
each one with a cocktail stick. Fry these in olive oil. Pour
the tomato sauce over the fish rolls and let them simmer for
a few more minutes over a low heat. Serve hot.

PESCE SPADA IN SALMORIGLIO
Grilled marinated swordfish
(Illustrated below, background)

For the mariade:
EXTRA VIRGIN OLIVE OIL
JUICE OF 1 LEMON
OREGANO
1 SMALL BUNCH OF PARSLEY, CHOPPED
1 CLOVE OF GARLIC, CHOPPED
SALT AND PEPPER
1 TBSP CHOPPED CAPERS
GRATED LEMON ZEST

1 3/4 LBS/800 G SWORDFISH, CUT INTO 4 STEAKS

Mix the olive oil, lemon juice, a generous amount of
oregano, chopped parsley, and the chopped garlic together
in a bowl to form a marinade and season with salt and
pepper. Add the chopped capers and a little lemon zest.
Sprinkle the swordfish steaks with olive oil and cook over a
very hot grill. Sprinkle with the marinade and serve hot.

PREPARING SEAFOOD

Squid

First of all, wash the squid and, starting at the bottom, peel off the outer skin toward the head.

Then, take hold of the body and tentacles and pull apart.

If you are careful, the head and innards can be removed from the sac-shaped body.

Take great care not to split the ink sac.

Using a sharp knife, separate the head from the tentacles.

Keep the silver-gray ink sac as this may be used in some recipes.

Finally, slide the translucent quill out of the body of the squid.

Lastly, after slicing the squid into rings, chop up any remaining edible parts into small pieces.

Shrimp

Take hold of the shrimp between the thumb and forefinger.

Remove the head by giving it a slight twist.

Break open the shell along the underside.

The tail can be left for decoration.

The body can now be removed from the shell intact.

The deliciously delicate meat is ready to eat.

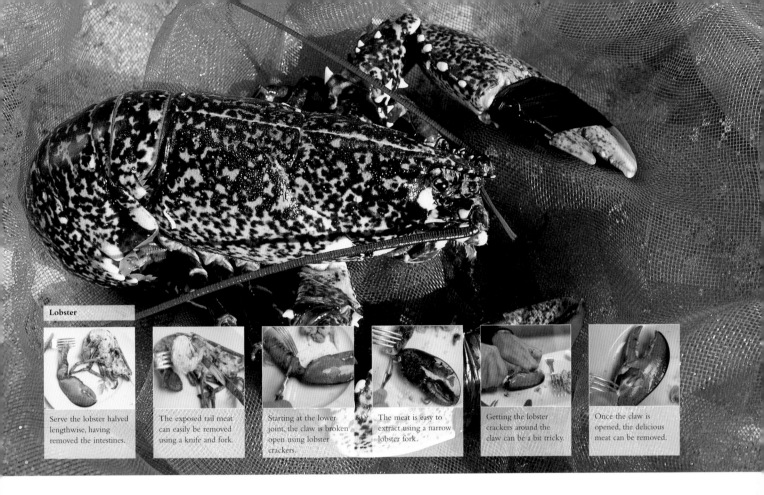

Lobster

Serve the lobster halved lengthwise, having removed the intestines.	The exposed tail meat can easily be removed using a knife and fork.	Starting at the lower joint, the claw is broken open using lobster crackers.	The meat is easy to extract using a narrow lobster fork.	Getting the lobster crackers around the claw can be a bit tricky.	Once the claw is opened, the delicious meat can be removed.

Rock or spiny lobsters

Halve the cooked lobster and remove the delicate roe.

With care the meat can be removed from the shell in one go.

Sea urchin

Carefully open up the mouth on the flat side of the sea urchin with a pair of scissors. Cut through the connective tissue beneath the prickly shell.

Once a large hole has been opened up using a pair of tweezers, the edible, orange-colored flesh can be scooped out with a teaspoon.

Spider crab

A fork is ideal for loosening the meat from the inside of the shell.

The meat can then be extracted bit by bit.

Cedro di Calabria, citron liqueur, can be used to add flavor to some desserts, such as *crema pasticcera*.

LIQUORE DI MANDARINI
Mandarin liqueur

RIND OF 5 MANDARIN ORANGES
2 CUPS/500 ML GOOD QUALITY CORN SCHNAPPS
1 1/2 CUPS/300 G SUGAR

Cut the mandarin orange peel into thin strips and leave to stand in the alcohol for two weeks in a dark place. Then, remove the peel and strain through a cloth, collecting the residual liquid which will then be returned to the alcohol. Stir the sugar into ¾ cup/200 ml boiling water and continue to boil until the sugar has dissolved. Leave to cool, then add to the flavored alcohol. Using a paper filter, strain the finished liqueur into bottles.

LIQUORE DI ZAGARE
Orange blossom liqueur

4 OZ/100 G ORANGE BLOSSOM
4 CUPS/800 G SUGAR
JUST OVER 4 CUPS/1 LITER GOOD QUALITY CORN SCHNAPPS

Layer the orange blossom and sugar in a brown, sealable glass container and leave for 12 hours in a cool, dark place. Add the alcohol, close the container, and shake until the sugar has completely dissolved. Strain the liquid through a paper filter into a bottle and seal. After a few more days, filter the liqueur into another bottle. Filter a few more times, as many times as necessary, until the liquid is completely clear.

LIQUORE DI LIMETTE
Lime liqueur

RIND OF 4 LIMES
JUST OVER 4 CUPS/1 LITER GOOD QUALITY CORN SCHNAPPS
4 CUPS/700 G SUGAR
JUICE OF 2 LIMES

Cut the lime peel into small pieces and leave to soak in the alcohol for a week. Stir the sugar into 4 cups/1 liter of boiling water and heat until the sugar has completely dissolved. Add the lime juice and allow to cool. Strain the alcohol into the sugar water through a sieve and discard the lime peel. Strain the liqueur into bottles through a paper filter.

LIQUORE DI LIMONI
Lemon liqueur

RIND FROM 5 VERY FRESH LEMONS
2 CUPS/500 ML GOOD QUALITY CORN SCHNAPPS
2 1/4 CUPS/450 G SUGAR

Remove the white pith from the lemon peel and cut the peel into small strips. Mix with the alcohol and leave to stand for 6 days in a dark place.
Stir the sugar into 1 ¾ cups/450 ml boiling water and boil until the sugar has dissolved before allowing to cool. Remove the lemon peel from the alcohol and add it to the sugar water, then leave to stand for 2 days before removing the peel from the syrup. Add the alcohol and strain the liqueur through a paper filter a few times before pouring it into bottles.

Below: Sicily and Calabria produce 75 percent of Italy's crop of clementine and mandarin oranges which are particularly in demand over the Christmas period.

CITRUS LIQUEURS

Sicily holds nearly all the records for growing and exporting citrus fruit, but Calabria occupies second place, albeit lagging a fair distance behind. Calabrian oranges, which are harvested from April to May, are characterized by their mild flavor, smooth peel, and firm, juicy, and almost completely seedless flesh. The main variety produced around Reggio Calabria is the Bergamotte orange. Although most of the fruit ends up in perfume manufacture or confectionery, some housewives still use it to make delicious marmalade.
Even the citron, which can grow up to more than two pounds (one kilogram) in weight, is used for perfumes and in the candy industry. The peel, which is around one inch (2.5 centimeters) thick, is made into candied lemon peel. Calabrians are particularly fond of making homemade liqueurs from citrus fruits. Nearly all varieties of fruits are suitable for this purpose, even the delicate orange blossom produces a delicious drink. The procedure is as simple as you could wish. The lemon, mandarin, lime, or citron peel has to stand in alcohol until the aromatic ethereal oils have been released. This takes one to two weeks. Sugar is then added to the flavored alcohol and the mixture filtered through a fine cloth. There is no need to worry about how long it will keep as the liqueur can have as high an alcohol content as you like.

SOMETHING SWEET

Like their counterparts from other southern Italian regions, Calabria's sweetmeats are aptly named, as sugar, honey, and candied fruit are used in huge quantities by Calabrian cake and candy confectioners. It is easy to spot Sicilian and oriental influences among the sumptuous delicacies available in this part of Italy. The *cubbaita*, for example, a soft nougat made from sugar and sesame seeds, is almost identical to the sesame sweetmeat found in Greece and Turkey.

Calabrians are also very fond of *cannoli*, or sweet pastry rolls, which stem from neighboring Sicily, as well as almond cookies and various kinds of almond nougat. One of the most popular sweetmeats is *torrone gelato*, which is not, as its name suggests, some sort of nougat ice cream. This cylindrical-shaped speciality does not need a refrigerator as it has nothing to do with ice cream. This sweet, sticky, and brightly colored confection can be bought in every cake-shop in and around Reggio Calabria. Chopped candied lemon peel, candied oranges, and mandarin oranges are held together by almond paste mixed with brightly colored dissolved sugar. The whole confection is finally covered with chocolate.

FICHI SECCHI RIPIENI
Stuffed dried figs
(Illustrated above)

2 OZ/60 G HAZELNUTS
2 OZ/60G ALMONDS
GRATED RIND OF 2 LEMONS
8 LARGE DRIED FIGS
HONEY

Toast the hazelnuts in the oven for 5–10 minutes at 375 °F (190 °C). Rub the skin off with a cloth and chop. Blanch the almonds, then take each almond between the thumb and forefinger and squeeze it out of its skin, and chop. Mix together the hazelnuts, almonds, and grated lemon rind. Make a cut through the middle of the figs and put some of the mixture in each. Place the stuffed figs on a greased baking tray, dribble honey over them, and bake in a preheated oven for about 10 minutes at 350 °F (180 °C).

MOSTACCIOLI CALABRESI
Calabrian honey cookies
(Pictured right)

1 1/2 CUPS/250 G ALL-PURPOSE FLOUR
8 LEVEL TBSP/250 G HONEY, PREFERABLY FIG HONEY
3 1/2 TBSP/50 G BUTTER
1 TBSP ANISE-FLAVORED LIQUEUR

Mix all the ingredients together and knead into a firm dough. Roll out to about ¼ inch (1 cm) thickness. Using a knife, cut out small animal shapes and figures. Place on a greased baking sheet and bake in a preheated oven at 300 °F (150 °C) until golden brown.

Of the altogether 700 or so varieties of fig, the Dottato di Cosenza is the most sought after. To preserve figs, they should be dried in the sun for two weeks.

Water melons are best eaten when thoroughly ripe. The color of the flesh indicates how ripe it is. The deeper red it is in color, the sweeter the fruit.

Large water melons can be as heavy as medicine balls. You should be prepared for this if your fresh purchase is thrown for you to catch.

The choice of melons is considerable. Not only are there various sizes of water melons to choose from but also different types of honeydew melons available.

Background: Franco Moriello's stall is located near a busy intersection linking Calabria and the Basilicata with Campania and Apulia. Here you can buy not only melons but all sorts of fruits, vegetables, various spices, and preserves. As a special service to long-distance truck drivers, not to mention local residents and their summer visitors, Franco stays open round the clock.

MELONS

Melons, like zucchini, belong to the pumpkin family. Various varieties of this fruit, which originally came from southern Asia and Equatorial Africa, are grown all over central and southern Italy as well as on the islands. It is often bought from a fruit-seller's stand as a refreshing snack on the way to the beach. Children, love biting into a slice of cool, juicy watermelon after a few hours playing in the sand or in the water.
Basically, melons can be divided into honeydew melons and watermelons. The flesh of honeydew melons is whitish, pale yellow, orange, or light green in color and their skins are yellow or green, sometimes criss-crossed with white or gray markings. The watermelon, which is usually somewhat bigger in size, has a green or greenish-white skin and bright red flesh with numerous seeds. Melon tastes best either eaten in slices with your fingers, in a *Macedonia di frutta* (fruit salad), or in its classical combination with Parma ham.

At around 30 lbs/15 kg, the **Charleston Gray** is not for the weak-hearted shopper.

Thanks to its high water content (95 per cent), the **watermelon** (*Anguria*) is wonderfully refreshing on hot summer days.

The **Cantaloupe** has orange-colored flesh.

The **Crimson Sweet** is another melon that came originally from America. It can weigh over 10 lb/up to 5 kg.

The flesh of the **Tendrale verde** is slightly green in color.

The **Piel de sapo** continues ripening on into the autumn. Its light-colored flesh is often diced and used in fruit salad.

The white-fleshed **Invernale Giallo** is harvested in the autumn.

WINES OF CALABRIA

Calabria is home to the Gaglioppo grape, otherwise known as Montonico nero.

The dark red wines produced here are full-bodied and rich in tannins. They not only form the basis for the majority of DOC wines, but are also good for blending with other types of wine. Although the region has a considerable winegrowing area of almost 71,630 acres (29,000 hectares) – equivalent to a quarter of Germany's vineyards – it does not play a significant role in the national or international wine market. There are both historical and social reasons for this: During the sixties and seventies, Calabria's population was considerably depleted by the exodus of Italian workers to other countries. As a result, it missed sharing in the country's general economic development and also failed to keep pace with advances in wine production.

This does not mean, however, that conditions here are not perfectly suited to producing top quality wines. It was not for nothing that Calabria's vintages enjoyed an outstanding reputation in ancient times – it was precisely this part of Italy which was originally named *Oinotria* by the Greeks before the term came to encompass the whole of the Italian boot. Admittedly, the climate produces difficult conditions over large parts of the region. With 90 percent of the area consisting of mountainous terrain, the vineyards are often perched so high up on the hills that frost is a frequent danger in winter and spring.

Cirò, Pollino, Savuto, and Greco di Bianco are the only labels which are reasonably well-known and the Cirò is virtually the only one of these wines to be exported, albeit in small quantities. Even then, it is consumed largely by Italian émigrés living abroad. There is also a handful of other DOC wines, such as Lamezia, Sant'Anna di Isola Capo Rizzuto, and Melissa, which are not even regionally well-known. Really good wines are rare in Calabria and are the product of isolated, individual efforts.

Background: Even the Ancient Greeks regarded the hills of Cirò as excellent winegrowing areas.

Cirò

Whether the Cirò is indeed a direct descendant of the Cremissa, the prestigious wine of antiquity which used to be presented to the winners of the Olympic Games, is open to debate. What is incontrovertible, however, is the fact that this dry red wine made from the Gaglioppo grape and grown on the terraces of the eastern slopes of the Sila massif is the best known of all Calabria's wines. A small number of producers have succeeded in improving what used to be a rather harsh and acidic wine by developing it into a modern, robust, and smooth product which is sometimes even put to mature in the barrique cask. The best wines are dark red, full-flavored, high in tannin and in some cases, good for laying down.

Pollino

The Gaglioppo grapes used for this dry red wine are grown on the southern slopes of the Pollino mountains. The grapes are pressed and the wine marketed almost exclusively by the region's main growers' cooperative. The swing in temperature between hot summer days and cool nights is what gives the wines their distinctive bouquet.

Savuto

Of all Calabria's DOC wines, it is probably not the successful Cirò but the virtually unknown Savuto grown on the western slopes of the Sila massif that has the greatest potential for being a quality wine.

The moderate climate enjoyed by the higher vineyards produces fine, expressive wines, particularly when the Gaglioppo grape is blended with other varieties, for example the Sangiovese. Unfortunately, there are only one or two producers in this area who are worthy of note.

Greco di Bianco

Calabria's choicest dessert wine comes from the extreme tip of Italy from the area around the little town of Bianco. This is a full-bodied, amber-colored wine with a pleasant fruity flavor and distinctive bouquet, which is made from semidried fruit of the Greco grape.

OINOTRIA – THE LAND OF WINE

The Ancient Greeks gave this southern part of Italy the name *Oinotria* and the Romans extended its Latin equivalent, *Enotria,* to encompass the whole boot of Italy. This is no coincidence, as we know, for Italy has been one of the world's most important winegrowing countries from ancient times right up to the present-day. There is scarcely a province in the country where grapes are not cultivated and in many of Italy's altogether 20 regions, winegrowing continues to be an important branch of industry despite industrialization and the postindustrial revolution.

With nearly 2.5 million acres (1 million hectares), Italy boasts the third largest winegrowing area in the world after Spain and France, and shares with France first place as the largest wine-producing nation. Depending on the vintage, 1.3 – 1.5 million U.S. gallons (50 to 60 million hectolitres) of wine are produced and, for the most part, consumed since Italy also shares the lead with France in per capita consumption. The average Italian drinks nearly 16 U.S. gallons (a good 60 liters) of wine every year, this is almost three times the amount consumed by the average German, twice the amount drunk by Austrians, and nearly eight times the

average consumption in the United States. Compared with the sixties, this actually represents a sharp drop as, up until that time, most Italians did not consider wine a luxury, but a daily source of calories and to this end drank on average more than 32 U.S. gallons (120 liters) per year.

Every Italian region and province can produce wine. The predominantly continental climate of the north is characterized by cold winters and warm summers and produces particularly aromatic wines. By contrast, the southern regions, with their hot, sunny days and nights with temperatures that do not drop very low, produce robust wines with a high alcoholic content.

Since Italy is covered to a great extent by hills and mountains, the grapes are often grown on slopes – in itself an important factor in producing high quality grapes. The diversity of soil types in the different cultivation areas of Italy, combined with the large variety of grapes, results in distinctive wines with a wide variety of flavor characteristics.

The most important winegrowing regions, as far as production quantities go, are Sicily and Apulia. However, central and northern Italy produce the most quality wines. Tuscany and Piemont undisputedly produce the country's most renowned wines – Barolo, Brunello, Chianti, and Barbaresco, to name but a few. Friaul, Trentino-southern Tyrol, the Veneto, Umbria, the Marche, and Lombardy come somewhat lower down the list while winegrowing in the rest of the regions is more geared to producing large quantities than to high quality.

Although the northern regions of Italy, in particular, produce a number of outstanding white wines from the Chardonnay, Sauvignon blanc, or Pinot grigio grape, the strength of Italian viniculture lies in its red wines. The country has two varieties of grape which are considered to be among the best in the world, the Nebbiolo and Sangiovese. The former is cultivated mainly in Piemont, while the latter is the main type used in the Chianti, Brunello, and Vino Nobile wines of Tuscany. The fact that a Barolo wine is made from Nebbiolo grapes, for example, is something that only dyed-in-the-wool wine connoisseurs would be aware of for it is rare in Italy for the variety of grape to be named on the label. Exceptions to this are varieties such as the Barbera d'Asti or Chardonnay Collio, which do have labels denoting origin.

During the eighties and nineties, Italy made great progress in developing its production of high quality wines. The country still has untapped reserves, however. Not only are there grape varieties like the Friaulian Schioppettino or Refosco, the Sicilian Grillo or Nero d'Avolo and the Apulian Primitivo or Negro-amaro, which have still to achieve their full potential, but Italy still has large winegrowing areas with great quality potential waiting to be developed, such as Sicily, the Marche, Campania, or Apulia. The future will show whether Italy's winegrowers will succeed in achieving a break-through with these high-quality varieties from lesser known regions and turn them into wines which can hold their own next to the popular Nebbiolo and Sangiovese.

Binding up the vines properly in winter is vital for the development of the grapes.

The vines are tied by hand using young, flexible willow branches or, more commonly, modern stapling pins.

To prevent wind damage, the branches are trained along a wire framework supporting the vines.

Nowadays vines are anchored by mechanical means instead of by an artistic knot like this.

At the end of April, new shoots sprout from the fruit-buds of the year-old wood.

In order to maintain strong growth, the vines must be pruned hard every winter.

SICILIA

SICILY

Tuna fish

Fish from three seas

Salt

Primi piatti from nine
provinces

Opulent cuisine

Pumpkins and zucchini

Sicilian vegetable dishes

Citrus fruits

Prickly pears

You'll be for it
tonight…

Sweet occasions during
the church year

Marzipan from
Martorana

Ice cream

Winegrowing

Marsala

Lipari Islands
(Aeolian Islands)

S.Vito
lo Capo

Palermo

Trapani

Favi-
gnana   Marsala

Mazara
del Vallo

Agrigento

Messina

Straits of Messina

Sicily

Etna
3350 m

Enna
Caltanisetta   Catania

Francofonte

Siracusa

Ragusa

As far as Sicilians are concerned, the best things in life include good company, family life, sunny days by the sea, and, above all, an appreciation of the culinary arts. Just how important good food and fine wines are here is obvious from the region's culture which exhibits a fair amount of preoccupation with matters of a gastronomic nature. In his novel entitled *The Leopard* – which is actually about something else entirely, namely the political turmoil within Italy prior to Unification – Giuseppe Tomasi di Lampedusa profiles the eating habits of Sicilian aristocracy in loving and minute detail. Similarly, Domenico Modugno, the singer – who despite his claims to the contrary, is not a native of Sicily himself – has immortalized in song the tradition of fishing for swordfish which goes on in the Straits of Messina. Sicilians have a long tradition of enjoying their culinary pleasures. Long ago in prehistoric times, when people still worshiped Dea Madre, ritual little cakes were baked in honor of the goddess who was, essentially, motherhood. Then came the Greeks, colonizing the eastern Mediterranean. They dispensed with these female goddesses and devoted themselves to the cult of the grape as personified by the god Dionysus. The Romans introduced elaborate goose dishes to the island, the Byzantines brought with them their fondness for sweet and sour and the Arab invasion between the 9th and 11th centuries brought about a minor culinary revolution: To this day, apricots, sugar, citrus fruits, sweet melons, rice, saffron, raisins, nutmeg, cloves, pepper, and cinnamon are cornerstones of Sicilian cuisine. The Normans and Hohenstaufen invaders, in turn, were fond of meat dishes and the Spaniards magnanimously shared their latest discoveries from the New World: cocoa, maize, turkey, tomatoes, and other produce of the Solanaceae family. They were followed by the Bourbons, the "continental" Italians, and many other races who helped fashion the Sicilian menu.

Eating and drinking in the heart of the Mediterranean, therefore, is always synonymous with a journey back in time to cultures of a bygone age. The ingenuity of Sicilian cooks ensures that the result will be a highly individual interpretation of a multicultural cuisine: colorful, sweet, hearty, aromatic, exotic, typical of the region, and sometimes very mysterious. Just like the island itself.

Previous double page: Sicily is not the only province where street stalls provide instant refreshment in the form of ice cream and *granita*.

Left: The Sicilian landscape, as pictured here near San Vito lo Capo, can appear harsh and romantic at the same time.

Tuna can grow up to 14 feet
(4 m) long and weigh several
tonnes.

TUNA FISH

There is an old fisherman's song which waxes lyrical about the seas off the coast of Scopello, Castellammare, and Magazzinacci as being Sicily's richest waters and pokes fun at the poor fishing grounds off Sicciara where fishermen wait in vain for fish from the Levant. Sadly, however, these former bastions of tuna fishing have themselves fallen on hard times and the song is now barely remembered among the few surviving fishermen. Growing environmental pollution along the coasts and the high-tech Japanese fishing fleets which constantly lie in wait just outside territorial waters mean that few tuna ever get as far as the warm spawning grounds off the Sicilian shores. Only in Favignano, the main town of the Egadi islands, does life still revolve around this great fish even though nowadays the catches are significantly smaller. In other words, the island is slowly but surely losing one of its oldest sources of employment, one which once provided a lot of people with a modest but secure existence: Nets had to be made, repaired, and eventually taken out to the fishing grounds, the fish trapped in the nets had to be killed, then cleaned and numerous factory workers were needed to process the rich meat into delicious specialities for international export. Despite present difficulties, the old traditional methods are still used to catch the coveted tuna. Tuna meat can be preserved in brine or oil as well as cooked fresh. *Tonno* is also very popular as a canned fish. People used to salt it down in huge vats to store for winter supplies.

THE MATTANZA

The Mattanza, the ritual tuna slaughter in Sicily, is a fairly bloody affair and definitely not for the faint-hearted. This ancient island tradition dates from the days of Spanish rule and is an important element of Sicilian culture and local identity.

The island's southern coastal waters with their strong currents are particularly well-stocked and provide the people living along their shores with an abundance of fish and seafood: shrimp, langoustines or crayfish, calamari, sea bass, and rays. Siracusa and the waters surrounding the Egadi islands off the western tip of Sicily play host to large shoals of tuna which arrive from the colder waters of Northern Europe to spawn in the warm waters. Local fishermen have, since time immemorial, used a clever system of nets to catch these fish. This is an ancient method of fishing, which involves no modern technology of any kind. Nowadays, however, the Mattanza is yielding fewer and fewer fish.

The Mattanza also provides an occasion for the whole village to celebrate a folklore festival. This major event in the calendar gets underway with a morning mass to bless the fishing boats before they sail out with the *rizza*, the system of nets. Singing old folk songs as they work, the fishermen start setting up the various corrals of netting in which the tuna will be trapped. These corrals are anchored by heavy stones to the sea bed. Now, all they have to do is wait. The *raís*, or most experienced fisherman, has the honor of signaling the actual start of the Mattanza. When the first shoals are sighted, the fishermen sail out early in the morning to start reducing the size of the corrals in which the tuna are now confined.

Eventually, the entire shoal ends up in the *camera della morte*. Once again, it is the *raís* who decides when to harpoon the fish. The sea runs with blood and the fish are heaved on board with nets. The procession of boats returns to shore where the fish are weighed, washed, and cleaned. Tuna has to be processed very quickly as it soon goes off. Favignana, along with several other villages around Siracusa, Marzamemi, Porto Palo, Sampieri and Donnalucata, are endeavoring to keep this ancient tradition alive.

The Mattanza is the traditional method of tuna fishing. To this day, food festivals are still celebrated in early summer in honor of this fish even if it no longer has the same importance for local industry that it once did.

Tuna fish can be cooked fresh or else the raw fish fillet can be eaten as *carpaccio* cut into thin slices. Other tuna fish delicacies include:

Bottarga di tonno
This speciality, also known as "Sicilian caviar," consists of roe from the female fish, carefully pressed and salted. *Bottarga* is cut into slices and can be eaten raw, fried, or steamed. Oil, parsley, garlic, and peperoncini can be used as accompaniments to this already salty delicacy.

Musciuma
Musciuma, or tuna fish preserved in salt, has to mature for 30 days before it is ready to use as an ingredient in certain salads.

Occhi rassi
The name refers to the solid blue bone surrounding the eye to which some of the choicest meat adheres. The *occhi rassi* are salted in barrels and are good served with pepper and wild fennel.

Curri, Surra, Vintrisca, Ventresca
The belly of the tuna fish, which is known by various names, is cut into long strips, salted, and pressed.

The "big" fish of the sea, like tuna and swordfish, are seldom sold whole. It is the fishmonger's job to clean the fish and cut it up.

Tonno alla palermitana
Tuna fish Palermo style
(Illustrated below)

1 GLASS OF DRY WHITE WINE
JUICE OF 1 LEMON
1 SPRIG OF ROSEMARY
1 GARLIC CLOVE, CRUSHED
SALT AND FRESHLY GROUND PEPPER
1 1/4 LBS/600 G FRESH TUNA FISH
4 TBSP EXTRA VIRGIN OLIVE OIL
3 SARDINE FILLETS

Combine the wine and lemon juice with the rosemary, garlic, a little salt and pepper to make a marinade. Slice the tuna fish and wash thoroughly, then leave to marinate in the mixture for several hours.
Remove the fish from the marinade, drain off excess liquid and broil on both sides, basting with the marinade from time to time.
Meanwhile, heat up the olive oil in the skillet, add the sardines, and mash into a paste using a fork. Spread this over the tuna fish and serve.

Tonno alla marinara
Tuna fish with olives

4 SLICES OF FRESH TUNA FISH
4–5 TBSP EXTRA VIRGIN OLIVE OIL
1 LB/400 G RIPE TOMATOES
1 BUNCH OF BASIL LEAVES, CHOPPED
GENEROUS 1/2 CUP/80 G BLACK OR GREEN OLIVES, PITTED
2 TBSP/30 G CAPERS
SALT AND FRESHLY GROUND PEPPER
2 TBSP BREADCRUMBS

Wash the tuna fish thoroughly, remove the skin, and pat dry. Pour half the olive oil into an ovenproof dish and arrange the slices of tuna on the bottom.
Blanche and skin the tomatoes, remove the cores and seeds and chop into small pieces. Add these to the fish together with the basil, diced olives, capers, some salt, lots of pepper, and the breadcrumbs. Sprinkle over the rest of the olive oil and bake in a pre-heated oven for about 30 minutes at 320 °F (160 °C) until the fish is cooked and the sauce has thickened. Serve hot.

Tuna fish is usually cut into steaks and broiled, but it is also delicious eaten raw as *carpaccio* and sprinkled with a lemon marinade.

Above: *Dentice al forno con cipolle e brodo di carne* –
Baked sea bream (dentex) with onions and bouillon.

FISH FROM THREE SEAS

Sicily has three main coastal areas. The eastern shores, which open onto the Ionian Sea, begin with the Straits of Messina, the traditional fishing grounds for sword-fish, and stretch down to the Capo Passero. The Riviera dei Ciclopi, the Cyclops coast between Aci Trezza, Aci Reale, and Catania, is abundant in sea bass, sea bream (also known as porgy), mussels, and a variety of mackerel known as alalunga. The southern coast between Pozallo and Marsala is home to the dentex fish (type of bream), which is prepared in Agrigentian style or served with orange mayonnaise. The waters off the western tip of Sicily offers a wealth of fishing opportunities: Here, where the Ionian and Tyrrhenian Seas unite, you can catch anything from tuna to sardines. The northern shores harbor the mormyr (type of bream), a popular edible fish which is caught all year round and lives all around the coast. Finally, cuttlefish, calamari, shellfish, and mussels complete the wide selection available from every fish market.

Fish and seafood are a major part of any Sicilian menu. It can be boiled, baked, or broiled – anything goes. Fish is not only served as the main course but often appears as a delicious starter, sometimes in a pasta sauce. *Pasta e pesce* is one of the islanders' favorite combinations – although sometimes, as the following story of an

unhappy Tuscan woman shows, an unusual dish can be the unwitting cause of a lot of trouble. A tragedy was indeed sparked off by the dark sauce made from squid ink. Around the turn of the century, Giselda, a young teacher from Florence, came to Catania with the Sicil-ian-born writer Giovanni Verga to teach at a girls' school. She soon attracted the attentions of the poet Mario Rapisardi, who began paying court to her. Eventually, they were married and the young bride was taken to live at her mother-in-law's house. Before the honeymoon was even over, she had committed the unforgivable faux pas of refusing with utter distaste to try even one mouthful of her mother-in-law's

The little town of Mazara del Vallo is one of Italy's main fishing ports.

spaghetti with dark squid sauce. All hell broke loose and in the end her poet husband – no doubt as a result of the deplorable situation on the domestic front – began a love affair with the Contessa Lara. Giselda, however, knew just what to do and remembered her old friend Verga. One day, Rapisardi discovered a passionate love-letter penned by the writer to his wife, Giselda. Verga had been foolish enough to send it wrapped only in newspaper. The family immediately convened a council of war at the Rapisardi house and unanimously decided to banish the faithless wife. Once again, Giselda sought and initially found conso-lation in the arms of Verga until he ditched her soon afterwards. The duel, so eagerly anticipated by every-one in Catania, failed to materialize, however. No doubt the two writers became reconciled over a large bowl of steaming *spaghetti al nero di seppia*.

DENTICE AL FORNO CON CIPOLLE E BRODO DI CARNE
Baked sea bream (dentex) with onions and bouillon
(Illustrated left)

1 SEA BREAM, ABOUT 1 LB/500 G IN WEIGHT
1 ONION
2 GARLIC CLOVES
1 SPRIG OF ROSEMARY
1 SPRIG OF THYME
OLIVE OIL
SALT
1 PEPERONCINO, DICED
1 ONION, SLICED INTO RINGS
1 LARGE POTATO, DICED
3/4 CUP/100 G CELERIAC, DICED
4 CUPS/1 LITER BOUILLON
PEPPER

Scale and clean the fish. Dice the onions and garlic, chop the rosemary and thyme, and mix together to make the filling. Drench the onions and herbs with olive oil, season with salt and pepper and stuff some of this mixture into the fish. Lightly sauté the onion rings in olive oil and place in an ovenproof dish with the rest of the filling and the oil. Lay the fish on this and place the diced potato and celeriac on top. Bake in a preheated oven for 25–30 mins at 350 °F (180 °C). Very gradually add 4 cups/1 liter of bouillon which has been seasoned with salt and pepper.

SARAGO DI PORTO ALLA BRACE O SULLA PIASTRA
Sea bream, barbecued or cooked on a hot stone

1 SEA BREAM
SALT

Salsa salmoriglio:
SCANT 1/3 CUP/50–100 ML OLIVE OIL
1 CLOVE OF GARLIC, CHOPPED
1 HANDFUL OF CHOPPED PARSLEY

1 LEMON, SLICED
1 BUNCH OF RADISHES

Clean the bream, but do not scale it. Season with salt. Cook on a hot stone or, better still, barbecue over charcoal. To make the *salsa salmoriglio*, stir 2–4 tablespoons hot water into the olive oil and season with garlic and parsley. Brush this mixture onto both sides of the barbecued bream. Serve with slices of lemon and radishes.

SPAGHETTI AL NERO DI SEPPIA
Black spaghetti

4 SQUID (CALAMARI), NOT CLEANED
14 OZ/400 G SPAGHETTI
2 CLOVES OF GARLIC, FINELY MINCED
1 ONION, FINELY MINCED
2 TBSP OLIVE OIL
2–3 TOMATOES, SKINNED AND FINELY DICED
SALT AND PEPPER

Clean the squid, being careful not to damage the ink sacs. Put the ink in a glass and set aside for the sauce. Cut the squid into small pieces. Cook the spaghetti *al dente* in plenty of salted water. Meanwhile, sauté the garlic and onions in hot oil until transparent. Add the tomatoes, squid and squid ink and season with salt and pepper. Simmer for a few minutes and then pour the sauce over the spaghetti.

White sea bream (sarago)
White bream is one of the most popular fish in the Mediterranean. In Catania the fish is known as the *sarago di porto*, harbor bream. It can be caught using simple bait such as prickly pear skin, instead of the usual cuttlefish bait. White bream is best cooked over a charcoal barbecue.

Dentix (dentice)
The dentix can grow up to 12 to 36 inches (30 to 90 cm) in length and weigh up to 22 to 27 pounds (10 to 12 kg). Its pleasant-tasting meat is particularly suitable for boiling. It can also be braised in the oven with onions and bouillon.

Sea bass (cernia di fondale)
This is a fish of the Serranidae family. It has a long, spiky dorsal fin and an extended lower jaw. Fisherman nicknamed it *a'ddottò*, "doctor", because its scale markings look like hieroglyphics. This very large species of sea bass can measure up to 6 feet (150 cm) and weigh up to 155 pounds (70 kg). The women turn its excellent meat into a delicious soup or use it for main dishes.

Mormyr (mormora)
This type of bream lives in the muddy, brackish coastal waters. It is caught all year round and can be identified by the twelve vertical stripes across its yellow or gray flanks. It can measure 10 to 14 inches (25 to 36 cm) and be used in virtually any fish dish.

Cuttlefish (seppia)
Cuttlefish and calamari (*calamaro*) are edible cephalopods with pear-shaped bodies and ten tentacles. They have a sac that contains an ink-like substance which they squirt out when threatened in order to disorientate their attacker and obscure visibility. They are popular in Sicily as ingredients in seafood salads but they can also be broiled, fried, or stuffed. The ink is used to color rice and pasta dishes. These oddly black-colored dishes are not to everyone's taste. If you are not put off by the unusual color, you should sample *Spaghetti al nero di seppia*.

Swordfish (pesce spada)
The swordfish is one of Sicily's most popular fish. It is mainly caught in the Straits of Messina. The traditional method of fishing by harpoon is also practiced around Bagnara in Calabria on the opposite shore. It can be a risky business as these creatures, which can be up to 13 feet (4 m) long and weigh around 440 pounds (200 kg), often attack the small fishing boats. Swordfish meat should be left to hang for a few days before eating to make it tender and more flavorsome. A typical swordfish dish is *Involtini di pesce spada*, stuffed swordfish rolls.

SALT

Man could not survive without salt. Sodium chloride keeps the body's muscles and nerves in working order, enables it to digest food and helps maintain a proper water balance. Without salt in his diet, he would suffer from tooth loss, heart disease, and general disability. Prehistoric man got what salt he needed from eating plenty of meat, but the quantities he required forced him to live the life of a hunter and nomad. Life depended on the salt and protein derived from animals. It was not until people discovered that the gray or white crystals obtainable from seawater or from natural deposits were equally capable of supplying the body's vital salt requirements that they could contemplate a change in their diet and life style. People began to settle, to live off the fruits of their land and they supplemented their daily food with salt. This reduction in meat consumption and a switch to a diet based on virtually salt-free grain and vegetables led inevitably to a dependence on the "white gold." Salt became the most important trading commodity in the early civilized world and the demand for it increased dramatically after resourceful cooks discovered that this crystalline substance with its characteristic taste could also keep meat, fish, and vegetables from spoiling – thus was born the art of preserving, an important new cultural advance as this also meant that salted food rations now made intensive military operations and invasion campaigns feasible. Towns along the salt routes flourished, a salt embargo could mean the ruin of an entire region, and the local princes were at pains to safeguard their access to salt resources. Salt was also used as currency – as the word "salary" reminds us.

Sicily is particularly blessed with salt. Sea salt is extracted around Trapani, Marsala, and Augusta while Cattolica Eraclea has extensive deposits of rock salt in its vicinity. In earlier days, large trading ships used to call at the western tip of the island to carry Sicilian salt all over the world.

The traditional methods of salt extraction have not changed all that much over the past 140 years and so it is well worthwhile recalling how Sicilian scholar Giuseppe Pitré described the Trapani salt pans in his book published at the end of the 19th century entitled *La famiglia, la casa, la vita del popolo siciliano* (Family, home and life of the Sicilian people). He wrote: "A large area to the east of Trapani is divided into numerous squares. These are linked by a system of small canals which gradually allow sea water to penetrate right the way inland to the salt pan farthest from the shore. Its color changes as it progresses, starting off a reddish color, then turning bluish, and finally ending up white after the water has been evaporated by the baking African sun, leaving a layer of salt crystals which gleam like glistening white snow."

Around a century earlier, an English traveler described the process of salt extraction at the salt-works in some detail: "The salt-works is divided into numerous pans. The cold seawater is pumped into the largest one, the so-called 'cold' basin or 'mother'. This is where the evaporation process begins. Once the

Background: The extensive salt extraction plants and windmills for crushing salt near Trapani lie on the Via del Sale, the salt route, which runs along the coast between Trapani and Marsala.

WHITE GOLD

Salt is mankind's oldest preservative. No other substance has had such a strong influence on cooking or life style. Transportable, salted provisions mean mobility, freedom from concerns about food shortages, and insurance against diseases caused by nutritional deficiencies. This was particularly crucial to seafarers, soldiers, and settlers in undeveloped areas. But those who remained close to home also benefited from the new kinds of preserved food. Salted cod and herring, vegetables salted down in barrels, and salted meat specialities like ham and sausage transformed the culinary landscape. Trapani assumed an important role in supplying this valuable commodity. The situation has changed somewhat since then. Nowadays, cheap industrial salt is produced all over the world. Gone are the days when the Phoenicians used to load up their maneuverable ships on Sicilian shores. The Greeks and Romans came next, followed by Arab feluccas and later the ocean-going vessels of the Normans. Valuable Sicilian salt was eventually introduced to Brittany, England, and later the towns of the Hanseatic League. It would have been impossible to process the large herring catches without salt and on Norway's Lofoten islands, it was used in the preparation of klipfish and stockfish. Cod, salted and dried in the cold northern air, soon became popular in the Mediterranean region and Sicilian salt, after this excursion to northern climes, returned home again. Norman ships brought consign-

ments of this hard but tasty fish to southern Italy and returned home again with cargoes of citrus fruits, Marsala, wine, and, of course, "white gold."

The advent of modern refrigeration methods and industrial preserving techniques, including sterilization and pasteurization, has meant that Trapani sea salt has lost its key role. It is, however, currently experiencing a small renaissance as more and more cooks are using these large crystals of coarse grain salt on focaccia or other types of flat bread.

water has had time to warm up a little, it is channelled into the next basin, known as the *frittedda* or 'no longer quite so cold': It remains here for two weeks before being channelled along a canal into a third chamber known as *ricauda* or *idicauda*, or 'lukewarm', which is further subdivided into three sections. Buckets and ladles are now used to transfer the water into a tub before being poured yet again into the *casa calda* or 'warm house', again divided into three sections. From here, it goes to the penultimate chamber, the *caldissima*, the 'hot basin'. The seawater's journey finally ends in the last pan where the water, five inches deep to start with, crystallizes into a roughly two-inch layer of salt. The water…is channelled along the canals into the respective basins by means of a system of sluice-gates. The resulting salt crystals are piled into pyramids away from the salt works and left to air-dry for a year. During this time, a crust forms which protects the salt underneath. The salt is crushed into coarse grains by means of a vertically-turning mill-wheel."

When the summer season is over, the pyramids of salt are protected by terracotta tiles.

PRIMI PIATTI FROM NINE PROVINCES

The first course, in other words, the one which follows an appetite-stimulating antipasto and is designed to take the edge off your hunger and at the same time increase anticipation of the main course, is a serious matter in Sicily. The *primi piatti* are something of a passion for Sicilians in general. However, or perhaps precisely for this reason, the culinary preferences of each of the island's nine provinces are easy to recognize from their different "first courses." In the province of Enna, the grain basket in the heart of the island, polenta with vegetables is the popular dish. Sicilians in nearby Caltanissetta also like local dishes and serve *gnocchetti* with a pork-based sauce. Messina, which has most of the local swordfish trade, specializes in an appropriate pasta sauce. Palermo is famed for its sardine dishes while Trapani's favorite is a simple, but extremely tasty pasta dish with sheep's cheese. Agrigento's speciality is homemade macaroni with red sauce and aubergines and Catania has its famous *pasta alla norma*. Beans are the key ingredients in Ragusa and Siracusa, for its part, boasts one of the oldest pasta recipes in Sicily, *pasta fritta alla siracusana*.

MACCARUNEDDI CON SALSA ROSSA E MELANZANE
Macaroni with tomato eggplant sauce

Agrigento

2 MEDIUM EGGPLANTS, DICED
SALT
FLOUR
OLIVE OIL
1 LB/500 G MACARONI
2 CUPS/500 ML TOMATO SAUCE

Sprinkle the diced eggplant with salt and leave to stand for about 1 hour to draw out excess moisture. Pat dry, sprinkle with a little flour, and fry in plenty of olive oil until golden brown. Cook the macaroni *al dente* in plenty of salted water, and serve immediately with the hot tomato sauce and the diced eggplant.

CAVATIEDDI – GNOCCHETTI DI SEMOLA AL SUGO DI MAIALE
Pasta with pork ragout

Caltanissetta

1 BUNCH OF SOUP VEGETABLES (2 CARROTS, 1 LEEK, 2 CELERY STALKS, PARSLEY), CHOPPED
OLIVE OIL
3/4 LB/300 G PORK, CUT INTO CUBES
1/2 GLASS RED WINE
4 TOMATOES, CHOPPED
SALT AND PEPPER
1 LB/500 G GNOCCHETTI
1/4 LB/100 G RICOTTA, SIEVED

Sauté the soup vegetables gently in olive oil. Add the meat and fry until brown on all sides. Pour in the red wine and add the tomatoes. Cover the pork ragout with a lid and cook until tender. Season to taste with salt and pepper. Cook the gnocchetti *al dente* in plenty of salted water. Mix the pasta with the ricotta and serve with the ragout.

SPAGHETTI ALLA TRAPANESE
Spaghetti Trapani style

Trapani

14 OZ/400 G SPAGHETTI
SALT
2 LB/1 KG RIPE, PEELED TOMATOES
2 GARLIC CLOVES, CHOPPED INTO SMALL PIECES
1 SMALL BUNCH OF BASIL LEAVES, ROUGHLY CHOPPED
SICILIAN SHEEP'S CHEESE, CRUMBLED
1 GLASS OF EXTRA VIRGIN OLIVE OIL
FRESHLY GROUND PEPPER
GRATED PARMESAN

Boil the spaghetti in salted water until it is cooked *al dente* and drain off the water. Finely dice the peeled tomatoes and mix them with the garlic, basil, sheep's cheese, and olive oil. Season to taste with salt and pepper and serve with the spaghetti. Sprinkle with grated parmesan.

RIGATONCINI CON MACCU DI FAVE
Rigatoncini with bean paste

Ragusa

3/4 LB/300 G FAT, DRIED BEANS
1/2 CELERIAC, DICED
1 TOMATO, PEELED
3/4 LB/350 G RIGATONCINI
OLIVE OIL
SALT AND PEPPER

Soak the beans in water overnight. Next day, boil them in fresh water with the celeriac and tomato. Once the beans are pulpy, mash them and add the *rigatoncini*. The dish should not be too runny. Add plenty of olive oil, salt and pepper to taste.

PASTA FRITTA ALLA SIRACUSANA
Fried vermicelli

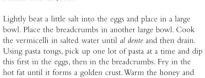
Siracusa

3 EGGS
SALT
2 CUPS/150 G FRESH BREADCRUMBS
1 1/4 LBS/600 G VERMICELLI
PORK FAT
5 TBSP/150 G THYME HONEY
1 GLASS ORANGE JUICE

Lightly beat a little salt into the eggs and place in a large bowl. Place the breadcrumbs in another large bowl. Cook the vermicelli in salted water until *al dente* and then drain. Using pasta tongs, pick up one lot of pasta at a time and dip this first in the eggs, then in the breadcrumbs. Fry in the hot fat until it forms a golden crust. Warm the honey and orange juice together in a bain-mairie and then pour over the fried pasta. An oriental delight!

Pasta alla norma
Pasta with eggplants

Catania

3–4 SMALL EGGPLANTS
4–5 TBSP OLIVE OIL
2 CLOVES OF GARLIC
L LB/500 G SIEVED TOMATOES
I SMALL BUNCH OF BASIL
SALT AND FRESHLY MILLED PEPPER
14 OZ/400 G RIGATONI, MACARONI, OR TAGLIATELLE
4 TBSP FRESHLY GRATED PECORINO

Wash and slice the eggplants into rounds roughly the thickness of a finger. Sprinkle with salt to draw out the slightly bitter juices. After 30 minutes rinse off under running water and pat dry with paper towels. Heat the olive oil in a skillet and sauté the eggplants. Slice the garlic very thinly and add to the eggplants along with the tomatoes and a few coarsely chopped basil leaves. Season with salt and pepper and simmer for a further 10–15 minutes.
Bring a large pan of salted water to a boil, toss in the pasta, and cook until *al dente*. Drain, cover with the tomato sauce, and sprinkle with pecorino.

Frascatula di polenta di grano e verdure
Vegetable polenta

Enna

Serves 6

I LB/500 G POLENTA (CORNMEAL PORRIDGE)
I LB/500 G BROCCOLI SPEARS
1/2 LB/200 G POTATOES, DICED
OLIVE OIL
2 ONIONS, SLICED INTO RINGS
I 3/4 LBS/800 G ZUCCHINI, DICED
1/2 LB/250 G TOMATOES, SKINNED
SALT AND PEPPER

Mix the cornmeal into a polenta with a good 6 cups/1.5 liters of water (cf. basic recipe page 19). Allow the cooked polenta to cool and cut into chunks.
Cook the broccoli and potatoes in about 10 cups/2.5 liters of lightly salted water, then drain. Heat the oil in a large skillet and sauté the onions along with the zucchini and tomatoes, season with salt and pepper, and simmer over a low heat. Place the polenta on plates and add the broccoli, potatoes and cover with the sauce made from onions, zucchini, and tomatoes.

Pasta ai quadrucci di pesce spada
Pasta with swordfish

Messina

Serves 6

2 TOMATOES
OLIVE OIL
2 CLOVES OF GARLIC, CHOPPED
I BUNCH OF PARSLEY, MINCED
SALT AND PEPPER
14 OZ/400 G SWORDFISH
1/2 GLASS OF WHITE WINE
I 1/2 LBS/600 G SEDANINI (SHORT PASTA)
12 LEAVES OF MINT, CHOPPED

Peel and quarter the tomatoes. Heat the olive oil in a saucepan and lightly sauté the tomatoes, garlic, and parsley. Season with salt and pepper. Cut the swordfish into small pieces, add to the sauce, and pour in the wine. Cover and simmer for about 20 mins.
Cook the pasta *al dente* in plenty of salted water, drain, add to the sauce. Garnish with chopped mint.

Pasta con le sarde
Pasta with sardines

4 FRESH SARDINES
1/2 LB/250 G FENNEL
SALT
2 ONIONS
EXTRA VIRGIN OLIVE OIL
A PINCH OF SAFFRON
SALT AND PEPPER
3 ANCHOVY FILLETS
14 OZ/400 G SPAGHETTI
1/3 CUP/50 G RAISINS
1/3 CUP/50 G PINE NUTS

Wash and fillet the sardines. Roughly chop up the fennel and cook in plenty of salted water. Remove the fennel from the water with a spatula and set aside; retain the cooking water. Dice the onions and sauté in olive oil. Pour about

Palermo

a cup of the "fennel water" over the onions and bring to a boil. Once the liquid has been almost completely reduced, stir in the saffron. Add just enough olive oil to make a thick sauce, then season with salt and pepper. Sauté the anchovy fillets in hot oil in a skillet until they disintegrate. Add the sardines to the anchovy mixture and cook over a fairly low heat.
Add the pasta to the "fennel water" and boil until *al dente*, topping up with more salted water if necessary, then drain. In a bowl, combine the pasta with the saffron sauce and the sardines. Add the raisins and pine nuts and make sure all the ingredients are thoroughly mixed. Allow to stand for a short while before serving.

Luchino Visconti's film version of *The Leopard*, based on the novel by Giuseppe Tomasi di Lampedusa, used spectacular sets and starred top names like Claudia Cardinale and Burt Lancaster.

Above: In the 19th century, the San Nicola monastery in Catania was the second largest monastery in the world.

OPULENT CUISINE

Until Italy became a liberal centralized state in the 1870s, Sicily's inheritance laws were based on primogeniture, the right of the firstborn to inherit. This meant that younger siblings were, to some extent, destined from the outset to have no financial means of their own, even if they came from rich, aristocratic backgrounds. The notion of earning money from gainful employment was, by and large, an unknown concept to them and often the only course left open to these lower-ranking nobles was to embark on a career in the church. In order to cushion their harsh fate a little, these sons and daughters of Sicilian princes, barons, and counts naturally made every effort to

provide themselves with a fitting life style within the monastery walls. It was for this reason that feudal cuisine in 19th-century Sicily branched off in two main directions which still retained many surprising similarities. On the one hand, there was the culinary magnificence seen in the great palaces, and on the other, the sumptuous cuisine of the monasteries which often employed their own French *monzu*, a type of latter-day gourmet chef.

One of the most powerful and richest monasteries was San Nicola, in Catania. This was the second largest monastery in the world after Cisnerros in Portugal. In 1894, Federico de Roberto, in his epic novel *The Viceroys*, painted a revealing portrait of monastic life: "The monks lived according to the motto 'Good food and drink, not forgetting a little gentle exercise.' On rising, every monk went to celebrate mass in church, usually behind closed doors so as not to be disturbed. After returning to his cell, he would partake of a small

bite to eat in anticipation of the midday meal, for which preparations would be underway in the vast kitchens, often staffed by no fewer than eight cooks and their helpers. To keep the fires in the kitchen ranges burning, 14 loads of oakwood charcoal were delivered each day. The cellarer also supplied four bladders of lard and two kafis of oil each day just for the fried dishes alone. Such quantities would have lasted a prince's household six months. Grills and fireplaces could accommodate half a calf or a whole swordfish at a time. Two kitchen boys would spend an hour grating two whole cheeses. Even the oak chopping board was so gigantic that two men could not reach around it with their arms. So heavily used was it that a carpenter had to be summoned once a week – in return for a fee of four taris and half a cask of wine – to plane off about an inch of wood from the surface to make it smooth again. The opulence of Benedictine cuisine was the talk of the whole town. It included *Timballo di maccheroni*, a baked pasta dish, topped with short pastry, *arancini*, so-called rice balls as big as melons, served with stuffed olives and honeysweet *crespelle*…And, believe it or not, for ice cream dishes like *spumone* and *cassata*, the monks would actually send to Naples for Don Tino, the young man from the Caffè Benvenuto." According to literary history, were it not for *The Viceroys*, there would have been no *Leopard*, in other words, no book by the Prince of Lampedusa about the life of the fictitious Prince Salina. Giuseppe Tomasi di Lampedusa obviously knew his subject well. Having been brought up by his maternal grandparents at the Palazzo Cutò-Filangieri in Santa Marìa Belice and at the castle of Palma di Montechiaro, Lampedusa was very well acquainted with the cuisine of his day. His novel consequently reads like a treatise on the gastronomic traditions of Sicilian aristocracy, which, after years of Bourbon rule, found itself on the threshold of a new, unified Italy. The Prince of Salina, the Leopard, is summoned to Naples by King Ferdinand because his nephew is propagating new-fangled, liberal ideas. Having aired his – entirely justified – displeasure, the king then amiably shows his Sicilian guest that there are no hard feelings by inviting him to a small, private repast – consisting, naturally, of macaroni and pleasant female company – thereby indicating that he wishes to let the matter rest.

When Garibaldi lands near Marsala with his famous "Thousand", the Salinas simply withdraw to their summer residence at Donnafugata, as if nothing has happened. A gala dinner is held on the evening of their arrival, given by the Leopard in honor of the mayor and local nobility. Lampedusa's description of the banquet reads like an excerpt from the culinary history of an Italy whose upper classes, though all for the sort of refined, aristocratic life style cultivated elsewhere in Europe, are more concerned with eating their fill and are not interested, therefore, in any kind of experimentation. The Prince of Salina takes account of this by unceremoniously ignoring existing rules of haute cuisine and instead, having nourishing, home-cooked Sicilian dishes served at his table. Lampedusa makes fun of the fact that the guests' sole concern as the banquet gets underway is that the first course might turn out to be the clear, pale soup that has gained popularity as the latest culinary fashion. Soup as a starter is an intolerable notion for the local dignitaries of Donnafugata and its environs and they mutter about such a "dreadful, foreign custom." However, all their fears prove unfounded as the liveried servants carry in a huge mountain of pasta which turns out to be *Timballo di maccheroni*. Unfortunately, Lampedusa did not provide a recipe for this work of art, but it is obvious from the story that it must have been quite a spectacular affair.

Il timballo del Gattopardo

Sicilian pie
(Illustrated below)

1/2 LB/250 G FROZEN PLAIN (SHORTCRUST) PASTRY
2 LB/1 KG DRIED BEANS

2 pints/1 liter Salsa spagnola:
1 LB/500 G VEAL ON THE BONE
4 PINTS/2 LITERS BOUILLON

For the sauce:
SCANT HALF CUP/100 ML MARSALA VERGINE SOLERAS
OLIVE OIL
1/4 CUP/25 G ONIONS, DICED
1/4 CUP/25 G CARROTS, DICED
2 SLICES/50 G RAW HAM, DICED
1 SMALL/50 G CHICKEN BREAST, SKINNED AND CUT UP INTO SMALL PIECES
1/8 CUP/25 G DICED LIVER
1/3 CUP/80 G DICED HARD-BOILED EGG
A GOOD PINCH OF CINNAMON
A FEW CLOVES
1 1/2 TBSP/30 G TOMATO PASTE
ALL-PURPOSE FLOUR
BUTTER
SALT AND PEPPER
TRUFFLES OR WILD MUSHROOMS

1/2 LB/250 G FROZEN PUFF PASTRY
2 LB/1 KG PENNE RIGATE
GRATED PARMESAN OR CACIOCAVALLO
1 EGG WHITE, WHISKED TO A FROTH
1 EGG YOLK
MILK
FRESH FLOWERS FOR DECORATION

Roll out the thawed out plain pastry to a thickness of just less than ¼ inch/1 cm and line the base and sides of a 13-inch/33-cm springform cake pan with the pastry. Cover the pastry with aluminum foil which has been pierced several times with a fork. To keep the pastry flat while baking, place about 2 lb/1 kg of dried beans on top of the base and bake blind in a preheated oven for 15 minutes at 350 °F (180 °C). Remove the beans and foil and bake for a further ten minutes. Leave to cool, then carefully undo the springform. Refrigerate the pastry base until required.
To make the *salsa spagnola*, first brown the veal in the oven, then add the bouillon and cook until the liquid is reduced to about 2 pints/1 liter.
To make the sauce, slowly reduce the 2 pints of *salsa spagnola* over a low heat. Remove from heat and leave to cool, then add the Marsala Vergine Soleras or any other good, dry marsala. Meanwhile heat the oil in a skillet and sauté the onions, carrots, ham, chicken, liver, and eggs. Season with cinnamon and cloves and add the tomato paste thinned down with a little water. Brown some flour in butter, add a little water and pour over the vegetable and meat mixture. Season with salt and pepper and add the reduced *salsa spagnola*. Simmer a while longer and allow the mixture to thicken further. Finally, fish out the cloves, then add the butter, truffles, or sliced wild mushrooms.
Roll out the layers of puff pastry to a thickness of about ⅛ inch/3 mm. Cook the pasta until *al dente* in plenty of salted water, drain, quickly sprinkle the cheese over and toss. Stir the sauce into the pasta.
Remove the baked pastry case from the refrigerator and fill with the hot pasta. When it is still just warm, brush the edges of the pastry with egg white. Cover the pasta with layers of puff pastry, pressing it down around the edges to hold it in place. The pie can be decorated with shapes, for example, Sicilian motifs, cut from the remaining plain pastry. Brush the lightly beaten yolk of an egg, mixed with a little milk, over the pastry lid and bake in a preheated oven for 45–50 minutes at 340–350 °F (170–180 °C). Decorate with a few small, fresh flowers.

Il timballo del Gattopardo – Sicilian pie

Farsumagru

Stuffed veal roulade
(Illustrated below left)

1/4 LB/100 G HAM OR BACON
3/4 CUP/175 G SALSICCIA, DICED
1/4 LB/100 G CACIOCAVALLO
2 CLOVES OF GARLIC
1 TBSP CHOPPED PARSLEY
1 EGG
SALT AND FRESHLY MILLED PEPPER
1 1/4 LBS/600 G PIECE OF VEAL FOR A LARGE ROULADE
2 HARD-BOILED EGGS
A PINCH OF DRIED MARJORAM
4 TBSP EXTRA VIRGIN OLIVE OIL
1 ONION
1/2 CARROT, DICED
1 BAY LEAF
1/2 CUP/125 ML BOUILLON
1 GLASS RED WINE

Dice the ham and cheese, and combine with the diced
salsiccia, one crushed clove of garlic, the chopped parsley
and the lightly beaten egg to make the filling. Season
with salt and pepper.
Carefully flatten the veal with a meat mallet and spread
the mixture over it. Slice the hard-boiled eggs and
arrange on top of the mixture. Roll up the meat and
secure tightly with kitchen string. Sprinkle with marjoram. Heat the olive oil in an ovenproof dish and sauté the
veal roulade on all sides. Add the onion, sliced into rings,
the diced carrot, bay leaf, and remaining garlic. Pour in
half the bouillon and cover. Cook the meat for about an
hour in a preheated moderate oven (about 340–350 °F/
170–180 °C) until tender, basting occasionally with the
meat juices. Top up the liquid with more bouillon if
necessary.
Place the meat on a warmed platter and keep warm. Put
the ovenproof dish back on the burner, pour in the wine,
and simmer until the liquid is reduced by half. Remove
the bay leaf. Cut the veal roulade into slices, arrange on a
warmed platter, cover with the sauce, and serve.

Arancini alla siciliana

Rice balls with ground beef
(Illustrated below center)

2 RIPE TOMATOES
1/2 ONION, DICED
EXTRA VIRGIN OLIVE OIL
1/2 CUP/100 G GROUND BEEF
1 1/2 CUPS/250 G FRESH PEAS
SALT AND PEPPER
1 CUP/250 G RICE
3 1/2 TBSP/50 G BUTTER
1/2 CUP/50 G PECORINO, GRATED
2 EGGS
1/2 CUP/50 G DRIED BREADCRUMBS
OIL FOR FRYING

Blanche and peel the tomatoes, then press them through a
sieve. Lightly sauté the onions in olive oil, add the ground
beef and peas and cook for a few more minutes. Add the
tomatoes, season with salt and pepper, and cook slowly over
a low heat.
Boil the rice in salted water, drain and mix with the butter,
the grated pecorino, and 1 egg. Allow the mixture to cool,
then, taking small amounts at a time, mold into small pockets and fill with the meat mixture. Firmly press the open
edges together to seal and shape into balls. Dip the rice balls
first in the beaten egg, then in breadcrumbs and fry in hot
oil. Drain off any excess fat on a paper towel and serve
warm or cold.

Farsumagru – Stuffed veal roulade

CANNELLONI RIPIENI
Stuffed cannelloni
(Illustrated below right)

Serves 4–6

For the dough:
1 GENEROUS CUP/150 G PLAIN FLOUR
1 CUP/150 G DURUM WHEAT SEMOLINA
2 EGGS
1/2 TSP SALT
FLOUR (FOR ROLLING OUT THE DOUGH)

For the filling:
1 LB/500 G BRAISED BEEF WITH A GOOD THICK SAUCE
SALT AND FRESHLY MILLED PEPPER
FRESH NUTMEG
1 CUP/100 G CACIOCAVALLO OR PECORINO, GRATED

5 TBSP OLIVE OIL
2 EGGS

To make the dough for the pasta, mix together the flour and durum wheat semolina and pile in a mound on a work surface. Make a well in the center. Break in the eggs and add salt, then add ⅓ cup plus 1 tablespoon of lukewarm water and knead by hand until the dough is smooth. Cover the dough with a cloth and set aside for 20 minutes. Sprinkle the work surface with flour and roll out the dough to form a flat sheet about ⅛ inch/2 mm thick. Using a pastry wheel, cut out 10 x 4-inch/10 cm squares. In a large saucepan, bring 6 ½ pints/3 liters of salted water to a boil with 2–3 tablespoons of oil and cook the squares of pasta, a few at a time, for 5 minutes. Remove with a spatula and hold under cold running water for a moment, then leave to drain.

Dice the braised beef into very small pieces or grind briefly in a food processor. Place in a saucepan with half the cooking juices and cook until a thick meat sauce is formed. Season with salt, pepper, and freshly grated nutmeg.

Grease a large, ovenproof dish with 3 tablespoons of olive oil. Pile 2 tablespoons of the meat sauce along one edge of a pasta square, sprinkle with grated cheese and roll up the pasta. Do the same with the other pasta squares. Lay the cannelloni side by side in the greased dish. If there is any meat sauce left over, pour this over the top and sprinkle with the remaining cheese. Finally, drizzle 2 tablespoons olive oil over the whole and cook in a preheated oven for 15 minutes at 390 °F (200 °C). Lightly beat the eggs, pour over the cannelloni, and bake for a further 5 minutes until a crisp golden crust has formed.

Canneloni ripieni –
Stuffed cannelloni

Arancini alla siciliana –
Rice balls stuffed with meat

PUMPKINS AND ZUCCHINI

The pumpkin family, which incorporates the various varieties of garden pumpkin as well as cucumbers, melons, and zucchini, plays a key role in Italian cooking. Whether it is braised, sautéed, tossed in flour and fried, broiled, stuffed, used as a salad or dessert ingredient, the possibilities are endless. And yet, the fruit got off to something of a shaky start when it was first introduced to Europe by the Spanish Conquistadores. Discovered in South America, it was initially regarded as no more than an ornamental feature for the flower garden – a fate which the pumpkin shared with the tomato and the eggplant. The latter was even given the name *mela insane*, unhealthy apple, from which the Italian word for eggplant *melanzana* is obviously derived.

The word *zucca* was not exactly flattering in meaning either. This word in local dialect meant "dimwit," "quarrelsome person" or "idiot". As is often the case, however, the palate eventually won the day and now that the pumpkin and its relatives have gained acceptance in the kitchen, people have forgotten that they were once viewed so derisively.

Zucchini flowers and other flowers of the pumpkin family can be bought all over Italy. They can be stuffed before frying or else simply sautéed just as they are.

The long, green zucchini, in particular, have had spectacular success – not just in Italy but all over the world where they are regarded by many people as a symbol of Mediterranean cuisine. They can be used in a wide variety of dishes.

ZUCCHINI AL POMODORO E BASILICO
Zucchini with tomatoes and basil

2 LB/1 KG RIPE TOMATOES
2 LB/1 KG ZUCCHINI
4 CLOVES OF GARLIC
1 BUNCH OF FRESH BASIL
OLIVE OIL
SALT

Blanch, peel, deseed, and dice the tomatoes. Wash and dice the zucchini. Peel and mince the garlic and chop the basil. Lightly sauté the garlic in hot olive oil. Add the tomatoes, basil, and cubes of zucchini. Cook over a low heat until the zucchini is cooked but still firm to the bite. Season with salt to taste.

FIORI DI ZUCCA RIPIENI
Stuffed pumpkin or zucchini flowers
(Illustrated left)

2 EGGS
1/2 CUP/50 G FLOUR
12 ZUCCHINI FLOWERS
10 OZ/275 G RICOTTA
A PINCH OF FRESHLY GRATED NUTMEG
1 BUNCH OF CHIVES, SNIPPED
1 EGG, LIGHTLY BEATEN
4 TBSP FRESHLY GRATED PARMESAN
SALT AND FRESHLY MILLED PEPPER
OLIVE OIL

To make the batter, lightly beat the two eggs in a bowl. Add the flour a bit at a time and mix in. Stir in 4 tablespoons cold water to make an even batter. Set aside.
Carefully clean the zucchini flowers, rinsing the outside under running water and removing any insects from the inside of the flower. Carefully pat dry.
To make the filling, combine the ricotta, nutmeg, chives, egg, parmesan, salt, and freshly milled pepper and spoon this mixture into the flowers. Carefully twist the tips of the flowers closed to prevent the mixture falling out.
Heat a generous amount of oil in a large pan. Dip the flowers in the batter and fry one at a time in the hot oil until golden brown in colour, turning occasionally. Drain off excess oil on paper towel and serve.

Assemble the ingredients for stuffing the zucchini flowers.

Lightly beat the cheese, chives, and egg together and season.

Dip the stuffed flowers in the batter and fry.

Use paper towels to absorb any excess oil before serving.

SICILIAN VEGETABLE DISHES

One of the oldest Sicilian recipes is the *Maccu di San Giuseppe*. Despite its Christian-sounding name, this dish was actually brought to Sicily by the Ancient Romans. The *Maccu* is made from dried, hulled lima beans which are mashed during cooking with a wooden spoon. It is said that the word *maccari*, Sicilian dialect meaning "to mash," was derived from this procedure and this led, in turn, to the term "maca-roni." If this is true, then *Maccu* is, if nothing else, the etymological forefather of our pasta. It was only later that "San Giuseppe" was added to its name in recognition of the St. Joseph's Day tradition in Siracusa of treating all the poor young women of the town to a plate of *Maccu*.

Another dish with a long, colorful past to its name is *Caponata* - another typically Sicilian dish. Nowadays, the *Caponata* is made exclusively from vegetables, but it originally started life as a fish dish, served in the *caupone*, the taverns around Sicily's ports, and consisted of squid, celery, and eggplants, served with a sweet-and-sour sauce. The most unusual variation of this is *Caponata San Bernardo*: The eggplants are combined with a sauce made from plain dark chocolate, almonds, sugar, vinegar, and toasted breadcrumbs.

CAPONATA

Eggplants with tomatoes and olives
(Illustration top right)

1 LB/500 G EGGPLANTS
SALT
1 LB/500 G ONIONS
4 STALKS/100 G CELERY STALKS
1 CUP/150 G GREEN OLIVES
1 LB/500 G TOMATOES
4 TBSP VEGETABLE OIL
6 TBSP EXTRA VIRGIN OLIVE OIL
FRESHLY MILLED BLACK PEPPER
2 TBSP/25 G SUGAR
7 TBSP WINE VINEGAR
2 TBSP CAPERS

Wash and slice the eggplants, sprinkle with salt and place in a sieve to allow the bitter juices to drain off. Finely dice the onions, blanch the celery and cut into small pieces. Cut the olives in half and remove the stones. Blanch the tomatoes and pass them through a sieve. Rinse the eggplants in cold running water, drain, and pat dry.
Heat the vegetable oil in a skillet and sauté the eggplants on both sides until golden brown. Place on paper towels to remove any excess oil.
Put the olive oil in a saucepan and gently sauté the onions. Add the celery, olives, and sieved tomatoes and season with salt and pepper. Simmer for 5 minutes. Add the sugar, vinegar, capers and eggplant and simmer for a further 10 minutes until the vinegar fumes have evaporated. Leave the vegetables to cool before serving.

MACCU DI SAN GIUSEPPE

Bean paste with fennel

1 LB/500 G DRIED LIMA BEANS
3/4 CUP/100 G DRIED LENTILS
3/4 CUP/100 G DRIED PEAS
5 OZ/150 G DRIED CHESTNUTS
1/2 LB/250 G FENNEL
1 CELERIAC
3 DRIED TOMATOES
1 ONION
SALT AND PEPPER
EXTRA VIRGIN OLIVE OIL

Soak the dried pulses and chestnuts overnight in water. Pour away the water and put the beans, lentils, peas, and chestnuts in a large pan of fresh water. Coarsely chop the fennel and celeriac, dice the tomatoes and onion, and add all these ingredients to the pulses. Season with salt and pepper and cook over a low heat for about 3 hours until it forms a paste.
Serve on deep plates, drizzling a few drops of olive oil on each portion, with white bread as an accompaniment.

CAPERS

The hardy and undemanding caper bush can be found all along the Italian coast and grows well on dry, stony soil, or even crumbling old brickwork. Capers are not actually the fruit of the caper bush but its as yet unopened buds.
After being picked in spring – the tiniest buds are best – the capers first have to be made edible. To eliminate their bitter taste, they are placed in vinegar water or brine for several days. Both solutions are also ideal for preserving the buds on a long-term basis. Before being eaten, the capers must be rinsed in order to remove most of the vinegar or salt which would otherwise overpower the other flavors of the dish. The little buds with their distinctive taste go well in salads, tomato sauces, pasta dishes, and vegetable specialties. They are a crucial ingredient of the tuna fish sauce in the famous *Vitello tonnato*. Capers should not be cooked along with the food, however, but should be added at the very last minute, or else they will lose their flavor. The best capers grow on the Aeolian islands and on Pantelleria which lies off Sicily's southern coast.

Goethe in Italy

Towards the end of the 18th century, Johann Wolfgang von Goethe, who loved traveling in Italy, kept a diary recording some of his impressions from his travels in southern Europe. In his *Italian Journey*, the entry for April 13, 1787, tells us about some of the thoughts that occurred to him during his visit to Palermo, about the weather, the culinary specialties and about Sicily's importance in general: "One cannot think of Italy without having a picture of Sicily in your heart: this is the key to everything. One cannot praise the climate enough: it is the rainy season at the moment, but even so, there are breaks in the rain; it is thundering and lightning today and everything is turning very green. Some of the flax is already in bud, the rest is in bloom. The flax in the fields below is such a beautiful shade of bluish-green that it looks as if there are little pools of water in the valleys. There are countless charming sights! …

Johann Heinrich Wilhelm Tischbein, *Goethe in Campania,* Oil on canvas, 164x206 cm. Städelsches Kunstinstitut, Frankfurt am Main.

I have as yet said nothing of the food and drink hereabouts despite the fact that this is a matter of some significance. The garden produce is wonderful – the lettuce, especially, is extremely tender and tastes like milk; you can see why the ancients called it Lactuca. The oil and wine are all very good and could be even better if more care were taken in their prepara-tion. Fish are of the best and tenderest. We have also enjoyed very good beef this time even if it is normally not much praised."

Eleven days later, on April 24, during a visit to Girgenti, Goethe observes the local method of pasta making: "Since there are no inns here, a hospitable family made room for us and accommodated us in a raised alcove in a large room. A green curtain separated us and our luggage from the other members of the household, who were preparing pasta in the main room. This was pasta of the finest, whitest and smallest kind, the most expensive kind, which, after first being shaped into long ribbons the length of an arm, were then twisted by nimble young girls' fingers into a spiral shape. We seated ourselves with the pretty children and had the process explained to us. We learned that they were made out of only the best and strongest wheat, *grano forte*. The process is done mainly by hand rather than by machine or mold. They then cooked us the most delicious pasta dish, whilst at the same time regretting that their stores did not include a dish comprising the most perfect of all pastas, a pasta that could not be made by anyone outside Girgenti, indeed anyone outside their own home. This was said to be unparalleled in whiteness and delicacy."

CITRUS FRUITS

If anyone who has been to Sicily is asked Goethe's question "Do you know the land where lemons bloom and grow, where amidst the dark foliage the golden oranges glow," he will answer with a very heartfelt "Yes, of course." No other Italian region has achieved such fame as a result of one single fruit. Even in the Middle Ages, if the citrus fruit was of Sicilian origin, then its quality was guaranteed to be of the best. This provided the island with a reliable source of income. The Arab poet, Ibn Zaffir, who resided at the court of the Hohenstaufen King Friedrich II, was very fond of extolling the citrus trees in the groves of Palermo: "The trees in Sicily have their heads in the fire and their feet in water." The Arabs were indeed proud of their irrigation methods, which they then bequeathed to the Sicilians when their rule came to an end. Cultivated with the aid of Arab know-how, lemon and orange trees caused a sensation on this Mediterranean island. The original home of citrus fruit is apparently China and Japan in the Far East, although the bitter tasting variety of orange probably stems from India and, along with the citron, was already familiar to the Greeks and Romans. The lemon may also come originally from northern India where it seems to have been known prior to the 8th century B.C.

Thanks to the Arabs, lemon and orange trees with their bitter-tasting fruit became firmly established in Sicily between the 11th and 12th centuries. Five hundred years later, monks planted sweet varieties for the first time. The plains of Palermo proved ideal for growing this fruit and became known from that time on as the *Conca d'Oro*, the golden basin. Cultivation of the mandarin orange, which originated on the island of Samoa, did not begin until the early 19th century. The grapefruit likewise was cultivated for the first time in East India during the same century and, along with the clementine, is still one of the comparatively new fruits to be found in Sicilian citrus groves.

Today, the island supplies 70 percent of Italy's oranges and 90 percent of its lemons. Despite the excellent reputation of its citrus fruit, however, Italy's lemon and orange growers are having to struggle harder and harder to survive. This is because imports from North Africa and other states with lower production costs, not to mention fruit from other European Community countries, keep forcing down the prices.

Biondo commune
The "common blond" is one of Sicily's most traditional orange varieties. Because of its numerous pips, however, it is being replaced more and more by the "Ovale" and "Washington navel" varieties.

Ovale
The "oval" with its compact, juicy flesh is good for storing. It ripens late, between April and May.

Sanguigno comune
This type of orange, found all over the island, is harvested from January to April.

Washington navel
This attractive, aromatic and almost seedless variety was introduced from Brazil during the 40s and 50s. It is grown largely around Ribera and Sciacca and can be harvested from November to January.

Tarocco
Blood oranges constitute more than three-quarters of Sicily's entire orange production. Tarocco is a popular, fast-growing variety, which can be cropped from November to January in Catania, Siracusa and Francofonte.

Tarocco dal muso
The Tarocco dal muso is recognizable from its distinctive bell shape. It is a fast-growing variety found mainly in the groves of Francofonte.

Although Sicily produces 90 percent of Italy's lemon crop, the best lemons are said to come from Amalfi in Campania.

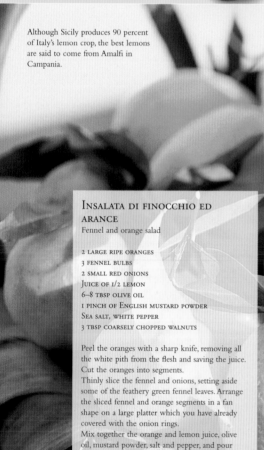

INSALATA DI FINOCCHIO ED ARANCE
Fennel and orange salad

2 LARGE RIPE ORANGES
3 FENNEL BULBS
2 SMALL RED ONIONS
JUICE OF 1/2 LEMON
6–8 TBSP OLIVE OIL
1 PINCH OF ENGLISH MUSTARD POWDER
SEA SALT, WHITE PEPPER
3 TBSP COARSELY CHOPPED WALNUTS

Peel the oranges with a sharp knife, removing all the white pith from the flesh and saving the juice.
Cut the oranges into segments.
Thinly slice the fennel and onions, setting aside some of the feathery green fennel leaves. Arrange the sliced fennel and orange segments in a fan shape on a large platter which you have already covered with the onion rings.
Mix together the orange and lemon juice, olive oil, mustard powder, salt and pepper, and pour over the salad. Allow to stand for at least 30 minutes before sprinkling finely chopped fennel leaves and chopped walnuts over the salad.

Sanguinello
The Sanguinello is an oval-shaped variety with a pleasantly bitter taste. It is harvested from January to April in Paternò Santa Maria di Licodia, Palagonia, Scordia, and Francofonte.

SORBETTO D'AGRUMI DEL SULTANO
Sultan's tropical sorbet

2 CUPS/500 ML MANDARIN JUICE
2 CUPS/500 ML ORANGE JUICE
2 CUPS/500 ML JUICE SQUEEZED FROM RIPE LEMONS
1 CUP/500 ML JUICE FROM GREEN LEMONS
2 CUPS/400 G SUGAR
3/4 CUP RUM

Strain the juices and mix together. Add 2 cups of water and stir in the sugar. Lastly, add the rum. Pour it all into an ice-making machine and leave to freeze.
If you do not have an ice-making machine, pour the liquid into a flat metal tray and place in the freezer for several hours. When the sorbet is half frozen, put it into a well cooled bowl and beat thoroughly. Put it back into the metal tray and return it to the freezer. Repeat this process once or twice more.

Valencia
The Valencia orange, which is also used for confectionery, is similar to the Ovale variety.

Moro
This variety has crimson-colored flesh and is grown around Lentini, Scordia, and Francofonte. It is harvested from mid-January to the end of April.

Femminello
This variety of lemon, which is mainly grown in Catania, Siracusa, Messina, and Palermo, constitutes 80 percent of Sicily's lemon crop.

Verdello
Thanks to intensive cultivation, this variety is ready to pick between May and September.

Monachello
The "little monk" is better able to withstand periods of drought than the Femminello variety and is harvested from October to March.

Comune
Comune is a common variety of mandarin orange.

Tardivo Ciaculli
Tardivo Ciaculli is the other type of mandarin in Sicily.

PRICKLY PEARS

The Italian word for prickly pear or Indian fig is *fico d'India*. This is because the variety of cactus on which it grows comes from Central America. The early botanists were not always so precise in differentiating between the two races of "Indian." This robust, long-lived cactus with its fleshy, prickly leaves spread quickly right across southern Italy and the islands. Not only did it provide delicious fruit but was also ideal for marking boundaries or forming a prickly hedge to protect home and garden from intruders. Sicily, where some villages even hold a special harvest thanksgiving festival in honor of the prickly pear, is home to various varieties, all of which bear different types of fruit. Surfarina is a common and very popular variety, Sanguigna has small, crimson, and very tasty fruit and the snow-white to light green fruit of the Muscaredda is best eaten ice cold. The bulk of prickly pears grown, however, are fruits with yellow flesh. Released from its prickly covering, the delicate fruit is often served sliced and drenched in dry Marsala. In Biancavilla, Belpasso, and San Cono, the main areas of cultivation at the foot of Mount Etna, the fruit is also made into a type of firm purée.

The prickly pear, whose botanical name is *Opuntia*, also grows in other Mediterranean regions. These plants were originally grown, not for their fruit, but for a special dye. The Opuntia is the natural host of the cochineal beetle, which produces a vivid red dye used in the textile industry.

Mosto di fico d'india
Prickly pear purée

8 LBS/4 KG RIPE PRICKLY PEARS, PEELED
2 PTS/1 LITER FRESHLY PRESSED GRAPE JUICE (GRAPE MUST)
3 1/2 CUPS/400 G ALL-PURPOSE FLOUR
1 CUP/100 G CORNSTARCH
1 CINNAMON STICK
PULP FROM 1 VANILLA POD
LEMON JUICE
CANDIED ORANGE PEEL, ACCORDING TO TASTE
ROASTED ALMONDS, ACCORDING TO TASTE

Press the flesh of the prickly pears through a sieve to remove the seeds. Bring the puréed flesh and the grape juice to a boil. Slowly add the flour and cornstarch to this and bring back to the boil, stirring constantly with a wooden spoon. Add the cinnamon and the vanilla. Do not add sugar! Once the mixture is no longer runny but before it begins to thicken too much, remove from the heat and extract the cinnamon stick. Pour into small ceramic molds which have first been sprinkled with lemon juice, then top this, as desired, with candied fruit and almonds. Once the dessert has cooled, it can be tipped out of the molds.

Right: The prickly pear is part of the Sicilian landscape: You will not find a more effective means of protecting property from intruders.

The best way to peel a prickly pear is to spear it on a fork.

Using a sharp, pointed knife, cut into the upper part of the fruit and …

…peel the skin in a spiral motion. Real pros can peel the entire fruit in one go.

The exposed fruit can be eaten as it is or be added to a fruit salad.

YOU'LL BE FOR IT TONIGHT…

On All Hallows' Eve, that is the night of October 31, it is harder than ever to get Sicilian *bambini* to bed as it is on this night, during the secret hours of darkness, that the ancestral dead are supposed to return to the homes of their loved ones. This might not in itself be a pressing reason to want to remain awake but these nocturnal visitors from beyond the grave also bring candies and gifts with them – which naturally makes the event interesting to even the smallest child. In the same way that children north of the Alps lie in wait, keen to catch a glimpse of St. Nicholas, Sicilian boys and girls likewise would really love to know what their ancestors look like. If truth be told, it is usually the parents who hide the little surprises all over the house for their offspring. Next morning, as they search for the hidden gifts, the children are delighted to find *ossa dei morti*, which are very sweet, hard cookies. Also popular are *pupi di zuccaro*, lifelike little figures of dolls, knights, or dancers, consisting of pure sugar. These are made by pouring liquid sugar into special molds, leaving them to set, and finally coloring them lovingly by hand.

Since Christmas celebrations in Italy, especially southern Italy, do not normally include the sort of large-scale present-giving seen in Central and Northern Europe, this last night of October, which is known as Halloween in the English-speaking part of the world, is a good opportunity to give the children a treat. The institution of Santa Claus is largely unknown in these southern parts. Christmas presents, if there are any, arrive not on December 25, but on January 6, the Feast of Epiphany. They are brought, not by a man with a white beard and wearing a red coat (although Babbo Natale, Father Christmas, is a well-known figure in northern Italy), but by La Befana, the Christmas witch. Instead of following the example of her northern counterparts and loading her presents on a practical sleigh, she whizzes through the air with them balanced on her broomstick.

Another favorite figure, who makes children's eyes light up, is Topolino. This little mouse, which like all the other magical figures has never actually been sighted and only operates in the dead of night, much to the children's annoyance, collects baby teeth which have come out. You have to put the tooth on the window-sill before you go to bed and then go to sleep as good as gold. The next morning there will be a little gift which Topolino has left in exchange for the tooth. This practice of "tooth exchange" still goes on in many parts of Italy as it does in Anglo-Saxon tradition.

PASTA GAROFOLATA PER OSSA DEI MORTI O AGNELLINI PASQUALI
Clove-flavored pastry for dead men's bones or Easter lambs (Illustrated below)

The quantities given are for both versions. Lambs are baked for Easter and the "bones" for Halloween.

2 LB/1 KG SUGAR
2 LB/1 KG ALL-PURPOSE FLOUR
10 CLOVES, MILLED
ALMOND OIL

In a saucepan, bring the sugar to a boil in a little water. When the sugar is dissolved, turn down the heat and sift in the flour, stirring constantly with a wooden spoon, taking care that no lumps form. On no account should the flour be allowed to turn brown but must remain snow-white. Add the powdered cloves and stir in. Once the flour has been thoroughly mixed in and the mixture is nice and white, remove from the burner.
As soon as it has cooled down enough for it to be handled, make lamb shapes or bones out of the dough. Alternatively, brush appropriately designed baking molds with almond oil and fill with dough. Leave for a few days in a dry place. Remove the shapes from the molds. Moisten the underside with water. Place on a baking sheet and bake in a preheated oven at 350 °F (180 °C). When the sugar has risen and turned the distinctive color of a monk's habit, the cookies are ready.

The *ossi dei morti* (dead men's bones) are a very sugary type of cookie which are given to children at Halloween. Another equally sugary confection are the little figures, knights, and dancers which are hand-painted in bright colors.

Cannoli, fried pastry rolls with a delicious filling made from sweet ricotta, chocolate, and candied fruits, were once a special treat at Carnival time – but why should people not enjoy them all year round?

SWEET OCCASIONS DURING THE CHURCH YEAR

Sicilians like to celebrate. In addition to the nationwide festivals which punctuate the church year, every district holds its own individual thanksgiving celebrations and commemorates the name days of its saints. In addition, there are the church ordinations and the popular village festivals which can be held on almost any pretext. All these celebrations would be nothing without special confectionery. In the dark days of the past, simple bread constituted the traditional votive offering. Nowadays, this tradition is echoed in cakes, gateaux, pastry rings, sugar figures, or almond confectionery as well as many other fairly sumptuous specialties which are reserved for special occasions.

At the *Circu di pani* in Calatafini, a rider on horseback rides through the village holding aloft a trophy of small loaves of bread and on November 11, St. Martin's Day, the people of Valle del Belice bake *muffulette*, little figures made of yeast dough, to serve with new wine. On December 8, the Day of the Immaculate Conception, *sfinci*, sweet lardy cakes, are served and five days later, on December 13, Santa Lucia's name day is celebrated with *Occhi di Santa Lucia.* "Lucia's eyes" are made from wheat cooked in milk, sweetened ricotta, and cubes of pumpkin. Between Christmas and New

CANNOLI
Stuffed pastry rolls
(Illustrated above)

Makes 16

5 TSP/25 G BUTTER
5 TBSP/25 G SUGAR
1 EGG
3 1/2 TBSP DRY WHITE WINE
2 TBSP SUGAR
1 TSP VANILLA ESSENCE
A PINCH OF SALT
5 OZ/150 G ALL-PURPOSE FLOUR
1 EGG, LIGHTLY BEATEN
SHORTENING OR VEGETABLE OIL FOR FRYING
CONFECTIONERS' SUGAR

For the filling:
1 LB/500 G FRESH RICOTTA
1/2 CUP/100 G SUGAR
2 TBSP ORANGE FLOWER WATER
2 TBSP/50 G MIXED CANDIED ORANGE AND LEMON PEEL,
FINELY CHOPPED
1 1/2 TBSP/40 G ANGELICA, FINELY CHOPPED
10/50 G GLACÉ CHERRIES, FINELY CHOPPED
3 OZ/90 G DARK CHOCOLATE, FINELY CHOPPED

Cream the butter and sugar together until light and fluffy. Mix in the egg, wine, sugar, vanilla essence, and salt. Add the flour a little at a time and knead the dough for 5 to 10 minutes until it is smooth and elastic. Cover and leave for at least two hours in a cool place.
Roll out the dough to a thickness of 1/16 inch/2 mm and cut into 16 x 5 inch/12-cm squares. Lay a bamboo or metal tube (6 inches by 3/4 inch/15 cm by 2 cm in diameter) diagonally across each square and fold the two opposite corners over the tube. Brush the corners with the beaten egg to stick them together. Heat enough shortening or oil in a large saucepan to completely cover the *cannoli.* When the oil is very hot, carefully place three to four *cannoli* side by side in the oil and fry until golden brown (approx. 1½–2 mins.) Drain the cooked *cannoli* on paper towel. Once they are completely cool, carefully remove the tubes.
For the filling, stir the ricotta with a fork, then add the sugar, vanilla sugar, and orange flower water. The ricotta should have creamy consistency. Mix in the candied orange and lemon peel, the angelica, glacé cherries, and chocolate. Fill the *cannoli* with this mixture and arrange on a plate. Sprinkle with confectioners' sugar and serve cold, but do not refrigerate.

Year, the bakeries and cake shops are working all out. *Cucccidatti di Natale* are pastry rings made from yeast dough and stuffed with figs and almonds and *mustazzoli*, traditional Christmas cookies popular throughout southern Italy, are often served in Sicily with freshly pressed prickly pear juice instead of grape must.

Once upon a time, *cannoli* were traditionally only eaten at carnival time. These fried pastry rolls, stuffed with sweetened ricotta, vanilla cream, or chocolate mixture, are so popular that bars and bakeries nowadays sell them all year round.

To mark St. Joseph's Day on March 19, lavish "Joseph loaves" and the *spera di pani*, an altar-piece of bread, are produced. The next ecclesiastical landmark is Easter, a holiday which would not be complete without sweet Easter cakes and lamb cookies. After this come the summer festivals and, in autumn, All Hallows' Eve.

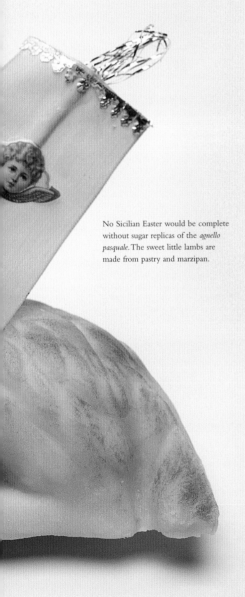

No Sicilian Easter would be complete without sugar replicas of the *agnello pasquale*. The sweet little lambs are made from pastry and marzipan.

CASSATA

The cassata, which we are generally familiar with as an ice cream dessert, is in fact a rich cake for special occasions, the authentic *Cassata alla siciliana*, which is served at Easter, for example, or at weddings and christenings. This artistic creation is made from layers of sponge, interspersed with a creamy mixture of sweetened ricotta, chopped candied fruits, slivers of chocolate, nuts, and melted sugar. Depending on the confectioner's individual recipe and preference, the cake can include additional layers of marzipan or else be covered with a final coating of marzipan. Otherwise, it is finished with a layer of thick icing. It is decorated with whole or attractively sliced candied fruits, the bright colors of which show up wonderfully well against the white sugar or marzipan. The original *Cassata alla siciliana* recently celebrated its 1000th anniversary. This delectable cake was first baked in its present form in the year 998 in Palermo, the town which the ruling Arab emirs of the time had proclaimed the island's capital. At that time, Palermo, which was then regarded as an area free from the rules and restrictions of the Koran, was host to more than 300 thriving night spots, serving alcoholic drinks, distillation being another Arab invention, and providing the spectacle of attractive belly-dancers. These competed successfully with the maidens, who, according to Islamic faith, supposedly awaited the faithful in Paradise. At a time when the western Christian world was approaching the new millennium with great trepidation and fear at the thought of "One thousand and no more," the Muslims of Palermo indulged themselves in a sort of fighting men's "time-out," tolerated by Islam. However, this cushy life was to be short-lived as the Arabs began fighting each other again, and this in turn left the field open for the Normans to gain control over Sicily. The Normans even succeeded in establishing Europe's first multicultural state in the late Middle Ages – and this applied similarly to culinary matters. Not only did they bring their own recipes with them, but they also retained the traditional Sicilian dishes, as well as the highly sophisticated skills of the Arab confectioners.

Eloisa Martorana, a noble Norman woman, was soon to make a name for herself refining marzipan production. Compulsive candy-eaters to this day are still addicted to *frutti di Martorana*.

CASSATA

Sponge cake with ricotta and apricot jam

1/3 CUP/100 G APRICOT JAM
1 SPONGE BASE WEIGHING ABOUT 3/4 LB/350 G
1 1/4 LBS/600 G RICOTTA
1 1/3 CUPS/300 G SUGAR
4 OZ/120 G PLAIN CHOCOLATE, BROKEN UP INTO SMALL PIECES
3/4 LB/350 G CANDIED FRUITS, FINELY DICED
1/3 CUP/40 G PEELED PISTACHIOS OR PINE NUTS
CINNAMON
1–2 GLASSES MARASCHINO
1 3/4 CUPS/200 G CONFECTIONERS' SUGAR

Line a cake pan with waxed paper and spread the apricot jam over the base. Cut the sponge base in two and lay one half on top of the apricot jam.

Mix the ricotta to a cream in a large bowl. Add the sugar, the plain chocolate, candied fruit, pistachios or pine nuts, and mix with the creamed ricotta. Flavor with a pinch of cinnamon and some maraschino. Spoon the cream mixture into the pan and place the other half of the sponge on top.

Refrigerate for at least two hours to allow the flavors to permeate, then remove from the refrigerator and tip out onto a cake plate. Carefully peel off the greaseproof paper and smooth out the apricot jam. Mix a little confectioners' sugar with the rest of the maraschino and drizzle over the cassata. Allow the glacé icing to set, then serve.

Various versions of cassata exist all over the world, but if you want to try a real cassata cake, a Sicilian *pasticcere* is the place to do so. Then you are sure to enjoy the genuine article.

MARZIPAN FROM MARTORANA

Sicilians learned the art of confectionery from the Arabs. After the departure of the Muslims, their recipes for sweetmeats were adopted and improved upon in mediaeval monastery kitchens. Luckily, the former occupiers left behind their distillation equipment. This useful apparatus made possible the manufacture of an essence, called "orange flower water," an essential ingredient in the making of marzipan. The pious confectioners pounded almonds in mortars, mixed the result with sugar, cooked the two together in orange flower water, flavored the result with some vanilla and the resulting product was Sicilian marzipan.

Its name comes from the Arabic word *manthaban*, which was originally just the container in which the sweet almond paste was stored. Later, this term was used for measuring the correct ratio of sugar and almonds used in the manufacture of marzipan. So quickly did marzipan become a regular fixture on the tables of kings that Sicilians gave it a fitting nickname: *pasta reale* or royal paste.

The Martorana cloister became particularly famous for producing this specialty. In 1143, George of Antioch, a trusted admiral of Roger II, the first Norman king, had a church built which he handed over to an order of Greek nuns. The nuns lived in a nearby convent where they devoted themselves primarily to producing sugar figurines for All Saints' Day and All Souls' Day. These already famous delicacies were colored with dyes made from roses, saffron, and pistachio. About 50 years later,

Eloisa Martorana built another cloister which was joined to the building belonging to the Greek sisters. The entire complex became known from that time on as "Martorana," the same name that was also given to the sweetmeats. Even after 1435, when the buildings were taken over by Benedictine monks, the name remained the same.

Although the secrets of marzipan making and confectionery made their way into ordinary households during the course of time, the sweetmeats produced in the cloisters retained their special reputation. So high was the demand that the nuns were kept busy round the clock, producing marzipan and other confectionery for special festivals. So much so that in 1575, the religious authorities of Mazara del Vallo were forced to prohibit the local nuns from making it so that they would not be distracted from their religious duties during Holy Week. These gentlemen had not reckoned with such resistance on the part of the holy sisters, however. Passionate confectioners all, they refused to obey the order from the synod, continued to manufacture their *frutti di Martorana*, and created new delicacies. Unfortunately, we have no record of what the Bishop said on the subject of the *minni di Virgine*, maiden's breasts, decorated with tiny glacé cherry halves!

The independent confectioners of Palermo meanwhile put their trust in lucky charms of a more pagan nature and competed with each other to see who would create the best marzipan pig for January 20, St. Sebastian's Day. These appetizing little pigs quickly found their way north across the Alps – today you can buy them in every confectioner's shop, especially at New Year and during carnival time.

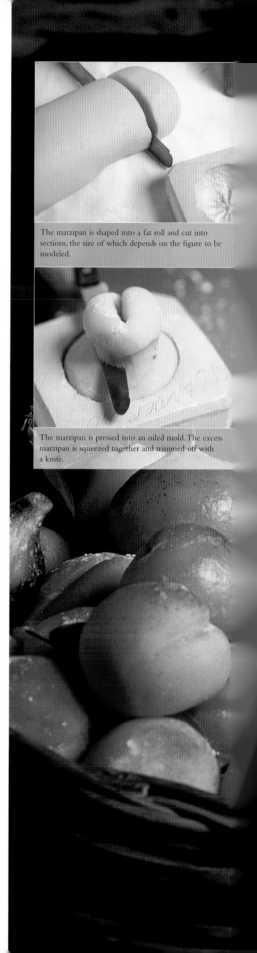

The marzipan is shaped into a fat roll and cut into sections, the size of which depends on the figure to be modeled.

The marzipan is pressed into an oiled mold. The excess marzipan is squeezed together and trimmed off with a knife.

Above: The Martorana cloister.
Background: The marzipan mandarin oranges are a source of fascination to young and old, alike.

Small amounts of marzipan are rolled by hand into smooth, round balls.

The marzipan fruit has to be left to dry for several days. Once a thin crust has formed, colors can be applied. Fresh marzipan would absorb the color.

Background: Giuseppe Caruso, the pastry chef of the Palermo bar, Italico, holds up a basket full of fresh fruit – or are they really marzipan fruits?

Ice cream carts have been a feature of Italian summers and on the beaches for years.

ICE CREAM

The origins of ice cream are just as disputed as those of pasta. Whereas Italians from the Dolomite region claim to have been the first to invent this ice-cold speciality, the Tuscans claim it as an invention of the Renaissance and maintain that Catherine de' Medici took it to Paris on the occasion of her wedding to Henry IV. Sicilians, on the other hand, proudly claim to have learned the original art of ice-cream making from the Arabs and to have added further subsequent refinements of their own.

Whatever the truth of the matter, ice cream started life as a sorbet. It was easy to make, simply by taking clean, white snow from the mountains – or from Mount Etna, if you were in Sicily – and mixing it with fruit juice, must, wine, or honey. The main problem in this prerefrigerator age was how to transport and store this refreshing commodity: Underground caves and subterranean ice caves were used, where these ice-based concoctions would keep at least for a while. The first "ice cream parlor" on the other side of the Alps was opened in 1668 by a native of Sicily, Francesco Procopio de' Coltelli: The elegant clientele of his Café Procope in Paris, a renowned restaurant which still exists to this day, soon developed a taste for the various ice specialties on offer.

As cooling techniques improved, ice-cream making was perfected more and more. The original sorbets, or

Above: There is hardly one Sicilian *gelataio* which has less than 30 sorts of ice cream.

types of fruit ice, were followed by the first milk-based ices. Experts still disagree as to whether the first ice cream, based on milk, cream, sugar, and eggs, is attributable to the legendary Procopio or to the favorite chef of Charles I of England, who is said to have introduced this revolutionary dessert in the middle of the 17th century.

The fact that ice cream became a familiar feature of the 19th and 20th centuries is not so much an achievement of English or Sicilian ice cream makers as a tribute to the hard work of many individual entrepreneurs from the Veneto region. As a consequence of industrialization, the traditional metal-processing industry was facing extinction. Without further ado, however, the unemployed metalworkers of the Dolomite valleys exchanged their hammers and anvils for cooking spoons and ice cream making machines

ICE CREAM VARIETIES

Gelato mantecato (ice cream)
This term covers any type of ice cream made from a basic recipe of milk, sugar, and egg yolk. The individual flavors are achieved by adding various flavorings.

Sorbetto (sorbet)
No milk or eggs are used to make sorbet. This low-calorie dessert is a water-based ice made from fruit juice, fruit purée, bits of fruit, syrup, wine, spirits, sugar, or other flavoring ingredients.

Gelato perfetto (parfait)
The difference between this and *gelato mantecato* is that cream is used instead of milk to create this deliciously smooth ice cream. It is flavored in the same way as milk-based ice cream.

Bomba (bombe glacé)
Bombes glacés combine several different flavours of ice cream. One northern version, which is fairly universally known, is the Prince Pueckler ice cream, which consists of layers of vanilla, strawberry, and chocolate ice cream. Sicily has its own lavish, imaginative creations which are sold under the name of *cassata gelato*

Frullato
This is a kind of milkshake which is a combination of cold milk and fruit or sorbet.

Frappé
This refreshing drink is made by pouring ice cold vanilla- or coffee-flavored milk over ice cubes.

Granita
The most refreshing combination of all: tart fruit juice, syrup, or black coffee poured over crushed ice.

and unexpectedly made a name for themselves producing ice creams.Every summer with their ice cream carts they visited towns and seaside resorts on either side of the Alps. Many of them made a small fortune. In places where the local authorities refused to tolerate itinerant ice cream sellers, the *gelatai* settled down and opened ice cream parlors. The names of these popular cafés recall the homelands of their owners: you will find a Venezia ice cream parlor or a Rialto ice cream shop in the remotest backwater. It has been estimated that businessmen from Veneto or Venice make up 80 percent of the ice cream trade. Compared to this, Sicilian ice cream has remained more of a local speciality. Apart from the familiar sorbet, granita, and ice cream, another popular specialty is the *gramolata*. If you are entertaining guests, just take a correspondingly generous amount and serve up this iced dessert, consisting of vanilla-flavored ice cream on an almond base, with some cookies. If you have guests in for coffee, they are unlikely to need a sumptuous evening meal after that. The large blocks of water-based ice, known since the 17th century as *acqui tesi* (stiff water), are likewise perfect for offering to visitors. They can serve eight to ten people and can be cut into slices and attractively arranged on ice plates.

In summer, when Riposto harbor at the foot of Etna fills up with holidaymakers' yachts, business booms for Costanzo, the ice cream maker. Every visitor wants to try his delectable *spumone*, chocolate ice cream with a golden center of zabaglione. *Cassata gelata* is the ice cream version of the famous Sicilian cake. Although there are several versions of this, they all contain vanilla ice cream, candied fruits, pistachio ice cream, and marzipan or almond essence. A very special delicacy from Trapani in the west of the island is jasmine ice cream, which is evocative of the scents of nearby North Africa. This exotic specialty is eaten as a morning pick-me-up in a sweet pastry, such as a brioche or croissant. Lemon or almond sorbet are also popular fillings for this ice-cold breakfast.

ITALIAN ICE CREAMS

Limone – lemon
Fragola – strawberry
Menta – mint
Arancia – orange
Mora di rovo – blackberry
Lampone – raspberry
Yoghurt – yogurt
Caffè – coffee
Mandorla – with slivers of almond
Pistacchio – pistachio

Amaretto – with almond liqueur
Cioccolato – chocolate
Stracciatella – vanilla ice cream with chocolate chips
Vaniglia – Vanilla
Amarena – sour cherry
Crema – extra creamy
Nocciola – hazelnut
Albicocca – apricot
Cassata – Cassata
Torrone – with nougat, almonds or Turkish honey

GELATO
Basic recipe for ice cream

4 EGG YOLKS
1/2 CUP/100 G SUGAR
2 CUPS/500 ML MILK OR CREAM

Beat the egg yolks with the sugar until light and fluffy. Pour into a saucepan and warm slowly over a low heat, stirring constantly. Add the milk a little at a time, still stirring constantly. Allow the mixture to cool completely, stirring occasionally. Place the creamy mixture in the ice cream maker or the freezer and leave to set.

GELATO DI GELSOMINO
Jasmine ice cream

Serves 6

2 OZ/50 G JASMINE BLOSSOM
3/4 CUP/150 G SUGAR
1 PIECE OF SCURSUNERA ROOT, OR 1 CINNAMON STICK
1 SMALL GLASS OF RUM
4 EGG WHITES

The scursunera root is known in the Trapani region as an antidote to snake bites. For this dish, a cinnamon stick can be substituted in its place. Soak the jasmine flowers without their stems in a bowl containing 2 cups of water. After three hours, strain the water into a saucepan. Add the sugar, scursunera root or cinnamon, and the rum and bring to a boil. Leave to cool. Whisk the egg whites until stiff and

gently fold into the mixture. Place the mixture in the freezer or ice cream maker.

GELATO DI CAMPAGNA
Sicilian ice dessert

Serves 6

SCANT 1/2 CUP/100 ML VANILLA-FLAVORED WATER
4 CUPS/1 KG SUGAR
1 1/4 CUPS/150 G ALMONDS, GROUND
1 CUP/150 G WHOLE ALMONDS, PEELED
1 CUP/150 G PISTACHIOS
1/2 CUP/80 G CANDIED FRUITS, DICED
A PINCH OF CINNAMON
FOOD COLORING (RED, GREEN, AND BROWN)

Pour the flavored water into a saucepan with the sugar. As soon as the sugar begins to form strands, add the ground almonds while stirring constantly. Reduce the heat and mix in the peeled almonds, pistachios, candied fruits, and cinnamon. Divide the mixture into four bowls and add coloring to three of them. Pour into molds and freeze for 24 hours.
Remove from the molds and cut into semicircular pieces. You can buy this ice dessert from street stalls at all Sicilian festivals.

GRANITA

Granita is a delicious refreshment which helps make a hot Sicilian summer tolerable. Like sorbet, it contains only frozen water and fruit juice, or other flavoring ingredients. Milk, cream, and eggs are only used in *gelati mantecati*, the ice cream dishes.
The simple but ingenious idea of pouring coffee over crushed ice has helped millions of Sicilians as well as many exhausted tourists to get back on their feet.

WINEGROWING AND MYTHOLOGY

Even in classical times, Sicily was well-known for its agricultural produce. Even before the Greeks, Phoenicians had introduced grape vines from the Middle East to this island where previously only wild grapes had grown. The Phoenicians were followed by Greek settlers who brought with them the latest grape-crushing technology as well as new varieties of grape, such as the Greganico. Greek mythology and its wines also came onto the scene. The cult surrounding Dionysus and his maenads, later called bacchantes by the Romans, began to spread and the poetess, Sappho, expelled from her native island of Lesbos, is also said to have cultivated wine here. Her famous nuptial songs celebrate the bridal pair who, at their marriage ceremony, drink wine out of the same goblet by way of asking for the blessings of Eros and Aphrodite. The

town of Erice, near to present-day Trapani, had a sacred place, a shrine to temple prostitution. As evidenced by large numbers of amphora shards, the priests and priestesses drank wine before the sacrifice. In the days of the Roman Empire, Sicilian wine was regarded as a welcome change from the Falerner wine and it is even claimed, though on no reliable evidence, that Caesar's favorite tipple was Mamertino wine from Capo Peloro.

Even Arab rule had no adverse effect on Sicilian viniculture. Despite the Koran's ban on alcohol, the new rulers not only tolerated the cultivation of the grape but even introduced the technique of distilling wine into alcohol with the aid of a still.

Hidden away in monastery cellars, Sicilians continued to brew secret elixirs which were sold to numerous customers. And yet there was no real need for the abbots to switch to distilling. The church's immeasurable wealth came not least from the vast vineyards in its possession and the monopoly that these gave it in producing and selling wine.

The wines' outstanding reputation soon extended far beyond the island's shores and Sante Lancerio, the cup bearer of Pope Paul III, praised them very highly

indeed in a letter sent to Cardinal Guido Ascanio Sforza in 1559. The star of Sicilian wine cultivation did not begin to set until the Spanish Viceroys took control. Instead of cultivating wine, they grew wheat. It was not until 1773 that Sicily managed to resume its accustomed place in the world of wine. Quite by chance, an Englishman, John Woodhouse, discovered Marsala and helped to make it popular. A further market for the island's wines opened up in 1870 when France's vineyards were so devastated by phylloxera that French vintners had to import wine by the barrel. All too soon, however, the pest crossed the Alps and continued its destruction in far off Sicily. Within a few years all hope of large and continuing profits was destroyed and once again wine cultivation had a hard struggle beginning all over again.

For a long time, Sicilian wine had a difficult time of it on today's world market with cheap mass-produced wines adversely affecting its reputation. Nevertheless, over the past few decades, some wine producers and wineries have managed to develop good quality wines of their own and gradually been able to establish themselves on the Italian market as well as some important foreign markets.

Initiation ceremonies into the mysteries of Dionysus, as depicted on a wall painting in the Villa dei Misteri in Pompeii, around 50 B.C.

THE ROAD TO MODERN WINE-GROWING TECHNIQUES

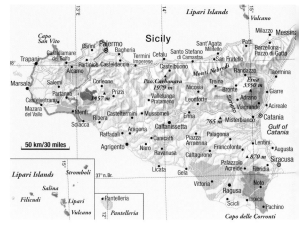

As far as winegrowing is concerned, Sicily is surely one of the most amazing regions in Italy. Not only does it share the lead with Apulia for the extent of its vineyards and the size of its grape harvest – each year 2.4 to 2.6 million U.S. gallons (9 to 10 million hectoliters) of wine are produced from an area extending over 321,100 acres (130,000 hectares) – but for more than a decade, it has been developing its potential as a producer of top-class wines. This is despite the fact that for decades, Sicily produced only the simplest mediocre wines and vast quantities of the popular sweet, sickly Marsala.

The region, whose most distant outposts of Pantelleria and Lampedusa are nearer to Tunisia than Italy, boasts perfect conditions for wine-growing: Barren soil, lots of sunshine, warmth, and low rainfall all conspire to create perfect growing conditions. At the same time, the winegrowing slopes of the central mountain region, which rise up to 3000 feet (900 m), experience sharp swings between daytime and nighttime temperatures, a factor which helps the grapes develop their fruity flavor. The main area of vineyards is situated in the westernmost province of Trapani, where Marsala, Sicily's most most famous wine, is produced. The countryside on the north and south of the island are also major wine-growing areas, whereas the eastern part is mainly given over to the production of dessert grapes.

Thanks to an enormous improvement in quality, the Sicilian wine industry now boasts a number of outstanding vintners and wineries – and this, despite the fact that only about 120 of the altogether 100,000 or more wine producers bottle and market their product themselves. The main varieties used are not only native grapes such as the white Catarratto, Inzolia, and Grillo or the red Nero d'Avolo and Nerello Mascalese but also so-called "international" varieties such as Cabernet Sauvignon and Chardonnay, which a small number of winegrowers are now turning into some of Italy's most coveted "modern" wines.

Catarratto and Grillo, which are mainly cultivated in the Trapani area and used for Marsala, can also be used for dry, fairly robust white wines. The white Inzolia grape has an even greater potential for quality wine and also does well in higher locations. Malvasia is an ancient Greek variety, or rather a whole family of vine stock with an endless number of different varieties, which can be found in nearly every region of Italy. It

The area between Selinunte and Castelvetrano, to the southwest of Marsala, produces more than 2.4 million U.S. gallons (9 million hectolitres) of wine.

forms the basis for a rare, top-quality dessert wine native to the Lipari islands. Of the native red grapes, it is the Nero d'Avolo, also known as Calabrese, which has the greatest quality potential. This produces a red wine that is both elegant and powerful.

Modern technology is the key word in winegrowing and wine-making. Consequently, extensive winegrowing areas can be seen to have departed from the traditional methods of growing vines where they were kept pruned into bush-type growths and have switched to modern techniques of training vines on wire trellis supports. Similarly, wine-making procedures have witnessed the advent of steel tanks, computers, and cooling systems, by means of which fermentation can be controlled with precision. Many of the top wines nowadays are produced in small, new wooden casks, so-called *barriques*, and these can easily hold their own against the best vintages of Tuscany or the Piedmont.

With regard to the groups of islands surrounding the Sicilian mainland, they have successfully continued the region's old traditions of sweet wine. Heavy, full wines with powerful bouquets and a rich, sweet flavor are produced here from Malvasia and Zibibbo (Moscato) grapes. As part of the general upturn in the wine industry, the producers of Marsala have also bethought themselves of their past glory and now boast a variety of fortified products. The fact that winegrowing in Sicily is becoming a booming industry again has come to the notice of winegrowers and wineries in northern Italy who, for some years now, have been investing heavily on the island. The region's future has only just begun!

	Marsala
	Alcamo
	Contessa Entellina
	Menfi
	Etna
	Cerasuolo di Vittoria
	Moscato di Noto
	Malvasia delle Lipari
	Moscato di Pantelleria, Moscato Passito di Pantelleria

SICILIAN WINES

Alcamo
Alcamo or Bianco d'Alcamo is the name given to wines produced from Sicily's largest DOC region covering more than 5200 acres (2.100 hectares) in the Trapani province. Although this area for a long time produced only fairly run-of-the-mill wine in barrels, a few wine producers have, over the past few years, gained a reputation for some pleasant, fresh new wines. The Catarratto variety of grape, which is fairly neutral in character and is one of the main ingredients of Marsala, is grown in most of the region's vineyards. If its yield is correspondingly limited, it can produce robust, full, dry white wines which are excellent served with fish and antipasto.

Cerasuolo di Vittoria
These red wines from Sicily's southeast corner are produced largely from the native varieties of Frappato – which can also be used on its own – and Calabrese. They are sometimes quite high in alcohol content and the best of them have a pleasant, fruity aroma that some drinkers find reminiscent of sour cherries.

Malvasia delle Lipari
The grapes with this DOC label of origin, which have experienced a dramatic comeback over the past decades, grow on the volcanic slopes of the Lipari islands situated off Messina. A variety of Malvasia and the native Corinto nero form the basis for this delicious dessert wine, the balsamic overtones of which are unmistakable. In its ordinary form, Malvasia delle Lipari has an alcohol content of just 8 percent but it also exists as a 20 percent proof fortified Liquoroso and Passito made from dried grapes. It is good either as an aperitif or dessert wine, depending on which type it is.

Moscato di Pantelleria
The Moscato di Pantelleria, which comes from the island of the same name situated half way between Sicily and Tunisia, is produced from the Moscato di Alessandria grape, known here as Zibibbo. This golden dessert wine, which is only produced in small quantities, has become so popular that the island's winegrowing industry is thriving once more. Like the Malvasia delle Lipari, it is also available as a fortified liqueur version, which can be powerful with an almost oily sweetness.

MARSALA

In 1770, a storm forced the young Englishman, John Woodhouse, to seek refuge in the port of Marsh-allà. This anchorage with its Arabic name, which roughly means the "port of God", belonged to the western Sicilian town of Marsala. Woodhouse was to make a discovery here that would fundamentally change the world wine market. This ambitious son of a Liverpool merchant had actually been on his way to Mazara del Vallo to purchase soda ash. After almost being shipwrecked, he now found himself stuck in Marsh-allà while the storms raged. What better way to pass the time than to go and explore the local inns? Sampling the native wine, he soon realized that this was a drink which could easily compare with expensive Spanish and Portuguese sherry or Madeira. Hoping to have his own impressions endorsed, he sent for his betrothed who worked for a wine producer on Madeira. After

some intensive sampling, they both agreed about the potential of Marsala wine: It could easily rival Madeira and sherry and thus finally break the Portuguese and Spanish monopoly on fortified wines. Woodhouse faced a fairly difficult task, however. Although Sicilian grapes were easy to obtain and local labor fairly cheap, a three-year trial period followed before the production of Marsala could get fully underway and Woodhouse could send the first shipment back to England where it quickly became popular. It was not longer before Woodhouse had to institute regular shipping runs between Marsala and Liverpool to cope with the growing demand.

After seven hard years, a breakthrough occurred in the form of a state order. In 1800, Admiral Nelson sent a written commission for 500 barrels of Marsala to be supplied annually to the English Mediterranean fleet based in Malta. Just five years later, His Majesty's navy, under Nelson, won the decisive victory of Trafalgar by destroying the united fleets of Spain and France. From then on, the Sicilian wine became known in England – as well as the rest of the world – as Marsala victory wine.

When the high demand began to lead to a shortage of grapes, Woodhouse had another ingenious idea. In order to encourage more wine production, he began to advance interested farmers the necessary capital. At the same time, he reserved the right to set the prices for any grapes or basic wines supplied. During his long sojourn on the island, he had obviously taken to heart

Marsala wine is often stored for many years in wooden barrels before it is finally bottled. It is then called Fine, Oro or Stravecchio.

the Sicilian saying *nenti ppi nenti nuddu fa nenti*, nothing comes from nothing. The farmers saw things in a similar light and were only too happy to cooperate with the Englishman.

Other English entrepreneurs tried to cash in on the success of Marsala victory wine. In 1806, Benjamin Ingham, a 22-year-old with an eye for business, arrived in Marsala. In 1812, he opened a new, bigger, and technically better equipped establishment at Lungomare Mediterraneo, situated a decent distance from the Woodhouse stronghold. Ingham knew that he was dependent on the farmers' cooperation so he began his own PR campaign: At harvest time, town-criers traveled all over the winegrowing areas around Marsala giving small-time farmers tips on harvesting intended to improve the quality of the wine. Ingham listed ten points for ensuring quality and some of these are still followed by the region's wine producers to this day.

In 1833, a Sicilian entrepreneur finally took the fate of marsala into his own hands. Using the name of a friend, Vincenzo Florio acquired a vast estate on Lungomare, which bordered Woodhouse's property on one side and Ingham's land on the other. Thus began the unstoppable rise of Marsala Florio S.O.M., with its familiar trademark of a drinking lion. The deeds founding the firm belonging to Vincenzo Florio and

his friend, Raffaele Barbaro, which were signed on October 20, 1834, curiously enough still refer to a Madeira-type wine. Even though it is John Woodhouse who is credited with discovering and marketing the wine, it was Ingham and Florio who first transformed Marsala into a really marketable product, the demand for which grew year by year. Despite initial difficulties, Florio was gradually able to win over the local grape producers and Marsala's worldwide success was thus guaranteed.

FINE, ORO, AND VERGINE STRAVECCHIO

There are various types of Marsala, some of which – such as the notorious and often inferior quality Marsala all'Uovo – have fortunately gone out of fashion. The varieties which have the lowest alcohol content are the Oro made from white grapes and the Rubino made from red. Cremovo is a variety aromatized by various means but the most interesting ones are called Fine, Superiore, Vergine, or Vergine Stravecchio. These wines are up to 18 percent proof and have matured for four, six, or even ten years in the cask before being bottled and sold. Marsala, in its various forms, is ideal to drink either as an aperitif or dessert wine.

Melone cantalupo al Marsala
Cantaloupe melon with Marsala
(Illustrated below)

Serves 2

1 CANTALOUPE MELON
DRY MARSALA, ACCORDING TO TASTE

Cut the melon horizontally through the middle, remove the
seeds and excess juice. Place the two halves of melon in
suitable dishes into which they fit snugly. Using a melon
baller, scoop out balls of melon and return them to the
melon halves. Pour over a measure of good-quality, dry
Marsala and refrigerate before serving.
Serve as a starter or a dessert.

Scaloppine al Marsala
Veal escalope in Marsala

1 LB/500 G VEAL, CUT INTO SLICES 1/4 INCH/5 MM THICK
FLOUR FOR DUSTING
6 TBSP EXTRA VIRGIN OLIVE OIL OR 4 TBSP/50 G BUTTER
2/3 CUP/150 ML GOOD QUALITY, DRY MARSALA
SALT AND FRESHLY MILLED, BLACK PEPPER

Toss the escalopes in flour, tap off any excess flour. Heat the
oil or butter in a large, heavy skillet. Sauté the escalopes one
at a time for several minutes on each side. Remove from the
pan and set aside.
When all the escalopes are cooked, put them back in the
skillet. Pour over the Marsala and season with salt and
pepper. Stir for a few seconds. The mixture of wine and
flour should coat the meat in a thin sauce.

SARDINIA

Sardinia, the island that lies farthest from the Italian mainland, is an isolated place. Surrounded by emerald green sea, blessed with majestic mountains and fertile plains, criss-crossed by cool mountain streams and clear rivers, this region, which is still relatively unblighted by tourism, must seem like paradise to the visitor – and Sardinians do indeed maintain that God was especially generous when creating their island, providing fishermen and farmers, shepherds and seafarers, all with a place where they could live happily and in harmony with each other.

Sardinia is far from being an "Elysian island," however. Its strategically favorable position has throughout history attracted invaders not just from the Mediterranean region but from even farther afield. Attacked by the Phoenicians and Carthaginians, occupied by the Romans, overrun by the Arabs, a bone of contention between Pisa, Genoa, the popes, Aragon, Austria, and Savoy, the Sardinians had good reason for coining the saying that "all evil comes from across the sea." Even if the comment is nowadays accompanied by a wink, external influences are still regarded with some suspicion. The same attitude applies to unfamiliar faces, but once these islanders are satisfied that the visitor has come, not out of some sinister ulterior motive, but simply to visit and enjoy their captivating island, their legendary hospitality knows no bounds.

However, as stated earlier, there was every reason in times gone by to avoid the proximity of the sea and to withdraw to the safe, mountainous regions of the hinterland which were almost impassable to strangers to the island. As a result, fish and seafood do not traditionally figure in Sardinian cuisine and came into the picture much later. The true original culinary specialties of the island are unmistakably biased toward traditional country dishes. Sucking pig and wild boar roasted on the spit, rustic stews with wild vegetables and hearty beans, *carta da musica*, the dry bread which keeps fresh for long periods, a distinct fondness for fresh herbs such as myrtle and mint – these are all traditional elements of a cuisine which dates back a thousand years and has remained unchanged throughout history in country villages.

Previous double page: A rich catch – typical of the splendid specimens which Luigi Ledda, a Bosa fisherman, takes from Sardinian waters.

Left: Daniele Licheri not only runs the Azienda Mandra Edera holiday farm near Abassanta with his wife Rita, but is also a shepherd and horse-breeder.

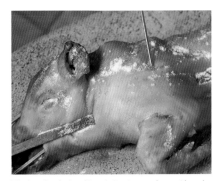

The heavily salted sucking pig is crispy on the outside and deliciously tender on the inside.

The cleaned-out sucking pig is skewered above the open fire on small spits.

Aromatic herbs and the smoky taste of the wood give the meat an unmistakable flavor.

SHEPHERDS' FARE

Whenever the shepherds went off on their wanderings with their herds, they often stayed in the mountains for months on end, far away from their families, not to mention well-equipped kitchens. Out in the wild, they had to use the most primitive facilities for cooking if they were not to live on cheese, sausage, and dry bread alone. Since the men could not take pans or skillets or special seasonings with them, they would roast the meat on a wooden spit over a fragrant wood fire. The flavor came from wild herbs gathered from the mountainside. This proved a tasty and, at the same time, simple way of cooking meat – pork, veal, kid, and lamb were all equally suited to this method. To this day, barbecued and roasted meat remains an important part of the menu, even for modern townsfolk, and a freshly roasted sucking pig is still the highlight of every Sardinian village festival.

The only dish that could possibly surpass such a delicacy is *carraxiu*, a specialty mainly found in and around Villagrande in the Nuoro province. This consists of a grass-fed male calf, stuffed with a whole kid, which in turn has been filled with a sucking pig, enveloping a hare, inside which is a partridge with a small bird tucked inside its breast. Before it can be cooked, the village cobbler is summoned to close up the calf using a big needle and strong thread. This extravagant specialty is consequently known in some regions as *toro del ciabattino* or cobbler's calf.

A much more modest affair is the *pastu mistu*. This "mixed dish" is simply a turkey stuffed with a mere chicken, hare, or rabbit.

Right: Sardinian cuisine is noted less for its fish dishes from the coast than for specialties from the country's hinterland. The sucking pig remains ever popular. If you are planning a celebration, you need to order your *porchetto* well in advance of the event.

This is how Sardinians like their *porchetto*: juicy pink meat which melts on the tongue and crispy crackling.

A sucking pig cannot be hurried. The meat has to smoke slowly rather than roast over a fairly low heat.

Costa Smeralda

Bitter experience has taught Sardinians to distrust anything that comes from across the sea. All too often, this island people has had to endure being ruled, exploited, or robbed by strangers. In the case of the Aga Khan Karim IV, this distrust was undeserved for when he came to the island in the sixties, it was certainly not with the aim of enriching himself at the expense of the islanders. This is a man who, it must be said, has never yet claimed his ancestral privilege of being paid his own weight in gold once a year by his subjects. On the contrary, the Aga Khan was more interested in the wallets of a clientele who were in the same league as himself as far as affluence is concerned. He opened their eyes to the island's beauty – at a price, naturally, since his plan was for these millionaires to enjoy the magic of Sardinia from 5000 hectares of his own land along the coast. He named this hitherto completely unknown stretch of coast "Costa Smeralda." In the years that followed, this attractively named region, which translates as "Emerald Coast," was a magnet for the sort of visitors whose names held as much attraction for readers of the international tabloid press as they did for the hoteliers of this exclusive holiday resort.

It probably did indeed take a man like the Aga Khan to create a holiday resort which was not only conceived with the Happy Few in mind, but which proved an immediate success with this elite group. This immensely rich prince was better acquainted with the preferences of the Agnellis and Flicks of this world than any marketing strategist could be – a luxurious beach paradise right at the gates of Europe, but a world away from the crowded coasts with names like "Blanca" or "Brava." The Aga Khan really did possess great farsightedness when, in 1963, he rejected plans for multistory buildings and insisted instead that his architects, Jacques Couelle and Luigi Vietti, come up with an architectural style that was in harmony with nature and in keeping with the landscape. Rich people also brought hard currency to the region and the Sardinians' fears that streams of foreigners would pour into the country in the wake of the Aga Khan proved groundless for the most part. The smart set on the Costa Smeralda tend to keep mainly to themselves and usually avoid any trips into the hinterland. Nevertheless, a few vestiges of Sardinians' inherent skepticism toward strangers still persists: Despite the fact that these rich people have brought a great deal of money to the island, they have not managed to buy the affections of the Sardinians. The islanders' almost sacred sense of hospitality, however, would ensure that these well-heeled holidaymakers never sensed this.

Prices are high in and around Porto Cervo but quality and service are guaranteed.

The "Emerald Coast" is not the only paradise Sardinia has to offer. There are hundreds of romantic, little bays awaiting discovery if you look a little farther afield off the beaten track and are prepared to explore.

SARDINIAN BREAD

Traditional Sardinian dishes were – and in some remote areas still are – based on practical considerations. In the same way that meat was mainly roasted on the spit because the herdsmen were unable to carry heavy cooking equipment around with them, many types of bread were likewise made with the needs of men in mind who often spent weeks on end in lonely mountain regions far away from the possibility of fresh supplies. The bread had to be light in weight with a low moisture content so that it would be less likely to go moldy and, at the same time, be versatile enough to form the basis for a variety of quick, complete meals. *Carta da musica* or *pane carasau*, as it is called in Sardinia, fitted the bill perfectly: The once-baked flat bread could be rolled up and carried in a shepherd's bag and the twice-baked version was practically immune to mold.

Pane fratau is the "filled" version of the *carta da musica*, whereby the crisp rounds of bread are turned into a nourishing meal with diced tomatoes, eggs, pecorino or other cheese, and herbs. Bread was also an important part of the menu of farmers and townsfolk except that they preferred heavier and doughier bread: *moddizzosu*- or *mazzosu*-loaves could weigh up to 22 pounds (10 kilograms).

Whether it is bread for wandering herdsmen or for townspeople, nothing much has changed with regard to the Sardinians' preference for country-style breads made from bread flour, wheat, or barley flour. One look inside local bakeries will dispel any idea that southern Europeans only eat white bread, as is commonly supposed.

Another very popular bread is *ciabatta*, which is now also fairly common north of the Alps. Although *ciabatta* is not really a typical Sardinian bread, there is hardly a bakery – either in Sardinia or the rest of Italy – which does not sell this aromatic wheat bread with its lightly floured, somewhat leathery crust. *Ciabatta* is made from "Grade 0" flour, in other words, not as fine or white as the bread made from "Grade 00" flour, but it does have more bite and flavor. This soft and fairly moist bread has large holes in it which are formed during the six hours in which the dough is left to rise. They give the bread its characteristic appearance.

CARTA DA MUSICA

This distinctive Sicilian bread is actually called *pane carasau*. Its old Sardinian name is becoming increasingly uncommon as visitors from the mainland call it *carta da musica*. These thin almost transparent rounds of bread resemble sheets of parchment-like music manuscript paper and the distinctive sound of these crisp sheets when they are broken also provides the *musica*.

Making *pane carasau* the traditional way is fairly expensive. First of all, a dough is made from durum wheat semolina, wheat flour, yeast, water, and a little salt. This is left to rise for half a day. Then it is kneaded again and left to rise a second time. The dough is then divided into balls and rolled out into wafer-thin rounds. After being left to stand for several more hours, the bread finally goes into the oven. As soon as the rounds of bread balloon up, they are removed from the oven and cut horizontally through the middle. The halved bread circles are then baked a second time until they are a delicious golden brown color.

Because the preparation is so time-consuming, most Sardinians leave it to the baker to make this musical bread. He sells it in stacks of ten or twenty, wrapping his delicate product in paper to protect it.

Carta da musica is a tasty snack just as it is, but it can also be brushed with oil and briefly reheated to make it even crispier. It can also be soaked in water to restore its original elasticity and then made into a type of lasagna by layering it with different fillings in an ovenproof dish. The most popular dish of all must be *pane fratau*. For this, the bread rounds are spread with tomato paste, layered with poached or fried eggs and then sprinkled liberally with grated cheese.

Pane carasau has even made a name for itself in the expensive restaurants of the famous tourist resorts. The bread is broken into pieces, brushed lightly with oil and sprinkled with coarse sea salt – this is as addictive as crackers or crisps. Once you start nibbling – as with *pane carasau* – you can't stop.

Civraxiu
This bread speciality from Cagliari is baked from bread flour. In order to get a smooth, homogenous dough, it must be well kneaded. As soon as it has risen, it is shaped into loaves, each weighing about two pounds (1 kilogram) and baked in a wood oven. Since the method of making it varies from place to place, *civraxiu* comes in strong and soft, thin, and thick versions.

Coccoi pintatus or pintau
The dough for this exceptionally attractive bread is made by mixing bread flour, lukewarm water, and yeast together. It is often decorated with a cross to ensure that it turns out well! It is then shaped by nimble fingers, using scissors, knives, and pastry cutters, into a vast number of figures ranging from plants to animals. You can see fish, birds, little pigs, turtles, roses, and many other things. These small works of art are mainly made for festival days.

Pistoccu
Pistoccu, which, like the *carta da musica*, is a snack for wandering herdsmen, is made from bread flour. The dough, which is mixed only with water, is shaped into small, rectangular loaves which are pierced several times with a fork to prevent air bubbles forming. They are then baked twice in succession. This bread is commonly found in and around Cagliari and the shepherds take it with them on their wanderings as it keeps fresh for long periods. It is often served with tomatoes, basil, oregano, garlic, and a strong local cheese.

Carta da musica

Flat rounds of bread
(Background illustration and below left)

1/2 LB/250 G ALL-PURPOSE FLOUR
1/2 LB/250 G DURUM WHEAT SEMOLINA
WATER
SALT
1 1/2 CAKES/20 G YEAST (IF USING ACTIVE
DRY YEAST, FOLLOW THE MAKER'S
INSTRUCTIONS)

Mix the flour and semolina into a dough
with lukewarm salted water, adding the
water a little at a time. Knead the dough
carefully with your hands and fists until
it is smooth. Add the yeast and continue
to knead until it has been completely
worked into the dough. Finally, cover the
dough with a cloth and leave to rise in a
warm place. Knead thoroughly one more
time and roll out the dough into a thin
round. Bake in a preheated oven at 465°F
(240°C) until the dough balloons.
Quickly remove it from the oven and
cut horizontally through the middle so
that you end up with two large rounds
of bread. Bake these briefly in the oven
for a second time.

Sardinian-born Anna Nieddu demonstrates in her own kitchen how authentic *malloreddus* are made.

First dissolve the saffron in water, then mix this water with the flour and salt.

Knead the dough in the bowl until the flour is completely mixed in.

Break off small pieces from the long rolls of dough and press into shell shapes.

The *malloreddus* get their pattern from being rolled across thin wires or a ridged board.

PASTA FOR HIGH DAYS AND HOLIDAYS

Pasta plays almost as big a role in Sardinian cooking as bread. Even now, no Sardinian cook would miss an opportunity – at least on special occasions – to serve traditional homemade pasta. The quintessential pasta for Sardinian feast days is known as *malloreddus*. It is claimed that *gnocchetti sardi*, as these small pasta specialties are called outside Sardinia, were already part of the island's cuisine in classical times.

The dough consists of durum wheat semolina, mixed with salt and lukewarm water. The *malloreddus* owe their distinctive yellow color to saffron. Once the dough has been thoroughly kneaded and is nice and elastic, it is divided equally into small portions, which are then rolled out into thin sausage shapes. Then comes the most challenging part of the operation, requiring a fair amount of skill. Small sections of pasta are nipped off the roll of dough. These are first pressed flat, then rolled lightly by thumb over a sieve or a grooved board in order to give them their characteristic ridged surface.

These little works of art are traditionally served with a simple tomato sauce or a lamb- or sausage-based ragout. If you prefer this dish in its more classical form, serve the *malloreddus* simply with a little butter and grated pecorino.

MALLOREDDUS
Semolina pasta with saffron
(Background illustration)

A PINCH OF SAFFRON
SALT
2 2/3 CUPS/400 G DURUM WHEAT SEMOLINA

Dissolve the saffron and a little salt in ⅔ cup/150 ml lukewarm water. Pile the semolina into a mound on the work surface and make a hollow in the middle. Pour in the saffron water and gradually knead into a dough.
Add a little more lukewarm water if necessary, but keep the dough fairly firm. Roll the dough into long lengths measuring about ¼ inch/0.5 cm in diameter and nip off small pieces just under ½ inch/1 cm in length. Using your thumb, roll these lightly over a grater, a grooved board, or the prongs of a fork to give them their curved shape and ridged pattern.
Leave the *malloreddus* to dry for at least half a day before cooking. Cook in boiling salted water until firm to the bite.

Background: *Malloreddus* go well with tomato sauce, but can also be combined with a hearty lamb ragout or served simply with butter and pecorino.

PASTA

Using the palm of your hands, roll out the dough into long narrow sausage shapes.

Use your thumbnail to roll the pasta shapes carefully over the grooves in a slow downward movement.

There is a kind of semolina in Sardinia known as *sa fregula*, which is used in North Africa and elsewhere to make couscous. In Sardinia, however, these tiny granules are added to soup or served as an accompaniment to braised meat. The dough is made from bread flour and water and then rolled by nimble fingers into little balls, no larger than peppercorns. These are then dried in the sun or in the oven. *Sa fregula* – like *malloreddus* – owes its yellow color to the addition of saffron.

A less common type of pasta is *filindeu*. This is mainly found in the Barbagia region where this paper-thin, almost transparent spaghetti is given each year to the pilgrims who come to Lula for the festival of St. Francis. The *filindeu* are cooked in a goat's meat broth into which pecorino is crumbled. Unfortunately, there are not many people left who are still able to make *filindeu* as it takes a lot of dexterity and skill to turn the dough, made from durum wheat semolina, olive oil, water, and salt, into such delicate pasta.

Culingionis (also known as *culurzones* or *culurgiones*) bear a remarkable resemblance, in shape at least, to the ravioli from Liguria or the Veneto. The filling used in Sardinia, however, is completely different from the northern version. The most popular fillings include young pecorino; Swiss chard and ricotta; mashed potato, ripe pecorino, and pork fat; minced lamb, pork, and veal; a mixture of ricotta, eggplants, and grated pecorino.

SA FREGULA
Couscous

2 1/2 CUPS/350 G DURUM WHEAT SEMOLINA FOR COUSCOUS
3 EGG YOLKS
SALT
A PINCH OF SAFFRON

Sa fregula is the Sardinian term for durum wheat semolina which is used to make couscous.
Pile the semolina into a large, deep bowl and make a hollow in the center. Mix the egg yolks with one glass of slightly salted water and the saffron. Pour a little of this into the hollow. Run your fingertips through this, rubbing the mixture off against the sides of the bowl to form small peppercorn-sized granules. Once a small amount of granules has accumulated, remove them from the bowl and set aside. Repeat this process until all the liquid and the semolina has been used up.
Leave the semolina granules to dry overnight on a linen cloth, turning occasionally.
Next day, continue to dry in the sun if the weather is fine, or else dry in a hot oven, leaving the oven door open to allow the steam to escape. These little balls will dry in a few minutes this way.

FILINDEU

The paper-thin *filindeu* are made by mixing durum wheat semolina with olive oil, adding salt and enough lukewarm water to make a smooth, but fairly firm dough.
The dough is cut, either by hand or using a pasta-making machine, into thin strips of spaghetti, which are then plaited together. It is then cooked in a mutton broth, in which chunks of sharp sheep's cheese are melted.

CULINGIONIS
Sardinian ravioli
(Illustrated below)

Serves 6 to 8

For the filling:
1 3/4 LBS/800 G POTATOES, BOILED AND MASHED VERY SMOOTH
2 CUPS/200 G FRESH MILD PECORINO, GRATED
1/2 CUP/50 G RIPE PECORINO, GRATED
1 1/2 CUPS/120 G PARMESAN, GRATED
2 1/2 TBSP OLIVE OIL
2 1/2 TBSP FINELY DICED MINT

For the dough:
2 1/2 CUPS/300 G ALL-PURPOSE FLOUR
1 EGG YOLK
1/2 CUP/120 ML WATER

3 1/2 TBSP/50 G BUTTER
8 SAGE LEAVES
A PINCH OF SAFFRON, DISSOLVED IN A LITTLE HOT WATER
FRESHLY GRATED PARMESAN OR PECORINO

To make the filling, mix the potatoes with the cheeses, olive oil and mint, and set aside.
To make the dough, pile the flour onto the work surface and make a hollow in the center. Pour the egg yolk and three-quarters of the water into this. Mix the egg and water together with a fork and gradually work in the flour. Add the remaining water, if required. Knead the dough for about 20 minutes until it is smooth and elastic, but not too firm. Roll out the dough very thinly by hand or using a pasta machine to a thickness of around ⅛ inch/2 mm, then cut out circles about 4 inches/10 cm in diameter. Knead the leftover dough together again and roll out once more. Continue cutting out circles. To make the *culingionis*, place a circle of dough on the palm of your hand and put a teaspoonful of filling in the center. Fold the circle in half over the filling and press the edges together. The *culingionis* should resemble little pockets. These also go well with tomato sauce.
Since the dough is very thin, it must be worked quickly. Once they have been cut out, the circles of dough should be covered with foil to prevent them drying out.
Slowly heat the butter, sage leaves, and saffron water in a large saucepan until the butter is melted. Meanwhile cook the *culingionis* in plenty of salted water until they are *al dente*. Drain, then carefully combine them with the sage, saffron, and butter mixture and serve.
Sprinkle with freshly grated Parmesan or pecorino, if desired.

CHEESE AND SAUSAGE

CASUMARZU

Casumarzu, the maggot cheese, is a Sardinian specialty which will definitely not appeal to vegetarians. This is basically a harmless, slightly mature pecorino. What causes this cheese to be viewed with suspicion, however, are the residents which are introduced into it. A small channel is bored through the rind on top of the cheese, into which small white maggots are inserted. To keep the new arrivals in tiptop condition, they are initially given a few drops of milk every now and again. After a few days, however, the maggots become accustomed to their new, not unappetizing, surroundings and begin to consume the pecorino from within. Once the maggots have worked their way through the whole cheese, the *casumarzu* aficionado breaks it open and scrapes out the mixture of cheese and maggots onto a chunk of bread.

The **Pecorino sardo**, with its own DOC label, is Sardinia's own version of the same sheep's cheese that is produced in central and southern Italy.

Some Sardinian cheese shops occasionally stock *pecorino romano*. If it has not actually been produced in Rome itself, it is called **Pecorino tipo romano**.

Calcagno is a strong, full-flavored cheese used for slicing, which is made from unpasteurized milk. It can be served as it is or be used in the kitchen for grating.

The milk for **Semicotto** is curdled with calf rennet. As a young cheese, it is quite mild, but it becomes stronger in flavor as it matures.

Pepato is a mild cheese, ideal for slicing, which develops a sharp taste as it matures. Goat rennet is used in its preparation and it gets its name from the peppercorns in its rind.

The **Dolce di Macomer** is a traditional cheese made from cow's milk which comes from Macomer, Sardinia's cheese-making center. This relatively low-fat specialty with its soft, light rind has a pleasantly mild flavor.

Sausage and air-dried salami from Macomer are among Sardinia's main meat products.

MACOMER

Every Sardinian is familiar with the little town of Macomer, which lies halfway between Oristano and Sassari. It is the island's equivalent of Tilsit – the only difference being that Macomer offers the visitor not one, but numerous different cheese specialties. The first cheese-producing cooperative is said to have been founded here back in 1907. This cheese-making industry, therefore, goes back a relatively long way – relatively, insofar as the actual town of Macomer boasts a much longer history. The parish church of San Pantaleo, for example, dates from the 16th century. Although there is no concrete evidence that the congregations of that time were already enjoying locally produced cheese, there seems every likelihood that they were.

Even several hundred years earlier, when Bernhard von Clairvaux dispatched Cistercian monks to Sardinia in the middle of the 12th century to found the Santa Maria di Corte monastery about six miles (ten kilometers) to the west of Macomer, it is likely that cheese products appeared on the monks' menu. In view of such an august past, the hundred or so years of history clocked up by the cheese-producing cooperative seems comparatively short. If measured in human terms, however, around four generations have enjoyed Macomer cheese since 1907. Its continuing popularity is the best proof of the quality which Macomer represents. Cheese is not the only specialty of this small town, however. If you like strongly flavored, air-dried salami or would like to sample other genuine Sardinian sausage varieties, Macomer is well worth a visit.

Left: The Buon Gustaio store in Macomer offers a large selection of cheese and sausage specialties.

PECORINO SARDO

About half the area of Sardinia is used for grazing. The island supports one third of all Italy's sheep, and livestock farming is the main source of income for the 1.6 million or so inhabitants. An offshoot of this is a very productive and renowned milk-processing industry: *Pecorino sardo* is one of the most sought-after cheeses "on the continent," as the Sardinians call the Italian mainland.

Background (left): After the whey has been skimmed off, the curdled milk is removed from the vat and pressed into a cylindrical sieve.

Only sheep's milk is used for *pecorino sardo*.

Calf rennet is added slowly and gradually mixed in.

The whey which has formed is skimmed off.

The curdled milk is pressed into a sieve.

Any remaining whey is drained off and the young cheese takes shape.

The pecorino is carefully rinsed in brine.

Gray mullet bottarga

Fishing for gray mullet is especially worthwhile in August and September when the female fish are full of eggs. The precious *bottarga di muggine* is somewhat more expensive than tuna *bottarga*, which is not exactly cheap itself. It is no wonder, therefore, that the female fish is opened with the greatest of care to avoid damage to the coveted eggs. The fish roe is salted to preserve it, and then pressed into characteristic oblong shapes using wooden paddles. After being stored for three to four months in cool, well-aired rooms, the blocks of pressed roe will have matured to a nutbrown or amber color. They are firm but not too dry and have an incomparable aroma of the sea. *Bottarga di muggine* is popular as an antipasto, served in thin slices with fresh white bread. Crumbled into small pieces and mixed with high-quality olive oil, this fine delicacy also makes a wonderful sauce for spaghetti or other long pasta. There are over a hundred species of gray mullet worldwide. They live in coastal waters and can even be found in brackish water or rivers near the coast.

There are over a hundred species of gray mullet worldwide. They live in coastal waters and can even be found in brackish water or rivers near the coast.

Nowadays, genuine *bottarga di muggine* is only found in selected delicatessens. The fish roe is removed immediately after the fish has been caught and placed in salt.

Muggini in teglia
Gray mullet in oil and vinegar

4 GRAY MULLETS, WEIGHING 3/4 LB/350 G EACH, READY TO COOK
3–4 TBSP OLIVE OIL, SALT
4 TBSP RED WINE VINEGAR
I GLASS OF DRY WHITE WINE
FRESHLY MILLED PEPPER

Rinse the mullet under running water, allow to drain and place in a lightly oiled, ovenproof dish. Salt the fish and brush with olive oil, sprinkle with 2 tablespoons red wine vinegar and bake in a preheated oven for about 15 minutes at 320 °F (160 °C). Pour over the remaining vinegar and white wine and cook the fish for a further 15 minutes. Remove the fish, fillet them with the aid of a spoon and arrange on a platter. Pour the cooking juice over the fish and season with freshly milled pepper. Serve with rice or a green salad.

FRESHLY CAUGHT FISH

Sardinian specialties are strongly biased toward the food popular with shepherds and farmers. Sardinians have never felt much affinity with the sea as they are not a seafaring people, although, being an island, it has always been and will always be home to fishermen. Sardinian fish dishes are simple and uncomplicated. They rely on the freshness and delicate flavor of the fish itself, as well they may, since the sea surrounding Sardinia, with the exception of the stretches of coast either side of the major ports, has very high water quality. Wherever you find the tourists recuperating from hectic everyday life on the fine sandy beaches and in the blue-green shimmering, crystal-clear waters of the bays around Sardinia, the fish, too, are similarly happy in their environment. Sardines, gray mullet, and tuna are the most commonly caught fish.

The Sardinian way of preparing the small, flavorsome sardines is just to wash them well without scaling or filleting them. Plenty of salt is rubbed in before they are barbecued. They are so tender that they can be eaten "top and tail." Local cooks have another clever tip for frying fish: semolina produces a much crispier coating than flour. Fresh gray mullet, the best specimens of which come from the waters around Cabras in the west of the island, are also prepared whole. Not only do they have tender, delicately flavored flesh, they are also the source of the valuable *bottarga*, which is rather like caviar and only found in the best delicatessens.

The southern side of the island used to depend on tuna fishing. The large shoals of tuna which existed in the past went to the local factories to be processed into canned fish. Nowadays, however, the conveyor belts have more or less come to a standstill: Tuna from the oceans, especially from Japan, has pushed Sardinian products into the background. A few family concerns, which concentrate on the small-scale manufacture of specialties for the gourmet market, have regained some of their importance over the past few years. *Ventresca*, the belly fat of this big fish, and *tarantello*, a type of salami made from belly fat, popular in Campania, Calabria, and Apulia, are now being rediscovered by chefs and gourmets alike.

At the Oristano fish market you will find imported fish as well as local Sardinian varieties, including gray mullet from the marshy areas of nearby Cabras – and *bottarga*.

SARDINE AL POMODORO
Sardines with tomatoes

1 ONION
EXTRA VIRGIN OLIVE OIL
3/4 LB/400 G TOMATOES
GENEROUS 3/4 LB/500 G SMALL SARDINES
SALT
FLOUR

Finely chop the onions and lightly sauté in a little olive oil. Peel and dice the tomatoes, add them to the onions, and continue to cook gently for about 20 minutes.
Wash and drain the sardines, season with a little salt and toss in flour. Heat plenty of olive oil in another skillet, fry the sardines in this and drain on paper towels. Arrange the sardines on a serving dish, cover with the tomato sauce, and leave to stand for 24 hours in the refrigerator. Serve cold.

TONNO ALLA CATALANA
Catalan style tuna fish

4 TUNA FISH STEAKS, EACH WEIGHING ABOUT 5 OZ/150 G
7–8 TBSP EXTRA VIRGIN OLIVE OIL
1 CUP/250 ML DRY WHITE WINE
3 RIPE TOMATOES, PEELED AND PURÉED
SALT
1 RED ONION, SLICED INTO RINGS
2 POTATOES
1/2 YELLOW BELL PEPPER
1/2 RED BELL PEPPER
1/2 PEPERONCINO

Rinse the tuna fish steaks under running water, then pat dry. Heat 2 tablespoons olive oil in a skillet and sauté the tuna on both sides. Pour in the wine and, after a few minutes, add the prepared tomatoes. Simmer for a further 10 minutes, season with a little salt and then stand in a warm place.

Heat the remaining olive oil in a skillet and lightly sauté the onion rings. Peel the potatoes and dice into small cubes, then add to the onions. Cut the peppers into strips and add these as well. Season with salt and add the half of the peperoncino. Simmer for a short while over a low heat. Arrange the tuna on plates with the vegetables, pour over some of the cooking juices and sprinkle with freshly milled pepper just before serving.

CASSOLA
Fish casserole

Serves 6

4 TBSP OLIVE OIL
1 ONION
1 CLOVE OF GARLIC
1 PEPERONCINO
GENEROUS 1 LB/500 G TOMATOES
1 GLASS DRY WHITE WINE
SALT AND FRESHLY MILLED BLACK PEPPER
1/2 LB/250 G BABY OCTOPUS
2 1/2 LBS/1.3 KG MIXED SEA FISH
6 SLICES OF WHITE BREAD

Heat two tablespoons of olive oil in a large saucepan. Finely dice the onion, garlic clove, and peperoncino and sauté for 5 minutes in the olive oil. Peel the tomatoes, dice, and add to the saucepan. Pour in the wine, season with salt and pepper, and slowly bring to the boil.
Cut the octopus into pieces and sauté in the remaining olive oil for 4 to 5 minutes, then add to the tomatoes in the saucepan and simmer with the lid on for about 30 minutes. Remove the bones from the sea fish, cut into pieces, add to the saucepan and allow to simmer for about 15 minutes. Toast the bread or bake it in the oven, arrange each slice on a deep plate, and pour over the fish casserole.

FISH PREPARATION

Round fish

Starting from the tail, remove all fins and any barbels with a kitchen knife.

Carefully trim the tail fin to make a perfect "fish-tail" shape.

Holding the fish by its tail, remove any scales with a fish scaler or a sharp knife.

Lift the gill flap and, using a small kitchen knife, loosen and carefully remove the gills.

Partially clean the fish through the gill opening, taking care not to damage the head or body.

Make a deep 1-inch/2–3-cm opening in the stomach cavity from the tail toward the head to clean out the rest of the fish.

Thoroughly rinse the cleaned fish inside and out under running cold water.

Drain the cleaned fish and carefully pat dry with paper towels.

Filleting salmon

Cut through the middle of the salmon just above the backbone.

Using a sharp knife, remove the skeleton together with the head.

Cut away any bones or fatty meat on the upper side.

Remove any small bones with tweezers.

Carefully remove the skin with a flat knife.

Finally, remove any remnants of skin or fatty meat.

UTENSILS USED IN FISH PREPARATION

Oyster tongs with curved grips (tenaglia Inox per ostriche)
These tongs are also useful for opening up crabs and lobsters.

Heavy cast-iron skillet (padella in ferro)
Fish can be cooked without oil in this non-stick skillet.

Heavy oval cast-iron skillet (padella in ferro nero ovale)
This is designed for cooking plaice and other flat fish.

Tweezers for removing bones (molla levalische)
These are useful for removing any bones left in the filleted fish.

Scaling knife with compartment to collect the scales (squamapesce)
The scales can be scraped off without getting sprayed all over the kitchen.

Scaling knife (squamapesce)
Only large fish like gray mullet or carp are scaled. Others have scales which are too small to be removed.

Sea urchin tongs (tenaglia per ricci di mare)
These tongs can be used to cut a sea urchin in half without injuring yourself on the sharp spines.

Lobster tweezero (pinza per astice)
Lobster crackers are used to break open the strong shell of the claws to expose the delicious meat inside.

Lobster crackers with tweezers (pinza per astice)
Once the claws have been broken open, the meat can be removed with the tweezers.

Deep-frying thermometer (termometro per frittura)
The temperature of the oil is important in deep frying.

Flexible spatula (spatola flessibile)
This is a useful kitchen utensil for turning the fish without it disintegrating.

Filleting knife with wooden handle and flexible blade (coltello per filettare)
This utensil is essential for filleting the fish cleanly.

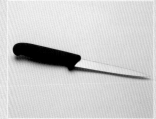

Filleting knife (coltello per filettare)
This knife can be used to open up shellfish.

ROCK LOBSTERS

There is only a small part of Sardinia that is renowned for its rock lobsters: namely, a strip of west coast, stretching from Capocaccia in the north, through Alghero, down to Bosa in the south. Here are found a wealth of delicious fish and a wealth, too, of rock lobsters which cling to the picturesque cliffs.

Capocaccia itself, surely one of the most beautiful spots of the Mediterranean, is a paradise for anyone looking for rock lobsters or sea urchins. Alghero, the main town of this bay, is likewise a real jewel where the blue of the sea meets the gold of the chalk cliffs; Bosa, in turn, with its colorful little houses, is a picturesque fishing village. This corner of the island seems more like Catalan than Sardinia in atmosphere. This is because a thousand years ago this area around Alghero was conquered by Catalonia invaders. Whereas the Sardinians are traditionally a pastoral folk and the Sardinian diet does not lean toward the sea and its inhabitants, the Catalans from Alghero – known as

Barcelloneta – Bosa, and Capocaccia have been fishermen since time immemorial and had always lived in close contact with the sea. Nowadays, fish is an important part of Sardinian cuisine.

Rock lobsters are traditionally caught with special nets, known as *nasse*. These are long nets drawn over a structure – formerly made from rushes, but nowadays constructed from wire – to make a tunnel. The rock lobsters swim into the wide opening, which eventually narrows into a funnel shape, lured in by small calamari bait. In days gone by, the fishermen used to tie the *nasse* containing the trapped shellfish to the boat, thus ensuring that the catch would remain alive and fresh until it was sold. Nowadays, however, modern ships have refrigeration equipment and the traditional methods of keeping the catch fresh have long since been replaced.

In Alghero, rock lobsters are prepared in many different ways. What to us is a rather expensive delicacy, was to the fisherfolk of Alghero a staple food, so much so that they sometimes wearied of it. It became imperative in Alghero kitchens to introduce some variety into the monotonous diet of rock lobsters – and anyone who could afford it, dished them up in a stew, enhanced by precious potatoes and vegetables, considered great delicacies.

Rock lobsters can be caught in fish-traps or nets. Here, Marco Sotgiu, is carefully hauling in the net, hoping for a catch.

To avoid damaging the catch, the net, up to 1 mile/1.5 km in length, is wound in over a spool (see also background illustration).

Skilled, experienced hands untangle the lobsters, which can weigh up to 1–1¼ lbs/400–600 g, from the net without damaging it.

Freshly caught rock lobsters are a delicacy. They are kept in water tanks at the market or fish counter until sold.

How do you tell whether seafood is really fresh?

The same rule that applies to fresh fish also applies to the sometimes very delicate and easily spoiled seafood, namely always buy it from a reliable source. Even then, it does no harm to check the merchandise.

Bivalves must always be firmly closed. Even a tiny gap between the two halves of the shell indicates that the creatures have dried out and spoiled after being caught. Any open shells should be thrown in the garbage, not in the cooking pot, as should any specimens that float to the surface in a bowl of water or do not open up during cooking.

Crabs, lobsters, or shrimps should have their shells intact, feel heavy, and smell fresh. Your nose is a reliable guide in this respect. The slightest hint of an unpleasant smell should make you wary. Never ever buy "fishy" smelling seafood. It is a sign that the fish is not fresh.

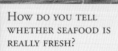

May is the best season for catching lobsters off the Sardinian coast. This prized catch does not need sophisticated preparation as its delicious meat already has a wonderful flavor of the sea of its own. Rock lobsters are delicious barbecued or baked in the oven with olives, salt, pepper, and rosemary, and need only a short cooking time.

Scampi a zuppetta
Scampi with tomato sauce

2 LBS/1 KG SCAMPI
1 ONION, DICED
1 GARLIC CLOVE, MINCED
4–5 TBSP EXTRA VIRGIN OLIVE OIL
2 BAY LEAVES
1 SMALL PIECE OF PEPERONCINO
1/2 CUP/100 G TOMATO SAUCE
SALT
1 GLASS OF DRY WHITE WINE
1 TBSP CHOPPED PARSLEY

Halve the scampi lengthwise and wash thoroughly under running water. Lightly sauté the onion and garlic in olive oil and add the bay leaves and finely chopped peperoncino. Pour in the tomato sauce and simmer for a few minutes over a low heat before adding the scampi and a little salt to taste. Pour in the wine and simmer for a few minutes, then add a little water and simmer with the lid on for about 10 minutes. Arrange the scampi on a plate, pour over some of the cooking juices, and garnish with the parsley.

Aragosta al forno
Baked rock lobster
(Illustrated below)

1 ROCK LOBSTER, ABOUT 2LBS/1 KG IN WEIGHT
1/2 CUP/50 G FLOUR
4 TBSP/100 G BUTTER
1 TBSP VEGETABLE OIL
SALT AND PEPPER
1 SPRIG OF ROSEMARY
1 GLASS OF DRY WHITE WINE

Halve the lobster lengthwise and remove the intestine, which runs from the tail end to the rump. Wash under running water, dry on paper towels and dust with flour.

Heat the butter and oil in a ovenproof dish. Add the lobster, season with salt and pepper and sauté on both sides. Add the rosemary, pour in the wine, and cook in a preheated oven for ten minutes at 350 °F (180 °C).
Serve immediately with the cooking juices.

Spaghetti all'aragosta
Spaghetti with rock lobster
(Illustrated right)

1 SMALL ROCK LOBSTER, ABOUT 1 LB/500 G IN WEIGHT
3–4 TBSP EXTRA VIRGIN OLIVE OIL
4 GARLIC CLOVES, MINCED
1 ONION, DICED
4 BAY LEAVES
1 GLASS OF DRY WHITE WINE
1/2 PEPERONCINO, GRATED
1 TBSP CHOPPED PARSLEY
1 CUP/200 G TOMATO SAUCE
14 OZ/400 G SPAGHETTI
SALT

Halve the lobster lengthwise and remove the intestine, which runs from the tail toward the rump. Cut the meat into small pieces, removing the shell where possible.
Heat the olive oil in a saucepan and sauté the onion and garlic together. Add the lobster meat and the bay leaves and sauté. Pour in the white wine, the grated peperoncino, chopped parsley and tomato sauce and simmer for 30 minutes over a low heat.
Cook the spaghetti in plenty of salted boiling water until *al dente*, drain into a bowl, and combine with the lobster mixture. Serve hot.

Calamari ripieni –
Stuffed squid

SEAFOOD

A wide variety of seafood can be found along the
Sardinian coast which boasts a total length of 830
miles (1340 kilometers) in all. You will find crabs and
shrimp everywhere and even a novice fisherman can
catch the delicate octopus – he virtually only needs to
dip his hand in the water to do so. The trattorias invite
visitors to the island to sample delicious mussels from
Marceddi and the squid season is a must for seafood
lovers. Artificial breeding grounds for common mussels
and, to a lesser extent, oysters produce top quality
seafood which is a crucial feature of a typical Sardinian
Antipasto misto di mare.

CALAMARI RIPIENI
Stuffed squid

1 3/4 LBS/800 G FRESH EQUAL-SIZED SQUID
JUICE OF 1 LEMON
SALT
2 EGGS
1 CUP/50 G BREADCUMBS
2 ANCHOVIES, CUT INTO SMALL PIECES
1 GARLIC CLOVE, MINCED
1 TBSP CHOPPED PARSLEY
1/2 CUP/30 G PECORINO, GRATED
PEPPER
2 TBSP/30 ML OLIVE OIL

Remove the ink sac, innards, and head from the squid.
Wash and pat dry. Cut the tentacles into small pieces
and cook in salted water, to which the lemon juice has
been added, for about 15 minutes, then drain. Place
the tentacles in a bowl with the eggs, breadcrumbs,
anchovies, garlic, parlsey, and cheese. Season with salt
and pepper and mix thoroughly. Stuff the squid with
this mixture and secure the openings with a skewer or
kitchen string. Place them on a greased baking sheet
and bake in a preheated oven for about 20 minutes
at 320 °F (160 °C). Leave to cool, then cut into
¾-inch/2-cm slices and serve.

FRUIT AND VEGETABLES

The fertile plains of Sardinia are ideal for growing fruit and vegetables. Every ingredient used in Mediterranean cooking is grown in small plots and fields, be they large or small, commercial or private. Even in the heart of towns, you can stumble upon hidden plots, surrounded by high walls. If you do succeed in getting a peep through the securely bolted wooden or iron door, you will glimpse a shady, cool, well-watered garden which supplies its proud owner with figs, oranges, lemons, cherries, plums, pomegranates, melons, chestnuts, hazelnuts, and also almonds.

No one actually needs to cultivate prickly pears, a fruit popular all over Sardinia, since these fleshy-leaved cacti grow wild by the wayside almost everywhere. If you want to pick any, however, you need to go armed with gloves. It is inadvisable to stand on a wobbly ladder when picking the fruit at the top for a tumble into this prickly plant is not one of the more enjoyable experiences in a gourmet's life.

Pomodori ripieni –
Stuffed tomatoes

SARDINIAN – A LATIN LANGUAGE

Est tundu e non est mundu,
est rubiu e non est fogu,
est birde e non est erba,
est abba e non est funtana.
(su forastigu)

Even if you paid only scant attention during Latin lessons at school, you can see from this old Sardinian riddle that this is a Latin-based language *par excellence*. You might almost think you were hearing a Roman from Ancient Rome. According to linguistic researchers, Sardinian is not just a dialect of Italian, but a language in its own right which, to this day, is still closely related to Latin. Words have been retained in Sardinian, for example, which have long since become obsolete in Italian in favor of other expressions. "House" is *domus* in Latin, *domu* in Sardinian and *casa* in Italian. The word for "door" is *janua* in Latin, *janna* in Sardinian, but *porta* in Italian. Similarly, the word for "large" likewise demonstrates the greater Latin bias of Sardinian compared with Italian: *magnus* in Latin, *mannu* in Sardinian, and *grande* in Italian.

For all non-Latin students, here is the translation of the riddle – with the answer, of course:

It is round, but it is not the earth,
It is red, but it is not fire,
It is green, but it is not grass,
It is water, but it is not a spring.
(Answer Watermelon)

Minestra di piselli con ricotta –
Pea soup with ricotta

Sardinian vegetable gardens are fully on a par with fruit as far as diversity is concerned. Artichokes are grown here; varieties such as the thornless Violetto di Provenzo and Violetto di Toscana or the thorny Spinoso sardo. The latter is particularly tender with a delicately pleasant flavor and is even shipped in large quantities to the mainland. Along with the artichoke, its relative the cardoon is also cultivated successfully on Sardinia. Over the past few decades, tomatoes have likewise become one of Sardinia's national products and have found their way to the markets of Turin and Milan. The fleshy, juicy, almost seedless fruit tastes exceptionally good and has a fine, smooth skin. Generally speaking, Sardinian vegetables do seem to develop a bit more flavor than their counterparts elsewhere. Many traditional salad recipes require only the addition of salt, since an oil and vinegar dressing is usually not necessary. Celery has so much flavor that it has to be used sparingly so as not to overpower the main dish. Radishes (particularly the long Arreiga variety) go well with a joint of meat – and only require a sprinkling of salt. Peas are particularly tender and juicy. The eggplants are just as good as those from Calabria and beans easily stand comparison with those from Apulia. Many herbs, such as the saffron crocus, mint, rosemary, basil, garlic, sage, bay, and marjoram also grow well here.

POMODORI RIPIENI
Stuffed tomatoes
(Illustrated above left)

4 LARGE, FIRM TOMATOES
2 EGGS
1/2 CUP/60 G PECORINO, GRATED
2 CUPS/100 G FRESH BREADCRUMBS
1 TSP SUGAR
SALT AND PEPPER
A PINCH OF NUTMEG
EXTRA VIRGIN OLIVE OIL

Wash the tomatoes, remove the tops, core, and deseed. Lightly beat the eggs in a bowl and add the grated pecorino, breadcrumbs, and sugar. Season with salt, pepper, and a pinch of nutmeg and mix together well. Fill the tomatoes with the mixture and replace the tops.
Put the tomatoes in an oiled pan and bake in a preheated oven for about 30 minutes at 320 °F (160 °C).

TORTINO DI CARCIOFI
Artichoke gratin

6 ARTICHOKES
JUICE OF 1 LEMON
4 EGGS
3–4 TBSP EXTRA VIRGIN OLIVE OIL
3 TBSP CHOPPED PARSLEY
1/2 CUP/50 G GRATED PECORINO OR GRANA
SALT AND PEPPER
BUTTER
BREADCRUMBS

Remove the tough outer leaves of the artichoke. Cut the tips off the remaining leaves and cut the artichokes into thin slices and place in a bowl containing the lemon juice and some water. In a second bowl, lightly beat the eggs and olive oil together. Add the parsley and cheese and season with salt and pepper. Grease an ovenproof dish and sprinkle in the breadcrumbs. Drain the artichokes, pat dry, and spread

Flavor-filled vegetables and garden fresh fruit continue to play a major role in Sardinian cooking. Since every housewife needs fresh supplies of these every day, the business of shopping is organized very simply – as it is all over the Mediterranean world. People shop either at the market or a nearby store. If you suddenly remember that you are short of an ingredient, you can always get it from a traveling tradesman by the roadside.

out in the dish along with the egg mixture. Sprinkle with more breadcrumbs and bake in a preheated oven for about 30 minutes at about 320 °F (160 °C). Cut the gratin into slices and serve warm or cold.

MINESTRA DI PISELLI CON RICOTTA
Pea soup with ricotta
(Illustrated below left)

1 LARGE ONION, FINELY DICED
3–4 TBSP EXTRA VIRGIN OLIVE OIL
4 LBS/2 KG FRESH PEAS
2 TBSP TOMATO PASTE
SALT
1/2 LB/200 G SMALL PASTA
8 OZ TUB/200 G RICOTTA

Lightly sauté the onions in olive oil. Shell the peas, add them to the onions, and sauté for about 15 minutes, stirring occasionally with a wooden spoon. Add the tomato paste and a little water. Season with salt and simmer for a further 20 minutes. Add the pasta and cook with the lid on until they are firm to the bite.
Crumble the ricotta onto deep plates. Pour the soup over the ricotta and stir together.

FAVATA
Bean stew

1/2 LB/250 G DRIED BEANS
1 ONION
1/2 STICK OF CELERY
1 CARROT
1/2 LB/250 G SAVOY CABBAGE
1–2/250 G PIG TROTTERS AND RIND
1/2 LB/200 G FAIRLY OLD SALSICCIA
1 VERY LOOSELY FILLED CUP/40 G DRIED TOMATOES
1 GARLIC CLOVE, CRUSHED
1 BUNCH OF DILL
SALT
TOASTED SLICES OF BREAD
GRATED PECORINO

Soak the beans overnight in water. Next day, put these into a large saucepan with about 12 cups/3 liters of water. Dice the vegetables and add to the beans along with the meat, tomatoes, and garlic. Cook for about 40 minutes over a low heat. Then, add the dill, season with salt and continue to cook until the beans are done. This bean stew improves in flavor if it is allowed to stand overnight. It should then be reheated and poured over pieces of toasted bread arranged on deep plates. Sprinkle with grated pecorino and serve.

For certain festivals in Sardinia, traditional costumes are still worn, as here in Cavalcata in the province of Sassari.

CAKES, CANDIES, AND COOKIES

Sweetmeats are very appropriately named in Sardinia for they really are extremely sweet. Different types of sponge and pastry, themselves already sweetened with honey or sugar and including a variety of ingredients, such as almonds, mixed spices, yeast, or marzipan, are used for the bases of little delicacies. This decorative confectionery, in the shape of cubes, balls, diamonds, or even animal and human figures, is similar to French *petits fours* and is covered with thick glacé icing or marzipan and decorated with candied fruit or sugar pearls in all colors of the rainbow – including real gold and silver.

Sardinian birthday cakes from the local bakery can also be wonderful works of art. Layers of sponge are liberally soaked in schnapps or other spirits before being alternately layered with sweet crème patisserie or cream. The color of the icing depends on who is celebrating the birthday: Adults get a white or pale lemon cake, while girls will find a pink and boys a blue creation to marvel at among their gifts. Cakes with an alcoholic content, however, are reserved exclusively for the adults. It will almost certainly have "Happy Birthday" written in icing on top. It is not only birthday cakes that are reserved for special occasions, however. The other *dolci* are likewise kept mainly for special events, but since even a neighbor dropping in can constitute such an occasion, some excuse can always be found for bringing out these sometimes costly sweet delights.

Sardinian confectioners are not only famous for their candies but also produce various kinds of small pastries which are sold in every bar, especially around breakfast time. These snacks of puff or yeast pastry are freshly baked every day and are available with a custard filling. Another very popular type of cookie is the so-called *ciambelle*, a cookie the size of a saucer, which is decorated in the middle with a dollop of bright red jelly. Anyone who does not trust the products from their local bakery can take their custom to a nearby convent: Even today it is quite common for people to buy their confectionery from convent bakeries. Many compulsive candy eaters would go so far as to say that the nuns, who depend on the income to keep their convents going, still bake the best *ciambelle*. Unfortunately, there is rarely an opportunity to compliment these pious confectioners on their art, since many Sardinian nuns belong to enclosed orders and maintain a strict vow of silence. Even the sale of the goodies is conducted in silence. Anyone wanting to buy cookies must knock at a certain door or window, which is opaque, naturally, The money is then placed in a sort of two-sided hatch. Once the outer door is closed, the nuns open up the inner door, collect the money and replace it with fragrant *ciambelle*, attractively wrapped in snow white paper and usually still warm from the oven. Only when the inner door is heard to close again may the outer door be opened and the delicious cookies removed. The very first bite will be enough to convince you that this silent purchase was definitely worth it.

AMARETTUS
Almond macaroons

1 LB/500 G SWEET ALMONDS
3 OZ/80 G BITTER ALMONDS
3–4 EGG WHITES
2 CUPS/500 G SUGAR
ALL-PURPOSE FLOUR

Soak the almonds for a while in boiling water, then peel and chop very finely. Whisk the egg whites until stiff, add the sugar and almonds and mix in well. If necessary, add 1 to 2 tablespoons of flour to make the mixture a little firmer. Shape small, light balls from the mixture and place on a baking sheet lined with waxed paper. Bake the macaroons until golden in a preheated oven for about 10 minutes at 300 °F (150 °C).

TORTA DI MANDORLE
Almond cake

4 EGGS
3/4 CUP/150 G SUGAR
1/2 CUP/50 G FLOUR
1/4 LB/100 G ALMONDS
2 1/2 LEVEL TSP BAKING POWDER
1 TSP VANILLA ESSENCE
GRATED ZEST OF 1 LEMON
1 TBSP BUTTER
FLOUR FOR DUSTING
CONFECTIONERS' SUGAR

Separate the egg yolks from the whites. Whisk the yolks with the sugar until frothy, then add the flour, the peeled and finely chopped almonds, baking powder, vanilla essence, and lemon zest. Whisk the egg whites until stiff and carefully fold in to the mixture. Grease a cake pan with butter and dust with a little flour. Pour the mixture into the pan and bake for about 40 minutes in a preheated oven at 350 °F (180 °C). Tip the cake out of the pan and leave to cool. Serve on a cake platter, liberally sprinkled with confectioners' sugar.

SEBADAS
Cheese ravioli with honey

1 1/3 CUPS/200 G DURUM WHEAT SEMOLINA
4 TSP/20 G SHORTENING (OR MARGARINE)
SALT
4–5 TBSP EXTRA VIRGIN OLIVE OIL
2 OZ/60 G FRESH CHEESE (CACIOTTA SARDA)
1 TBSP ALL-PURPOSE FLOUR
2 LEVEL TBSP HONEY

Mix the semolina with the shortening, a little water, salt, and one tablespoon of olive oil to make a soft, smooth dough. Roll out the pastry very thinly and cut out circles measuring about 2½–3 inches (6–7 cm).
Cut the fresh cheese into pieces and add to a saucepan with some water and one tablespoon of flour. Melt over a low heat until the mixture is thick and creamy. Drop a small amount of melted cheese onto half of the dough circles, using the remaining half as lids. Press the edges together firmly and fry in hot olive oil. Drizzle honey over the *sebadas* and serve hot.

GATTÒ AND OTHER WORKS OF ART

The festival calendar inspires Sardinian confectioners to greater and greater heights of achievement. Every year, a *gattò* is produced for the festival in honor of the local saint. This is more than just a confection of almonds and sugar – it is almost an architectural work of art. Great efforts are made to reproduce in cake form the town's main church or the leading convent and this scale-size replica is given pride of place at the celebrations. Nor would carnival time be complete without the saffron-yellow, deep-fried *zipulas*. Sumptuous cakes, as well as modest quark or ricotta tartlets called *pardulas*, are traditional features of the Easter table. All Saints' Day is an occasion to serve colorful confectionery and at Christmas and New Year, every region creates its own individual candy specialties.

Bianchini

Pardulas

Amarettus

Pabassini

Aranzadas

Pistoccheddus

Gueffos

Pastissus

WINEGROWING ON THE SUNSHINE ISLAND

Situated just 125 miles (200 kilometers) from the Italian mainland and on the same latitude as Campania and Basilicata, Sardinia, boasts one of the oldest wine industries in the country. In the course of history, it has been occupied by Byzantines, Arabs, and Catalans and the Spanish influence on wine cultivation is still evident to this day. The most important grape varieties in Sardinia, such as Cannonau and Carignano, originate from the Iberian peninsula. Winegrowing in Sardinia, far more so than in the rest of Italy, is dominated by large cooperatives of growers.

Apart from these, there are just a few wineries and a handful of talented vintners who have achieved a degree of success, both nationally and internationally. A large proportion of the island's wine production is still for domestic consumption or sent for blending with other wines on the mainland.

Only a few of Sardinia's DOC wines, therefore, can really be classed as quality wines, including, as mentioned above, Cannonau di Sardegna, the Vermentino di Gallura, Vernaccia di Oristano as well as Carignano del Sulcis.

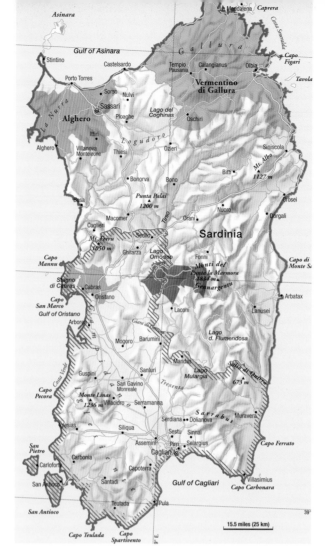

Legend:
- Cannonau di Sardegna, Malvasia di Cagliari, Monica di Cagliari, Moscato di Cagliari
- Vermentino di Gallura (DOCG)
- Moscato di Sorso-Sennori
- Alghero
- Nuragus di Cagliari
- Giro di Cagliari
- Vernaccia di Oristano
- Mandrolisai
- Carignano del Sulcis

15.5 miles (25 km)

Cannonau di Sardegna

In its Spanish homeland, the Cannnonau, sometimes written Cannonao, is known as Garnacha. This is the second most common variety of grape in the world and covers 20 percent of Sardinia's grape-growing area. It forms the basis of many a famous Spanish wine, such as the Rioja. It has also become one of the main grapes grown in southern France – under the name of Grenache – where it is also used in the production of many excellent Châteauneuf-du-Pape wines. It can also be found here and there around Maremma on the Tuscan coast, where it is called Alicante. It produces deeply-colored, strong, full-bodied red wines which are also popular for mixing with other varieties, like the Cabernet Sauvignon, for example. The best Cannonau

wines go well with roast meat and game dishes and are produced in the province of Nuoro in eastern Sardinia.

Vermentino di Gallura

The island's best Vermentino, a lively fresh white wine, which is an excellent accompaniment to simple fish dishes, comes from the Gallura province in the northern tip of Sardinia. This grape is also widely cultivated on the neighboring island of Corsica and in the Liguria region as well as in southern France, where it is known as Rolle. The best results are really only obtained if the winegrower is meticulous about restricting the yield – a crucial factor in producing flavor-intensive wine.

Carignano del Sulcis

The Carignano, known as Carinena or Marzuelo in Spain and Carignan in southern France, is primarily a simple mass-produced wine without much character or distinguishing features. In Sardinia, however, it can, in the right hands, produce some interesting wines, which can be seductive with their lingering bouquet and round, full flavor.

Monica, Vernaccia, and Malvasia

In addition to several native grape varieties, Sardinia also grows many unusual types of some of the more widely cultivated Italian vines. These include the Monica (M. di Cagliari or M. di Sardegna), a dry red with an intense bouquet, the Vernaccia (V. di Oristano), which produces strong, dry, white wines and can also be used in a kind of liqueur, similar to sherry, as well as the Malvasia.

The Cantina Sociale della Vernaccia in Oristano was founded in 1953. It has always been the winery's aim to combine the traditional hand methods of Vernaccia production with up-to-the-minute winemaking techniques – the result is a high-quality DOC wine.

The large, bulbous Vernaccia bottles used in Oristano resemble the wicker bottles once used to collect wine from the *cantina sociale*.

IL VINO DELLO ZIO

Even up to 20 years ago, *il vino dello zio*, in other words, wine made by your winegrowing uncle – and nearly every family had one among its relatives – was still what Italians drank as an everyday wine. You brought it home with you in a wicker bottle from a visit to your relatives and if you lacked the necessary *zio*, uncle, or *nonno*, grandfather, in the family, then you simply took your empty bottle to the wineshop round the corner or went to the nearest *cantina sociale*, one of the numerous cooperatives, armed with a plastic canister or wicker basket, and filled this up for a few lire from large storage tanks.

In those days, cheap wines did not afford much enjoyment, however. Badly made from inferior grapes, they frequently did not withstand the long journey back from holiday and by the time they reached home, had a distinct vinegary taste and a similarly unappealing bouquet. By and large, only a sumptuous family meal in the countryside or a sunny day on the beach in holiday mood could make them reasonably palatable to most people.

The picture began to change somewhat in the eighties. As the production of top quality wines began to increase throughout Italy, Italian wine drinkers became correspondingly more demanding. Holidays were no longer spent exclusively on the Adriatic or Riviera, but people began instead to explore the fascinating world of foreign travel. Young Italians, in particular, returned home from increasingly exotic destinations with newly discovered tastes and higher expectations in wine drinking.

It is true that even today, a large proportion of everyday wine, especially in the less renowned winegrowing areas of Italy, is still collected in canisters from the filling point at the nearest *cantina sociale*, as is also the practice in France, Germany, and elsewhere in the world. During the past two decades, however, Italy has developed a really distinguished viniculture. Fine, perfectly made wines from best-quality grapes, which are bottled in modern designer bottles and sold in elegant stores and restaurants at uniformly steep prices, have taken the place of the *vino dello zio*, once the Italians' everyday tipple.

Left: The Vernaccia di Oristano is one of the best Sardinian DOC wines. Here we see Giuseppe Atroni of the Cantina Sociale della Vernaccia tapping the wine straight from the stainless steel tank.

WATER

The interior of Sardinia has a wealth of high mountains and unspoilt landscapes. The many mountain streams are sources of clean, clear drinking water for which there is widespread demand.

Even though nowadays a large amount of spring water is bottled and sold in supermarkets with a laboratory analysis on the label, some Sardinians still like to go, or rather drive, to "fetch water," in other words, they take their own containers to fill from accessible streams or springs. Since some spring water is said to have special curative properties, people are skeptical as to whether the supermarket water possesses the same powers.

If you have the time and suitable transport, you can collect your own drinking water fresh from the famous mountain springs. Many people mistrust the plastic bottles that are widely sold in the supermarket.

San Leonardo has long been one of the most popular and frequented Sardinian springs. The local authorities have even had to improve the access road to the spring.

WELL-KNOWN ITALIAN MINERAL WATERS

The **Rochetta** spring in Umbria produces water with a low mineral and carbonic acid content.

Levissima comes from Italy's highest spring in the Bormio mountains of Lombardy.

Water rich in potassium bubbles up from the **Sangemini** spring in Umbria.

Ferrarelle still water comes from the Riardo source in Emilia Romagna.

Vera comes from the Veneto and is said to stimulate the metabolism.

The **San Pellegrino** from Val Brembana has been famed for its healing powers since around 1200.

Uliveto a still water from Vico Pisano in Tuscany, is low in natural carbonic acid.

Monteforte comes from the Coveraie spring, situated high in the Apennines.

Boario originates from four springs in a Lombardy nature reserve.

The province of Orvieto in Umbria is home to **Panna**, a completely uncarbonated water.

Cerelia water from Emilia Romagna is said to be good for bladder infections.

Fiuggi water from Lazio is recommended for disorders of the urinary tract.

The **Limpia** source in Lombardy produces water with a low mineral content.

Lora Recoaro comes from the Veneto. The spring lies at an altitude of 2625 ft/800 m.

San Francesco from Caslino al Piano (Como province) rises from a spring deep underground.

Tavina mineral water comes from a spring in Salò on Lake Garda.

GLOSSARY

abboccato — medium sweet
acciuga/alice — anchovy
aceto balsamico — balsamic vinegar
aceto di vino — wine vinegar
acqua di rose — rose water
acquavite — schnapps
affettato — cold cuts
affogare — poach
affumicare — smoke
affumicato — smoked
agarico delizioso — saffron milk cap
aglio — garlic
agnello da latte — sucking lamb
agro — sour
agrodolce — sweet-and-sour
aguglia — needlefish
al dente — firm to the bite
al forno — baked in the oven
alalunga — mackerel
albicocca — apricot
alborella — whitefish
alcolici — alcoholic drinks
alice — anchovy
alimentari — foodstuffs
all'arrabbiata — spicy, with peperoncino
alla casalinga — homemade
alla griglia — broiled
alloro — bay leaf
amabile — sweet
amanita cesarea — imperial mushroom
amaretto — almond macaroon
amaro — bitter
aneto — dill
anguilla — eel
anice — aniseed
anice stellato — star anise
antipasto — antipasto
aperitivo — aperitif
aragosta — rock/spiny lobster
arancia — orange
aromatizzato/aromi — seasoned/herbs
arrosto — roasted
artemisia, assenzio — artemisia
arzilla — flat fish
asparago selvatico — wild asparagus
astice — lobster
attaccarsi — burn
baccalà — dried salt cod
baccello — pod
bacca — berry
bagnare — soak
bagnomaria — bain-marie
bevanda — drink
bietola — Swiss chard
bisso — beard (of a mussel)
bistecca — steak
bocconcino — nibbles
bollito — boiled (especially meats)
borragine — borage
branchie — gill breather
branzino — sea bass
brasato — braised
brodo — bouillon/broth

bruschetta — toasted bread
buccia — peel, skin
budino — pudding
bulbo, tubero — bulb
burro — butter
caffè — espresso
caffè corretto — espresso with almond liqueur, grappa, or Sambuca
caffè latte — coffee with milk
caffè macchiato — espresso with a dash of milk
caffè ristretto — doubly concentrated espresso
calamaro — squid
camomilla — chamomile
canederlo — dumpling
cannella — cinnamon
cannocchia — Mantis shrimp
cantarello — chanterelle
cappero — caper
cappone — capon
carciofo — artichoke hearts
cardo — cardoon
carne d'asino — donkey meat
carne di camoscio — chamois meat
carne di cavallo — horse meat
carne di montone, di castrato — mutton
carota — carrot
carpa — carp
caviale — caviar
cavolfiore — cauliflower
cavolino di Bruxelles — brussels sprout
cavolo — cabbage
ceci — garbanzo bean/chickpea
cedro — citron
cereali — cereals
cerfoglio — chervil
cernia di fondale — sea bass
cervella — brain
cetriolo — cucumber
chiodi di garofano — cloves
chiodino — honey agaric mushroom
cibo kascer — kosher food
ciccioli — crackling
cicoria — chicory
cieca — glass eel
ciliegia — cherry
cime di rapa — turnip tops
cinghiale — wild boar
cipolla — onion
cipollotto — scallions
cirenga — sea bass
coccio — clay pot
colazione — breakfast
concentrato di pomodoro — tomato paste
conchiglia di San Giacomo — pilgrim scallops
condire — season
confetto — dragée
congelato — frozen, iced
coniglio — rabbit

conservabile — keeps well
contorno — vegetables
coriandolo — coriander
corteccia — bark
coscia — leg, haunch
costola — rib
co(s)toletta — cutlet
cotechino — pork sausage
cotenna — rind
cotto — well done
cozza — common mussel
crauti — herbs
crema — cream
cren — horseradish
crespella — pancake
croccante — crisp
crocchetta — croquette
crosta — crust
crosta di sale — salt crust
crostacei — crustaceans
crostino — toasted bread
crudità — crudités
crudo — raw
crusca — bran
cucinare — cook
cucinato al forna — baked in the oven
cumino — caraway
cuocere e far addensare — thicken
dattero di mare — date mussels
dentice — dentix (sea bream)
di giornata — fresh each day
digestivo — digestive
disossare — bone
disporre a strati — layer
dolce — candy, dessert
dorare — sauté until transparent
dragoncella — tarragon
eleta — morel mushroom
erba cipollina — chive
erbette aromatiche — herbs
estragone — tarragon
estratto — extract
evaporare — evaporate
fagiano — pheasant
fagioli — beans
famigliola buona — honey agaric mushroom
far legare — bind
faraona — guinea fowl
farina di riso — rice flour
farina di segale — rye flour
faro — spelt
fatto in casa — homemade
fegato — liver
fegato d'oca — goose liver
fermentare — ferment
fetta biscottata — crispy, toast-like bread
fico d'India — prickly pear
filettare — fillet
filetto — fillet
finferlo — chanterelle
finocchio — fennel
fiore di sambuco — elderberry blossom

focaccia — focaccia
fonduta — cheese fondue
formaggio di pecora — sheep's cheese
formaggio duro — hard cheese
formaggio fresco — soft cheese
formaggio fresco tipo ricotta — curd cheese
fragola — strawberry
frattaglie — innards
fresco — fresh
friggere — fry
frigorifero — refrigerator
fritto — fried
frizzante — sparkling (wine)
frutta secca — dried fruit
frutta di bosca — fruits of the forest
frutti di mare — seafood
fungo imperiale — imperial mushroom
fungo ostrica — oyster mushroom
fuoco, piastra — hot plate
gamberetto — shrimp
gambero — (king) prawn
gelato — ice cream
ginepro — juniper
girare, voltare — turn
gnocchi — little semolina or potato dumplings
gocciolare — sprinkle
grancevola — spider crab
granchio — crab
grano duro — strong wheat
grano integrale — wholegrain
grano saraceno — buckwheat
grano tenero — wheat
grano turco — maize
grassetti — crackling
grasso del pesce — fish fat
gratinato — gratin
grattugiato — grated
grissino — bread stick
impanato — breaded
impastare — knead
in agro — marinated in vinegar
in agro-dolce — marinated in sweet and sour
in brodo — in a broth
in marinata — marinated
in padella — in a skillet
in umido — braised in sauce
indivia — endive
insalata brasiliana — iceberg lettuce
integrale — wholemeal
involtino — roulade
lampone — raspberry
larderellare — grease
lardo — lard
lasca — roach
lasciar andare — leave to rise
lasciare in concia — allow to stand
latte di bufala — buffalo milk
latte intero — full-cream milk
lattuga — lettuce
lavarello — whitefish
legumi — pulses
lenticchie — lentils
lepre — hare

Italian	English
lessato	boiled
lievito	yeast
lime	lime
limone	lemon
lingua	tongue
liquirizia	liquorice
liquore	liqueur
lisca	fish bone
lombo	loin
lumaca di mare	sea snail
macerare	steep, soak
macinato	ground meat
maggiorana	marjoram
magro	lean
maiale	pork
maionese	mayonnaise
mandorla	almond
manzo	beef
marinare/marinata	marinate, marinated
marmora	mormyr (bream)
marrone	chestnut
marzapane	marzipan
mazzetto	bouquet
mazzetto di aromi	bunch of herbs and vegetables for soup-making
mela	apple
melanzana	eggplant
melograno	pomegranate
menta	mint
meringa	meringue
merluzzo	cod
mescolare	stir
mettere ammollo	soak
mettere in concia	pickle
miele	honey
miglio	millet
minestra	minestrone
mirtillo rosso	cranberry
misto	mixed
molluschi	mollusks
mora di rovo	blackberry
mostocotto	fruit syrup
muggine	gray mullet
nasello	hake
nocciola	hazelnut/filbert
noce	nut
noce moscata	nutmeg
orata	gilthead
origano	oregano
orzo	barley
orzo perlato	pearl barley
osse con il midollo	marrow bone
pagello	bream
palombo	shark
pan grattato	fresh breadcrumbs
pancetta	belly fat
pane	bread
panino	bread roll
panna	cream
passato	sieved, puréed
passera di mare	flounder
pasta	pasta
pasta asciutta	lit.: dried pasta = pasta with tomato sauce
pasta frolla	plain pastry
pasta leggera tipo biscotto	sponge mixture
pasta lievitata	yeast dough
pasta sfoglia	puff pastry
pasticcio	paté
patata	potato
patata dolce	sweet potato
pelato	peeled
pepe	pepper
peperoncino	chili pepper
peperone	bell pepper
pera	pear
pernice	partridge
pesare/pesato	weigh/weighed
pesca	peach
pesce	fish
pesce persico	perch
pesce San Pietro	John Dory
pesce spada	swordfish
pestello di legno	wooden pestle
petto di pollo	chicken breast
piatto da magro	Lenten fare
piccante	spicy, hot
piccione selvatico	wood pigeon
pietanza	dish
pimento	pimento
pinna	fin
pinolo	pine nut
piselli	peas
pizzoccheri	buckwheat pasta
pleuroto	oyster mushroom
polenta	polenta
pollame	poultry
pollo	chicken
polpa	pulp
polpa di pomodoro	canned chopped tomatoes
polpo	octopus
pomodoro	tomato
pompelmo	grapefruit
porcellino da latte	sucking pig
porcino	boletus mushroom
porro	leek
pralina	praline
prataiolo	field mushroom
preparazione	preparation
presa	pinch
prezzemolo	parsley
primo piatto	first course
prodotti caseari	dairy produce
prosciutto	dry-cured ham
prugna	plum
pulire	clean
quaglia	quail
rafano	horseradish
raffreddare	cool
raffreddare in acqua	cool in water
ragù	ragout
rapa	turnip
ravanello	radishes
reni	kidneys
residuo, fondo	residue
resistente alla fiamma	heat resistant
riccio di mare	sea urchin
ripieno	stuffed
riscaldare	heat up
riso commune	rice
riso fino	medium-grain rice
riso semifino	round-grain rice
riso superfine	arborio rice
rombo	turbot
rosmarino	rosemary
rospo/rana pescatrice	monkfish
rucola	garden rocket (hedge mustard)
salame di fegato	liver sausage
salamoia	brine
salato	salted, seasoned
sale	salt
salmone	salmon
salsa	sauce
salsiccia	pork sausage
salsiera	sauceboat
salsina	dip
salvia	sage
sanguinella	blood orange
sarago	white bream
sardina	sardine
savoiardo	sponge finger
sbollentare	blanche
scalogno	shallot
scaloppina	escalope
scampi	langoustines
scavare	scoop
schiacciare	mash, pound
sciogliere	dissolve, melt
sciroppo	syrup
scorzonera	black salsify
scottare	overheat
scremato	semi-skimmed
secco	dry
secondo piatto	second course
sedano	celeriac
selvaggina	game
seme, nocciolo	seed, kernel
semi di finocchio	fennel seed
semi-secco	semi-dry
semolina	semolina
seppia	squid
servire	serve
sesamo	sesame
sformato	flan
sgocciolare	drain
sgombro	mackerel
sobbollire	sieve
soffriggere	sauté
sogliola	sole
soppressata	pressed meat
sorbetto	sorbet
sott'aceto	marinated in vinegar
sott'olio	preserved in oil
spalla	shoulder
spalmare	smooth
spazzolare	brush off
spennellare	brush
spezzettare	dice
spianare	roll out
spiedo	kebab
spigola	sea bass
spinaci	spinach
spolverare	sprinkle
spugnola	morel mushroom
spumante	sparkling wine
squama	(fish) scales
stagionato	mature
storione	sturgeon
stufare	stew
succo d'arancia	orange juice
succo di limone	lemon juice
sventrare	clean
svuotare, scavare	hollow out
tacchino	turkey
tagliare, tagliato	cut/sliced
tagliare a dadini	diced
tagliare a tranci	sliced
affettare	
tagliuzzato	cut into small pieces
tarassaco	dandelion
tartaruga	turtle
tartufo bianco	white or Alba truffles
tartufo nero	black, winter or Norcia truffles
temolo	mullet
temperatura di cottura	cooking temperature
timballo	timbale
timo	thyme
tinca	tench
tonno	tuna
tordo	thrush
tortelli	ravioli
tortino	tartlet
tramezzino	sandwich
triglia	red mullet
trippa	tripe
tritare	ground
trota	trout
tuorlo	egg yolk
uovo all'occhio di bue	fried egg
uovo	egg
uva	grape
uvetta	raisin
vaniglia	vanilla
verdura	vegetables
versare	pour in
vinacce	marc
vino da tavola	table wine
vino liquoroso	liqueur
visciola	wild cherry
vitello	veal
vongola	clam
zafferano	saffron
zampone	pig trotter
zenzero	ginger
zucca	pumpkin
zuccherare	sugar
zucchero a velo	confectioners' sugar
zucchero di canna	cane sugar
zucchero vanigliato	vanilla sugar
zuppa densa	thick soup

COOKING TECHNIQUES

Artichokes

Cut off the stem of the artichoke. Only stalks from very tender artichokes are edible, but even they must be peeled. Remove the tough outer leaves and, using kitchen scissors, cut a generous amount off the tips of the remaining leaves. Place the prepared artichokes in a water and lemon juice mixture to prevent discoloration. Use according to the recipe instructions. Before eating, remove the choke from the base of the artichoke, taking care not to damage the delicate heart, the choicest part of the vegetable.

Blanching

This entails cooking the ingredients for a few moments in plenty of boiling water, then plunging them into cold water. This not only partly precooks the food, but also helps it retain its color and, in the case of soup bones, removes protein, fat, and foreign particles.

Braising

Cooking food in its own juices or in a small amount of fat and/or liquid over a constant, moderate heat. Some vegetables, such as onions, are lightly sautéed until they are translucent.

Calf's sweetbreads

Soak the sweetbreads for 2 hours in cold water to remove any traces of blood, frequently changing the water. Blanch in boiling water for about 5 minutes and then plunge in cold water. Use a knife to peel off the skin, removing any blood vessels, then prepare according to the recipe.

Cannelloni

Roll the fresh pasta dough into a thin sheet and cut into small squares. Pipe a small amount of filling in the center of each square and moisten the edges with water and roll up into tubes. Place the cannelloni in a dish with the join facing downward.

Carpaccio

To slice carpaccio, wrap the loin of beef in foil and place in the freezer compartment for about 1 hour, after which the meat can be cut into paper-thin slices using a large, sharp kitchen knife or an electric carving knife.

Chestnuts

To roast chestnuts, first make a small incision in the shell of the chestnut to prevent it bursting during roasting. Chestnuts should be roasted for 30 minutes at most in a hot oven. Any longer than this and they become hard.

Coating with breadcrumbs

Season meat, fish, or other ingredient, toss in flour, then dip in egg yolk and coat with breadcrumbs before frying.

Coloring pasta

Add the following ingredients to egg-based pasta dough (See: Pasta dough):

For green pasta, substitute about ¼ lb/100 g well drained spinach purée for one egg. For red pasta, add 2–3 tablespoons tomato paste or 1 small puréed beetroot; for golden yellow pasta, 1 small packet of saffron strands, ground in a mortar, and for black pasta, use the ink from about 1 lb/500 g squid.

Crabs

These must be boiled for about 20 minutes and then left in the cooking water for a further 15 minutes. The best way to open them is to press firmly between their eyes which will cause the shell to lift like a lid. Remove the gills and extract the meat from the body and claws.

Dried beans and pulses

Dried beans and pulses are generally soaked for 8–12 hours before use. In this way, they cook faster and are easier to digest. Any beans that float to the surface during soaking should be discarded as these could contain insects. Drain off the water they have soaked in, as this contains indigestible substances. Rinse the beans or pulses well in fresh water and cook for up to 3 hours, depending on variety. Beans are cooked when they have doubled or trebled in size. Do not add salt until the beans are nearly cooked (as adding it early on will make the beans tough).

Eggplants

Slice the eggplant, sprinkle with salt and leave to stand until the salt has drawn out the bitter juices and excess moisture. After 15–30 minutes, rinse the salt off under cold running water and pat the eggplants dry. Before frying, blanch the eggplants briefly to prevent them absorbing too much oil.

Excess fat removal

Remove excess fat from broths, soups, and sauces by pouring or skimming it off, soaking it up into paper towels or lifting off the solidified layer of cold fat.

Farfalle

Roll the pasta dough out thinly and cut into small squares using a pasta wheel. Squeeze these together in the middle between thumb and forefinger to make little "bows."

Gnocchi

Boil about 2 lbs/1 kg of potatoes, peel them while they are still hot and mash them straight onto the work surface. Gradually knead in 1 teaspoon salt and about ½–1 lb (250–500 g) flour. The amount of flour required depends on how floury the potatoes are. The resulting dough should be smooth without being sticky. Leave to stand covered for about 15 minutes. Mold the dough into rolls each about the thickness of a finger. Cut these into pieces about ¼ inch/2–3 cm in length. Using a fork, press in both sides to give the gnocchi their characteristic shape. Leave for a further 15 minutes. Cook in gently (not fast) boiling water for about 5 minutes.

Gratin

This means cooking a dish under a high top heat in the oven or broiling under a high temperature so that a brown crust forms. To form the crust, sprinkle small amounts of butter, grated cheese, breadcrumbs, or a creamy sauce over the surface.

Kidneys

Peel off the thin outer skin of the kidneys. Halve them and cut out the white core, taking care not to damage the kidneys.

Marinating

This means placing food in any seasoned liquid to give it flavor, or, in the case of meat, to tenderize it. Game can be treated similarly.

Marinating and preserving vegetables in vinegar

Vegetables and mushrooms need to be precooked but must remain *al dente* at all costs. To ensure that the vegetables remain crisp and retain their color, they should be plunged into ice-cold water. To marinate about 2 lbs/1 kg vegetables (e.g. zucchini, eggplants, bell peppers, green beans, carrots, fennel, or mushrooms), peel and quarter 4 cloves of garlic and crumble 2 dried bay leaves. Finely chop a bunch of parsley and half a bunch each of marjoram and thyme. Pour a little olive oil into a large glass jar, add a layer of prepared vegetables, season with salt and pepper and some of the herbs. Sprinkle over some white wine vinegar and cover the whole lot with plenty of oil. Repeat this process until the jar is full, ending with a thick layer of oil. Leave the vegetables to stand for a week in a cool place (ideally in a cellar or cool pantry). Mushrooms should be left to stand for two days in the refrigerator. Following this, vegetables can be kept for a further week, mushrooms for about another two days. The ingredients must always remain well covered with the marinade

Mushrooms

Avoid washing mushrooms if at all possible as they soak up water. To clean them, wipe with a damp cloth or paper towels, scratching off any particles of dirt left with a small knife and cutting away any unwanted parts. Morel and chanterelle mushrooms, however, do need rinsing to remove any sand or grit from the lamella.

Mussels

Wash and brush mussels thoroughly under running water and scrape off any calcium deposits with a knife. Remove the beards by giving them a sharp twist. Discard any open mussels as they will have gone off. Cook the mussels over a high heat for about 5 minutes until they open up. Discard any unopened shells.

Omelets

To make an omelet for 2 people, lightly beat 4 eggs with 1 tablespoon milk, water, or cream and season the mixture with salt and pepper. Melt some butter in a large skillet and cook the egg mixture gently over a moderate heat. Keep stirring with a fork without disturbing the bottom layer. When the omelet is almost set, but still runny on the surface, remove the skillet from the heat and fork along the edge, while simultaneously shaking the skillet, so that the front edge of the omelet folds over slightly. Important: remove the skillet from the heat while the surface of the omelet is still runny as it will carry on cooking in the hot pan. This ensures the omelet retains its perfect consistency and is not too dry.

Pasta

Pasta must be cooked in a large saucepan in plenty of water. Use 4 cups/1 liter of water and one generous teaspoon of salt for every ¼ lb/100 g of pasta. Do not add the salt until the water is boiling. A dash of oil in the water will prevent fresh pasta and lasagna sheets from sticking together. Oil is not necessary with other types of pasta. Once the pasta has been added to the boiling water, cover with a lid for a moment until the water returns to a boil. Stir briefly with a wooden spoon to prevent the pasta from sticking to the base of the saucepan, then continue to cook in rapidly boiling water without the lid. Check the pasta a couple of minutes before the end of the recommended cooking time to see if it is *al dente*, firm to the bite. It should be soft on the outside but still firm inside. Drain in a sieve. Pasta should not be rinsed in cold water as this would wash out the flavour and nutrients. Mix immediately with a prepared sauce.

Pasta dough

To make egg pasta, mix 2½ cups/300 g all-purpose flour with 3 eggs, 1 tablespoon oil, and a little salt and knead for at least 5 minutes until the mixture forms a smooth elastic dough. Wrap the dough in foil or plastic wrap and leave to stand for 30–60 minutes. Either using a pasta-making machine or a rolling pin, roll out the dough into a thin sheet, dusting with more flour as necessary. This amount makes about 1 lb/500 g (enough for 4 portions).
To make pasta without eggs, mix 3⅓ cups/400 g flour with 3 eggs, ⅞ cup/200 fl. oz lukewarm water and a little salt and knead for at least 5 minutes until the mixture has formed a smooth, elastic dough. Wrap in foil and leave for 30–60 minutes. Using a pasta machine or a rolling-pin, roll out into a thin sheet, dusting as required with a little flour. The pasta dough will make about 1¼ lbs/600 g (enough for four portions).

Pizza

To make pizza dough, dissolve 30 g/1¼ cakes compressed yeast in some hand-hot water, add 2–3 tablespoons flour and mix to a smooth paste. Leave to rise for 30 minutes. (If using active dry yeast follow maker's instructions.) Mix a generous 4 cups/500 g of flour with the paste and add ½ teaspoon of salt. Knead well for at least 10 minutes, adding a scant ½ cup/100 ml hand-hot water a little at a time. Divide the dough into four, sprinkle with flour. Cover and leave to rise in a warm place for two hours. Roll out the four pizza bases and cover with the desired ingredients. The best pizzas are baked in Italian stone ovens over a wood fire. These reach a temperature of 340 °C (620 °F) and the pizza is cooked within minutes. If using an electric or gas oven, bake for about 20 minutes on the second shelf from the bottom at 220–250 °C (430–480 °F) until the base of the pizza is crisp and the cheese has melted.

Pizza dough preparation

Whether you use fresh or dried yeast: pizza dough must be thoroughly kneaded for a good 10 minutes until it is smooth and elastic. Then, it has to be covered and left to rise in a warm place for about two hours until it has doubled in volume. Knock back the dough once more and knead again. Sprinkle a little flour on the work surface and roll out the dough. Cover and leave to rise for a further 12 to 15 minutes.

Polenta

Slowly sprinkle 1 cup/250 g polenta flour into boiling salted water (3 cups/750 ml) or boiling broth, stirring all the while to prevent any lumps forming. Cook over a low heat, stirring constantly, for about 45 minutes. When air bubbles begin to form, remove the saucepan from the heat, otherwise the mixture will start to splash. Press any clumps that form against the side of the saucepan to dissolve them.

Ravioli

Roll out some fresh pasta dough (See: Pasta dough) into a thin sheet. Pipe equal amounts of filling onto one half of the sheet of dough. The distance between the mounds of filling depends on the size of ravioli required. Brush the spaces in between with water and carefully place the other half of the sheet on top of the first, firmly pressing the sheets together around the filling. Cut out the ravioli with a pastry wheel, or with metal ravioli shapes or a wooden ravioli press, which is even easier. Cooking time: about four minutes.

Risotto

Always add risotto rice to the saucepan without washing it so that none of the starch is washed out. About 7 cups/1.75 liters of liquid (broth) is required for 2½ cups/500 g of rice. Lightly sauté the rice in butter and oil with finely diced onion and herbs and spices until the onion is soft and translucent. Gradually add the hot liquid a bit at a time, stirring constantly. More or less liquid may be used but test from time to time to see if it is cooked. The rice must be soft on the outside but still be firm inside.

Salt (dried) cod

Leave the fish in water for 24 hours, changing the water three to four times. Very thick specimens should be soaked for 36 hours. For the last two hours of this procedure, use warm water in order to ensure that all the salt has been dissolved out of the fish. Pat the fish dry and it is ready to use.

Shrimp

Twist the heads off and remove the tail flesh from the shell. Using a sharp knife, lift and remove the threadlike black intestine which is visible along the back.

Sieving

Strain soups, sauces, or puréed food through a sieve or muslin cloth to get a fine, even consistency.

Skinning bell peppers

Cut the peppers in half and lay on a baking sheet lined with waxed paper. Bake in the oven until the skin turns dark brown and begins to blister. Remove from the oven, cover with a damp dish cloth, and leave to cool. Carefully scrape off the skin with a sharp knife.

Squid (calamari)

Remove the innards along with the tentacles from the body. Separate the tentacles from the head, leaving them still joined together at the top end. Remove the cartilage from the tentacles. Peel off the outer skin from the body sac and slide out the translucent bone. If you wish to use the ink, carefully remove the ink sac from the innards and set aside.

Steaming

To steam food, it is placed in a colander, covered, and cooked over boiling water. This method of cooking is ideal for retaining vitamins and other nutrients, as well as preserving the natural taste.

Tagliatelle

Even without a pasta machine, tagliatelle is simple to make from fresh pasta dough: Roll the dough out thinly into a roughly rectangular shape. Starting from both sides, roll the dough up towards the middle and then cut into strips with a sharp knife. Cooking time: about 2 minutes for narrow, and 6 minutes for wide ribbon pasta.

Thickening

Sauces, soups, and creamy mixtures can be thickened by stirring flour, cornstarch, cream, eggs, butter, roux, grated potatoes, or puréed vegetables into the liquid.

Tomatoes

To preserve tomatoes, pour boiling water over about 2 lbs/1 kg of tomatoes, peel off the skins, cut them in half, and remove the core. Lightly sauté one shallot and one stick of celery in one tablespoon olive oil. Add the tomatoes, a pinch of sugar, salt and freshly milled pepper, and cook for about 20 minutes uncovered in a saucepan. Pour the hot tomatoes into a clean glass jar, screw the lid closed, and stand upside down for 5 minutes. If the tomatoes are to be stored for any length of time, the jars should first be sterilized by standing them in boiling water for one hour. Makes about 2½ cups/600 ml.

Tortellini

Roll out fresh pasta dough (See: Pasta dough) into a thin sheet and cut out circles. Place the filling in the center of each circle and fold in half. Wrap these semicircular shapes around your forefinger and press the ends firmly together. Cooking time: about 6 minutes.

Trimming and dicing

Cut off the fat, sinews, and skin from pieces of meat or fish and cut into equal sized pieces. These discarded bits can be used for stock or go into the cooking juices.

Vegetables in sweet and sour marinade (in agrodolce)

Prepare about 1 lb/500 g of eggplants (See: Eggplants) and dice into cubes. Sauté in 2 tablespoons olive oil and dry on paper towels. Sauté several tender stalks of celery in the oil, then remove them from the skillet. Cut an onion into rings and fry in the oil for a few minutes along with 4 cored and seeded tomatoes. Add one tablespoon of pine nuts and soaked raisins, respectively, and one teaspoon of sugar, a little red wine vinegar, the eggplants, and celery. Cook over a moderate heat for about 30 minutes. Sweet and sour zucchini can be prepared in the same way. To preserve it, see Marinating.

Zucchini flowers

To stuff the flowers, cut off the stem and dip the flowers briefly into cold water, drain, and pat dry with paper towels. Carefully open up the center of the flower and cut out the pistil with a sharp knife. Pipe the filling into each flower cup and twist the ends closed to seal in the filling.

BIBLIOGRAPHY

PICTURE CREDITS

Accademia Italiana della Cucina: Cucina Italiana. Das große Buch der italienischen Küche. Cologne 1993

Alessi, Alberto: Die Traumfabrik. Alessi seit 1921. Milan 1998

Apicius, Marcus Gavinus: De re coquinaria. Über die Kochkunst. Stuttgart 1991

Artusi, Pellegrino: Von der Wissenschaft des Kochens und der Kunst des Genießens. Munich 1998

Assine, Jérome: The Book of Bread. Paris/New York 1996

Beusen, Paul/Ebert-Schifferer, Sybille/Mai, Ekkehard (Hrsg.): L'Art Gourmand. Stilleben für Auge, Kochkunst und Gourmets von Aertsen bis Van Gogh. Essen 1997

Bugialli, Giuliano: Classic Techniques of Italian Cooking. New York 1989

Capalbo, Carla: The Ultimate Italian Cookbook. London 1994

Carluccio, Antonio: Antonio Carluccio's Italian Feast. London 1996

Carluccio, Antonio/Carluccio, Priscilla: Carluccio's Complete Italian Food. London 1997

Christl-Licosa, Marielouise: Antipasti. Munich 1991

Cipriani, Arrigo: La leggenda dell'Harry's Bar. Milan 1991

Cùnsolo, Felice: Italien tafelt. Munich 1971

Davids, Kenneth: Espresso – Ultimate Coffee. Santa Rosa 1993

Davidson, James: Courtesans and Fishcakes. London 1997

Degner, Rotraud: Fische und Meeresfrüchte. Munich 1989

Donovan, Jane: Pasta. London 1997

Enciclopedia della cucina. Novara 1990

Freson, Robert: Italien – Eine kulinarische Entdeckungsreise. Munich 1992

Goethe, Johann Wolfgang: Italienische Reise. Cologne 1998

Harris, Valentina: Italian Regional Cookery. London 1990

Hess/Sälzer: Die echte italienische Küche. Munich 1990

Kaltenbach, M./Simeone, Remo: Italienische Küche. Niedernhausen 1996

Levi, Carlo: Christ Stopped at Eboli. Munich 1982

Löbel, Jürgen: Parmaschinken & Co. Düsseldorf 1989

Marchesi, Gualtiero: Die große italienische Küche. 1984

McNair, James: Pizza. Berlin 1990

Medici, Lorenza de' (Hrsg.): Italien – Eine kulinarische Reise. Munich 1989

Meuth, Martina/Neuner-Duttenhofer: Venetien und Friaul. Munich 1990, 1996

Meuth, Martina/Neuner-Duttenhofer: Piemont und Aostatal. Munich 1996

Moisemann, Anton/Hofmann, H.: Das große Buch der Meeresfrüchte. Füssen 1989

Monti, Antonia: Il nuovissimo cucciaio d'argento. Rome 1991

Muus, B.: Collins Guide to the Sea Fishes of Britain and Northwest Europe. London 1974

Paolini, Davide: Peck. Milan 1998

Peschke, Hans-Peter von/Feldmann, Werner: Kochen wie die alten Römer: 200 Rezepte nach Apicius, für die heutige Küche umgesetzt von Hans-Peter von Peschke und Werner Feldmann. Zürich 1995

Peschke, Hans-Peter von/Feldmann, Werner: Das Kochbuch der Renaissance. Düsseldorf/Zürich 1997

Simony, Pia de: Köstliches Italien. Munich 1995

Supp, Eckhard: Enzyklopädie des italienischen Weins. Offenbach 1995

Supp, E.: Wein für Einsteiger – Italien. Munich 1997

Teubner (Hrsg.), C.: Das große Buch vom Fisch. Füssen 1987

Teubner (Hrsg.), C.: Das große Buch vom Käse. Füssen 1990

Vollenweider, A.: Italiens Provinzen und ihre Küche. Berlin 1990

Wolter, Annette: Geflügel. Munich 1987

l. = left; r. = right; c. = center; a. = above; b. = below

All illustrations – Könemann Verlagsgesellschaft mbH, Cologne/Foto: Ruprecht Stempell, Cologne

With the exception of:

Alessi Information Bureau c/o Integra Communication GmbH, Hamburg: 154/155 (except a.)

Alinari 1999, Florence 42 b., 214 a.r., 294 a., 306 (Pope Boniface IX), 338, 446 (Martorana)

Archiv Alessi, Crusinallo: 154 a.

Archive for Art and History, Berlin: 40 a., 153 b., 170 a., 306 (Pope Alexander VI), 306 (Pope Leo X), 306 (Pope Julius III); Erich Lessing: 306 (Pope Pius V)

Archivio Fotografico e Copyright Sacro Convento, Assisi: 264 a.r.

Archivio Storico Barilla, Parma: 197 a.r., 197 a.c.

Arnaldo Forni Editore, Sala Bolognese (Bologna)/ Foto: Württemberg Regional Library Stuttgart: 111 l.

Artothek, Peissenberg/Foto: Blauel/Gnamm: 88 l., 438 l.

Picture Archives Foto Marburg: 306 (Pope Martin IV)

Picture Archives of Prussian Cultural Heritage, Berlin: 356

Cafarell S.p.A., Luserna S. Giovanni (Turin): 153 a.

Casa Buonarroti, Florence/Foto: Archivio Buonarroti: 103 r.

Cintetext, Frankfurt: 145, 389 b.r., 432 l.

Civico Museo Bibliografico Musicale, Bologna: 278

Ente Sardo Industrie Turistiche, Cagliari: 477 a.l.

Mary Evans Picture Library, London: 344 a.

Faber & Partner, Düsseldorf: 142 l.

Food Foto, Cologne: 299 a.l.

Foto Archives, Essen/Foto: Jörg Meyer: 247 a.l., 247 (3. Row r.), 247 b.r.; Jörg Sackermann: 246 a.r.; Andreas Riedmiller: 247 a.c., 247 (2. Row r.), 261 a.

Paroli Galperti: 402 (Nubia); © Lomonaco: 386 b.r.; Granata Press, Milan/Foto: Luigi Galperti: 402 (Asmara); Herzog August Library, Wolfenbüttel: 306 a.

Helga Lade Photographic Agency, Frankfurt/Foto: Willi Arand: 72/73 (Gerstenfeld)

Gisela Jahrmärker, Berlin: 237 r., 238 l., 320 l.

Rainer Kiedrowski, Ratingen: 74 r.

© Tandem Verlag GmbH/Foto: 50 l.; Günter Beer: 18 b.l., 26/27, 29, 30/31, 34 b.l., 43, 44/45, 47 a., 51 (Bream, sardine, gray mullet, eel, shark, turbot, John Dory, monkfish); 52 (calamari, clams, common mussel, razor shell, scallop, shrimp, spider crab, crab), 64/65, 66/67, 69 a., 70 b., 71 b., 72 l., 73 r., 75, 76, 77 b., 78 (Golden Delicious, apple tree, Canada Renette, Royal Gala, Elstar), 79 b., 80 r., 81, 82, 84/85, 94/95, 96/97, 98, 100, 104–107, 109 (cookies), 118 a.r., 119, 126 a.l. 126 a.r., 136/137, 141, 142 r., 144, 146 l., 147 r., 151 (sweet chestnut), 152, 156/157, 160, 162 b., 168 (all fish), 170 c., 172, 173 (background), 174 b., 177 r., 177 (Trofie), 192 (except Abissina rigate, Bucatini, Capellini, Capunti, Cavatellucci, Cinesini, Ditali rigati, Fenescècchie), 193 (Fusilli pugliesi, Genzianelle, Gramigna, Maccheroni), 194 (Orecchiette, Panzerotti di magro, Pappardelle, Passatelli, Ravioli, Ravioli alle noci, Riscossa), 195 (Spirali, Taglierini, Tortelli, Tortellini, Tortiglioni, Triangoli al salmone, Trucidi pugliesi), 198, 199 l., 200 (except a.), 211 r., 213 r., 214 l., 215 (background), 216/217 c., 218/219, 220/221, 223 (except Pan de ramerino), 225 (box), 226 (all except a.),

217 a.r., 231 (basil, rosemary), 240 (except Sbricciolana, Salsiccia), 241 a., 241 c., 245 l., 248/249 c., 259, 284 (3 and 4), 285 a.r., 301 a.l., 301 c.l., 301 a.r., 308 (lettuce, Roman salad, chicory, curly lettuce, endive), 310 (bunches of herbs, capers), 311 (coriander, tarragon, majoram, chili pepper, rosemary, sage, thyme, vanilla), 326 a., 340 a.l., 369 b.r., 372 (background), 386 a., 412 (all except background), 413 (all except background a.), 427 (bream, dentex, sea bass), 428 b.l., 437 a., 443, 444/445, 462, 463 l., 464 m.l., 469, 481 (water 5–12); Christoph Büschel: 113 (perch), 262 l.a., 263 (tench, perch, eel, whitefish, roach 373 a., 373 c., 417 (water melon); Sonja Büschel: 113 (sturgeon); Helmut Claus: 345; Eduard Noack: 109 b.r. (reproduction)

laif, Cologne/Foto: Luigi Caputo: 246 c. 246 b., 247 a.r., 247 b.c.; Celentano: 264 (background), 352/353 a.c.; Hedda Eid: 247 (2. row l.), 250 b.l.; Achim Gaasterland: 244; Fulvio Zanettini: 247 (3. row l.)

H.E. Laux, Biberach an der Riß: 235 (all mushrooms except Funghi Misti)

Fondazione Lungarotti/Foto: Archivio Fotografico: 268 b.

Milko Marchetti, Gallo (Ferrara): 58

Marka, Mailand/UBIK: 328 a.

Melitta, Minden: 300 a.

© Federico Meneghetti: 55 (Asparagus)

Nationalmuseum, Stockholm: 242 b.r.

Werner Neumeister, Munich: 235 a., 277, 432 (background)

Okapia, Frankfurt/G. Büttner/Naturbild: 78 (Gloster, Jonathan), 176 b.; Günter Kiepke/Naturbild: 437 b.; E. Weiland: 135 a.

Österreichische Nationalbibliothek, Vienna/Photo: Picture Archives ÖNL, Vienna: 206

Owen Franken: 326 b., 327 a.l.

Giovanni Panarotto, Cola di Lazise (Verona): 392 a.l.

Picture Press, Hamburg/Mondadori: 108 a.r., 108 b.l.

Piemme, S. Agnello di Sorrento: 357 r.

Poccard-Chapuis, Y./Delmas, L., Paris: 468 (except background)

Molinari Pradelli Collection, Castenaso (Bologna)/ Foto: Mario Bernardi: 243 b.

Prima Press, Milan: 258 b.l., 341 (Pomodoro di Cerignola, Marena, Roma, Perino, Sardo, Ramato, Napoli, Palla di Fuoco), 348 r., 440 a., 440 c.r., 441 (all b.r.)

Scala S.p.A., Antella (Florence): 40 b., 110, 228 a.l., 228 b.l., 242 a., 242 b.l., 276 a., 279 b.l., 292, 450

SIPA Press, Paris/Foto: Yaghobzadeh: 41

Franca Speranza, Milan: 424 b.

Stock Food, Munich/Maximilian Stock LTD: 51 (Salmon)

Eckhard Supp, Offenbach: 80 a.l., 117, 158/159, 217 b.r., 247 (2. row c.), 248 l., 250/251 a.c., 268 a., 269 a., 286/287, 332/333 (except b.r.), 379 l., 396 a., 418, 452

Teubner Foodfoto, Füssen: 302 (box), 348 r., 372 a.l., 377 (Regina), 417 (Charleston Gray, Crimson Sweet), 440 c.l., 441 (oranges a.l.)

© Sandro Vannini/CORBIS, Düsseldorf 122/123

Visum, Hamburg/Foto: Günter Beer: 236/237 a.c.

Voller Ernst, Berlin/Foto: Pfeiffer: 448 a.l.

TEXT CREDITS   ACKNOWLEDGMENTS

This project represents collaboration between several authors in producing the text and compiling the recipes.

Pino Correnti (Sicily)
Andrea Maestrelli (Val d'Aosta, Piedmont, Veneto)
Flavia Marin (Emilia-Romagna, Liguria)
Eugenio Medagliani (Abruzzi, Friuli, Lombardy, Sardinia, Trentino)
Eugenio Medagliani and Laura Niccolai (Basilicata, Calabria, Campania)
Simone Medagliani (Apulia, Lazio)
Marzia Tempestini (Marche, Tuscany, Umbria)

The following texts are attributed to Marina Collaci: "Prosciutto baciato" (p. 149), "Tonno del Chianti" (p. 239), "Puntarelle and Other Vegetables" (p. 303), "Tiella di verdure" (p. 366), "Vegetables and Pulses" (p. 368), "Lamb" (p. 393), "Sicilian Vegetable Dishes" (p. 437), "Rock Lobsters" (p. 470).

The text on Barilla (p. 196) was written by Bettina Dürr.

The text on the still lifes (p. 242–243) is by Roswitha Neu-Kock.

The author of the sections on wine is Eckhard Supp (p. 22–23, 60–61, 80–83, 114–117, 132, 158–161, 216–217, 246–251, 268–269, 286–287, 314–315, 332–333, 356–357, 378–379, 396–397, 418–419, 451, 478–479).

The text on the Romanengo confectionery and cake store (p. 181) is by Cornelia Zingerling.

The recipes for "Fish in batter," "Tortellini with pork meat filling," "Mushroom soup" and "Pumpkin tart" (p. 229) are from: The Renaissance Cookbook by Hans-Peter von Peschke/Werner Feldmann. Düsseldorf/Zürich 1997. The recipes for "Chicken salad à la Apicius," "Sauce for boiled eggs," "Pear patina" (p. 293) are from: Cooking Ancient Roman Style: 200 Recipes by Apicius, Adapted For Modern Cuisine by Hans-Peter von Peschke and Werner Feldmann. Zürich 1995. All seven recipes have been reprinted with the kind permission of the publishers Artemis & Winkler Düsseldorf/Zürich.

Editing and research by:
Marina Collaci (Apulia, Basilicata, Calabria, Lazio, Sardinia, Sicily)
Bettina Dürr (all chapters)
Cornelia Zingerling (Val d'Aosta, Emilia-Romagna, Friuli Venezia Giulia, Liguria, Lombardy, Piedmont, Trentino/Southern Tyrol, Veneto)

The publishers would also like to extend their thanks to all those unnamed persons whose kind cooperation made this project possible. Special thanks is owed to Kyra and Lilly Stempell who, for the sake of this book, were obliged to do without their Ruprecht, and to Carolin Büns, who looked after more than just the props and stores, as well as Bernhard Roetzel, who kept Claudia's strength up with food and drink. Thanks go also to the Verna family for allowing us to photograph a considerable number of the Italian dishes at Masseria Modesti. This book would not have been possible without the commitment and assistance of Birgit Beyer, Sabine Blemann, Stefan Marzak (Olive e più, Cologne), Gisela Jahrmärker, Henning Mader, Ruth Mader, Sandra Schauerte, Sabine Schwarz and Dott. Scianella (Ist. Di Commercio Estero, Rome).

The publishes also wish to thank the following manufacturers, restaurants, and institutions for their kind assistance:

Friuli – Venezia Giulia
Casa del Prosciutto, San Daniele del Friuli; Trattoria-Osteria Grappolo d'Oro, Arba

Venice – Veneto
The Cantina Ca'Salina vineyard, Valdobbiadene; Francesco Cavalerin, Sottomarina; Harry's Bar, Venice; the Gianni Seguso glass-blowing works, Murano; Unioncop fish cooperative, Chioggia; Gastronomia Volpato food store, Mestre

Trentino – Alto Adige
Casa del formaggio, Bolzano; Forst Brewery, Algund-Merano; Peter Egger foods, Bolzano; the Franciscan bakery, Bolzano; Buschenschank Gruber, Vorderafing

Lombardy
Salumeria Corte dell'Oca, Mortara; Claudio Faccoli vineyard, Coccaglio; Restaurant Giannino, Milan; Bar-Pasticceria Marchesi, Milan; Eugenio Medagliani, Milan; Peck Foods, Milan

Val d'Aosta
La Cascina Vollget cheesemakers, Brissogne; Maison de la Fontine food store, Aosta; Valdotaine distillery, Saint-Marcel

Piedmont
Dei Cacciatori Restaurant, Alberetto della Torre; Azienda Agricola Dove osano le aquile, Castelmagno; Consorzio del Gorgonzola, Novara; Il Rondò della frutta fruit and vegetable store, Novara; Sibona distillery, Piobesi d'Alba

Liguria
Gianpiero Navone, Villanova d'Albenga; Romanengo confectionery and cake store, Genoa

Emilia-Romagna
Barilla, Parma-Pedrignano; Caffè Commercianti, Bologna; Trattoria Cantarelli, Samboseto; Il Coccio Ceramics, Bologna; Falegnami Bar and Patisserie, Bologna; Restaurant Fini, Modena; Anna Nieddu, Bologna; Osteria del Sole, Bologna; La Salumeria di Bruno & Franco, Bologna; Scaramagli Spirits and Delicatessen, Bologna; Salumeria Serra e Tamerlani Foods, Bologna; Nicola Tassinari asparagus growers, Altedo; Il Temperino household goods, Bologna

Tuscany
Chini Butchers and Pig-Breeders, Gaiole in Chianti; Panificio Giorgio Franci, Gaiole in Chianti; Forno Marcello Pugi bakers, Florence; Vivaio Sabatini tree school, Mercatale Val di Pesa

Umbria
L'Artigiano dei Salumi, Norcineria Ansuini, Norcia; Fondazione Lungarotti Museo del Vino, Torgiano; Pasticceria Sandri, Perugia

Marche
Il Bocconcino sausage and cheese store, Pesaro; Re Formaggio Antonio Budano cheese store, Ancona; Azienda Conca d'Oro, Agriturismo Villa Cicchi, Abazia di Rosara; Enoteca Vino Vip, Pesaro

Lazio – Rome
Bar Arcioni, Rome; Trattoria La Carbonara, Rome; Pasticceria Faggiani, Rome; Caffè Greco, Rome; Apistica Romana, Rome

Abruzzi – Molise
Confetti D'Alessandro Lo Scrigno, Sulmona; Gabriele Colasante rolling-pin maker, San Buceto near Pescara; Ristorante Italia, Sulmona; Franca Leone of the APT Sulmona, Sulmona; Patisserie-Caffè Fratelli Nurzia, L'Aquila; Confetti Ovidio, Sulmona; Soldo di Cacio sausage and cheese shop, Sulmona

Campania
Baffone Fruit and Vegetables, Naples; Gran Caffè Gambrinus, Naples; Pescheria Sasà + Peppe, Naples; Felicitas Sonnenberg, Naples, Azienda Caseificio Vannulo buffalo and cheese farm, Capaccio

Puglia
Panificio Angelini Bakers, Martina Franca; Fratelli Continisio, Altamura; Panificio Dimarno, Altamura; Fratelli Ricci butchers and snack bar, Martina Franca; Masseria Serra dell'Isola, Mola di Bari; Caffè-Pasticceria Tripoli, Martina Franca; Hotel dei Trulli, Alberobello

Basilicata
Fornaio Arena, Trecchina; La Caffetteria, Maratea; Farmacia dei Sani herb and delicatessan store, Maratea; Restaurant Antica Osteria Marconi, Potenza; Armando Martino vineyard, Rionero; Osvaldo Palermo "Il Patriarca" distillery, Marina di Maratea; Lo Sfizio, Potenza

Calabria
Pasticceria Francesco Careri, Bagnara Calabra; Fornaio Albino Mandera, Rende; Franco Mariello; Agenzia Pro Loco, Bagnara Calabra; Fratelli Rocco, Angiolino De Biasi, Bagnara Calabra

Sicily
Bar Italico, Palermo; Fattoria Montalto farm, Castelvetrano, Baglio Santa Teresa

Sardinia
Il Buongustaio, Macomer; Maddalena Carta, Abbasanta; Azienda Agrituristica Mandra Edera holiday farm, Abbasanta; Enodolci, Salumi e Formaggi, Da Carmelo, Alghero; Lacesa, Bortigali; Luigi Ledda and Franco Sotgiù, Bosa; Azienda Franco Meloni, Selargius near Cagliari; Pescheria del Golfo, Oristano; Pescheria Urgu-Lai, Bosa

INDEX

RECIPE INDEX

Recipes with illustrations have page number in bold type.